Encyclopedia
of
Chart Patterns

WILEY TRADING ADVANTAGE

Encyclopedia
of
Chart Patterns

Thomas N. Bulkowski

John Wiley & Sons, Inc.
New York • Chichester • Weinheim • Brisbane • Singapore • Toronto

Published by John Wiley & Sons, Inc.
Published simultaneously in Canada.

This publication is designed to provide accurate and authoritative information in regard to the subject matter covered. It is sold with the understanding that the publisher is not engaged in rendering professional services. If professional advice or other expert assistance is required, the services of a competent professional person should be sought.

Library of Congress Cataloging-in-Publication Data:

Bulkowski, Thomas N., 1957–
      Encyclopedia of chart patterns / Thomas N. Bulkowski.
         p.   cm.—(Wiley trading advantage)
      Includes index.
      ISBN 0-471-29525-6 (alk. paper)
      1. Stocks—Charts, diagrams, etc.   2. Commodities—Charts, diagrams, etc.   3. Technical analysis.   I. Title.   II. Series.
      HG4638.B85   2000
      332.63'222—dc21   99-15789

Printed in the United States of America.
10 9 8 7 6 5 4

*To **my parents**, who continued to love me even after my homemade rocket set the lawn on fire, and to my four-legged best friend, **Rusty**, who saved my life; it grieves me that I couldn't save yours.*

Preface

When I was a little tyke I decided the easiest way to riches was to play the stock market. It was, after all, a level playing field, a zero-sum game with somebody winning and somebody losing (hint: The winner is always the broker). All one had to do to win was pick the stocks that went up and avoid the stocks that went down. Easy.

I kept this in mind when I graduated from Syracuse University with an engineering degree and showed up early for my first professional job. Each morning I cracked open the newspaper and plotted my stock picks on a piece of paper taped to the wall. Bob, my office mate, used the same newspaper to select his stocks. I chose my selections using strict and exhausting fundamental research, but Bob simply closed his eyes, twirled his hand around, and plunged his finger into the newspaper. When he opened his eyes and removed his finger, he announced another pick.

After several months of tracking both our selections, I made a startling discovery: I was getting creamed. Bob's random selections were beating the tar out of my carefully researched choices. I also discovered something else: I was learning a lot by paper trading.

With the hesitancy and distrust inherited from my parents, I studied two dozen firms before making my final selection and first purchase: I opened a money market account. The timing was excellent; I was earning over 17% on my cash. At first glance, the return might imply a very risky investment but it was not. The prime rate was, after all, at 21%.

Flush with success, I gathered my courage and opened a brokerage account and began investing with the few pennies I saved. Again, the timing was excellent as I caught the beginning of a major bull market. I bought a stock near $3\frac{1}{2}$ and watched it go to $46\frac{1}{2}$—my first ten-bagger.

Lest you think that everything was easy, consider what happened. My stock portfolio was growing by leaps and bounds, but my professional career was about to take a turn for the worse. After switching careers more often than I sometimes like to admit, I landed at a job with a company I could finally call home—a job that would last a lifetime, or so I thought. Almost six months *after* my 10-year anniversary with the company, I received a letter from the chairman. He congratulated me on my decade with the company and looked forward to even more success for me in the coming years. Six weeks later I was laid off.

I took stock of the situation and decided that, at the age of 36, I had had enough. Newspapers term guys like me *The Missing Million*. We are the ones who, for whatever reason, leave their jobs and decide not to go back into the workforce. We retire. Everyone, and I mean *everyone* (with the notable exception of my cousin Mary Ann—bless her heart), thinks we are nuts. They are right, of course!

For the longest time, I have been fascinated with technical analysis of stocks. In the early years, I considered the little squiggles to be nothing short of voodoo. Still, I was curious as to why the major brokerage houses were hiring technical analysts in droves. But I did not dare take my eye off the fundamentals simply because I did not know anything about the technicals. Then I discovered *Technical Analysis of Stocks and Commodities* magazine. During my lunch hour, I would take the elevator down to the library and read back issues. Although I had seen chart patterns in the stocks I bought, I never really attached much significance to them. As some of my selections went sour, I began to view chart patterns with more respect. The fundamentals always looked good, but the technicals were signaling a trend change just as I was about to pull the trigger. The stocks I bought either lost money outright or I sold them too soon and cut my profits short.

Perhaps this has happened to you. You do your fundamental research on a stock, then buy it only to watch it go nowhere for a year or more. Even worse, once you get in, the stock tumbles. Had you looked at the chart the answer was always there. Prices pierced a trendline, a head-and-shoulders top appeared out of nowhere, the relative strength index signaled an overbought situation. In short, any number of technical indicators were screaming that a buy now would cost you your shirt. But you never saw the signs because you had your eyes closed.

You are not alone; I did the same thing for years. I eventually got so frustrated with the performance of my stock selections that I decided to do my own research on technical analysis. I went to the library and read the same thing in many books: A head-and-shoulders formation works *most of the time*. What does that mean? Does it mean they are successful 51% of the time or 90% of the time? No one had the answer. I was not willing to risk my hard earned dollars on simple bromides. As an engineer I wanted hard, cold facts, not fuzzy platitudes. So, I wrote this book.

At the back of the book is an Index of Chart Patterns. If you suspect your stock is making a chart pattern but do not know what to call it, the Index of Chart Patterns is the first place to look. Page numbers beside each pattern direct you to the associated chapter.

The chapters are arranged alphabetically, making it easy to locate the chart pattern of interest. Within each chapter, you are first greeted with a "Results Snapshot" of the major findings followed by a short discussion. Then, a "Tour" invites you to explore the chart pattern. "Identification Guidelines," in both table form and in-depth discussion, make selecting and verifying your choices easier. For simpler chart patterns, the "Tour" and "Identification Guidelines" have been combined into one section.

No work would be complete without an exploration of the mistakes, and the "Focus on Failures" section dissects the cause of failures. The all-important "Statistics" section follows. Once you can identify a chart pattern, know how it is likely to perform, and are alert to possible failure indications, how do you trade it? That is what the "Trading Tactics" and "Sample Trade" sections explore.

If you have ever worked on a car or done some woodworking, then you will recognize the importance of selecting the right tool for the job. You would not want to use a flat-head screwdriver when a Phillips works better. Both do the job but they are hardly interchangeable. Sometimes it is not a screwdriver you should be using, but a chisel. Selecting the proper tools and knowing how to use them is half the battle. This book is a lot like that, helping to sort the wheat from the chaff. Sometimes a chart pattern is frightening enough that you will want to take profits. At other times, the best trade that you can make is none at all.

I cannot give you the experience needed to make money in the stock market using chart patterns. I can only give you the tools and say, "Go to work on paper first." That is the first step in developing a trading style that works for you, one you are comfortable with, one that improves as you do. If you review your paper trades, you will understand why a stop-loss order is more than a necessary evil: It is a useful tool. You will improve your ability to predict support and resistance levels that will, in turn, allow you to tighten your stops and get out near the top, cut your losses short, and let your profits ride. Simple.

You will discover why the measure rule is so important, especially in turbulent markets. Unless you are willing to suffer a 20% drawdown, you will understand why the average gain quoted so often in this book may be a best-case scenario and will come to grips with why you are still struggling to make it above the most likely gain. You may discover that your girlfriend loves diamonds, but as a chart pattern, you cannot seem to make them pay. One word says it all. Experience.

Good luck.

Thomas N. Bulkowski
December 1999

Acknowledgments

Perhaps several times in your life, something happens that alters the direction your life is taking. That happened to me several years ago when I brashly submitted my first article to *Technical Analysis of Stocks and Commodities*. Much to my surprise and delight, the editor at the time, Thom Hartle, published the work. That single event sent me spinning off in a new direction.

Nearly a dozen articles later, I called Thom and chatted with him about an idea for a book. He steered me to Pamela van Giessen, senior editor for John Wiley & Sons, Inc., publisher of this book. A single e-mail of my idea to her put a new set of wheels in motion.

Simple words cannot express my thanks to these two outstanding individuals. Of course, there are many others such as my younger brother, Jim, the unsung heroes that sometimes gave me a helping hand, formed my support group, or gave me a good, swift kick in the butt. They are not forgotten.

T. N. B.

Contents

Encyclopedia
of
Chart Patterns

Introduction

Jim is struggling.

He is the owner of JCB Superstores and his competitor across town is beating him up; there is blood all over Jim's ledger. He decides it is time to take off the gloves: JCB goes public. He uses the money from the initial public offering to buy his competitor and add a few more stores around town.

With a growing sales base, Jim's clout allows him to negotiate lower prices for the office supplies he is retailing. He passes on part of the savings to his customers, while watching his margins widen, and plows the profits back into building more stores.

Jim calls his friend, Tom, and tells him of his plans to expand the operation statewide. They chat for a while and exchange business tactics on how best to manage the expansion. When Tom gets off the phone, he decides to conduct his own research on JCB. He visits several stores and sees the same thing: packed parking lots, people bustling around with full shopping carts, and lines at the checkout counters. He questions a few customers to get a sense of the demographics. At a few stores, he even chats with suppliers as they unload their wares. Back at the office, he does a thorough analysis of the financials and looks at the competition. Everything checks out so he orders his trading partners to buy the stock at no higher than 10.

When news of the expansion plan hits the wires, the Street panics. It is, after all, a soft economy and expanding willy-nilly when a recession looms is daft, maybe even criminal, according to them. The stock drops below 10 and Tom's crew makes its move. They quietly buy as much as they can without raising suspicion. The stock rises anyway. It goes back up to 11, then 12, and rounds over at 13 before heading back down.

Several months go by and the economic outlook is as bleak as ever. The stock eases down to 9. After Tom checks in with Jim for the latest public news, Tom's team buys more. It is an easy score because investors are willing to dump the stock especially as year-end tax selling approaches.

Six weeks later the company releases the sales numbers for JCB; they are better than expected. The stock rises 15% in minutes and closes at 10¾. And that is just for starters. Six months later, it's clear the economy was never in danger of entering a recession and everyone sees boom times ahead. The stock hits 20.

Years go by, the stock splits a few times, and the holiday season looms. Tom interviews a handful of customers leaving JCB Superstores and discovers that they are all complaining about the same thing: The advertised goods are missing. Tom investigates further and discovers a massive distribution problem, right at the height of the selling season. JCB has overextended itself; the infrastructure is simply not there to support the addition of one new store each week.

Tom realizes it is time to sell. He tells his trading department to dump the stock immediately but for no less than 28¼. They liquidate about a third of their large holdings before driving the stock down below the minimum.

Since it is the holidays, everyone seems to be in a buying mood. Novice investors jump in at what they consider a bargain price. The major brokerage houses climb aboard and tout the stock, but Tom knows better. When the stock recovers to its old high, his trading partners sell the remainder of their holdings. The stock tops out and rounds over. During the next month and a half, the stock drifts down, slowly, casually. There does not appear to be a rush for the exits—just a slow trickle as the smart money quietly folds up shop.

Then news of poor holiday sales leaks out. There is a rumor about distribution problems, merchandising mistakes, and cash flow problems. Brokerage firms that only weeks before were touting the stock now advise their clients to sell. The stock plummets 39% overnight.

One or two analysts say the stock is oversold; it is a bargain and investors should add to their positions. Many bottom fishers follow their brokers' recommendation and buy the stock. Big mistake. The buying enthusiasm pushes the price up briefly before a new round of selling takes hold. Each day the stock drops a bit lower, nibbling away like waves washing against a castle of sand. In 2 months' time, the stock is down another 30%.

The following quarter JCB Superstores announces that earnings will likely come in well below consensus estimates. The stock drops another 15%. The company is trying to correct the distribution problem, but it is not something easily fixed. They decide to stop expanding and to concentrate on the profitability of their existing store base.

Two years later, Tom pulls up the stock chart. The dog has been flat for so long it looks as if its heartbeat has stopped. He calls Jim and chats about the outlook for JCB Superstores. Jim gushes enthusiastically about a new retailing concept called the Internet. He is excited about the opportunity to sell office supplies on-line without the need for bricks and mortar. There is some risk because the on-line community is in its infancy, but Jim predicts it will quickly expand. Tom is impressed, so he starts doing his homework and is soon buying the stock again.

Investment Footprints

If you picture in your mind the price action of JCB Superstores, you should recognize three chart patterns: a double bottom, a double top, and a dead-cat bounce. To knowledgeable investors, chart patterns are not squiggles on a price chart; they are the footprints of the smart money. The footprints are all they need to follow as they line their pockets with greater and greater riches. To others, such as Tom, it is hard work and pavement pounding before they dare take a position in a stock. They are the ones *making* the footprints. They are the smart money that is setting the rules of the game—a game anyone can play. It is called investing.

Whether you choose to use technical analysis or fundamental analysis in your trading decisions, it pays to know what the market is thinking. It pays to look for the footprints. Those footprints may well steer you away from a cliff and get you out of a stock just in time. The feet that make those footprints are the same ones that will kick you in the pants, waking you up to a promising investment opportunity.

This book gives you the tools to spot the footprints, where they predict the stock is heading, how far it will travel, and how reliable the trail you are following really is. The tools will not make you rich; tools rarely do. But they are instruments to greater wealth. Use them wisely.

The Database

If you want to discover how much you do not know about a chart formation, try teaching a computer to recognize one. I spent several months doing that preparing for this book. The program helped me locate, analyze, and log well over 15,000 formations. It is not a substitute for my eyes or my brain, just another tool to augment my talent. Consider it another set of dispassionate eyes, a friend nudging you and saying, "Look at this one here. It's a bump-and-run reversal."

When the starting gun went off, I selected 500 stocks, all with durations of 5 years (each from mid-1991 to mid-1996) of daily price data on which to collect statistics. I included the 30 Dow Jones industrials and familiar names with varying market capitalizations. Stocks included in the study needed a heartbeat (they were not unduly flat over the 5-year period) and did not have consistently large daily price ranges (too thinly traded or volatile).

I usually removed stocks that went below a $1.00, assuming bankruptcy was right around the corner. Most of the names in the database are popular American companies that trade on the NYSE, AMEX, or NASDAQ. The numerous illustrations accompanying each chapter give a representative sample of the stocks involved.

Occasionally a chart formation came along that presented a problem. It was so scarce that 2,500 years (500 stocks times 5 years) of daily price data were simply not enough. So I pulled from the database I use on a daily basis. It contains about 300 issues and begins where the other one ends.

Stock Performance from 1991 to 1996

Before reading about the various chart patterns in this book, it is wise to review the performance of the stock market during the period. Figure I.1 shows a monthly price chart of the Standard & Poor's 500 stock index. Beginning in mid-1991, you can see that the market hesitated until January 1992. It had a wild burst upward, perhaps due to the January effect, but trended downward until May. (In case the January effect is unfamiliar to you, it is commonly attributed to investors selling their stocks for tax reasons near year end then buying back during January. The selling may or may not depress prices, whereas the January buying gives them a temporary lift.) Toward the end of 1992, it looks as if the January effect occurred early, in December, when prices broke through their malaise of consolidation and reached new highs. Then it was off to the races, and prices rose on a steady tear until March 1994. The market stumbled and moved up for 5 months then declined for 4 months. Beginning in 1995, the race resumed, but the pace accelerated. The slope of the trend tilted upward noticeably until running into some turbulence in early 1996.

What does all this mean? Viewed as a whole, the market during the 5 years used in my analyses plus the 2 or 3 additional years used sporadically but not shown in Figure I.1, marks a very bullish environment. While the market as a whole was going up gangbusters, many individual stocks were not so fortunate. Some had steady downward trends. Others moved up smartly, rolled over, and died (check out most semiconductor and semiconductor capital equipment stocks in 1995).

During a soaring bull market, bullish chart patterns are more successful by having fewer failures and longer uphill runs. They perform better, chumming along on a rising tide that lifts all boats.

Common sense suggests that bearish formations might fail more readily with stunted declines. More likely, though, is that bearish patterns just disap-

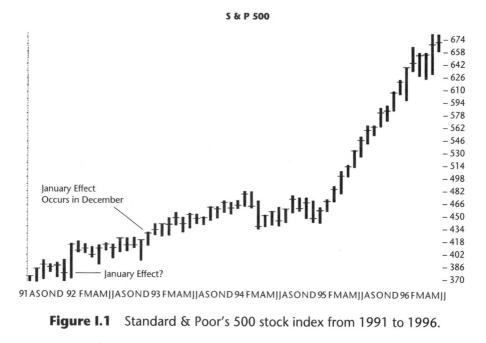

Figure I.1   Standard & Poor's 500 stock index from 1991 to 1996.

pear; they never happen. You might think that stocks moving up would form bearish reversals. Instead, they just keep moving up, now and again pausing to catch their breath before continuing the rise.

You can see this trend in the statistics. Bullish formations, those that typically occur after a downward price trend and signal an upward reversal, happen more often than bearish ones. Symmetrical triangles are a good example. Triangles with upside, bullish breakouts occurred 225 times, whereas downside breakouts happened 176 times. A favoring of the bullish trend is also evident in many paired formations. Consider double bottoms and double tops. There were 542 bottoms (bullish) and *only* 454 tops (bearish).

Even the statistics favor a bull market. A stock moving up can advance 50%, 100%, or even 1,000%. The gains can be unlimited, but what of the declines? A stock can only lose 100%, or all of its value, and nothing more.

Averages and the Frequency Distribution

The frequency distribution mentioned so often in this book deserves special attention. Before I discuss it, however, let me explain averages. An average is the sum of the numbers divided by the number of samples. If you measure the returns from five chart patterns and they are 30%, 40%, 50%, 60%, and 120%, then the average is 60%. That is the sum of the numbers (300) divided by 5 samples.

This example shows the effect large numbers have on the average. If the 120% gain is not in the series, the average drops to 180/4 or 45%. The single large gain pulls the overall average upward, distorting the result. This distortion is important when discussing bullish formations. A 600% gain in one chart formation can make a chart pattern appear more successful than it really is. Instead of dropping off samples (by arbitrarily removing the large returns), I use a frequency distribution.

The esoteric name *frequency distribution* is appropriate. To create a frequency distribution, find the highest and lowest values to give you the range. Divide the range by 10 because you want to sort the numbers into 10 bins (10 is arbitrary, but commonly chosen). Then, you do just that—sort the numbers into one of 10 ranges and place them in the bins. When finished, count how often the numbers appear in each bin (the frequency). Note that you do not add up the numbers, you just count how often they appear. It is a lot like seeing troops on a battlefield. You really do not care how tall each one is, only that they outnumber you. The results are the same: You wet your pants and run!

An example makes this clear. Look at Table I.1. Suppose I am studying a chart formation and have the gains for 50 patterns. For simplicity, suppose the gains range from 5% to 95%. The first column in the table holds gains less than 10% and the last column holds gains over 90%. I do not show them all in the table, but I begin placing the gains into the different bins, and the first 10 gains are 8%, 35%, 70%, 13%, 95%, 9%, 6%, 33%, 3%, and 63% (see Table I-1). When I finish placing the gains from the 50 formations into the table and sum the columns, I see which column has the highest frequency. A count of each column appears as the last row in the table and assumes all 50 formations were sorted.

From the numbers in the bottom row, we see that the first column has the highest frequency and represents those formations with gains of less than 10%. We might conclude that if you invested in a similar chart formation, your gain is likely to be between zero and 10%, since that is where most (40%) of the formations reside. The average of the 50 gains will likely be higher than 10%, especially if the higher ranges show either a large number of entries or represent large gains.

I call the column with the highest frequency "the most likely gain." Sometimes the sum of the columns are near to one another and so the most likely gain is a range of values, such as 10% to 20%. Just because a chart pattern has a *most likely gain* of 10% does not mean that you will have a 10% gain from trading your chart pattern. After all, if you trade the pattern well enough and often enough, you should approach the results represented by the average. However, I feel that the most likely gain gives the investor a better understanding of the performance or reliability of the chart pattern.

I use a frequency distribution any time I want to see which range occurs most often (or any time I think outliers distort the average). It is just another perspective, a useful tool in the hands of an investor.

Table I.1
Some Entries in a Frequency Distribution for a Chart Pattern

<10%	11–20%	21–30%	31–40%	41–50%	51–60%	61–70%	71–80%	81–90%	>90%
1									
	1		1			1			1
1									
1			1						
1						1			
...	...	...	...	...	...	...	...	...	...
20	8	6	5	5	1	2	0	0	3

Note: A count of each column, assuming all 50 entries are in the table, appears as the last row.

Investing Using Chart Formations

I could give a dentist's drill to any person walking by, but I would not let him or her near my teeth. This book is just like that. *It gives you the tools to invest successfully.* It suggests which chart patterns work best and which ones to avoid. Whether you can make money using them is entirely up to you.

I call this book an encyclopedia because that is how I use it. Whenever I see a chart pattern forming in a stock I own, or am thinking of buying, I read the applicable chapter. The information refreshes my memory about identification quirks, performance, and any tips on how I can get in sooner or more profitably. Then I search for similar patterns in the same stock (using different time scales), and if that does not work, I search for similar patterns in stocks in the same industry. I look at them closely to determine if their secrets are applicable to the current situation. I try to learn from their mistakes.

At the same time, I am paper trading chart formations in the 250 or so stocks I follow on a daily basis (relax, a review only takes me an hour). Even though I consider myself an experienced investor (after nearly 20 years, what do you think?), the constant paper trading keeps me sharp. It has moved pulling the trigger (buying or selling a stock) from a conscious effort to a rote reflex. The constant checking on how the chart pattern is faring forces me to develop an intuitive feel for the formation, the stock, and the market.

Developing an Investment Style

The question I am asked most often is, *how do I develop an investment style?* It is usually not asked like that. Most take a more direct approach: *How do I make money trading stocks?* When first asked this question, I stumbled over the answer. I think it is like showing four people the color blue and asking them to describe it. One person is color blind so you automatically throw out whatever he says. One says it is solid blue. Another says it is not blue at all but green, while the third says it looks like a combination: blue-green. To each individual, blue looks like blue—just do not try to compare answers.

Developing a trading style is a lot like that. It is an individual endeavor that has a lot in common with experience. I cannot give you experience; I can only suggest ways to acquire your own.

If you read a chapter on a chart pattern and buy the first stock showing the pattern, you will probably be successful. The first trade nearly always works for the novice, maybe even the second or third one, too. Eventually, though, someone is going to pull the rug out from under you (who knows, maybe it occurs on the first trade). You will make an investment in a chart pattern and the trade will go bad. Maybe you will stumble across a herd of bad trades and get flattened. You might question your sanity, you might question God, but one thing is for certain: It is not working!

Most people buy stocks like they buy fruit. They look at it, perhaps sniff it, and plunk down their money. We are not talking about $1.59 here. We are talking about thousands of dollars for part ownership in a company.

If you have ever been a board member, you know what I am talking about. You have a fiduciary responsibility to the people who elected or appointed you to that position. Not only should you study the material handed to you by the staff, but you have to get out in the field and kick the tires. Do not assume that what the staff says is always correct or represents the best solution. Question everything but learn in the process and try to be helpful without being a pest (I always seem to fall into the pest category). As a shareholder—an owner of the company—should it be any different?

I recently was considering buying a position in a company showing an upside breakout from a symmetrical triangle. My computer program told me the company is a member of the machinery industry and further research revealed that it makes refractory products. I continued doing research on the company until the message gnawing at me finally sank in. I did not have the foggiest idea of what a *refractory product* was. Despite my search for an answer, I was not getting the sort of warm fuzzies I usually get when researching a possible investment. So, I passed it over. I am trading it on paper, sure, but not in real life. Call it the Peter Lynch Syndrome: Do not invest in anything you cannot understand or explain in a paragraph. Good advice.

Of course, if you blindly invest in chart squiggles and it works for you, who am I to tell you you are doing it wrong? The fact is, you are not. If you consistently make money at it, then you have developed an investment style that fits your personality. Good for you!

My investment style, as you might have guessed, combines fundamental analysis, technical analysis, emotional analysis, and money management. Just because I rely on technical analysis does not mean I do not look at the price-to-earnings, price-to-sales, and other more esoteric ratios. Then there is the emotional element. After going for months without making a single trade, suddenly a profitable opportunity appears and I will take advantage of it. Three days later, I will want to trade again. Why? Am I trading just because it feels good to be finally back in the thick of things? Am I trading just because the single woman living nearby does not know I exist and I am acting out my frustrations or trying to impress her with the size of my wallet? That is where paper trading comes in handy. I can experiment on new techniques without getting burned. If I do the simulation accurately enough, my subconscious will not know the difference and I will learn a lot in the process.

Once I come to terms with any emotional issues, I look at money management. How much can I realistically expect to make and how much can I lose? What is the proper lot size to take? When should I add to my position? How long will it take for the stock to reach my target and should I invest in a less promising but quicker candidate?

Investing using chart formations is an exercise in probability. If you play the numbers long enough, you will win out. Sure, some of your investments will fail, and you must learn to cut your losses before they get out of hand. But the winners should serve you well, providing you let them ride. Just do not make the mistake of watching a stock double or triple only to reverse course and drop back to where it started. Or worse.

Day Traders, Position Traders, Buy-and-Hold Investors

As I was writing this book, I kept asking myself *what is the time horizon for chart patterns?* Are they best for day traders, position traders, or buy-and-hold investors? The answer I kept coming up with is: Yes! Chart formations can be profitable for day traders—those people who are in and out of a trade during a single day. Many day traders have trading styles that depend on chart formations, support, and resistance. They concentrate on reliable formations that quickly fulfill their measure rule predictions.

For position traders, those who hold the trade longer than a day but not forever, chart patterns offer convenient entry and exit points. I put myself in this category. If the trade goes bad, I am out quickly. If it is profitable, I see no need to cut my profits short. When the gains plateau, or if the stock has moved about all it is going to, I consider moving on. Like the day trader, I try to maximize turns by buying formations that promise reliable returns and reach the ultimate high quickly.

For the long-term investor, chart patterns also signal good entry and exit points. I recently purchased an oil services company knowing that the investment would not make a significant return for 2 or 3 years (I was wrong: It doubled in 3 weeks). It is my belief that in 3 years' time, the stock will be in the 30s, a sixfold increase from its low. It probably will not qualify for a ten-bagger, but it is not small change either. In the short term, the road is going to be rocky and I have added to my position as the stock has come down. Since I am in it for the long term, I have an outstanding order to buy more shares. If this stock goes nowhere, then my analysis of the market trends was wrong, and I will have learned a valuable lesson.

The Sample Trade

The Sample Trade sections that are included in many of the chapters in this book are fictitious except for one: the trade I made using a symmetrical triangle bottom. Each sample trade uses techniques I wanted to illustrate, incorporating fictitious people in sometimes unusual circumstances. Call it poetic license, but I hope they give you some ideas on how to increase your profits or to minimize your losses.

If You Like This Book . . .

When I plunk down my hard-earned money for a book, I expect to get a good value. Many times I have complained that I did not learn anything from a book. At other times, the information is exciting and new, but I cannot use it because the tools the author presented are either too esoteric or too expensive.

I vowed to give the reader real value in this book. The information is easy to find, from the alphabetical chapter layout, to the statistical snapshot at the start of each chapter, to the advice and suggestions all laid out in easy reference tables. The chapters are replete with pertinent illustrations. However, I fear that if you try to read this book from cover to cover, it surely will put even the most hardened insomniac to sleep. Use this book as a reference tool. Refer to it before you make a trade.

If this book saves you money, gives you the courage to pull the trigger with a little bit more confidence, or makes you a whopping profit, then I will have done my job.

1

Broadening Bottoms

Upside Breakouts

Appearance	Price trend is downward, leading to the formation. Megaphone appearance with higher highs and lower lows that widen over time. Breakout is upward.
Reversal or consolidation	Short-term (less than 3 months) bullish reversal
Failure rate	2%
Average rise	25%, with most likely gain less than 10%
Volume trend	Ragged, but usually follows price: rises as prices rise, falls when prices fall.
Percentage meeting predicted price target	59%
Surprising finding	Partial rise at the end of the formation predicts a downside breakout 67% of the time and partial declines predict an upside breakout 80% of the time.
See also	Broadening Formations, Right-Angled and Ascending; Broadening Formations, Right-Angled and Descending; Broadening Tops; Broadening Wedges, Ascending; Broadening Wedges, Descending

Downside Breakouts

Appearance	Price trend is downward, leading to the formation. Megaphone appearance with higher highs and lowered lows that widen over time. Breakout is downward.
Reversal or consolidation	Short-term (less than 3 months) bearish consolidation
Failure rate	6%
Average decline	27%, with most likely decline between 15% and 20%
Volume trend	Ragged, but usually follows price: rises as prices rise, falls when prices fall.
Percentage meeting predicted price target	70%
See also	Broadening Formations, Right-Angled and Ascending; Broadening Formations, Right-Angled and Descending; Broadening Tops; Broadening Wedges, Ascending; Broadening Wedges, Descending

When I compiled the statistics for broadening bottoms, I had to double check the results because they were unusual. Broadening bottoms with downside breakouts outperform those with upside breakouts. Bullish formations typically have gains averaging about 40%; broadening bottoms have gains of just 25%. Bearish formations decline about 20%, on average, but bearish broadening bottoms show losses of 27%. This information tells me that even though you can have an upside breakout, the chart pattern is essentially a bearish one. Prices do not rise all that far before retreating, and when they do break out downward, the decline is above average in severity.

The most likely gains—computed using a frequency distribution of the returns—are about what you would expect: 10% for upside breakouts and a relatively high 15% to 20% for broadening bottoms with downside breakouts.

The failure rates are also remarkably small: just 2% and 6% for upside and downside breakouts, respectively. Anything that is under 20% I consider acceptable.

One surprising finding concerns partial rises and declines, where prices begin moving across the formation to the opposite side, reverse course, and stage a breakout. When prices begin moving down from the top and reverse, 80% of the formations stage an upside breakout. For downside breakouts, the score is a respectable 67% (two out of three show this behavior).

Tour

You may be wondering what differentiates a broadening bottom from a broadening top. A broadening bottom has a price trend leading down to the start of the formation; a broadening top has prices trending up. This differentiation is an arbitrary designation I made to separate the two formation types. I could have used their location in the 12-month price range (those located in the upper half are tops, the rest are bottoms). However, this methodology poses a problem when the formation is near the center of the yearly price range: Is it a top or a bottom?

Using a price trend leading to a formation is no sure-fire solution either. If the price trend is nearly horizontal or changes abruptly just before the formation starts, then I pretend I am a moving average. Would a 90-day moving average be trending up or down? Once you know the trend, you can then figure out whether you are dealing with a broadening top or bottom.

Some maintain that a broadening bottom does not exist. They simply lump every broadening pattern into the broadening top category. I decided to separate the two on the off chance that their performance or behavior differs. You may want to combine the statistics or do your own research.

Figure 1.1 is an example of a broadening bottom. This particular one is called a five-point reversal because there are five alternating touches, two minor lows and three minor highs. A five-point reversal is also rare: I located

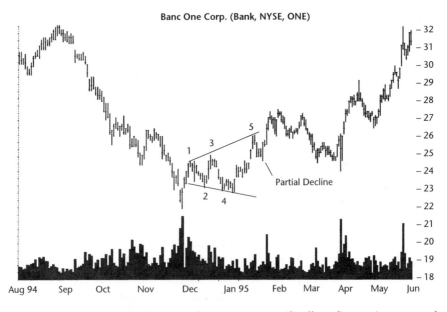

Figure 1.1 A broadening bottom formation, specifically a five-point reversal, so called because of the two minor lows (the even numbers) and three minor highs (the odd numbers).

only 5 in the 77 broadening bottoms I examined. The price trend begins moving down in late August and reaches a low 2 days before the formation begins. Yes, prices do move up for several days, leading to the first touch of the top trendline, but I still consider the overall price trend to be moving down to the formation.

This particular chart pattern shows the partial decline I mentioned earlier. Prices move down from 26 to 24½, then reverse course and shoot out the top. The stock reached a high of 38½ just over a year later.

Identification Guidelines

Table 1.1 lists the identification guidelines for broadening bottoms. As mentioned earlier, a declining price trend precedes a broadening bottom. Even if prices rise just before the formation begins, ignore it. It is still a bottom. This arbitrary designation also makes intuitive sense: A bottom should appear at the end of a downtrend, not when prices are climbing to the moon.

The shape of the formation is distinct. It reminds me of chaos theory where small disturbances oscillate back and forth, then sometimes grow unbounded, wreaking havoc. In the stock market, prices reach new highs then cross over and make new lows. When you draw a trendline across the minor highs and another connecting the minor lows, the formation looks like a megaphone.

The two trendlines drawn across the minor highs and lows are important. The top trendline should slope up; the bottom one should slope down. The diverging trendlines distinguish the broadening bottom from other types of

Table 1.1
Identification Characteristics of Broadening Bottoms

Characteristic	Discussion
Price trend	The intermediate-term price trend should be downward leading to the formation.
Shape	Megaphone shape with higher highs and lower lows.
Trendlines	Prices follow two trendlines: The top one slopes up and the bottom one slopes down.
Touches	Should have at least two minor highs and two minor lows, but not necessarily alternating touches.
Volume	Irregular but usually rises as prices rise and recedes as prices fall.
Breakout	The breakout can occur in either direction and, in some cases, prices move horizontally for several months before staging a definitive breakout.

formations, such as the right-angled broadening formation (which has one horizontal trendline) or the broadening wedge (both trendlines slope in the same direction). So it is important that both trendlines have a slope that is opposite each other (that is, the top slopes up and the bottom slopes down).

A broadening bottom needs at least two minor highs and two minor lows to be a valid formation. Anything fewer means you are incorrectly identifying the formation. What is a minor high or low? A minor high is when prices trend up, then drop back down, leaving a clearly defined peak. A minor low is just the same thing flipped upside down: Prices move lower, then head back up leaving a clearly defined valley. Figure 1.1 shows five minor highs or lows, labeled by numbers. The odd numbers tag the minor highs and the even numbers are the minor lows. Let me stress that the minor highs and lows need not be alternating, as in Figure 1.1. Just as long as you can count at least two peaks and two valleys—wherever they may appear—that is fine.

There is nothing magical in the volume trend. I performed linear regression from the start of each formation to the end point (not the breakout point that is usually a month beyond the end of the formation) and found that volume rises about 58% or 59% (upside and downside breakouts, respectively) of the time. That is just a little better than a coin toss, certainly not strong enough to make a definitive statement.

If you look closely at most broadening bottoms, you will find that volume usually follows price. In Figure 1.1, the price decline between peak 1 and trough 2 shows a receding volume trend. When prices head up from point 2 to point 3, so does volume. One thing is certain: Volume is irregular and the rising-falling trend is only a general guideline often broken. When selecting a broadening bottom, I ignore the volume pattern.

The breakout point is difficult to identify in a broadening formation as it is developing. In retrospect, it is easier. I look for the place where prices pierce the up or down trendline or make an extended move. If prices pierce the trendline, then the penetration point becomes the breakout point. If prices move up and follow along the top trendline without piercing it, then I backtrack to the prior minor high and draw a horizontal line forward in time until prices cross it. When that happens, that is the breakout point.

Let me give you an example. Consider the broadening bottom shown in Figure 1.2. The price trend over the preceding month leading to the formation is downward. The two trendlines outline a widening price pattern as you would expect from a broadening formation. There are more than two minor highs and two minor lows pictured, meeting another criterion mentioned in Table 1.1.

Where is the breakout? This formation is particularly easy. If you extend the top trendline upward, you find that prices rise well above the line, signaling an upside breakout. Then it is just a matter of backtracking to the highest minor high and drawing a horizontal line to determine the actual breakout price. Point A marks the highest high in the formation.

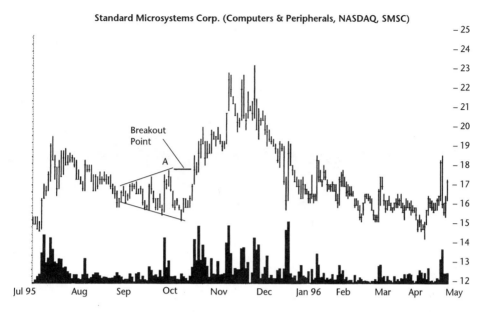

Standard Microsystems Corp. (Computers & Peripherals, NASDAQ, SMSC)

Figure 1.2 A breakout from the broadening bottom occurs when prices rise above the highest high in the formation, shown as point A.

This formation is typical of broadening bottoms. The breakout is upward and occurs at a price of 18. Soon, the stock moves up to $23\frac{1}{2}$, a rise of 23% or nearly the 25% average rise for broadening bottoms with upside breakouts.

Focus on Failures

The good news is that with only three formation failures there is little to worry about. The bad news is that with only three failures there is not much to learn. Figure 1.3 shows one of the three broadening bottom failures. Prices head down and appear to suffer a dead-cat bounce lasting from April to August. I do not recommend taking a position in any stock that shows a dead-cat bounce regardless of how attractive the formation looks. Obey this recommendation for 6 months to a year while the stock recovers and management gets its house in order (or solves the cause of whatever is ailing the stock).

In the 3 weeks before the formation appeared, prices were heading higher in reaction to the dead-cat bounce. In June they moved horizontally from the formation top for over a month before easing down. It was during this time that prices rose above the high of the formation (see point A).

I do not consider prices to break out above or below a formation until the *closing* price moves beyond the formation high or low, which is the case with point A. It is not an upside breakout because the close is at $33\frac{7}{8}$, well below the

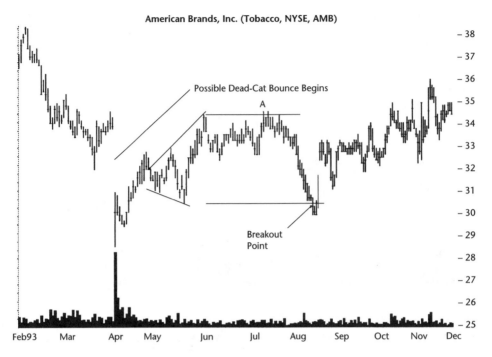

American Brands, Inc. (Tobacco, NYSE, AMB)

Figure 1.3   This broadening bottom forms as part of the recovery process from a dead-cat bounce. When prices close below the formation low, a downside break-out occurs. Point A shows where prices move above the high but do not close higher. The formation is a failure because prices do not move down by more than 5% below the breakout point before reversing.

formation high of $34\frac{1}{4}$. Two days later, it peaks above the high, but the close is also below the formation high.

However, look what happens when prices begin sinking in mid-July. They drop below the formation and close even lower. The price needs to drop below $30\frac{3}{8}$. At its lowest point, it closes at $29\frac{7}{8}$. That is just fifty cents below the low, but it is enough to signal a downside breakout. Within a week of moving below the formation low, prices shoot to 33 and continue up using a slower trajectory.

Figure 1.3 represents what I call a 5% failure. Prices break out lower but fail to continue moving in the breakout direction by more than 5% before heading back up. The reverse is also true for upside 5% failures: Prices move up by less than 5% before turning around and tumbling.

Statistics

Table 1.2 shows general statistics, which I separated into two types: upside and downside breakouts. Since there is a dearth of broadening bottoms in my usual database of 500 stocks over 5 years, I searched the database that I use on a daily

Table 1.2
General Statistics for Broadening Bottoms

Description	Upside Breakout	Downside Breakout
Number of formations: 35 in 500 stocks from 1991 to 1996; 42 in about 300 stocks from 1996; to 1999	45	32
Reversal or consolidation	45 reversals	32 consolidations
Failure rate	1/45 or 2%	2/32 or 6%
Average rise/decline of successful formations	25%	27%
Most likely rise/decline	10%	15% to 20%
Of those succeeding, number meeting or exceeding price target (measure rule)	26 or 59%	21 or 70%
Average formation length	2 months (61 days)	2 months (57 days)
Partial rise but ended down	12/18 or 67%	12/18 or 67%
Partial decline but ended up	16/20 or 80%	16/20 or 80%
Percentage of time there was a trend reversal within 3 months	48%	52%

basis. About 3 years long, it covers approximately 300 stocks and picks up from where the other database ends, so there is no overlap in dates. It is noteworthy that I uncovered more formations (42 versus 35) in the most recent 3 years (900 years of daily price data) than in the prior 5 years (2,500 years of daily price data).

Broadening bottoms with upside breakouts act as reversals of the prevailing trend, whereas those with downside breakouts act as consolidations. This observation makes sense when coupled with the provision that the trend leading to the formation must be downward. Under those circumstances, an upward breakout will be a reversal, whereas a downward breakout is a consolidation.

The failure rate is very low: 2% and 6% for the two breakout types. I think the reason for this occurrence is that at its widest point, a broadening formation represents a strong trend as prices move from one side of the formation to the other. Once this momentum gets under way, it seems likely to continue, and not falter after a breakout occurs (leading to a 5% failure). As the saying goes, a trend in motion tends to remain in motion.

The average rise and decline is 25% for upside breakouts and 27% for downside ones. Both statistics are unusual. The upside breakout is below the usual 40% or so for well-behaved bullish formations. The 27% decline is well above the usual 20% norm for bearish formations. The numbers suggest the broadening bottom is predominantly a bearish formation, resulting in short upside gains or extended downside losses.

The most likely rise or decline is about average: 10% for upside breakouts and a stronger than normal 15% to 20% for downside breakouts. Figure 1.4 shows the results from a frequency distribution of the gains and losses. I call the tallest columns the *most likely gain* or *loss* because they have the highest frequency (the most formations in a given percentage range). It is the return an investor is likely to experience most often.

The figure looks quite irregular with returns forming two humps: one from 10% to 25% and a second from 35% on upward. A small sample size is probably the reason, with just 45 or 32 formations to divide between 10 categories, so view the results with skepticism.

I explain the measure rule in the Trading Tactics section, but it involves computing the height of the formation and adding or subtracting it from the breakout price. The result gives the target price to which the stock will move. For upside breakouts, prices reach the target just 59% of the time, whereas downside breakouts score much better, at 70%. Still, the values are a bit shy of the 80% benchmark I consider a minimum for reliable formations.

The average formation length is remarkably close for both types of breakouts: about 2 months. Since this is an average, the actual lengths can range all over the place. If you can state one thing about broadening formations, it is that they take time to form. The oscillating movements from one side of the formation to the other do not happen overnight.

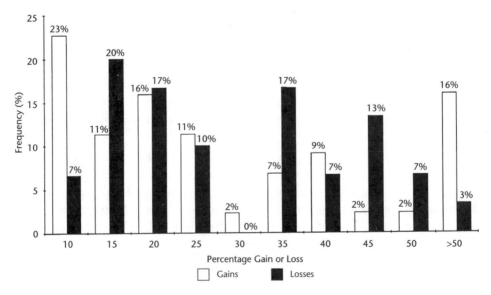

Figure 1.4 Frequency distribution of returns for broadening bottoms.

An interesting anomaly I noticed when scanning broadening formations is the partial rise or decline. Figure 1.1 shows a good example of what I am talking about. Prices begin to move down across the formation to the opposite side, turn around, and break out. When a partial rise occurs, a downside breakout follows 67% of the time—that is two out of three. A partial decline does even better: 80% of the formations showing a partial decline break out upward. So, if you see a partial rise or decline in a broadening bottom, you might want to jump in and trade the stock with the expectation that a breakout will follow.

Some have said that when a broadening formation has an upside breakout (usually a bullish scenario), then the ultimate high is not far away. Soon, they maintain, the stock will reach its high and make an extended downward move. I tested this premise and found that it basically is not true. Only 48% of the formations have the ultimate high (a trend reversal) appear within 3 months of the breakout point. I think anything more than 3 months places a company into another fiscal quarter, and a different dynamic is probably responsible for any downturn.

Table 1.3 shows breakout statistics for broadening bottoms. There were 45 formations with upside breakouts and 32 with downside breakouts. Once a formation ends, the actual breakout occurs about a month later. As explained, I consider a breakout to occur when prices pierce one of the trendlines (and closes outside the trendline) or continue moving along a trendline for an inordinate amount of time. Once a breakout occurs, it takes 4 months for those formations with upside breakouts to reach their ultimate high and 3 months for chart patterns with downside breakouts to reach their ultimate low.

Where in the yearly price range do breakouts occur? To find the answer, I divided the yearly price range into thirds and sorted each formation into the appropriate range. Those formations with upside breakouts appear most often in the center or lower third of the price range, suggesting that the chart pattern itself resides rather low in the price range. This occurrence makes sense

Table 1.3
Breakout Statistics for Broadening Bottoms

Description	Upside Breakouts	Downside Breakouts
Number of breakouts	45 or 58%	32 or 42%
Formation end to breakout	28 days	36 days
For successful formations, days to ultimate high/low	4 months (123 days)	3 months (95 days)
Percentage of breakouts occurring near 12-month low (L), center (C), or high (H)	L40%, C42%, H19%	L78%, C15%, H7%
Percentage gain/loss for each 12-month lookback period	L26%, C23%, H26%	L30%, C28%, H22%

because a requirement of a broadening bottom is that prices trend downward to the start of the formation. Since the breakout point is at the top of the formation, it sometimes pokes the breakout point into the center third of the yearly price range. For downside breakouts, the breakout point is usually in the lowest third of the yearly price range.

Mapping the performance of the chart patterns over the same price range shows that those with upside breakouts split evenly: The lowest and highest thirds of the yearly price range score best with gains averaging 26%. For downside breakouts, those in the lowest third of the yearly price range have the highest average decline: 30%. This percentage tapers off with those formations in the highest third of the range showing the worst returns at 22%.

Table 1.4 shows the last group of statistics—all the formations broken down by alternating touches. This is not the same as the requirement of having two minor highs and two minor lows in each broadening bottom. Two minor highs, for example, can occur without prices declining fully to the opposite side. I counted the number of alternating touches for each formation to see if there is a pattern to the number of touches and the breakout point. As you can see in Table 1.4, formations with four alternating touches break out most often, 13 each. However, formations with upside breakouts commonly range from three to five alternating touches per chart pattern.

What does this mean? If you find a broadening bottom in a stock you own or are considering purchasing, you might try counting the number of alternating touches. If the stock has four touches, then it is more likely to break out on the next crossing of the formation. The table suggests that the likelihood of an upside break out after four alternating touches is 52%, and a downside breakout is 57% (the side of the first touch gives the breakout direction: If the first touch is on the top, then an upside breakout is likely after four touches).

Table 1.4
Frequency Distribution of Successful Formations by Number of Alternating Touches with Cumulative Percentage of Total

Number of Alternating Touches	Number with Upside Breakouts	Number with Downside Breakouts
3	10: 23%	4: 13%
4	13: 52%	13: 57%
5	10: 75%	8: 83%
6	6: 89%	2: 90%
7	3: 95%	3: 100%
8	1: 99%	0: 100%
9	1: 100%	0: 100%

To count the number of touches, refer to Figure 1.1 where I labeled the touches. I do not consider the initial entry point to be a touch. In the figure, the entry point is on the bottom of the formation at about $23\frac{1}{8}$. Prices move to the top and reverse course. That is the first touch. Then prices descend to the opposite side, making another touch. You can see on the fourth touch that prices touch the bottom trendline twice. Between the two touches is a minor high, but since prices did not touch or near the top trendline, no additional touch scores.

Trading Tactics

Table 1.5 shows trading tactics for broadening bottoms. The first tactic is to determine how much money you are likely to make in a trade. The measure rule helps with the prediction. Subtract the highest high from the lowest low in the formation to give you the formation height. Then add the value to the highest high to get the target price for upside breakouts and subtract the height from the lowest low for downside breakouts.

Figure 1.5 makes the computation clear. Point A shows the highest high in the chart pattern at $14\frac{1}{8}$. The lowest low is point B at 12. The formation

Table 1.5
Trading Tactics for Broadening Bottoms

Trading Tactic	Explanation
Measure rule	Compute the difference between the highest high and the lowest low in the formation. Add or subtract this value from the most recent minor high or low, respectively. The result is the target price for upside and downside breakouts.
Go long at the low	Once recognizing a broadening formation, buy after the stock makes its turn at the low.
Long stop	Place a stop-loss order $\frac{1}{8}$ below the minor low to protect against a trend reversal.
Go short at the high	Sell short after prices start heading down at the top.
Short stop	Place a stop $\frac{1}{8}$ above the minor high to protect against an adverse breakout. Cover the short when it turns at the trendline and starts moving up. For a downside breakout, cover as it nears the target price or any support level.
Move stops	Raise or lower the stop to the next closest minor low or high once prices pass the prior minor high (for long trades) or low (for short sales).
Other	If a broadening bottom shows a partial decline or rise, trade accordingly (on a partial decline, go long; on a partial rise, short the stock).

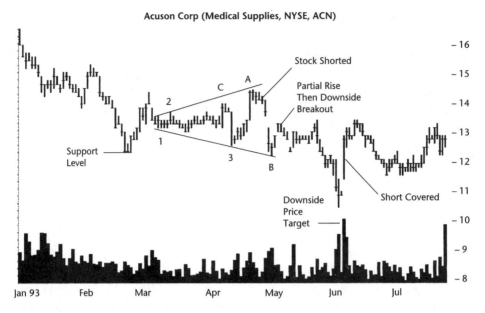

Acuson Corp (Medical Supplies, NYSE, ACN)

Figure 1.5 A broadening bottom with five alternating touches. Expect a downward breakout because a partial rise appears.

height is the difference between the two or $2\frac{1}{8}$. Add the value to the high to arrive at the upside price target. This turns out to be $16\frac{1}{4}$. I compute the downside target by subtracting the height from the lowest low (that is, $12 - 2\frac{1}{8}$ or $9\frac{7}{8}$). You can see in Figure 1.5 that the price never quite reaches the downside price target. For downside breakouts, prices fulfill the measure rule 70% of the time but only 59% of the time for upside breakouts. Both values are shy of the 80% that I like to see for reliable formations.

Once you have uncovered a broadening bottom, with two minor highs and two minor lows, you can think about trading it. When the price bounces off the lower trendline, buy the stock. Sell when it turns down. The downturn may occur as a partial rise partway across the formation or prices may cross completely to the other side, touch the top trendline, and head down. Remember, the formation may stage an upside breakout, so do not sell too soon and cut your profits short.

In a rising price trend, place a stop-loss order $\frac{1}{8}$ below the minor low. Should the stock reverse and head down, you will be taken out with a small loss. As the stock rises to the opposite side of the formation, move your stop upward to $\frac{1}{8}$ below the prior minor low. The minor low may act as a resistance point, so you will be giving the stock every opportunity to bounce off the resistance level before being cashed out.

The trading tactic for downside breakouts is the same. When prices touch the top trendline and begin moving down, short the stock. Place a stop-loss order $\frac{1}{8}$ above the highest high in the formation, then pray that prices decline.

If luck is on your side and the stock heads down, move your stop lower. Use the prior minor high—place the stop $\frac{1}{8}$ above it.

If the stock makes a partial rise or decline, consider acting on it. This is a reliable breakout signal. For partial rises, the signal is right 67% of the time, and for partial declines, it works 80% of the time. Take advantage of it but make sure you place a stop-loss order $\frac{1}{8}$ beyond the nearest resistance point in case the trade goes bad.

Once prices break out and leave the broadening pattern, consider selling if the price nears the target. There is no guarantee that the price will hit or exceed the target, so be ready to complete the trade, especially if there is a resistance level between the current price and the target. The stock may reach the resistance point and turn around.

Sample Trade

Susan likes to think of herself as the brains in the family. While her husband is suffering in foul weather as a carpenter, she is toiling away at her keyboard, a slave to her computer masters. She is an active position trader who is not afraid to short a stock, given good profit potential and an especially weak fundamental or technical situation. It is a stressful life but making money often is.

When she spotted the broadening bottom shown in Figure 1.5, she began her analysis. The stock reached a high of $37\frac{3}{8}$ in early November 1991 and has been heading down ever since. Now, with the formation trading at 14, she wondered how much downside remained. She drew the two trendline boundaries and counted the number of alternating touches (in Figure 1.5, three are labeled as numbers and Point A is the fourth touch).

Since most broadening formations tend to break out after four alternating touches and since the price was near the top of the formation heading down, she guessed that the stock would break out downward on the next crossing. So she sold the stock short and received a fill at $13\frac{7}{8}$. It was a gamble, sure, but one she was comfortable making. In any case, she immediately placed a stop at $14\frac{1}{4}$, or $\frac{1}{8}$ above the high at point A.

Susan was overjoyed to see the stock plummet 2 days later and race across to the other side of the formation, touching the bottom trendline at point B. Usually, her trades are not that easy. She decided to protect her profit and lowered the stop to the nearest minor high, shown as point C, at $13\frac{3}{4}$ or $\frac{1}{8}$ above the high. Then she waited.

The stock bounced off the lower trendline instead of busting through as she hoped. She decided to be patient and see what the stock did next. With her stop-loss order in place at the break-even price, she felt protected and comfortable in letting the trade ride.

The stock bounced off the $12\frac{1}{8}$ support level and did a partial rise before it met resistance and headed back down. Two days after cresting, she made the determination that on the next touch, the stock would pierce the lower trend-line and continue down. She doubled her stake by selling more stock short at $12\frac{3}{4}$. She was wrong. The stock continued down 1 more day before moving up again. Susan adjusted her stop-loss order to include the additional shares, but kept it at the same price level ($13\frac{3}{4}$). Again she waited. The stock slowly climbed and reached a minor high of $13\frac{1}{8}$ before heading down again. This time the decline was swift enough to punch through the resistance zone at the lower trendline.

When the stock descended below point B, Susan lowered her stop-loss order to $\frac{1}{8}$ above that point or $12\frac{1}{8}$. Then she looked at the measure rule for the price target. She calculated a target of $9\frac{7}{8}$ and wondered if the stock would really reach that point. To be safe, she decided to cash out if the stock reached $10\frac{1}{8}$, or $\frac{1}{8}$ above a common support price of 10 (a whole number typically shows support).

When the stock plunged to $10\frac{3}{8}$ on high volume, she wondered if she was looking at a one-day reversal chart pattern. With those formations, it is difficult to be sure if prices would reverse or not. She decided to hold on to her original target.

Two days later, prices zoomed upward and her stop closed out the trade at $12\frac{1}{8}$. She did not make much money (about 9% with a hold time of just over a month), but she gained experience and a few pennies to put in the bank.

2

Broadening Formations, Right-Angled and Ascending

RESULTS SNAPSHOT

Appearance	Horizontal bottom with higher highs following an up-sloping trendline
Reversal or consolidation	Short-term (up to 3 months) bearish reversal
Failure rate	34%
Failure rate if waited for breakout	9%
Average decline	18%, but most likely decline is about 10%
Volume trend	Irregular
Pullbacks	72%
Percentage meeting predicted price target	43%; using half of formation height gives 91% success rating

Before I began studying this formation, I assumed prices would climb away from it, simply because the word *ascending* is in the title. However, that is not how the formation performs. It is a bearish reversal of the short-term price trend. This is not a novel finding, as others have discussed the bearish behavior of ascending broadening formations. The word *ascending* in the title refers to the minor highs that rise over time. The base of this formation is flat but the tops widen out, generally following an up-sloping trendline.

There are a few surprises highlighted by the Results Snapshot. The failure rate falls from 34% to 9% if you wait until after a downside breakout before buying the stock. An improvement is not unusual but such a large one is. The large gain is because I ignore all upside breakouts, and only a few downside breakouts fail, leaving a small failure rate.

The other interesting statistic is the number of pullbacks to the formation base. This number is due, in part, to the messy looking breakout that seems to be quite common with this reversal. After a breakout, prices move horizontally and bounce around a bit before continuing down. The decline is sometimes over quickly as a 10% to 20% decline is easy to erase, fostering a 72% pullback rate.

Tour

Right-angled ascending broadening formations: What does the name mean? *Right angle* implies that it is a member of the triangle family. A horizontal base with an up-sloping hypotenuse forms a right triangle. The third side drops down from the hypotenuse to the base and intersects it at a 90 degree angle, forming the so-called right angle. *Ascending* means that the hypotenuse ascends over time as contrasted with descending broadening formations. *Broadening formation* means that prices make higher highs. Ascending and descending triangles, in contrast, have narrowing price movements.

Figure 2.1 puts the formation in perspective. There are two formations shown in the chart. The first one is somewhat ill-formed but better performing than the second. Both formations have a base outlined by a horizontal trendline connecting the minor lows. The up-sloping trendline skirts the tops of the minor highs. The result is a triangle-appearing formation with prices that broaden out, but do not let the ascending price pattern fool you. This formation is bearish: Prices plummet through the base of the formation most of the time.

Why do right-angled ascending broadening formations form? Consider Figure 2.2. The rise began in mid-December 1991 on volume that was higher than anything seen in almost 2 months. By late February, the stock had reached a new high and was rounding over after meeting selling resistance at 14. The stock returned to the 12¼ level where it found support. At that point, it paused for about 2 weeks and established the base on which a horizontal trendline appears.

The reason for the horizontal trendline is one of perceived value. As the stock approached the $12 level, more investors and institutional holders purchased the stock. The desire to own the stock at what they believed a good

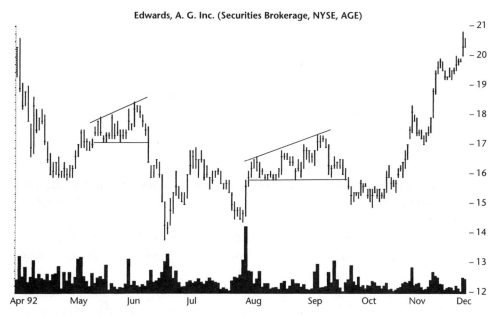

Figure 2.1 Two right-angled ascending broadening formations bounded by a horizontal base and up-sloping trendline. Prices decline after a downside breakout.

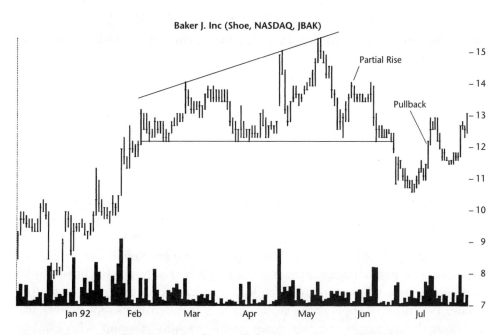

Figure 2.2 A pullback to the base of the formation. Pullbacks occur often in ascending broadening formations.

value outweighed the reluctance of sellers to part with their shares. The demand halted the decline in the stock and eventually sent it skyward again. This happened in mid-April as volume spiked along with the price. The enthusiasm caused the stock to reach a new high. Momentum was high enough so that the next day, prices rose even further before closing lower. With the second peak, a tentative trendline drawn along the tops of the formation sloped upward and gave character to the broadening formation.

The stock moved rapidly back down even as volume increased. This decline stopped before it reached the lower trendline, signaling continued enthusiasm. Prices pushed higher and reached a new high, this one at 15½ on May 6. The up-sloping trendline resistance area repelled any further advance. The stock simply did not have enough upward momentum to push through the selling pressure at the new level.

The next day volume dried up, but there was enough momentum remaining for another try at the summit. When the attempt failed, the smart money headed back for base camp and volume receded even further. As prices collapsed, other investors joined in the retreat and volume moved up. In less than 2 weeks, prices were back at the lower trendline.

Another feeble attempt at a new high floundered on unremarkable volume. The stock moved horizontally and stalled out—a partial rise that often spells trouble for a stock. On June 4, prices dropped on high volume and returned to the horizontal trendline. The stock paused there for just over a week before moving down and punching through the support level at 12¼.

A pullback is quite common for ascending broadening formations, so it is no surprise that the decline quickly faded. After a rapid 13% retreat, the stock turned around and pulled back to the base of the formation. Although it is not shown in Figure 2.2, the stock continued moving up until it began forming another ascending broadening formation in late October with a base at 16½.

The ascending broadening formation represents the desire of investors and traders to own the stock at a fixed price, in this case about 12¼. Their buying enthusiasm pushes prices higher until mounting selling pressure causes a halt to the rise and sends the stock tumbling. With each attempt, fewer people are left willing to sell their shares until they receive an even higher price, so a broadening range of prices appears at the top. Eventually, the buying enthusiasm at the base of the formation collapses and removes the support for the stock. When that happens, the stock punches through the support level and declines. It continues moving down until reaching a point where other investors perceive significant value and buy the stock.

Identification Guidelines

What are the characteristics of an ascending broadening formation? To answer the question, peruse the selection guidelines outlined in Table 2.1. While con-

Table 2.1
Identification Characteristics of Right-Angled Ascending Broadening Formations

Characteristic	Discussion
Shape	Looks like a megaphone with the base of the formation horizontal and bounded on the top by an up-sloping trendline.
Horizontal bottom support line	A horizontal, or nearly so, trendline that connects the minor lows. Must have at least two distinct minor lows before drawing a trendline.
Up-sloping top trendline	An up-sloping trendline bounds the expanding price series on the top. Must have at least two minor highs to create a trendline.
Volume	Irregular with no consistent pattern.
Premature breakouts	Very rare. A close below the horizontal trendline is most likely a genuine breakout.
Price action before breakout	Prices sometimes move horizontally for many months before moving outside the formation high or low. After a breakout, expect a pullback to the base of the formation.
Downside breakout	Prices drop below the horizontal trendline usually accompanied by a surge in volume.
Support and resistance	Follows the two trendlines into the future.

sidering the table, look at Figure 2.3, an ascending broadening formation on a weekly scale. The overall shape of the formation looks like a megaphone with one side horizontal. The bottom of the formation follows a horizontal trendline, while an up-sloping trendline bounds the top side. The top trendline touches at least two minor highs. A minor high refers to a distinct peak that is clearly visible and well separated from other peaks on the chart. The horizontal trendline also shows two minor low touches as prices descend to the trendline. The phrase *minor low* refers to valleys separated and distinct from other troughs. The various touch points help define the boundary of the formation.

As you can see from Figure 2.3 and the preceding charts, the volume pattern is irregular. However, in a majority of cases, volume picks up after the breakout. Although this formation fails to descend, you can still see the volume rise in early 1993.

I define premature breakouts to be prices that close outside the formation boundary but return before the formation ends. Premature breakouts for this formation are rare enough that they should not be of concern.

In some ascending broadening formations, prices make higher highs and form a solid, horizontal base at the start but then move sideways for many

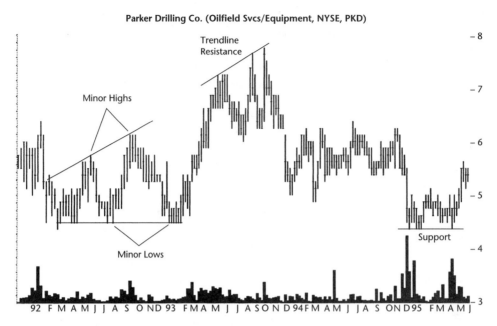

Figure 2.3   Support and resistance areas on a weekly time scale. They appear along the trendline axis and can extend far into the future, as in this case.

months. Eventually, prices rise above the formation top or slide through the bottom trendline and stage a breakout. Once a breakout occurs, typically downward, expect a pullback. A pullback is when prices move lower, then turn around and touch the bottom trendline. Prices may continue moving up but they usually bounce off the trendline and continue back down. A pullback gives investors another opportunity to short the stock or add to their short position. Before investing, however, make sure the pullback is complete and prices are declining once again.

I chose Figure 2.3 because it shows the two common areas of support and resistance. These areas follow the trendlines. Along the base of the formation projected into the future, the support area repels the decline over 2 years after the formation ends. The rising trendline tells a similar tale; it repels prices three times nearly a year later. The implications of this observation can be profound. If you own a stock and it is breaking out to new highs, it would be nice to predict how high prices will rise. One way to do that is to search for formations such as this one. Many times, extending the trendline into the future will predict areas of support and, in this case, resistance.

Although the trendline did not predict the absolute high, it did suggest when prices would stall. The resistance area turned out to be a good opportunity to sell the stock.

Focus on Failures

What can we learn from a review of the failures of this formation? Figure 2.4 shows two broadening formations, the one on the left fails to descend but the one on the right makes up for it. The figure makes one lesson clear: Always wait for a confirmed breakout before taking a position in a stock; that is, wait for prices to fall below the lower trendline before selling your long position or selling short. Even though most ascending broadening formations break out downward, the failure rate is too high to hazard an investment before knowing the outcome. Had you sold the stock short during the first formation, your position would not have made money for almost half a year. Look back at Figure 2.3. A short position in the stock at the low would have lost money for years.

Selling a stock prematurely is just as bad. If you held a long position in the stock shown in Figure 2.4 but sold it during June, you would have regretted your trade until December when the footwear company slipped. Had you waited for a downside breakout, you would have remained in the stock as it ascended. Once the second broadening formation took shape, a sale after prices pierced the horizontal trendline would have gotten you out at a better price.

Figure 2.4 Two broadening formations. The formation on the left fails to descend below the lower trendline. You should wait for the breakout before investing in ascending broadening formations.

Statistics

Table 2.2 shows general statistics. Just like other broadening formations in this book, I did not feel comfortable basing the statistics on my 5-year database alone, so I incorporated my more recent database for 35 additional formations. This gives a total of 216 formations, making ascending broadening formations one of a rare breed. An examination of the formation reveals that 81 are consolidations of the prevailing trend, but the vast majority are reversals, with 135 falling into that category.

I measure the failure rate in two ways. Since I expect a downward breakout, I counted the number of formations in which that is not the case. There are 74, giving a failure rate of 34%. What if the investor waits for a downside breakout? This is called breakout confirmation. It lowers the failure rate to just 9%, well below the 20% maximum I consider reliable formations to possess. That is how I suggest you trade this formation: Wait for a confirmed downside breakout before selling short.

Table 2.2
General Statistics for Right-Angled Ascending Broadening Formations

Description	Statistic
Number of formations in 500 stocks from 1991 to 1996	181
Number of formations in 296 stocks from 1996 to 1998	35
Reversal or consolidation	81 consolidations, 135 reversals
Failure rate	74/216 or 34%
Failure rate if waited for downside breakout	13/151 or 9%
Average decline of successful formations	18%
Most likely decline	10%
Average rise for failed formations	32%
Most likely rise for failed formations	20%
Of those succeeding, number meeting or exceeding price target (measure rule)	60 or 43%
Use measure rule based on half height	125 or 91%
Average formation length	3 months (86 days)
Days to ultimate low	3 months (81 days)

Note: Only two out of three ascending broadening formations work as expected and the most likely decline is meager at 10%.

What is the average decline for formations with downside breakouts? The average is 18%, but the most likely decline is less than 10%. I measure this by sorting the percentage losses into 10 bins and counting the results. The resulting frequency distribution reveals that the most likely loss is narrower than the average, due to a few large declines and several in the 15% to 20% range. Together, they skew the average upward.

I use a similar method for rises from failed formations. A failed formation is one with an upside breakout or downside breakout that fails to continue moving down by more than 5%. The average gain is 32%, with the most likely rise being about 20%. Over a quarter of the formations with upside breakouts (27%) rise over 50%.

The measure rule, which predicts a target price, is disappointing for ascending broadening formations. With only 43% of the formations meeting or exceeding the target, I decided to compute a new measure rule that gives a higher success rate. I computed the formation height by subtracting the lowest low from the highest high and then dividing by two. The target price is the height subtracted from the breakout price. Dividing the height by two is the only change in the formula, and it results in 91% of the formations meeting their price targets.

The average formation length is just under 3 months, long enough to be visible on weekly charts. I also computed the average duration from the end of the formation to the ultimate low. This turns out to be about 3 months.

Table 2.3 shows statistics related to the breakout. There are only 13 formations that break out downward but fail to continue moving down by more than 5% (the so-called 5% failure). This statistic coupled with only three formations breaking out upward and then moving lower suggests that once the formation breaks out, it will likely continue in the breakout direction. For investors, this is worth knowing. Simply trade with the trend.

Almost a quarter (24%) of the formations break out upward, 6% have horizontal breakouts, and the remainder are downside ones (70%). I define a breakout either as prices closing below the lower trendline and moving down or as rising above the highest high in the formation and continuing up. Often prices just meander between the two points for several months before finally staging a breakout.

Throwbacks are prices that break out upward and return to the top trendline. They occur 44% of the time for those formations with upside breakouts. The average time to complete a throwback is less than 2 weeks (11 days). That is the time it takes to flip around and touch the top trendline. I exclude any throwback taking longer than 30 days. If it takes over a month for prices to return, I consider it normal price action and not due to a throwback.

Pullbacks are more prevalent. A pullback is when prices break out downward and quickly return to the formation base. Seventy-two percent of the formations with downside breakouts experience pullbacks. The average time to

Table 2.3
Breakout Statistics for Right-Angled Ascending Broadening Formations

Description	Statistic
Downside breakout but failure	13 or 9%
Upside breakout but failure	3 or 6%
Upside breakout	52 or 24%
Horizontal breakout	13 or 6%
Downside breakout	151 or 70%
Throwbacks	23/52 or 44%
Average time to throwback completion	11 days
Pullbacks	109/151 or 72%
Average time to pullback completion	12 days
For successful formations, days to ultimate low	2 months (69 days)
For failed formations, days to ultimate high	3 months (96 days)
Percentage of downside breakouts occurring near the 12-month price low (L), center (C), or high (H)	L22%, C42%, H36%
Percentage loss for each 12-month lookback period	L17%, C18%, H18%
Volume for breakout day and next 5 days compared with day before breakout:	157%, 170%, 122%, 107%, 99%, 102%
Percentage of successful breakouts occurring on high (H) or low (L) volume	H74%, L26%
Percentage of failed breakouts occurring on high (H) or low (L) volume	H80%, L20%

Note: Downside breakouts experience pullbacks 72% of the time.

complete a pullback to the formation base is 12 days. Again, I remove any pullback over 30 days.

Ascending broadening formations reach their ultimate low or high quickly, in about 2 or 3 months, respectively. The abruptness of the decline is due in part because these formations do not decline very far (the most likely decline is just 10%), so it takes less time to reach the ultimate low.

Most ascending broadening formations occur near the middle of the 12-month price range, as measured from the base of the formation. The largest declines split evenly at either 17% or 18% throughout the various yearly price ranges. In essence, it does not matter where in the yearly price range the formation occurs; the performance is the same (unlike some other formations that show definite trends).

Although volume appears irregular throughout the formation, I did examine the volume surrounding the breakout day. When compared with the day before the downside breakout, the day after the breakout typically shows the largest volume. It measures 70% above the benchmark but recedes as the week wears on. This pattern is not unusual as investors seem to sell once they realize a confirmed breakout is underway.

I next wanted to know if there is a relationship between high and low breakout volume and the success or failure of the formation. In both upside and downside breakouts, high volume is present. Thus, breakout volume, by itself, is not a key to the success or failure of a particular formation. Put another way, just because you see a low-volume downside breakout is no reason to suspect prices will soon recover.

Trading Tactics

Table 2.4 lists trading tactics. The measure rule predicts the price to which the stock will decline. Compute the difference between the highest high and the horizontal trendline in the formation. Subtract this value from the value of the horizontal trendline, and the result is the target price. The target should serve as a minimum price move to expect, but with ascending broadening formations, prices *usually* miss the target (only 43% of the time is the target met).

For a more conservative approach, try calculating the formation height and dividing by 2, then subtract the value from the horizontal trendline. Prices reach the nearer target almost all the time (91%). The closer target value also serves as a wake-up call indicating that the formation is probably not worth trading—at least on the downside.

Table 2.4
Trading Tactics for Right-Angled Ascending Broadening Formations

Trading Tactic	Explanation
Measure rule	Compute the formation height from highest high to the horizontal trendline. Subtract the height from the value of the horizontal trendline and the result is the target price. More accurate targets use a formation height divided by 2.
Wait for confirmation	Since this formation has a comparatively high failure rate (34%), you should always wait for the breakout to drop (close) below the horizontal trendline or above the up-sloping trendline.
Buy upside breakouts	Once a breakout occurs, prices continue in the direction of the breakout. Buy an upside breakout and expect a 20% gain.
Ignore downside breakouts	Most breakouts occur downward but the resulting loss is about 10%. Such a small decline is usually not worth the risk of a short sale.

Note: The best approach is to buy after an upside breakout.

Figure 2.5 Ascending broadening formation. Predicted price targets using half and full formation heights. A broadening top formation appears in late October.

Figure 2.5 makes the measure rule clear. The height of the formation is the difference between the highest high (34⅛) and the trendline price (29¼), or 4⅞. Subtract the result from the trendline price, giving a target price of 24⅜. Since prices only reach the target 43% of the time, I show a second one. The nearer target uses half the formation height, or 2.44, to give a price target of 26.81. Prices reach the closer target 91% of the time after a downside breakout.

With an overall failure rate of 34%, there is a high likelihood of an adverse breakout from this formation. Therefore, an investor should always wait for a breakout before making a trade.

Although the formation usually breaks out downward, you can try buying the stock on an upside breakout. This approach allows you to go with the usual trend in prices (up), and the most likely gain is about 20%. Again, be sure to wait for the upside breakout (when prices close above the up-sloping trendline) since only one in three breakouts is upward.

I do not suggest trying to capitalize on a downward breakout by shorting the stock. Although the likelihood of a decline is good, the most likely decline is only 10%, hardly enough to warrant the extra risk of a short sale. If you already own the stock and do not want to experience a 10% or perhaps larger decline, then you can either wait for a confirmed downward breakout (wait for prices to *close* below the lower trendline) or sell the stock as it nears or touches the upper trendline and begins heading down.

Sample Trade

Palmer is a wiry sort of guy, one who acts as if he has swallowed too much caffeine. I am sure you have met the type. Faced with the situation shown in Figure 2.5, he took swift, decisive action. At point A, where the stock touched the top trendline, he quickly sold it short and received a fill at $33\frac{3}{8}$. He placed a stop at 34 in case the trade went against him. Then he waited.

It did not take long for the stock to cross the formation and reach the horizontal trendline. Unfortunately, Palmer did not use an order to automatically cover his short at $29\frac{3}{8}$ (the value of the trendline). So when prices bounced off the low, he covered his short the following day, shown as point B, at $30\frac{1}{2}$. Immediately, he went long and bought the stock at the same price.

Palmer placed a stop-loss order just below the horizontal trendline, at $29\frac{1}{4}$, just in case. Then he extended the top trendline but worried that the stock might not reach its predicted high. He opted to put a target price at $\frac{1}{8}$ below the old high at point A. In less than a week, the stock reached his target and sold at $33\frac{1}{2}$ (point C). Since the stock was still showing an upward bias, he laid back for a bit and waited for the trend to reverse. Three days later he sold the stock short again at 33. This time, he put a sell order at $\frac{1}{8}$ above the lower trendline at $29\frac{1}{2}$. The trade went against him. It rose to 34 and oscillated up and down for nearly 3 weeks, never quite reaching his stop-loss point of $34\frac{3}{8}$. Then the stock plunged and zipped across the formation. It hit his target price at point D, and he covered his short.

Sensing a shift in the investment winds, he went long on the stock at the same price but put a stop loss $\frac{1}{8}$ below the lower trendline. The following day prices hit his stop at $29\frac{1}{4}$ and he took a small loss. For some unexplained reason, Palmer walked away from the stock at this point. Perhaps it was the small loss he incurred on his last trade, or perhaps he was just running low on caffeine.

3

Broadening Formations, Right-Angled and Descending

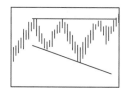

RESULTS SNAPSHOT

Appearance	Horizontal top with lower lows following a down-sloping trendline
Reversal or consolidation	Short-term (up to 3 months) reversal
Failure rate if waited for downside breakouts	3%
Failure rate if waited for upside breakouts	19%
Average rise	27%, but most likely rise is between 20% and 30%
Average decline	19%, but most likely decline is about 10% to 15%
Volume trend	Irregular
Pullbacks	33%
Throwbacks	23%
Percentage meeting predicted price target	69% for successful downside breakouts, 89% for successful upside breakouts

Before I begin studying a particular formation, I review the available literature and determine in which direction the breakout is likely to occur. For the general class of broadening formations, the breakout pattern is said to be down: Broadening formations are apparently bearish. After I completed the statistics for this formation, however, I surprisingly found that more right-angled descending broadening formations broke out upward than downward. At first I logged the upside breakouts as failures since I expected the correct breakout to be down. I was wrong. I reexamined the literature and discovered that descending broadening formations could break out either way. So I reworked the statistics and scanned all the formations again to make sure that they agreed with the new methodology.

The first thing you may notice in the Results Snapshot is that the reversal or consolidation line does not say whether the formation is bullish or bearish. That is because it depends on the breakout direction. If the breakout direction is up, which it is 57% of the time, the formation is bullish. For downside breakouts, which occur 37% of the time, the formation is bearish. The balance have horizontal breakouts or no specific breakout direction.

Only those formations that break out and continue in the opposite direction classify as failures (the so-called 5% failures). I consider failure rates below 20% acceptable, so the rates for both breakout directions score well.

The average rise (27%) or decline (19%) are both below par. Bullish formations usually have gains of about 40% and bearish ones decline about 20%, on average. However, the most likely rise for upside breakouts is reassuring, at 20% to 30%. Since the tabulation uses a frequency distribution of gains, the numbers imply that the returns distribute evenly. In other words, there are few large gains to skew the average upward. Unfortunately, with a small sample size, the numbers are suspect. I believe the most likely rise is probably in the 10% to 15% range, as it is for most other bullish formations.

The measure rule works out better for this formation than for the ascending broadening formation. For downside breakouts, almost 7 in 10 (69%) meet or exceed their price targets, whereas 89% of upside breakouts reach theirs. The first statistic is borderline, but the second is reassuring. The meaning is also clear: Wait for the breakout, then place a trade in the direction of the breakout.

Tour

What do descending broadening formations look like and why do they form? Figure 3.1 is an example of the chart pattern. The characteristic flat top and down-sloping bottom are apparent in the figure. These are the two key ingredients. Prices at the top of the formation reach the same price level before declining. Over time, a horizontal trendline can be drawn connecting them.

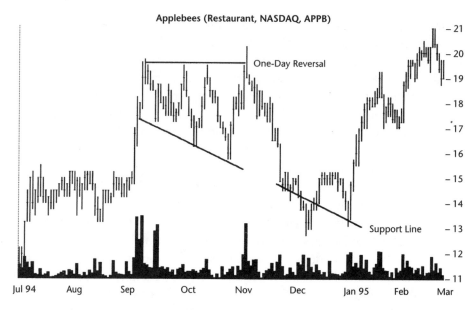

Figure 3.1 Descending broadening formation. A horizontal trendline along the top and a down-sloping trendline connecting the minor lows is characteristic of this chart pattern. The extended, down-sloping trendline shows future support and resistance zones. A one-day reversal appears on November 3 when prices pushed above the formation top on high volume, but closed at the low for the day.

Along the bottom of the formation, the minor lows touch a down-sloping trendline before prices rebound. Eventually, prices break out of the formation by either closing above the top trendline or below the bottom one.

In Figure 3.1, the breakout is downward since prices close below the lower trendline. I require prices to *close* outside the trendline so that is why the peak on November 3 does not classify as an upside breakout. On that day, prices close at 19, the low for the day, and below the top trendline value of about 19½.

I mentioned in the Results Snapshot discussion that most descending broadening formations have upside breakouts. Figure 3.2 shows an example. The top of the formation is well formed with several minor peaks reaching the same price level. However, three one-day touches compose the lower trendline. A trendline touch is a trendline touch regardless of whether it is composed of one-day spikes or many days of consecutive touches.

Figure 3.2 shows a broadening formation with an upside breakout providing a 10% rise in just over 2 weeks. During May 1996, the stock reached 29, for a 25% gain. The figure also shows one of the few throwbacks to the top of the formation. This one occurs almost 4 weeks after the breakout. I consider throwbacks or pullbacks that occur later than 30 days to be just normal price action, not due to the throwback or pullback. This one just makes the cut at 27 days.

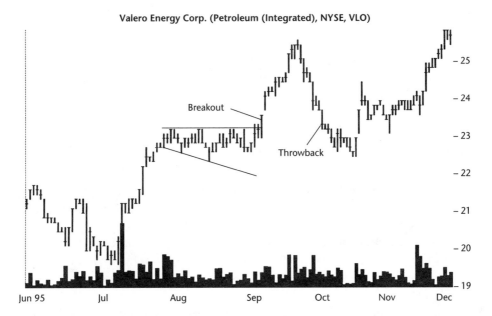

Figure 3.2 Another descending broadening formation but this time the breakout is upward. Almost 4 weeks after the breakout, prices throw back to the formation before ultimately moving higher.

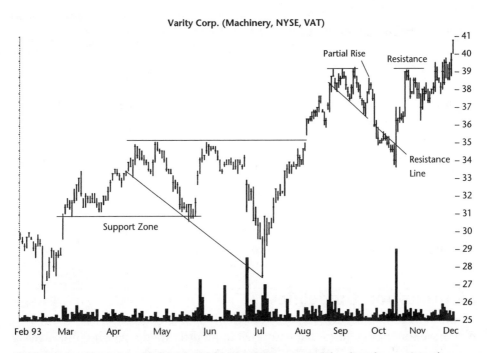

Figure 3.3 Two descending broadening formations. The first formation shows a trendline rebound resulting from an earlier support zone. The second formation shows a partial rise that often precedes the ultimate breakout. Shown are two resistance areas that parallel the trendlines.

Why do these chart patterns form? Look at Figure 3.3. During 1993, the stock entered the first formation in early April and moved higher on moderate volume until it reached about 35. There, investors selling the stock matched buyers eager to own the security and the rise stalled. It traveled sideways until May 10 when it moved below the prior minor low. As the stock approached the 31 level, it entered a support zone set up by the retracement in mid-March. The decline stalled and moved sideways for several days. Due to the support level, many investors believed that the decline was at an end and the stock would move higher. It did. As volume climbed, the price gapped upward and quickly soared back to the old high.

The stock ran into selling pressure from institutions and others trying to sell a block of shares at a fixed price. The available supply halted the advance. Prices hung on for a few days, moved a bit lower, and paused before beginning a rapid decline to a new minor low.

As volume climbed, the stock declined until it touched the lower trendline, a region of support. Suspecting an oversold stock, investors bought and forced it higher again. When the stock reached the old high, there were fewer shares available for purchase. Apparently, those investors and institutions who were trying to get 35 a share for their stock sold most of their shares in the preceding months. Soaking up the available supply, the stock gapped upward and closed above the old high. An upside breakout was at hand.

The stock moved higher but soon formed another descending broadening formation. This one was compact and tight but had bearish implications. When the stock tried to reach the top trendline but could not, the partial rise foretold the coming decline. The stock plunged through the lower trending in late September and continued lower.

If you look at both formations, their stories are nearly the same. There is a supply of stock available at a fixed price. After exhausting the supply, prices either rise above the top trendline or decline below the lower one. The determination on which way things will go is not clear. Sometimes the supply overwhelms buyers and the stock declines, unable to recover as it pierces the lower trendline. At other times, the supply gives out and enthusiastic buyers jump in and push the price higher.

Identification Guidelines

Are there some guidelines that can assist in identifying descending broadening formations? Yes, and Table 3.1 outlines them. The shape of the formation looks like a megaphone with the top held horizontal. Prices climb until they touch the top trendline, then reverse direction. On the lower edge, prices decline making a series of lower lows until they touch the lower trendline.

When two minor highs achieve the same, or nearly the same, price level, you can draw a horizontal trendline connecting them. The same applies to the

Table 3.1
Identification Characteristics of Right-Angled Descending Broadening Formations

Characteristic	Discussion
Shape	Looks like a megaphone, tilted down, with the top of the formation horizontal and bounded on the bottom by a down-sloping trendline.
Horizontal top resistance line	A horizontal line of resistance joins the tops as a trendline. Must have at least two distinct touches (minor highs) before drawing a trendline.
Down-sloping trendline	The expanding price series is bounded on the bottom by a down-sloping trendline. Must have at least two distinct minor lows to create a trendline.
Volume	Irregular with no consistent pattern.
Premature breakouts	Very rare. A close outside the trendline is most likely a genuine breakout.
Breakout	Prices can break out in either direction, usually accompanied by a rise in volume that soon tapers off.
Partial rise or decline	For an established formation, when prices climb toward the top trendline or decline toward the lower one but fail to touch it, prices often reverse direction and break out of the formation.
Support and resistance	Follows the two trendlines into the future but is sporadic.

down-sloping trendline: It requires at least two distinct touches before drawing the trendline. There is usually ample time to recognize a broadening formation, and many times there are more than two touches of each trendline.

There is no consistent volume pattern for this formation. Sometimes volume tapers off, then explodes on the breakout day, just like its triangle cousins. At other times, volume starts slowly and rises as the breakout nears. Of the two scenarios, the first is slightly more likely than the second, at 53% versus 47%. Since the numbers are so close, I attach no significance to them.

A partial rise, as shown in Figure 3.3, or a partial decline is often a clue to the ultimate breakout direction. When prices curl around on a partial rise or decline and return to the trendline, they usually break out immediately (that is, without crossing the formation again). We will see in the Statistics section that this behavior is more reliable for upside breakouts than downside ones.

The trendlines, when projected into the future, can sometimes act as areas of support or resistance, depending on which side prices are approaching (Figures 3.1, 3.3, and 3.7 show examples). Sometimes the support or resistance level is active for months or even years at a time.

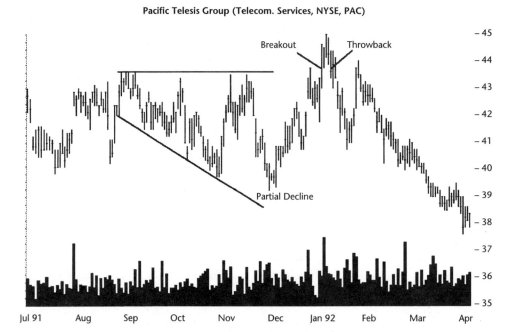

Figure 3.4   A descending broadening formation with prices that fail to continue moving up. The partial decline suggests the ultimate breakout will be upward, but the rise falters and prices move downward instead.

Focus on Failures

Since descending broadening formations can break out in either direction, I show both views of failed breakouts. The first one, Figure 3.4, is characterized by the telltale partial decline in late November. From there, the stock climbs and eventually pierces the top trendline. Once prices close above the trendline, you would expect them to throw back to the formation top then continue higher or simply move upward from the start. In this situation, prices stall at 45 and return to the formation proper—a classic throwback. Unfortunately, instead of rebounding and heading higher like a typical throwback, the stock continues down. It does some more work inside the formation before shooting out the other side in a straight-line run.

Had you purchased after the upside breakout, you would have seen the stock decline from a purchase point of about $44\frac{1}{2}$ to a low of $36\frac{7}{8}$. Even a stop at the lowest point of the formation would have gotten you out at 39, still a hefty decline. However, if you held onto the stock (not recommended, by the way), it would have been rewarding. The low occurred on April 8 (not shown), and it turned out to the be the lowest price reached during the next 2 years. The stock hit its peak in early November 1993 at a price of nearly 60.

Healthcare Compare (Medical Services, NASDAQ, HCCC)

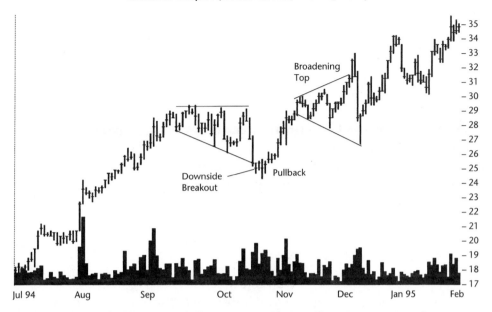

Figure 3.5 A downside breakout failure. Prices decline by less than 5%, turn around, and eventually hit 42. Such failures are rare, but they do occur, so stop-loss orders are always important. A broadening top formed in early November.

Figure 3.5 shows a more harrowing tale because it involves a short sale. Investors watching the sharp 2-day decline beginning October 14, 1994, would be tempted to short the stock the next day. Had they done so, or even waited a few days, they would have bought near the low. From that point on, the stock moved higher before it pulled back into the formation where it meandered before ultimately soaring out the top. If you were a novice investor and had not placed a stop on your short sale, your loss would have taken you from a low of $24\frac{3}{8}$ to 53, where it peaked near the end of the study.

Figure 3.5 represents a failure type I call 5% *failures*. That is when prices break out in a given direction and move less than 5% before moving substantially in the direction opposite the breakout. It is the type of failure that can turn a small profit into a large loss if stops are not used.

If there is a bright side to the situations shown in Figures 3.4 and 3.5, it is that failures do not occur very often. The statistics follow, but for now let me point out that 8 of every 10 formations continue moving in the direction of the breakout. The two figures should also provide a warning to make sure you use stops to limit your losses. Even if you choose to hold a mental stop in your head, be sure to pull the trigger once things begin to go bad.

Statistics

Table 3.2 shows the general statistics for the descending broadening formation. Of the broadening formations studied so far, this one is the most rare. I used two databases and still found only 82 formations in over 3,000 years of daily price data. Rare indeed!

There are 6 more reversals (44) than consolidations (38) of the trend. Like most formations, I compare the trend before entry to the chart pattern to the trend after the breakout.

A formation classifies as a failure if prices do not continue in the breakout direction by more than 5% before reversing course. Table 3.2 provides the failure rate for the two breakout directions. Upside breakouts show failure

Table 3.2
General Statistics for Right-Angled Descending Broadening Formations

Description	Statistic
Number of formations in 500 stocks from 1991 to 1996	69
Number of formations in 296 stocks from 1996 to 1998	13
Reversal or consolidation	38 consolidations, 44 reversals
Failure rate for upside breakouts	9 or 19%
Failure rate for downside breakouts	1 or 3%
Average rise for successful upside breakouts	27%
Most likely rise	20% to 30%
Average decline of successful downside breakouts	19%
Most likely decline	10% to 15%
Of those succeeding, number meeting or exceeding price target for upside breakouts (measure rule)	34 or 89%
Of those succeeding, number meeting or exceeding price target for downside breakouts (measure rule)	20 or 69%
Average formation length	3 months (88 days)
Days to ultimate high, upside breakouts	5 months (148 days)
Days to ultimate low, downside breakouts	3 months (86 days)
Success rate of partial rises	7/12 or 58%
Success rate of partial declines	18/23 or 78%

Note: This rare formation does better on an upside breakout, scoring an average 27% gain.

rates of 19%, whereas downside breakouts fail 3% of the time. I consider values below 20% to be acceptable, so both directions score well.

The average rise from an upside breakout is 27%, but the most likely rise is between 20% and 30%. Since I base the most likely rise on a frequency distribution of the gains for each formation, I must caution you not to place too much emphasis on this particular statistic. There are simply too few samples in the study on which to base any firm conclusions. The highest frequency, for example, is seven hits in the 30% range followed by five hits in the 20% category. A frequency of 30 or higher, by comparison, is reliable. Other formation types typically have likely rises in the 10% to 15% range, and, if enough samples were present in this formation, that is the performance I would expect.

The average decline from a downside breakout is 19%. This figure is close to the range (20%) of most bearish formations. The most likely decline is in the 10% to 15% range, and the same warning applies to the sample size. Even though the samples may be few, the results are typical and there appear to be no surprises.

Use the measure rule to predict the target price for the formation after a breakout. The Trading Tactics section of this chapter explains the calculation more thoroughly, but the measure rule simply computes the height of the formation and adds or subtracts the result from the breakout price. Often, the target price serves as a minimum expected price move. For this formation, upside breakouts hit or exceed their targets 89% of the time and downside breakouts reach or decline below their targets 69% of the time. I like to see values above 80%, so the downside target performance is low.

The average formation length is about 3 months (88 days), and takes between 3 months (for downside breakouts) and 5 months (for upside breakouts) to reach their ultimate price values. The longer time it takes to reach the ultimate high makes sense since the percentage gain (27%) is larger than the decline resulting from downside breakouts (19%). In short, it takes longer to go further.

A partial rise, where prices begin heading up from the lower trendline and approach but do not touch the top trendline before turning down, results in a downside breakout 58% of the time. That is not much higher than guessing the result of a coin toss. However, partial declines—which is the same curling action only from the top of the formation—result in an upside breakout 78% of the time. That is high enough on which to base a trading strategy: If you see a partial decline that begins heading up, buy the stock.

Table 3.3 outlines the breakout statistics. Since this formation can break out either way, the failure statistics appear in two categories: upside and downside failures. Only 19% of the formations breaking out upside fail to continue moving up by more than 5%. For downside breakouts, only one formation fails to continue moving down. Remember, the sample size is only 47 and 30 samples for upside and downside breakouts, respectively.

Table 3.3
Breakout Statistics for Right-Angled Descending Broadening Formations

Description	Statistic
Upside breakout but failure	9 or 19%
Downside breakout but failure	1 or 3%
Upside breakout	47 or 57%
Horizontal breakout	5 or 6%
Downside breakout	30 or 37%
Throwbacks	11 or 23%
Average time to throwback completion	11 days
Pullbacks	10 or 33%
Average time to pullback completion	14 days
Percentage of upside breakouts occurring near 12-month price low (L), center(C), or high (H)	L0%, C26%, H74%
Percentage gain for each 12-month lookback period	L0%, C41%, H25%
Percentage of downside breakouts occurring near 12-month price low (L), center (C), or high (H)	L40%, C40%, H20%
Percentage loss for each 12-month lookback period	L31%, C14%, H10%
Volume for breakout day and next 5 days compared with day before breakout	143%, 105%, 96%, 92%, 83%, 71%
Percentage of successful breakouts occurring on high (H) or low (L) volume	H76%, L24%
Percentage of failed breakouts occurring on high (H) or low (L) volume	H70%, L30%

Note: For a traditionally bearish formation, there are more upside breakouts than downside ones—57% versus 37%.

There are three types of breakouts: up, horizontal, and down. Most of the formations (57%) break out upward. Downside breakouts are next at 37%, with the remainder breaking out horizontally. If you are wondering what a horizontal breakout looks like, see Figure 3.6. As shown, after the formation ends, the stock moves horizontally for about 6 months before closing above the top of the formation. Even so, in about 4 months, prices dip below the formation top again. Not until July 1994 do prices stage a strong rally and move decidedly higher.

Throwbacks and pullbacks are rare, being found in only 23% and 33% of the formations, respectively. The duration of pullbacks, at 14 days, is slightly above normal (10 to 12 days) for all formation types. I ignore any throwback or pullback beyond 30 days because I consider it normal price action and not due to a throwback or pullback.

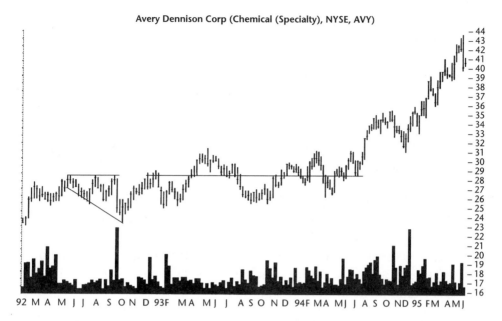

Avery Dennison Corp (Chemical (Specialty), NYSE, AVY)

Figure 3.6 A horizontal breakout. Prices do not rise above or fall significantly below the formation for months on end, shown on a weekly scale.

Most of the upside breakouts (74%) occur near the yearly high. This observation suggests descending broadening formations appear at the end of an upward trend. Note that there are no formations appearing near the yearly low. Since I use the top of the formation as the benchmark, this result is not unusual.

The best performance from upside breakouts occurs when the breakout is in the middle third of the yearly price range; why is unclear. In other formations, the tendency is for the upper range to perform best, possibly due to momentum players taking hold of the stock and bidding it higher after an upside breakout. Since this formation broadens downward, it might scare off investors even after an upside breakout.

Downside breakouts tell a different tale. Most breakouts split between the lower and center third of the yearly price range. The highest price range garners only 20% of the formations since I use a breakout below the lowest formation low in the computation. True to form, formations breaking out downward in the lowest third of the yearly price range perform best, with an average decline of 31%. This performance suggests that it is better to short stocks making a new yearly low than a yearly high.

Breakout volume is surprising in that it peaks then quickly recedes. The breakout volume is, on average, 43% above the prior day (or 143% of total volume) and diminishes rapidly and steadily to 71% a week later. I did not separate the volume numbers into the two breakout types; the numbers apply to all descending broadening formations.

The breakout volume for successful breakouts is indistinguishable from unsuccessful ones. Both occur on high volume about three-quarters of the time. So, if you see weak volume on an upside breakout, do not be too concerned about an impending failure.

Trading Tactics

Table 3.4 outlines trading tactics for descending broadening formations. Figure 3.7 illustrates the computation of the measure rule. Compute the formation height by first taking the difference between the highest high ($49\frac{1}{2}$) and the lowest low ($43\frac{1}{2}$). Add the result (6) to the value of the horizontal trendline to get a target price of $55\frac{1}{2}$. Prices reach this target during mid-March 1996 as the stock climbs on its way to 60.

Table 3.4
Trading Tactics for Right-Angled Descending Broadening Formations

Trading Tactic	Explanation
Measure rule	Compute the formation height by taking the difference between the horizontal top and the lowest low in the formation. For upside breakouts, add the result to the value of the horizontal trendline. For downside breakouts, subtract the value from the lowest low. The result is the expected target price.
Wait for confirmation	It is unclear which way prices will break out, so it is best to wait for prices to close outside the trendlines. Once they do, expect prices to continue moving in the direction of the breakout. Place your trades accordingly.
Stops	Once a breakout occurs, consider the opposite side of the formation as the stop-loss point. However, in many cases you will want something closer to your purchase price so look for nearer support or resistance zones. Once the stock moves substantially, advance the stop to the break-even point.
Intraformation trading	Once you recognize a broadening formation, consider placing a trade as prices reverse course at the trendline. Go long at the bottom and short at the top but be sure to use stops to protect against an adverse breakout.
Partial decline	Buy a stock if you see a partial decline once prices curl around and begin heading back up.

Note: Always wait for the breakout, then trade with the trend.

If the stock breaks out downward, the measure rule computation is nearly the same. Subtract the formation height from the lowest low giving a target price of 37½. Be aware that upside breakouts are more likely to reach their targets (89%) than downside ones (69%).

Once you know the target price, you can make a profit and loss assessment for the trade. What is the likely downside move compared with the target price? Does the potential profit justify the risk of the trade? For Figure 3.7, there is support in the 46 to 47 area. Examining the peaks and valleys of the prior price action determines support and resistance levels. In March 1995 (not shown in Figure 3.7), there is an area of congestion bounded by a symmetrical triangle with an apex at about 46. Additional resistance appears in July and October, as shown in Figure 3.7. Together, the 46 to 47 area makes a good location for a stop-loss order.

Let us say the stop is 45¾, just below the bottom of the support area. If the trade happens at 50½, which is the close the day after the upside breakout, that gives a potential loss of less than 10%. With a target price of 55½, or 10% upside, the win/loss ratio is an unexciting one to one. In such a situation, you

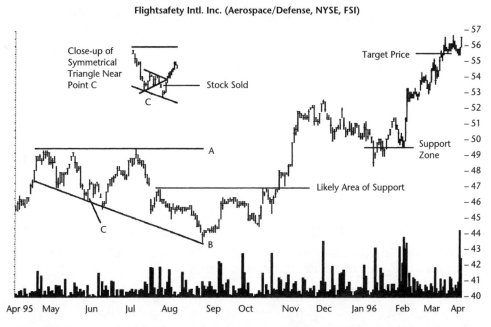

Figure 3.7 An upside breakout from descending broadening formations. To compute the measure rule for upside breakouts from descending broadening formations, find the difference between the high and low in the formation, denoted by points A and B. Add the result to point A to get the target price. It took almost 7 months for prices to exceed the target. A small symmetrical triangle appears at point C.

could either tighten your stop by moving it higher (and risk getting taken out by normal price action) or look elsewhere for a more profitable trade. Remember there is no rule that says you have to place a trade.

The Statistics section of this entry introduces you to partial declines—78% of the time an upside breakout follows. That is high enough to risk a trade. If you see a partial decline occur (and it really does not matter how far down it dips, so long as it is not touching or coming too close to the lower trendline) and it begins heading back up, buy the stock. With any luck, it will shoot out the top of the formation and continue higher. As always, be sure to place a stop-loss order and raise it as prices climb.

Sample Trade

Ralph is a formation trader with a measure of experience milking chart patterns for all they are worth. When he noticed what he thought was either a descending broadening wedge or a right-angled descending broadening formation, he bought the stock. His order, placed at point C in Figure 3.7 (46⅜), was just after the stock bounced off the lower trendline.

He monitored it closely, and watched the stock move up the very next day, then ease lower. After a few days, Ralph saw a symmetrical triangle form and he became worried. Those formations, he reasoned, usually follow the trend and the trend was downward. When the stock moved below the lower triangle trendline, Ralph sold the stock and received a fill at 46½.

When he erased the lines from his computer screen and looked at the fresh price chart, he knew he had made the right decision because a partial rise, such as where the triangle formed, usually portends an immediate, downside breakout.

Sure enough, the following day prices dropped even further, tagging the broadening formation trendline again. Then they rebounded. In the coming days, he watched as prices surprisingly zipped across the formation and touched the top trendline. Ralph took a small loss after factoring in commissions. Did he sell too soon or was he just being cautious, and what lessons did he learn? Spend some time searching for the answers in your own trades and you will rapidly become a better investor.

4

Broadening Tops

RESULTS SNAPSHOT

Upside Breakouts

Appearance	Price trend is upward, leading to the formation. Megaphone appearance with higher highs and lower lows that widen over time. Breakout is upward.
Reversal or consolidation	Short-term (less than 3 months) bullish consolidation
Failure rate	4%
Average rise	34%, with most likely gain between 10% and 15%
Volume trend	Ragged, but usually follows price: rises as prices rise, falls when prices fall.
Percentage meeting predicted price target	75%
Surprising finding	Partial rise at the end of the formation predicts a downside breakout 65% of the time and a partial decline predicts an upside breakout 86% of the time.
Synonyms	Expanding triangle, orthodox broadening top, and five-point reversal
See also	Broadening Bottoms; Broadening Formations, Right-Angled and Ascending; Broadening Formations, Right-Angled and Descending; Broadening Wedges, Ascending; Broadening Wedges, Descending

Downside Breakouts

Appearance	Price trend is upward, leading to the formation. Megaphone appearance with higher highs and lower lows that widen over time. Breakout is downward.
Reversal or consolidation	Short-term (less than 3 months) bearish reversal
Failure rate	4%
Average decline	23%, with most likely decline between 10% and 20%
Volume trend	Ragged, but usually follows price: rises as prices rise, falls when prices fall.
Percentage meeting predicted price target	64%
See also	Broadening Bottoms; Broadening Formations, Right-Angled and Ascending; Broadening Formations, Right-Angled and Descending; Broadening Wedges, Ascending; Broadening Wedges, Descending

Broadening tops, not surprisingly, act a lot like broadening bottoms. What separates a top from a bottom is the price trend leading to the chart pattern. For tops, the intermediate-term price trend is upward; for broadening bottoms, it is downward. This is an arbitrary distinction I made just to see if the two formations act differently. In answer to the question you have probably posed right now: The two formations act similarly, but their performance differs slightly.

Broadening tops divide into two types: those with upside breakouts and those with downside ones. You can see in the Results Snapshot that the failure rates are the same for both: 4%. That is a very good number. I consider failure rates below 20% to be acceptable.

The average gain for upside breakouts is subpar at 34%. Well-behaved bullish formations usually score about a 40% rise. Downside breakouts from broadening tops perform better than normal with a 23% loss. The usual loss for all bearish chart patterns is about 20%.

The broadening top formation performs better than some chart patterns regarding the measure rule. The rule estimates a target price for the stock. Three out of every four broadening tops (75%) with upside breakouts meet or exceed their price targets, whereas 64% of those formations with downside breakouts meet or exceed theirs. Still, I consider values above 80% to be reliable, so the formation comes up a bit short.

This formation does excel in predicting the breakout direction. When a partial rise or decline occurs—that is, when prices move toward the opposite side, then reverse before touching the trendline—it is a breakout signal. For partial rises, the breakout direction is downward. A downside breakout follows those formations showing a partial rise 65% of the time. Partial declines score even better when they break out upward. Almost all the formations (86%) showing a partial decline correctly predict an upside breakout.

Tour

Broadening formations come in a variety of styles and names. There are the broadening tops and bottoms, right-angled ascending and descending, expanding triangle, orthodox broadening top, and five-point reversal. The last three, expanding triangle, orthodox broadening top, and five-point reversal, are synonyms of the broadening top formation, with the last two being based on five turning points.

For a quick tour of the formation, look at Figure 4.1. The stock began an uphill run in December 1994 and paused for about 2 months in May and June. Then it continued its climb and reached a high in mid-September at a price of 53¾. Holders of the stock, witnessing the long run, decided to sell their shares and the stock headed lower. On September 25, 1995, volume spiked upward and halted the decline. Investors, seeing a 40% retrace of their gains from the

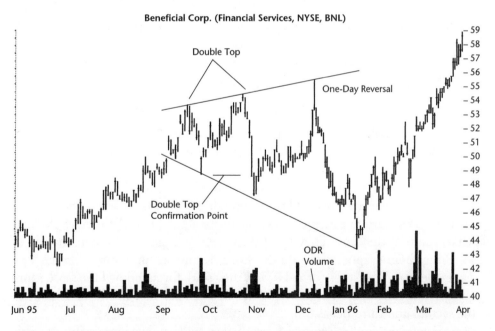

Figure 4.1 A double top changed into a broadening formation. The one-day reversal appeared as the third peak after an unsustainably quick price rise. The broadening top formation marked a struggle between eager buyers and reluctant sellers at the lows and the quick-to-take-profit momentum players at the peaks.

June level, apparently thought the decline overdone and purchased the stock, sending prices higher.

Prices peaked at a higher level, $54\frac{1}{2}$, on October 19. Many diligent investors probably suspected that a double top was forming and promptly sold their holdings to maximize their gains, sending the price tumbling. Prices confirmed the double top when they fell below the confirmation point, or the lowest low between the two peaks, at $48\frac{3}{4}$.

Volume picked up and the struggle between supply and demand reasserted itself. The decline stalled as traders willing to buy the stock overwhelmed the reluctance to sell. The stock turned around and headed higher. By this time, chart followers could draw the two trendlines—one across the twin peaks and another below the two valleys. The broadening top formation was born. Astute traders probably jumped on the bandwagon at this point and purchased the stock. They wanted to play the anticipated rise as the formation broadened out. The stock cooperated and moved higher, reaching the top trendline once again at a new high of $55\frac{1}{2}$.

The steepness of the ascent in the latter stages was unsustainable. The peak looked like a one-day reversal, with a close near the low of the day and a wide daily price swing. However, volume was unconvincing. It was higher that day than during the prior week, but it certainly was not of the caliber of the late November spike. In any case, the stock tumbled downward and soon reached a new low of $43\frac{1}{2}$, stopping right at the down-sloping trendline. Once the stock began moving higher, the momentum players jumped on board and volume increased along with the price. Buying enthusiasm and rising momentum pushed the stock higher, climbing through the top trendline. An upside breakout occurred.

Throughout the various peaks and troughs of this formation, there was a struggle between buyers and sellers. Near the lows, the buyers believed the stock was oversold and they eagerly bought it. At the top, they quickly sold their shares and pocketed their handsome profits. This selling, of course, sent the stock back down.

Some investors, seeing the stock decline below their purchase price and still believing that the stock had value, bought more. The behavior also helped turn the stock around at the lows and probably explained their heightened nervousness at the tops. They wanted to keep their gains this time, instead of watching them evaporate should the stock decline again. Once a higher high was evident and the stock turned lower, they sold, forcing down the stock more quickly this time and on higher volume. You can see this on the declines after the second and third peaks.

The formation in Figure 4.1 also makes evident that identifying the ultimate breakout is exceedingly difficult. It appears that each new high or new low may be the final breakout. Only when prices move in the opposite direction is it clear that prices will not break out. We explore ways to profit from this behavior in the Trading Tactics section.

Table 4.1
Identification Characteristics of Broadening Tops

Characteristic	Discussion
Price trend	The intermediate-term price trend leading to the formation should be up.
Shape	Megaphone shape with higher highs and lower lows. Five-point reversals have three peaks and two troughs.
Trendlines	Prices are bounded by two trendlines: The top one slopes up and the bottom slopes down.
Touches	Should have at least two minor highs and two minor lows, but not necessarily alternating touches.
Volume	Irregular but usually rises as prices rise and recedes as prices fall.
Breakout	The breakout can occur in either direction and, in several cases, prices move horizontally for several months before staging a definitive breakout.

Identification Guidelines

Table 4.1 shows the identification guidelines for the broadening top formation. The first criterion is the price trend leading to the formation. This price trend is what differentiates a broadening top from a broadening bottom. For a broadening top, the price trend should be leading up to the formation, not down as in its bottom counterparts. This is just an arbitrary designation I have chosen to distinguish the two formations.

Trendlines drawn across the peaks and valleys resemble a megaphone. Higher highs and lower lows make the formation obvious to those versed in spotting chart patterns. The slope of the trendlines is what distinguishes this formation from some others. The top trendline must slope up and the bottom one must slope down. When one of the two trendlines is horizontal or nearly so, the formation classifies as a right-angled ascending or descending broadening formation. When the two trendlines slope in the same direction, the formation is a broadening wedge.

There should be at least two minor highs and two minor lows before the chart pattern becomes a broadening top. A minor high is another name for a distinct price peak. A minor low refers to the valley pattern as prices descend to a low then turn back up. Again, the minor low should be a distinct trough that is easily recognizable. Figure 4.1 shows three minor highs touching the top trendline and four minor lows either nearing or touching the bottom trendline. The minor highs and minor lows need not alternate as prices crisscross the formation.

Linear regression on the volume trend shows it splitting evenly between trending up and trending down. If you look closely at most broadening top chart patterns, you will see that volume typically follows price. When prices rise, so does volume; when prices fall, volume recedes. In Figure 4.1, volume rises as prices climb into the beginning of the formation and round over at the peak. Then volume declines, following prices lower. However, I attach no real significance to volume in a broadening top formation.

A breakout happens when prices move outside the trendline boundaries or follow a trendline for an extended time. In Figure 4.1, if you extend the top trendline upward, it will intersect prices at about 58. Prices push through this level and move higher. When a breakout occurs, I consider the actual breakout price to be the value of the highest peak in the formation. In Figure 4.1, for example, the breakout price is $55\frac{1}{2}$, or the high at the early December peak.

For an example of how to apply the various guidelines, consider the broadening top shown in Figure 4.2. At first glance, it looks like a large megaphone with price trends that generally follow two sloping trendlines. The top trendline slopes upward and the bottom one slopes downward, each intersecting the minor highs or lows at least twice. Prices, over time, form higher highs and lower lows until they breakout of the formation, generally moving beyond the line of trend before retracing.

The volume pattern is irregular but generally rises as prices move up and recedes as prices move down. Figure 4.2 shows this quite clearly. During the rise in mid-November, for example, volume jumped upward as prices peaked, then just as quickly receded as prices declined.

Where in the yearly price range does the formation appear? Broadening tops, as you would expect, appear near the top of a price range or near the top of an upward trend.

The only characteristic not discussed so far is that the formation is usually horizontal and symmetrical. The formation does not appear as an ascending or descending broadening wedge, with both trendlines either sloping up or both sloping down. In broadening formations one trendline *must* slope up while the other *must* slope down.

Orthodox broadening tops and five-point reversals describe the same type of formation. They are simply broadening tops that have three minor highs and two minor lows. Figure 4.3, for example, falls into this category. Other than the name, I found no substantial difference between broadening tops and orthodox broadening tops or five-point reversals.

Some analysts say five-point reversals are bearish indicators, that the formation predicts a downward breakout. My statistics, admittedly on only 30 formations, suggest this is untrue. Sixteen break out upward and the others break out downward. The sample size is too small to make a definitive statement, but the numbers do reflect the general trend of upside breakouts for all broadening top formations, that is, slightly more than half (53%) break out upward.

Figure 4.2 The broadening top has higher highs and lower lows as the price action widens over time.

Figure 4.3 A weak example of a five-point reversal or orthodox broadening top. It has three minor highs and two minor lows composing the five turning points.

Focus on Failures

What does a failure look like? Look at Figures 4.3 and 4.4, two examples of broadening patterns that fail to continue in the expected direction. Figure 4.3 shows a sharp downward thrust that pierces the trendline on high volume. Since this is clearly outside the lower trendline, and coupled with the failure of prices to attain the upper trendline, a downside breakout is at hand. But the downward movement stalls on very high volume, turns around, and moves higher. This is an example of a 5% failure, that is, prices break out then move less than 5% in the direction of the breakout before heading substantially in the other direction. In this case, the breakout direction is downward, but prices recover before moving lower than 5% below the breakout point.

Contrast the behavior shown in Figure 4.3 with that shown in Figure 4.4. I include this chart because I have noticed that a large number of broadening formations act this way. Instead of making a clear up or down thrust that pierces the trendline, prices move horizontally for months on end before finally moving above or below the formation highs or lows.

In the case of Figure 4.4, prices decline below the low in early July and halt. They climb for a bit then recede again and reach a new low in early August. Another recovery sees prices rise no higher than 44 for about half a year before finally staging an upside breakout.

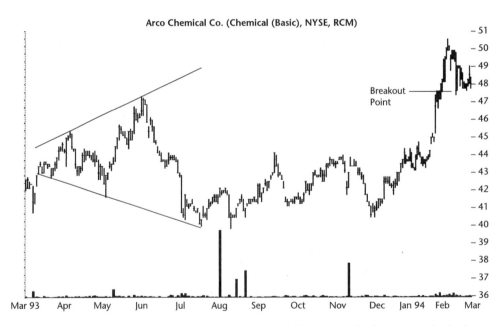

Figure 4.4   Prices in this broadening top moved horizontally for 6 months before staging an upward breakout. This is a common occurrence with broadening tops.

Even Figure 4.3 shows a consolidation pattern for 6 weeks after prices pierce the trendline. Prices do not move very high before stalling and essentially travel sideways for an extended period. Then a new trend sets in and prices finally break out in the genuine direction.

The last point I want to make is that failures are rare. Only 8 occurred in nearly 200 formations. Once a broadening formation breaks out, it continues moving in the same direction.

Statistics

As I completed my first pass through my main database, it became clear that I was not finding many broadening formations. Only about 25% of the stocks I examined had usable formations. So I expanded the sample size by adding the database that I use on a day-to-day basis. This latter database is smaller, with nearly 300 stocks, but it is only about 3 years long. This compares with the 5-year, 500 stock database used throughout this book. Together, there still were not that many formations, only 189, but the sample size is sufficiently large enough to draw valid conclusions. Table 4.2 shows the general statistics.

Does the formation perform as a reversal or consolidation of the existing trend? Just over half (100) are continuations of the trend (consolidation) and

Table 4.2
General Statistics for Broadening Tops

Description	Upside Breakout	Downside Breakout
Number of formations: 132 in 500 stocks from 1991 to 1996, 57 in about 300 stocks from 1996 to 1999	100	89
Reversal or consolidation	100 consolidations	89 reversals
Failure rate	4/100 or 4%	4/89 or 4%
Average rise/decline of successful formations	34%	23%
Most likely rise/decline	10% to 15%	10% to 20%
Of those succeeding, number meeting or exceeding price target (measure rule)	72 or 75%	54 or 64%
Average formation length	2.5 months (72 days)	2 months (67 days)
Partial rise but ended down	45/69 or 65%	45/69 or 65%
Partial decline but ended up	25/29 or 86%	25/29 or 86%
Percentage of time there was a trend reversal within 3 months	41%	47%

the others (89) are reversals. The formation's behavior depends on the direction of the breakout. Formations with upside breakouts act as consolidations of the trend because one of the criteria for a broadening top is that the price trend leading to the formation is upward. Thus, they continue the upward trend; broadening tops with downside breakouts act as reversals.

Some analysts say that broadening top formations are inherently bearish reversals, but I found little to support that claim. I prefer to think of them as weakly performing bullish patterns (those with upside breakouts) or mildly strong bearish patterns (downside breakouts).

The failure rate is not easy to determine since the formation has no indication in which direction it will ultimately break out, so I used a 5% price movement as the benchmark. This breakout means that if prices decline below (or rise above) the lowest (highest) point in a formation by less than 5%, then turn around and head in the opposite direction, the formation is a failure.

The reasoning for this approach is simple. If you purchased the stock after an upside breakout but the stock failed to continue rising, then you would be disappointed and may even take a loss. Given such constraints, out of 189 formations, only 8 fail to continue moving in the direction of the breakout. That is a good score.

Once a breakout occurs, what is the average move? For formations with upside breakouts, the average rise is 34%, whereas formations with downside breakouts decline by 23%. The average gain is a bit under the 40% that bullish formations exhibit, but the average decline is above the 20% loss for bearish chart patterns.

Large percentage moves can skew the overall average, so I computed the most likely rise and decline using a frequency distribution. Figure 4.5 shows a graph of the results. Large gains are the case with upside breakouts as you can see in the figure. Twenty-one percent of the formations with upside breakouts have gains over 50%. If you ignore this column, then the next highest one is for returns in the 10% to 15% range. I consider this range to be the most likely return that investors can expect. If you are lucky, you will have a formation that does considerably better, just do not bet that farm that it will happen.

For downside breakouts, the most likely loss ranges between 10% and 20%, which includes the three tallest columns in the graph; they are near enough to one another that I lump them together. Over half the formations (56%, or the sum of the first three columns) with downside breakouts have returns less than 20%.

The measure rule applies just as it does for most formations. Find the formation height and add the result to the highest point in the formation for the upside target and subtract the result from the formation low for the downside target.

You can see in Table 4.2 that 75% of the upside breakouts reach the target price. However, downside breakouts fare much worse, with 64% reaching or exceeding their targets. I consider values above 80% to be reliable, so the

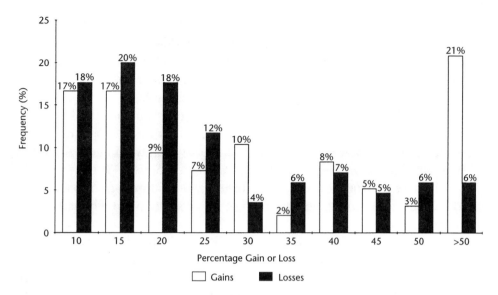

Figure 4.5 Frequency distribution of returns for broadening tops. The most likely gain for upside breakouts is 10% to 15%, and the loss is likely to be in the 10% to 20% range after a downside breakout.

broadening top does not quite make the grade. I explain the measure rule further in the Trading Tactics section.

The average formation length is nearly the same for both of the breakout types at 72 and 67 days. The formation is long enough to show up on the weekly charts.

Partial rises and declines are a reliable way to determine the breakout direction and they allow an investor to take a position in the stock early. Figure 4.3 shows a partial rise that correctly predicts a downside breakout. For broadening tops that show a partial rise, where prices leave the lower trend and rise up but do not come close to the top trendline, a downside breakout follows 65% of the time. The results are even better with partial declines, which are dips from the top trendline that move downward without coming close to the lower trendline. Partial declines correctly predict an upside breakout 86% of the time.

Some analysts suggest that broadening formations are bearish formations. Even when they do not work, analysts maintain, a trend reversal soon appears. I scanned my database and looked at all formations to see if this is true. Only 41% of the formations with upside breakouts reach their ultimate high in less than 3 months. This means that less than half suffer a trend reversal in under 3 months. Downside breakouts perform marginally better, at 47%, but still not high enough to support other analysts' premise. It is my belief, supported by the statistics, that even when things do not work out as expected, a broadening top does not presage the end of the trend.

Table 4.3 shows breakout statistics. Figure 4.4 is a good example of the distance between where the formation ends and where the breakout occurs. For both breakout types, it takes over a month to reach the breakout point, on average. I consider the breakout to be where prices either rise above the highest high in the formation or drop below the lowest low.

In the 100 formations I examined with upside breakouts, it takes nearly half a year (166 days) to reach the ultimate high. Downside breakouts, on the other hand, reach their ultimate low much more quickly, in about 4 months (129 days). This makes sense because it takes longer to rise 34% than to fall by 23% (the average gain or loss from Table 4.2). Both durations measure from the breakout point to the ultimate high or low point (a point where a significant trend change occurs).

Where in the prior 12-month price range do breakouts occur? Most (94%) upside breakouts happen in the upper third of the price range. Although this may sound suspicious, it is reasonable. Consider that upside breakouts occur along the top of the formation placing them closer to the top of the yearly price range. Since broadening tops occur near the end of an upward trend, it should come as little surprise that most (49%) downside breakouts from broadening tops appear in the center third of the yearly price range. The highest third follows with 40%.

Substituting the gains or losses for prices shows interesting results. Upside breakouts from broadening tops climb 35% on average when they occur in the upper third of the yearly price range. Downside breakouts split evenly with about 22% in each category (with a slight edge, 24%, going to the center third).

Table 4.3
Breakout Statistics for Broadening Tops

Description	Upside Breakouts	Downside Breakouts
Number of breakouts	100 or 53%	89 or 47%
Formation end to breakout	46 days	34 days
For successful formations, days to ultimate high/low	5.5 months (166 days)	4 months (129 days)
Percentage of breakouts occurring near 12-month low (L), center (C), or high (H)	L0%, C6%, H94%	L10%, C49%, H40%
Percentage gain/loss for each 12-month lookback period	L0%, C24%, H35%	L22%, C24%, H22%

Note: The best performing broadening tops with upside breakouts are those that appear in the upper third of the price range.

Table 4.4 shows statistics for alternating touches. I wanted to determine if there is a relationship between the number of alternating touches and the breakout. A frequency distribution of the number of alternating touches reveals that most formations have four alternating touches before staging a breakout (either upward or downward). Some, however, go on to cross the formation several more times before ultimately breaking out.

How did I count the number of alternating touches? Look back at Figure 4.2. The numbers represent the alternating touches. I usually tag the first touch on the side opposite the entry point. In Figure 4.2, the entry is from the bottom, but it almost makes its way to the top, so I decided to call the first alternating touch on the bottom. Figure 4.3 shows an easier example of counting alternative touches.

Returning to Table 4.4, turning the numbers into percentages gives an investor a better feel for how likely a breakout will be. For example, if you have a formation with the first touch on the top and a total of five alternating touches, then the likelihood of a downside breakout (since the last touch is also on the top) is 95% should prices cross the formation again. That is a safe bet, but it does not mean that the formation will break out downward. Since prices are already at the top, they could do a partial decline, turn around, and break out upward.

There is also the belief among some technical analysts that the breakout will occur opposite the side with the most touches. For five-point reversals (which have three touches on top and two on the bottom), the breakout should be downward. Of the 30 five-point reversals in my database, only 47% breakout downward.

What about inverted five-point reversals? Such a formation has two minor highs and three minor lows. The statistics do show that these formations break out upward twice as often as downward (68% versus 32%). However, I

Table 4.4
Frequency Distribution of Successful Formations by Number of Alternating Touches with Cumulative Percentage of Total

Number of Alternating Touches	Number with Upside Breakouts	Number with Downside Breakouts
3	8: 8%	8: 9%
4	42: 52%	35: 51%
5	31: 84%	21: 75%
6	12: 97%	17: 95%
7	3: 100%	4: 100%

Note: The table indicates that most successful broadening tops have four alternating touches before breaking out.

hasten to add that there are 36 additional formations that have more than 5 touches. Some five-point reversals, inverted or not, go on to bounce off the opposite side several more times. Once that happens, of course, they are no longer five-point reversals. My conclusion is that there is nothing magic about five-point reversals or their inverted brethren. They are all broadening formations and there is really nothing special about them that I have been able to determine.

Trading Tactics

Table 4.5 outlines trading tactics for broadening top formations. The first thing to consider about trading tactics is the measure rule. The measure rule predicts the price to which the stock will move. For many formations, one simply computes the height of the formation and adds the result to the breakout price. Broadening formations are not much different. Consider Figure 4.6. The height of the formation is the difference between the highest high ($12\frac{1}{8}$) and the lowest low (10), or $2\frac{1}{8}$. For upside breakouts, add the height to the

Table 4.5
Trading Tactics for Broadening Tops

Trading Tactic	Explanation
Measure rule	Compute the height between the highest high and the lowest low in the formation. Add or subtract the height from the highest high or lowest low, respectively. The results are the target prices for upside and downside breakouts.
Go long at the low	Once a broadening top appears, buy after the stock makes its turn at the low.
Long stop	Place a stop-loss order $\frac{1}{8}$ below the minor low. Should the stock reverse course, you will be protected.
Go short at the high	Sell short after prices start heading down at the top.
Short stop	Place a stop $\frac{1}{8}$ above the minor high to protect against an adverse breakout. Cover the short when it turns at the bottom trendline and starts moving up. For a downside breakout, cover as it nears the target price or any support level.
Move stops	Raise the stop to the next lowest minor low (for prices moving up) or next highest minor high (for prices moving down) as prices cross the formation.
Other	Go long if a broadening top shows a partial decline. Consider adding to your position once it makes an upside breakout.

highest high in the chart pattern giving a minimum price move of 14¼, as shown in the figure.

How do you make use of the measure rules? Imagine that you are considering purchasing the stock. Since it is never clear which way a broadening formation will ultimately break out, it is difficult to pick a good long-term entry point. The easiest way to invest using the formation is to buy just after the stock turns at the bottom trendline.

Since a broadening formation requires two points along the top trendline and two along the bottom before the formation appears, point A in Figure 4.6 shows one likely investment location. Before placing the buy order, compute the target price using the measure rule. The target price will help you determine if the potential gain is worth the risk. In the example shown in Figure 4.6, the purchase price is about 10⅜ and the target price is 14¼, a 37% move. The stop loss should be 9⅞, for a potential loss of 5%, which gives a reward-to-risk ratio of 7 to 1, more than enough to risk a trade.

On an upside breakout, prices reach the target 75% of the time, on average. This means you need not feel pressured to sell too early. Let the stock wind its way upward while you watch your profits grow.

Buy the stock as soon after it touches the lower trendline and moves higher. Place a stop-loss order ⅛ below the lowest low (⅛ below point A). Should prices drop, your position will likely be sold before a large loss occurs.

Figure 4.6 Use the measure rule to compute the target price. First, compute the formation height from the highest high to the lowest low then add or subtract the height from the highest high or lowest low, respectively. Depending on the breakout direction, the result is the expected target price.

If the stock fails to break out upward, perhaps you can capture the ride up to the upper trendline for a 20% rise. Buy when prices turn upward at the lower trendline, then be ready to sell once prices reach the old high. Prices may pause for a bit before moving higher and tagging the top trendline or they may reverse at this point. Make sure your stops have been raised to protect some of your profits.

What about the measure rule for downside breakouts? Again, the formation height is $2\frac{1}{8}$. Subtract $2\frac{1}{8}$ from the lowest low (10) to arrive at the target price of $7\frac{7}{8}$. If prices break out downward, they should reach $7\frac{7}{8}$. However, the reliability of the target price for downside breakouts is just 62%—not very reassuring.

For short positions in broadening tops, open the short after the price touches point B and begins heading down. Place a stop $\frac{1}{8}$ above the highest high ($12\frac{1}{4}$ in this case) to limit your losses. Lower your stop to the next minor high or apex of the broadening top (either $11\frac{7}{8}$ or $11\frac{1}{8}$ in this case) once the stock nears point A. Sometimes the stock will not make it down to the trendline before beginning to move up. At other times, there is a lengthy pause before prices turn around or continue down. A lower stop-loss point helps you achieve at least some measure of profit.

The last trading tactic is to look out for partial rises or declines, which occur when prices begin to cross the formation but do not come close to the opposite side. Instead, prices reverse course and break out soon after. When you see a partial rise or decline, place a trade once the stock reverses course. If a breakout happens, then consider adding to your position.

Sample Trade

Sandra has always taken a liking to the stock market but never had enough money to jump into the game. Still, she paper traded stocks just to get a feel for the markets and dreamed of one day trading for real. Then her parents died in a tragic car accident with a drunk driver.

The year that followed was tough for Sandra because she was close to them and missed them dearly. She bought a dog to help fill the void in her life, but it was not the same. Fortunately, her parents had insurance and a few savings, all of which she inherited. After paying taxes to the government, she suddenly realized there was no need to continue working. "Why wait till I'm older when my health might be gone or I might die young like my parents?" She retired at 29.

Sandra knew that if she cut her expenses to the bone she could live off the savings. She paid off the mortgage, the car loan, credit card balances, and stopped going out to eat in restaurants. Her lifestyle changed to accommodate the limited income but one thing she would not compromise: her paper trading.

After opening a brokerage account, she waited for the perfect trade and finally found it; the one shown in Figure 4.6. She saw the broadening top formation early enough to buy into the stock before the breakout. Two days after the stock reached point A, she placed her order and received a fill at $10\frac{1}{2}$. Immediately, she placed a stop $\frac{1}{8}$ below the lowest low, or $9\frac{7}{8}$ for a potential loss of 6%.

Sandra applied the measure rule and was looking at an upside target of $14\frac{1}{4}$. If everything worked as expected, that would give her a return of over 35%. After she placed the trade, she sat back and waited but kept an eye on the price action. When prices paused at the high of the formation, she wondered if the trend was going to reverse course. She considered taking her profits and running but decided against it. After a few days, she recognized a flag formation and hoped that it represented a half-mast move (the flag being a halfway point in the upward move). If that was true, she could expect a climb to $13\frac{1}{4}$ (that is the distance from the top of the flag ($12\frac{1}{8}$) to the start of the move at 10 projected upward using the lowest low in the flag at $11\frac{1}{8}$).

A few days later, the stock not only fulfilled the measure rule for the flag formation, but for the broadening top as well. Did Sandra sell? No. Since the stock was moving up, she wisely decided to let her profits ride. However, she did raise her stop to $11\frac{7}{8}$, or $\frac{1}{8}$ below the formation high. She viewed this point as a support zone and hoped that should the stock retreat to that level, it would rebound before taking her out.

In mid-February, just after the second peak around 17 appeared, she recognized a double top formation. She moved her stop to $\frac{1}{8}$ below the confirmation point, or $14\frac{1}{4}$. About two weeks after raising her stop, her position sold when the stock plunged from the prior close at $15\frac{5}{8}$ to $12\frac{1}{8}$. After commission costs, she made 33% in less than 4 months

5

Broadening Wedges, Ascending

RESULTS SNAPSHOT

Appearance	Price action follows two up-sloping trendlines that broaden out.
Reversal or consolidation	Short-term (up to 3 months) bearish reversal
Failure rate	24%
Failure rate if waited for downside breakout	6%
Average decline	20%, with most likely decline being 10%
Volume trend	Slight tendency to increase over time
Pullbacks	21%
Throwbacks	7%
Percentage meeting predicted price target	61%
Surprising finding	A downside breakout follows a partial rise 84% of the time.

I call this formation an ascending broadening wedge because it resembles a rising wedge formation with a broadening price pattern. I first noticed it when searching for the symmetrical variety of broadening formations. Symmetrical broadening formations have a price pattern that revolves about the horizontal axis—prices form higher highs and lower lows and two sloping trendlines outline the formation; one trendline slopes up and the other slopes down.

The ascending broadening wedge is different from a rising wedge. Both ascending broadening wedge and rising wedge trendlines encompass price action that slopes upward. However, that is where the similarity ends. The top trendline of ascending broadening wedges slopes upward at a higher rate than the bottom one, giving the appearance of a broadening price series.

Volume of ascending broadening wedges is also opposite that of rising wedges: Volume for the ascending broadening wedge is slightly higher as the breakout nears, but in a rising wedge volume typically recedes.

The Results Snapshot shows some statistics for ascending broadening wedges. This chart pattern sports a relatively high, 24%, failure rate that reduces to 6% if one waits for a downside breakout. Failure rates below 20% I consider to be acceptable, so the rule is, wait for a downside breakout before selling this one short.

Pullbacks (21%) and throwbacks (7%) are rare, which is somewhat unusual for broadening formations. The numbers suggest that once a breakout occurs, there is no looking back; prices break down cleanly and continue down. This is not strictly true as the chart patterns accompanying this entry attest. There is some hesitancy when the stock nears the lower trendline.

The 61% result for meeting the predicted price target is lower than I like to see in a formation (which is at least 80%). It is even weaker after revealing the computation. The computation is not based on the formation height as you would expect. Rather, the target is the lowest point in the formation. The measure rule is similar to the wedge family. Prices decline to, or below, the start of the formation about two-thirds of the time.

A surprising finding for ascending broadening wedges is the partial rise. A partial rise is when prices lift off the lower trendline but curl around and head down before coming near the top trendline. When a partial rise occurs, a downside breakout follows 84% of the time.

Tour

What does an ascending broadening wedge look like? Consider the chart pattern in Figure 5.1. The first thing you will notice is the two sloping trendlines; the top one has a slightly steeper slope than the bottom one. Together, the two trendlines spread out over time but both slope upward. Once prices pierce the

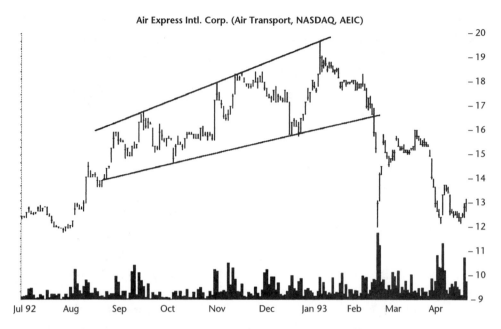

Figure 5.1   An ascending broadening wedge. Two up-sloping trendlines contain prices that broaden over time.

bottom trendline, they drop rapidly. The chart looks like a pie-shaped wedge that slopes uphill. That is why it is called an ascending broadening wedge. The price action alternates and is contained by the two trendlines. The two trendlines are not parallel. If they were parallel, you would have a channel or rectangle (when both trendlines are horizontal).

Figure 5.2 shows a better example of a broadening wedge, with two upsloping trendlines where the slope of the top trendline is much steeper than the bottom one.

Figures 5.1 and 5.2 both show a similar situation. The formation appears at the end of a rising price trend and signals a reversal. Although a reversal is not always the case, nor is the formation required to be at the end of a rising price trend, both situations occur more often than not.

Figure 5.2 also shows an interesting pattern that is key in identifying the start of a new price trend: the partial rise. After touching the lower trendline, prices again move up but fail to touch the higher trendline. As prices descend, they pierce the lower trendline and continue moving down. The chart also shows a similar situation that occurs earlier in the price pattern, around the start of the new year. There is a rising price trend that fails to touch the upper trendline. In this case, prices return to the lower trendline, then rebound and zoom up again to touch the higher trendline. The partial rise fails to predict a change in trend. We further explore partial rises later.

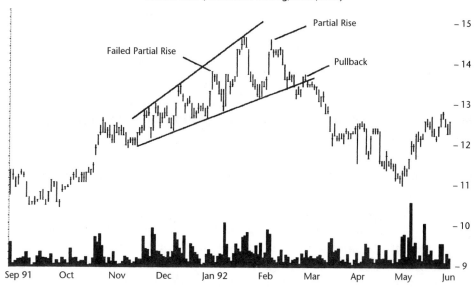

Figure 5.2   An ascending broadening wedge. The broadening feature is clear in this chart. The partial rise and failure to touch the upper trendline is a signal of an impending trend change.

Why does a broadening wedge form? Pretend for a moment that you are the head of an investment conglomerate that has big bucks to spend and wants to buy shares in another company. When the price is low, you instruct your trading department to begin its buying spree. The sudden buying demand forces the price to climb even though the trading department spreads its orders over several days and through several brokers. The trading department tries to keep its buying quiet, but the word gets out that you are in the market. The momentum players jump on your coattails and ride the stock upward by buying into the situation. This sends the stock higher than you expected, so your trading department stops buying for the moment.

Value investors, sensing an overbought situation developing, are willing to sell their shares at the higher price. Soon the stock is moving down again. But before it can reach its old low, the buy-the-dip crowd jumps in and halts the decline. Your trading department, seeing a higher low form, jumps back in and buys while the price is still reasonable. Some new value investors also decide the stock is worthy of a flyer and add to the buying pressure. The company itself gets into the act and buys shares authorized by the board of directors as a share-buyback program announced long ago. The buyback program is nearing the expiration date and the company feels it is the right time to buy to complete their promise to shareholders.

The stock makes a new high. When it climbs high enough, the selling pressure overwhelms the buying demand and sends the shares lower, but the price will not drop far—not with everyone trying to buy at a good price. What you have then are much higher highs from the unbridled buying enthusiasm and higher, but more sane, lows as your conglomerate and the company itself try to buy near a fixed low price. You never quite succeed and pay higher and higher prices as the minor lows move up.

Soon, however, the stock is too pricey even for your tastes. You may even decide it is time to sell some, or all, of your holdings. Meanwhile, the momentum players send the stock coasting higher, but this time the price does not come close to the upper trendline.

Everyone has his or her ear to the ground listening, trying to figure out what all the buying enthusiasm is about. In the distance, a rumble sounds. The same-store sales numbers are going to be lower this quarter, the shorts say. This time the rumor finds sympathetic ears. The rumble heard earlier is the stampede of the smart money running for the exits. The price drops quickly. It may hover for a bit around support zones while novice investors, who have not gotten the word, buy the stock. When they finish placing their trades, the meager buying demand abates and the stock crashes through the lower trendline and heads down further.

Identification Guidelines

There are a number of identification guidelines, outlined in Table 5.1, that make this formation unique. As I discuss the different guidelines, consider the ascending broadening wedge depicted in Figure 5.3. This formation is different from Figures 5.1 and 5.2 in that it is born from a region of consolidation. From the beginning of the study in July 1991, prices move generally horizontally and do not fall much below the $15\frac{3}{8}$ level (Figure 5.3 shows only a portion of the prior price action).

The situation changes just before the new year. Prices start moving up on December 23. They reach a new high in mid-January but soon move down. At that point, two tentative trendlines connect the highs and lows. Although it is too early to form a definitive conclusion, a broadening wedge appears to be taking shape. After prices move up and touch the upper trendline then pull back to the lower one again, the broadening wedge formation is clearly visible. At the start of March, prices move higher but quickly stall, turn around, and pierce the lower trendline. The partial rise and trendline penetration suggest a change in trend is at hand.

It is a false breakout. Prices travel higher for 3 days in a tight, narrow pattern then zoom upward and touch the upper trendline. The bottom trendline has to be redrawn to accommodate the slight decline below the old trendline. Clearly, prices have more work to do before declining below the lower trendline.

Table 5.1
Identification Characteristics of Ascending Broadening Wedges

Characteristic	Discussion
Shape	Looks like a megaphone, tilted up, with price action that outlines two up-sloping, trendlines.
Trendlines	The top trendline has a steeper upward slope than the lower one and neither is horizontal.
Touches	There should be at least *three* distinct touches (or near touches) of the trendlines on each side. This helps assure proper identification and performance of the formation.
Volume	Irregular with a slight tendency to rise over the length of the formation.
Premature breakouts	Very rare. A close below the lower trendline is usually a genuine breakout.
Breakout	The breakout direction is downward the vast majority of times, but an upside breakout is not unheard of.
Partial rise	Prices touch the lower trendline, climb toward the top trendline, but fail to touch it. Prices reverse direction and break out downward from the formation.

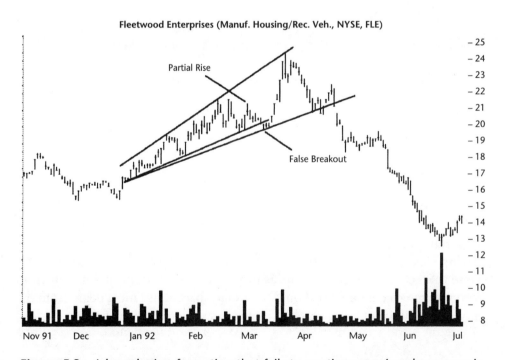

Figure 5.3 A broadening formation that fails to continue moving down, requiring a redraw of the formation boundaries. The internal partial rise is rare, occurring in just 18% of the formations.

A month later, prices return to the lower trendline and move higher for a few days. However, the rise stalls and prices pierce the lower trendline. Like a replay of the price action a month earlier, prices return to the trendline and start moving higher. However, this rise falters on low volume and quickly returns to the lower trendline. When prices gap down on April 16, the genuine breakout occurs. In rapid fashion, prices plummet to below $12\frac{3}{4}$, nearly a 50% decline from the high.

Looking back at Figures 5.1, 5.2, and 5.3, there are several characteristics that ascending broadening wedges have in common. The overall shape appears as a megaphone. This appearance is not uncommon for broadening formations except that this megaphone tilts upward: both trendlines slope higher. The upper trendline has a higher slope than the lower one, giving the formation a broadening appearance. The lower trendline also slopes upward separating the formation from the right-angle and symmetrical varieties of broadening formations.

In my studies of ascending broadening wedges, I select formations that have at least *three touches of each trendline* (or at least come close). The three-touch minimum helps remove consideration given to normal price action and helps identify reliable chart patterns.

The volume pattern is irregular but generally rises as prices move up and recedes as prices decline. Although it is not clear from the charts, volume tends to rise over time. However, this tendency is slight when considering all ascending broadening wedges and is not a mandatory selection guideline.

Figure 5.3 shows an exceptional premature breakout. Usually, prices follow the lower trendline and do not penetrate it until very near the breakout. When prices do break out, the price action can be messy, as shown in the figure. Sometimes the price runs straight through the lower trendline without pausing, and sometimes it weaves around the trendline before finally continuing down. In either case, the breakout is usually downward.

The partial rise, already mentioned, occurs in nearly half of the ascending broadening wedges. Since it usually occurs just before a breakout, it is an important trend change indicator. In a partial rise, prices start moving up, after having touched the lower trendline, then stop before touching (or coming close to) the upper one. Prices return to the lower trendline and usually head lower, staging a genuine breakout. Note that a partial rise must begin from the lower trendline, not as an upward retrace from the top trendline.

Focus on Failures

Figure 5.4 shows what a failure looks like. Although prices break out downward, they fail to continue moving down by more than 5%. The breakout occurs at a price of $50\frac{1}{8}$ and prices move to a low of $48\frac{5}{8}$ about 2 weeks later, resulting in a 3% decline—too small to register as a success.

Eaton Corp. (Auto Parts (OEM), NYSE, ETN)

Figure 5.4 An ascending broadening wedge that fails to continue moving down. Prices decline less than 5% below the breakout point before moving higher.

Only 7 out of 126 or 6% of the formations breaking out downward fail to continue moving down by more than 5%. This is an exceedingly low figure. However, it does not mean that failures do not occur. If you blindly invest in an ascending broadening wedge, there is a 76% likelihood that the formation will break out downward. This is a reasonably good number and it improves if you wait for an actual breakout. Although 76% may head down, that still leaves 24% that either move up or move horizontally. A failure rate of 24% is not something that you should take lightly. As with most formations, it pays to wait for a confirmed breakout before investing.

Statistics

Table 5.2 shows general statistics for ascending broadening wedges. The formations are more plentiful than other types of broadening chart patterns. I located 157 in 500 stocks over a 5-year period. Out of those formations, 118 or 75% act as reversals of the prevailing trend.

The failure rate is comparatively high at 24%, meaning that one out of every four formations has an upside breakout. If you wait for the breakout to occur, the failure rate drops to a more palatable 6%. Only 7 out of 126 formations fail to continue moving down by more than 5% after a downside breakout. These 5% failures are rare and not worth worrying about.

Table 5.2
General Statistics for Ascending Broadening Wedges

Description	Statistic
Number of formations in 500 stocks from 1991 to 1996	157
Reversal or consolidation	39 consolidations, 118 reversals
Failure rate	38/157 or 24%
Failure rate if waited for downside breakout	7/126 or 6%
Average decline of successful formations	20%
Most likely decline	10%
Of those succeeding, number meeting or exceeding price target (measure rule)	73 or 61%
Average formation length	4 months (116 days)
For successful formations, days to ultimate low	3 months (95 days)
Partial rise followed by a downside breakout	63/75 or 84%
Partial rise as a percentage of all formations	48%
Partial rise not at formation end	29 or 18%
Percentage with rising volume trend	59%

Note: Most formations break out downward and a partial rise is often a clue to a downside breakout.

How far will a stock decline after a downside breakout? On average, the decline is 20%. However, a frequency distribution of the declines tell a slightly different tale (see Figure 5.5). The vast number of hits occur in the 10% category, suggesting that the most likely decline is about 10%. The 15% to 25% categories have a rather steady but declining trend, leading me to believe the likely decline is probably understated at 10%. The likely decline is probably higher, perhaps in the 15% to 20% range.

For a bearish formation, the measure rule usually is the height of the formation subtracted from the breakout point. However, for wedges, the price target is the lowest low in the formation, which is what I use for this formation too. I compare the ultimate low price with the formation start. Only 61% of the time is the ultimate low price below the formation low. This is not a very reassuring figure; I consider values above 80% to be reliable.

I compute the average formation length by subtracting the date of the formation end from the beginning. On average, the formation is about 4 months long (116 days), and it takes almost as long (95 days) to reach the ultimate low.

A frequency distribution of the days to the ultimate low helps determine in which investment category the formation belongs: short, intermediate, or

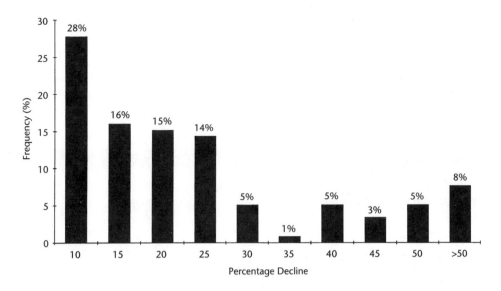

Figure 5.5 Frequency distribution of declines for ascending broadening wedges. The most likely decline is 10%, followed by the 15% to 25% range.

long term. There are 81 formations with durations less than 3 months and the remainder of the formations split evenly, at 19 each, for intermediate and long term, suggesting that the investment implications of this formation are short term. If you short a stock showing this formation, the odds favor you closing out your position in less than 3 months.

One set of exciting statistics my research reveals is the behavior of partial price rises. A partial rise, such as that shown in Figure 5.2, occurs nearly half the time (48%) but when it does occur, it is followed by a downside breakout 84% of the time. In only 18% of the formations does a partial rise within a formation occur, such as that shown in Figure 5.3. If you choose not to take advantage of the partial rise, you are still being alerted to a possible trend change. Sometimes that in itself is worth knowing, especially if you are about to buy a stock.

The volume trend, as measured by the slope of a line found using linear regression, indicates 59% of the formations have an increasing volume trend. This result is weak and suggests volume is probably not meaningful as an indicator of the validity of this formation. Observation of volume indicates that the volume series is irregular in appearance.

Table 5.3 lists statistics pertaining to breakouts. Out of 29 upside breakouts, only 1 formation breaks out upward but fails to move higher than 5%. Downside breakouts (126) are much more plentiful. Even so, there are only seven failures of downside breakouts. These are 5% failures, meaning that the stock fails to continue moving down by more than 5% after a downside breakout before recovering substantially. The remainder (2 or 1%) of the formations have horizontal breakouts.

Table 5.3
Breakout Statistics for Ascending Broadening Wedges

Description	Statistic
Upside breakout but failure	1 or 3%
Downside breakout but failure	7 or 6%
Upside breakout	29 or 18%
Horizontal breakout	2 or 1%
Downside breakout	126 or 80%
Throwbacks	2 or 7%
Average time to throwback completion	7 days
Pullbacks	26 or 21%
Average time to pullback completion	9 days
Percentage of breakouts occurring near the 12-month price low (L), center (C), or high (H)	L9%, C27%, H64%
Percentage loss for each 12-month lookback period	L25%, C21%, H19%
Volume for breakout day and next 5 days compared with day before breakout	165%, 134%, 116%, 96%, 114%, 109%

Throwbacks and pullbacks are rare for ascending broadening wedges. Since there are so few upside breakouts, it is no surprise that there are only two throwbacks to the top of the formation. The time between a breakout and completion of a throwback is just a week. Other formations usually have throwback durations of about 10 to 12 days. Again, the short throwback time is probably due to the low number of throwbacks.

Pullbacks, at 26 or 21%, are more plentiful but still rare when compared with other types of formations. The pullback completion time is just 2 days longer (9 days total) than its throwback brethren. For this formation, the numbers imply that throwbacks and pullbacks are not reliable and should not be depended on to initiate a trade. If your stock does pull back, consider adding to your position once prices begin falling again.

For downside breakouts, I examined where the breakout occurs over the prior 12-month period. The formation appears most often (64%) within one-third of the yearly price high. This may sound surprising since the breakout is on the bottom of the formation. However, since the wedge rises over time, the breakout point lifts into the higher ranges. In essence, you will find ascending broadening wedges breaking out near the yearly high, probably near the end of an uptrend.

I divided the yearly price range into thirds and distributed the percentage declines over the range, depending on where the breakout occurs. The largest declines occur in the lower third of the price range with an average decline measuring 25%. This is larger than normal, but the largest decline occurring near the yearly low is not surprising. Other bearish formations show this tendency. This behavior reinforces the belief that you should short a stock making new lows, not new highs.

Table 5.3 shows the volume for the week after a breakout as compared with the day before the breakout. There is high volume on the breakout day, as expected, and it measures 65% above the prior day (or 165% of the prior day's total). Throughout the following week, volume remains relatively high, although inconsistent.

Trading Tactics

Table 5.4 lists trading tactics. The measure rule for this formation is different from most other formations in that it is based on the lowest daily low, not on the height of the formation.

Figure 5.6 shows two ascending broadening wedges and application of the measure rule. Both formations are well formed, but the first one has a tendency to rise slightly above the top trendline before beginning its downhill run. The chart marks the lowest low in each formation. The low serves as the expected minimum price move. The formation on the left shows prices reaching the target price in mid-November just as prices turn around and rebound. The formation shown on the right has prices hitting the target when they plummet.

The reason for choosing the lowest low in the formation is simply for performance. Using the formation low as the target price allows 61% of the formations to achieve the target. This means that almost two out of every three formations decline below the formation low. I like to see performance numbers

Table 5.4
Trading Tactics for Ascending Broadening Wedges

Trading Tactic	Explanation
Measure rule	Use the lowest price in the formation as the minimum price move to expect. Do not use the formation height subtracted from the breakout point as the result overstates the anticipated decline.
Wait for confirmation	Although this formation breaks out downward 80% of the time, it is best to wait for a downside breakout before shorting the stock.
Partial rise	If a stock shows a partial rise and begins to head back toward the lower trendline, consider selling short. A downside breakout follows a partial rise.

Note: Wait for the breakout then trade with the trend.

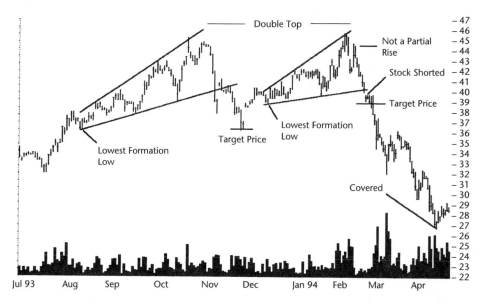

Centex Corp. (Homebuilding, NYSE, CTX)

Figure 5.6 The measure rule as it applies to two ascending broadening wedges. Astute investors will recognize the twin peaks as a double top.

above 80%, so the 61% value is poor. As you look at the formation on the right, you can see how close the price target really is to the breakout price.

If you were to compute the formation height and subtract it from the breakout point, there would be even fewer formations meeting the price target. Only 27% would meet the new, lower, price target, which is very different from 80%. What about computing a target price that is nearer the breakout, say, using half the formation height subtracted from the breakout? This computation only results in a 64% success rate. The number is certainly better than 27% but is not much of an improvement over the 61% number using the lowest formation low.

This formation has a good track record of downside breakouts. However, 20% of the time prices either move horizontally or break out upward. If you wait for a breakout before investing, you substantially increase your chances of a profitable trade. Once prices decline below the lower trendline, sell the stock short. Be prepared to cover the short as prices near the target, especially if the price approaches an area of support.

The most likely decline from an ascending broadening wedge is just 10%, but it could be substantially higher. In computing the most likely decline, you can use the measure rule. However, consider that support areas are probably better places to close out the trade. In Figure 5.6, the lowest formation low on the left is also a support point. Prices decline to the low in early August then head up and create the formation. Several months later, prices decline to that level and turn around. As prices decline after the second formation, the support level at 36 changes into resistance. During March, prices try to rebound but turn away near the 36 level.

An exception to the wait-for-breakout-confirmation rule is if a partial rise occurs. Looking again at Figure 5.6, you might conclude that there is a partial rise in the right formation. You would be wrong. I define a partial rise as when prices touch the lower trendline, move up, then return to the lower trendline. The figure shows prices starting from the *top* trendline, not the lower one. Figure 5.2 shows a properly identified partial rise.

If you detect a partial rise, consider shorting the stock. In 84% of the cases, a downside breakout follows a partial rise. Since you are getting a quicker jump on the stock, your profits should be larger. When the stock declines to the lower trendline, move your stop-loss order to break-even. If the stock should turn around at the trendline and head up, consider closing out your position.

Sample Trade

Curtis works the night shift at a large bakery near his home. Working at night frees up the daylight hours for other activities, such as sleep. Occasionally, he spots a situation such as that shown in Figure 5.6, one that makes the morning sun seem even brighter.

Each day before he hit the sack, he plotted the stock and watched with amusement the first broadening wedge form. When the second one appeared, he wiped the sleep from his eyes and took notice. It was not so much the broadening wedge that excited him; it was the wedge coupled with the double top. Together, they spelled an especially bearish situation, one that he was willing to shell out his hard earned money to trade.

The day after the stock closed below the lower trendline, Curtis sold the stock short and received a fill at $39\frac{1}{2}$. He used the double top measure rule to estimate his target price. With a top at $45\frac{3}{4}$ and a valley low of $36\frac{1}{4}$, the target turned out to be $26\frac{3}{4}$ (that's $45\frac{3}{4} - 36\frac{1}{4}$). He decided to place an order to cover the short at $27\frac{1}{8}$, just above the whole number and just above where everyone else was likely to place theirs. Then he went to bed.

Each day, before he closed the curtains to get some sleep, he would check on his stock. To him, it was pleasing to see the stock begin moving down immediately and sailing below the nearest broadening wedge target price ($38\frac{7}{8}$). He lost some sleep worrying about the upward retrace in March, and wondered if the party were over.

Curtis hung in there and the stock eventually pierced the resistance zone and kept moving down. He hoped that the March resistance zone was just the corrective phase of a measured move down, which would place the target price at $22\frac{1}{2}$, well below his target at $27\frac{1}{8}$. He decided not to be greedy and lower his target. Instead, he moved his stop-loss price down to just ⅛ above the resistance zone high at 36⅜.

On April 18 he was rudely awakened from his REM state by a phone call from his broker. The short was covered at his target price. He got up and started his computer and checked out the situation. All told, he made about $12 a share. That put a smile on his face and he went back to his dream of telling his boss what he could do with the night shift

6

Broadening Wedges, Descending

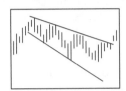

RESULTS SNAPSHOT

Appearance	Price action follows two down-sloping trendlines that broaden out.
Reversal or consolidation	Long-term (over 6 months) bullish consolidation
Failure rate	37%
Average rise	46%, with most likely rise being 20%
Volume trend	Usually increases over time
Throwbacks	40%
Percentage meeting predicted price target	81%
Surprising finding	An upside breakout follows a partial decline 76% of the time.

What a surprise! When I discovered this formation, I thought it would act like a falling wedge, but it did not. Falling wedges are reversal formations, whereas descending broadening wedges act as a consolidation of the prevailing trend. The volume pattern is also different from falling wedges. In the descending broadening wedge formation, the volume tends to increase over time but with falling wedges, it decreases.

During my search through the various stocks in the database, I noticed that this formation appears most often after an uptrend. Prices move down in a broadening wedge for several months then return to their original direction: up. The pattern is representative of a trend consolidation, reaffirming the statistics.

How do you measure the failure rate of this formation? Once I knew that the formation acts as a consolidation of the trend, then trend reversals become failures. Also, formations that are consolidations but fail to move more than 5% in the breakout direction (after a breakout) are also failures. Altogether, 37% of the formations fail. That is well above the maximum 20% that I consider reliable formations to possess.

Being a consolidation in a bull market, the average rise is a very high 46%. The most likely rise is 20% and an astounding 40% of the formations have gains above 50%! With bullish numbers like these, it makes the failure rate seem tolerable.

The measure rule stacks up well, but that is no surprise considering the performance is so good. Unlike ascending broadening wedges, this formation uses the formation height added to the breakout price to predict the target. Over 80% of the formations with upside breakouts meet or exceed their price targets.

One surprise is really not a surprise at all for broadening formations: the partial decline. When prices move down from the top trendline then rebound, an upside breakout occurs 76% of the time.

Tour

What does the formation look like? Figure 6.1 shows a well-formed descending broadening wedge. The stock begins rising in June 1994 and rounds over at the top a year later, in August. In September, the stock starts down in tight oscillations that broaden over time. A month later, two trendlines drawn across the highs and lows make the wedge shape clear.

Volume at the start of the formation is well below normal. As the formation develops, volume is erratic, but trends higher. Computing the slope of the volume line using linear regression confirms the result; the slope is positive, which indicates volume is getting heavier.

In mid-October, prices gap up and shoot above the upper trendline. A breakout occurs. Volume spikes upward also and continues to be heavy for several days as prices climb.

As you look at the chart, you may make an interesting observation. The price trend has three stages: The first stage is the long bull-run from June 1994 to August 1995, leading to a consolidation or retrace for 2 months (second stage), then prices move higher (third stage). In Figure 6.1, the broadening formation is a consolidation of the upward trend. Taken as a whole, it looks like the corrective phase of a measured move up chart pattern.

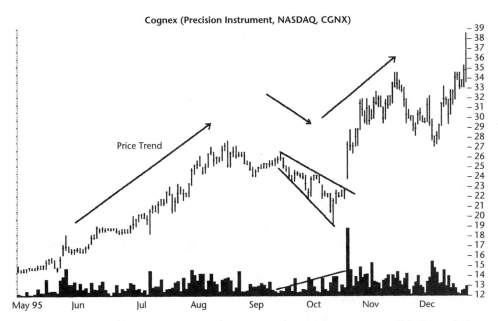

Figure 6.1 The descending broadening wedge acts as a consolidation of the upward trend. Two down-sloping trendlines outline price action that broadens out. Volume usually increases over time.

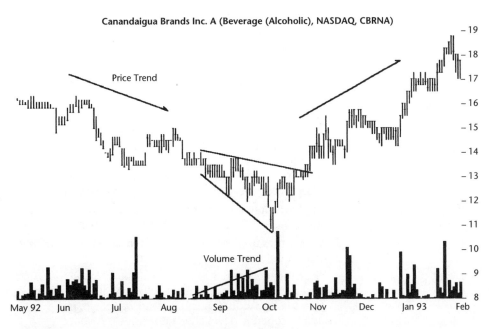

Figure 6.2 The descending broadening wedge formation acts as a reversal of the intermediate-term downward trend.

Contrast Figure 6.1 with Figure 6.2, where a descending broadening wedge acts as a reversal of the intermediate-term price trend. Prices peak in May 1992 and head lower. During August, prices begin to broaden out as they continue their downward spiral. By mid-September, a descending broadening wedge forms.

Volume is low at the start of the formation but does have a few spikes. Into September, volume moves up and becomes even more irregular. At the start of October, as prices begin moving up, volume recedes. Prices pierce the top trendline on negligible volume and head higher. A trend reversal is at hand.

Up to October, prices have been trending down rather steadily, then prices reverse course and start climbing. By January prices reach the old high. During late January and early February, prices pierce the old high and record a new one. A year later, prices soar to a high of 32, almost triple the low achieved during the formation ($10\frac{3}{4}$).

Identification Guidelines

Table 6.1 outlines the identification guidelines for the formation, and Figure 6.3 shows another example of a descending broadening wedge. Figure 6.3 shows two down-sloping trendlines that encompass a series of oscillating prices. The two trendlines look like a megaphone, tilted down. The chart pat-

Table 6.1
Identification Characteristics of Descending Broadening Wedges

Characteristic	Discussion
Shape	The formation looks like a megaphone tilted down. Two down-sloping trendlines outline the price action.
Down-sloping trendlines	Both trendlines slope downward, with the lower trendline having a steeper slope. Thus, the two lines broaden out over time. Neither trendline is horizontal.
Trendline touches	The formation requires at least two distinct touches of each trendline.
Volume	Usually rises over the length of the formation. However, the volume pattern is not a prerequisite.
Breakout	Since the formation acts as a consolidation of the trend, if prices were moving up, they usually continue moving up after the breakout. If the price trend was down, prices usually continue down after a downside breakout.
Partial decline	For a partial decline, prices must touch the top trendline and move down, turn around, then head higher without coming close to the lower trendline. An upside breakout usually follows a partial decline.

tern is narrow at the start but gets wider over time. Neither trendline is horizontal, which is a key consideration since it differentiates this formation from other types of broadening formations.

There are a number of touches of the minor highs against the top trendline and the minor lows against the bottom one. There should be at least two distinct touches—two minor highs and two minor lows—of each trendline to correctly define a broadening formation.

The slope of the volume trend is usually upward, unlike formations from the narrowing wedge family: They have volume trends that recede over time. The increasing volume pattern seems to catapult prices higher, sending them out the top of the formation. Volume at the breakout is usually high but need not be. As long as demand exceeds supply, prices will rise.

Since the formation represents a consolidation of the prevailing trend, prices continue in the same direction they were traveling before the formation began. As shown in Figure 6.3, if prices are heading up, they will continue moving up after the formation completes.

Sometimes, however, the formation acts as a reversal of the trend. Figure 6.2 is an example of a reversal. There is no easy way to differentiate a budding consolidation from a reversal. Both often occur at the end of a rising price trend. In a consolidation, the breakout is usually upward and prices resume climbing. In a reversal, the breakout is downward and prices head lower. Only the breakout direction decides whether the formation represents a consolidation or a reversal of the prior price trend.

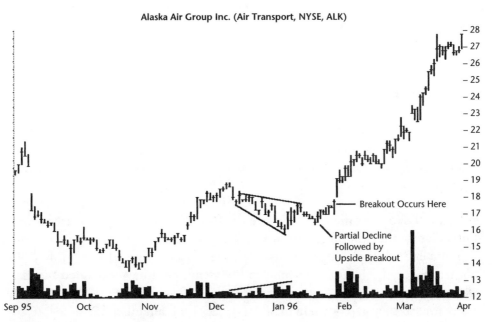

Figure 6.3 A descending broadening wedge as a consolidation of the rising trend. Volume moves higher even as prices head down. A partial decline signals that an upside breakout is coming.

The partial decline, such as that shown in Figure 6.3, often indicates an impending upside breakout. This works quite well for consolidations or reversals. However, the success rate appears much lower for downside breakouts that follow partial rises. I discuss statistics in more detail later, but there are too few samples to really make a definitive statement about partial rises.

Why do these formations form? The chart pattern, as do many formations, illustrates the struggle between supply and demand. In Figure 6.3, after attempting to close the September gap in early December, the stock stalls. Buying enthusiasm dries up and the stock heads lower.

Volume sometimes rises as prices near whole dollar amounts and at 40%, 50%, or 60% retraces of the prior rise or fall. At those points, prices are somewhat more likely to stage a rebound. That is what occurs in Figure 6.3. Prices rise from a low of 13⅝ to a high of 18⅞. A 40% retrace of this range takes prices back to 16¾. This is quite close to 17, and you can see some hesitation in the stock at that level. However, once the stock approaches the 60% retrace level (15¾), the smart money knows the jig is up. They start buying heavily for the 5 days surrounding the new year. Prices halt their decline and move higher. However, sellers are not sitting by idly. They sell into the rally and prices eventually stall and drift lower, forming the partial decline highlighted in Figure 6.3.

As it happens, volume dries up as prices trace a V-shaped pattern. Low volume before an upside breakout reminds me of the calm before an approaching storm. Formations such as ascending and descending triangles commonly have low volume just before a breakout. Volume spikes upward the day prices close above the prior minor high (where the top trendline ends in January). The momentum players take the upper hand, and prices surge higher on very high volume.

Focus on Failures

I classify a failure two ways. First, when the formation acts as a reversal—that is, a failure of the formation to continue the direction of the prior trend. Since descending broadening formations usually act as consolidations of the prevailing trend, a reversal is a failure. Figure 6.2 shows this type of failure.

Figure 6.4 shows a second way for a failure to occur, a formation that acts as a consolidation of the trend. Before the formation begins, prices are rising. Immediately after the breakout, prices are also rising. The process starts on September 3 when prices punch through the top trendline. However, they do not travel very far before returning to the trendline. I have extended the top trendline in Figure 6.4 to make the throwback clear. You see that prices ride along it until they gap down (a breakaway gap) on September 17.

This formation is what I call a 5% failure, that is, when prices breakout and move less than 5% before reversing course. Failures to act as a consolidation of the trend are common; failures to continue moving by more than 5%

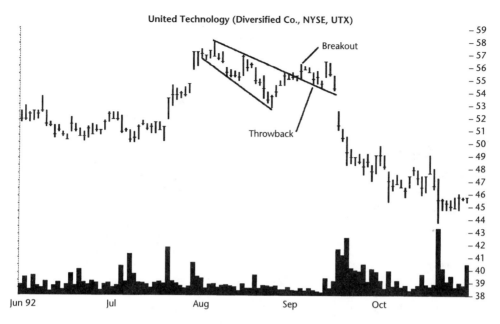

Figure 6.4 This formation is a failure according to the 5% rule. Prices fail to move away from the formation by more than 5% before moving down.

are not. Only four formations, or 3%, do not pass the 5% rule. The lessons from this analysis suggest that it is imperative that you wait for a breakout before placing a trade. Once a breakout takes place, prices will continue moving in the direction of the breakout.

Statistics

The descending broadening wedge is a rare formation, being found in only 101 unique stocks (117 formations) over a 5-year span. Of those formations, 66% act as consolidations of the current trend. Table 6.2 shows general statistics for this formation.

As explained earlier, trend reversals count as failures of the formation to consolidate, so the failure rate is high at 37%. Also included in the rate are four 5% failures, where prices move less than 5% after a breakout before reversing.

Upside breakouts have an average gain of 46%, which is very high, but it is not so surprising when you consider that this formation acts as a consolidation of the trend. In a bull market, the trend is inherently upward, and this formation simply underscores that fact. Still, many bullish formations have gains of about 40%, so this one scores well.

The most likely rise from this formation is 20%, suggesting that there is an inordinate number of large gains. The number derives from a frequency distribution and a review confirms this suspicion. Forty percent of the chart

Table 6.2
General Statistics for Descending Broadening Wedges

Description	Statistic
Number of formations in 500 stocks from 1991 to 1996	117
Reversal or consolidation	78 consolidations, 39 reversals
Failure rate	34 or 37%
Average rise of successful formations	46%
Most likely rise	20%
Of those succeeding, number meeting or exceeding price target (measure rule)	47 or 81%
Average formation length	2.5 months (76 days)
For successful formations, days to ultimate high	6.5 months (190 days)
Volume trend	64% have a rising volume trend
Partial decline followed by upside breakout	35/46 or 76%

Note: The formation acts most often as a consolidation of the long-term bullish trend.

patterns with upside breakouts have gains over 50%. Since large gains tend to pull the overall average up, I ignore the category and choose the bin with the next highest total. That turns out to be the 20% category.

I computed the price target using several different rules and discovered that the traditional way works best for upside breakouts. The Trading Tactics section explains this more thoroughly, but it involves computing the formation height and adding the result to the breakout price. This results in 81% of the formations meeting their target prices (for successful, upside breakouts only). I consider formations with values above 80% to be reliable.

The average formation length is about 2½ months and results in a long-term move (6 months or longer). This formation is one of the few that have long-term, bullish implications. The long-term category is a reinforcement of the tenet that large rises take longer than shorter ones.

The upward volume trend is stronger in this formation than its brother, the ascending broadening wedge. Almost two out of three formations (64%) experience heavier volume over time. The slope of a line found using linear regression on volume determines whether volume is trending up or down over the length of the formation.

Partial declines and rises are important clues to the performance of this formation. An upside breakout follows a partial decline 76% of the time (Figure 6.5 shows a good example of this).

A partial decline must always begin after touching the *top* trendline. Prices then head down toward the lower trendline but do not touch it (or come that close). The stock curls around and moves back up and pierces the top trendline, usually immediately. The piercing results in an upside breakout.

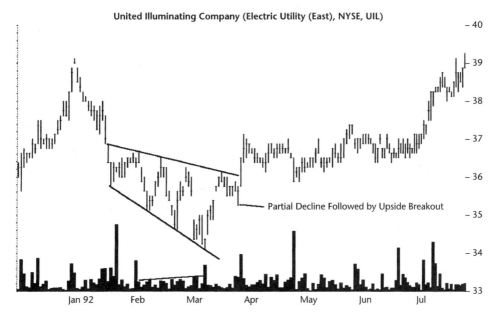

United Illuminating Company (Electric Utility (East), NYSE, UIL)

Partial Decline Followed by Upside Breakout

Figure 6.5 A descending broadening wedge with an upside breakout follows a partial decline 76% of the time. The stock must always touch the top trendline before beginning the partial decline and must not come too close to the lower trendline before reversing.

Downside breakouts also follow a partial *rise*. However, due to the scarcity of downside breakouts and even fewer partial rises (there are only 5 out of 22), only two partial rises have downside breakouts. The sample size is just too small on which to base any conclusions.

Table 6.3 shows breakout-related statistics. Premature breakouts are when prices close outside the formation boundary (that is, a close above or below the trendline) and return to the formation before the genuine breakout. Due to the broadening nature of these formations, you would expect few premature breakouts. That is exactly what happens. There are only seven premature breakouts, six of them occurring as premature upside breakouts.

Thirty-four formations with upside breakouts fail. Most of these failures are due to the formation acting as a reversal instead of a consolidation of the price trend. If the price trend is downward and the breakout is upward, for example, then the chart pattern is a failure because it does not act as expected. There are nine formations with downside breakouts that fail in a similar manner.

Most of the formations (79%) have upside breakouts, 19% have downside ones, and the remainder are horizontal (no breakout for months).

Throwbacks, when compared to pullbacks, are much more numerous at 37 versus 8 simply because there are more upside breakouts. On a percentage basis, throwbacks and pullbacks are about even at 40% and 36%, respectively, for upside and downside breakouts. The average time to complete a throwback

Table 6.3
Breakout Statistics for Descending Broadening Wedges

Description	Statistic
Premature upside breakouts	6 or 5%
Premature downside breakouts	1 or 1%
Upside breakout but failure	34 or 37%
Downside breakout but failure	9 or 41%
Upside breakout	92 or 79%
Horizontal breakout	3 or 3%
Downside breakout	22 or 19%
Throwbacks	37 or 40%
Average time to throwback completion	11 days
Pullbacks	8 or 36%
Average time to pullback completion	14 days
Percentage of breakouts occurring near the 12-month price low (L), center (C), or high (H)	L16%, C45%, H39%
Percentage gain for each 12-month lookback period	L51%, C53%, H44%
Volume for breakout day and next 5 days compared with day before breakout	136%, 152%, 101%, 103%, 89%, 109%

Note: Upside breakouts are the most plentiful, occurring 79% of the time.

to the formation top is just 11 days. Pullbacks take 2 weeks, on average, to return to the lower trendline axis.

Most formations (45%) have breakouts in the center third of the yearly price range. To determine this, remove any formation with a breakout less than a year from the start of the study. Then sort the breakout price (using the daily low) into three categories, low, center, and high, according to where it appears in the yearly price range. The results indicate where in the yearly price range the breakout is most likely to occur.

Since descending broadening wedges trend downward over time, it should come as no surprise that relatively few breakouts occur in the highest third of the price range. A formation probably has its start in the highest range but trends down and moves into the center third of the range before the breakout. Mapping performance over the yearly price range shows where the best performing breakouts occur. The gains are highest in the center third of the range with scores averaging 53%. This compares with a 46% gain for all descending broadening wedges with upside breakouts. So if you have a choice between two chart patterns, one with a breakout near the yearly high and one with a breakout in the center of the yearly price range, go with the center one. Chances are, it will perform better.

Volume on the day of the breakout averages just 36% above the prior day (136% of the volume figure). However, a day later, the volume rises to 52% above the day before the breakout. We have seen this pattern before. Presumably, once investors recognize a breakout, they jump on the bandwagon. That is why the day after a breakout sometimes has a higher average volume.

Trading Tactics

Table 6.4 outlines trading tactics for descending broadening wedges. Use the measure rule to predict the minimum price to which the stock will move. First, subtract the lowest price in the formation from the highest. This gives the height of the formation. Once prices break out upward, add the result to the breakout price to arrive at the target price.

Figure 6.6 makes the computation of the measure rule clear. The highest price in the formation is at the start: $47\frac{1}{4}$. The lowest low is near the formation end at $42\frac{1}{8}$. Add the difference, $5\frac{1}{8}$, to the low of the breakout price ($44\frac{1}{2}$) to get the target of $49\frac{5}{8}$. Consider the target a minimum price move. The daily highs and lows used in the height calculation represent the widest points. I use the daily low at the breakout as a conservative measure.

Table 6.4
Trading Tactics for Descending Broadening Wedges

Trading Tactic	Explanation
Measure rule	Compute the formation height by taking the difference between the highest high and the lowest low in the formation. For upside breakouts, add the result to the breakout price to achieve the target price.
Wait for confirmation	This formation has too many failures (trend reversals) to risk taking a position before a breakout. Wait for prices to *close* beyond the trendlines before placing a trade.
Partial decline	If a stock shows a partial decline from the top trendline and begins to head back up, consider going long. An upside breakout most often follows a partial decline.
Trade the trendlines	If the formation is especially broad, buy at the lower trendline and sell at the top. If the stock executes a partial rise and begins falling, close out the position as it may breakout downward. Alternatively, sell short at the top trendline once prices are heading down and close the position after it rebounds off the lower trendline.
Stops	For intraformation trading, place a stop on the other side of the trendlines, just to catch an adverse breakout. Move the stop as prices cross the formation. Pick areas showing support or resistance.

Note: Unless trading the trendlines, always wait for the breakout then trade with the trend.

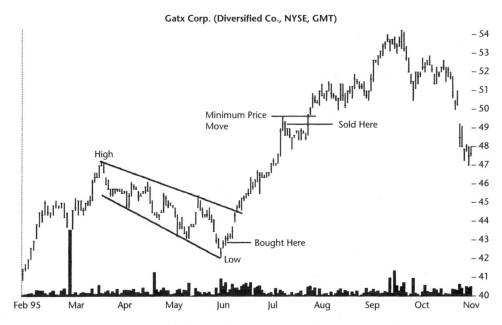

Figure 6.6 Calculated minimum price move using the measure rule. Take the difference between the high and low in the formation and add the result to the breakout price. The target price is the minimum you can expect, and prices reach the target over 80% of the time.

If you are considering buying this stock, it is not obvious at first that a broadening wedge is forming. Over time, once enough minor highs and lows appear, draw the two trendlines. Then, it becomes a matter of waiting for a breakout. Since most descending broadening wedges break out upward, that is the way to trade it. However, with a failure rate of 37%, you really need to wait for prices to close above the top trendline before buying.

An exception to this rule is the partial decline. As prices move down from the top trendline, watch them closely. If prices reach a support zone and begin moving up, buy because that is a partial decline, and it usually signals an impending upside breakout. Place a stop ⅛ below the curl low, just in case.

If the formation is especially wide, try an intraformation trade. Buy at the lower trendline and sell at the top one, or sell short at the top and cover near the bottom. With the trendlines sloping downward, a short sale will be more profitable. Use a stop ⅛ beyond the appropriate trendline in case of an adverse breakout. Adjust your stop as prices move in your favor. Place them ⅛ below a support zone (long trades) or above a resistance area (short trades).

Sample Trade

"Do you feel lucky, punk?" Mary growls as she looks at her computer screen (Figure 6.6). She just finished watching a Dirty Harry movie and is feeling ornery.

She decides to buy the stock as an intraformation trade once it rebounds off the lower trendline. When it is clear the stock is climbing again, she pulls the trigger and receives a fill at 43. Immediately, she places a stop-loss order $\frac{1}{8}$ below the lower trendline, at a price of 42. If things go wrong, she only will lose 3%. Then she waits.

The stock cooperates by moving higher each day. Soon it is at the top trendline, and she waits for it to ricochet off the line and begin heading down. It does not. Prices close above the top trendline, signaling an upside breakout. She calculates the price target using the measure rule, $49\frac{5}{8}$, and that is where she places her sell order. She raises her stop-loss point to 44, $\frac{1}{8}$ below the minor low in mid-April.

As the stock advances each day, she keeps wondering why it has not paused. She shrugs her shoulders and does not worry about it. When the stock makes a new high at $47\frac{3}{8}$, she raises her stop to $45\frac{1}{4}$, slightly below the two minor highs in late April and mid-May.

In a burst of energy, the stock zooms up over a 2-day period and reaches her sell point. The stock sells at the high for the day, $49\frac{5}{8}$. She has cleared over $6 a share on her trade. Even better, the stock moves lower for several days, reinforcing her sell decision.

It turns out that she sold too soon, but she does not care. She spots another promising formation in a stock she has been following for quite some time. She leans back in her chair, smiles and mumbles something about luck, then runs to the VCR and plugs in another Dirty Harry movie

7

Bump-and-Run
Reversal Bottoms

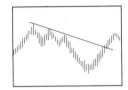

RESULTS SNAPSHOT

Appearance	Looks like a frying pan with the handle on the left following a trendline down until a large decline ensues.
Reversal or consolidation	Short-term (up to 3 months) bullish reversal
Failure rate	19%
Failure rate if waited for upside breakout	9%
Average rise	37%, with most likely rise being 20%
Volume trend	High volume at formation start, bump start, and breakout
Throwbacks	38%
Percentage meeting predicted price target	92%
See also	Cup with Handle; Rounding Bottoms

More than a year after I discovered the bump-and-run reversal (BARR) top, I decided to look for its complement: the BARR bottom. The reasoning is simple. Many formations, such as double tops, ascending triangles, and triple tops

100

all have bottom versions. Why not the bump-and-run reversal? It never dawned on me to look for the formation before then. As I searched through the 2,500 years of stock data looking for candidates, I was skeptical that the formation added real value. Some looked like cup-with-handle formations with the handle coming first, whereas others looked like rounding bottoms. Only after I compiled the statistics did my thoughts change.

If you wait for a breakout, the failure rate drops from 19% to 9%. I consider anything less than 20% to indicate a reliable formation. The average gain is 37%. This is a bit shy of the usual 40% for bullish formations, but the most likely rise, at 20%, is quite good.

The percentage of BARR bottoms meeting the price target is exceedingly high, at 92%. I consider anything over 80% to be reliable. Of course, the measure rule sets the price target. We see how to do that in the Trading Tactics section of this chapter.

Tour

What is a bump-and-run reversal, anyway? If I had to name this formation independent of all others, I would probably call it the frying pan or spoon formation because that is what it looks like. However, the formation is just a BARR top flipped upside down, so I call it a BARR bottom. I guess a more accurate description is an inverted BARR. Even the word *bottom* is a misnomer since the best performing BARRs appear in the middle of the yearly price range.

Why do BARR bottoms occur? Like the top version, the BARR bottom is a study in momentum. Consider the chart shown in Figure 7.1 on a weekly scale. Since late 1991, the stock was moving sideways—a trading range between 6½ and 11. However, that changed during the last week of October 1993, when the stock moved up and closed higher than the prior week. At first, this did not seem unusual since many weeks close higher than the prior week, but this one was different. It initiated a long climb to the highs of early January. On the highest volume that the stock had seen in years, the stock hit a new high of 14⅜ during the week of January 14, 1994. Volume began tapering off, although it was still high, and prices tagged a much smaller peak during the week of March 25, at 14. The two minor highs, one in mid-January and another in late March, formed the basis of a down-sloping trendline.

As the weekly volume trended lower, so did enthusiasm for the stock. Eventually, bullish sentiment could not sustain the high price and the stock collapsed. As it headed down, volume continued to taper off. The upward momentum experienced during the rise to the highs in January was now working against the stock. Over the course of a year, the stock gave back all its gains and, by mid-February 1995, it started sinking to new lows.

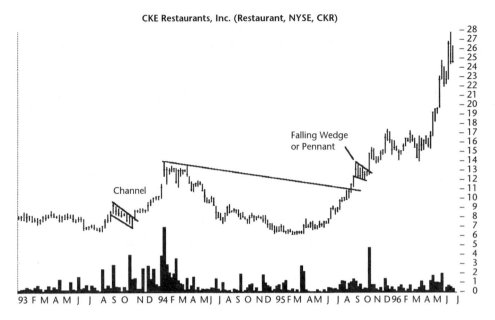

Figure 7.1 Bump-and-run reversal bottom. Upward momentum propels prices higher during late 1993 then stalls at the start of the new year. Volume tapers off and prices follow. A cup-with-handle formation or rounding bottom takes shape and prices climb 350% from the 1995 lows. A channel appears in late 1993 and a falling wedge in late 1995.

High volume a month later was a key as it signaled a turning point. A week later, again on high volume, the stock closed higher by over 10%. The upward move had begun but soon stalled out. The stock moved sideways for another 2 months, gathering strength for the uphill run. Then it took off, not jumping up, but slowly moving higher, almost week after week. When the stock reached the trendline in mid-August, it was clear that it had executed a massive rounding bottom—a turn in the trend that signaled higher prices.

The stock pushed through the trendline on relatively high volume, then paused for a month, and formed a falling wedge or pennant. Following that, on very high volume, prices jumped up to new highs, but this did not last very long as the stock entered a consolidation phase just below 18. There it stayed for many months before the stock jumped up and ran still higher. By late June, the stock had touched 28³⁄₄, a rise of about 140% from the breakout, and 350% from the low.

Many would recognize this formation as a cup-with-handle, and indeed it is. But it is also a BARR bottom, as a cup does not depend on a down-sloping trendline and a larger handle on the left such as that shown in Figure 7.1. Whatever you call the formation, the result is still the same: Prices move higher.

Identification Guidelines

Table 7.1 shows a host of characteristics that correctly identify a BARR bottom. Figure 7.2 illustrates the various characteristics outlined in Table 7.1. Overall, the formation appears as a frying pan. The handle, or lead-in phase, forms a trendline that slopes downward at an angle of about 30 degrees to 45 degrees, sometimes more and sometimes less. Draw the trendline along the daily high prices as the line signals a buying opportunity once it is pierced.

Unlike BARR tops, sometimes *horizontal* trendlines in the lead-in phase contain valid BARR bottoms. Such situations are rare, though, and should probably be avoided. The trendlines in this study are higher on the left and slope downward—these give the best performance.

Table 7.1
Identification Characteristics of Bump-and-Run Reversal Bottoms

Characteristic	Discussion
Frying pan shape	The formation looks like a frying pan with the handle on the left sloping downward to the pan. After a deepening decline that takes prices into the pan base, prices level out and eventually soar out the right side.
Down-sloping top trendline, lead-in height	The handle forms a down-sloping trendline that approximates 30–45 degrees (but this varies with scaling). The handle portion of the formation is called the lead-in as it leads in to the bump phase. The lead-in height measures from the trendline drawn across the highs to the low (not necessarily the lowest low) of the formation. Select the widest distance from the trendline to the low, measured vertically, in the first quarter of the formation. The duration of the lead-in should be at least a month, but varies depending on the situation.
Bump phase	The bump is analogous to the frying pan base. The down-sloping trendline deepens to 60 degrees or more. Prices drop rapidly then level out and turn around, usually forming a rounded turn. After the turn, prices move up and sometimes pause at the 30 degree trendline before moving higher. The bump height, as measured from the trendline to the lowest low, should be at least twice the lead-in height. Strict adherence to this rule is not required, but it serves as a good, general guideline.
Uphill run	Once prices lift out of the bump phase, they begin an uphill run that carries prices higher.
Volume	Volume is typically high during the three critical parts of the formation: formation start, bump start, and upside breakout. However, high volume is not a prerequisite.

Note: The frying pan shape and descending trendline is a study in bearish momentum.

Bethlehem Steel Corp. (Steel (Integrated), NYSE, BS)

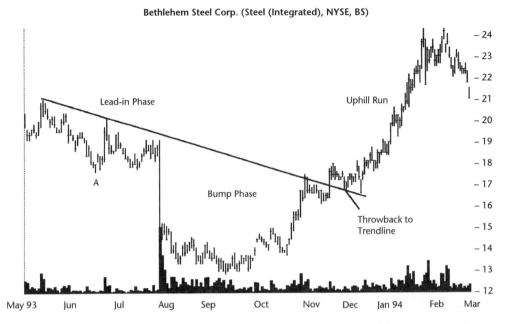

Figure 7.2 Various components of a bump-and-run reversal bottom. A price drop-off follows the lead-in phase where prices move in a narrow range. The bump forms, then rounds upward as prices leave the bowl and move higher on the uphill run to new highs.

Calculate the lead-in height once a trendline forms. Do this by finding the widest distance from the trendline to the daily low, measured vertically, in the first quarter of the formation. In Figure 7.2, the lead-in height calculation uses prices on June 16 (point A). On that day, the low is $17\frac{5}{8}$ and the trendline has a value of about $20\frac{3}{8}$. Thus, the lead-in height is the difference between these two, or $2\frac{3}{4}$. Both the minimum bump height and the target price use the lead-in height, so the calculation is important.

After the lead-in phase comes the bump phase. Prices decline rapidly, although usually not quite as rapidly as that shown in Figure 7.2, and form a new trendline that slopes down at about 45 degrees to 60 degrees or more. Volume is noticeably higher at the start of the bump, but selling pressure overtakes buying demand and the truth finally comes out: There are problems with the company. The stock continues down as the smart money and the momentum players leave the stock in droves.

Eventually, downward pressure abates allowing the stock to recover. It rounds over and touches the original 30 degree trendline. Here, it may move lower for a while or it may sail right through the trendline. About a third of the time, prices start moving higher, then throw back to the trendline before continuing up.

Volume picks up as prices break out of the formation and move higher. Rising prices characterize the uphill run phase. Within 3 months, about half the formations will have hit their ultimate high and started moving down again.

Focus on Failures

Figure 7.3 shows what a BARR bottom failure looks like. The stock starts its ascent in June 1994 when it hits a low of $24\frac{1}{2}$ (not shown). Although the rise is not a straight-line path, prices reach a new high a year later (the highest peak on the left). Then it is downhill from there. The decline is quite orderly with peaks that follow the trendline down. During early September, however, prices drop rapidly on high volume as the bump forms. Prices quickly reach a low of $33\frac{5}{8}$ before rebounding. Having sliced through the trendline and moving just a bit higher, prices throw back and follow the trendline lower. Prices following a trendline lower are not unusual, but what is unusual is that prices do not continue their climb. Instead, they drop off the end of the trendline and plummet. By late June, they slip to under $20 a share, less than half what they were at the high.

Why did the BARR fail? This formation is not a perfect example of a BARR bottom, but few formations are. In this case, the bump height is less

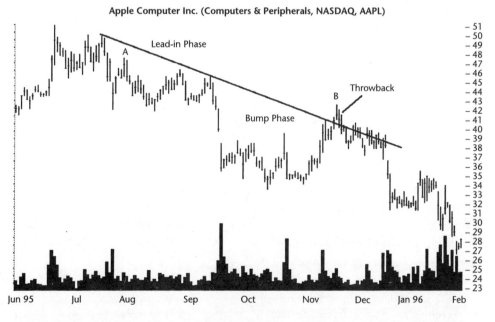

Apple Computer Inc. (Computers & Peripherals, NASDAQ, AAPL)

Figure 7.3 A bump-and-run reversal bottom failure (less than 20% fail). The bump height is less than twice the lead-in height, a clue that the pattern probably is not worth investing in. A trendline drawn from point A to B (not shown) satisfies the bump to lead-in height guideline. Using the new line, an investor waiting for prices to move above the trendline would not buy this stock.

than twice the lead-in height. However, this depends on how the trendline is drawn. Drawing a trendline beginning from the peak at point A, the bump to lead-in height is about 2 to 1. The new trendline also touches the peak at B. So, if you wait for prices to move above the new trendline before investing, you would not purchase this stock. Sometimes it is wise to draw alternative views just to see how the chart pattern behaves (do not forget to draw the pattern on logarithm-based scales).

Statistics

To determine how the average BARR bottom performs, I searched the hundreds of stocks in the database and tabulated their performance statistics. Table 7.2 shows the results. Compared with other formations, the BARR bottom is plentiful, appearing 360 times in 2,500 years of daily price data. When the BARR bottom appears, it acts like a reversal of the prevailing trend 55% of the time and a consolidation the remainder of the time.

The BARR bottom performs well with 81% of the formations moving upward at least 5% after the breakout. If an investor waits for an upside breakout, the performance is even better, with 91% of the formations moving higher. This performance corresponds to a failure rate of 19% and 9%, respectively. Failure rates below 20% are acceptable.

Once an upside breakout occurs, how high does the price rise? On average, prices climb by 37% as measured from the low of the breakout to the

Table 7.2
General Statistics for Bump-and-Run Reversal Bottoms

Description	Statistic
Number of formations in 500 stocks from 1991 to 1966	360
Reversal or consolidation	161 consolidations, 199 reversals
Failure rate	67 or 19%
Failure rate if waited for upside breakout	32 or 9%
Average rise of successful formations	37%
Most likely rise	20%
Of those succeeding, number meeting or exceeding price target (measure rule)	271 or 92%
Average formation length	5 months (157 days)
Number of rounded appearing bumps	279 or 78%
Number of multiple bump formations	52 or 14%

Note: This formation sees prices rise 37% above the breakout, on average.

ultimate high. This is a very good number but is even higher if you happen to catch the rise sooner. From the low during the bump phase, the rise is an astounding 57%. Of course, trying to predict the bottom is exceedingly difficult and I would not use the 57% figure as anything but a statistical observation.

Undo influence by a number of large gains can affect the average, so I created a frequency distribution of gains to check the result (Figure 7.4). The graph shows that the most likely rise is 20%. The graph also shows the relatively high number of large gains (41 formations or 14% with gains over 90%). The many outsized gains apparently pull up the overall average.

If you trade this formation, you might be lucky to have a large gain, but you probably will not. Instead, expect a more reasonable rise and use the likely gain of 20% as the benchmark. That is the tallest column in Figure 7.4—the one with the highest frequency—and it represents the most likely gain.

The measure rule, which predicts the target price, works 92% of the time when using the lead-in height as the benchmark. Simply add the largest height found during the first quarter of the formation to the breakout price. The result is the target price to which prices rise, at a minimum. Later (see Trading Tactics), I discuss details on how to do this.

Substituting the bump height (the widest distance between the trendline and price low, measured vertically) for the lead-in height, results in a performance drop to 67% of formations meeting the predicted price. This is still a good number, but if you depend on it as part of your risk-reward ratio, it might disappoint when your gains fall short.

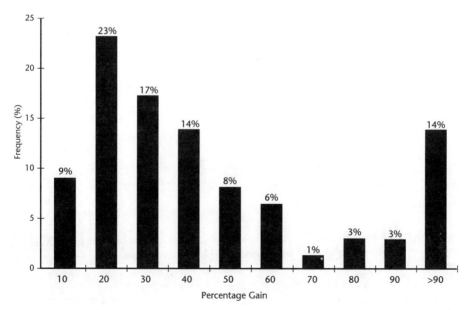

Figure 7.4 Frequency distribution of gains for bump-and-run reversal bottoms. The relatively high number of large gains tends to pull up the average.

It takes about 5 months for the formation to complete, but this varies widely. At a minimum, each formation is a month long as that is what is required of the lead-in duration. When you add in the bump phase, the duration grows.

Three out of four times (78%), the bump appears rounded. Only 52, or 14%, of the BARR bottoms have dual or multiple bumps. Dual or multiple bumps are significant declines after the main bump touches the trendline. Most of the time, the second or later bumps do not decline to the low seen during formation of the main bump. The actual number of secondary bumps declining below the main bump are few but not tabulated.

Figure 7.5 shows a good example of a multiple bump BARR. The first bump completes in mid-August 1993 when prices touch the down-sloping trendline. If you purchased the stock at any time during the first bump, you would have been toast. From the high of $22\frac{3}{4}$ on August 19, the stock declined to $17\frac{3}{8}$ on October 1, nearly a 25% fall.

After that, it is all uphill. The stock moves up smartly and crests at $28\frac{1}{2}$ in mid-January 1994. From the bump low, that is a 64% move and a 33% rise from the breakout. Figure 7.5 imparts a valuable lesson: Consider waiting for the upside breakout before buying into a situation. Not surprisingly, this lesson applies to many formations, not just the BARR bottom.

The dual bump is unusual in that the second bump is lower than the first. As mentioned, dual bumps are a rarity, occurring only 14% of the time. Of

Figure 7.5 A dual bump-and-run reversal bottom. Consider waiting to buy the stock until after it breaks out upward. Had you bought into this situation during July, you would have lost money in the short term.

course, that is scant comfort if you already bought into a situation and it begins declining again.

Table 7.3 shows breakout statistics. Of the 360 formations I examined, only 9% have upside breakouts with prices that fail to move meaningfully (more than 5%) upward. I discovered no formations that break out *downward*, quickly turn around, and move meaningfully higher. That is not to suggest such a scenario will never happen; it simply means it did not happen on my shift. Upside breakouts occur most of the time (90%) with downside breakouts responsible for the remainder.

Once a stock moves above the trendline, it throws back to the trendline about a third (38%) of the time. To accomplish the maneuver, it takes slightly less than 2 weeks. Some throwbacks finish within a few days and others take almost a month before they touch the trendline and start rising again. Excluded from the tally are throwbacks over 30 days as I consider them to be due to normal price action and not part of a throwback.

Once prices begin moving up, it takes slightly over 5 months (160 days) to reach the ultimate high. This sounds about right as a 37% average rise does not happen overnight.

To gauge where in the yearly price range the breakout occurs, I exclude any formation that occurs less than a year from the start. Then I sort the gains into three bins each representing a third of the yearly price range. The resulting frequency distribution shows that most of the formations have breakouts in the center third of the range. Only 20% fall into the high category.

Due to the way the BARR bottom forms, with a down-sloping trendline, one can infer that BARRs start near the yearly high, then move down in price

Table 7.3
Breakout Statistics for Bump-and-Run Reversal Bottoms

Description	Statistic
Upside breakout but failure	32 or 9%
Upside breakout	325 or 90%
Downside breakout	35 or 10%
Throwbacks	136 or 38%
Average time to throwback completion	13 days
For successful formations, days to ultimate high	5 months (160 days)
Percentage of breakouts occurring near the 12-month low (L), center (C), or high (H)	L38%, C43%, H20%
Percentage gain for each 12-month lookback period	L39%, C42%, H28%
Start high to bump low	28% decline
Start high to breakout low	17% decline

Note: Nearly all the BARR bottoms break out upward, with over a third throwing back to the trendline.

to the center range before the breakout. To test this assumption, I compared the price at which the formations start (the daily high) with the yearly price range. Over 8 out of 10 formations (82%) have their start at the top of the price range and decline into the center of the range. The implications of this statistic are significant: *BARRs begin life near the yearly high.* After reviewing the charts, this clearly is the case. BARRs often start just after prices climb to a new high. Prices drift lower and make another try at a new high but fail. The two peaks, the first one higher than the second, set the stage for a down-sloping trendline. Prices then move down and a BARR forms when prices suddenly drop during the bump phase.

Is there a difference in performance among the three price ranges? I computed the gains for the formations that fall into each of the three bins. Formations in the center price range have an average rise of 42%, followed closely by the lower third at 39%. In last place is the highest third, with a 28% average gain.

I expected formations in the lowest grouping to place first and they almost did. I reasoned that the most beat-up stocks would rise furthest. On the other hand, failed momentum stocks, those that are in the highest third of their price range, would have the most difficult time recovering. That is exactly what appears to be happening.

How far down from the formation start are the bump low and breakout points? The statistics say that, on average, the low that occurs during the bump phase is 28% below the high. Since the breakout is above the bump low, it is still 17% below the start.

Many times, prices rise up to their old highs and stop near that level then decline. Several formations base their performance on this assumption, including double and triple tops. I set out to determine if there is any significance to the rise in the stock after a breakout when compared with the starting point for BARRs. Figure 7.6 shows the results of the analysis. I compared the daily high price at the start of the formation with the ultimate high after the breakout. Pictured are the results of a frequency distribution of the percentage gains in the stock price as compared with the starting point. Positive values mean the stock climbs above the starting price (on its way to the ultimate high), whereas negative values mean it falls short. There are a number of points with rises above 25%, but each bin contains less than half the number contained in the 25% category and are not shown for clarity.

The graph suggests that 34% of the formations stop rising within plus or minus 5% of the starting price. Almost two-thirds (61%) are within 15% of the start. Since these are averages, your results may vary, but it does suggest that a measure rule based on the attainment of the old high would work well. If prices rise to the formation starting point (or the nearest high), that may be as far as they go.

Nine months after reaching a low, the stock in Figure 7.7 climbed to its highest price but closed lower for the day. For the next 6 weeks or so, it moved

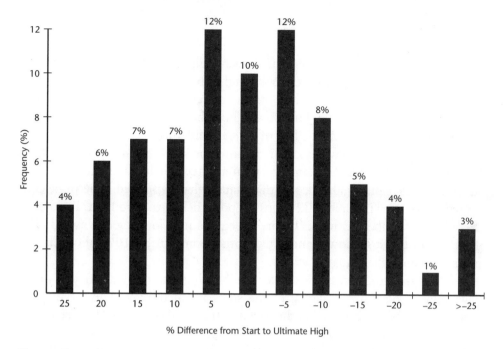

Figure 7.6 Price start versus ultimate high. Comparison between the ultimate high after a bump-and-run reversal bottom compared with the daily high at the start of the formation. Does the stock rise up to the old high and stop? A value of zero means the two points are at the same price level. You can see that many bump-and-run reversal bottoms have prices that are within 5% of each other.

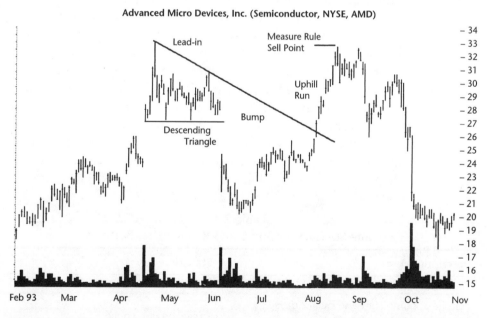

Figure 7.7 Bump-and-run reversal that stopped rising within 15% of its old highs. Sixty-one percent of bump-and-run reversal bottoms perform this way.

in a descending triangle shape, with lower highs and higher lows, until late May 1993. Prices moved up marginally higher but were still below the peak in late April. Then parts began falling off the semiconductor stock. It plummeted over $4 to close at 23¾ on June 7. On high but receding volume the price moved lower until it reached a low of 20⅜ in mid-June.

After spending a few days near the low, the stock began climbing: It was leaving the bump phase. On August 5 it intersected the down-sloping trendline signaling higher prices ahead, and that is just what happened. The price continued rising until it reached 32⅝, just ¼ point below the old high. Its sojourn there lasted for about 2 weeks before it began a new journey downward. The decline sent the stock lower and it did not stop until it hit 16¾, about half its prior level, in early January 1994.

If you used the measure rule (see the Trading Tactics section), you would have sold at the top, the day after the stock reached 32⅝. The target price exactly matched the lead-in height added to the breakout price. This fact, coupled with matching the old high, reinforced the sell signal. Together, the two signals would have taken you out of the stock before the 50% decline began, potentially saving you a bundle.

The last statistics table, Table 7.4, shows the results of the volume study. I examined the most important points in the pattern: formation start, bump start, and breakout. Volume at the start of the formation is 20% above the day before (or 120% of the prior figure), on average. This is only marginally higher than normal and you might not even notice it, since volume tends to bounce around a lot anyway. However, upon entering the bump phase, when prices decline drastically, the volume tells a different tale. It rises 75% on the day of the break and more than doubles (223%) the next day and remains high. In many of the charts that accompany this chapter, you can see high volume surrounding the bump phase. The breakout day also exhibits high volume, but it quickly tapers off. On the day of the upside breakout, volume is 39% above the prior day, on average, and trends downward from there.

Figure 7.8 shows a typical volume pattern. At the start of the formation, volume is quite high for a few days but quickly recedes. As prices move down,

Table 7.4
Volume Statistics for Bump-and-Run Reversal Bottoms

Description	Statistic
Volume at formation start versus day before	120%
Volume at bump start and next 2 days versus day before bump start	175%, 223%, 192%
Breakout day (and succeeding days) volume compared with day before breakout	139%, 130%, 115%, 109%, 99%, 96%

Note: Volume is heavy during the formation start, bump start, and breakout.

General Housewares Corp. (Household Products, NYSE, GHW)

Figure 7.8 Volume pattern. Volume is usually high at the start of the formation, during the beginning of the bump phase, and during the breakout. Only during the start of the bump is the volume in this chart muted.

volume follows. Even at the start of the bump, volume is quiet. Once prices begin descending more rapidly, volume rises a bit overall, especially near the minor lows (late October and December). During the breakout, volume spikes upward and propels the stock higher. Enthusiasm is high enough that the stock gaps upward, not once, but several times. From the bump low, the stock climbs almost 80%, or 50% from the breakout.

Trading Tactics

Table 7.5 outlines trading tactics for BARR bottoms. After properly identifying a BARR bottom, you will want to compute how profitable the formation is likely to be. You do that using the measure rule. Compute the lead-in height by measuring the widest distance from the trendline to the daily low, vertically, in the first quarter of the formation. This is before the bump phase. Add the difference to the breakout price to get the target price. Over 90% of the time prices reach the target, and so the measure rule should serve as a minimum move estimate.

The measure rule relies on knowing the breakout price. Even without the breakout price, you can still see how profitable the formation is likely to be by

Table 7.5
Trading Tactics for Bump-and-Run Reversal Bottoms

Trading Tactic	Explanation
Measure rule	Compute the lead-in height and add it to the breakout price (use the daily low to be conservative). The result is the minimum price to which the stock will rise.
Wait for confirmation	Waiting for the breakout improves investment performance. The close should be above the down-sloping trendline before you buy the stock.
Sell at old high	When prices rise to the old high, consider selling if the stock shows weakness.
Stops	Place a stop $\frac{1}{8}$ below prior resistance. As prices rise, raise the stop.

Note: Profitabilitiy improves if you wait for breakout confirmation.

computing the lead-in height as a percentage of the current price. If the number is small, consider looking elsewhere for a more promising trade.

If the stock looks as if it might be profitable, then it is wise to wait for breakout confirmation. The confirmation point is when prices rise above the trendline formed during the lead-in phase. Should the price close above the trendline, buy the stock.

A second corollary to the measure rule is to sell at the old high. I have discussed how often a stock showing a BARR bottom stops near the old high (which is the start of the formation). Place a sell order near the price level of the old high. That will keep your profits intact should the stock then turn down. If you are reluctant to sell your holdings, why not sell half when the stock reaches the old high, then see what happens?

As always, place a stop-loss order $\frac{1}{8}$ below the nearest support zone. Move the stop upward as the stock advances. That way, when prices turn down, you will not lose too much. There is nothing worse than riding a stock up and following it all the way back down.

Sample Trade

Perhaps the most interesting way to illustrate trading tactics is by example. John is new to investing and he did not take the time to learn thoroughly about BARR bottoms. As he flipped through his stock charts one day, he noticed an intriguing situation developing in the stock depicted in Figure 7.9. During August, the stock peaked, declined a bit, then formed a second minor high. As the stock declined from the second high, John drew a tentative trendline down connecting them. Soon, he noticed that the stock was descending in a sort of channel. He drew a second trendline, parallel to the first, that connected the lows.

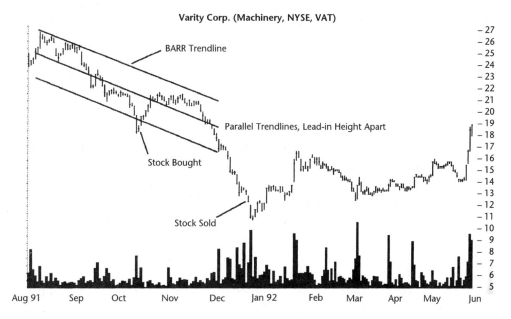

Figure 7.9 A bump-and-run reversal bottom failure in which John invested. He finally sold the stock just 2 days before it reached its low.

However, the stock soon pierced through the second trendline and moved lower. When it declined even further, John thought he recognized a BARR bottom forming. He drew a third trendline, parallel to the other two and lead-in height apart.

As the stock dipped below the lowest trendline, he believed that the decline was at an end. So, the following day he pulled the trigger and bought 100 shares at 18¼. He was pleased to acquire the stock a bit below the closing price for the day.

For the next week, the stock shot upward and pierced the second trendline. John was brimming with enthusiasm and believed that picking stocks was an *easy game*, as he put it. As the stock moved into a consolidation period, John showed no concern. Flat periods of trading often follow quick rises.

When the stock neared the top trendline, John calculated the target price. He computed the lead-in height by subtracting the daily low from the trendline at its widest part in the first quarter of the formation. He used the low of August 20, at 24, and subtracted this from the trendline value of 26, measured vertically. This left him with a lead-in height of $2. John believed that the stock would likely break out at about 21¼, so this gave him a target price of 23¼, which is the lead-in height added to the breakout price.

John recalled that this was a minimum price move achieved by the vast majority of BARR formations, so he was confident that he could hold out for larger gains. From his purchase point, he calculated that he would receive at least a 25% return if everything worked out as planned.

For about a month, the stock moved sideways but this did not alarm him. He even expected the stock to decline a bit and recapture some of its quick gains. Secretly, he hoped that the stock would soon break out of its trading range and head higher. He was confident that it would move up—it was only a question of when.

He was wrong. Indeed, the stock *did* break out of its trading range, but it headed *lower*, not higher. After it approached the top trendline, the stock continued down and touched the middle trendline. John knew that a stock often retraces 40% to 60% of its gains. He grabbed his calculator and computed the retrace value.

The stock reached a high of 21.43 in a straight-line run from the low at 18, a rise of about $3\frac{1}{2}$ points. Now the stock was retracing the gains and had moved down to $18\frac{3}{4}$, a 78% retrace. Clearly, this was out of the realm of a simple retrace. John suspected that a trend change had occurred, but hoped that the pause he was seeing as it touched the middle trendline would give the stock support and call an end to the decline. For a while, it did. The stock paused for 3 days at the trendline then started moving lower again. It quickly fell below the purchase price and headed down.

Although John had purchased the stock as a short-term play, he convinced himself that he really liked the company and would not mind holding it for the long term. Now, at least, that is what it would take for him to recoup his losses and get out at break-even.

The stock quickly moved down through the third trendline, heading lower. The *easy game* was now turning into a disaster. John first considered selling on December 11, when the stock reached $12\frac{3}{4}$, for a 30% loss. He delayed the selling decision by saying that the holding was a long-term one and he should expect to come across such declines in the short term.

The next day, the stock closed higher and it gave him renewed hope. Indeed, it closed even higher the following day. But the 2-day recovery was an illusion and the stock declined again. As it plunged below $12\frac{3}{4}$, John threw up his hands and told his broker to dump the dog. He received a fill at $12\frac{1}{4}$, the low for the day. Two days later, the stock bottomed out at about $10\frac{3}{4}$. From the buy point, John lost 35%.

As upset as this made John, the stock was not finished tormenting him. He continued to follow the stock and watched it move higher. He extended the BARR trendline downward (Figure 7.10) and noticed that a new, larger BARR had formed. After suffering through the large bump, the stock moved higher until it touched the BARR trendline. Then, the stock followed it lower, unable to pierce the resistance line.

Varity Corp. (Machinery, NYSE, VAT)

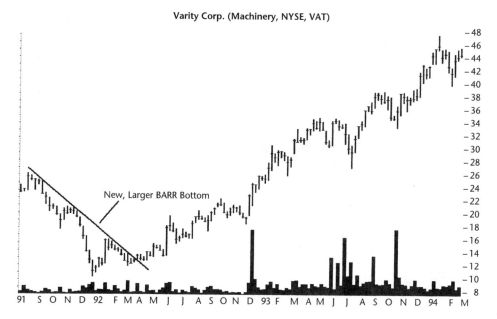

Figure 7.10   A bump-and-run reversal bottom on a weekly scale. After the breakout, the stock climbed over 350%.

During the week of March 27, 1992, the stock closed above the trendline for the first time in months. The BARR was complete and a confirmed breakout was occurring. Did John buy the stock? No. For several months, he watched its progress as it moved higher almost week after week. Disgusted, he quit following the stock.

In April 1994, John took another look at the stock and was surprised to see that it continued moving higher. It had just reached a high of 50⅛, a climb of almost 370%. He grabbed his calculator and realized that his mistake cost him gains of over $3,000.

What did he do wrong? Several things. He did not wait for the BARR to pierce the trendline and move higher. If he had, he would have purchased closer to the low, saving him precious capital. Next, he did not cut his losses short. After he bought the stock, he should have determined his sell point. The middle trendline would have been a good place for a stop-loss order. In this case, it would have taken him out of the stock at about 17⅞, a small decline from the purchase price of 18¼. Instead, he followed the stock down and changed his investment philosophy from a short-term trade to a long-term investment.

When he finally gave up all hope of recovering from this trade, the stock was near the low. Apparently other investors felt the same way as the high volume peaks during late November and through most of December attest. That is a common scenario: Novice investors buy near the top and sell near the bottom, exactly the opposite of what they should be doing.

But there is good news. John has learned from his mistakes. Since that trade, he has learned to wait for a confirmed breakout before placing a trade and now uses stop-loss orders to limit his downside exposure. Does this mean he is a model trader? No. Now he is making other types of mistakes.

8

Bump-and-Run
Reversal Tops

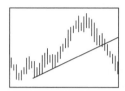

RESULTS SNAPSHOT

Appearance	Prices rise steadily along a trendline, bump up, round over, then decline through the trendline and continue down.
Reversal or consolidation	Short-term (up to 3 months) bearish reversal
Failure rate	19%
Average decline	24%, with the most likely decline between 15% and 20%
Pullbacks	39%
Percentage meeting predicted price target	88%
See also	Rounding Tops

If you were thinking of buying stock in a company, wouldn't it be wonderful if you knew the purchase price would be less tomorrow? Of course! But how do you predict tomorrow's price? That is the question I was working on when I discovered this formation. I was trying to figure out a reliable way to determine if tomorrow's price would be higher or lower than today's and by how much.

I tried all sorts of mathematical games to boost the accuracy of the prediction with only limited success. Then I moved to the visual world. I drew a trendline along a stock chart and wondered if I could determine how far prices would decline below the line. I looked at many stock charts and trendlines trying to see if there was a relationship between a trendline and the breakdown of the trend. That is when I discovered it: the bump-and-run formation—BARF for short. I toyed with the idea of leaving the name as is but decided that the investment community would not believe the veracity of the new formation. So, I changed the name to bump-and-run reversal (BARR), a slightly more descriptive and palatable acronym.

Tour

As I looked at the various trendlines, I discovered that pronounced breakdowns share several characteristics. Look at Figure 8.1, a good BARR example. The overall formation reminds me of a mountain range. The foothills at the start of the formation are low and subdued, not venturing too far above the up-sloping plain. Volume at the start of the formation is high but quickly recedes. The mountains themselves rise up well above the foothills on high volume. Investor enthusiasm continues high as prices round over at the top, then diminishes on the far side. When the mountains end, prices decline sharply and continue moving down. That is a BARR. Prices bump-up, round over, and run back down again. The formation is the visual representation of momentum. The base of the formation follows a trendline that always slopes upward. It signals investors' eagerness to acquire the stock. As each day goes by, investors bid higher to reluctant sellers and the price rises.

Other momentum players eventually notice the rise in the stock price. Many jump on the bandwagon the day after a surprisingly good earnings announcement. That is when the bump begins. Volume spikes upward along with the stock price. Quickly rising prices entice others to join the fray and that, in turn, sends the stock even higher. As momentum increases, prices jump up to form a new, higher-sloping trendline. Then things start going wrong.

Upward momentum continues until supply catches up with demand. As that happens, the rise slows and the smart money turns cautious. Investor enthusiasm wanes and the war between supply and demand turns. The stock rounds over and starts heading down. When the smart money sees prices falling, they sell and the decline picks up speed. Downward momentum increases and returns prices to the trendline. At this point, buying enthusiasm may increase and send prices back up for one last try at a new peak. Usually, however, prices do not bounce off the trendline but continue moving down. Sometimes there is a pause and sometimes prices just plunge straight through the resistance line, as illustrated in Figure 8.1.

Fieldcrest Cannon Inc. (Textile, NYSE, FLD)

Figure 8.1   Good example of a bump-and-run reversal. Prices move up along the trendline in the lead-in phase, jump up during the bump phase, then crash down through the trendline during the downhill run. Volume at the start of the formation and again at the start of the bump is usually high but tapers off as the bump rounds over. About half the time volume picks up as prices pierce the trendline.

Once prices pierce the trendline, volume increases as investors dump the stock. This selling alarms more investors and the downward trend feeds on itself. Eventually, after several months of declining prices, the selling pressure abates and buying enthusiasm halts the downward slide. Prices tentatively level out and perhaps even rebound a bit. Once the cause of the reversal fades from memory, prices start rising again and the process begins anew.

Identification Guidelines

Table 8.1 outlines the various parts of the formation that are illustrated in Figure 8.1. In the figure, a trendline drawn below the lows in the stock extends until it intersects prices as they decline in May. Volume is high at the start, and the trend is up. That is a key consideration: Prices must be rising. The trendline should be approximately 30 degrees, but the degree of slope depends on the scaling used to view the chart. *If the trendline is flat or nearly so, it is not a good BARR candidate.* A rising trendline shows investor enthusiasm for the stock. However, the trendline should not be too steep either. Steep trendlines (over 60 degrees or so) do not allow enough room for the bump to complete properly.

Table 8.1
Identification Characteristics of Bump-and-Run Reversal Tops

Characteristic	Discussion
Rising trendline	A trendline connecting the lows rises steadily: no horizontal or near-horizontal trendlines. The trendline usually rises at about 30–45 degrees (although this varies with scaling). Avoid trendlines that are too steep (over 60 degrees): There is not enough room for the bump.
Lead-in, lead-in height	The lead-in is the section just before prices move up sharply in the bump phase. Lead-in prices should have a range of at least \$1 (preferably \$2 or more), as measured from the highest high to the trendline, vertically, during the first quarter of the overall formation length. Minimum lead-in length is 1 month with no maximum value.
Rounded bump	Prices rise up (trendline slope is 45–60 degrees or more) on high volume usually after a favorable event (unexpectedly good earnings, an analyst recommends or upgrades the stock, higher store sales, that sort of thing). Prices eventually round over and decline back to the 30 degree trendline. The bump must be at least twice the lead-in height, measured from highest high to the trendline, vertically.
Downhill run	After returning to the trendline, prices may bounce back up and form a second bump or slide along the trendline. Eventually prices drop through the trendline and continue down.

The first part of the formation, called the lead-in phase, leads to the bump phase. The lead-in phase should be at least 1 month long and usually falls in the 2- to 3-month range, but can be considerably longer. Prices oscillate up and down in this phase and have a range of at least \$1 as measured from the highest high to the trendline. This range, called the lead-in height, is calculated using prices from the first quarter of the formation.

Figure 8.1, for example, shows that the highest high during the first quarter of the formation occurs on January 12, 1994, at $25\frac{5}{8}$. The trendline directly below this date has a value of about $24\frac{1}{4}$, giving a lead-in height of $1\frac{3}{8}$. The height is important because the minimum bump height and target price, calculated later, use this value. A more accurate approach is to use the *largest* distance from the trendline to the high, which is not necessarily found between the *highest* high and the trendline. Use whatever method makes you feel comfortable.

During the lead-in phase, subdued price action looks as if the stock is gathering strength for the bump phase. Prices do not move very far away from the trendline and usually appear rounded. If you visualize the formation as a mountain range, the lead-in phase represents the foothills.

Volume during the lead-in phase is high at the start. Often this is due to events that occur just before the formation begins. Volume drops off until the start of the bump, when it suddenly rises. The higher share turnover and expanding enthusiasm for the stock forces prices up. In Figure 8.1, this price rise occurs on February 17 and is accompanied by volume that is the highest in half a year.

Prices jump up at the bump start and quickly rise from a low of $26\frac{1}{2}$ to a high of $34\frac{3}{8}$ during late March. Volume remains high throughout this period then quickly tapers off as prices round over at the top. Many times, the top takes on the appearance of a head-and-shoulders formation or a double or triple top. If you recognize any of these formations on your chart, ignore the BARR top formation and obey the implications of the individual formations.

The bump height, as measured from the highest high to the trendline, should be at least twice the lead-in height. In this example, the bump height is 8 (that is, $34\frac{3}{8} - 26\frac{3}{8}$). This is more than twice the lead-in height of $1\frac{3}{8}$.

The reason for the minimum two-to-one ratio is arbitrary. The idea is to make sure that investor enthusiasm and, hence, momentum are getting carried away. An up-sloping trendline that turns into a bump with a higher sloping trendline emphasizes the rising momentum. Sustaining such unbounded enthusiasm for too long is difficult and the stock price eventually declines. In Figure 8.1, that is exactly what happens. Prices round over and start heading down. Sometimes the decline is orderly and sometimes it is choppy. In nearly all cases, prices return to the trendline. Once there, the stock may do several things. Fairly often prices bump up again, and that is called a BARR with a dual bump or a dual BARR. Occasionally, a dual BARR consists of several bumps but the result is still the same. Prices eventually fall below the trendline.

Sometimes prices slide up along the trendline for a month or so before continuing down. At other times, prices drop straight through the trendline, turn around and climb again, before ultimately dropping. In a few rare cases, prices descend from the bump high and never make it back to the trendline before moving higher. These cases commonly appear on weekly or monthly price charts.

Focus on Failures

In Figure 8.2, a weekly chart, the first BARR on the left shows high volume during the initial stages of the bump, as you would expect. The bump height to lead-in height ratio looks good (over 2:1) and clearly investor enthusiasm is high. However, prices continue climbing instead of rounding over and heading down.

Contrast the failed BARR with the one in the center. The middle BARR has a nicely rounded appearance. The volume pattern is what you would expect: high at the start, at the start of the bump, and when prices cross the

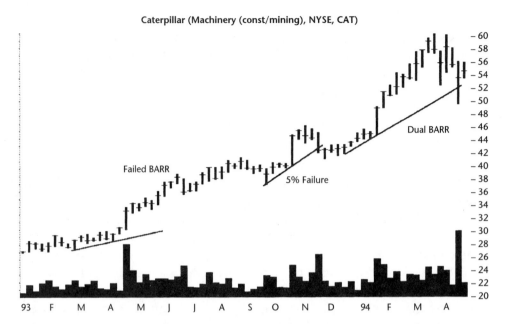

Caterpillar (Machinery (const/mining), NYSE, CAT)

Figure 8.2 A bump-and-run reversal on a weekly chart. The formation on the left fails as prices climb away instead of moving below the trendline. The rounded-appearing center bump-and-run reversal has good volume characteristics—high volume at the formation start, bump start, and trendline crossing. However, prices decline below the trendline just 4%. That is called a 5% failure. The right bump-and-run reversal is a dual bump-and-run reversal formation because prices approach the trendline in March, form a second peak, then drop below the trendline.

trendline. However, prices drop below the trendline by just 4%. Any formation recovering after moving less than 5% below the breakout point is called a 5% failure.

The BARR on the right is a dual BARR. Prices near the trendline in late March 1994, then just as quickly climb again forming a second peak before dropping through the trendline. Often the peak of the second bump is below the first.

On weekly and monthly price charts, you often see prices moving up steadily over time. However, without the sharp bump-up of prices, the rising trend should not be labeled a budding BARR. The slope of the price trendline should rise from about 30% at the start to 60% or higher during the bump phase.

As you look at Figure 8.2, you might think that many BARR formations appear as the failure on the left. However, the statistics show that that is not the case. Ten percent have upside breakouts like the one shown. The other 90% make it to the trendline and begin moving down. Of those heading down, 10% will move down less than 5% before recovering and moving back up substantially. They appear as the BARR in the center and are 5% failures. Together, the two failure types cause the formation to fail 19% of the time. That is still below the 20% maximum that I consider reliable formations to possess.

To reduce the failure rate to just 9%, wait for prices to close below the trendline. Waiting boosts the success rate to 91% but reduces the profit that you would make if you sold near the top. In the Trading Tactics section of this chapter, I show you how to sell near the top before the decline really begins. That way you can keep more of your profits or make even more by shorting.

Statistics

Table 8.2 shows general statistics for BARR tops. Most of the formations (531 or 82%) qualify as reversals of the upward trend. A substantial number (81%) perform as expected, which is to say that prices decline below the trendline by at least 5%. For those formations that succeed, the average decline is 24% as measured from the breakout point to the ultimate low.

Since averages can be misleading (because a few high numbers can pull the average up), I graphed the frequency distribution of declines from the *bump high to the ultimate low*. Figure 8.3 shows the result. A frequency distribution gives a good indication of what the most likely decline will be for a stock in which you invest. The numbers are free of the distorting effects that large returns can have on averages. Figure 8.3 shows that the most likely decline is in the 30% to 40% range.

Figure 8.4 shows a frequency distribution of declines as measured from the high price at the *breakout to the ultimate low*. I use the high price because it

Table 8.2
General Statistics for Bump-and-Run Reversal Tops

Description	Statistic
Number of formations in 500 stocks from 1991 to 1996	650
Reversal or consolidation	531 reversals, 119 consolidations
Failure rate	123 or 19%
Average decline of successful formations	24%
Most likely decline	15% to 20%
Of those succeeding, number meeting or exceeding price target (measure rule)	462 or 88%
Average formation length	7 months (213 days)
Number of rounded-appearing bumps	493 or 76%
Number of multiple bump formations	166 or 26%
Higher second (or later) bump	55 or 8%

Note: More than 80% of the formations studied have downside breakouts with an average decline of 24% below the breakout point.

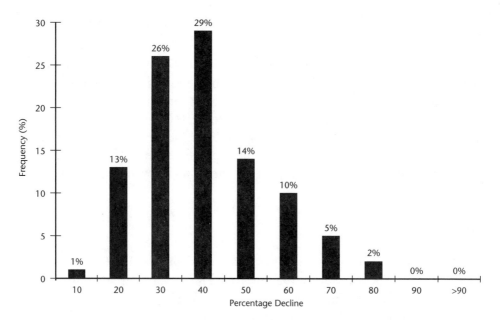

Figure 8.3 Frequency distribution of declines measured from bump high to ulti-mate low. Most of the stocks in the study suffer declines between 30% and 40%, as measured from the highest high during the bump phase to the ultimate low.

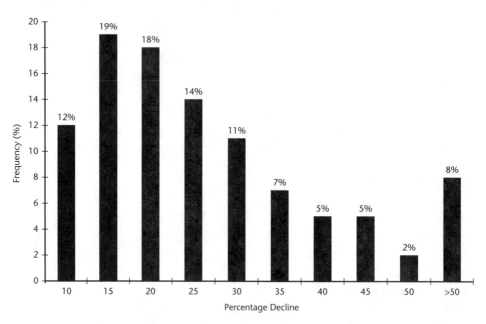

Figure 8.4 Frequency distribution of declines measured from breakout high to ultimate low. Looking at the decline after a downside breakout shows additional declines of 15% to 20% as measured from the high at the breakout (the point clos-est to the trendline) to the ultimate low.

is closest to the trendline on the day of the breakout. Figure 8.4 shows that the most frequent declines occur in the 15% to 20% range. Depending on when you take your profits, you can do exceedingly well with this formation. In the Trading Tactics section, I show you a technique to assist you in selling near the top instead of waiting for prices to plunge to the trendline (the breakout point).

For this formation, I designed the measure rule so that more formations meet the price target. I use the height of the lead-in subtracted from the breakout point to predict the minimum price move. The Trading Tactics section of this chapter explains this more thoroughly, but the approach means 88% of the stocks meet or exceed their price targets, on average.

BARRs take time to form, about 7 months on average. When they form and move into the bump stage, the bump appears rounded 76% of the time.

Compare Figure 8.5 with Figure 8.6. The stock in Figure 8.5 has a bump with a rounded appearance, giving investors plenty of time to sell the stock near the high. Figure 8.6, on the other hand, shows a chart pattern with a much narrower peak. Investors had only a few days to catch the top before prices moved down quickly. The chart in Figure 8.6 is also a dual BARR. There is a second smaller bump just before prices head below the trendline. Dual or multiple bump BARRs occur 26% of the time with only 8% of second or additional bumps having peaks that rise above the first bump.

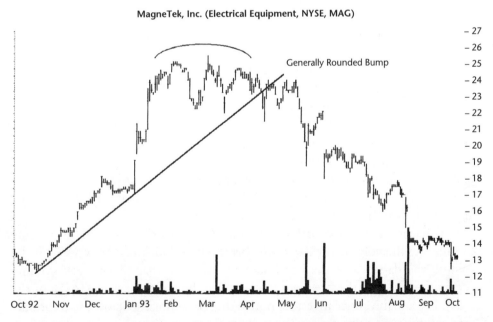

Figure 8.5 A bump-and-run reversal with a rounded bump occurs 76% of the time, on average. Notice the premature downside breakouts in mid-April, a week or two before the actual breakout. The ultimate low reached in October is at a price of 12¼, a decline of over 50%.

Figure 8.6 A bump-and-run reversal with a pointed-looking first bump, leaving investors precious little time to get out of the stock. Many semiconductor stocks showed similar price patterns in late 1995, setting the stage for an industry-wide downturn. The ultimate low reached in mid-January 1996 comes after a decline of nearly 70%.

Table 8.3 shows statistics related to breakouts. Only 9% of the formations have premature breakouts. As you would expect, prices stay at or above the trendline until the genuine downside breakout occurs. Only 9% of the formations studied break out downward and, without declining meaningfully, move back up. These are 5% failures.

Most of the BARR formations have downside breakouts: 584 or 90% move lower with only one moving horizontally. Over a third (39%) of the formations show a pullback to the formation base. Pullbacks occurring over a month after a breakout are removed. Such price movements are really changes in the trend and not pullbacks at all. Pullbacks complete their return to the formation base within 2 weeks (12 days), on average.

What is the volume pattern like on the day of the downside breakout? Comparing the volume the day of the breakout and for the next week with the volume the day before the breakout, you can see that the highest volume occurs the day *after* the breakout (64% above the benchmark, or 164% of the total). Presumably, once investors notice the stock moving below the trendline, they sell the next day, sending the volume figure soaring.

On average, it takes 3 months (94 days) for prices to reach the ultimate low. The ultimate low is the lowest price before a significant trend change occurs.

Table 8.3
Breakout Statistics for Bump-and-Run Reversal Tops

Description	Statistic
Premature downside breakouts	58 or 9%
Downside breakout but failure	57 or 9%
Upside breakout	65 or 10%
Downside breakout	584 or 90%
Horizontal breakout	1 or 0%
Pullback	226 or 39%
Average time to pullback completion	12 days
Breakout day (and succeeding days) volume compared with day before breakout	136%, 164%, 126%, 118%, 116%, 115%
For successful formations, days to ultimate low	3 months (94 days)
Percentage of breakouts occurring near the 12-month low (L), center (C), or high (H)	L12%, C43%, H46%
Percentage decline for each 12-month lookback period	L46%, C37%, H30%

Note: The most significant declines occur near the yearly price low, but BARRs do not often occur there.

At what point in the yearly price range do downside breakouts occur? I removed breakouts that occurred less than 1 year after the start of the study and compared the price on the breakout day with the range over the prior year. I divided the yearly price range into thirds and compared the breakout price with three categories: the lowest third, center, and highest third. The results show that only 12% break out near the yearly low, 43% are in the middle, and the rest occur near the yearly high. These results make sense. The highest enthusiasm for a stock is when it reaches new highs. Such bullish enthusiasm feeds momentum and propels the stock even higher. Eventually, supply rises along with the price and quenches demand. When that happens the stock rounds over and heads down. Even though the stock declines, there are still many investors who try buying on the dips or who believe the decline will be short. They help slow the decline and may even turn it around.

Mapping the performance over the three categories results in some surprises. For those formations breaking out near the yearly low, prices decline by an average of 46%. Breakouts in the highest third of the yearly price range decline by only 30%. I expected the reverse. I assumed that you would get the largest declines near the yearly high, not the yearly low.

Upon reflection, this makes sense. Since the BARR is a representation of momentum, upside momentum carries prices upward. Even after a reversal, some investors continue to hope (by buying more shares as prices decline) that the stock is only retracing its gains and will soon rebound.

When a BARR occurs near the yearly low, presumably the stock is already in the doghouse. Although some investors are exuberant about the rising price, once it begins to descend, they quickly run for cover. Bad news follows bad news and sends the stock down even further.

On the basis of the results in Table 8.3, you could argue that you should short stocks that appear on the new low list in the newspaper and not on the new high list. In any case, the largest declines from BARR formations occur with breakouts in the lowest third of the yearly price range.

Trading Tactics

Table 8.4 lists tools to help judge when to sell a stock that contains a BARR as well as the minimum price decline to expect from such a formation. As you view your stock charts periodically, some stocks will follow trendlines upward. These are the ones to monitor closely. Occasionally, one will begin a rapid climb on high volume and enter the bump phase.

By definition, a BARR is only valid when the bump height, as measured from the highest high to the trendline, is at least twice the lead-in height. Two

Table 8.4
Trading Tactics for Bump-and-Run Reversal Tops

Trading Tactic	Explanation
Measure rule	Compute the lead-in height (see Table 8.1 for the definition) and subtract the result from the value of the trendline where prices cross the trendline moving down (end of the bump). The result is the *minimum price* move to expect. Almost 9 out of 10 stocks meet their price targets.
Warning line	Drawn parallel to the trendline and lead-in height above it. The line warns that the stock is making a move and is entering the sell zone, an area between the warning and sell lines.
Sell line	A second trendline parallel to the warning line and lead-in height above it. Consider selling when prices touch the sell line, especially if the bump is narrow. Delay selling if prices continue moving up. Draw additional lines parallel to the original trendline and lead-in height above the prior line. When the stock rounds over and touches the lower trendline, sell the stock.
Sell zone	The zone alerts the investor to begin doing research to determine if taking profits is wise. Since valid bumps always touch the sell line (by definition, the minimum bump height is twice the lead-in height, and that is where the sell line appears), an investor should be ready to make a sell decision.

Note: Consider selling when prices rise above the sell line.

lines parallel to the trendline assist in that determination. The first line, called the warning line, is lead-in height above the trendline. A second trendline, parallel to the first two and lead-in height above the warning line, is the sell line.

The warning line serves as a signal that a BARR may be forming. Once prices move solidly above the line, consider doing any fundamental or technical research on the stock to prepare yourself for a sale.

By the time prices touch the sell line, you should have a firm grasp of the company, industry, and market outlook. The sell line is not an automatic sell trigger, but it does confirm that a BARR is present. The sell line touch indicates that the momentum players have the upper hand. The game could continue for several weeks or months before the downhill run phase sets in, so do not be in too much of a rush to sell. Since most bumps appear rounded, there is ample time to sell the stock. By waiting, you are giving the momentum players additional time to push the stock even higher.

However, there are situations when you will want to pull the trigger quickly. If the company, industry, or market look dicey, then perhaps it is time to take profits. You might not be selling at the exact top, but you never go broke taking a profit. Also, if the bump does not appear rounded, then consider selling. A quick decline often follows a quick rise.

Figure 8.7 shows the BARR trendline and the two parallel warning and sell lines, each line lead-in height from the other. The chart is on a weekly scale

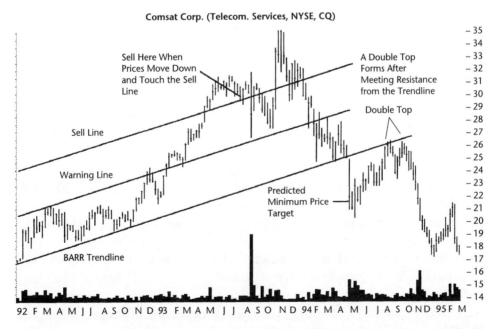

Figure 8.7 Bump-and-run reversal trendline and two parallel warning and sell lines. There is plenty of time to take profits in this bump-and-run reversal. The stock reached a low of 17½ in December, a 40% decline from the sell point in July. Also shown in the July to September period is a double top.

and emphasizes the relaxed nature of some BARRs. If you owned the stock depicted in Figure 8.7 and sold it when prices pierced the sell line moving down, you would not have sold at the top. However, you would have avoided the 40% decline that followed. The decline also points out that it can be easy to make money, on paper, in the stock market but difficult to keep it.

Figure 8.7 also shows the measure rule in action. The measure rule is a method used to predict the *minimum* price decline of the stock. For BARRs in this study, almost 9 out of 10 stocks decline below the predicted price.

To compute the predicted minimum decline, calculate the lead-in height by splitting the formation along the trendline into four equal parts. In the first quarter of the formation, compute the height from the highest high to the trendline, measured vertically (or use the widest distance between the two). Subtract the result from where the trendline is pierced, heading down. In Figure 8.7, the lead-in height is $3\frac{1}{2}$ (that is, $21\frac{1}{2} - 18$). The target price is thus $21\frac{5}{8}$ ($25\frac{1}{8} - 3\frac{1}{2}$), reached during the week of the breakout.

After the breakout, the stock rises back up to meet the trendline before resuming its decline. Since a trendline denotes a resistance area when approached from below, it is no surprise prices turn away. Prices form a double top in the July to September period and plunge downward.

Sample Trade

Jenny is a librarian. Before she goes home at the end of each day, she logs onto the Internet and checks her stock portfolio. She did not notice it at first, but by mid-September, Jenny spotted a BARR forming in a stock she owned (Figure 8.8). She spent an hour searching the Internet for anything she could find about the company. She checked the fundamentals, analysts' recommendations, insider buying and selling patterns, and anything else she could think of.

She reviewed the reasons she bought the stock. Using the Peter Lynch style of investing—that of buying a stock one is familiar with—held a special appeal to her. She liked shopping at the grocery store chain and the products they sold were something she could really sink her teeth into. She felt comfortable owning the stock.

Jenny printed out the price chart and examined the BARR in detail. She drew the trendline along the bottom, divided the length of it into four equal parts, and computed the lead-in height. Then she drew the warning and sell lines parallel to the trendline, each separated by the lead-in height. She computed the minimum target price to which the stock was likely to decline. From the current price of 30, the target price was 23, a decline of almost 25%. Even though she still liked the stock, such a large decline made her nervous.

She looked back through the chart price history and searched for support zones so she could better gauge the area where any decline might stop. The first support area was in the 23 to 24 zone, where a prior advance had paused.

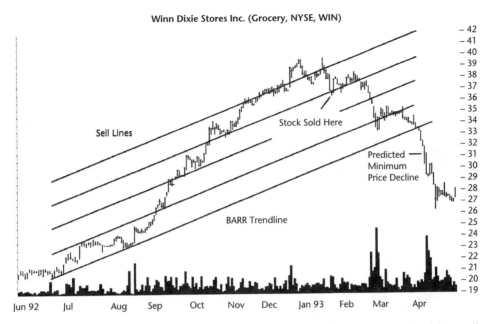

Figure 8.8   Detailed bump-and-run reversal with sell lines. Jenny raised her sell point as the stock climbed. Eventually, she sold the stock the day after it pierced a lower sell line.

Interestingly, that was also the predicted decline point for the stock. If the stock fell below the support point, she noticed a second, more robust support area between 20 and 22.

What of the possible reward? How high could she expect the stock to rise? Long-term price charts were no help as the stock was making new highs almost daily. Jenny shrugged her shoulders as there was no way to determine where the rise would stop. Her only guess was that it might pause at 35, 40, or 45, price points where investors might decide to sell. Any one of those points could turn the stock downward, she decided. Even the current 30 level might be the highest price the stock sees.

After her analysis was complete, she was still confident that the stock held promise of additional gains. As with any stock caught by upward momentum, there was no telling how high the stock would climb before it stopped. She decided to hang on to the stock. If the stock declined to the warning line, she would sell it. She placed a stop-loss order at 27½, the current value of the warning line.

During late September and into the start of October, the stock followed the sell line upward. On October 12, the stock jumped upward again. After a week or so, Jenny was able to draw another sell line parallel to the original BARR trendline that intersected stock prices. She decided that should the stock fall to the lower sell line, she would dump the stock. She raised her stop-loss point to 31. But the stock did not return to the lower sell line.

The stock reached a minor high of 34⅜ on October 19, then retraced some of its prior gains. It curled around and reached a low of 32⅞ before turning around. Jenny printed out another price chart and drew a new trendline. This line had a slope of about 60 degrees. She smiled as the BARR was performing exactly as predicted.

During the first part of December, prices pierced the 60 degree trendline when the stock began moving sideways. Jenny suspected that the rise was nearly over, but one could never tell for sure until it was too late. She decided that should the stock decline below the latest sell line, she would close out her position.

The stock moved up again. A few days after Christmas, the stock reached a new high of 39¾ and Jenny was able to draw another sell line. During the next 2 weeks, the stock declined to the lower sell line, then rebounded to challenge its recent high. On January 15, it peaked at 39⅞, a smidgen below the 40 resistance number she estimated earlier.

To Jenny, the day looked like a one-day reversal, but she could not be sure. Taken together, the two highest points looked like a double top but the recession between them was not deep enough to qualify and the two peaks were a bit too close together. Still, it was a warning sign and it made her nervous.

Less than a week later, the stock declined below the lower sell line. Should she sell or hold on for additional gains? She looked back at the profit she had made so far and decided not to be greedy. She sold the stock at 36¾ on January 22. The next trading day, the stock closed up 1¼ at 38, and she was crestfallen.

She continued to monitor the stock and watched it hesitantly move higher over the next 2 weeks. She tried to take solace in the large profit she achieved, but it was little comfort in the face of missed gains. Did she sell too soon? Should she have held on? On February 23, her questions were answered when the stock dropped below her sell point, heading down.

Jenny watched the stock drop to 35 and find support at that level. Then, it continued moving down. In early April, the stock declined below the original trendline and she calculated the minimum target price of 31. This was reached within the week and the stock continued falling.

She turned her attention to other interesting situations and forgot her trade until July 1994. By chance, she pulled up a chart of the company and was horrified to see that the stock had declined to a low of about 21, almost a 50% decline from the high.

9

Cup with Handle

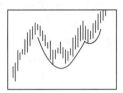

RESULTS SNAPSHOT

Appearance	Looks like a cup profile with the handle on the right
Reversal or consolidation	Short-term (up to 3 months) bullish consolidation
Failure rate	26%
Failure rate if waited for breakout	10%
Average rise	38%, with most likely rise between 10% and 20%
Throwbacks	74%
Percentage meeting predicted price target	49% using full formation height, 73% using half formation height
Surprising finding	Cups with a higher right lip perform better, 40% versus 35% average gain.
See also	Bump-and-Run Reversal Bottom; Rounded Bottom

Shown above are the important statistics for the cup-with-handle formation. The failure rate is 26%, above the 20% that I consider acceptable. However, if you wait for an upside breakout, the failure rate drops to 10%. The average gain is 38%, which is good, but below the 40% garnered for most bullish formations. The most likely rise ranges between 10% and 20% and it is evenly distributed. A closer examination of the results shows that 39% of the formations have gains less than 20%, whereas the outliers, those with gains over 50%, represent 27% of the formations.

Throwbacks after an upside breakout occur in nearly three out of four chart patterns. This suggests an interesting way to play the cup-with-handle pattern: Wait for the throwback before buying the stock. This technique also boosts the average gain by a small amount. I discuss this further in the Trading Tactics section of this chapter.

The percentage of formations meeting the predicted price target is a pathetic 49%. Most measure rules, which predict the target price, involve computing the formation height and adding the result to the breakout price. With this pattern, the cup height can be considerable so it should come as no surprise that only half the formations meet their price targets. I explore changes to the measure rule in the Trading Tactics section that improve the price prediction.

A surprising finding that is discussed in the Statistics section is a tendency for cups with a higher right lip to outperform those with a higher left lip. The difference, an average gain of 40% versus 35%, is statistically significant.

Tour

The cup-with-handle formation was popularized by William J. O'Neil in his book, *How to Make Money in Stocks* (McGraw-Hill, 1988). He gives a couple of examples such as that shown in Figure 9.1. The stock climbed 345% in less than 2 months (computed from the right cup lip to the ultimate high). This was the best performing stock in this study. Unfortunately, it does not meet O'Neil's criteria for a cup-with-handle formation. I discuss my interpretation of his criteria in a moment, but let us first take a closer look at the chart pattern. The stock began rising in early August at a price of about $5\frac{1}{2}$ and climbed steadily until it bumped up in early December. Volume, incidentally, was very high for the stock at this stage. The stock climbed robustly then rounded over and plunged back through an earlier trendline. It completed a bump-and-run reversal (BARR). During its climb, the stock reached a high of $26\frac{7}{8}$ during late December and a low of $12\frac{3}{8}$ after the BARR top—a loss of 54%. The rise and decline formed the left side of the cup. Over the next 2 months, prices meandered upward and pierced the old high during late March. The rise to the old high completed the right side of the cup.

Profit-taking stunted the climb and prices moved horizontally for almost 2 weeks before resuming their rise. This formed the cup handle (incidentally, the handle in this formation is a high, tight flag formation). Volume during formation of the handle was down sloping—higher at the start and trending lower. When prices rose above the cup lip, a breakout occurred. This accompanied a surge in volume that propelled prices higher. However, a week after the breakout, prices threw back to the handle top before continuing upward.

Diana Corp. (Telecom. Services, NYSE, DNA)

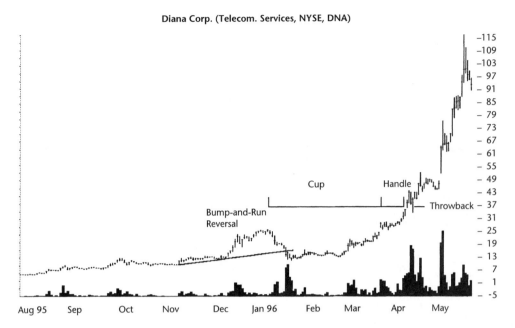

Figure 9.1 Bump-and-run reversal that leads to a cup-with-handle formation. Note the price scale as the breakout occurs at about 30 and the stock climbs to 120 in less than 2 months. The cup handle is a high, tight flag formation.

This throwback allowed nimble investors the opportunity to enter long positions or add to existing ones. By late May, just 44 days after the breakout, the stock reached the ultimate high of 120.

Identification Guidelines

In the study of chart formations, when I search a database for various patterns, I ignore most conventional selection criteria. I let the formations determine their own characteristics. That is the approach I used in selecting the cup-with-handle formation. After making my selections, I sorted the database according to my interpretation of O'Neil's selection guidelines and compared the performance. Table 9.1 shows the O'Neil selection criteria, the guidelines I used to select formations, and my interpretation of his criteria.

O'Neil outlines many selection guidelines in his quest to find suitable cup-with-handle patterns. He found that the performance of a stock, relative to the performance of other stocks, is important. A stock with improving relative strength helps weed out underperforming situations.

I do not know which stocks he used to compute his relative strength characteristics, so I did not use relative strength as a selection rule. If I had, the number of stocks meeting O'Neil's guidelines may have decreased further (just

Table 9.1
Two Different Approaches to O'Neil's Cup-with-Handle Pattern

O'Neil Criteria	Unfiltered Selection Guidelines	Filtered Selection Guidelines: The O'Neil Interpretation
Improving relative strength	None	None, information unavailable
Substantial increase in volume during prior uptrend	None	Very high volume during rise to cup
Rise before cup is at least 30%	Same	Same
U-shaped cup	Same	Same
Cups without handles allowed	Cups must have handles	Cups must have handles
Cup duration: 7 to 65 weeks	Same	Same
Cup depth: 12% or 15% to 33%. Some decline 40% to 50%	None	12% to 33%
Handle duration: usually at least 1 to 2 weeks	1 week minimum	1 week minimum
Handle downward price trend	None	Same
Handle downward volume trend	None	Same
Handles form in upper half of cup	Selected if handle *looks* like it formed in upper half; 16% failed but were close and used anyway	Same
Handle forms above 200 day price moving average	None	Handle low above 200 day moving average
Handle price drop should be 10% to 15% from high unless stock forms a very large cup	None	Handle decline from right cup high to handle low must be 15% or less
High breakout volume, at least 50% above normal	None	Breakout volume at least 50% above 25-day moving average
Saucer with handle price pattern has more shallow cups	None	No distinction made
None suggested	Cup edges should be at about the same price level	Cup edges should be at about the same price level

Note: The best performance comes from the unfiltered selections in the center column. The word *same* refers to the guideline shown in the left column.

9% meet his guidelines as it is) and the impact on performance is unknown. For those stocks that meet his selection criteria, I looked at each cup-with-handle formation and verified that there is very high volume somewhere on the rise leading to creation of the cup. Of the formations obeying the O'Neil criteria, only one successful formation was excluded as a result.

As I was selecting cup-with-handle formations, it became apparent that locating cups during an uptrend is important. So, I adopted O'Neil's criteria of a minimum 30% rise leading up to the cup.

All the cups are U-shaped (V-shaped ones being removed). Also removed from the study were cups without handles. To me, a cup without a handle is a rounding bottom. I discuss rounding bottoms in Chapter 34.

I use a strict interpretation of O'Neil's cup depth. A maximum depth of 50%, although increasing the number of cups meeting his guidelines, raises the failure rate along with the average gain. However, neither the failure rate nor the average gain changes significantly, so I used a range of 12% to 33%.

O'Neil specifies a number of guidelines for the handle. He says the handle should be a minimum of 1 to 2 weeks long, but does not set a maximum duration. In my observation of the formation, prices can, and often do, move horizontally for several months before staging a breakout.

As I examined each chart for the pattern, I eliminated those with handles that form well below the midpoint. However, I was not concerned if my casual observations included a few cups with handles that fell below the center. Removing all handles that are lower than the cup midpoint boosts the average gain just 1% to 39%.

As you can see from Table 9.1, I ignore many of the O'Neil criteria when selecting cup-with-handle formations for further analysis. Once I collected the chart patterns, I filtered the cups through my interpretation of the O'Neil criteria. This grouping of methods, unfiltered and filtered, yielded two sets of performance statistics. But first, let us take a look at a few examples of cup-with-handle patterns.

As mentioned before, the cup pattern shown in Figure 9.1 does not meet the O'Neil criteria. Why? The cup depth, at 54%, is too deep to qualify. Additionally, the handle price trend is upward, not downward. Price and volume trends were evaluated using linear regression from the day after the right cup lip to the day before the breakout. Excluding those 2 days helps remove possibly large price moves. I used closing prices in the calculation on the remaining data (for the handle price trend).

Figure 9.2 shows another good example of the cup-with-handle pattern. The cup gently rounds over and climbs just beyond the old high then pauses. Prices drift down in the handle, along with a down-trending volume pattern before the breakout. Then volume surges and prices move smartly upward. Two days after the breakout, prices move marginally lower again and enter the region of the right cup lip. It is a brief throwback and prices are soon on their way again. Less than 2 months later, the stock tops out at $15\frac{1}{2}$ for a rise of 22%.

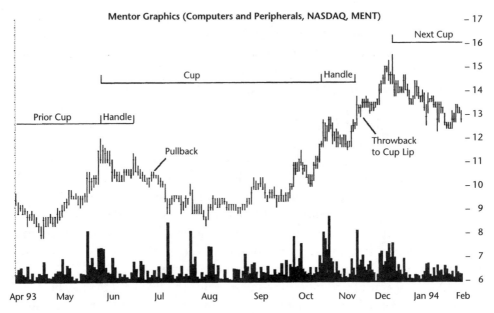

Figure 9.2 A cup-with-handle pattern. The cup and handle are shaped nicely with the right cup lip slightly higher than the left.

If you look on either side of the cup in Figure 9.2 you will find two additional cups (portions of which are shown) that fail. The one on the left breaks out downward and the one on the right fails to continue rising by more than 5%, so it too is a failure. Only the center cup works as expected but even it shows muted gains. We see in the Statistics section that a significant number of cup-with-handle formations fail to rise very far.

Figure 9.3 also shows a cup-with-handle formation but on the weekly time scale. When I was searching for the various formations, I found that weekly scales provide an easy way to identify many of the formations. Of course, I also looked at daily price data to refine the weekly patterns and identify new formations that I may have missed.

The chart in Figure 9.3 shows an example of a cup-with-handle formation in which the rise falters after rising just 11%. Fortunately, after declining back to the handle base, the stock recovers and goes on to form new highs. Ultimately, the stock gains 52%.

Figure 9.3 also highlights an incorrectly selected cup: an inner cup. There is no 30% rise leading up to the formation (since prices are trending downward) and the handle lasts just 2 days. However, inner cups offer wonderful trading opportunities as they allow you to get in on the ground floor of an impending rise. Even if prices only rise to the height of the outer left cup lip, the move can be significant. A discussion of trading tactics occurs later in this chapter.

Figure 9.4 shows another example of an errant cup selection. The rise from point A to point B is less than 30%. Had you invested in this pattern after

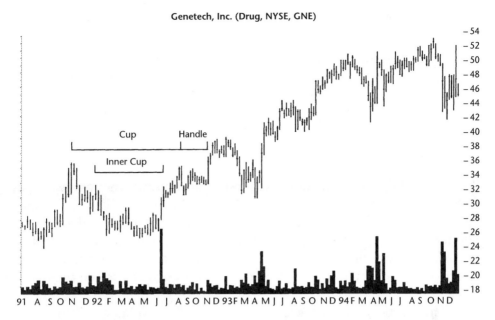

Figure 9.3 Cup-with-handle pattern on a weekly scale. The failure at 10% to 15% above the breakout is quite typical for this formation. However, this stock recovered and continued upward.

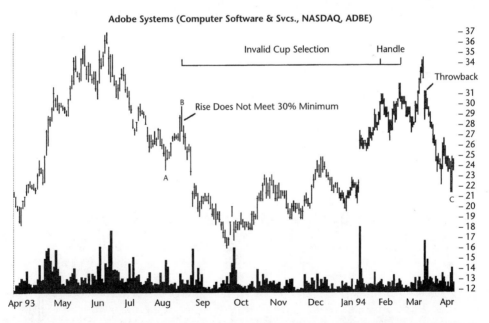

Figure 9.4 An invalid cup-with-handle pattern. The rise from point A to point B is less than 30%. The two outer peaks (in June and March) do not create a cup either because the handle drops down too far (point C)—well below the cup midpoint.

prices rose above the cup lip, you would have seen the stock climb to 34½, an increase of just 11%. After it reached the high, the stock plummeted. In less than a month, prices declined to 21½, a loss of 38%.

Focus on Failures

The cup-with-handle formation, like most formations, suffers from two types of failures. The first type of failure is shown in Figure 9.5. The cup formed after an extended rise that began in mid-December 1993 at 15½ and rose to the left cup lip at 24⅜. Prices quickly reversed course and moved lower, then became choppy as they traversed the cup bottom. Once an upward trend was underway, the choppiness smoothed out and prices soared to the right edge of the cup.

The day before prices reached a new high, high volume soaked up the demand for the stock. The stock coasted to a new high the next day then moved lower. A handle formed about a week later in the 22–23 range. The volume trend during this time was sloping downward, as you would expect. However, prices dropped through the handle low, pulled back into the handle, then dropped away again. From that point on, it was all downhill. A low reached in late January at 14½ shows a decline of 42% from the cup lip.

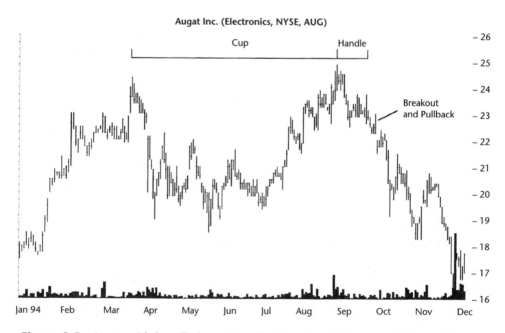

Figure 9.5 A cup-with-handle formation that breaks out downward. It should serve as a reminder to always wait for the breakout to move above the cup lip before buying the stock. This cup-with-handle formation turned into a double top.

As you look at the cup-with-handle formation in Figure 9.5, you see little that is out of the ordinary. The right edge of the cup is somewhat above the left edge. Minor differences between the two cup edges are normal. Sometimes the left edge is higher and sometimes the right one is higher.

Volume during formation of the cup is about average for this stock. Instead of a cup-with-handle formation, what you really are looking at is a double top. The two widely spaced peaks, the first in March and the second in August, predict a decline in the stock.

The vast majority of cup-with-handle formation failures break out downward. Of the formation failures identified in the database, 74 have downside breakouts and only two of those turn around and finish higher by more than 5%.

The second type of failure is the inability of the stock to rise by at least 5% before declining. Figure 9.6 shows this situation. The nicely shaped cup forms after an extended price rise from 33 to 45. The two cup edges are at about the same price level. The handle seems to form a small cup of its own. Prices move up sharply in late September and break above the right cup lip and continue higher, but only briefly. The stock tops at $47\frac{7}{8}$, moves horizontally for about 3 weeks, then starts down. Two months later, the stock hits a low of $37\frac{5}{8}$. The rise after the breakout is slightly less than 5%. I classify as a failure a stock that does not continue moving more than 5% in the direction of the breakout. Of the formations with upside breakouts, only 10% or 30 failed because they did not continue climbing by more than 5%. It seems that once an upside breakout occurs, prices generally continue climbing—at least 5% anyway.

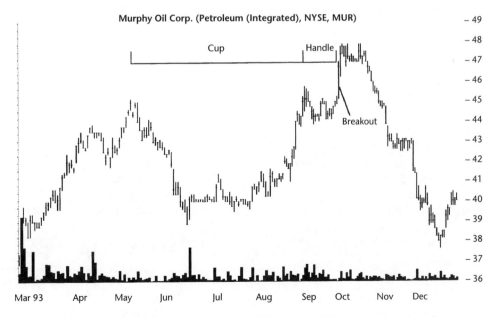

Figure 9.6 A cup-with-handle formation 5% failure. Although prices break out upward, they move less than 5% away from the cup lip before plunging downward.

Statistics

As mentioned earlier, I first selected the cup-with-handle formations then filtered out those chart patterns that did not obey my interpretation of O'Neil's criteria. Listed in Table 9.2 are the results. Just 9% of the selected patterns met his selection criteria (outlined in Table 9.1). Of those meeting the criteria, only 62% perform as expected. That is to say, 38% either break out downward or fail to rise by more than 5% before reaching the ultimate high. The average rise of successful formations is 34%, but the most likely rise is just 15%. Since only 23 formations were successful (a small sample count), the frequency distribution used to determine the most likely rise is suspect but it does agree with the unfiltered (non-O'Neil) formations.

O'Neil suggests that there should be a substantial increase in volume somewhere during the rise to the cup. I excluded only four formations because

Table 9.2
Statistics and Results for Cup-with-Handle Formations Filtered by Many
of O'Neil's Rules

Description	Statistic or Result
Number of formations	37 out of 391
Failure rate	14 or 38%
Average rise of successful formations	34%, but most likely rise is 15%
Is *substantial increase* in volume during prior uptrend important?	No. Only 4 formations were excluded (if included, performance deteriorates).
Is cup length from 7 to 65 weeks important?	Unknown. All selected cups fall in this range.
Is cup length related to ultimate gain?	No. Relationship is random.
Does cup depth (12% to 33%) improve performance?	No. It is detrimental and limits performance.
Is a handle duration (1 week minimum) important?	Unknown. Cups with shorter handles were eliminated.
Do down-sloping handle price trends improve performance?	No. They are detrimental.
Does a down-sloping handle volume trend improve performance?	No. It is detrimental.
Is it important that a handle be above cup midpoint?	Yes, but most formations were selected with this in mind.
Is handle low above 200-day moving average important to performance?	No. Has no bearing on performance.
Is it important that handle low is 15% or less from cup lip?	No. Has no bearing on performance.
Is high breakout volume important to performance?	Yes, but only minimally.
Is cup depth related to ultimate gain?	No. Relationship is random.

of this item (three formation failures and one 22% gain). However, including all four formations would increase the failure rate. I did not include this requirement in the unfiltered cup selections.

Is the cup length important to performance? All the cup-with-handle patterns I selected fall within the range of 7 to 65 weeks. However, I did a scatter plot to determine if shallow cups perform better than deep ones. The plot suggests the relationship is random.

Does cup depth improve performance? Placing specified limits on the cup depth is detrimental to performance. Changing the minimum depth to 30% from 12% and the maximum depth to 55% from 33% improves both the failure rate (to 33% from 38%) and the average gain (to 36% from 34%). I chose not to specify any cup depth in the unfiltered cup selections.

All the cup-with-handle formations I chose had handles that were at least 1 week long. Shorter handle cups were removed from the statistics so it is not clear if this rule is important.

Rules regarding down-sloping price and volume trends were found to limit performance. Removing the two rules decreases the failure rate and improves the average rise. These two factors are primarily responsible for the relatively poor performance of the filtered cup selections.

Is it important how low a handle goes? Yes, and no. I found it important that the handle remain above the midpoint (although most cups were selected with this in mind, so a fair analysis cannot be performed) but it is irrelevant that it remain above the 200-day price moving average or within 15% from the right cup lip.

Is breakout volume important? Removing this selection rule hurts performance but the change is slight.

O'Neil made a distinction between cup-with-handle patterns and saucer-with-handle patterns. I believe that the difference between the two is only a matter of cup depth, already addressed by the cup depth rule. However, I wondered if cup depth played an important part in determining the average gain. A scatter plot of the cup depth versus percentage gain for unfiltered cups suggests the relationship is random. The scatter plot for the filtered cups also suggests the relationship is random, but samples are too few to be meaningful.

Table 9.3 shows statistics for the unfiltered cup-with-handle formations. Only those rules outlined in Table 9.1 for *unfiltered* selections apply. There are 391 formations identified, with 302 of them acting as consolidations of the prevailing trend. Eighty-nine formations act as reversals, with the vast majority of them being failures to perform as expected. The failure rate is 26%, well below the 38% found for the filtered variety. The failure rate improves dramatically (to 10%) if you wait for the upside breakout before investing.

The average rise at 38% handily beats the filtered-cup average rise of 34%. However, the most likely rise is between 10% and 20%. Figure 9.7 shows that most likely gain splits evenly between the first three columns (10% through 20%). The tallest column suggests that large gains skew the average

Table 9.3
General Statistics for Unfiltered Cup-with-Handle Formations

Description	Statistic
Number of formations in 500 stocks from 1991 to 1996	391
Reversal or consolidation	302 consolidations, 89 reversals
Failure rate	102 or 26%
Failure rate if waited for upside breakout	30 or 10%
Average rise of successful formations	38%
Most likely rise	10% to 20%
Of those succeeding, number meeting or exceeding price target (measure rule using full cup height)	151 or 49%
Of those succeeding, number meeting or exceeding price target (measure rule using half cup height)	223 or 73%
Average formation length	7 months (208 days)
Do short handles show larger gains?	Yes, but relationship may be weak
Does a higher right cup lip mean larger gains?	Yes, with gains of 40% versus 35%

Note: Both the failure rate and average gain improve over the filtered variety.

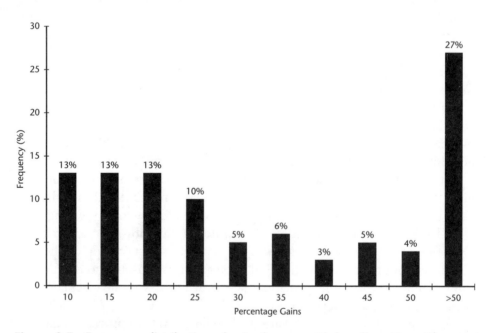

Figure 9.7 Frequency distribution of gains for cup-with-handle pattern. The most likely rise is between 10% and 20%, but the outsized gains over 50% distort the average.

rise upward. A quarter of the formations have a rise of less than 15%, whereas half the formations top out with less than 25% gains. The message from the frequency distribution graph is clear: If you think investing in a cup-with-handle formation will yield outsized gains, you should think again. The statistics suggest that you have only a 27% chance of selecting a cup formation that yields a gain over 50%. The chances of doubling your money are just 7%.

A discussion of the measure rule occurs in the Trading Tactics section, but it involves adding the formation height to the breakout price (the right cup lip is the breakout point) to predict the target price. The target price serves as a minimum price move. Only 49% of the formations climb to the target price. If you use half the cup height in the calculation, then 73% of the formations reach their price targets.

The average formation length is 7 months, as measured from the left cup lip to the breakout.

O'Neil suggests that the handle should be at *least* 1 to 2 weeks long but he did not specify a maximum length. I looked at a scatter plot of handle length versus percentage gain for successful formations (see Figure 9.8). There are a few formations with short handles (about 3 weeks) and large gains (over 200%) and there are longer handles with shorter gains.

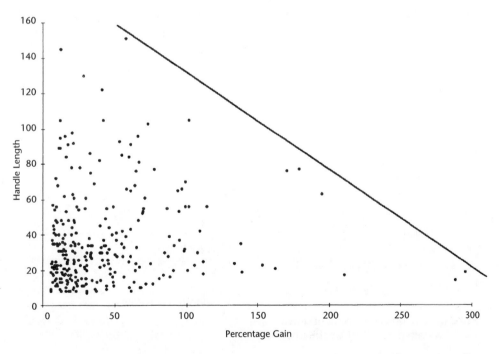

Figure 9.8 Handle length versus percentage gain. Cups with shorter handles seem to perform better but the relationship may be weak. The line emphasizes the relationship but has no statistical significance.

Do cups with higher right sides rise further? Yes. The average gain is 40% for cups with a higher right lip versus 35% for those with higher left lips. The differences are statistically significant meaning that the results are probably not due to chance.

Table 9.4 shows breakout statistics for unfiltered cups. Most (79%) of the cup-with-handle formations have upside breakouts. Only 10% of the formations break out upward but fail to rise by more than 5%. This suggests that once a cup-with-handle formation breaks out upward, it generally continues moving upward (but not necessarily very far; the most likely gain is only 10% to 20%).

Almost three out of every four formations (74%) experience a throwback to the price level of the right cup lip. This is a very high number and it suggests a way to improve performance. A discussion of this follows in the Trading Tactics section.

The average time to complete a throwback is 12 days, which seems to be about the number that many of the formation types in this book achieve. None of the throwbacks takes longer than 30 days. Although several formations do return to the cup top after 30 days, this behavior is normal price action, not a throwback. Figure 9.3 shows this extended behavior during the February to April 1993 period (remember, the scale is weekly).

It takes 6.5 months for the average formation to reach the ultimate high. However, a frequency distribution of the duration shows that almost half (47%) of the formations reach the ultimate high quickly (less than 3 months). Over a third (35%) take longer than 6 months. This pattern parallels the most likely rise and average rise for the formations. The most likely rise lands within the 10% to 20% range while the average gain is 38%. A frequency distribution

Table 9.4
Breakout Statistics for Unfiltered Cup-with-Handle Formations

Description	Statistic
Upside breakout	307 or 79%
Downside breakout	74 or 19%
Horizontal breakout	10 or 3%
Upside breakout but failure	30 or 10%
Throwbacks	226 or 74%
Average time to throwback completion	12 days
For successful formations, days to ultimate high	6.5 months (196 days)
Percentage of breakouts occurring near the 12-month price low (L), center (C), or high (H)	L0%, C0%, H100%
Volume for breakout day and next 5 days compared with day before breakout	180%, 151%, 127%, 112%, 108%, 108%

of the gains over the short-, intermediate- and long-term periods shows that the longer it takes to reach the ultimate high, the larger the average gain.

I compared the breakout price level with the yearly price range. Every formation has a breakout in the highest third of the range. You might consider this surprising except that one selection criterion says that the cup occurs after a minimum 30% price rise. This uptrend forces the breakout (which is itself at the top of the formation) into the upper price range.

Breakout volume on the day of the breakout is quite high—registering 80% above the prior day (or 180% of the prior total). Volume remains high throughout the following week.

Trading Tactics

Table 9.5 lists trading tactics. The measure rule predicts the price to which the stock will rise, at a minimum. The traditional method involves determining the height of the formation from lowest low in the cup to the high at the right cup lip. Adding the difference to the high at the right cup lip results in the target

Table 9.5
Trading Tactics for Cup-with-Handle Formations

Trading Tactic	Explanation
Measure rule	Compute the formation height by subtracting the lowest low reached in the cup from the high at the right cup lip. Add the difference to the high at the right cup lip and the result is the target price to which prices will climb, at a minimum. Only 49% of the formations rise this far. Use half the cup height to get a more realistic price target (met 73% of the time).
Use unfiltered criteria	To achieve the best performance, use the unfiltered criteria when selecting formations.
Buy after throwback	Do not buy the stock until after the throwback occurs. Once prices slip below the right cup lip *after* an upside breakout, which occurs 74% of the time, wait for prices to close above the lip before buying. This technique reduces failures and improves performance.
Buy inner cup	If you discover a cup within a cup, buy on the breakout of the inner cup (when prices rise above the inner cup lip). Be prepared to sell at the price of the old high.
Watch for 15% failure	Many cups fail after rising only 10% to 15%. Be sure to use stop-loss orders to limit losses or to maximize gains.
Stop loss	Place a stop-loss order $\frac{1}{8}$ below the handle to limit losses. Raise the stop to break-even or just below the nearest support zone when prices rise.

price. However, this method only has a 49% success rate (less than half the formations reach their price targets). For a better target, compute the cup height and take half of it. Then continue as before. The stock reaches the new, lower-priced target 73% of the time. This is still shy of the 80% number I consider reliable, but it gives a more accurate indication of the likely price rise.

Figure 9.9 is an example of the two measure rules in practice. Compute the cup height by taking the difference between the right cup high (point A at 19) and the cup low (point B at 10). Add the difference (9) to the right cup lip to get the price target (28). Mid-May sees prices hit the target but plummet the following week.

A more conservative price target uses half the formation height. This gives a target of just 23½, reached during early July. The stock climbs to the nearer target quickly and without the severe declines experienced on the way to the more risky price target.

When selecting cup-with-handle formations, use the unfiltered selection guidelines outlined in Table 9.1. When compared with the filtered selection guidelines, they improve performance.

Usually, I recommend buying a stock once it breaks out, but with 74% of the formations throwing back to the right cup lip, you might as well wait for the throwback. Buy after it throws back to the right cup lip *and once it rises above the lip* again. This technique improves the percentage gain from 38% to 39%.

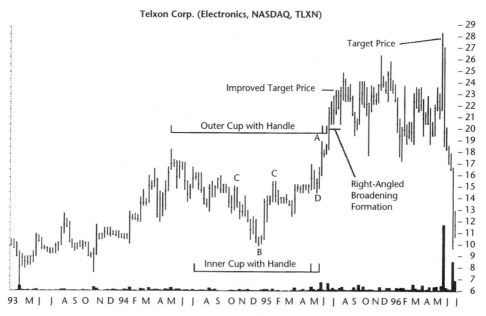

Figure 9.9 Example of the two measure rules in practice. Compute the formation height, divide by 2, and add the value to the right cup lip to get a conservative price target. Trade the inner cup-with-handle formation for a better entry price. A right-angled ascending broadening top appears during June and July 1995.

Consider applying this technique to the stock shown in Figure 9.4. Assume for a moment that the chart shows a valid cup-with-handle pattern. If you bought the stock after the breakout, you would have received a fill between 30¼ and 32 (which was the price range the day after the stock rose above the right cup lip). The stock reached a high of 34½ before throwing back.

Perhaps you would have held onto the stock and watched your gains evaporate. However, had you waited for the throwback, you would not have purchased the stock at all. Why? First you would have waited for the throwback that eventually occurred on March 16 (the day prices gapped down). Then you would have waited for prices to close above the right cup lip. This never happened, so you would not have purchased the stock.

To be fair, this technique means you will miss some opportunities. Figure 9.9, for example, shows a stock without a throwback (remember, throwbacks occur within a month of a breakout and the chart uses a weekly scale). This means you would not have bought the stock.

Figure 9.9 also shows an inner cup. If you are going to trade this formation and can identify an inner cup, buy it. An inner cup appears as two widely spaced minor highs that are at about the same price level. You score as the stock advances to the old high (the outer, left cup lip) and further if the outer cup-with-handle formation succeeds. Playing the inner cup shown in Figure 9.9 would have boosted profits about $2 a share or 12%.

Once you initiate a trade, place a stop-loss order ⅛ below the handle low. The handle is a place of support and sometimes declines will stop at that point. Placing a stop just below the low point will get you out of those situations when the stock continues tumbling.

When the stock rises, move your stop to ⅛ below the support zone nearest your break-even point. That way, if the stock declines, you will be protected. Continue raising the stop as prices climb. This technique forces you to eventually take profits but saves you from watching them fritter away during a reversal.

Sample Trade

Cody is in high school. He is not sure what he wants to do for a living, but he still has a few years to figure it out before he graduates. When he is not chasing after cheerleaders, he either has his nose buried in the financial pages or is reviewing charts on the computer screen. His interest in stocks follows in his father's footsteps: The man works for a brokerage firm and taught Cody the ropes.

Although Cody does not belong to the investment club at school, he pals around with the players. One day, he overheard them talking about the stock pictured in Figure 9.9. At first he did not think much about it until he looked deeper. That is when he saw it: a cup-with-handle pattern.

He was not convinced the stock was a good trade, but did not have the money to buy it anyway. He decided to paper trade it to see what he could learn. On the daily time scale, he saw an inner cup forming at point C, so that is the one he decided to trade.

Week after week, he waited for the buy signal but it did not come. Eventually, the stock climbed above the right cup lip but he missed it. When he pulled up the stock chart on the computer, a throwback had already occurred. So, he waited for prices to climb above the cup lip again.

That happened on May 9, his girlfriend's birthday. Sensing a positive omen, he made a notation to buy the stock, on paper, at the closing price the following day (filled at $15\frac{1}{4}$). When he met his girlfriend the next day, she was not impressed with the birthday present he gave her, and the stock closed lower as well.

Two weeks later, the stock was moving up. Cody placed his stop $\frac{1}{8}$ below the handle low, at $14\frac{3}{8}$ (point D, which also marks the purchase point). When the stock climbed above the outer cup, he raised the stop to $\frac{1}{8}$ below the handle low or $17\frac{1}{2}$. Then, he noticed a problem forming: a right-angled broadening top formation. To him that was a bearish signal, so he moved his stop up to just below the base at $20\frac{1}{4}$. Then he waited.

He got word that the stock was in trouble from his pals. They were not too happy with the company for some reason. When he pulled the stock up on his computer screen, he noticed that it had hit his stop in late August when prices momentarily dipped. Cody whipped out his calculator and tallied up his gains. He made $5 a share for a gain of over 30%. He chuckled to himself that next time he would use his paper profits to buy his girl something other than cubic zirconium.

10

Dead-Cat Bounce

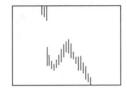

RESULTS SNAPSHOT

Appearance	An upward bounce and a declining price trend follow a dramatic decline.
Reversal or consolidation	Long-term (over 6 months) bearish reversal
Failure rate	10%
Event decline	25%, with most likely decline being 20%
Postevent decline	15%, with most likely decline between 5% and 25%
Surprising findings	The larger the event decline, the larger the bounce. The larger the event loss, the quicker the bounce reaches its high.

If you trade stocks long enough, you will probably run across this puppy: the dead-cat bounce. (I could not resist the pun). It is not so much a chart formation as it is a warning to exit the stock quickly after a dramatic decline.

The event decline, which is the decline that spawns the dead-cat bounce, averages 25%. After the event decline, prices bounce up, round over, and continue down another 15%, on average (measured from the event low to the ultimate low). Together, the two declines see prices move lower by an average of 37%.

The Results Snapshot outlines several unusual findings. The first one reminds me of a bouncing ball: The larger the event decline, the larger the bounce. When an event sends prices tumbling rapidly and severely, the bounce, while correspondingly higher, occurs quicker. Short duration bounces (to the recovery high, anyway) follow large event losses; smaller event losses are more shallow and take longer to reach their bounce high.

Tour

What is a dead-cat bounce? The name comes from the behavior of a stock after an unexpected negative event. Figure 10.1 shows a typical example of a dead-cat bounce. In late September, the smart money started selling their holdings, driving down the price and pushing up the volume trend. Prices declined from a high of $42\frac{7}{16}$ to $35\frac{13}{16}$ in just over a week. On October 9, a major brokerage house lowered its intermediate-term rating on the stock. Down it went. In 2 days the stock dropped from a high of $37\frac{13}{16}$ to a low of 26, a decline of over 30%.

For the next week and a half, the stock recovered somewhat, rising to $32\frac{13}{16}$ and enticing novice investors to buy the stock. The stock moved lower, then climbed again to form a double top. This was the end of the good news. From the second peak, it was all downhill until mid-January, when the stock bottomed at $18\frac{13}{16}$. From the high before the event began to the ultimate low, the stock plunged 50%! Welcome to the dead cat bounce.

Figure 10.1   Typical example of a dead-cat bounce. A major brokerage firm lowered its rating on the stock, sending it tumbling 50% in about $3\frac{1}{2}$ months. The dead-cat bounce allowed astute investors to sell their holdings and minimize their losses before the decline resumed. The twin peaks in mid-October and early November are a double top signaling further declines.

Table 10.1
Identification Characteristics of a Dead-Cat Bounce

Characteristic	Discussion
Price gap	The daily high is below the prior day's low, leaving a price gap (breakaway) on the chart.
Plunge	On the negative announcement, prices gap down and plunge, usually between 20% and 30% but can be as much as 70% covering 2 or 3 days.
Bounce	Prices recover somewhat and move upward. Do not be fooled; the decline is not over.
Decline	After the bounce finishes, another decline begins. This one is more sedate but prices typically decline another 5% to 25%.

Identification Guidelines

Are there characteristics common to the dead-cat bounce? Yes, and Table 10.1 lists them. Consider Figure 10.2, a 47%, 1-day decline. The stock peaked in early February at 28½. It moved lower following a down-sloping trendline until late April. Then, it curled around at a low of 15¾ and moved to reach a new minor high at 21⅞. Then the Food and Drug Administration's advisory panel rejected Cephalon's Myotrophin drug application. When the news hit the Street, the stock gapped down and traded at almost half its value. Volume was a massive 8.4 million shares, more than 15 times normal. During the next 3

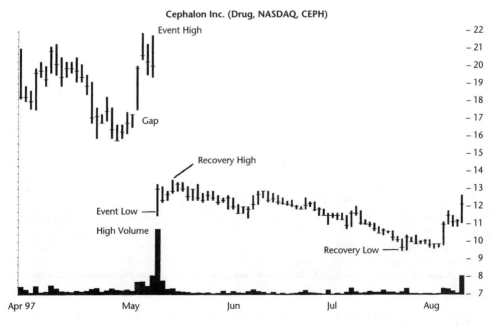

Figure 10.2 A negative announcement triggered the dead-cat bounce, which began when prices gapped down, bounced upward, then trended lower.

days, the stock recovered a portion of its decline by gaining $2 a share (low to high). Then the remainder of the decline set in. As if rubbing salt in the wound, the stock moved down again in an almost straight-line fashion. From the recovery high of 13½ to the new low of 9½, the stock declined another 30%.

Figure 10.3 shows an even more alarming decline. Just 3 days before the massive decline, a brokerage firm reported that it believed the company would continue seeing strong sales and earnings trends. Perhaps this boosted expectations, but when the company reported a quarterly loss—instead of the profit the Street was expecting—the stock dropped almost 43 points *in 1 day*. That is a decline of 62%.

The stock gapped downward, a characteristic that most dead-cat bounces share. A negative news announcement is so surprising that sell orders overwhelm buying demand. The stock declines and opens at a much lower price. Volume shoots upward, typically several times the normal rate. Figure 10.3 shows that 49 million shares exchanged hands on the news, about 20 times normal.

Usually the 1-day decline establishes a new low and prices begin recovering almost immediately. Figure 10.3 shows that the stock made a new low the following day but then closed up a day later.

After a massive decline, the bounce phase begins. Most of the time, a stock will rise up and retrace some of its losses. However, the bounce phase for Oxford Health Plans was brief—only 1 day. The stock closed higher, but the downward trend resumed the next day. In less than 2 months, the stock dropped by half, from a high of 28⅝ to a low of 13¾.

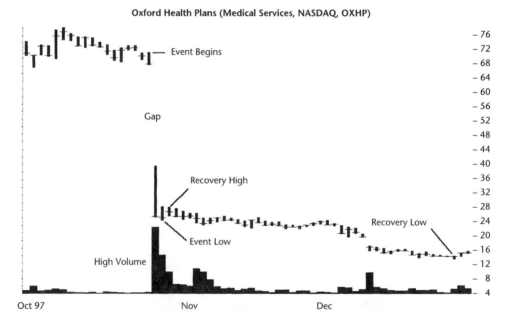

Figure 10.3 Negative news announcement triggered the massive 1-day decline, which saw prices drop by 43 points or over 60%, but the decline was not over as the stock fell an additional 43%.

What types of events cause these massive declines? Almost all the events are company specific: negative earnings surprises, bad same-store sales numbers, failed mergers, accounting sleight of hand, outright fraud—that sort of thing. Sometimes the news affects more than one company. Figure 10.2 shows what happened to Cephalon, but Chiron stock was not immune. Chiron has a joint development and marketing agreement with Cephalon for the Myotrophin drug, so its stock also took a hit, but not nearly as large (less than 5%) as Cephalon.

Most of the time investors cannot predict the event. If you own the stock, you will lose your shirt. The question then becomes, how much of your remaining wardrobe do you want to lose? We see in the Trading Tactics section that it pays to sell quickly.

Focus on Failures

Not all massive declines end in a dead-cat bounce. Consider the event shown in Figure 10.4. On April 3, 1997, the company released earnings that fell short of expectations and announced that its merger with another company was terminated. Several brokerages downgraded the stock. It tumbled from a high of $17\frac{1}{4}$ to a low of $9\frac{5}{8}$, a decline of 44%. Like all dead-cat bounces, the stock recovered. However, instead of bouncing up then turning down and moving lower, this stock continued trending up. In less than 3 months, the stock recovered its entire loss.

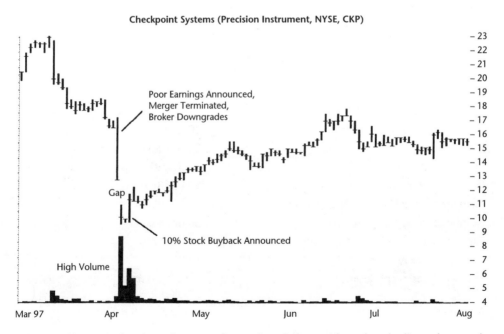

Figure 10.4 A dead-cat bounce formation failure. After the decline, the stock moved higher and kept rising instead of moving back down.

Why did the stock fail to bounce and head lower? Events that take place just after the negative news announcement explain the stock's behavior. Several insiders bought the stock. Even the company got into the act and announced it was purchasing 10% of the stock. Together, the news sent the stock moving higher. Subsequent events kept the momentum building and the stock continued rising.

A survey of all 24 failures in the database reveals that 83% have stock trends that continue moving lower without any significant upward bounce. The remainder (4 formations) are similar to that shown in Figure 10.4, that is, prices rebound and move up.

Statistics

Table 10.2 contains the general statistics for the dead-cat bounce. I located 244 formations in 500 stocks over 5 years. Of these formations, 54% act as reversals of the prevailing trend, and the remainder act as consolidations. Almost all the formations (90%) perform as expected. That is to say, after a major decline, the stock bounces and heads lower. Only 20 move lower without a significant bounce and 4 trend upward; they are the failures.

The average decline, as measured from the high the day before the major decline to the recovery low, is 37%. The recovery low is usually the same as the

Table 10.2
General Statistics for the Dead-Cat Bounce

Description	Statistic
Number of formations in 500 stocks from 1991 to 1996	244
Reversal or consolidation	113 consolidations, 131 reversals
Failure rate	24 or 10%
Average decline of successful formations (event high to recovery low)	37%, with most likely loss between 30% and 40%
Average event decline	25%, with most likely loss 20%
Average event duration	2 days; 92% last 4 days or less
Number of formations with price gap	194 or 80%
Number of gaps closed during recovery	48 or 22%
Number of gaps closed in 3 months	80 or 36%
Number of gaps closed in 6 months	119 or 54%
Average recovery bounce height	19%
Additional postevent decline	15%, with most likely loss between 5% and 25%
Average postevent duration	3 months (90 days)
Number of formations declining below event low	198 or 81%

ultimate low. After the stock completes its major decline and bounces upward, the recovery low is the lowest price before any significant rise signals a trend change.

The most likely decline is in the 30% to 40% range. This is unusual as most formations have a few large declines that skew the overall average upward. With the most likely decline near the average, the declines are well spread as seen in Figure 10.5. Notice the bell-shaped graph. The graph shows the results of a frequency distribution of losses from the high price the day before the decline to the recovery low.

The average event loss is 25%. The event loss is the difference between the high the day before the large decline to the lowest low before the bounce begins, expressed as a percentage. A frequency distribution of the event loss shows that the most likely event loss is 20%.

The event loss happens quickly, usually in just 2 days. This is the massive decline that gets the ball rolling. Most times the stock suffers a large 1-day loss then makes a lower low the next day before entering the bounce phase (a 2-day decline occurs 71% of the time). Sometimes the stock will continue moving down for a few days, but most (92%) begin rebounding in 4 days or less.

Most market participants find the negative news surprising. As such, prices gap lower (that is, the current day's high is below the prior day's low, leaving a gap on the price chart). Only 22% of the formations showing a gap close them (prices rising far enough to fill the gap) during the bounce or recovery phase. Even in 3 months, only 36% close the gap and slightly over half (54%) close in less than 6 months. Since 80% of the formations show gaps and only half

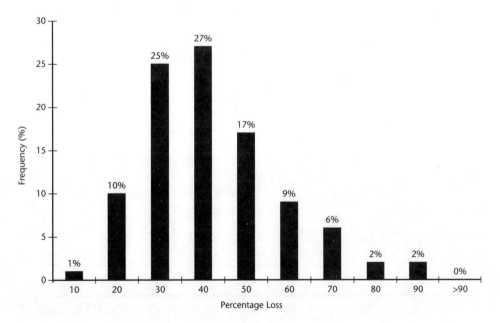

Figure 10.5 Frequency distribution of total loss. Note the bell-shaped graph of total losses from the high the day before a large decline to the recovery low. The most likely decline is 30% to 40%.

close within 6 months, the long-term bearish implication of this formation becomes obvious.

During the bounce phase of a dead-cat bounce, the stock rises 19%, on average (as measured from the event low to the recovery high). Does the bounce height relate to the severity of event loss? Yes. In simple terms, the larger the event loss, the larger the bounce. Figure 10.6 shows the relationship.

An additional 15% loss (as measured from the event low to the recovery low) occurs after the recovery bounce completes and prices start declining again. Prices usually fall below the event low and continue moving down. A frequency distribution of the postevent loss ranges from 5% to 25% and is evenly distributed. This wide range suggests that even though the event decline may be massive, sometimes substantial additional losses follow. The postevent loss occurs much more slowly, averaging about 3 months (90 days) in duration, as measured from the event low to the recovery low.

Figure 10.7 shows the relationship between event loss and the number of days to the recovery high (the highest high reached during the bounce). Although it may be difficult to see the relationship, one can generally say that as the size of the event loss grows, the days to the recovery high lessen. In other words, the bounce becomes steeper (occurring quicker). This seems to be contrary to what you would expect.

Taken together, Figures 10.6 and 10.7 suggest that short duration, high recoveries (to the recovery high, anyway) follow large event losses. Smaller losses are more shallow and take longer to reach their bounce high.

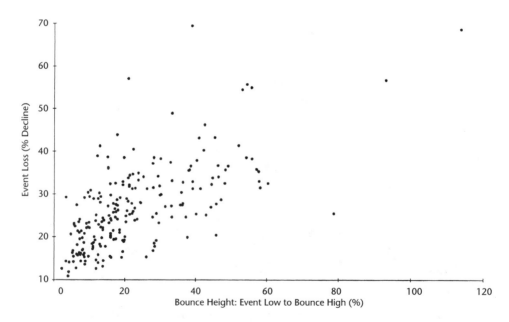

Figure 10.6 Relationship between event loss and bounce height. Like a ball, the larger the loss the larger the bounce.

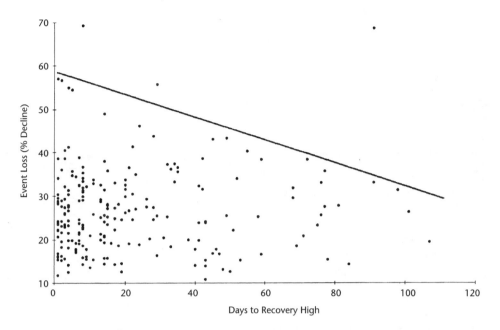

Figure 10.7   Relationship between the event loss and days to the bounce high. The line helps describe the relationship but has no statistical significance.

Over 8 out of 10 (81%) formations decline below the event low. The event low is the low price reached after the massive decline but before the bounce. This statistic emphasizes that even though you have suffered a painful loss (or had your profits trimmed), you should still sell your position because further losses are coming.

Table 10.3 shows additional statistics related to the dead-cat bounce. Every formation showed extraordinarily high volume on the day the event occurred. After prices decline, they recover and reach a bounce high in less than 3 weeks (19 days).

Where in the yearly price range does the event occur? A frequency distribution of the day before the event indicates that most stocks (40%) are within a third of their yearly high. The center third of the yearly price range follows closely with 39%. When you substitute the percentage loss into the yearly price range, you find returns behave about the same. The average formation declines between 35% and 37% regardless of where it begins in the yearly price range (as measured from the day before the event begins).

Breakout volume is massive (596% of the prior day's volume) and continues to be high for the next week.

I looked at gaps and tried to discover if they hold any special significance. Do formations with gaps have larger event losses? No, since the average decline is 24% for those formations with gaps and 27% without. Do formations with gaps have a better recovery (that is, do they bounce higher)? Again, the answer is no as the recovery rise is 18% for those formations with gaps versus 20% without.

Table 10.3
Additional Statistics Related to the Dead-Cat Bounce

Description	Statistic
High volume event (at least 50% above prior day)	238 or 100%
For successful formations, days to recovery high (from event end)	19 days
Percentage of dead-cat bounces occurring near the 12-month low (L), center (C), or high (H)	L20%, C39%, H40%
Percentage loss for each 12-month lookback period	L37%, C35%, H37%
Volume for breakout day and next 5 days compared with day before breakout	596%, 304%, 177%, 154%, 140%, 125%
Percentage of formations with gaps having larger event declines than formations without gaps	24% versus 27%
Percentage of formations with gaps having better recovery (a higher bounce) than formations without gaps	18% versus 20%

Note: The negative event occurs on high volume, the bounce occurs quickly, and the recovery is slow.

Trading Tactics

There is not much that can be said for trading the dead-cat bounce unless you are shorting the stock (see Table 10.4). For long positions, wait for the bounce then sell. About a third of the time (36%), prices reach the bounce high in the first week. Over half the formations (56%) take 2 weeks or less. When the stock peaks and rounds over, dump it. If you choose to hang onto your position, you will likely incur further losses and it may take well over 6 months before you come close to recovering them. Why not invest your remaining capital in a more promising situation?

If you are considering selling the stock short to profit from the impending decline, look at Figure 10.8, which shows the percentage decline from the bounce high to the recovery low. On average, the most likely decline is between 15% and 25%, large enough to risk a trade.

The last trading tactic is to be aware of the dead-cat bounce and its effect on prices. When a severe decline takes hold of a stock, the cause is not trivial. It takes time for the company to fix the problem and recover. Ignore any bullish chart formation occurring in a stock in less than 6 months (even up to a year). The chart pattern will likely fail or, if it works, the rise may be short-lived when the company announces more bad news (such as poor quarterly earnings).

Table 10.4
Trading Tactics for the Dead-Cat Bounce

Trading Tactic	Explanation
Wait for rise, then sell	The stock will make a new low then begin to bounce. Sell after the bounce rounds over, usually in 1 to 2 weeks. The worse the event decline, the quicker the bounce high appears, and the higher prices bounce.
Short sales	Sell short after the bounce rounds over. Expect a decline to at least the event low. Most of the time (81%), the stock continues lower by another 15%, on average.
Avoid formations	Avoid all bullish chart formations for at least 6 months (or even up to a year) in a stock showing a dead-cat bounce. If they work at all, the gains are below average.

Note: Wait for the bounce, then sell or sell short.

Sample Trade

Once satisfied that you know the implications of the bad news and the reasons for the stock's massive decline, short the stock. Consider Figure 10.9, a dead-cat bounce in Cerner Corporation. The stock dropped five points (25%) after the company said earnings would fall short of expectations and the outlook for

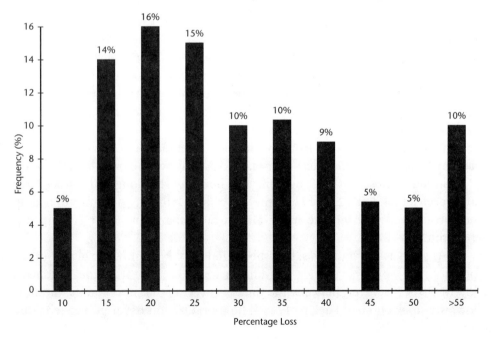

Figure 10.8 Frequency distribution of declines from the bounce high to the recovery low. If you time your short sale correctly, the profits can be rewarding.

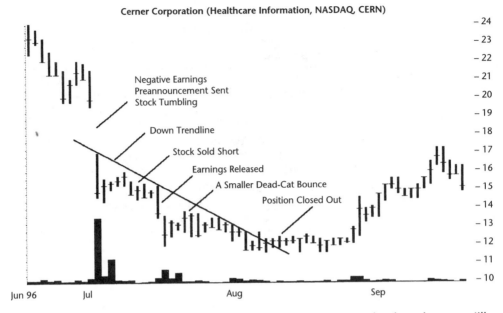

Figure 10.9 A negative earnings announcement triggers a dead-cat bounce. Jill sold the stock short just after the bounce high then covered when prices closed above the trendline. The trade resulted in a 20% gain in 1 month.

the remainder of the year was grim. The stock closed higher on each of the next 4 days then closed lower. Jill, after seeing the stock climb the hill, sold the stock short and received a fill at the closing price of 15. She then waited, watching the stock closely. It continued moving down—as predicted.

The earnings announcement forced the stock down another 20% in 2 days. Expecting another dead-cat bounce, Jill held on to her position. The stock rose in an uneven fashion over then next week or so, then rounded over and headed lower.

Jill connected the tops from the preannouncement day onward in a downsloping trendline. When prices eventually closed above the trendline, she knew it was time to close out the position. The next day she bought the stock back and received a fill at 12, ¼ below the daily close. She sat back and totaled up her profits and realized she made almost $3 a share, or about 20% in just 1 month.

As good as the trade was, had she waited until November to close out the position, she would have made an additional $1.50 a share (the stock reached a low of 10½). However, between the time of covering the short and the ultimate low, the stock climbed back to 17¼. The moral is, you never go broke taking a profit.

11

Diamond Tops
and Bottoms

RESULTS SNAPSHOT

Diamond Tops

Appearance	Diamond pattern forms after an upward price trend.
Reversal or consolidation	Short-term (up to 3 months) bearish reversal
Failure rate	25%
Average decline	21%, with most likely decline being 20%
Volume trend	Downward until breakout
Pullbacks	59%
Percentage meeting predicted price target	79%
See also	Head-and-Shoulders Tops

Diamond Bottoms

Appearance	Diamond pattern forms after a downward price trend.
Reversal or consolidation	Short- to intermediate-term (up to 6 months) bullish reversal
Failure rate	13%
Average rise	35%, with most likely rise being 15%
Average volume trend	Downward until breakout

Throwbacks	43%
Percentage meeting predicted price target	95%
See also	Head-and-Shoulders Bottoms

The Results Snapshot shows the important results of diamond tops and bottoms. In appearance, the only difference between the two diamond patterns is the price trend leading to the formation. For diamond tops, the prior price trend is upward, whereas diamond bottoms have price trends that lead down to the formation.

The performance of the two types is similar. Both act as reversals of the prevailing price trend with a volume trend that diminishes over time. Volume on the day of the breakout is also high.

The failure rate for tops, at 25%, is more than double the rate for bottoms. I consider failure rates above 20% to be alarming, so you might consider tops unreliable.

The average decline (21%) and rise (35%) is about what you would expect for reversals, with bottoms a bit shy of the usual 40% rise for bullish formations. However, the most likely decline for tops is near the average, suggesting that there are few large declines to distort the average. Diamond bottoms, with a likely rise of just 15%, are well away from the 35% average gain. This suggests there are a high number of formations with smaller gains that balance a few larger ones.

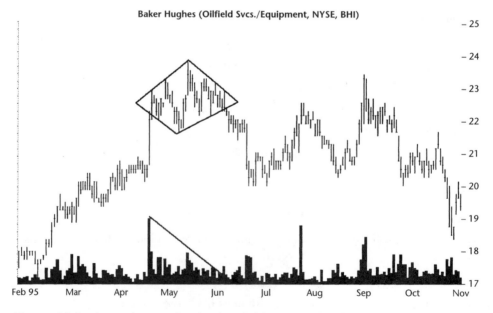

Figure 11.1 A good example of a diamond top. Notice that prices quickly return to the $20 level.

Tour

What does a diamond top or bottom look like? Figure 11.1 shows a good example of a diamond top. After rising steadily since mid-February, the stock jumps 1½ points on April 20. Volume on that day is well above average. Then, the stock forms higher highs and lower lows, as if it is tracing a broadening top pattern. Volume diminishes throughout the early pattern development. Then, things reverse. The third minor high calls the top and prices decline. The minor lows begin moving higher even as the tops are descending. This phase of the pattern looks like a symmetrical triangle. However, volume continues receding, albeit at an irregular rate.

Prices break down out of the pattern on June 8 accompanied by volume that is about average. Prices meander sideways for about 2 weeks before plunging and retracing all the gains since the mid-April, 1-day rise.

The pattern is a diamond top; it signals a reversal of the prevailing price trend. The chart in Figure 11.1 shows the typical behavior of a top: Prices return to the level before the diamond begins. In this regard, the reversal stands out like a sore thumb. Of course, not all tops act this way. Some signal a reversal of the primary trend and prices not only retrace their recent gains but continue moving down.

The diamond bottom, shown in Figure 11.2, is similar to the top version with the exception of the prevailing price trend. In Figure 11.2, prices are trending down toward the diamond bottom. In Figure 11.1, prices are trending upward before the start of the formation.

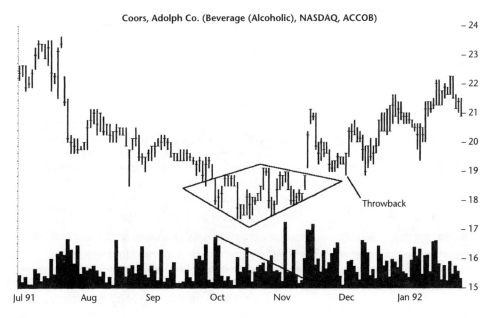

Figure 11.2 A diamond bottom reversal. Volume typically recedes through the formation until the breakout day.

The diamond bottom begins by widening out and tracing higher highs and lower lows, then the process reverses. The price range narrows until the breakout occurs.

Volume throughout the formation is diminishing. The breakout usually sports a significant rise in volume. Figure 11.2 shows high volume on the breakout when prices gap through the diamond boundary. In less than 3 months, the stock climbs over 20% to a high of 22¼.

Identification Guidelines

Table 11.1 lists the identification guidelines for diamond tops and bottoms. Consider the diamond top pictured in Figure 11.3. The short-term price trend is up just before the formation, leading to the minor high on the left. Then prices decline and form a minor low before moving higher again. In late September, prices reach a new high before cascading downward to finish below the prior minor low. Again, prices rise up and form another minor high before breaking down through the upward trendline on the right. The fluctuations of minor highs and lows form a diamond shape when the peaks and valleys connect such as that shown in Figure 11.3. Notice that the diamond is not symmetrical; irregular diamond shapes are common for diamonds.

Table 11.1
Identification Characteristics of Diamond Tops and Bottoms

Characteristic	Discussion
Prior price trend	For diamond tops, prices usually trend *up* to the formation, whereas bottoms usually form at the end of a downward price trend. With this definition, diamond tops (or bottoms) need not form at the top (or bottom) of a price chart—they can form anywhere.
Diamond shape	Prices form higher highs and lower lows (widening appearance), then lower highs and higher lows (narrowing appearance). Trendlines surrounding the minor highs and lows resemble a diamond. The diamond need not appear symmetrical.
Volume trend	Diminishing over the length of the formation
Breakout volume	Usually high and it can continue high for several days
Support and resistance (SAR)	The formation creates a location for support or resistance. Diamond tops usually show SAR near the top of the formation, whereas diamond bottoms show SAR near the formation bottom. SAR duration can last up to a year or more.

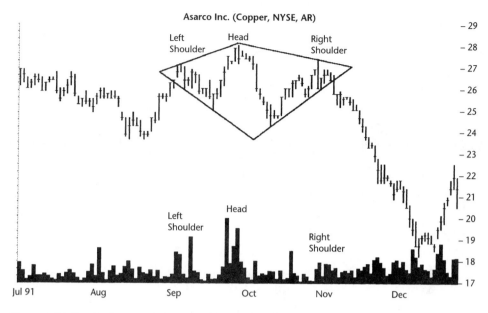

Figure 11.3 A diamond top masking a head-and-shoulders top. In either case, the bearish outlook is certain.

The volume trend is receding, especially in the latter half of the formation when the price range is narrowing (and the chart pattern resembles a symmetrical triangle). The breakout volume is usually high but is not a prerequisite to a properly behaved diamond. In Figure 11.3, the volume on the breakout day and succeeding days is tepid at best but trend upward as prices fall.

The pattern is a head-and-shoulders top, with the left shoulder, head, and right shoulder marked on Figure 11.3. The volume pattern is typical for a head-and-shoulders top, with the right shoulder volume vastly diminished when compared to the left shoulder or head volume.

Should you locate a diamond pattern and discover that it may be a head-and-shoulders top, do not worry. In both cases, the formation is bearish. When such a collision occurs, choose the formation that gives you the more conservative performance results (see the measure rule).

Support and resistance for diamond tops commonly appear at the top of the formation, as seen in Figure 11.4. The diamond reversal forms a resistance level, repelling prices during the rise in March and April 1993, and is not pierced until a year later.

A congestion zone forms in October 1993 and lasts through March of the following year before prices climb convincingly above the resistance area. Even then, during April and May 1994, prices are buoyed by the support zone at 31 created a year and a half earlier.

Figure 11.5 shows a diamond bottom. The price trend is downward for nearly 2 months, leading to the formation. Prices rebound slightly and the

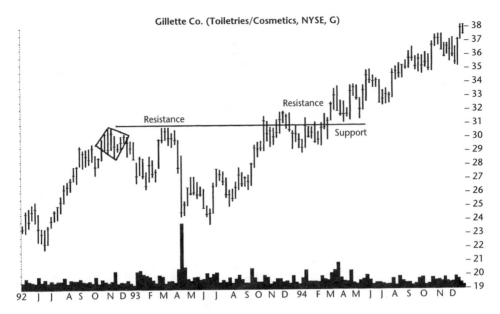

Figure 11.4 Support and resistance for diamond top appears at top of formation. A support and resistance zone at 31 created by the diamond top lasts for a year and a half. Note the weekly time scale.

range widens as higher highs and lower lows appear. Then the tide turns and the range narrows; higher lows follow lower highs. The diamond pattern takes shape after connecting the boundaries of the price movements.

Trading volume throughout the formation is receding. This is typical but not a prerequisite for a well-formed diamond bottom. As in diamond tops, there are wide variations in the volume pattern. Overall, however, the volume trend diminishes over time until the breakout, then volume usually jumps upward. Figure 11.5 shows that breakout volume is four times the prior day but is just slightly above average for the stock.

Figure 11.6 illustrates the support area often promoted by diamond bottoms. The figure shows support at the $10 level on a weekly scale. Although support varies from diamond to diamond, when it appears after a diamond bottom, it is usually near the base of the formation. Another area of support commonly appears when the stock throws back to the level of the breakout. Figure 11.6 shows an example of this. After climbing away from the formation after the breakout, a stock sometimes pauses, reverses course, and heads lower. Support meets prices that decline into the formation area, usually stopping briefly near the breakout price, then prices turn around again and head back up. This throwback to the formation happens more than a third of the time (43%) and represents another opportunity to initiate a trade or add to a position.

Figure 11.5 A diamond bottom with receding volume trend. Prices quickly recover and reach new highs.

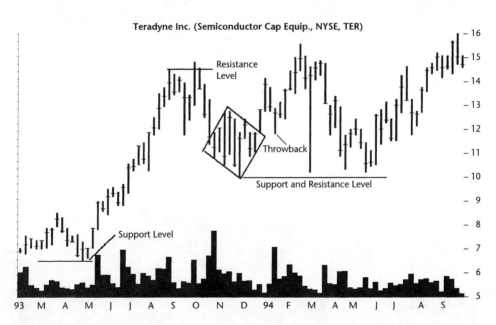

Figure 11.6 Support areas for diamond bottoms are near the base of the formation. Shown here is support at 10 on a weekly scale.

Focus on Failures

Not all diamond tops and bottoms work out as expected. Figure 11.7 shows a diamond top that fails to breakout downward. As in Figure 11.1, I would expect the stock to return to its jump-off point, that is, the 108 level. Instead, the stock breaks out upward and continues moving higher until it reaches a high of 127¾. The move, which occurs less than 2 weeks after the breakout, signals a peak for the stock. From that point, it is all downhill. In early April 1994, the stock touches bottom at 92½, well below the breakout price of 118⅜. If you sold the stock before the breakout, you may be upset that it continues higher, but eventually your tactic pays off. The stock declines 22% from the breakout low to the ultimate low in 1 year.

Is there a reason the stock continues higher? Certainly the breakout volume is not supportive of an upward move. Although volume on the day of the breakout is 69% above the prior day, there is no significant volume spike shown on the chart (translation: breakout volume is not above average). This weak volume is unusual but not unheard of. The weak volume breakout and decreasing volume trend over the next week or so, even as prices climb, is a warning that the upward momentum is running out of steam.

Although it is not clear from looking at Figure 11.7, the volume trend, measured by the slope of a linear regression line of volume, is downward. This is typical for most diamond tops and bottoms but offers no clue to the eventual failure of this situation. I can see no reason why this diamond fails to breakout

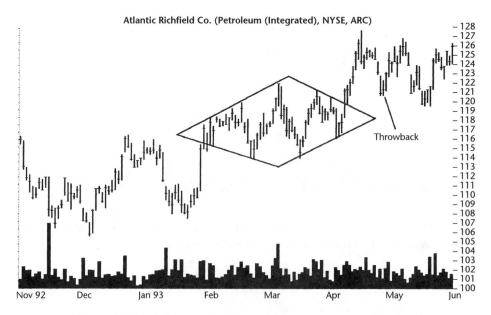

Figure 11.7 A failure of a diamond top to reverse direction.

downward. The lesson is that you should wait for the breakout before trading your position.

Figure 11.8 is an example of a failed diamond bottom. The stock reaches a high in early February at a price of 32¼, then heads lower. The diamond forms at about the level where the prior downtrend stops descending (in early April). One could expect the stock to stop falling when it meets support. For almost 2 months (April and May), that is exactly what happens. The stock moves horizontally, forms the diamond bottom, but then breaks out downward. Briefly, the stock pulls back to the breakout price then heads lower. It reaches a low of 10½ in mid-June then moves sideways for 5 months (not shown). By the end of this study, the stock is trading at less than $1.

Breakout volume is above average and remains high for several days. The pullback to the breakout level gives investors the opportunity to sell their positions before the downhill run resumes.

The diamond low, at 16¼, approximates the low in early April. These two lows, when taken together, initially appear to be a double bottom. Volume is higher on the left side of the double bottom than the right. The rise between the two troughs is sufficient to validate a double bottom. However, prices fail to rise above the confirmation point (21¼, or the highest high between the two bottoms) so the formation is not a double bottom. This failure suggests prices will move lower.

Double bottoms and diamond bottoms are both bullish formations, so why did the stock fall? I could find no technical evidence to suggest why the

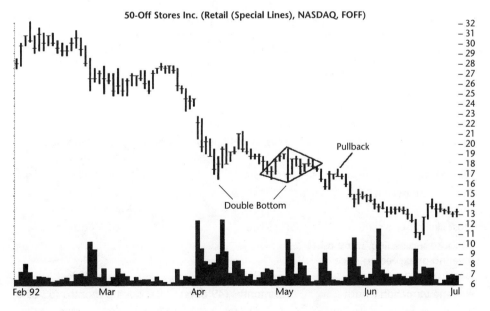

Figure 11.8 A diamond bottom failure. The diamond bottom fails to reverse as prices break out downward and continue moving down. The double bottom is unconfirmed; it is not a true double bottom.

two formations fail to perform as expected. However, since the stock continues down to less than $1, this decline suggests that the fundamental situation is decidedly weak. This alone may explain the stock's behavior.

Statistics

Table 11.2 contains general statistics for diamond tops and bottoms. Due to the dearth of formations located in 2,500 years of daily price data, I reviewed a more recent database to augment the statistics. The numbers of formations uncovered indicate diamond tops and bottoms are a rare breed. Most of the time, they act as reversals of the prevailing price trend (80% for bottoms and 78% for tops).

The failure rate is higher for diamond tops than bottoms (25% versus 13%). Failure rates above 20% suggest an unreliable formation, so, if you decide to trade a diamond top, be extra careful. Only diamond tops suffer from 5% failures. That is when prices move less than 5% in the breakout direction before reversing. With just 45 diamond bottoms, the sample size is not large enough to really determine the 5% failure rate.

The average rise after a bottom is 35%, although the most likely rise is just 15%. Figure 11.9 shows the most likely rise and it is computed using a fre-

Table 11.2
General Statistics for Diamond Tops and Bottoms

Description	Bottoms	Tops
Number of formations in 500 stocks from 1991 to 1996	34	111
Number of formations in 299 stocks from 1996 to 1998	11	27
Reversal or consolidation	9 consolidations, 36 reversals	31 consolidations, 107 reversals
Failure rate	6 or 13%	35 or 25%
Average rise/decline of successful formations	35% rise	21% decline
Most likely rise/decline	15% rise	20% decline
Of those succeeding, number meeting or exceeding price target (measure rule)	35 or 95%	86 or 79%
Average formation length	1.5 months (49 days)	1.5 months (52 days)
Volume for breakout day and next 5 days compared with day before breakout	151%, 174%, 151%, 123%, 137%, 139%	152%, 200%, 177%, 160%, 160%, 179%

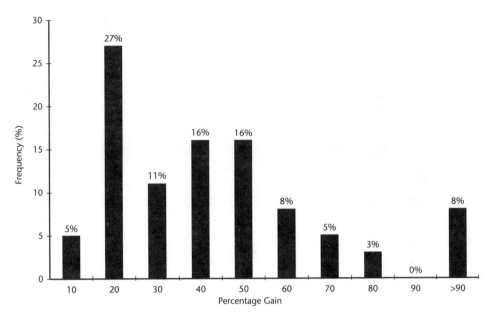

Figure 11.9 Frequency distribution of gains for diamond bottoms. The chart suggests the most likely rise after a breakout from a diamond bottom is 20%, but the actual value is 15% (using a finer scale than the one shown).

quency distribution of gains. The column with the highest frequency becomes the most likely rise. Only 37 formations qualify for the chart. Still, the 20% column stands out as the one with the highest frequency. Scaling the columns in 5% increments (instead of 10%) shows that the 15% column has the highest frequency. Even though the 20% column is highest in the chart, the most likely rise is really 15%.

The average decline from a diamond top is 21%, although the most likely decline is 20%. Figure 11.10 shows a frequency distribution of the losses. There are a larger number of samples and the bell-shaped curve is smoother. Diamond tops are one of the few cases where the average decline is near the most likely decline. This suggests the declines are evenly distributed about the average (there are few large declines that pull the average upward).

The 35% rise for diamond bottoms is below the average 40% return for other types of bullish formations. Diamond tops, on the other hand, show declines (21%) similar to other bearish formation types.

The measure rule, discussed in the Trading Tactics section of this chapter, involves calculating the formation height and either adding or subtracting the difference from the breakout price. The result is the minimum target price. For bottoms, nearly all (95%) of the formations reach the predicted target prices. However, tops have a success rate of 79%. I consider values above 80% to be reliable.

The formation length from start to breakout is similar for both diamond types, at about 7 weeks (49 and 52 days). That is comparatively short.

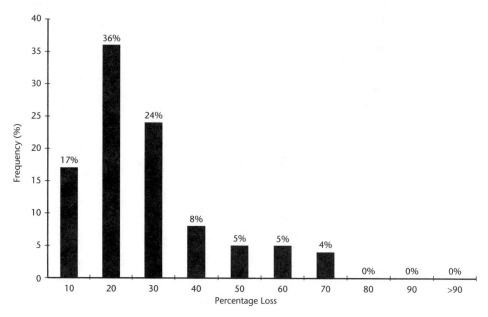

Figure 11.10   Frequency distribution of losses for diamond tops. The most likely decline after a diamond top is 20%.

Table 11.3 shows breakout statistics for diamond tops and bottoms. Both tops and bottoms have breakout volume that is half again has much as the prior day, on average. It remains high throughout the next 5 trading days. Ten diamond top formations have downside breakouts that fail to continue declining by more than 5%. Since this represents only 9% of the formations, the result is quite good. There are no diamond bottoms that have upside breakouts

Table 11.3
Breakout Statistics for Diamond Tops and Bottoms

Description	Bottoms	Tops
Upside/downside breakout but failure	0	10 or 9%
Upside breakout	37 or 82%	29 or 21%
Downside breakout	7 or 16%	109 or 79%
Horizontal breakout	1 or 2%	0
Throwbacks/pullbacks	16 or 43%	64 or 59%
Average time to throwback/pullback completion	11 days	11 days
For successful formations, days to ultimate high/low	4 months (122 days)	2 months (65 days)
Percentage of breakouts occurring near 12-month low (L), center (C), or high (H)	L16%, C56%, H28%	L7%, C24%, H69%
Percentage gain/loss for each 12-month lookback period	L30%, C37%, H35%	L26%, C15%, H20%

that fail to rise by more than 5%. As explained earlier, this is probably due to the small sample size.

The significance of this result is that once prices break out of the formation, they continue moving in the same direction (by at least 5% anyway), suggesting that a trader should wait for the breakout, then trade with the trend.

Breakout statistics listed in Table 11.3 show bottoms having upside breakouts 82% of the time and tops having downside breakouts 79% of the time.

Bottoms have throwbacks to the price level of the breakout (where prices pierce the diamond boundary) 43% of the time, whereas pullbacks after a diamond top reversal occur just over half the time (59%). Throwbacks allow investors another opportunity to either place a trade or add to their position. Pullbacks are an opportunity to exit the position before the decline resumes or to initiate a short sale. If you are on the wrong side of a trade and are given another opportunity to leave the trade, take it. If you do not, things only get worse.

For both throwbacks and pullbacks, the average time for prices to return to the breakout point is 11 days. In all cases, the throwback or pullback occurs in less than 30 days. Anything taking longer than a month classifies as normal price action and is not a throwback or pullback.

For successful formations, the average time to reach the ultimate low or high is almost twice as long for bottoms (122 days) than it is for tops (65 days). This makes sense when coupled with the average price rise and fall. Bottoms rise almost twice as far (35%) as tops fall (21%), so it is not unusual for bottoms to take almost twice as long to cover almost twice the distance.

Where do breakouts occur in the yearly price range? For bottoms, 56% of breakouts occur in the center third of the yearly price range. For tops, 69% of breakouts happen in the top third of the price range. Considering these numbers, you may wonder how a diamond *bottom* can occur in the *top* of the price range or a diamond *top* can occur in the *bottom* of the price range.

I base my definition of a bottom or top on the price trend leading to the formation, not the price itself. Diamond bottoms have price trends that decline to the start of the formation; diamond tops have price trends that lead up to the formation at its start. If this is still confusing, review Figures 11.1 and 11.2.

The formations are grouped according to the price trend because they share the same characteristics. When prices rise up to a formation (as in the case of a diamond top), expect a reversal to send prices declining once the formation completes. If you classify a formation based on price, then tops will form at the top of the yearly price range and bottoms will form at the bottom. How do you classify a formation that appears in the middle of the range? It can be either a top or a bottom. See the dilemma?

Substituting the percentage gains or losses in the yearly price range, we find most successful bottom reversals rise by 37% (and they have breakouts that occur in the center third of the yearly price range). Since all three of the gains (30%, 37%, and 35%) are relatively close, and since the frequency distribution used to gather these statistics rests on a few samples (5, 18, and 9, respectively), do not read too much into the numbers.

Tops tell a similar story. The statistics suggest tops occurring in the lower third of the price range decline further. This may or may not be true since it is based on only five samples (the other two categories have 17 and 50 samples, respectively).

Trading Tactics

Table 11.4 shows trading tactics for diamond tops and bottoms. Use the measure rule to predict the minimum price move. Consider Figure 11.11, a chart of a diamond top and diamond bottom. Compute the measure rule by first finding the formation height. Locate the lowest low in the formation (shown as point B) and subtract it from the highest high (point A). Subtract the difference (in the case of diamond tops) or add it (for bottoms) to point C—the breakout price. The result is the minimum target price.

For the diamond top, the formation height is $7\frac{5}{8}$ (that is, $79\frac{1}{4} - 71\frac{5}{8}$). Subtract the difference from point C to get the target price of $65\frac{7}{8}$ (or $73\frac{1}{2} - 7\frac{5}{8}$). Point C, incidentally, is where prices pierce the diamond trendline. Prices meet the target just 1 week after the breakout.

Calculation of the measure rule for diamond bottoms proceeds in a similar manner. The height turns out to be $3\frac{3}{4}$ (that is, $71\frac{3}{4} - 68$). Add the difference to point C, the location where prices pierce the diamond boundary. The target price is $74\frac{1}{2}$ (or $70\frac{3}{4} + 3\frac{3}{4}$). Prices meet the target in just 3 days.

As noted in the Statistics section of this chapter, prices fulfill the measure rule 95% of the time for diamond bottoms and 79% for tops. Both these num-

Table 11.4
Trading Tactics for Diamond Tops and Bottoms

Trading Tactic	Explanation
Measure rule	Compute the formation height by subtracting the lowest low from the highest high in the formation. For tops, subtract the difference from the location where prices pierce the diamond boundary. For bottoms, add the difference to the breakout price. The result is the minimum price move to expect. Alternatively, formations often return to price levels from which they begin. The base serves as a minimum price move.
Wait for breakout	For best results, wait for prices to close outside the diamond trendline before placing a trade.
Risk/reward	Look for support (risk) and resistance (reward) zones before placing a trade. These zones are where the trend is likely to stop. From the current closing price (before the breakout), compute the difference between the zones and the current price. The ratio of the two must be compelling enough to risk a trade.

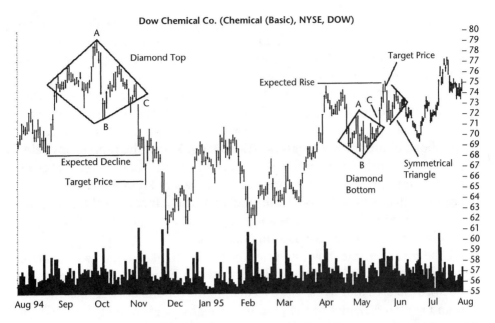

Figure 11.11   A diamond top and a diamond bottom. Compute the measure rule using the formation height by subtracting point B from point A. For diamond tops, subtract the difference from point C and for bottoms, add the difference. The result is the expected minimum price move. Diamonds often return to their base. The Expected Decline and Expected Rise lines are another way to gauge the minimum price move. A symmetrical triangle appears in late May.

bers are high enough that you should consider the measure rule a reliable price prediction mechanism.

However, there is an alternative method that sometimes yields more accurate results. The method involves looking at the price chart and seeing if there is something to reverse. By this I mean diamonds sometimes form after a quick run-up in prices. The reversal will usually erase these gains and return prices to where they were before the run-up.

Figure 11.1 is a good example of this. Prices make a 1-day jump from the 20 area. After the reversal completes, prices quickly return to the same level. Figure 11.11 also shows the two jump-off points. The diamond top starts climbing from the 68 level. Prices quickly return to this level after the reversal (see the *Expected Decline* line shown in Figure 11.11).

The diamond bottom has a start from the 74 level (see the *Expected Rise* line in the figure) to which prices quickly return after the reversal. After reaching that level, prices do not exceed it for almost 2 months.

When trading technical formations like diamond tops and bottoms, it is always safest to wait for the breakout. Although failures from bottoms occur only 13% of the time, tops are more error prone (with a failure rate of 25%).

If you do not wait for the breakout, you may face a situation similar to that discussed in the Focus on Failures section of this chapter. Instead of reversing, prices resume their original trend and the investor misses out on additional gains or suffers larger losses.

Before placing a trade, consider the risk/reward ratio. In essence, you first identify the support and resistance levels and calculate the difference between those levels and the current price. Trades that result in risk/reward ratios of one to four or higher are worth making. When the ratio drops below one to four, the risk may be too high to warrant a trade. An example makes the calculation clearer. For the diamond bottom shown in Figure 11.6, assume the figure is all that is known about the stock. On the left side of the figure, the stock descends to $6\frac{1}{2}$ before rebounding. The stock bounces from this level, suggesting that the price level is a support zone.

The measure rule suggests prices will rise to $14\frac{5}{8}$, about where prices topped out recently (the resistance level shown in Figure 11.6). The close the day before the breakout, is $11\frac{13}{16}$. Calculating the differences between the support and resistance zones to the closing price gives a ratio of ($11\frac{13}{16} - 6\frac{1}{2}$) to ($14\frac{5}{8} - 11\frac{13}{16}$) or 5.31 to 2.82. The ratio is slightly less than two to one and it warns that the risk of failure is higher than the potential reward. The 2:1 ratio is well outside the 1:4 minimum. You would be taking on twice as much risk as potential reward. You could always tighten up the risk by placing a stop-loss order at the base of the diamond or even closer to the purchase point. The closer the stop is to the buy point, the more likely normal price fluctuations will take you out.

Sample Trade

Scott recently graduated from engineering college and took his first professional job at a growing software company. The job pays well, but he has many school loans and a mountain of debt. He thought of using his paycheck to keep ahead of the bills while depending on the bull market to furnish the luxuries.

He had his eye on a new stereo system and wanted it for a party he was hosting during the Fourth of July festivities. That did not leave him much time, so he searched for a chart pattern he could trade profitably. He chose the diamond bottom shown in Figure 11.11. Scott first noticed the diamond in May, a few days before the breakout. He believed that the price would not decline below $69\frac{7}{8}$, $\frac{1}{8}$ below the round number of 70 and at the same level as a couple of price peaks in January.

Risking just $0.75 with a possible reward of $3.75 gave him a risk to reward ratio of 1:5, he calculated. If everything worked as planned, he would make a tidy sum, enough to buy the stereo.

The day after the stock broke out upward, he bought and received a fill at $71\frac{3}{4}$ (near point C in Figure 11.11). That was higher than he liked, but with the strength shown, he was sure the trade would work out. Scott dutifully placed his stop-loss order at 69⅞ with his broker. Three days later the stock closed at 75, above the target price. He dropped by the music store just to fondle the knobs and flip the switches of his dream machine.

Then things began going wrong. The stock closed down nearly $3 to 72⅛. It dropped to 71⅜ the next day and made a lower low a day later. Suddenly, Scott was losing money and his stereo pipe dream was in danger of plugging. Should he sell the stock and put off the party for another time?

Luck was on his side and prices began climbing again. Soon, they were at 74, but the honeymoon did not last long. Prices completed a symmetrical triangle but Scott did not see it. They broke out downward through the support trendline (extend the lower right diamond diagonal toward the triangle). The stock even gave him another chance to get out at a profit when it attempted a pullback to the triangle boundary. Scott was busy making party plans and missed the signal. When he received a call from his broker in mid-June reporting that the stop took him out at 69⅞, Scott scratched his head and wondered what went wrong. Do you know the answer?

12

Double Bottoms

RESULTS SNAPSHOT

Appearance	A downward price trend bottoms out, rises, then bottoms again before climbing.
Reversal or consolidation	Short-term (up to 3 months) bullish reversal
Failure rate	64%
Failure rate if waited for breakout	3%
Average rise	40%, with most likely rise between 20 and 30%
Volume trend	Downward until breakout
Throwbacks	68%
Percentage meeting predicted price target	68%
Surprising finding	Bottoms closer together show larger gains
See also	Head-and-Shoulders Bottoms, Complex; Horn Bottoms

Perhaps the biggest surprise with double bottoms is the high failure rate at 64%. Only a third of the formations classify as true double bottoms. They are the ones that have prices rising above the confirmation point, which is the highest high between the two lows. The failure rate tumbles to just 3% if one waits for confirmation. *Only those formations with confirmed breakouts are evaluated in this study.*

The average rise is 40% but is tempered by a third of the formations having gains less than 15%. These small rises are balanced by a third of the formations showing gains over 45%. The most likely rise is between 20% and 30%, relatively high for bullish formations.

Throwbacks occur 68% of the time, suggesting it is wise to wait for a throwback and invest once prices turn upward. In some cases, waiting for a throwback can save you from making an unprofitable trade.

A surprising finding is that bottoms closer together outperform those spaced farther apart. The Statistics section of this chapter examines this in more detail.

Tour

What does a double bottom look like? Figure 12.1 shows a good example of a double bottom. Prices reach a high in mid-March then head lower. For the next 3 months, prices continue down in a steady decline to the low in June.

Volume picks up as prices near the low then peg the meter at over 1.1 million shares on June 18, the day prices reach a low of 12.69. From the March high, the stock declines 47% in 3 months. The high volume marks the turning point and the stock moves upward. However, a retest of the low is in store and prices round over and head down again. In late August, prices make another low when the stock drops to 13.06, also on high volume.

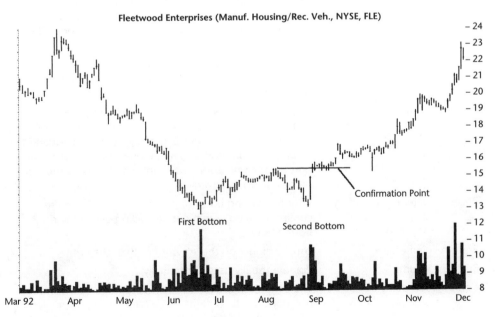

Figure 12.1 A double bottom occurs after a downward price trend. High volume commonly occurs on the first bottom.

The day after the low, on a burst of buying enthusiasm, the stock jumps up and reaches the confirmation point in just 2 days. Instead of continuing upward, however, the stock throws back to the breakout point and moves horizontally for just over a week before resuming its move upward. By late January, the stock reaches a high of 26⅞, a gain of 75% from the breakout price.

Figure 12.1 shows a double bottom and the gains achieved by such a formation. Are there key elements that make up a double bottom? Yes, and a discussion of the key elements follows in the next section.

Identification Guidelines

Not any two bottoms at the same price level will suffice for a double bottom. Listed in Table 12.1 are a number of guidelines that make correct selection easier. While considering the guidelines, look at Figure 12.2. The stock begins declining in mid-October 1993 from a price of about 56½. It bottoms out at

Table 12.1
Identification Characteristics of Double Bottoms

Characteristic	Discussion
Downward price trend	Prices trend down (short term) and should not drift below the left bottom.
Rise between bottoms	There should be a 10% to 20% rise (or more) between the two bottoms, measured from low to high. Peaks close together tend to be at the lower end of the range. The rise usually looks rounded but can be irregular.
Dual bottoms	Bottom to bottom price variation is 4% or less. This is not crucial except that the two bottoms should appear near the same price level.
Bottom distance	Bottoms should be at least a few weeks apart (many consider a month to be the minimum), formed by two separate minor lows (not part of the same consolidation area). Minimum bottom separation is not critical as the best gains come from formations with bottoms about 3 months apart, on average.
Prices rise after right bottom	After the second bottom, prices must rise above the confirmation point without first falling below the right bottom low.
Bottom volume	Usually higher on the left bottom than the right.
Breakout volume	Volume usually rises substantially.
Confirmation point	The confirmation point is the highest high between the two bottoms. It confirms that a twin bottom formation is a true double bottom. A breakout occurs when prices rise above the confirmation point.

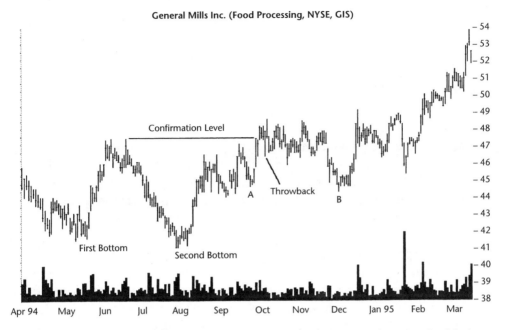

General Mills Inc. (Food Processing, NYSE, GIS)

Figure 12.2 Invalid double bottom. Points A and B do not depict a double bottom because there are lower lows to the immediate left of point A.

about 41½ in mid-May. Prices never drop below the left low on the way to the bottom. The reason for this guideline is that you should use the two lowest minor lows on the price chart. Do not try to select one low then a nearby low just to satisfy the guidelines. The two points marked A and B in Figure 12.2 represent an incorrectly selected double bottom because point A has lower lows to the left of it.

The rise between the two bottoms should climb at least 10%, as measured from the low at the bottom to the rise high. The confirmation point is the highest high between the two bottoms, and it is used to calculate the measure rule and to gauge the breakout price (more about that later). Figure 12.2 shows a rise from the right bottom, at 41$\frac{5}{32}$, to a high of 47½. That is a rise of 15%, well above the 10% threshold.

The bottom to bottom price variation should be 4% or less. The basic rule is that the two bottoms should appear to be near one another on the price scale. Figure 12.2 shows a price variation of about 1%.

The two bottoms should be at least a few weeks apart but are often separated by many months, as shown in Figure 12.2. I set a 10-day minimum as the standard for selections in this study (15 days between turns out to be the measured minimum for all double bottoms in this study). A month is the minimum separation that many professionals view as leading to powerful rallies. I set a lower standard to help verify that this is true. It turns out that peaks close together perform better than those spaced farther apart. I limited the maximum separation to about a year (the widest had a separation of 374 days).

Many of the identification guidelines are arbitrary and the classic definition of a double bottom has different ones. The classic definition says that the two bottoms should be at least 1 month apart, separated by less than a 3% price variation, and have a confirmation point that rises 20% above the low (bottoms closer together have somewhat lower confirmation points). The rise between the two troughs should look rounded.

I examined the performance difference between my definition and the classic one and optimized the parameters to achieve the best performance. What I discovered is that there is no meaningful performance difference between the various settings, so I used the less stringent guidelines in the statistical evaluation (10-day minimum separation, 4% price variation, 10% minimum rise to the confirmation point).

A double bottom is not a true double bottom until prices rise above the confirmation point. In tabulating the statistics, *I only count those double bottoms in which prices rise above the confirmation point.* Why? Because of the high failure rate: 64%. There were 980 formations that looked like double bottoms, but their price trends eventually moved below the second bottom. An additional 525 formations performed as expected by rising to the confirmation point and continuing higher. If you buy a stock just after it touches the second bottom, your chances of having a successful trade are one in three. In other words, wait for prices to rise above the confirmation point.

The volume chart for double bottoms usually shows the highest volume occurring on the left bottom. Diminished volume appears on the right bottom, and the volume trend of the overall formation is downward. None of these are absolute rules. Sometimes volume is highest on the right bottom instead of the left. However, on average, most of the formations obey the guidelines.

The breakout volume is high, usually well above the prior day's volume and above the average volume as well. Again, this is not an inviolate rule so expect exceptions.

Why do double bottoms form? To answer that question, consider the double bottom shown in Figure 12.3. Prices reach a high in mid-April 1993 and move horizontally until nervousness sets in during September. Then prices start moving down, sliding from a high of 33⅞ to 20¼ by late June 1994, a 40% decline in 9 months.

After reaching a multiyear low in June, prices recover some of their losses by moving upward. After reaching a new low, a rebound is quite common with a retest of the low typically following. A retest is just like it sounds; prices return to the low and test to see if the stock can support itself at that price level. If it cannot, prices continue moving down. Otherwise, the low usually becomes the end of the decline and rising prices result.

Such is the case depicted in Figure 12.3. It seems clear from the volume pattern that many investors believe the low, shown as point B, is a retest of

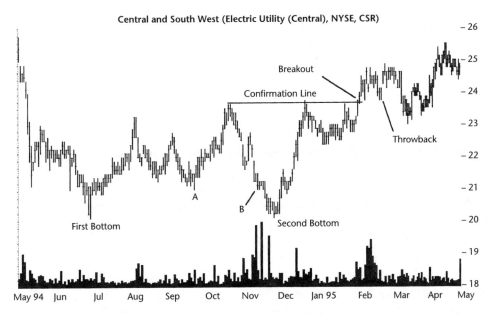

Figure 12.3 Prices confirm the breakout once they close above the confirmation point, shown here as the horizontal line. The confirmation point is the highest high reached between the two bottoms. Prices often throw back to this level after the breakout.

point A. Volume surges on two occasions in the vain hope that the decline has ended. Investors are wrong.

Prices hold at 21 for about a week before continuing down. As prices head toward the level of the June low, volume surges again. This essentially marks the end of the downward plunge. Prices hesitate at that level for slightly less than 2 weeks before turning around and heading upward.

A double bottom is nothing more than a retest of the low. Investors buy the stock in the hope that the decline has finally ended. Sometimes they are right and sometimes they are not, which leads us into the next section: failures.

Focus on Failures

It is obvious that the formation pictured in Figure 12.4 is a double bottom. The first bottom occurs after a downward price trend, as you would expect. The two bottoms are far enough apart, the rise between them is sufficient to delineate two minor lows, and the price variation between the two bottoms is small. The volume pattern is unusual in that the second bottom has a higher, denser volume pattern than the first. However, this is not significant. After the second bottom, prices rise at a steady rate until the confirmation point. Then prices jump up and pierce the prior minor high at about 40⅝. When prices *close* above the confirmation line, it signals a valid breakout and confirms the double bottom formation.

In this case, as is common for most double bottoms, prices throw back to the breakout point. However, prices continue moving down. Scrolling Figure 12.4 to the left, you would see prices making a new low in September 1993 at $31\frac{5}{8}$, below the February low of 34.

Had you purchased this stock on the breakout and held on, you would have lost money. I call this type of failure a 5% failure. Prices do not rise by more than 5% above the breakout before heading lower. Fortunately, 5% failures are also rare; they occur only 17 times in this study. To put that statistic in perspective, it means that on 525 separate occasions prices continue upward by more than 5%.

Figure 12.5 shows an example of a second type of failure that perhaps you, too, have seen. Ted is a novice investor with an attitude. He looks at the stock chart, checks the identification guidelines, and believes that the stock is making a double bottom. When prices rise after the second bottom, Ted decides to pull the trigger early and buys the stock, receiving a fill at $42\frac{5}{8}$. He reasons that all the indications suggest the stock has completed a valid double bottom. That being the case, why not get in now while the price is still low instead of waiting for prices to rise above the confirmation point ($46\frac{1}{4}$)? Ted makes a good point. He is pleased with the stock's performance until it begins to round over. Does he sell out now at a small profit or should he hold on and risk a downturn while waiting for additional gains? This is a recurring investor dilemma.

He decides to hang on to his position. During May, the stock surges upward again before beginning a downhill run. Ted watches in horror as his profit vanishes and losses mount. Eventually, when prices spike downward, he sells at the opening the next day and closes out his position.

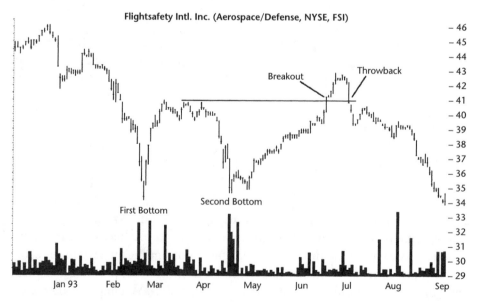

Figure 12.4 Example of a 5% failure. This rare occurrence happens when prices plummet after rising less than 5%.

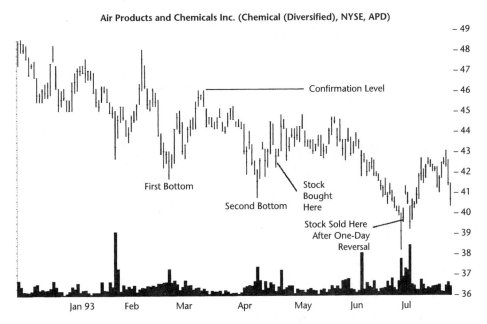

Air Products and Chemicals Inc. (Chemical (Diversified), NYSE, APD)

Figure 12.5 Example of second type of failure—failing to wait for breakout confirmation. Ted decided to get an early start on the double bottom but ended up losing money.

What did he do wrong? He failed to wait for breakout confirmation. Prices must close above the confirmation point before a trade is placed. Otherwise your chances of success are only one in three. We discuss how to trade this formation properly in the Trading Tactics section of this chapter.

Statistics

The statistics shown in the following tables only refer to formations that qualify as being true double bottoms. This means prices must close above the confirmation point (the highest price between the two bottoms). Table 12.2 shows the general statistics for double bottoms. There are 542 formations in 2,500 years of daily price data. Of these formations, 372 or 69% act as reversals of the prevailing trend.

Nearly all the formations (97%), continue moving above the confirmation point after an upside breakout. The remainder fail to continue upward by more than 5% before heading back down. This statistic suggests that you should buy the stock after an upside breakout. In all likelihood, prices will continue rising.

The average rise for formations with successful upside breakouts is 40%. However, the most likely rise is between 20% and 30%. Figure 12.6 shows a graph of the gains. The chart is built by sorting the gains into various bins and counting the number of entries in each bin. The resulting frequency distribution

Table 12.2
General Statistics for Double Bottoms

Description	Statistic
Number of formations in 500 stocks from 1991 to 1996	542
Reversal or consolidation	170 consolidations, 372 reversals
Failure rate	17 or 3%
Average rise of successful formations	40%
Most likely rise	20% to 30%
Of those succeeding, number meeting or exceeding price target (measure rule)	370 or 68%
Average formation length	2 months (70 days)
Average price difference between bottoms	2%
Average rise between bottoms	19%
Percentage of times left bottom price is lower than right	52%
Gains for lower left versus lower right bottom	39% versus 39%

shows the influence large gains have on the overall average. You can see in the chart that there are a significant number of large gains. If you consider anything above 50% a large gain, then almost a third of the formations fit into this category. The large gains tend to pull the overall average upward.

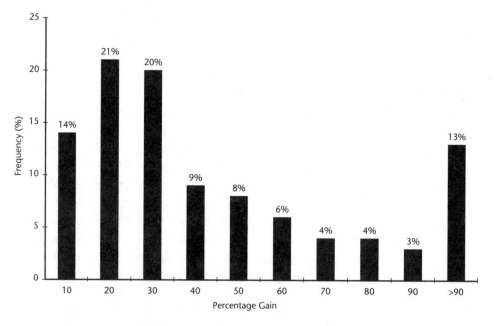

Figure 12.6 Frequency distribution of the gains for double bottoms. The most likely rise is between 20% and 30%.

The measure rule, discussed at length in the Trading Tactics section of this chapter, is a method used to predict the minimum price rise for a stock. One simply computes the formation height and adds the value to the confirmation point. The result is the price level to which it is hoped the stock will rise, at a minimum. Using this method, two-thirds (68%) of the formations meet or exceed their predicted price targets. This 68% value is low, as I consider values above 80% to be reliable.

The average formation length is just over 2 months (70 days) as measured from bottom to bottom. The minimum length is arbitrarily limited to 10 days as a selection guideline. Although I formally established no maximum length, there were a few formations well over a year long. I removed them from consideration. As a result, the formation length ranges from 15 to 374 days.

The average price variation measured between the two bottoms is 2%, half the 4% guideline maximum. The intent of this statistic is to show that the two bottoms appear to be on or near the same price level.

The rise between the two bottoms averages 19%, with a 10% minimum set as a guideline. The confirmation point is the highest price reached between the two bottoms. It is used to compute the formation height and to confirm an upside breakout.

The two bottoms are at nearly the same price level, with slightly more left bottoms at a lower price (52%) than right bottoms (48%). I checked the gains for formations with either a lower left or lower right bottom and both types perform equally well (in other words, formations with a lower left bottom have gains of 39%, the same as those with a lower right bottom).

Do bottoms spaced closer together show larger gains than those spaced farther apart? Yes. Consider Figure 12.7, a chart of the gains mapped onto a frequency distribution of the distance between the two bottoms. The chart says that if you have a bottom separation of 3 weeks, the average gain is 42%. A larger separation, say about 4 months, gives an average gain of just 23% for those formations in this study.

Table 12.3 shows breakout statistics for double bottoms. There is a time delay between the second bottom and the actual breakout. The reason for the delay is that it takes time for prices to rise from the second bottom to the confirmation point. For the formations in this study, the delay is about a month and a half (43 days).

Since this study only considers true double bottoms, those with prices rising above the confirmation point, all 542 formations have upside breakouts. Once an upside breakout occurs, 17 formations initially move higher but throw back to the formation and continue down. In these cases, prices did not rise by more than 5% before returning to the formation. This 5% failure, like that shown in Figure 12.4, is quite rare and should not be of major concern.

There are a significant number of throwbacks to the breakout price (68%). Such a high throwback rate suggests an investment strategy: Wait for

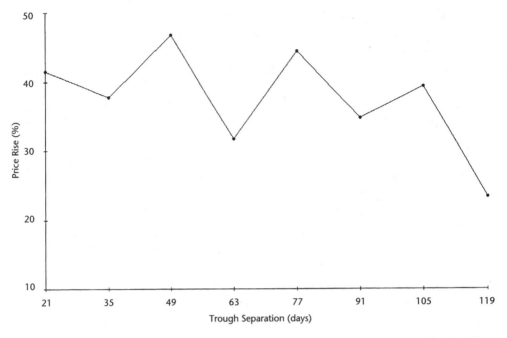

Figure 12.7   Price rise versus trough separation. Do bottoms closer together result in the larger gains? The graph suggests the answer is yes.

the throwback, then invest after prices recover. The Trading Tactics section of this chapter discusses this strategy further.

The average time for prices to return to the breakout price is 11 days, which is about the same value for many formation types. No throwbacks occur over 30 days. Throwbacks occurring beyond a month are not throwbacks at all, just normal price fluctuations.

Table 12.3
Breakout Statistics for Double Bottoms

Description	Statistic
Average days after right bottom to breakout	43 days
Upside breakout	542 or 100%
Upside breakout but failure	17 or 3%
Throwbacks	366 or 68%
Average time to throwback completion	11 days
For successful formations, days to ultimate high	7 months (204 days)
Percentage of breakouts occurring near 12-month low (L), center (C), or high (H)	L28%, C46%, H25%
Percentage gain for each 12-month lookback period	L42%, C38%, H41%

Once an upside breakout occurs, how long does it take to reach the ultimate high? Although the average time is about 7 months (204 days), one should temper this value by realizing it is an average. Should your particular formation rise by only 10% or 15%, the time to reach the ultimate high likely will be shorter—probably about 2 months.

Where in the yearly price range do double bottoms occur? Surprisingly, most (46%) occur in the center third of the range. Mapping the percentage gain into the yearly price range shows the average gain is about equal for all three ranges. The result suggests that most double bottoms occur after a run-up in prices. Once prices back off their yearly high and trend down for a while, they form a double bottom and begin climbing again.

You might expect that formations falling furthest (those in the lowest third of the yearly price range) rebound higher. That appears to be the case, with a 42% gain. You might also expect that those double bottoms occurring near the yearly high would get caught in upward momentum and soar even higher. Those formations with breakouts in the upper third of their price range show gains of 41%.

Table 12.4 contains volume statistics for double bottoms. The first bottom has higher volume 58% of the time, whereas the right bottom has higher volume 42% of the time. About two-thirds of the time (65%), the volume trend throughout the formation is downward. I computed this by finding the slope of the linear regression line of volume over the formation from the left to right bottom. Excluded from the calculation is the run-up from the right bottom to the breakout point because it often results in above average volume.

After a breakout, volume usually surges for a few days but quickly returns to normal. Table 12.4 shows the average volume for the day of the breakout until a week later. You can see how quickly the volume drops, from 165% of the prior day's value to 18% below a week later.

Are low volume breakouts more likely to throw back to the breakout price? No. Both high and low volume breakouts throw back to the breakout price 65% of the time.

Table 12.4
Volume Statistics for Double Bottoms

Description	Statistic
Percentage of left bottoms having higher volume	58%
Number showing downward volume trend	351 or 65%
Volume for breakout day and next 5 days compared with day before breakout	165%, 133%, 105%, 92%, 89%, 82%
Percentage of high and low volume breakouts subject to throwback	65%

Trading Tactics

Table 12.5 shows trading tactics for double bottoms. The measure rule predicts the minimum price move expected once a double bottom experiences an upside breakout. Consider the chart pictured in Figure 12.8. To calculate the predicted price, first determine the formation height by subtracting the lowest low from the highest high in the formation. In Figure 12.8, the lowest low occurs at the right bottom, with a price of 27.57. The highest high, marked on the figure by point A, is 31.09. Add the difference, 3.52, to the confirmation point, or the highest high between the two bottoms (that is, 31.09 + 3.52). Again, the highest high is point A. The result, 34.61, is the expected minimum target. You can see in the chart that prices meet the target in late December. A few days after meeting the target, prices momentarily descend before resuming their climb. During mid-April, the stock reaches its ultimate high price of 40.26 before declining.

After you locate a potential double bottom, review the selection guidelines before placing a trade. Figure 12.8 shows a declining price trend leading to the first bottom. The rise between the two bottoms is about 13%, just above the 10% threshold. The two bottoms are at nearly the same price level and several months apart.

Very high volume appears on the left bottom with substantially reduced volume on the right bottom, which is typical. The overall volume trend slopes downward from the left bottom to the right, as expected.

Once the second bottom of a double bottom occurs, you can use the measure rule to estimate the minimum price move. If the potential profit is large enough, then wait for the breakout. This cannot be overemphasized. With a dismal failure rate of 64%, you *must* wait for an upside breakout. Figure 12.5 is an example of what happens if you do not.

Table 12.5
Trading Tactics for Double Bottoms

Trading Tactic	Explanation
Measure rule	Compute the formation height by subtracting the lowest low from the highest high in the formation. Add the difference to the highest high between the two bottoms (the confirmation point). The result is the expected minimum price move.
Wait for breakout	Since only 36% of the formations break out upward, you must wait for an upside breakout before placing a trade.
Wait for throwback	Two-thirds of the formations throw back to the breakout price. Therefore, consider waiting for the throwback and for *prices to head upward again.*

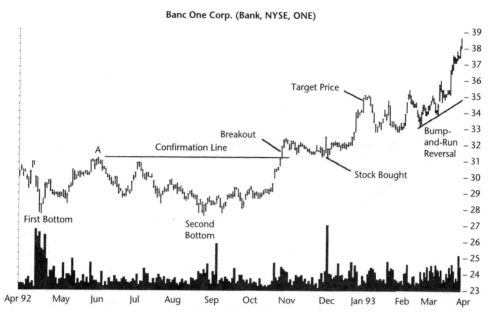

Banc One Corp. (Bank, NYSE, ONE)

Figure 12.8 Double bottom trading dilemma. How do you trade this double bottom? Do you buy just after the second bottom or wait for prices to rise above the confirmation point? You wait for prices to recover after the throwback, then buy. A rounding bottom appears from point A to the breakout.

A *close* above the confirmation point signals a breakout. The confirmation point is simply a fancy way of saying the highest high reached between the two bottoms. Shown is the confirmation point, marked point A in Figure 12.8, and a line extending to the breakout point.

Once prices close above the breakout point, should you buy the stock? Probably not. Since two-thirds of the formations rise up, then quickly return to the breakout price, it is wise to wait. Once prices complete the throwback to the breakout point, they may continue moving down. Usually, however, they turn around and start heading higher. In either case, wait for prices to stop descending and begin climbing again. When that happens, buy the stock. However, following this guideline means that you will miss some potentially profitable opportunities.

For short-term gains, sell as prices near the target price. Only 68% of the formations meet their price targets, so be ready to take profits as the target nears or if weakness intervenes.

For intermediate- and long-term investors, you can hold on to the stock and hope for an extended upward move. Of course, a review of the fundamental factors supporting the price rise is often a key to large gains. Use the double bottom formation to time your entry and the fundamentals to justify a continued presence in the stock.

Sample Trade

Lauren is a school teacher. Although she loves teaching kids, she would much prefer raking in the dough by day trading stocks over the Internet. Until that time, she shoehorns her investment activities into the few hours of free time she has each week.

When she spotted the double bottom shown in Figure 12.8, she knew it was love at first sight. The rounding bottom pattern (from point A to the breakout) suggested higher highs were in store. However, she resisted the temptation to get in early because she could not guarantee prices would continue moving up. She justified her action by pretending that she was teaching her students how to trade. If she could not do it properly, how could they?

When prices reached the high between the two bottoms, Lauren decided to buy. Just before she placed her order, the broker read off the current quotation. It was well above the confirmation point. So she decided to wait and pray for a throwback.

About 4 weeks after the breakout, prices dipped to the buy point, but would they continue down? She had to wait until she felt confident that prices would rise. To her, this occurred a day later, on November 27. That day prices made a higher low and she felt comfortable buying the stock. It was a gamble, because 2 days of rising prices hardly make a trend. Still, she was getting antsy and did not want to wait too long and watch prices rise above the level that she could have bought a month before. So, she bought the stock and received a fill at $31\frac{3}{8}$.

The following day, volume spiked to over three million shares and prices jumped over $\frac{3}{4}$ of a point. The spike made her nervous as it reminded her of a one-day reversal, but the stock closed at the high for the day, which is odd for the formation. That is when she remembered to place a stop. She chose a price of $30\frac{7}{8}$, about $\frac{1}{4}$ below the recent minor lows, an area of prior support.

The following day prices moved down but succeeding days saw them rebound. In mid-December, the stock went ballistic and fulfilled the measure rule. She could not make up her mind if it was worth selling at that point. By the time she decided to sell, the stock had returned to the up-sloping trendline (drawn connecting the lows in September through January), so she held on.

The stock moved up. In late March, the stock jumped sharply, climbing almost $1\frac{1}{2}$ in 1 day. That was a big move for the stock and she wondered what was going on. She followed the stock closely and it became obvious the stock had entered the bump phase of a bump-and-run reversal. Periodically, as the stock climbed, she penciled in the sell lines parallel to the original bump-and-run reversal trendline. As she looked at the chart, she saw the narrow peak appear and knew the end was near. When the stock dropped below the nearest sell line, she placed an order to sell her holdings and received a fill at $38\frac{5}{8}$.

She cleared 22% on the trade, but on an annualized basis, she made 60%. She smiled, knowing that annualized numbers were something her math class needed to learn. Now she had the perfect example.

13

Double Tops

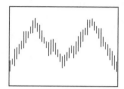

RESULTS SNAPSHOT

Appearance	Two well-defined peaks, separated in time but at nearly the same price level
Reversal or consolidation	Short-term (up to 3 months) bearish reversal
Failure rate	65%
Failure rate if waited for breakout	17%
Average decline	20%, with most likely decline between 10% and 15%
Average volume trend	Downward until breakout
Pullbacks	69%
Percentage meeting predicted price target	39%
Surprising findings	Tops closer together, deep troughs, and high volume breakouts all show larger losses.
See also	Head-and-Shoulders Tops, Complex; Horn Tops

The study of double tops results in several surprises. The failure rate at 65% is worse than just tossing a coin. If you blindly sell your holdings before the breakout, you will likely miss out on some handsome upside gains. If, instead, you wait for the breakout, then you will be correct in dumping your shares 83% of the time. However, almost half the formations decline less than 15%, and nearly two out of three formations fall shy of their predicted price targets.

Such poor performance statistics might make you think seriously about hanging onto your shares.

Pullbacks to the breakout point are high at 69%. Once a breakout occurs, you can probably safely wait for the pullback to complete and prices to head down again before selling.

Double tops spaced closer together have larger losses than those with peaks spaced farther apart. With peaks close together, investors are more likely to recognize a double top and try to take advantage of it.

There is also a relationship between the size of the decline between the two peaks and the resulting percentage loss. Formations with large peak-to-trough declines also have large losses when compared to small trough declines.

High volume breakouts result in statistically significant performance differences than those with low volume breakouts. In other words, formations with high volume breakouts decline further. The Statistics section of this chapter explores these findings.

Tour

Along with the head-and-shoulders formation, double tops are perhaps the most popular. Many novice investors see a dual peak on the stock chart and proclaim it to be a double top. It probably is not. There are a number of characteristics that compose a true double top and I discuss them in a moment, but, first, what does a double top look like?

Consider Figure 13.1, a double top in Pacific Scientific. The first thing one notices are the twin peaks. They are near the same price level and widely spaced. The price trend leading to the first peak is upward and prices fall away after the second peak.

The intervening valley is just that: a valley that sees prices decline by 10% or 20%, sometimes more. The valley floor forms the confirmation level or point. The confirmation point is the lowest price between the two peaks and signals a downside breakout once prices close below it. A twin peak formation can only classify as a true double top once prices close below the confirmation point.

There is usually a pullback such as that shown in Figure 13.1. A pullback allows investors another opportunity to exit their position before the decline resumes. For more adventurous traders, the pullback is a chance to make a short sale in the hope that prices will continue falling.

Identification Guidelines

Table 13.1 contains a host of guidelines that assist in correctly identifying double tops. The general price trend is the first guideline. Prices should be trending upward on their way to the first summit. The price trend should not be a retrace in an extended decline but generally has the stair-step appearance such

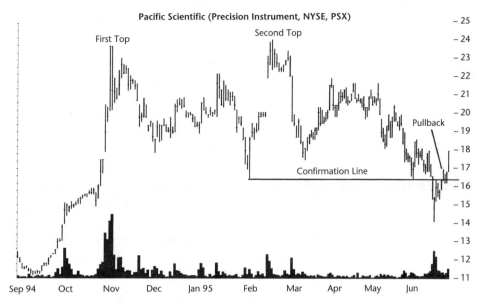

Figure 13.1 A double top has twin peaks that are usually several months apart but quite near in price. Only when prices decline below the valley floor is a double top confirmed as a valid formation.

Table 13.1
Identification Characteristics of Double Tops

Characteristic	Discussion
Upward price trend	Leading to the formation, prices trend upward over the short to intermediate term (3 to 6 months) and usually do not rise above the left top.
Decline between tops	There should be at least a 10% decline between the two tops, measured from high to low. Some analysts require a 20% decline with peaks spaced a month or more apart (the deeper the trough the better the performance). The valley is usually rounded looking but can be irregular.
Dual tops	Two *distinct* tops with a price variation between peaks of 3% or less. This is not crucial except that the two tops should appear near the same price level and not be part of the same consolidation pattern.
Top distance	Tops should be a few weeks to a year apart. For widely spaced peaks, use weekly charts.
Prices decline after right top	After the second top, prices must *close* below the confirmation point without rising above the right top high.
Volume	Usually higher on the left top than the right. Overall volume trend is downward.
Breakout volume	Volume is usually high but need not be. High volume breakouts decline further.
Confirmation point	The confirmation point is the lowest low between the two tops. Prices closing below the confirmation point confirm a double top and the breakout.

as that shown in Figure 13.2. Of course, rapid rises occur. The guideline is that the rise should happen over several months and culminate in a top.

Figure 13.2 shows a rise that begins in October 1993 and peaks during the following March. The climb takes prices from a low of 25½ to a high of 40. Then prices descend for a few months before climbing to the second peak. The second peak tops out at 39, just 2.5% below the first peak.

The time between the two peaks is about 5 months, far enough apart to form two distinct peaks with an intervening rounded, valley. The valley floor bottoms out at 32½, far below the highest peak of 40. The decline, at 19%, is well above the 10% minimum.

After the second peak tops out, prices decline away from it at a steady rate. Soon prices close below the confirmation point, which is the lowest low in the valley, and continue moving down. When that happens, it confirms both the downside breakout and the formation as a double top. *Prices must close below the confirmation point before the formation becomes a true double top.* This qualification cannot be overemphasized.

Prices often will decline below the second peak then turn around and continue rising. Sometimes a third peak forms and sometimes prices just sail away. In two out of three instances, prices will not descend to the confirmation point at all—they just rise above the twin peaks and continue moving higher. The Focus on Failures section discusses this behavior in more detail.

The volume pattern is what you would expect. It is usually higher on the left peak, diminished on the second peak, and above average on the breakout.

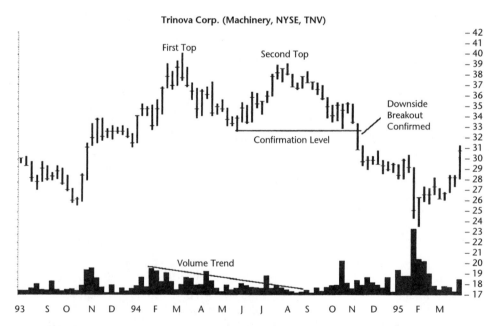

Figure 13.2 Double top on the weekly scale. Prices in this double top rise from a floor of 25½ to 40 in about 5 months. Prices closing below the confirmation level confirm a downside breakout and the formation itself.

Higher volume on the left peak and lower volume on the right peak help support the overall receding volume trend of the formation. Figure 13.2 shows higher volume on the left top and very low volume on the right one. Breakout volume is at about the same rate as the first peak—high but not as enthusiastic as it could be. Breakout volume is not a crucial factor in the validity of the formation, but formations with high volume breakouts tend to decline further.

Why do double tops form? Consider Figure 13.3, a well-shaped double top that satisfies all the identification guidelines. The stock essentially begins rising in October 1992 at a price of $9\frac{7}{8}$. At the start, volume is unremarkable but does have its moments. On spurts, like that shown during March and again in April, volume spikes upward and helps propel the stock higher.

Many unfortunate investors bought near the left top hoping prices would continue higher—a momentum play. However, astute technical investors recognized the price pattern for what it really was: a measured move up. The first up-leg occurs in just 3 days. It is followed by horizontal movement for several weeks and another swift rise to the first top.

Once the measured move completes, volume dries up and the upward movement stalls. Prices move down and form a base in early May that sees a low of $15\frac{3}{4}$. The consolidation lasts almost 2 months on light turnover.

The price decline from peak to trough is not much in dollars, but it represents a 20% decline. Comparatively few investors take advantage of the price lull to add to their position or place new trades. Those investors that buy in at the top swear they will sell just as soon as they get their money back. When

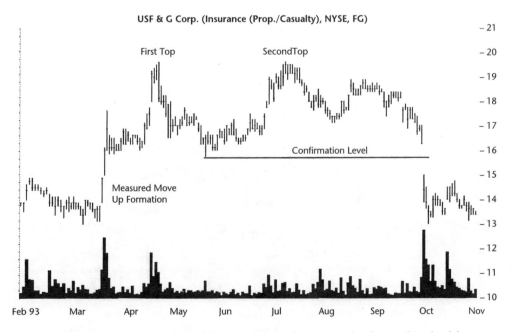

Figure 13.3 Well-shaped double top. Prices do not push above this double top for over 3 years. A measured move up formation forms the rise to the left top.

prices start to rise again, many of them pull the trigger and sell their shares. The volume pattern, which up to this point has been flat, bumps up and takes on a more rugged appearance (during late June and into July). Other investors, believing that the consolidation is over, buy for the first time.

As prices round over and form the second peak during July some investors correctly assume that a double top is forming. They sell their shares near the top, content with the profits they have locked in. Other intrepid traders sell short and hope prices fall. Prices do fall but stop at the top of the consolidation area formed between the peaks a few months earlier.

After a prolonged attempt at creating a third peak in late August and into September, prices gap below the confirmation point at 15¾. A downside breakout begins. The smart money sells their shares immediately and licks their wounds. Others hope the selling is overdone while still others sell short.

The stock attempts a pullback in mid-October but gives up. For the next 3 years, until the end of this study, prices fail to rise above the high established by the double top.

Focus on Failures

What does a double top failure look like and can anything be learned from it? Consider Figure 13.4, a common failure of a double top. The twin peaks satisfy all the identification guidelines outlined in Table 13.1 with two exceptions.

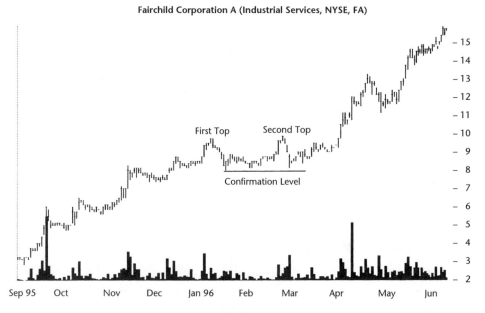

Fairchild Corporation A (Industrial Services, NYSE, FA)

Figure 13.4 A common double top failure. Prices decline after the second peak then rise before reaching the confirmation point.

First, the volume pattern is suspect. Volume on formation of the left top is high but lasts only 1 day. The right top volume is dense, high, and remains high for about a week as the top forms. However, in defense of the formation, the volume pattern often varies from the norm and offers little clue to the eventual outcome.

The second guideline violated is the more important of the two. Prices fail to close below the confirmation point. When considering all twin peak chart patterns in this study, two out of three (65%) perform as the one shown in Figure 13.4. In other words, they move higher. Why?

Expect top reversals (such as the double top) to perform poorly in a bull market, whereas bottom reversals should excel. That appears to be the case with many of the formations covered in this book. The key point to remember about Figure 13.4 is that you must wait for prices to drop below the confirmation point before placing a trade. Otherwise, you stand a good chance of cashing out too soon or getting taken to the cleaners if you sell short.

If you do wait for confirmation, then the probability rises to 83% that prices will continue moving down. Of course, that is small comfort if you happen to run into a 5% failure. Consider Figure 13.5, a double top that obeys the identification guidelines including closing below the confirmation level.

The uphill run starts in May 1992 and culminates in the top during March 1993, representing a rise of over 60%. Prices retreat for a month before gathering steam and trying for a new high. They succeed at the beginning of June, when prices crest the old high by $\frac{5}{8}$.

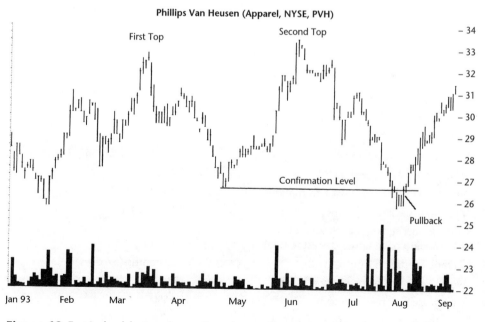

Figure 13.5 A double top formation that suffers a 5% failure. Prices fail to continue moving down by more than 5% before rebounding.

However, the celebration is short and prices tumble. They drop over 20% before meeting support at 26. The new low is below the valley low, the so-called confirmation point, but prices quickly turn around. Prices move up at a smart pace and do not stop until they touch 39. That is a 50% move from the low. If you sold your shares once prices closed below the confirmation point, you would walk away from a chunk of money.

This type of failure is called a 5% failure. Prices break out downward but fail to descend by more than 5% before turning around. Fortunately, 5% failures are relatively rare for double tops but still represent 17% of all formations with confirmed breakouts.

Statistics

Table 13.2 shows general statistics for double tops, but it does not tell the complete story. There are 1,280 formations identified in 500 stocks over 5 years. Out of these formations, 65% or 826 continue moving *higher* without first descending below the confirmation point. *Since a double top is only valid after a confirmed breakout, excluded from the statistics are the 826 formations.* In short, they are not double tops.

The remaining 454 formations separate into reversals (75%) and consolidations (25%) of the prevailing trend. The failure rate of these formations is 17%, meaning that 75 reverse course before moving down more than 5%. I view failure rates below 20% as belonging to reliable formations. However, I must emphasize that you have to wait for the breakout before investing.

Table 13.2
General Statistics for Double Tops

Description	Statistic
Number of formations in 500 stocks from 1991 to 1996	454
Reversal or consolidation	113 consolidations, 341 reversals
Failure rate	75 or 17%
Average decline of successful formations	20%
Most likely decline	10% to 15%
Of those succeeding, number meeting or exceeding price target (measure rule)	177 or 39%
Average formation length	2 months (57 days)
Average price difference between tops	1%
Average decline between tops	15%
Percentage of left tops higher than right	56% versus 44%

The average decline for successful formations is 20%, but the most likely decline is between 10% and 15%. Figure 13.6 shows this relationship. I created the graph by sorting the percentage losses into ten bins and counting the entries in each bin. The resulting frequency distribution shows an alarming trend. Almost half the formations (47%) descend less than 15% below the confirmation point before reaching the ultimate low.

The question then becomes, is it worth taking profits on a confirmed double top? If prices continue down an additional 15% and then turn around, why not just wait for prices to recover? Those are good questions. If you sell when the double top is confirmed, you may be selling near the ultimate low.

The average decline from the highest peak to the ultimate low is 32%. Why not sell at the top? Why not take profits sooner, before the formation is confirmed? If you do that, then you will most likely be giving up additional profits as prices rise after you sell (remember, two out of three twin peak formations never fall below the confirmation point). Of course, you can always sell and, if the stock does turn around, you can buy back in.

The measure rule estimates the price to which the stock will fall, at a minimum. In the Trading Tactics section of this chapter I discuss the measure rule further, but suffice it to say you simply compute the formation height and subtract the value from the confirmation point. The result is the minimum price move expected.

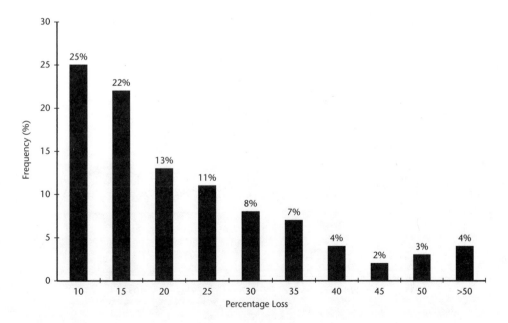

Figure 13.6 Frequency distribution of losses for double tops. The figure shows that almost half the confirmed double tops have declines less than 15%.

For double tops, only 39% of the formations decline far enough to fulfill the prediction. Reliable values are above 80%. The poor showing of this formation further emphasizes that many double top patterns do not decline far and this formation may not be worth trading at all.

Table 13.2 presents a few statistics related to the appearance of the double top. The average formation, as measured from peak to peak, is about 2 months (57 days) long. The average price difference between the two tops is just $0.30 and the valley is 15% below the highest peak, on average. The left top is usually higher than the right one but it is almost a wash (at 56% of formations versus 44%).

In an earlier study on a much smaller scale, I noticed a tendency of double tops to perform better with peaks closer together than with those spaced farther apart. This study supports those findings.

I measured the time difference between peaks and created a frequency distribution of the results. Then I mapped the corresponding losses for the formations and graphed the numbers in Figure 13.7. The graph suggests that peaks closer together have higher losses (they perform better) than those spaced more widely apart.

As with the earlier study, the sample size is a problem. The number of entries in the bins is quite good until the interval gets above 77 days between peaks. At 91 days, there are only 16 formations in that bin (followed by 15, 8, and 8 for the next three larger intervals, respectively). Even though the 4 bins

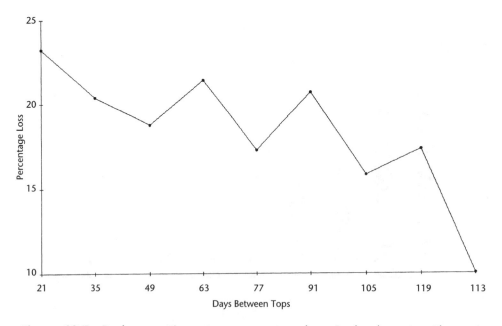

Figure 13.7   Peak separation versus percentage loss. Peaks closer together perform better than those spaced farther apart.

are below the minimum standard 30 entries, there are enough entries in the other bins to show the downward trend.

The reason for the improved performance of tops that are close together is probably one of recognition. It is simply easier for investors to recognize twin peaks that are 2 or 3 months apart than those that are separated by a year. Once investors recognize a double top, they act on it as a group, sending prices lower.

In another statistical oddity, I measured the depth of the trough between the two peaks and compared it with the ultimate loss. I discovered that double tops with large trough declines have larger losses than those with shallower troughs. Figure 13.8 shows the relationship. For example, formations with trough declines of 11% show an average loss of 15%, whereas formations with trough declines of 18% have losses averaging 27%. The 18% trough value is quite near the classic selection guideline of a 20% decline between tops.

Table 13.3 shows breakout statistics for double tops. After two peaks occur, it may be many days before prices decline to the confirmation point. The formations in this study take an average of about 5 weeks to make the journey from the right top to the confirmation or breakout point.

As mentioned earlier, included in this study are confirmed double tops only, which are formations in which prices close below the lowest price measured between the two peaks. As such, all 454 formations have downside

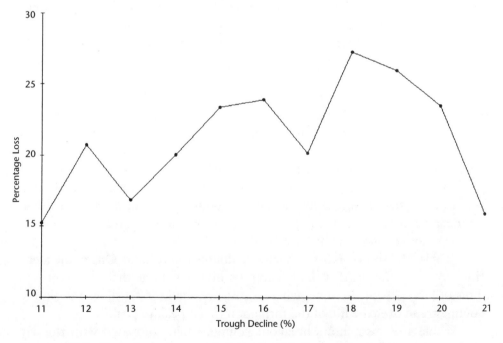

Figure 13.8 Trough decline versus loss. Double tops with deep troughs perform better than those with shallow ones.

Table 13.3
Breakout Statistics for Double Tops

Description	Statistic
Average days after right top to breakout	39 days
Downside breakout	454 or 100%
Downside breakout but failure	75 or 17%
Pullbacks	314 or 69%
Average time to pullback completion	10 days
For successful formations, days to ultimate low	3 months (83 days)
Percentage of breakouts occurring near 12-month price low (L), center (C), or high (H)	L24%, C50%, H26%
Percentage loss for each 12-month lookback period	L17%, C20%, H20%

breakouts. There are, however, 75 formations that break out downward but do not continue moving down by more than 5% before turning around. These 5% failures are somewhat rare, occurring only 17% of the time.

About two-thirds (69%) of the formations have pullbacks to the breakout price. This is a high number and it suggests some reluctance of prices to continue moving below the breakout point. This belief is strengthened further by the most likely decline being just 10% to 15%. Many times prices will drop by 10% or 15%, then pull back to the breakout point and continue higher. For this reason, it is probably wise to place a trade *after* a pullback and *after* prices begin heading down again. The average time for prices to pull back to the breakout point is 10 days, which is about average for many formations in this book.

Once a breakout occurs, it takes about 3 months (83 days) to reach the ultimate low. The vast majority (70%) of formations reach the low in 3 months or less. An additional 18% complete their descent in under 6 months. Thus, I classify double tops as having short-term investment implications.

Where in the yearly price range does the breakout occur? Most of the formations have breakouts in the center third of the price range. Substituting performance figures in the frequency distribution, we find there is really no clear-cut winner. The percentage loss is about the same regardless of where in the yearly price range the breakout occurs.

Table 13.4 shows statistics related to double top volume. One of the identification guidelines is that the left top has higher volume than the right top. This occurs 57% of the time, whereas just over half (56%) show a declining volume trend over the life of the formation (from peak to peak).

Table 13.4 also shows breakout volume when compared with the day before the breakout. It starts out high (191% of the prior day's value) and gradually diminishes.

Table 13.4
Volume Statistics for Double Tops

Description	Statistic
Percentage of left tops having higher volume	57%
Number showing downward volume trend	256 or 56%
Volume for breakout day and next 5 days compared with day before breakout	191%, 158%, 124%, 113%, 116%, 112%
Percentage of low volume breakouts subject to pullback	65%
Percentage of high volume breakouts subject to pullback	67%
Percentage of high volume downside breakouts resulting in larger price declines compared to low volume breakouts	21% versus 15%.

Are low volume breakouts more likely to pull back than high volume ones? No. Only 65% of low volume breakouts have pullbacks, whereas 67% of high volume breakouts have pullbacks.

I define high volume as 150% of the day before the breakout, whereas low volume is 75% of the prior day. If the low volume threshold drops from 75% to 50% of the prior day's volume, then 62% of the low volume breakouts have pullbacks. As such, you can probably argue that high volume breakouts are more likely to pull back than low volume ones. This makes sense. When everyone sells their shares soon after a breakout, what is left is an unbalance of buying demand (since the sellers have all sold), so the price rises and pulls back to the confirmation point.

Do high volume breakouts send stocks lower? Yes, and the results are statistically significant. Stocks with high volume breakouts suffer larger losses (21%, on average) than do low volume breakouts (with an average 15% loss).

Trading Tactics

Table 13.5 contains suggested trading tactics. The first tactic is the measure rule. The rule helps predict the price to which the stock will decline, at a minimum. An example of the measure rule as it applies to double tops is shown in Figure 13.9. The double top forms after a climb from $9\frac{1}{4}$ to $15\frac{1}{8}$ before descending and climbing again to the top area. In this regard, the double top is unusual as prices are higher 2 months before the formation tops out. Still, an investor willing to trade this formation would first consider whether it is profitable to do so. That is where the measure rule comes into play.

First, compute the formation height by subtracting the highest high from the lowest low in the formation. The highest high is the left top, at $14\frac{3}{8}$, and

Table 13.5
Trading Tactics for Double Tops

Trading Tactic	Explanation
Measure rule	Compute the formation height by subtracting the lowest low from the highest high in the formation. Subtract the difference from the lowest low between the two tops (the confirmation point). The minimum price move results. Better performance (70% versus 39% reach the target) occurs by dividing the height in two before subtracting from the confirmation point.
Do not trade	With a likely decline of just 10% to 15%, is it really worth selling your shares? If the answer is yes, then sell near the second peak and buy back should prices close above the higher peak (or begin a sustained uptrend).
Tops close together	For better performance, select tops that are closer together, say, 60 days apart or less.
Deep troughs	For better performance, the valley between the two tops should be deep, 15% or more.
Wait for breakout	Since 65% of the formations break out upward, you must wait for a downside breakout before placing a trade. On a confirmed downside breakout, prices continue down 83% of the time.
Wait for pullback	Two-thirds of the formations pull back to the breakout price. Therefore, consider waiting for the pullback and for *prices to head downward again.*

the lowest low is $12\frac{1}{8}$ (in the valley between the two peaks). Subtract the difference, $2\frac{1}{4}$, from the confirmation point ($12\frac{1}{8}$) to arrive at the target price of $9\frac{7}{8}$. Prices reach the target in late March.

Since the measure rule has a success rate of just 39%, meaning that only about a third of the formations decline to the predicted price, it is worth considering using half the formation height in the calculation. Doing so boosts the success rate to 70%. For Figure 13.9, a new target price using half the formation height is 11. Prices meet the new target the same day as the breakout.

It is always wise to check the fundamentals before placing a trade. Most formations making a double top on weak fundamentals are ripe to fall. Unfortunately, the news from a company and from brokerage firms following the company may be glowing just as the situation is about to change. You may find brokerage firms upgrading the company or boosting earnings estimates near the top. That is not their fault; it is just that earnings are notoriously difficult to predict and brokerage firms get caught up in the enthusiasm.

For any trade, it is critical that you understand why the stock is performing as it is. This understanding is even more important for double tops because of the poor *most likely* decline (just 10% to 15%). If you discover in your research that the fundamental factors are changing for the worse, then it gives you added confidence to risk a trade.

With such poor performance of double tops, one has to ask, why risk the trade? Should you decide not to trade, prices will probably continue moving higher after the second peak—especially in a bull market. About a third of the time, prices continue down. Sometimes stocks suffer agonizing declines, but Figure 13.6 shows that only 4% (17 out of 379) of the formations with confirmed downside breakouts have declines over 50%. Of course, a 30% decline is nothing to sneeze at either.

A way to improve the performance of double tops is to sell just after the second top forms. Most of the time, prices will rebound and move higher. If so, you can always repurchase your shares and ride the stock up. Should prices move down then you got out at the best time.

As mentioned earlier, the better performing double tops are those that have peaks closer together with deep troughs. Figure 13.9 is an example. The peaks are just 35 days apart and the valley descends 16% from the highest peak. For this situation, the measure rule implies a minimum decline of 2¼ points or 19% below the confirmation point, large enough to risk a trade.

When should you place the trade? Prices must close below the confirmation point before the double top is confirmed. In Figure 13.9, the little downside spike to the left of the breakout point is not a breakout because prices do not *close* below the confirmation line. Prices close below the line on February 2, a day of very high volume.

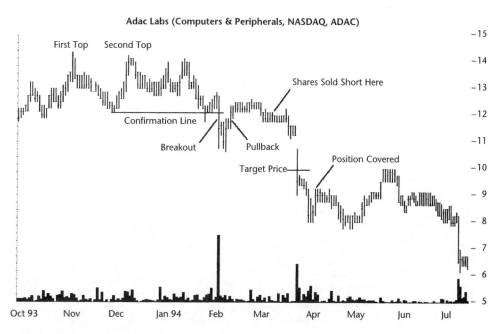

Figure 13.9 Measure rule as it applies to double tops. Sell short after the pullback once prices begin declining again.

With pullbacks occurring 69% of the time, it may pay to wait for a pullback before investing. You can see in Figure 13.9 that the stock pulls back to the confirmation point and continues moving upward for several days. Once prices begin dropping again, place the trade.

Sample Trade

Rachel is an executive secretary for a mutual fund company, one that is prospering. She has the intelligence and good fortune to date a few of the managers running the funds. Along the way, she has picked up several investment tips and speaks the lingo. Best of all, her buddies are still friends and willing to help her.

When she spotted the situation shown in Figure 13.9, she asked her friends if shorting the stock was a good idea. With their encouragement and further research on her own, she decided to sell the stock short on March 8 and received a fill at 12. In short order the stock drifted downward, easily fulfilling the target price. Since prices were moving down, she felt no rush to cover her position.

That changed on March 31 when prices closed higher. Since she usually reviews her stocks at the end of the day, there was nothing to do but wait until the stock opened in the morning. The following day, prices moved back down again and she decided to wait another day.

When prices again moved up, she covered her short and received a fill at 9. She made almost $3 of profit for each share (after commissions) or 25% in 3 weeks. Had she held on, her profits would have been even better. The stock moved sideways for about 3 months before reaching an ultimate low of 6⅛.

14

Flags and Pennants

RESULTS SNAPSHOT

Flags

Appearance	A short sloping rectangle bounded by two parallel trendlines
Reversal or consolidation	Short-term (up to 3 months) consolidation
Failure rate in uptrend	13%
Failure rate in downtrend	12%
Average rise in uptrend	19%, with most likely rise being 20%
Average decline in downtrend	17%, with most likely decline being 15%
Volume trend	Downward
Pullbacks	20%
Throwbacks	10%
Percentage meeting predicted price target in an uptrend	63%
Percentage meeting predicted price target in a downtrend	61%
See also	Rectangle Bottoms; Rectangle Tops

Pennants

Appearance	A short sloping triangle bounded by two converging trendlines
Reversal or consolidation	Short-term (up to 3 months) consolidation
Failure rate in uptrend	19%
Failure rate in downtrend	34%
Average rise in uptrend	21%, with most likely rise between 15% and 20%
Average decline in downtrend	17%, with most likely decline being 25%
Volume trend	Downward
Pullbacks	17%
Throwbacks	16%
Percentage meeting predicted price target in an uptrend	58%
Percentage meeting predicted price target in a downtrend	52%
See also	Triangles, Symmetrical Bottoms; Triangles, Symmetrical Tops; Wedges, Falling; Wedges, Rising

Flags and pennants look alike and in many ways their performance is similar, too. The formations are usually very short in duration, from a few days to 3 weeks, and mark the halfway point in a quick price move. These formations can be profitable short-term investments, but you must be nimble and attentive to take full advantage of them. Pennants, with a failure rate of 34% in downtrends, are above the 20% rate I consider acceptable. Flags at 12% to 13% and pennants in a uptrend (19%) perform better.

The percentage of formations that meet or exceed their predicted price targets is disappointing for both flags and pennants. I view values above 80% to be reliable, but the results show values that range from 52% to 63%, suggesting that you should trade these formations with caution as your profits may not be as large as you expect.

The most likely rise or decline is deceptive for these formations. When the likely rise or decline value is above the average, it simply means that a frequency distribution shows more hits at a particular value, but the bin totals of the prior columns are high, pulling the average downward.

Tour

Figure 14.1 shows a good example of a flag. It is bounded by two parallel trendlines and usually is less than 3 weeks long (sometimes as short as a few days). You see these formations appearing in strong uptrends or downtrends (such as that shown in Figure 14.1), usually near the halfway point in the move. This particular flag goes against the grain in the sense that prices rise in a downtrend. This is the most common behavior—a retrace in a downtrend—but it is not unusual for flags to appear horizontal (as short rectangles) or slope downward (following the trend). Since flags can also appear in an uptrend, they usually slope downward, but can be horizontal or slope upward too.

The volume trend is downward. As we see in the Statistics section of this chapter, a receding volume trend usually accompanies flag formations.

Figure 14.2 shows what a pennant looks like. The only visual difference between a flag and a pennant is the shape of the formation. Two sloping trendlines that eventually meet outline a pennant formation, resembling a small wedge. Sometimes the trendlines slope upward, as in Figure 14.2, and sometimes they do not. Usually, they slope upward in a downtrend and downward in an uptrend.

Like the flag formation, the volume pattern recedes. For pennants, the receding volume trend is more prevalent, occurring in nearly all the formations in this study.

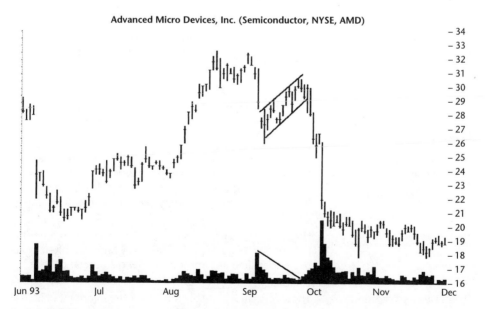

Figure 14.1   A flag bounded by two, parallel trendlines usually has a receding volume pattern.

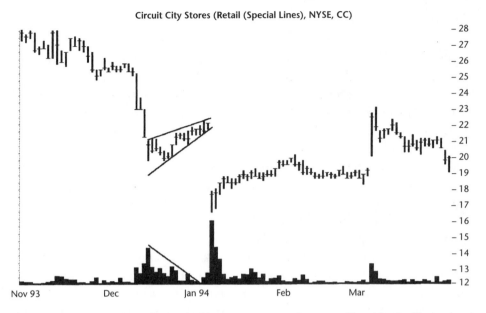

Figure 14.2 A pennant bounded by two converging trendlines looks like a short rising wedge.

Identification Guidelines

Table 14.1 outlines the identification characteristics for flags and pennants. Two parallel trendlines bound the price action for flags as shown in Figure 14.3. Two converging trendlines outline the boundaries for pennants as shown in Figure 14.4. In both figures the formations are short compared with many

Table 14.1
Identification Characteristics of Flags and Pennants

Characteristic	Discussion
Prices bounded by two trendlines	Flags: price action bounded by two parallel trendlines. Pennants: the two trendlines converge. For both patterns, prices usually go against the prevailing trend: They rise in a downtrend and fall in an uptrend, but exceptions are common.
Three-week maximum	Flags and pennants are short, from a few days to 3 weeks. Formations longer than 3 weeks may fail more often or are better classified as symmetrical triangles, rectangles, or wedges (rising or falling).
Steep, quick price trend	These formations usually form near the midpoint of a steep, quick price trend. If you do not have a strong advance or decline leading to the chart pattern, ignore the formation.
Downward volume trend	Volume usually trends downward throughout the formation.

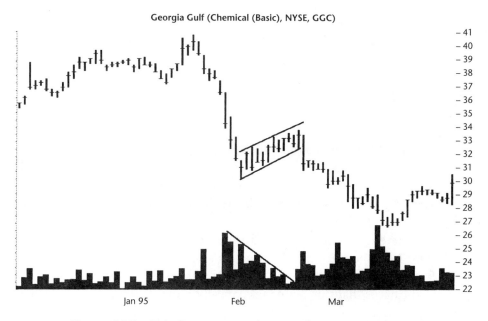

Figure 14.3   This flag appears about midway in a downtrend.

other chart patterns in this book. In the case of Figure 14.3, the formation is 12 trading days long, whereas the pennant in Figure 14.4 is just 8 trading days long. Many times when a formation is very short, such as 3 or 4 days, it appears as a horizontal rectangle—a dark blob in the middle of a fast price trend. The

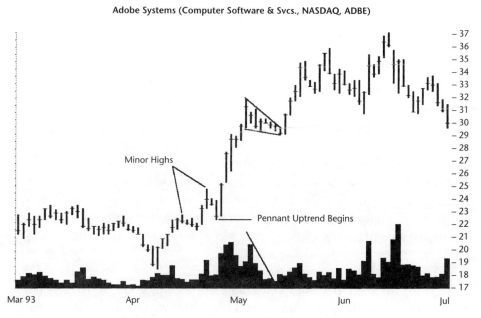

Figure 14.4   A short pennant forms after a quick price rise. The pennant slopes downward and prices move upward after leaving the formation.

formations usually are shorter than 3 weeks but this is an arbitrary limit. Sixteen formations in this study (6%) have durations greater than 3 weeks (the longest flag is 32 days and the longest pennant is 28 days).

Reliable flags and pennants appear during steep, quick price trends. The trends might be up or down, but prices rise or fall quickly, moving several points in just a few days to a few weeks. In Figure 14.3, for example, the downtrend begins on January 18 and the flag begins on February 1. In that short time, prices tumble from a high of $40\frac{3}{4}$ to a low of $30\frac{1}{8}$.

Although one might argue the uptrend in Figure 14.4 begins in early April, I suggest the rise leading to the pennant begins later, on April 26, from a low price of $22\frac{3}{8}$. Six trading days later, the price climbs to the top of the pennant at $31\frac{1}{4}$. The later starting point is after the two minor highs and it serves as a reference point for the measure rule.

Figure 14.3, the price trend in the flag slopes upward, whereas in Figure 14.4 the pennant slopes downward. This behavior is typical for the prevailing price trend (that is, flags or pennants typically move against the trend). The chart patterns usually appear near the midpoint of the move. As such, they are often termed half-mast formations.

The volume trend nearly always recedes over the course of the formation. However, this is not an inviolate rule but usually is the case. I should point out that rising volume is no cause for alarm. Of the 45 formation failures, only 4 have rising volume trends.

When selecting a flag or pennant to trade, the most important guideline is the rapid, steep price trend. If prices are meandering up or down and form a flag or pennant, then look elsewhere. The flag or pennant must be a place where the stock can take a breather from its rapid pace. Prices move against the short-term trend for several days before continuing on.

Focus on Failures

Like all formations, flags and pennants are not immune to failure. Figure 14.5 shows a flag failure. The flag, while obeying the confines of the two downsloping trendlines, has a good volume trend. Prices should continue higher after the flag completes but do not. Why? One explanation is that the formation is just too long at 26 days. Sometimes an excessively long formation suggests an impending failure or a weak price move (after the breakout). Trade flags or pennants more than 3 weeks long carefully or pass them up entirely.

Figure 14.6, another flag formation, is also a failure. Prices should continue rising after the flag completes. The duration is good, at 10 days (about average for flags), and the volume trend is downward. However, the formation has an inadequate price rise leading to it. The difference between the take-off

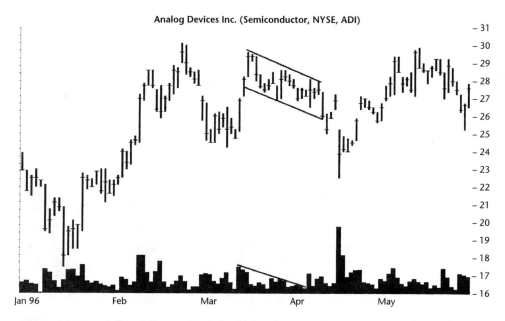

Figure 14.5 A flag failure. The failure of prices to continue rising is probably due to two factors: The price rise leading to the formation is short and the flag is longer than normal.

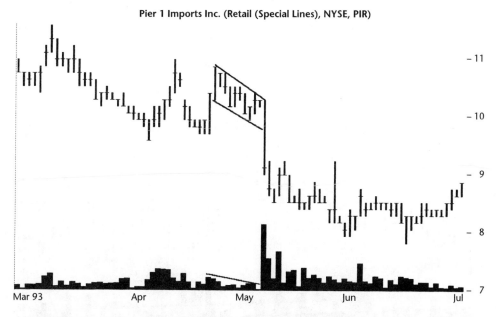

Figure 14.6 Another flag formation failure. Prices rise for just 1 day before this flag develops, much too short a rise to support a good formation.

point and the formation high is just over a dollar, well short of the 19% average rise. There is probably little danger that you would select this formation to trade. Since flags and pennants signal the halfway point, the predicted rise in this example is just too small to take advantage of. An investor viewing this formation for trading would likely pass it by.

Figure 14.7 shows a failure of a pennant in a downtrend. The formation probably reminds you of a short symmetrical triangle—one that acts as a reversal (which is unusual for a symmetrical triangle). The volume trend is receding, as you would expect. The formation price trend, bounded by the two sloping trendlines, looks good too. The price trend leading down to the formation represents an 18% decline, exactly the average for a pennant in a downtrend. Prices should continue moving lower after this formation completes but they do not. Why?

You can see in Figure 14.7 that prices loop around the formation end then head lower (a throwback). If you held onto your short position, you would eventually make money. However, I still classify this formation as a failure. Prices should continue down immediately after piercing the trendline boundary. The reason prices ascend immediately is not clear. A scan of the database reveals 66% of the formation failures (30 out of 45) fail in this manner. That is to say, they move briefly in the wrong direction (a breakout failure) but soon turn around (by throwback or pullback) and complete properly.

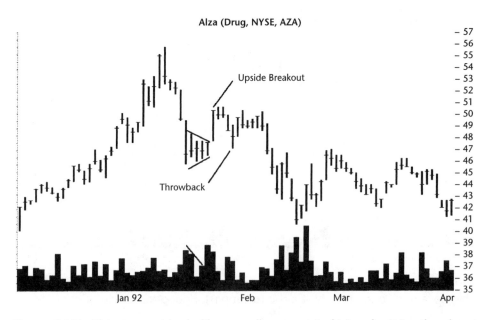

Figure 14.7   This pennant looks like a small symmetrical triangle. Prices break out upward, throw back to the formation, and head lower.

Statistics

Table 14.2 shows the general statistics for both flags and pennants. I uncovered 144 flags and 106 pennants over 5 years in 500 stocks. This is fewer than I expected.

All formations except 23 act as consolidations of the prevailing trend. Those acting as reversals are also formation failures. Most of the failure rates are quite reasonable. For flags, they are 12% and 13% for down and up trends. Pennants have a wider spread, 34% and 19%, respectively. Pennants in a downtrend fail more often than the 20% benchmark for reliable formations, so you might consider avoiding trading them.

Nearly all the flags (87%) and many of the pennants (75%) behave as expected, that is, prices continue in the same direction after the formation completes as they were moving before the formation began.

Table 14.2 lists throwbacks and pullbacks for flags and pennants. Ignore the possibility of a throwback or pullback when pondering a trade because both happen so infrequently.

The average length, at 11 and 10 days for flags and pennants, respectively, is quite short. As described in the Identification Guidelines, these formations usually range from just a few days to about 3 weeks.

Seventy-eight percent of the flags and 90% of the pennants have volume trends that recede over the course of the formation. I confirmed this by examining the slope of the line formed using linear regression on the volume data from the formation start to its end. As I mentioned earlier, just because a formation shows rising volume is no reason to ignore it. Only 4 formation failures (or 9%) and 41 successful formations have rising volume trends.

Table 14.3 shows the statistics for flags and pennants when the prevailing price trend is *upward*, which means the trend leading to the formation is rising

Table 14.2
General Statistics for Flags and Pennants

Description	Flags	Pennants
Number of formations in 500 stocks from 1991 to 1996	144	106
Reversal or consolidation	130 consolidations, 14 reversals	97 consolidations, 9 reversals
Failure rate in uptrend	10 or 13%	12 or 19%
Failure rate in downtrend	8 or 12%	15 or 34%
Throwbacks	7 or 10%	8 or 16%
Pullbacks	12 or 20%	5 or 17%
Average formation length	11 days	10 days
Downward volume trend	112 or 78%	95 to 90%

Table 14.3
Statistics for Flags and Pennants When Price Trend Is Rising

Description	Flags	Pennants
Percentage beginning near 12-month price low (L), center (C), or high (H)	L7%, C18%, H76%	L7%, C9%, H84%
Price trend duration	62 days	53 days
Average rise leading to formation	19%	22%
Average rise after formation	19%	21%
Most likely rise after formation	20%	15% to 20%
Of those succeeding, number meeting or exceeding price target (measure rule)	63%	58%

even though the chart pattern may have a falling price trend within the confines of its boundary.

Where in the yearly price range do flags and pennants usually form? Most flags begin life near the yearly high, with 76% of the formations falling into this category (I divided the yearly price range into thirds). For pennants, 84% are within one-third of the yearly high.

The trend duration, from the prior minor low before the formation begins to the minor high after the formation ends, is 62 days for flags and 53 days for pennants. Since flags and pennants are half-mast formations, and should you enter a trade after a flag or pennant completes, you should be out of the trade in about a month, on average. This quick investment turn means you can make a decent profit in a short time, then look elsewhere for another trade.

To assess how steep the price rise *leading* to the formation is, I calculated the average for the chart patterns. Both flags and pennants have rises near 20%, as measured from the low at the trend start to the highest high in the formation. I include these values in Table 14.3 because it is important to select flags and pennants that form after a large, quick price move.

A similar move, as you would expect, completes after the breakout. Flags (19%) and pennants (21%) show rises that almost exactly match the gain leading to the formation. As such, these formations live up to the nickname of half-mast formations (they mark the halfway point).

Since the numbers are averages, it pays to check what the most likely rise is by using a frequency distribution of the gains. For both flags and pennants, the most common rise is in the 15% to 20% range, about where you would expect.

The measure rule, which says that the move after a flag or pennant completes will meet or exceed the trend leading to it, succeeds 63% of the time for flags and 58% for pennants. I consider values above 80% to be reliable. While both values are over 50%, meaning that these chart patterns do act as half-mast formations most of the time, the values suggest that you should be conservative when gauging the eventual price move.

Table 14.4 shows behavior statistics for flags and pennants in *downtrends*. Where in the yearly price range do flags and pennants in a declining price trend occur? Both types typically form in the center third of the range, suggesting that prices are near the yearly high then begin heading lower. As they tumble into the center third of the yearly price range, a flag or pennant forms. Then, after the formation completes, prices continue lower.

The average trend duration, at 50 days for flags and 52 days for pennants, needs explaining. It is the average time from the beginning of the price trend to the end. It is measured from the nearest minor high before the formation forms to the minor low afterward. Where a trend starts and where it ends is sometimes difficult to ascertain, so I adopted the minor high-low scheme but allow some variation when necessary.

The average decline *leading* to a formation is 18% for flags and 17% for pennants. It is measured from the highest price where the trend begins to the lowest price at the start of the formation. The decline *after* a formation completes is similar (17%) for both formation types.

Taken together, we discover that both chart patterns appear to form in the center of a decline (roughly 17% on either side) that occurs over about 6 weeks, on average. Such a large decline in such a short time suggests a profit opportunity. Trading tactics are discussed in the next section.

The most likely decline is 15% (measured from the high at the end of the formation to the trend low) for flags and 25% for pennants. Although the pennant value is large, it simply means that there are more samples in the 25% range but the prior ranges have a fair number of samples, too. The many small numbers pull the overall average downward.

Table 14.4
Statistics for Flags and Pennants When Price Trend Is Declining

Description	Flags	Pennants
Percentage beginning near 12-month price low (L), center (C), or high (H)	L24%, C60%, H17%	L23%, C66%, H11%
Price trend duration	50 days	52 days
Average decline leading to formation	18%	17%
Average decline after formation	17%	17%
Most likely decline after formation	15%	25%
Of those succeeding, number meeting or exceeding price target (measure rule)	61%	52%

The measure rule, in which the price trend after a formation meets or exceeds the prior trend, is met 61% and 52% of the time for flags and pennants in a downtrend, respectively. I consider values over 80% to be reliable so these results fall short. Most alarming is that pennants perform so poorly. If you are considering trading a pennant in a declining price trend, be aware that prices may not reach the target.

Trading Tactics

Table 14.5 shows trading tactics for flags and pennants. Consult Figure 14.8 as I review the tactics listed in Table 14.5. The measure rule gauges the minimum price move. It is the same for both flags and pennants. First, determine where the trend begins, which is usually the minor high (for downtrends) or low (for uptrends) preceding the formation. Figure 14.8 shows the trend beginning at point A. Subtract the low at the formation start (point B at $42\frac{3}{4}$) from point A ($47\frac{1}{2}$), giving a difference of $4\frac{3}{4}$. Subtract the difference from the high at the formation end (point C at 43) to give the target price of $38\frac{1}{4}$. Prices reach the target 13 trading days after they move below the formation trendline.

When trading flags and pennants, you must first be sure you have a valid formation. Use the identification guidelines outlined in Table 14.1 to ensure that you have correctly identified a flag or pennant.

Use the measure rule to gauge the amount of profit likely from the trade and weigh the amount of profit against the possible risk of failure. Look for support and resistance levels where price trends were repulsed in the past. Many times prices will pause or turn around at these junctions. These values become the risk points for a trade. You can compare the risk with the reward by computing the current price with the measure rule target and the first or second level of support or resistance. A ratio of reward to risk should be four to one (or higher) for highly profitable trades.

For the stock shown in Figure 14.8, the potential reward is $4\frac{3}{4}$ (that is, 43 – $38\frac{1}{4}$). The first resistance level is at 44 and there is another at 45 (assuming the trade goes against you and prices rise). The risk is one or two, that is, 44 – 43 or 45 – 43. The ratio, at 4.75 to 1, suggests this formation is worth trading,

Table 14.5
Trading Tactics for Flags and Pennants

Trading Tactic	Explanation
Measure rule	Calculate the price difference between the start of the trend and the formation. Prices should move at least this amount above (if in an uptrend) or below (for downtrends) the end of the formation.
Wait for breakout	Once prices move outside the trendline boundaries, place the trade.

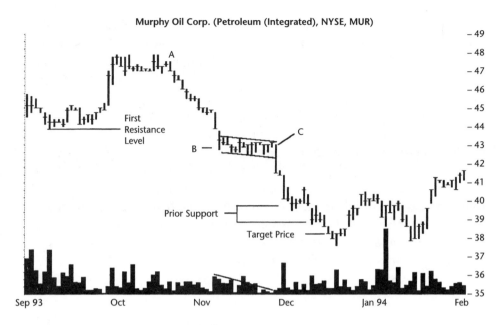

Murphy Oil Corp. (Petroleum (Integrated), NYSE, MUR)

Figure 14.8   Flags and pennants measure rule. Use the measure rule to gauge the decline in this stock. Take the difference between the prior minor high (point A) to the formation low at the start (point B). Subtract the value from the high at the formation end (point C) and the result is the expected minimum price move.

providing you limit your losses. A stop placed at $44\frac{1}{8}$ or so, slightly above the first resistance level, works well.

Take a position in the stock after a breakout, once prices move outside the formation boundary. As prices near the target price, as predicted by the measure rule, consider closing out the trade. Since the statistics regarding the success of meeting the predicted price target are so poor for these formations, be ready to close out the trade sooner than expected. If you wait for prices to reach the target, you might turn a profitable trade into a losing one.

Sample Trade

For example, let us say you are considering shorting the stock shown in Figure 14.8. Since the price trend is downward and it is a flag formation, the statistics suggest that 61% of the formations will meet their price targets, on average. That is a poor showing and deserves caution.

As the chart pattern forms, you monitor the price closely by not only charting the end-of-day price but also checking it at midday. When you dial into your broker for a midday price quote and discover that prices have moved outside the bottom trendline, you decide to pull the trigger. You sell short and receive a fill at 42, just above the closing price of $41\frac{1}{2}$.

You follow the stock closely as prices decline. You look back through the prior year's trading history and discover two support levels at about 40 and 39. You believe, and hope, that the stock will fall through the first support level but the second one may be more difficult. It is, after all, closer to the $38\frac{1}{4}$ target price and more robust than the first level.

When the stock moves sideways at the first support level, you check your work and reexamine the fundamentals and technical indicators. Everything seems good so you remain in the trade.

Eventually the stock pierces the first support level and declines to the second one, where it gets stuck. It closes at 39 but the next day moves up. So the following day you decide to close out your position, believing that the risk of a price rise now far exceeds the possible gain. Your short sale covers at 39 and you receive almost $3 a share. That is not a bad profit for a hold time of just 2 weeks. On an annualized basis, the return is . . . wonderful!

15

Flags, High and Tight

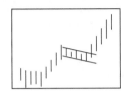

RESULTS SNAPSHOT

Appearance	A consolidation region of several days to several weeks long after a stock doubles in price
Reversal or consolidation	Short-term (up to 3 months) bullish consolidation
Failure rate	32%
Failure rate if waited for breakout	17%
Average rise	63%, with most likely rise between 20% and 30%; 44% have gains over 50%
Volume trend	Downward
Throwbacks	47%

Having recently completed the chapter on flags and pennants, I was surprised to discover an abundance of high, tight flags. Even more surprising is their performance. The 32% failure rate is poor, but if you wait for an upside breakout, the rate drops to 17%. Reliable formations have failure rates below 20%, so high, tight flags score well providing you wait for the breakout.

The average rise, at 63%, is among the highest I have seen for any formation. A frequency distribution suggests that the most likely rise is a more sedate 20% to 30%. However, 33% of the formations have gains over 90% and 44% have gains above 50%. A 50% gain in about 2 months is a formation worth exploring!

Tour

Figure 15.1 is a classic example of a high, tight flag. The quick rise from the low point at 14 to the flag high at 30¾ takes less than 2 months. The volume trend is downward throughout the formation. After the slight pause, the stock continues rising. In another 2 months, it reaches a peak of 120.

The high, tight flag is a play on momentum. When a stock doubles in a short time, it usually takes a breather and consolidates. When it does, it gives the trader the opportunity to buy the stock before the rise resumes. How do you correctly identify a high, tight flag?

Identification Guidelines

The phrase, *high, tight flag* is a misnomer as the formation usually does not resemble a flag formation at all. Sometimes prices move up slightly as the flag progresses, such as shown in Figure 15.1, but more often prices spike down briefly (a day or two) then return and move downward or horizontally before breaking out and heading up.

The formation was popularized by William J. O'Neil in his book, *How to Make Money in Stocks* (McGraw-Hill, 1988). In his brief introduction to the formation, he identifies many characteristics that high, tight flags share. Table 15.1 lists them.

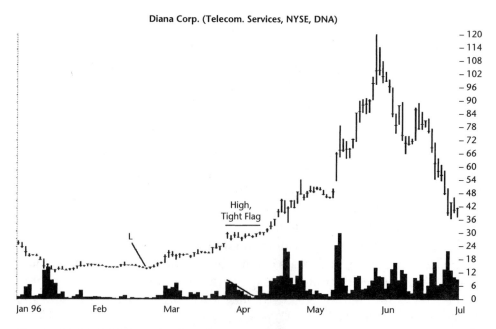

Figure 15.1 A high, tight flag that sees prices rise from about 30 to 120 in 2 months.

Table 15.1
O'Neil Identification Characteristics of High, Tight Flags

O'Neil Characteristic	Discussion
Substantial rise	A rise lasting less than 2 months carries prices upward approximately 100% to 120%.
Flag duration	Prices move sideways usually for 3 to 5 weeks.
Flag correction	During the flag phase, prices drift down a maximum of 20%.

Note: These guidelines select formations with an average gain of 69%, but only 6 formations out of 81 qualify.

O'Neil's description is quite specific but it is interesting for what is does not say. He does not mention that prices should be moving horizontally for an extended time before the stock doubles. Some have said that this is a prerequisite, yet the charts accompanying the O'Neil text show at least one stock in a steady uptrend well before the 2-month rise to the flag begins. The chart shows a price low of about 26 while the flag forms at nearly 100.

I view this extended price rise as a key. It suggests that you need only look for a stock that doubles in 2 months, then consolidates. By extension, you could have a stock double, consolidate (forming a high, tight flag), then double and consolidate again, forming another higher flag. I found several stocks in the database to which this situation applies. In my selections of this formation, I made no assumptions about the prevailing trend (in other words, the chart pattern need not form from a long, flat base).

Some analysts suggest volume should trend downward during the flag phase then spurt upward when prices break out of the formation. Again, O'Neil does not state this as a prerequisite and I do not consider it in my selection criteria. However, the statistics show a downward volume trend *does* improve performance.

The last omission of interest is how to trade the formation. Presumably, once you spot a high, tight flag you would buy into the situation. Unfortunately, with a 32% failure rate, you may be taken to the cleaners on numerous occasions if you follow this approach. It is safer to wait for a breakout before trading this and most other chart patterns.

How did I select the flags in this study? I programmed my computer to identify all stocks that have a minimum price rise of 100% in 2 months or less. Then I manually went through each stock and looked for a nearby consolidation region. If the region was close to the 100% price gain, then I accepted it as a high, tight flag. I ignored the flag duration and correction guidelines outlined in Table 15.1. The statistics later would show that these guidelines *do* contribute to performance but only to a minor degree.

Figure 15.1 passes all the O'Neil guidelines, whereas Figure 15.2 does not (if you apply them strictly). The stock in Figure 15.2 reaches a low of $5\frac{1}{4}$ in

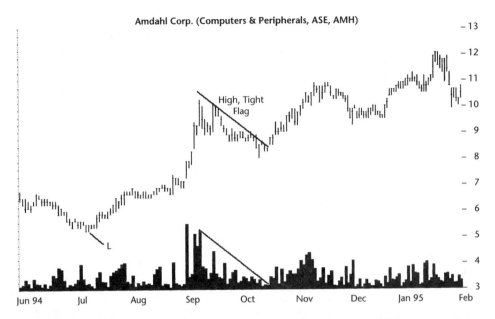

Figure 15.2   If interpreted strictly, this high, tight flag misses all but one of the O'Neil guidelines. It sports a rise of 95% in less than 2 months (measured from the low marked L) leading to the flag. The flag descends 22% in 38 days before breaking out and rising 33% above the highest high in early September.

early July then starts moving up. In early September, it reaches a price of 10¼, just shy of doubling. Admittedly, the 95% price gain is less than a strict interpretation of the O'Neil guidelines, but it comes close. The high, tight flag slopes downward for 38 days, 3 more days than the maximum and declines by 22%, 2% over the threshold. You could argue that the numbers are close enough to the O'Neil guidelines to qualify as a high, tight flag. I accept it as a flag but not under the O'Neil criteria for performance testing purposes. By necessity, I changed the fuzzy phrases, such as *approximately*, into hard rules. Then I compared the performance of those flags passing his guidelines with all the high, tight flags. A discussion of statistics appears later in this chapter. Returning to Figure 15.2, the gain from this flag registers 33%, well short of the average for all high, tight flags.

Table 15.2 shows the guidelines that should be used in selecting and evaluating high, tight flags. First and most importantly there must be a short, quick rise. A handful (10) of the flags in the database have rises of less than 100% but none are below 90%. Most of the stocks make the journey in less than 2 months with the longest taking an extra week (67 days). Again, the key is a short, quick doubling of the stock price.

Once the stocks are selected on a price-rise basis, then look for the nearest consolidation area. Most of the time, it will be quite near. In my selections, I did not care how long the stock consolidated nor how far the flag descended

Table 15.2
Identification Characteristics of High, Tight Flags

Characteristic	Discussion
Substantial rise	A rise lasting less than 2 months carries prices upward at least 90% (shoot for a doubling of the stock price). Stocks with 2-month rises over 115% perform best.
Find consolidation	Locate a consolidation area, an area where prices pause in the prevailing uptrend.
Receding volume trend	The volume trend in the flag should be receding for best performance.

Note: My guidelines result in nearly as good performance as O'Neil's but more than six times the number of formations qualify.

before turning upward. All that mattered was that the consolidation area was plainly visible to the casual observer.

The final identification guideline is not really for identification as much as it is for performance. Flags with a receding volume trend handily outperform those without. However, I would not ignore a high, tight flag simply because volume is rising. Rather, I would recognize that its performance may be subpar.

Focus on Failures

Investing in a stock showing a high, tight flag is not without risk. Figure 15.3 shows a flag that suffers from what I call a 5% failure. Almost a dozen formations (17%) have upside breakouts but do not continue rising by more than 5%. Since one would expect a stock to move up substantially after the breakout, I consider this behavior a failure of the stock to perform as expected.

Figure 15.3 shows a quick, nearly vertical rise, leading to formation of the flag. As the rise falters, high volume tapers off. When prices head lower in the flag portion of the formation (marked in this case by two down-sloping trendlines), volume recedes. The flag drifts lower for almost a month before breaking out of the trend and heading up. After rising for just over a week to a new high, the stock curls around and meanders lower. It throws back to near the base of the formation, then moves horizontally for several months before dropping lower again.

If you consider the highest point in the formation as the breakout point, then this formation is a failure (because it fails to continue rising by more than 5%). However, if you mark the point where prices pierce the top trendline boundary as the breakout point, then this formation is a success. If we use such breakout points in this study, then all 11 of the 5% failures disappear (in other words, the formations are no longer failures).

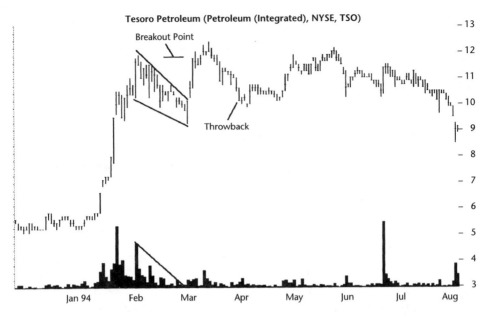

Figure 15.3 A 5% failure of a high, tight flag. Prices fail to continue moving up by more than 5% above the high reached in the flag before heading down in failure. These types of failures occur 17% of the time for high, tight flags.

Sometimes, however, the flag portion of the formation is irregular and the breakout point is not clear, so I decided to use the highest point in the formation as the breakout point. This prejudiced the performance statistics somewhat but is more conservative.

Incidentally, the high, tight flag shown in Figure 15.3 obeys all the O'Neil guidelines. Unfortunately, prices rise by just 4% before tumbling.

Figure 15.4 shows a blatant failure of a high, tight flag to rise. At first, the stock looks like a good candidate. From its low of 12½ in early October, the stock moves up and hits a high of 27 in early December—a double in 2 months. Then prices drift lower in the flag phase . . . and continue moving down. Even though it meets all the O'Neil guidelines, this stock fails to break out upward and move higher. By late March, the stock hits a new low of 11½ retracing all the gains and a little more. The figure should emphasize how risky high, tight flags can be. Unless you wait for the upside breakout, you may be setting yourself up for a losing trade.

Statistics

It is difficult to interpret the O'Neil guidelines to assess performance. At first, I believed I read them wrong and thought the flag length was fine unless it grew too long (over 5 weeks). Reading his guidelines again, it appears the flag

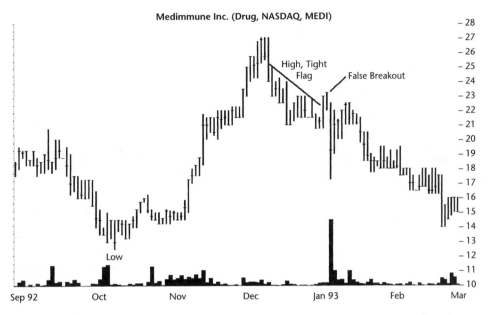

Figure 15.4 This high, tight flag meets all the guidelines, but it fails to break out upward. By late March, it has given up all its gains and then some.

length should be between 3 and 5 weeks long. Others have interpreted the guideline in a similar manner.

Table 15.3 shows the performance for the O'Neil selected high, tight flags with various interpretations of his definition along with my own variations. The first table entry stipulates that a flag occurs after the stock doubles and rises by no more than 120% of its base value in 2 months or less, has a flag length from zero to 5 weeks, and a flag that declines by no more than 20%. There are 38 formations in the database that meet these criteria. Nine of them are failures but the remaining 29 show a rise averaging 47%.

If you use the same guidelines and wait for an upside breakout (one that rises above the highest high in the flag), then all the failures are eliminated and the average gain rises to 64%.

When you place a minimum limit on the flag length, your performance rises to 69%, but you only have six formations that qualify. I do not view this as a positive step since this formation is scarce enough without making it less likely to occur. If you remove the minimum flag length and substitute a receding volume trend, then the average gain becomes 68% with 20 formations reporting in and no failures.

Scrapping many of the selection guidelines except for a minimum 90% rise in 2 months or less, a receding volume trend, and an upside breakout, I found the average gain to be 65% with 40 formations qualifying. Then I changed the minimum price rise in 5% intervals. The performance dips at

Table 15.3
Performance Statistics under Various Selection Criteria

O'Neil Criteria	Gain (%)	Failures/Formations
100–120% rise, up to 5-week flag, maximum 20% flag decline	47	9/38 or 24%
100–120% rise, up to 5-week flag, maximum 20% flag decline, wait for breakout	64	0/29
100–120% rise, up to 3–5 week flag, maximum 20% flag decline, wait for breakout	69	0/6
100–120% rise, up to 5-week flag, maximum 20% flag decline, wait for breakout, receding volume	68	0/20
My Criteria	**Gain (%)**	**Failures/Formations**
Minimum 90% rise, receding volume, wait for breakout	65	0/40
Minimum 95% rise, receding volume, wait for breakout	63	0/36
Minimum 100% rise, receding volume, wait for breakout	63	0/35
Minimum 105% rise, receding volume, wait for breakout	75	0/29
Minimum 110% rise, receding volume, wait for breakout	84	0/24
Minimum 115% rise, receding volume, wait for breakout	93	0/15

95% and 100% but then rises steadily to an average gain of 93% at the 115% interval. The performance deteriorates beyond this point.

You can see in Table 15.3 that the number of qualifying formations also drops from 40 to 15. Of course, you must recognize that the selection criteria is simply tuning the performance of the database. As such, your results will vary.

If I can locate more high, tight flags by using fewer guidelines and not suffer any meaningful performance degradation, then why not do so? Put another way, I removed each selection criterion from the stocks that passed the O'Neil guidelines and found their influence to be positive but less than 4%. For example, when I removed the stipulation that a flag must have a maximum 20% correction, the performance drops from 64% to 63%. The guideline adds value, but it limits the number of stocks qualifying without significantly boosting performance.

The only guideline that improves performance when it is removed is the 100% to 120% price rise stipulation. The best range turns out to be between 110% and 140% for the stocks *in this database*.

What do all these statistics mean? I view an average price rise of 65% with 40 formations qualifying as better than a 69% rise with only 6 formations making the grade (because you have more opportunities to make a killing). The statistics in Tables 15.4 and 15.5 refer to my guidelines outlined in Table 15.2, not to the O'Neil criteria.

Table 15.4 shows the general statistics for high, tight flags that follow my guidelines outlined in Table 15.2. I located 81 formations in 2,500 years of daily price data—a rare formation indeed.

Most of them (78%) are consolidations of the prevailing trend. The remainder are reversals and every reversal is also a failure.

The failure rate at 32% is quite high. However, when you wait for an upside breakout, the failure rate drops to 17%. I view failure rates below 20% to be reliable, so you really should wait for an upside breakout before taking a position in a stock.

The average rise is an exceedingly high 63%. This value does not include the idea that the flag should show receding volume as a selection guideline to improve performance. If you include such a guideline, then your performance rises to 65%, as measured from the highest high in the flag (or the highest high leading to it). This penalizes performance since you could compute the results using the breakout low instead of the flag high. Doing so reduces the number of 5% failures from 11 to zero while boosting the average gain. You would still have four regular failures, so even this method is not perfect.

Figure 15.5 is a graph showing the frequency distribution of gains. If you ignore the right-most column for a moment, then the columns with the high-

Table 15.4
General Statistics for High, Tight Flags

Description	Statistic
Number of formations in 500 stocks from 1991 to 1996	81
Reversal or consolidation	63 consolidations, 18 reversals
Failure rate	26 or 32%
Failure rate if waited for upside breakout	11 or 17%
Average rise of successful formations	63%
Most likely rise	20% to 30%
Average formation length	20 days
Average volume trend	60 or 74% down

Note: These general statistics follow the guidelines in Table 15.2 with the exception of a downward volume trend.

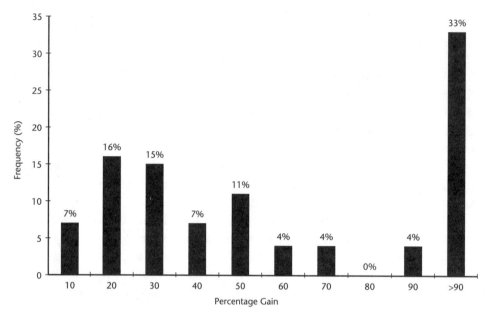

Figure 15.5 Frequenty distribution of gains for high, tight flags. The gains over 90% skew the overall average upward.

est frequencies are 20% and 30%. I consider these two ranges the gain an investor is likely to make. However, since 33% of the formations have gains over 90%, the most likely gain may be higher.

The average formation length is 20 days, suggesting that many of the formations do not meet the O'Neil guidelines of 3 to 5 weeks for flag length.

Many of the formations (74%) have receding volume trends. Six out of 21 failures (or 29%) have volume trends that are rising. About half (53%) of the successful formations having rising volume trends also show below average percentage gains. These statistics further support the notion that a receding volume trend is beneficial.

Table 15.5 shows breakout statistics for those formations obeying my guidelines. Most of the formations (81%) have upside breakouts and only 17% of these fail to continue moving higher than 5%.

The percentage of throwbacks, at 47% of formations with upside break-outs, is not high enough to formulate any sort of trading policy. If you discover a high, tight flag that is throwing back to the formation, then wait for the throwback to complete. The throwback must reverse and prices must move up before you buy in, otherwise the trend may not reverse and you will end up with a loss. The time to throwback completion is 11 days, about average with other formations in this book.

The number of days to reach the ultimate high is a very short 2 months (70 days). This follows the quick 2-month price rise that initiated the trend. After the stock consolidates from a few days to several weeks, the upward trend

Table 15.5
Breakout Statistics For High, Tight Flags

Description	Statistic
Upside breakout	66 or 81%
Downside breakout	15 or 19%
Upside breakout but failure (5% failures)	11 or 17%
Throwbacks	31 or 47%
Average time to throwback completion	11 days
For successful formations, days to ultimate high	2 months (70 days)
Percentage of breakouts occurring near 12-month price low (L), center (C), or high (H)	L0%, C8%, H92%
Percentage gain for each 12-month lookback period	L0%, C34%, H70%

resumes. Thus, the high, tight flag behaves like a regular flag or pennant. It is a half-mast formation (at least in terms of time—2 months before and 2 months after the formation).

Most of the formations (92%) occur near the yearly high. Dividing the yearly price range into thirds and distributing the performance, we find that those formations in the highest third of the price range perform best, with gains averaging 70%. The poor showing, at 34%, of those formations in the center third of the yearly price range offers a stark contrast. There are no formations in the lowest third, as you would expect.

Trading Tactics

Table 15.6 outlines trading tactics for high, tight flags. There is no measure rule for high, tight flags. However, almost a quarter of the formations (13 or 24%) have gains after the breakout that exceed the rise leading to the formation. In other words, the high, tight flag may be near the halfway point in the rise.

There is really only one trading tactic for high, tight, flags. Figure 15.6 shows an example of this tactic. Take a position in the stock after it breaks out

Table 15.6
Trading Tactics for High, Tight Flags

Trading Tactic	Explanation
Measure rule	None. The formation can act as a halfway point. Use that as the benchmark but be conservative in your estimate.
Buy after breakout	If prices break out of the flag portion, buy the stock. If you cannot tell if a breakout has occurred, wait for prices to rise above the highest high in the flag.

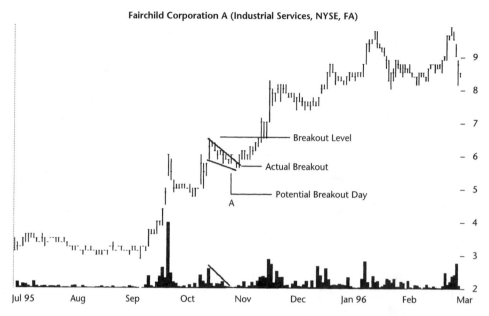

Figure 15.6 A high, tight flag with prices stair-stepping higher. How do you trade this high, tight flag? Buy into the situation once prices rise above the break-out level. You may buy sooner, once prices stage a breakout by piercing the top trendline, but you increase your risk of failure.

of the flag formation. This breakout is not always clear. In Figure 15.6, if you look closely, the stock appears to break through the top trendline 3 days before the actual breakout. In many cases, you cannot draw a straight trendline throughout the flag formation, making it difficult to gauge when a breakout occurs. For this reason, I use the top of the formation as the breakout point (shown in Figure 15.6 as the breakout level). If you are skeptical of this guide-line, look back at Figure 15.2. Five days after the stock reaches a new high and a flag begins forming, the stock spikes upward. Then, just as quickly, prices turn down again. It is over a month before prices rise above the highest high and a lot can happen in a month! Better yet, look back at Figure 15.4 and look at the false breakout. If you had taken a position in the stock when prices pierced the trendline, you would have ended with a loss. This trading tactic would have prevented you from investing in the stock.

After you take a position in the stock, hang on for the ride. The rise usu-ally will not be a straight-line advance but more like a staircase. The stock rises, consolidates, then rises again. Figure 15.6 shows this behavior. In mid-Sep-tember, just after the volume spike, prices retrace a bit before advancing again. Then they move up to the flag and pause. Another advance and pause brings higher prices into December. And so on. As long as the stock is stair-stepping higher, hang onto it.

Sample Trade

John is nuts. I say that in a friendly, good sort of way. He is unreliable, sure, but a blast to be around. Always effervescent, bubbling with enthusiasm, he trades stocks just as he runs his life: carefree, pedal to the metal.

When he spotted the high, tight flag shown in Figure 15.6, he wasted no time in taking a position. When prices pierced the down trendline, he bought in *big* (above point A on the chart).

He placed a stop $\frac{1}{8}$ below the formation low at $5\frac{5}{8}$. Two days later, he was stopped out.

"A billion here, a billion there, and pretty soon you're talking real money!" he grunted as he told me about the trade.

He backed off for a few days and waited for the stock to climb above the high ($6\frac{1}{2}$). When it did, he bit and piled into the stock again at $6\frac{1}{2}$. He considered the bottom of the flag a support area, so that is the price he used as his stop loss. This time, however, he used a mental stop, one that is not placed with a broker but kept in his head. There is really no problem with a mental stop providing an investor is willing to pull the trigger when prices hit the stop. With unreliable John, that is always a problem.

Now and again, John looked at the price chart just to see how the trade was doing. The stock climbed to a support zone at 8 and went horizontal for 3 months. Toward the end of that time, he raised his mental stop to $7\frac{3}{4}$.

Then, the stock climbed again. It ignored the double top formed by peaks in early January and late February, and so did John. By April the stock posted a new high, quietly disclosing that the double top turned out to be false. As the stock passed 13 in mid-April, John started to pay attention. He saw it reach $13\frac{1}{4}$ and back off for a bit, sinking to a low of $11\frac{1}{8}$. Then it spurted up again. John drew a trendline upward following the latest move and when prices pierced the line, he called his broker. He sold at $13\frac{5}{8}$, not close to the high of $15\frac{7}{8}$, but "close enough for government work," he chortled. After commissions, he made 108% in slightly less than 8 months.

16

Gaps

RESULTS SNAPSHOT

Appearance	A gap appears in the price because the current low is higher than the prior high (for uptrends) or the current high is below the prior low (downtrends).
Reversal or consolidation	Short-term (up to 3 months) consolidation
Area, common, or pattern gaps	90% close in 1 week. The average close time is 6 days.

Uptrends

Gap Type	Close within a Week (%)	Average Days to Close
Breakaway	1	83
Continuation	11	70
Exhaustion	58	23

Downtrends

Gap Type	Close within a Week (%)	Average Days to Close
Breakaway	6	86
Continuation	10	43
Exhaustion	72	17

There are five types of gaps, four of which I review in this chapter. The remaining gap, the ex-dividend gap, is not considered because it rarely happens and has no investment significance. The ex-dividend gap usually occurs in utility stocks or stocks with high-paying dividends. On the day of dividend distribution, the price sometimes moves downward leaving a gap in the price chart. Even though the price of the stock after distribution reduces by the dividend amount, the day's trading range often fills the gap so no actual gap appears on the chart.

I define *closing the gap* to be when prices return and span the gap completely. The area or common gap closes quickest, with 90% of those gaps closing within a week.

Listed in the Results Snapshot tables are the average days for the gap to close. Sometimes gaps close quickly (such as exhaustion gaps) because they are found near the ends of trends where prices reverse and fill the gap. Other gaps take much longer since they mark the start of a strong trend (breakaway gap). The continuation gap is a combination of the two because it commonly appears in the middle of trends.

Tour

A gap appears in an uptrend price series when yesterday's daily high is below today's low price. A downtrend gap is similar, being created when yesterday's low is above today's high. In both cases, some type of exuberance is driving the stock to create a gap. It sometimes is nothing more than the stock being worth less simply because of a dividend distribution. At other times, the repercussions are more severe. An earnings surprise, either positive or negative, often causes a gap and the stock to rise by 10% or 15% or to decline by 30% or more, depending on the severity of the news.

Figure 16.1 shows a plethora of different gap types. Area or common gaps occur in areas of congestion, usually when prices are moving sideways. They gap up or down and close quickly. Of all the gap types, area or common gaps are, well, common—appearing all over the place. Breakaway gaps appear at the start of trends. They, too, are quite numerous and accompany high volume. Usually there is some fundamental event driving the stock, creating a breakaway gap. Continuation gaps are relatively rare because they appear in the middle of strong trends. Those trends themselves do not occur very often and even less often do they contain a gap. Exhaustion gaps signal the end of trends. They are the last jump up or down before the trend either reverses or moves sideways.

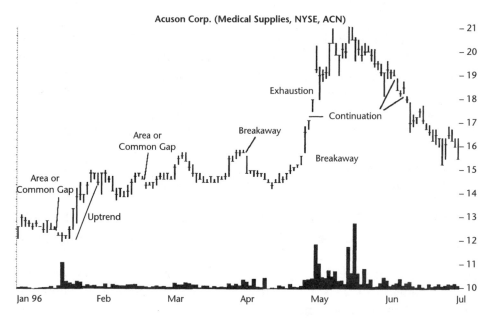

Figure 16.1 Plenty of gaps appear in a daily price chart. The most numerous are the area or common gaps.

Identification Guidelines

Table 16.1 lists identification guidelines for gaps. *Area*, *common*, or *pattern* gaps are all names for the same type of gap. The gap forms inside a consolidation region. It is easy to spot as prices seem to hook around and close the gap in less than a week. Figure 16.2 shows many examples of this hook feature. For example, you can see in late March that prices gap down and the next day the high closes the area gap. A quick hook such as that is characteristic of area gaps. Usually, few or no new highs (for uptrends) or lows (when prices gap lower) occur immediately after the gap.

Volume may be high on the day prices gap but usually settles down quickly. You can see this in late January. The volume spikes on the gap day then returns to normal the next day.

Breakaway gaps highlight the start of a new trend. Volume rises substantially above the prior day and prices gap upward and continue rising (or falling in the case of a descending price gap) forming new highs (or lows).

Consider the breakaway gap in early January shown in Figure 16.2. You can see prices moving up for 3 days accompanied by a rising volume trend. Then prices level out and move horizontally for several weeks before gapping down in an area gap. Two days later, another breakaway gap (not labeled on the chart) appears and prices reach new daily highs for 3 days in a row before settling back.

The large breakaway gap in mid-April, accompanied by a high volume spike, might be an exhaustion gap. Since prices soon continue rising (making

Table 16.1
Identification Characteristics of Gaps

Gap Type	Discussion
Area, common, or pattern	Occur in areas of congestion (trendless markets) and close rapidly. Volume on the day of the gap may be high but returns to normal in a day or two. No new highs (uptrends) or lows (in downtrends) occur after the gap. A distinctive curl as the gap closes is a key indication of this gap type.
Breakaway	Identifies the start of a new trend and usually occurs after breakout from a consolidation region. Is accompanied by high volume on the day of the gap, which continues for several days. The trend continues long enough for several new highs (for uptrends) or new lows (downtrends) to occur after the gap.
Continuation, measuring, or runaway	Happens in the midst of a straight-line advance or decline. Prices continue making new highs or lows without filling the gap. Volume is usually high, propelling prices in the direction of the trend.
Ex-dividend	Is triggered by a dividend distribution. Prices move down by the amount of the dividend and a gap appears if the day's trading range does not close it.
Exhaustion	Occurs at the end of a trend on high volume. The gap is not followed by new highs or lows and the gap itself may be unusually wide. After the gap, prices enter a consolidation region. Commonly occurs after a continuation gap. The gap closes quickly, usually within a week.

new highs), I have chosen to label it a breakaway gap. The same situation occurs in early June on the way down. Volume spikes upward as prices make a large gap. Usually large gaps are associated with exhaustion gaps, but prices continue moving lower after just a few days, so, again, I call it a breakaway gap.

Continuation gaps occur in the middle of price trends. They do not happen often since it takes a sharp rise followed by a gap and a continued rise in the stock (the reverse for downtrends, too). In Figure 16.2, you can see two continuation gaps in August when prices zoom from a low of $23\frac{1}{2}$ to $32\frac{5}{8}$ in about 2 weeks. Two continuation gaps appear in the quick, sharp price rise on high, but not unusually high, volume. The quick rise forms new highs and the gap remains open (compare these continuation gaps with how quickly the area gap closes). Of course, in a downtrend, prices gap downward and form new lows.

Exhaustion gaps commonly follow continuation gaps. The highest gap in the August uptrend is an exhaustion gap. At first I thought it was another continuation gap, but the gap is slightly larger than normal and prices pause for 2 days before making new highs. Those are some key factors associated with exhaustion gaps. Excessively wide gaps are most likely exhaustion gaps when they appear near the end of a trend. Two exhaustion gaps appear on the chart,

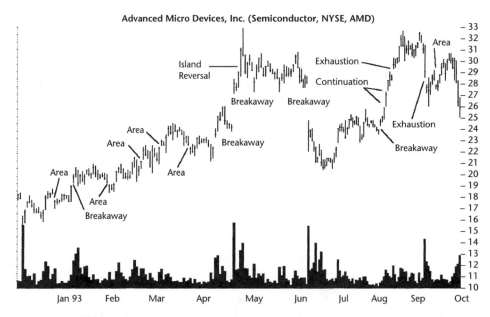

Figure 16.2 Various gap types with area gaps illustrating the hook feature. Volume pattern and position within the trend are the main keys to identify correctly the different gap types.

one in August and one in September. The September gap closes quickly, which is typical for exhaustion gaps.

Most exhaustion gaps occur on high volume; it is like the last gasp before prices end the trend. You can see in Figure 16.2 that both exhaustion gaps have high volume, but the September one takes the cake. Volume spikes upward even as prices descend, then volume recedes but remains high for several days after the gap. The high volume highlights the struggle of investors who want to purchase the stock at a good price with those who are trying to get out of the situation at the best offer.

Statistics: Area Gaps

Table 16.2 shows statistics for area gaps. After 25 stocks, I stopped logging the formations since they are so numerous. I uncovered 174 in the 5-year time span. Since these formations offer little investment interest, many performance statistics were not collected. However, 98% of the formations have gaps that close within 1 year. Most of them (90%) close within a week. The average time to close the gap is a very short 6 days.

Due to the short nature of gaps, I chose to compare the volume figures using a 25-day moving average of volume. On the day prices gap, the volume is 135% of the average volume. The following day, and for succeeding days, it is below average. This only emphasizes the belief that many area gaps may

Table 16.2
Statistics for Area Gaps

Description	Statistic
Number of formations in 25 stocks from 1991 to 1996	174
Number of gaps closed in 1 year	171 or 98%
Average time to close the gap	6 days
Percentage of gaps closed in 1 week	90%
Volume for gap day and next 5 days compared with 25-day moving average	135%, 90%, 89%, 96%, 87%, 86%

Note: I needed only 25 stocks to record a representative sample.

show high volume during the gap but then volume fades quickly. The volume pattern often becomes an important clue to the type of gap that is forming.

Statistics: Breakaway Gaps

Table 16.3 shows statistics for breakaway gaps. Of all the various gap types, the breakaway gap is perhaps the most important. I uncovered 199 of them in 50 stocks over 5 years, more than enough for a good sampling. Since breakaway gaps occur near the start of a trend, the average rise for gaps appearing in

Table 16.3
Statistics for Breakaway Gaps

Description	Uptrends	Downtrends
Number of formations in 50 stocks from 1991 to 1996	98	101
Average rise or decline	25%	20%
Most likely rise or decline	10% to 20%	10% to 15%
Days to ultimate high, low	77 days	52 days
Percentage of gaps occurring near 12-month low (L), center (C), or high (H)	L21%, C27%, H52%	L23%, C29%, H48%
Percentage gain or loss for each 12-month lookback period	L26%, C31%, H24%	L25%, C18%, H19%
Number of gaps closed in 1 year	74 or 76%	67 or 66%
Average time to close the gap	83 days	86 days
Percentage of gaps closed in 1 week	1%	6%
Volume for gap day and next 5 days versus 25-day moving average	197%, 144%, 133%, 139%, 120%, 143%	260%, 183%, 156%, 139%, 126%, 113%

uptrends is 25% and in downtrends 20%—both quite large for gaps. The most likely rise and decline is similar, about 10% to 15% or 20%, depending on whether the gap occurs in an uptrend or downtrend. I arrive at the most likely rise or decline by using a frequency distribution of the gains or losses. The bin with the highest frequency becomes the one with the most likely gain or loss. This method helps evaluate the skewing of the average due to a number of outsized gains or losses. The most likely gain or loss gives a more realistic performance expectation.

The average number of days to the ultimate high or low is 77 and 52 days for up and down trends, respectively. Both periods are quite short, indicating that to profit from gaps, you have to act quickly.

Separating the yearly price range into three categories, high, center, and low, provides a way to assess where most breakaway gaps occur. Most gaps happen in the upper third of the yearly price range, even for those that trend downward. When the performance overlays the yearly price range, we find that the best performing uptrend gaps occur in the center third of the yearly price range, with gains averaging 31%. For gaps in a downtrend, those gaps occurring in the lowest third of the yearly price range perform best, with an average loss of 25%.

Breakaway gaps close within 1 year 76% of the time in uptrends and 66% in downtrends. The average time to close the gap is similar for breakaway gaps in up and down trends, at almost 3 months each. The number of gaps closing understates the actual value since some gaps occur with less than a year remaining in the study. Many of them close anyway, but a few remain open at the end of the study, and no attempt was made to determine if they close within a year.

Only 1% (uptrend) and 6% (downtrend) of the gaps close in 1 week. This should come as no surprise as breakaway gaps often start a trend. Prices move up or down rapidly and do not look back. With average gains or losses of 25% and 20%, it takes quite a while for prices to return and close the gap—certainly more than just a week in most cases.

You can see in Table 16.3 that the volume trend for breakaway gaps remains high throughout the week after a gap. The day on which the gap occurs, volume essentially doubles above the average and remains high. High volume is a key factor in identifying breakaway gaps, so consult volume if there is any doubt about your identification.

Statistics: Continuation Gaps

Table 16.4 shows statistics for continuation gaps. As gaps go, these are somewhat rare, occurring only 160 times in 100 stocks over 5 years. Perhaps the most remarkable facet of continuation gaps is that they occur near the middle of a trend. As such, their average rise is about half that of breakaway gaps, at 11% for both up and down trends (compared with a 25% and 20% for breakaway gaps, respectively).

Table 16.4
Statistics for Continuation Gaps

Description	Uptrends	Downtrends
Number of formations in 100 stocks from 1991 to 1996	85	75
Average rise or decline	11%	11%
Most likely rise or decline	10%	10%
Days to *trend* high, low	14 days	11 days
Percentage of gaps occurring near 12-month low (L), center (C), or high (H)	L11%, C17%, H72%	L26%, C48%, H26%
Percentage gain or loss for each 12-month lookback period	L10%, C6%, H11%	L12%, C11%, H10%
Number of gaps closed in 1 year	74 or 87%	71 or 95%
Average time to close the gap	70 days	43 days
Percentage of gaps closed in 1 week	11%	10%
Volume for gap day and next 5 days versus 25-day moving average	223%, 165%, 144%, 143%, 135%, 133%	242%, 149%, 118%, 99%, 105%, 97%
Position of gap in time trend (trend start to gap start)	48%	58%
Position of gap in price trend (trend start to gap center)	48%	50%

The most likely rise or decline is 10% for both up and down trends. Again, a frequency distribution of performance removes any skewing caused by large numbers in the average.

The days to the trend high or low is about 2 weeks, quite short when compared with breakaway gaps. You might think that since continuation gaps appear in the middle of trends, they would be about half the trend distance to the ultimate high (when compared to a breakaway gap that starts a trend). With continuation gaps, I did not search for the ultimate high or low but the *trend* high or low—to prove or disprove that continuation gaps appear in the middle of trends.

Many times a short trend ends even though the overall trend is upward. In Figure 16.1, for example, the short uptrend in the middle of January ends a week after it begins even though the upward bias of the stock carries prices higher until mid-May. The ultimate low and high on the chart occurs in mid-January (for the low) and mid-May for the high. The *trend* low and high both occur in January.

For uptrends, gaps occur in the upper third of the yearly price range, whereas for downtrends, they happen in the center third. Overlaying the performance figures on the frequency distribution of gaps in the yearly price range shows that gaps occurring in the highest third of the price range perform best with average gains of 11%. For downtrends, the best performing gaps occur in the lowest third of the price range, scoring losses averaging 12%.

Nearly all the gaps (87% and 95%) close within 1 year. Again, some gaps do not have a chance to close before the end of the study so the value may understate the actual results. The average time to close the gap varies quite substantially for gaps in uptrends (70 days) versus those in downtrends (43 days). It appears easier for a falling stock to turn around and rise, thereby closing a downward gap, than it is for a stock in a bull market to suddenly decline and go against the flow to close an uptrend gap.

The percentage of gaps closing within 1 week is just 11% and 10%. This is normal since continuation gaps occur and prices continue moving along the prevailing trend and do not curl around and quickly close.

The volume figures in Table 16.4 compare with a 25-day moving average of the volume. On the day of the gap, volume is more than twice normal and remains high.

Compared with the overall trend, I measured the position of the gap in both time and price. Timewise, the gap occurs 48% of the way to the end of the uptrend and 58% of the way to the end for downtrends. For both up and down trends, the trend length is computed, in days, and compared with the trend start to the day before the gap opens.

With price, the gaps occur 48% and 50% of the way from the trend start to the gap center for up and down trends, respectively. The numbers support the theory that a continuation gap occurs near the middle of trends. In uptrends, prices move a little further after the gap. Since the numbers are averages, your result will vary.

Statistics: Exhaustion Gaps

Table 16.5 shows statistics for exhaustion gaps. I uncovered 159 exhaustion gaps in 100 stocks, comparatively few for all gap types. From the gap to the end of the trend, the gain is 6% for uptrends and the loss is 5% for downtrends. Since the exhaustion gap marks the end of the trend, these low numbers make sense. It also follows that the most likely rise, 3%, and decline, 3% to 4%, is small.

Where in the yearly price trend do exhaustion gaps occur? Most gaps in an uptrend occur in the upper third of the yearly price range, whereas the lowest third of the range scores best for exhaustion gaps in a downtrend. This makes intuitive sense as uptrends may set a new yearly high and downtrends a new yearly low before the trend ends. The performance of the gaps over the yearly price range was not measured because of the small average gains or losses registered.

Table 16.5
Statistics for Exhaustion Gaps

Description	Uptrends	Downtrends
Number of formations in 100 stocks from 1991 to 1996	63	96
Average rise or decline	6%	5%
Most likely rise or decline	3%	Between 3% or 4%
Percentage of gaps occurring near 12-month low (L), center (C), or high (H)	L9%, C14%, H77%	L41%, C37%, H22%
Number of gaps closed in 1 year	62 or 98%	94 or 98%
Average time to close the gap	23 days	17 days
Percentage of gaps closed in 1 week	58%	72%
Volume for gap day and next 5 days compared with 25-day moving average	280%, 144%, 120%, 121%, 108%, 95%	295%, 172%, 127%, 108%, 105%, 117%

Nearly all (98%) of the gaps close in just 23 days (uptrends) and 17 days (downtrends). The high closing value in such a short time reinforces the belief that exhaustion gaps occur near the end of trends. The number of gaps closed in a week ranges between 58% for uptrends and 72% for downtrends.

Table 16.5 shows gap volume and volume up to a week later. At the start, volume is almost triple the average but drops to just slightly above normal a week later.

Trading Tactics and Sample Trade

Table 16.6 lists trading tactics for gaps. To successfully trade gaps you have to be quick, making sure to use stops, and you have to be ready to close out a trade at a moment's notice. Still, they can be profitable. Consider what Gina did with the situation shown in Figure 16.3.

As a seasoned investor, Gina knew all about gaps and practiced trading them on paper until she was successful most of the time. The practice honed her skills and pulling the trigger seemed rote. With a focus on limiting her losses, she was growing confident that her trading style was one that would allow her to succeed in the markets, so she took the leap and decided to trade her system for real.

She followed the stock for quite a long time and was both familiar and comfortable with the fundamentals of the company. When she noticed the breakaway gap occur on May 10, she quickly checked the identification guidelines. Volume was above average (although it may not be clear from the chart)

Table 16.6
Trading Tactics for Various Gaps

Trading Tactic	Explanation
Area gaps	These gaps are too short-lived to be traded profitably, consistently.
Breakaway gaps	If high volume is present at the start of a trend, then trade with the trend. Verify gap type by reviewing the identification guidelines before trading.
Continuation gaps	Continuation gaps usually mark the halfway point so you can gauge the eventual price move. Measure from the trend start to the gap center and project the difference from the gap center to the predicted high or low.
Exhaustion gaps	If an abnormally wide gap occurs or a gap occurs at the end of a trend, then close out your position when the trend reverses. After a trend reversal, consider trading the new trend (shorting the stock if the prior trend was up). Violent reversals often follow exhaustion gaps. Close out the trade the day after new highs (for uptrends) or new lows (downtrends) fail to occur.
Stop loss	The lower rim (for uptrends) or the higher rim (for downtrends) of a gap is a good place to put a stop ($\frac{1}{8}$ or so away from the rim). Gaps provide near-term support or resistance, so this works well with those gaps that do not close quickly.

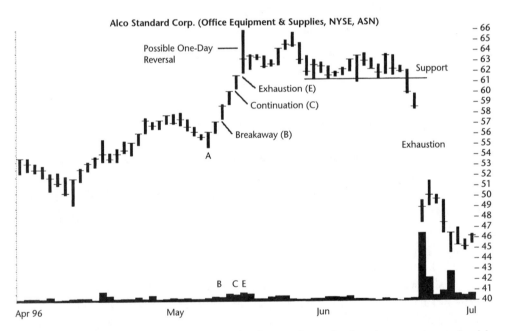

Figure 16.3 Gap trading. Gina bought the stock on the breakaway gap and sold it a few days later for a $7,500 profit. Then she shorted the stock as the exhaustion gap turned into a dead-cat bounce.

and a new upward price trend seemed to be forming. She called her broker and bought 1,000 shares receiving a fill at 58 that day.

She placed a stop-loss order at 57, $\frac{1}{8}$ below the lower gap rim just to be safe. If this turned out to be an area gap, she would probably be stopped out for a small loss. During her paper trading days, she discovered that most gaps provide near-term support or resistance, so she was confident that her stop would hold.

She watched the stock closely. Two days later the stock gapped again. It could either be a continuation gap or an exhaustion gap, she decided. Volume was heavy, about twice the 25-day moving average, so that offered no clue. The following day, when prices gapped again, she knew that the prior pattern was a continuation gap.

Gina checked the price chart and using the center of the continuation gap as a midpoint, she measured from the trend low (point A in the figure) to the center of the gap. The difference was $5\frac{1}{2}$ (that is, $60\frac{1}{4} - 54\frac{3}{4}$). Adding the difference to the middle of the continuation gap predicted that prices would top out at $65\frac{3}{4}$, so she placed a stop at $65\frac{1}{2}$ and moments later, the stock was sold. That day, the stock climbed to a high of 66, slightly above the predicted price, and closed the day at $63\frac{1}{4}$.

Not including commission charges, she made $7,500 in just 3 days. But she was not done. The large daily price range on high volume when she sold reminded her of a one-day reversal, but she was unsure. She decided to keep her options open and look for an opportunity to sell short. She followed the stock daily and when it closed below the support level at 61 she decided to sell the stock short and received a fill at 59.

The next day she was surprised to discover that a large exhaustion gap had formed, dropping the stock down to 49, a $10,000 gain overnight. Knowing that the gap was in reality a dead-cat bounce, she changed tactics and did not immediately close out her position. Instead, she watched the stock bounce upward for a few days then continue lower (as the formation predicts). Instead of getting greedy, she decided to close out her position and received a fill at 45, for an easy $14,000 profit in less than 2 weeks.

If you think Gina was lucky, netting over $21,000 in 2 weeks, you are probably right. But her ability to correctly size up an investment opportunity and act on it quickly while taking steps to minimize losses goes a long way to explaining her luck. Some call it skill.

Gina is a serious investor who leaves nothing to chance. She did not just jump in and start trading gaps after reading about it in some book. Instead she researched the formation and developed a successful trading style that incorporates gaps.

17

Hanging Man

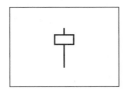

RESULTS SNAPSHOT

Upside Breakout

Appearance	An opening and closing price that is at or near the daily high with a significantly lower intraday low
Reversal or consolidation	Short-term (up to 3 months) bullish reversal
Failure rate	Since the breakout should be downward, in a rising price trend, 67% have upside breakouts. The 5% failure rate is 11%.
Average rise	40%, with the most likely rise being 10%

Downside Breakout

Appearance	An opening and closing price that is at or near the daily high with a significantly lower intraday low
Reversal or consolidation	Consolidation with short-term (up to 3 months) bearish implications
Failure rate	Not applicable. By definition, the breakout should be downward. The 5% failure rate is 22%.
Average decline	16%, with the most likely loss between 5% and 10%

There are conflicting definitions of a hanging man formation. As I define it in this chapter, many would call it a doji, or even a dragonfly doji, candlestick pattern. The two sources I used call it a hanging man. After reviewing additional sources, it is probably better called a doji. However, the name is less important than the performance, which this chapter describes. There are two main theories about how this formation works. One is that when the closing price is "near" (whatever that means) the daily high, then there is an 80% chance the following day will see a higher high. The statistics later in this chapter show that the best performance I could come up with is between 55% and 57%. Perhaps the theory relates to security types other than common stocks. For stocks held overnight anyway, the 55% chance that tomorrow's high will exceed today's is slightly better than a coin toss and is probably a wash if you compensate for the upward bias of the stock market over time.

The other theory, and one that the 67% failure rate pertains to in the Results Snapshot, is when both the daily open and close are "near" the daily high but the stock trades "significantly lower" intraday in a rising price trend. A hanging man formation under those conditions supposedly signals a bearish trend reversal. This only works a third of the time—a huge disappointment.

I looked at the failure rates in the more traditional sense and came up with better values. For those formations with upside breakouts, just 11% of the formations fail to move higher than 5% before changing direction and heading down. On the flip side, 22% of the formations with downside breakouts are 5% failures. This is above the suggested maximum failure rate of 20% that I consider acceptable.

Hanging man formations with upside breakouts show gains averaging 40%, which is quite good, but the most likely gain is 10%—comparatively poor. For downside breakouts, the average loss is 16% with a likely loss between 5% and 10%. If you decide to trade this formation, do not expect a large price move.

Tour and Identification Guidelines

Table 17.1 shows the identification guidelines for the hanging man formation. If you have the four daily prices available—open, high, low, and close—that is all you need. The open, high, and close should all be the same. This means that the horizontal bar on the chart will be at the top of the figure (it will look like the capital letter T). This formation also goes by the candlestick name of dragonfly doji.

Table 17.1
Identification Characteristics of Hanging Man Reversal

Characteristic	Description
Open = high = close	The daily open, high, and closing prices must be the same value. On an open-high-low-close chart, it looks like the letter T. Some call this a dragonfly doji.
Significantly lower low	The intraday low price must be significantly lower than the intraday high price. This means 5% or more.
Rising price trend	The price trend must be rising

The intraday low should be *significantly lower* than the intraday high. I interpret the phrase *significantly lower* to mean more than 5%. This arbitrarily chosen value results in a decent sample size for the statistics. If you do not like 5%, then choose another value. The results do not vary that much. Changing the benchmark from 5% to 2.5%, 7.5%, or even 10% causes the failure rate to vary from 59% to 75%. No matter how you slice it, it is still terrible—well above the 20% maximum.

The final criterion for selecting hanging man reversals is to find them during an uptrend. Since we are dealing with a formation that has a lifetime (width) of 1 day, I do not think the trend need be a large one. As long as prices have been rising noticeably, that is good enough for me.

Figure 17.1 shows what I am talking about; there are a number of hanging man formations highlighted. Each daily price move in the chart shows as a high-low-close figure; the opening price is not shown. Those prices highlighted by the black circles have the opening price at the daily high.

In early August, for example, you can see that a hanging man formation surfaces a day after prices peak at 3. The open (not shown), high, and close are all at the same value, 3. The daily low, at 2.81, is more than 5% below the daily high (it is *significantly lower* by 6.3%). The prices leading the way up either do not have the open at the daily high or do not have an intraday low 5% below the high. They are not hanging man formations (since the chart does not show opening prices, you will just have to trust me).

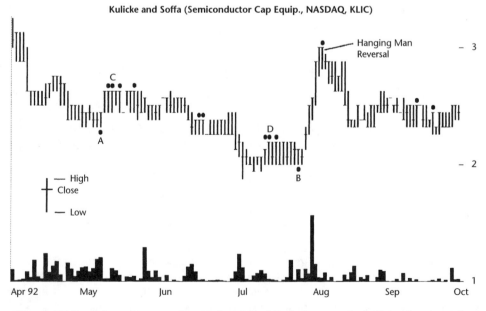

Figure 17.1 A hanging man formation. The black dots mark the hanging man formations. While only the high, low, and closing prices show in the graph, the black dots mark the days in which the opening price also matches the intraday high.

The price trend, having spurted from a low of 1.88, forms a rising trend. That is a key element in the formation; the reversal needs something to reverse. Point A, however, shows that the price trend leading to it is downward. Others, like point B, suggest the beginning of an uptrend (albeit, 2 days later). Point C is a hanging man formation that just marks time. This is probably the most common. Point D, arguably, is a successful hanging man reversal. Prices rise for 3 days then move flat. It is a change in trend, from a rising trend to a horizontal one or consolidation. The move from point D to B is downward, further suggesting a true reversal of the upward trend (although stretched out somewhat).

Of course, my favorite is the August reversal. Unfortunately, as you can see by the many black dots, the formation rarely works as expected even during a rising price trend.

Focus on Failures

Figure 17.2 shows two types of hanging man failures. The first one, on the left, I use to illustrate the belief that a hanging man formation should show a higher high the next day. In this example, it does not. Prices continue their downward trend. A higher high happens only 44% to 57% of the time, depending on whether you include the opening price in the formation or not, respectively. The Statistics section further describes this behavior.

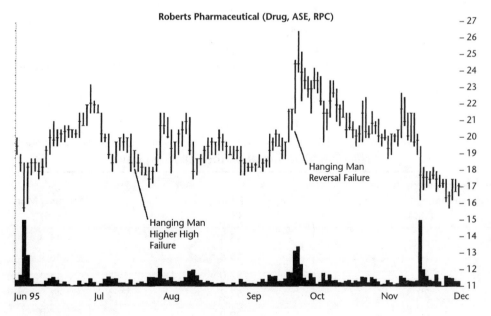

Figure 17.2 Two types of hanging man failures. A higher high is expected the day after a hanging man formation, or it should result in a reversal of the upward price trend.

The right formation failure illustrates a failure of the price trend to reverse. You can see that the hanging man formation has a high of 21¾ but 2 days later the high reaches 26½. This performance is hardly what I would call a reversal of the upward price trend. In this example, the formation acts as a continuation of the short-term uptrend.

Failures of the second type, where a price reversal is predicted but does not appear, happen 67% of the time. To flip this around, it is more accurate to say that prices will continue moving upward two-thirds of the time. With such a poor showing, I can only infer that the hanging man formation does not apply to stocks. Maybe it works better with other security types.

With such an astronomical failure rate, I rechecked my work. In a few formations, the hanging man pattern appears a few days before a peak (such as that shown in Figure 17.2). Most of the time the hanging man appears in the middle or near the beginning of an uptrend. Prices simply do not reverse after the formation—they continue moving higher.

There is one simple thing you can do to drop the failure rate to zero. Simply do not trade this one (or rely on it).

Statistics

Table 17.2 shows the first batch of statistics. Since many of the descriptions about a hanging man formation say the opening or closing price should be near the intraday high, I provided a range of distances to work from. The closing price ranges from 0% to 25% below the intraday high.

Table 17.2 provides two types of formations, a T-bar (my name for it) and a hanging man. A T-bar formation is one that looks like a hanging man except the opening price is disregarded. In the hanging man formation, the opening

Table 17.2
Statistics Showing Number of Times the Daily High Price Rises above T-Bar or Hanging Man Formation the Following Day

Closing Price Below Intraday High (%)	T-Bar (%)	Hanging Man (%)
0	55.4	44.4
10	56.4	44.7
15	57.0	45.4
20	57.2	47.0
25	56.6	48.0

Note: A T-bar formation is a hanging man with the opening price ignored. A hanging man allows the opening and closing prices to drift lower but has a significantly lower intraday low.

price is the same as the intraday high price with a significantly lower low (but a rising price trend is not a requirement).

The statistics in Table 17.2 show how often the daily high price rises above the T-bar or hanging man formation the following day. In the T-bar column, the number of samples is huge—the *smallest* sample size is over 78,000. Of course, that is on 500 stocks over a 5-year period of daily price data (2,500 years). When the closing price is at the intraday high, a higher high occurs the next day 55.4% of the time. Even when the closing price drifts lower, the percentage remains nearly the same with a best case of 57.2%. This is only slightly better than a fair coin toss (50%) and probably allows for the historical upward trend in the markets over time.

I evaluated the hanging man column on those formations where both the opening and closing prices are near the intraday high. In the case of 0%, the open and close match the daily high. Only 44.4% of the time is a higher high made the next day. Performance improves after allowing the open and close to drift downward. Almost half (48%) the formations have higher highs the next day. Incidentally, the minimum sample size is still a massive 27,600 plus.

I created Table 17.2 to specifically test the theory that a closing price near the daily high suggests a higher high the next day. From the results shown in the table, I consider the theory to be unreliable—certainly nowhere near the predicted 80% success rate. A close near the intraday high is no guarantee of a higher high tomorrow, as far as common stocks are concerned.

Table 17.3 shows general performance statistics for the hanging man formation. The price trend leading to the formation is generally ignored when examining the formation (except for failure rates discussed in a moment). I separated the chart pattern into two types: upside and downside breakouts. With over 56,000 hanging man formations in 2,500 years' worth of daily price data, I had to make some changes to drop the sample size to a reasonable amount.

I used the same procedure for the hanging man formation as I have for other chart patterns (such as inside and outside days). For those stocks that have more than 10 formations, I ration the number I accept. If a stock has 100 formations, for example, I accept 1 in every 10 so that 10 formations remain, sprinkled throughout the 5 years of daily price data. You can see in the table that these are about evenly split (by chance) between upside breakouts (274) and downside breakouts (261). Those formations with upside breakouts are predominantly reversals of the short-term price trend, whereas those with downside breakouts act as consolidations of the trend.

The failure rate, at 67%, is the worst I have seen for any formation. In order for the formation to qualify as a failure, it must first be a hanging man chart pattern passing these three criteria:

1. Intraday open, high, and close are all the same value
2. Intraday low is at least 5% below the high
3. Occurs during a short-term (or longer) rising price trend

Table 17.3
General Statistics for the Hanging Man Formation

Description	Upside Breakout	Downside Breakout
Number of formations in 400 stocks from 1991 to 1996, limited to about 10 formations per stock	274	261
Reversal or consolidation	104 consolidations, 170 reversals	210 consolidations, 51 reversals
Failure rate (good formation: an upward trend reversal)	104/155 or 67%	N/A
5% failure rate	29 or 11%	58 or 22%
Average rise/decline for successful formations	40%	16%
Most likely rise/decline	10%	5% to 10%
For successful formations, days to ultimate high/low	2.5 months (78 days)	1.5 months (41 days)
Percentage occurring near 12-month low (L), center (C), or high (H)	L66%, C17%, H17%	L77%, C16%, H6%
Percentage gain/loss for each 12-month lookback period	L41%, C26%, H53%	L15%, C12%, H17%
Volume day before to day after versus 25-day moving average	107%, 115%, 102%	107%, 115%, 102%
Percentage gain/loss for volume 1.5× 25-day moving average	28%	16%
Percentage gain/loss for volume 0.5× 25-day moving average	45%	15%
Number of high volume failures (1.5× 25-day moving average)	19 or 18%	N/A
Number of low volume failures (0.5× 25-day moving average)	42 or 40%	N/A

After meeting the three conditions (it is just a hanging man formation in a rising price trend), I examine the following days to see if the trend reverses (in other words, a downside breakout). Most of the time (67%) prices keep rising. There is no corresponding failure rate for downside breakouts because, by definition, a hanging man formation that works has a downward breakout (prices move lower the next day). There are only 155 formations (of the stocks I examined) that meet the three criteria just described and of these, 104 have upside breakouts (the breakouts should be down, so they are failures).

Since such a high failure rate is suspicious, at least in my mind, I looked at all hanging man formations with the 5% failure rate in mind. A 5% failure is when prices break out in a given direction and move less than 5% before reversing and moving significantly in the other direction. For upside breakouts, this happens 11% of the time, whereas downside breakouts have double the failure rate (22%). I consider anything less than 20% to be acceptable.

To assess the average rise or decline of the two breakout types of hanging man formations, I looked at the breakout direction and removed those 104 formations that fail. The remaining formations show gains of 40% for upside breakouts and losses averaging 16% for downside ones.

Shown in Figures 17.3 and 17.4 are frequency distributions of gains and losses, respectively. For upside breakouts, the most likely gain is less than 10%. You can see in Figure 17.3 that 15% of the formations have gains over 90% and a third of the formations have gains over 50%. These large gains pull the average upward.

Figure 17.4 shows the results for downside breakouts. The horizontal scale is in 5% increments and the tallest column, the largest loss, is 10%. Since the 5% column is quite close, I consider the most likely loss to be between 5% and 10%.

Successful formations with upside breakouts take 78 days to reach the ultimate high. Downside breakouts reach the ultimate low in about half the time, 41 days. Both numbers, in comparison, make sense because it takes upside breakouts about twice as long to go twice as far.

I determine the ultimate high or low by a significant change in trend, an adverse move of at least 20%. Finding the ultimate high for upside breakouts, for example, means prices rise then decline by 20% or more (from the high). On occasion, the 20% figure is excessive, and I override it when necessary. The

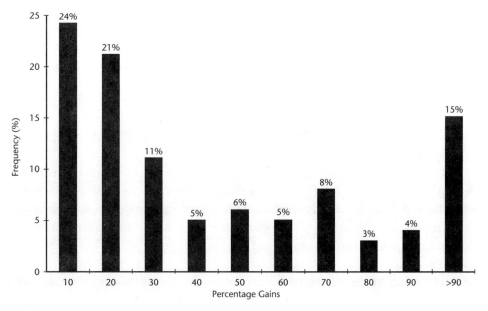

Figure 17.3 Frequency distribution of gains for hanging man formations with upside breakouts. The most likely gain is 10%, the tallest column on the chart.

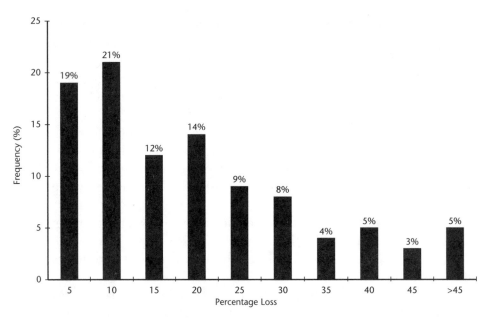

Figure 17.4 Frequency distribution of losses for hanging man formations with downside breakouts. The most likely loss is between 5% and 10%.

same methodology applies to downside breakouts. Such a large swing accommodates normal price behavior and quickly identifies significant trend changes.

Does a hanging man formation occur near the yearly high or low? Both upside and downside breakouts occur most frequently within a third of the yearly low. When you overlay performance on the yearly price range, the best performing upside breakouts are those occurring within a third of the yearly high, scoring average gains of 53%. Downside breakouts are more evenly split but the highest return made by those formations appears within a third of the yearly high (with an average 17% loss).

The volume during a hanging man formation is higher than average. You can see in Table 17.3 that the formation itself has a volume trend that is 15% above normal (115% of the 25-day moving average). Both the day before and the day after the formation show high volume.

Do hanging man formations with high volume produce superior results? No. When volume is 50% (1.5× in the table) or more above average, the average gain is only 28%, well below the 40% scored for upside breakouts. However, when the volume is 50% below average, the performance improves dramatically: 45%. For downside breakouts, the performance hovers around the 16% average gain.

Does volume relate to the failure rate? To answer this question, I separated the formations with upside breakouts into three categories: volume that is 50% above average, 50% below average, and everything else. The majority of the failures occur between the two 50% ranges. When volume is 50% below the 25-day moving average, 40% of the formations fail. Only 18% fail with high volume. These numbers suggest that you should be watchful of a hanging man formation in a price uptrend that shows below average volume. It may continue moving up instead of reversing.

Trading Tactics

After careful consideration, I cannot recommend trading this formation. The primary belief behind this chart pattern is that prices will reverse the uptrend. They do not. Just a third of the formations reverse, whereas the others see prices continue higher.

The only advice I can offer is when you are considering buying or selling a stock and see a hanging man formation. It is probably best if the opening price is well below the intraday high but the stock closes at the high, suggesting upward momentum. The following day, there is a very slight tendency to post a higher high. So, if you are selling, you might wait for the new high or at least follow the stock closely throughout the day.

If you are buying just before the close and the price is at or near the intraday high (again, with the opening price near the intraday low), you might take comfort in believing tomorrow's price will be higher—at least sometime during the day. The odds suggest a higher price, but the odds are not much better than a coin toss, certainly not worth betting the farm on.

18

Head-and-Shoulders Bottoms

RESULTS SNAPSHOT

Appearance	Three-trough formation with center trough lower than the others
Reversal or consolidation	Short-term (up to 3 months) bullish reversal
Failure rate	5%
Average rise	38%, with most likely rise between 20% and 30%
Volume trend	Downward; usually higher on the left shoulder than the right
Throwbacks	52%
Percentage meeting predicted price target	83%
See also	Head-and-Shoulders Bottoms, Complex

I find it easier to pick out tops than bottoms. Perhaps this is because I spend so much time worrying about when to sell. Placing a trade is easy but getting out is the tough part. In my quest to sell at the appropriate time, I have often overlooked the buy side: bottom reversals. Head-and-shoulders bottoms are just such a formation. They are quite easy to spot and can be very profitable.

The Results Snapshot highlights statistics for this bullish reversal. Like the top version of the formation, the bottom sports an exceedingly low failure rate of 5%. Only a few formations either fall or climb by less than 5%. Those that do experience an upside breakout continue rising by an average 38%.

Like many bullish formations, the head-and-shoulders bottom meets its price target often: 83% of the time. I consider values above 80% to be reliable.

Tour

What does the formation look like? Figure 18.1 shows a good example of a head-and-shoulders bottom. The stock starts rising in November 1993 and peaks during February, where the figure begins. From that point, the stock moves downward and makes a lower low in late March before moving up. The turn marks the left shoulder. The stock declines again and reaches a new low during late April, forming the head. The right shoulder appears as the stock recovers then continues moving down along the trendline (shown in Figure 18.1 as the neckline).

The stock advances above the neckline and stages an upside breakout. However, the rise does not last long. Prices soon decline below the level of the right shoulder. The stock moves sideways over the next 4 months. Then the stock enters another head-and-shoulders bottom and the upside breakout proves more lasting. By mid-August 1995, the stock is trading just below 60.

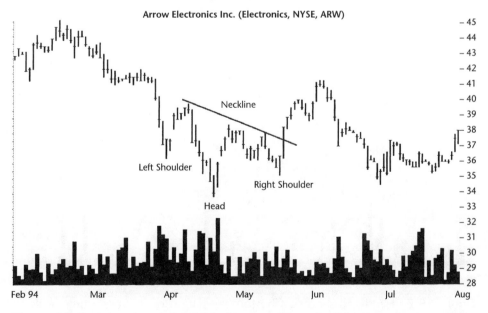

Figure 18.1 A head-and-shoulders bottom. Two shoulder troughs surround a lower head. Volume is usually higher on the left shoulder than on the right shoulder.

The head-and-shoulders bottom shown in Figure 18.1 has a somewhat unusual volume pattern. Volume is usually highest on the left shoulder, diminished on the head, and even lower on the right shoulder. The rise from the head to the right shoulder accompanies a rise in volume as does the actual breakout.

In contrast, the formation shows little increase in volume during the rise from the head to the right shoulder. Volume on the breakout is unexciting and that helps explain why the stock stalls. Upward momentum fails to happen quickly enough to propel the stock higher; the stock rounds over and heads back down.

Figure 18.2 shows a head-and-shoulders formation on a weekly time scale. I chose this chart to show you the typical trend of head-and-shoulders bottom reversals. They usually form after an extended downtrend in prices. As a reversal, once they complete, prices rise.

Why do head-and-shoulders bottoms form? The formation represents a struggle to find the bottom, the lowest price that represents the best value. As the stock descends during February 1994, investors nibble at the stock in increasing numbers. Volume climbs even as the stock descends until it spikes upward for 1 week during formation of the left shoulder. Buying demand puts a crimp on the downward slide and prices move up but only for a week. The following week, prices move lower. Again, volume spikes as the stock makes a

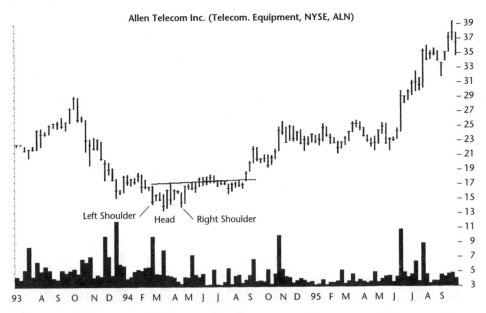

Figure 18.2 Head-and-shoulders bottom formation on a weekly time scale. It takes several months before this head-and-shoulders bottom stages an upside breakout. Volume is characteristic: highest on the left shoulder, diminished on the head, and exceedingly low on the right shoulder.

new low and this becomes the head. The smart money is accumulating the stock in anticipation of an eventual rise or a change in the fundamentals. The stock moves up on receding volume then retreats and forms the right shoulder.

Volume on the three troughs is diminishing. The left shoulder has very high volume, the head exhibits somewhat less volume, and the right shoulder records the lowest volume up to that point. Only after prices start moving up from the right shoulder does volume spike upward.

Breakout volume, depending on where you determine the breakout occurs, is unconvincing. In late August, prices move decidedly above the neckline and stage a definitive breakout. Even so, it is not until 2 weeks later that volume advances noticeably.

Identification Guidelines

Table 18.1 encapsulates the identification guidelines for a head-and-shoulders bottom. Consider Figure 18.3, a head-and-shoulders bottom. The formation does not appear at the end of a long-term downtrend but at a short-term one (up to 3 months). The uptrend begins the prior June with another head-and-shoulders bottom. The formation reverses the slight short-term downtrend but continues the long-term uptrend.

Overall, the formation sports the three telltale troughs: left shoulder, head, and right shoulder. The left shoulder is at about the same price level as

Table 18.1
Identification Characteristics of a Head-and-Shoulders Bottom

Characteristic	Discussion
Shape	A three-trough formation with the center trough below the other two. It looks like a head-and-shoulders bust flipped upside down. The three troughs and two minor rises should appear well defined.
Symmetry	The left and right shoulders should be opposite one another about the head, somewhat equidistant in both time and price. There are wide variations but the formation is noticeably symmetrical about the head.
Volume	Usually highest on the left shoulder or head and diminished on the right shoulder.
Neckline	A line that connects the rise between the two shoulders. A piercing of the neckline signals an upside breakout. Ignore the neckline if the slope is too steep. In such a case, use the highest rise between the shoulders as the breakout level.
Upside breakout	The breakout is upward, usually on high volume that powers prices upward. A low volume breakout is *not* an indicator of an impending failure.

Figure 18.3   A rare head-and-shoulders consolidation of the primary uptrend.

the right one and appears to be about the same width. Such symmetry is common in head-and-shoulders formations (tops, bottoms, and the complex variety). If the left shoulder is sharp or pointed, the right shoulder will be too.

The head is below both shoulders by a reasonable amount. By this characteristic I mean the formation is not a triple bottom—three troughs at about the same price level.

In Figure 18.3, the left shoulder suddenly declines for 3 days, then reverses and climbs to a minor high. Similarly, the rise between the head and right shoulder climbs almost to the height of the rise between the left shoulder and head then descends to the right shoulder. All five features, the three troughs and two minor rises, appear well defined and distinct. The features are important as you scan your charts looking for head-and-shoulders bottoms.

Symmetry is another important key to selecting a valid head-and-shoulders bottom. The right side of the formation usually mimics the left side. The right shoulder declines to about the price level of the left shoulder and the distances of both from the head are similar. Of course, there are many variations, but symmetry should make a head-and-shoulders bottom stand out from a sequence of any three depressions.

Volume represents another clue to the validity of a bottom. The left shoulder typically has the highest volume, followed by the head, with diminished volume on the right shoulder. Thus, overall, the volume trend is downward; higher on the left side of the formation than the right—until the breakout.

The neckline is an imaginary line connecting the two rises between the shoulders and the head. It can slope downward or upward. In well-formed formations, the slope of the line is not very steep, but a steep neckline should not be a disqualifier of a head-and-shoulders bottom (see Figure 18.1—it has a rather steep neckline).

Irregular volume patterns should also not disqualify the formation. Figures 18.1 and 18.3, for example, have volume that is highest at the head.

Breakout volume is usually high as it pushes prices above the neckline. However, in a quarter of the formations where prices continue higher, breakout volume is well below the day before the breakout. We see in the Focus on Failures section that high breakout volume accompanies most failures. As a rule, volume will rise on the day of the breakout, but it need not.

Focus on Failures

Like most formations, there are two types of failures. The first type, shown in Figure 18.4, is a failure of the head-and-shoulders bottom to pierce the neckline and move higher. As you would expect, the formation appears after a downtrend in prices. The highest price peak is partly visible in the upper left corner of Figure 18.4. From the high of 38¾, prices fall to the low at the head, 21¼, a decline of 45%. When the bottom forms, it should signal a trend reversal.

An interesting thing about the formation in Figure 18.4 is that the left shoulder is almost the same shape as the right. Only a dollar separates the

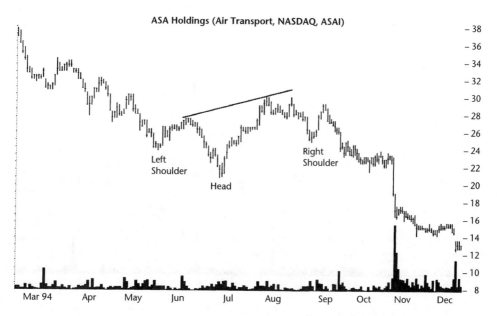

Figure 18.4   Failure of a head-and-shoulders bottom to stage an upside breakout.

two shoulder lows and the head is well below both shoulder troughs. The right shoulder is somewhat farther away from the head than the left. This characteristic is typical.

Volume is suspiciously low throughout the formation. The left shoulder and head register about the same level of volume. The right shoulder volume, however, is higher than the other two. Of course, an irregular volume pattern is no reason to discard a formation—but it serves as a warning.

After the right shoulder forms and prices begin rising, volume tapers off rapidly and the attempt to pierce the neckline fails. The rally attempt does not even come close to the neckline.

Looking at the overall formation, there is no one item that signals an impending failure. There is some suspicious activity, principally the abnormal volume pattern, but nothing to deter an investor.

Figure 18.5 shows a slightly different type of failure. This is what I call a 5% failure. The two shoulders and head appear well formed and distinct. The left shoulder looks different from the right, but the twin rises between the shoulders are similar. The price level of the two shoulders is not suspiciously out of line.

Volume is unusual. The only heavy volume appears near the head as prices rise away from it toward the right shoulder. The right shoulder volume looks like something you would want to tackle with your shaver: annoying but not high enough to be alarming.

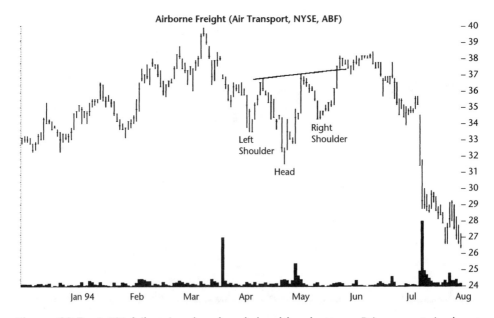

Figure 18.5 A 5% failure in a head-and-shoulders bottom. Prices must rise by at least 5% before the formation is a success. A 5% rise should take prices to $39\frac{3}{8}$ but it does not happen.

Prices advance smartly after the right shoulder forms. Once prices rise above the stair-step incline, they zoom upward for 3 days and then stop. The stock moves essentially sideways for 2 weeks before starting back down.

Although this formation does have an upside breakout, prices fail to rise by more than 5% above the neckline. Prices should reach $39\frac{3}{8}$ to meet the 5% threshold, but they do not. The result is a failure of the 5% rule: Prices must rise by more than 5% after a breakout or the formation is a dud.

I went through the various failures in the database and examined them to see if there is any truth to the notion that low volume breakouts are subject to failure. I found that this simply is not true. Of the 18 formation failures, only 8 (44%) occur after a low volume breakout. However, the sample size is small (30 samples usually provides reliable results). These numbers conveniently bring us to the next section: Statistics.

Statistics

Table 18.2 contains general statistics for head-and-shoulders bottom formations. There is a good assortment of formations, 330 to be exact, in 2,500 years of daily price data. Most of the formations, 85%, act as reversals, whereas the remainder are consolidations of the prevailing trend. Almost all the formations (95%) perform as expected. This means they break out upward and continue higher by more than 5%. The average rise after an upside breakout is 38%.

Table 18.2
General Statistics for Head-and-Shoulder Bottoms

Description	Statistic
Number of formations in 500 stocks from 1991 to 1996	330
Reversal or consolidation	49 consolidations, 281 reversals
Failure rate	18 or 5%
Average rise of successful formations	38%
Most likely rise	20% to 30%
Of those succeeding, number meeting or exceeding price target (measure rule)	258 or 83%
Average formation length	2.5 months (73 days)
Number of successful formations showing downward volume trend	193 or 62%
Average rise of up-sloping neckline versus down-sloping neckline	38% versus 40%
Average rise of higher right shoulder versus higher left shoulder	36% versus 41%

Note: With a 5% failure rate and an average rise of 38%, the head-and-shoulders bottom is a formation worth considering.

Since large numbers can skew averages, I computed a frequency distribution of the percentage gains. Figure 18.6 shows the results. The lopsided bell-shaped curve seems to be typical for most formations and the head-and-shoulders bottom is no exception. Notice the large number of gains over 90%. These tend to pull the overall average upward. The frequency distribution shows the most likely rise is between 20% and 30%, down slightly from the average gain of 38%.

In the Trading Tactics section of this chapter I explain the measure rule. It is a way for a formation to predict the minimum price move. For the head-and-shoulders bottom, the prediction succeeds 83% of the time, a comforting number (I view anything above 80% to be reliable).

The formation length from left shoulder trough to right shoulder trough is 2½ months. This understates the formation length somewhat because it does not include the run down to the left shoulder and the rise to the breakout. Occasionally, it can take several weeks or months before prices stage a breakout.

About two-thirds (62%) of the formations show a downward volume trend. The slope of the linear regression line between the shoulder lows measures this. The result fits with casual observation in that the left shoulder usually has the highest volume, followed by the head and greatly diminished right shoulder volume.

Does the slope of the neckline or the shoulder height predict the magnitude of the resulting rise? I looked into these questions and found results different from what I expected. For necklines in which the slope of the line is

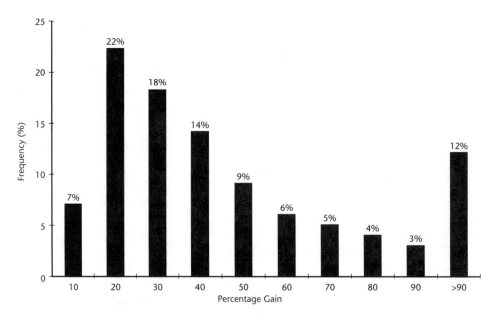

Figure 18.6   Frequency distribution of gains for head-and-shoulders bottoms. The most likely rise is between 20% and 30%.

upward (the rise on the left is below the rise on the right), the stock has an aver-age gain of 38%, versus 40% for those stocks with down-sloping necklines.

In a similar manner, I looked at the higher of the two shoulders. Does a higher right shoulder suggest a larger gain? No. The average rise of stocks with higher right shoulders is 36% while those with higher left shoulders gain an average of 41%.

For both necklines and shoulder height the results are not statistically sig-nificant. This means the results could be due to chance, or there could be some veracity to the difference.

Table 18.3 shows statistics related to the breakout. Nearly all (98%) of the head-and-shoulders bottoms have upside breakouts. There are only eight formations that have downside breakouts. Of those formations with upside breakouts, 10 fail to rise by more than 5%.

Throwbacks, when prices break out upward then return to the neckline, occur 52% of the time. This suggests some hesitancy of the formation to rise. It takes, on average, 11 days for the stock to return to the neckline and com-plete a throwback. This seems to be about average for many formations in this book.

Is a formation more likely to throw back after a low volume breakout? No. I separated the formations into two columns: those that have breakouts with high volume (over 125% of the prior day) and those with low volume (less

Table 18.3
Breakout Statistics for Head-and-Shoulders Bottoms

Description	Statistic
Upside breakout	322 or 98%
Downside breakout	8 or 2%
Upside breakout but failure	10 or 3%
Throwbacks	167 or 52%
Average time to throwback completion	11 days
Is a formation more likely to throw back after a low volume breakout?	No
For successful formations, days to ultimate high	7 months (215 days)
Percentage of breakouts occurring near 12-month low (L), center (C), or high (H)	L29%, C41%, H30%
Percentage gain for each 12-month lookback period	L37%, C34%, H44%
Volume for breakout day and next 5 days compared with day before breakout	163%, 125%, 104%, 95%, 97%, 95%
Successful breakouts on high volume	164 or 74%
Successful breakouts on low volume	59 or 26%
Formation failures on low volume	8 or 44%

Note: The vast majority of breakouts are upside breakouts.

than 75% of the prior day). Then I matched the throwbacks with the two columns. The results split evenly at 49% for each column. The results suggest that a throwback is independent of breakout volume.

After a breakout occurs, it takes about 7 months to reach the ultimate high. However, a frequency distribution of the time to reach the ultimate high shows that most formations land in the short-term category (up to 3 months). I therefore classify this formation as having short-term trading implications.

Where in the yearly price range does the formation occur? Most breakouts from a head-and-shoulders bottom occur in the center third of the yearly price range. The breakout happens near the top of the formation and explains why there are not more occurrences in the lowest third of the price range. When we distribute the percentage gains over the same yearly price range, we find that formations with breakouts in the top third of the yearly price range tend to gain the most, 44%. This finding suggests that momentum players grab hold of the stock and bid it up.

Average breakout volume is 63% above the prior day (163% of the total) but rapidly recedes over the course of a week. I looked at breakout volume as a function of high volume (125% of the prior day) and low volume (75% of the prior day). Almost three out of four breakouts occur on high volume. Still, that leaves 26% of the formations with successful upside breakouts on low volume. Even though a formation may break out on low volume is no reason to suspect the formation will ultimately fail. As mentioned previously, I looked at the 18 formation failures and 44%, less than half, have failures occurring after a low volume breakout.

Trading Tactics

Table 18.4 discusses trading tactics for head-and-shoulders bottoms. Use the measure rule to predict the minimum price move once prices break above the neckline. In Figure 18.7, the head marks the lowest price in the formation. Subtract its price from the value of the neckline at that point. In this example, the head has a daily low price of $13\frac{1}{8}$ and the neckline, measured vertically, is at $17\frac{1}{2}$. Add the difference, $4\frac{3}{8}$, to the price where the stock closes above the neckline. This occurs on March 28. I use its daily low price of $15\frac{1}{2}$ on that day to get a target price of $19\frac{7}{8}$. Prices reach the target in mid-July.

If you can determine that a head-and-shoulders bottom is forming, then there is no need to wait for confirmation (that is, for prices to close above the neckline) before placing a trade. With a failure rate of 5%, your guess will get you in at a lower level and yield higher profits. However, this all hinges on the validity of a head-and-shoulders bottom. If you guess wrong, you could see your profits rapidly turn into a loss. If you are unsure whether the price series is indeed a head-and-shoulders bottom, wait for prices to move above the neckline before investing.

Table 18.4
Trading Tactics for Head-and-Shoulders Bottoms

Trading Tactic	Explanation
Measure rule	Compute the formation height by subtracting the value of the lowest low reached in the head from the neckline, measured vertically. Add the difference to the point where prices pierce the neckline. The result is the target price to which prices will rise, at a minimum. For steep, up-sloping necklines, substitute the rise between the head and right shoulder (that is, the highest price in the rise) for the neckline breakout price.
Do not wait for confirmation	If you can determine that a head-and-shoulders formation is completing, consider buying the stock. This formation rarely disappoints and the rise is worth betting on. However, you must be sure that a head-and-shoulders bottom is present. Otherwise, wait for prices to rise above the neckline.
Stop Loss	Place a stop-loss order $\frac{1}{8}$ below the lower of the two shoulders. Often, prices drop to the shoulder lows before meeting support. Raise the stop as prices climb.
Watch for throwback	If you miss the upside breakout, wait. Half the time, the stock will throw back to the neckline. Once it does, buy the stock or add to your position.

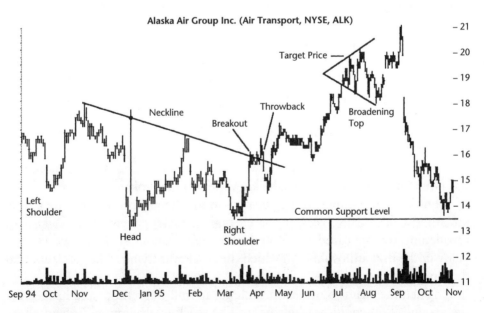

Figure 18.7 A head-and-shoulders bottom. Compute the measure rule by subtracting the lowest low from the neckline vertically to find the formation height. Add the difference to the point where prices close above the neckline. The result is the target price to which the stock will climb, at a minimum. A broadening top appears in July.

Also, since about half of all bottoms throw back, you can wait for a throwback before placing the trade. Although this will get you in at a higher price, the likelihood of the trade being profitable also rises. If you have already placed a trade, consider adding to your position once a throwback completes and prices move higher.

The two shoulders are common support areas. Figure 18.7 shows an example of this. The lower of the two shoulders, in this case the right shoulder, supports the stock in late October.

After placing a trade, consider setting a stop-loss point ⅛ or so below the lower of the two shoulders. Should prices decline, they often turn back before declining below the shoulder lows. If this is too far away from the purchase point, place your stop ⅛ below at the closest support zone. Raise your stop as prices climb.

Sample Trade

Some people might consider Bob unlucky, but he has an adoring wife and two children. Employed as a blue collar worker in a nearby auto plant, he is happy when he is working. Unfortunately, strikes by the union have taken their toll on his savings and he has been looking for ways to supplement his income.

Ever since he was a boy, Wall Street has held his fascination. He has wanted to play the market and when he saw the head-and-shoulders bottom pictured in Figure 18.7, he decided to deploy some of his savings. He bought at 16, the day after prices pushed through the neckline.

For over a week, he did all right. Prices slowly moved up and reached a high of 16⅝, then reversed. The stock threw back to the neckline and continued lower. Suddenly, he was losing money. Should he sell and take a loss or hang on because he knew it was going higher?

He decided to tough it out. The stock bottomed at 14½ and quickly recovered. It reached a higher high, then moved sideways for over a month, drifting slightly lower. Bob was not worried because he was making money. It was not a lot, but with patience, he knew he would do okay.

During the summer, things heated up for the airline and the stock took off. Almost on a daily basis, it soared higher, making new highs. A bearish broadening top appeared but Bob did not know about such things. He felt giddy in the thin atmosphere in which the stock was flying. The stock entered the clouds at 21⅜.

When the airline stock hit turbulence in mid-September and headed for the ground, Bob could not believe it. The stock was plummeting and all he could do was watch his profits spin lower like the stock's altimeter. He talked it over with his wife and they decided to hold on. "It'll come back to its old high and when it does, I'll sell it," he grumbled.

The stock continued down. Soon, his profits gone, he was posting losses. He maintained his firm stance that he would not sell until the price climbed back to the old level.

During October, things changed. The stock pulled up just before nosing into the ground, at 13⅝, and not only leveled out, but started climbing again. In a month he was at break-even.

At the start of the new year, a descending broadening wedge took prices lower as it widened but turned out to be a bullish omen. In mid-January, on unremarkable volume, the stock turned the corner. Volume climbed, helping prices reach a higher altitude.

As the stock closed in on his target of 21⅜, Bob called his broker and placed an order to sell at that price. In late February, the stock began a straight-line run. It soared through 21⅜, hitting his sell order but kept climbing. In just over a month it reached 30.

Bob no longer invests in stocks.

19

Head-and-Shoulders Bottoms, Complex

RESULTS SNAPSHOT

Appearance	An inverted head-and-shoulders formation with multiple heads, shoulders, or both
Reversal or consolidation	Long-term (over 6 months) bullish reversal
Failure rate	6%
Average rise	37%, with most likely rise between 20% and 30%
Volume trend	Downward
Throwbacks	47%
Percentage meeting predicted price target	82%
Surprising findings	Formations with down-sloping necklines perform better. High volume breakouts propel stocks to perform better.
See also	Cup with Handle; Double Bottoms; Head-and-Shoulders Bottoms; Horn Bottom; Rounding Bottom

I find that a complex head-and-shoulders bottom is more difficult to recognize than a normal head-and-shoulders bottom but not alarmingly so. After all, if you can locate a normal head-and-shoulders bottom, then there is a decent chance that you are also looking at a complex one. If you look to the left and right of the two shoulders, you might see additional shoulders. Multiple shoulders are one indication of a complex formation. But before I delve too far into pattern recognition, let me briefly review the important snapshot statistics.

The failure rate at 6% is outstanding. Only 15 formations out of almost 240 fail to perform as expected. The average rise is a reassuring 37%, and 82% of the formations experiencing an upside breakout meet or exceed their price targets. These figures are all excellent and they imply that this formation is worth trading.

Two interesting findings relate to the formation appearance. When the neckline slopes downward, the stock performs better, with gains averaging 39% versus 34% (for those formations with up-sloping necklines). Formations with high volume breakouts also perform better, with gains averaging 39% versus 32% for low volume breakouts. We explore these results in the Statistics section.

Tour

There are two types of complex head-and-shoulders bottoms: those with multiple shoulders and those with multiple heads. Consider the chart in Figure 19.1, a complex head-and-shoulders bottom. The chart pattern has two left shoulders, a single head, and two right shoulders. If you were scanning your

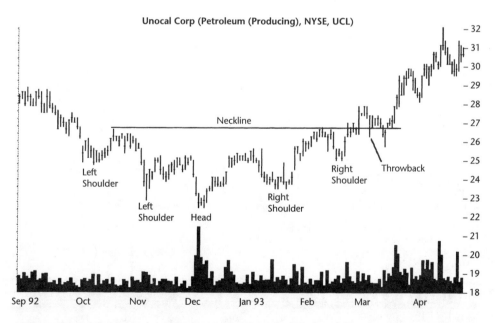

Figure 19.1 A dual shoulder complex head-and-shoulders bottom. Notice the horizontal neckline and throwback to it. The formation is part of a rounding bottom chart pattern.

charts for normal head-and-shoulders bottoms, this one would probably pop up. The left and right shoulders are well defined and the head is below them. As you widen your view, you see an additional pair of shoulders; the left shoulder is about the same distance from the head as the right one. The two outermost shoulders are near the same price level too.

Looking at all the shoulders and the head together, the chart is a good example of a complex head-and-shoulders bottom. However, the volume pattern is unusual as it is heavier on the right than on the left. Most of the time, the left shoulders show higher volume than the right pair.

If you ignore the various labels, you can see a rounding bottom. Although the volume pattern is not a characteristic bowl-shaped pattern, the gentle turn of prices (if you connect the minor lows) supports a bottom formation. However you choose to classify this pattern, the bullish reversal is clear.

Shown in Figure 19.1 is a throwback to the neckline, a common occurrence for the head-and-shoulders family, especially the complex variety. Although it takes a week or two before prices really begin moving up, the stock climbs to a high of $32\frac{5}{8}$ before retracing its gains.

Compare Figure 19.1 with Figure 19.2, a complex bottom with two heads. Overall, the formation is quite symmetrical. There are two shoulders and two heads. A neckline connects the highs in the formation and projects forward in time until prices close above it. The penetration of the neckline is the breakout point.

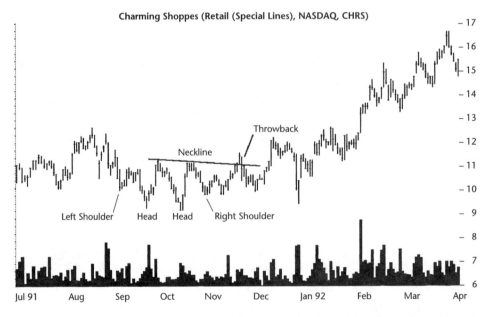

Figure 19.2 A dual head reversal. Volume on the left side of the formation is higher than on the right.

In Figure 19.2, the breakout in mid-November quickly throws back to the neckline and moves lower for a week or two. The stock rises but throws back again before finally breaking away and heading higher. By late March the stock reaches a high of $16\frac{5}{8}$, well above the head low of $9\frac{3}{16}$.

Volume on the left side of the formation is heavier than on the right. In this regard, the formation is more typical than that shown in Figure 19.1.

Identification Guidelines

Are there certain characteristics that make head-and-shoulders bottoms easy to identify? Yes, and they are outlined in Table 19.1. As discussed before, there are two general types of complex head-and-shoulder bottoms: those with multiple shoulders and those with multiple heads (rarely do you have both). Figure 19.3 shows a complex bottom with multiple shoulders. The head is distinctly below the shoulders, far enough below to distinguish the chart pattern from a triple bottom. In this case, there is a normal head-and-shoulders bottom flanked by an additional pair of shoulders. The overall formation appears symmetrical. The two left shoulders match the two on the right in distance. Figure 19.3 shows a far right shoulder that is higher than its corresponding left

Table 19.1
Identification Characteristics of Complex Head-and-Shoulders Bottoms

Characteristic	Discussion
Shape	A head-and-shoulders bottom with multiple shoulders, multiple heads, or (rarely) both. The head is lower than the shoulders but generally not by very much.
Symmetry	The tendency for the shoulders to mirror themselves about the head is strong. The price level of the shoulders and time distance from the shoulder to head is about the same on either side of the head. The shoulders also appear to be the same shape: narrow or wide shoulders on the left mirror the right.
Volume	Usually higher on the left side than the corresponding shoulders on the right. Overall, the volume trend recedes.
Near horizontal neckline	Connects the highest rise on the left and right of the formation center. Most formations have near horizontal necklines.
Upside breakout	A breakout occurs when prices close above the neckline. For those cases with a steep, up-sloping neckline, use the highest price between the head and rightmost shoulder as the breakout price.

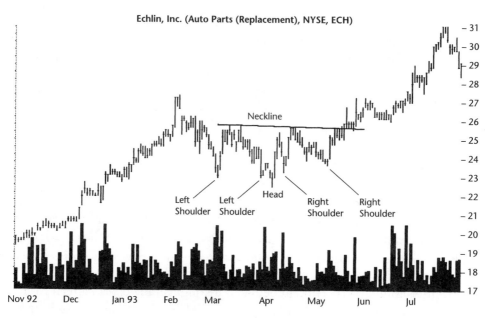

Figure 19.3   A complex head-and-shoulders consolidation. The trend resumes moving up once the formation completes.

one. However, the basic symmetrical pattern is typical for nearly all complex head-and-shoulders bottoms.

Figure 19.3 also shows the usual volume pattern: The two left shoulders show higher volume than the two right ones. Overall, the volume trend is a receding one.

The neckline connects the highest peak on the left with the highest peak on the right. Most of the time the line is nearly horizontal. Although this is subjective, a scan of all the formations indicates that 74% obey this guideline. Many of the formations shown in this chapter have near horizontal necklines.

For those with steep necklines (that slope upward), consider using the highest high in the formation as the breakout price. Using a steep-sloping neckline to gauge the breakout point is risky. Prices may never close above the neckline.

Once prices close above the neckline, a breakout occurs. Quite often, prices throw back to the neckline and perhaps move lower before ultimately continuing higher. Figure 19.2 shows an example of this behavior during late December when prices plunged from a high of $11\frac{1}{2}$ to $9\frac{7}{16}$, a decline of almost 20% in just 2 days! When the decline ended, prices recovered quickly.

The formation shown in Figure 19.3 is unusual because it acts as a consolidation of the uptrend. Prices from November through January climb steadily and then resume moving up after the breakout. The formation is a consolidation region, where prices move horizontally for a spell.

Most of the time you will find complex head-and-shoulders bottoms at the end of a downtrend. Figure 19.1 is an example of this. Although I discuss statistics later, the study reveals that 75% of the formations act as reversals of the prevailing trend and most of the heads (the lowest low in the formation) occur near the yearly low.

Focus on Failures

If making money in the stock market is important to you, it pays to study your failures. The lessons you learn will serve you for many years. When you look at your failures as a group, you may begin to see trends. Such is the case with chart formations.

Although there are only 15 failures out of 239 formations, 66% of the failures act as consolidations of the trend. Of course, this is really no help at all since you can only determine if the formation is a consolidation or a reversal after the breakout. Many of the failures occur after an extended run-up in prices (then prices backtrack to the formation). After the breakout, the ultimate low is nearby, usually within 10% below the lowest price reached during formation of the head. There are a few cases where the decline is over 25%, so you should still place a stop-loss order to limit your losses.

Figure 19.4 shows a typical failure of a complex formation to reverse the downtrend. The stock peaks during September 1991 at a price of $106\frac{3}{8}$. From that point, it is a slow decline at first but picks up speed after the minor high during mid-July 1992. By the following January, the stock reaches a low of $45\frac{7}{8}$ and forms the dual head.

After the head-and-shoulders formation completes, prices *do* climb, but only to $57\frac{1}{8}$. Prices squeeze above the neckline and close there for just a handful of days before sliding below the neckline in early March. Ultimately, the stock reaches $40\frac{5}{8}$ in August.

The volume pattern is nearly perfect for a head-and-shoulders formation. The left shoulder shows tremendous volume. Volume diminishes at the dual heads, and the right shoulder shows even less volume. Breakout volume is anemic and may explain why the formation fails. On closer examination, I found that only 3 of the 15 failures (20%) show low volume breakouts. It appears that breakout volume is not a predictor of the success or failure of a formation. After all, the statistics show 41 successful low-volume breakouts.

I count any formation with prices that fail to rise by more than 5% as a failure. About half the failures fall into this 5% failure category (the other seven formations have downside breakouts). Figure 19.4, for example, falls under the 5% rule. The breakout is upward, but it fails to climb very far before reversing direction. Once prices decline below the head, I know that there is no hope and mark the formation a failure.

Figure 19.4 A failure of the complex head-and-shoulders formation to climb more than 5% after an upside breakout. Just 6% of the formations fail in this manner or have downside breakouts.

In sum, I found no reliable clues that indicate an eventual failure of a complex head-and-shoulders bottom. This should not be alarming since failures represent only 6% of the formations. In essence, you should be able to trade this formation without worrying about a possible failure. Yes, failures will occur, but with a 94% success rate, why worry?

Statistics

Table 19.2 outlines general statistics for complex head-and-shoulder bottoms. I uncovered 239 formations in 500 stocks over 5 years. This number of formations is on the low side but quite respectable for a somewhat rare formation. Of the formations I reviewed, the vast majority (181 or 76%) act as reversals of the prevailing trend, meaning that once the formation breaks out, prices move in the direction opposite to that before the formation began. In the vast majority of cases prices head higher.

The failure rate is 6%. Nearly all the formations I looked at have upside breakouts in which prices rise by more than 5%.

After a breakout, the average rise is 37%. However, the most likely rise is lower—20% to 30%. Figure 19.5 shows how I arrived at this range. I created

Table 19.2
General Statistics for Complex Head-and-Shoulders Bottoms

Description	Statistic
Number of formations in 500 stocks from 1991 to 1996	239
Reversal or consolidation	58 consolidations, 181 reversals
Failure rate	15 or 6%
Average rise of successful formations	37%
Most likely rise	20% to 30%
Of those succeeding, number meeting or exceeding price target (measure rule)	184 or 82%
Average formation length	3.5 months (105 days)
Number of successful formations showing downward volume trend	150 or 63%
Average rise of formations with down-sloping necklines versus up-sloping necklines	39% versus 34%
Average rise of formations with higher right shoulders (furthest on left versus furthest on right) versus higher left shoulders	38% versus 36%
Near horizontal neckline	176 or 74%

Note: Complex head-and-shoulders bottoms have a 94% success rate and stocks climb 37% after an upside breakout.

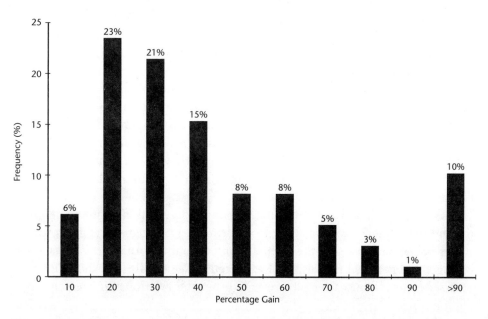

Figure 19.5 Frequency distribution of gains for complex head-and-shoulders bottoms. The chart shows the most likely gain is 20% to 30% for the stocks in the database.

a frequency distribution of the percentage gains for the stocks in the database. The chart shows two columns with the highest frequency, 20% and 30%, close together and well above the surrounding columns. You can also see how the *over 90%* column tends to pull up the overall average. The tendency for large numbers to skew an average adversely is the reason I use a frequency distribution.

The measure rule predicts the price move after a breakout. The rule involves computing the formation height and adding the value to the breakout price (see Trading Tactics). The result is the expected minimum move. For complex head-and-shoulders bottoms, 82% of the formations in the database meet or exceed their price targets. I consider anything above 80% to be reliable.

The average formation length is about 3½ months, which understates the actual length because it measures the distance between the two outermost shoulders. The descent to the left shoulder and rise to the breakout point are not included in the average.

I use the slope of the linear regression line on volume data to determine whether volume is trending up or down. In almost two out of three cases (63%), the volume trends downward. Many times it is easiest to see this trend by viewing the shoulders. The left shoulders will have higher volume than the corresponding right pair.

Some analysts suggest that the neckline slope and shoulder height show the strength of the formation. I looked into this and found that formations with down-sloping necklines have a tendency for larger gains than up-sloping ones. The average price rise is 39% for formations with down-sloping necklines and 34% for up-sloping ones. The difference is statistically significant, meaning the results are probably not due to chance.

In a similar manner, I looked at the shoulder height. Do formations with a higher right shoulder rise further? Yes. The average rise is 38% versus 36%. By *higher right shoulder*, I mean a right shoulder that does not decline as far as the left one. Although the difference is not statistically significant, it does stand to reason. When prices do not decline as far as they did in a prior minor low, then the trend is in the process of changing (from down to up). Investors notice this strength and purchase the stock.

Is there a relationship between the gain after a breakout and the height of the right shoulder? Not that I could determine. I calculated the gains for the stocks in the database and the right shoulder height, both expressed as a percentage, and graphed the results. I expected to see small right shoulders with outsized gains. The scatter plot revealed that the relationship is essentially a random one.

Do complex head-and-shoulders bottoms have mostly horizontal necklines? Yes, with 74% falling into that category. This is a subjective measure and I define the term *mostly horizontal slope* to mean less than 30%. The results support using the characteristic as an identification guideline.

Table 19.3 shows breakout statistics. Most of the formations (97%) have upward breakouts with the remainder showing downward ones. Eight formations have upside breakouts that fail to climb by more than 5%. Together with the 7 that have downside breakouts, this accounts for the 15 formation failures.

In almost half (47%) the formations, prices return to the neckline within 30 days (if they take any longer, it is not a throwback but normal price action). These are called throwbacks and it takes only 12 days, on average, for prices to return to the neckline.

For those formations with successful upside breakouts, it takes 8 months to reach the ultimate high. This places the formation in the long-term category. However, I use a frequency distribution of the time to reach the ultimate high to get a more realistic distribution. The results do not change. Most of the formations take over 6 months (which is the threshold between intermediate and long term) to reach the ultimate high.

Where in the yearly price range do formations occur? Most of the formations (44%) have their breakout in the center third of the price range. This makes sense because prices rise from the shoulder lows to the neckline. That rise alone often shifts the formation into a higher category. Mapping the percentage gains over the yearly price range shows that there is little difference in performance: 34% to 38%. The best gains occur when the breakout is within a third of the yearly high. It seems to me that the momentum players grab hold of the stock and bid it up faster when it is near the yearly high.

· **Table 19.3**
Breakout Statistics for Complex Head-and-Shoulders Bottoms

Description	Statistic
Upside breakout	232 or 97%
Downside breakout	7 or 3%
Upside breakout but failure	8 or 3%
Throwbacks	108 or 47%
Average time to throwback completion	12 days
For successful formations, days to ultimate high	8 months (241 days)
Percentage of breakouts occurring near 12-month low (L), center (C), or high (H)	L20%, C44%, H37%
Percentage gain for each 12-month lookback period	L34%, C37%, H38%
Volume for breakout day and next 5 days compared with day before breakout	163%, 138%, 115%, 103%, 98%, 99%
Average rise of high volume breakouts versus low volume breakouts	39% versus 32%

Note: Nearly all the breakouts are upward and reach the ultimate high in 8 months.

Another interesting statistic I developed relates to high volume breakouts. Do high volume breakouts propel stocks higher? Yes, with gains averaging 39% versus 32% for low volume breakouts. The differences are statistically significant.

In the calculation, I used the breakout day plus the next 2 days and averaged the volume of those three together (since a high volume breakout might be delayed). Then I compared the volume with the day before the breakout. I considered values over 25% above the benchmark as high volume and 25% below the benchmark as low volume. I computed the percentage gains for those stocks with high volume breakouts and compared them to those stocks with low volume breakouts to derive the results.

Trading Tactics

Trading tactics are outlined in Table 19.4. The measure rule predicts the expected minimum price move and is best explained by an example. Figure 19.6 shows a complex head-and-shoulders bottom on a weekly time scale with the head reaching a low of 13½. Directly above that point, the neckline has a value of 18⅝. The difference, 5⅛, is the formation height. Add the difference to the breakout point (17) to get the minimum price move (22⅛).

Table 19.4
Trading Tactics for Complex Head-and-Shoulders Bottoms

Trading Tactic	Explanation
Measure rule	Compute the formation height by subtracting the lowest low reached in the head(s) from the neckline, measured vertically. Add the result to the breakout price where prices pierce the neckline. The value is the minimum target price.
Do not wait for confirmation	If you can determine that a complex head-and-shoulders formation is completing, consider placing a long trade or cover any short commitments.
Stop loss	Stocks sometimes decline to the lowest of the right shoulders then turn around. Look for support areas near the shoulders. Place a stop-loss order ⅛ below the lowest shoulder or head.
Watch for throwback	Buy or add to the position during a throwback. Wait for prices to finish falling before placing the trade as prices sometimes throw back and continue moving down.

It took just 2 weeks after the breakout to reach the target, but the stock was not done climbing. It moved sideways for almost a year before continuing higher. The stock reached a high of 39⅜, nearly triple the head low of 13½ and more than double the breakout price.

The chart in Figure 19.6 shows a complex head-and-shoulders bottom that forms after nearly a 2-year run-up in prices. The formation marks a reversal of the 6-month retrace. Once a breakout occurs, prices quickly climb to fulfill the measure rule and then stall. Prices then move horizontally for almost 2 months before climbing to the next level. There the stock consolidates for 7 months before shooting upward in mid-June 1995.

Since complex head-and-shoulders bottoms reliably break out upward, there is little need to wait for the actual breakout. Once you determine that a complex formation is present, buy the stock. Of course, the key is that you must be sure a complex head-and-shoulders formation is present. Many times this is made easier when the formation looks like the one in Figure 19.6, where a normal head-and-shoulders pattern is flanked by two or more shoulders. If you can identify the inner head-and-shoulders pattern, then you need only widen your vision and look for additional shoulders.

With dual heads, the pattern is somewhat different. The dual-head formation usually has head lows that are less than a month apart. Two heads that

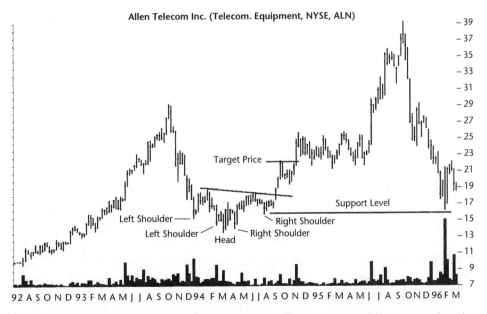

Figure 19.6 Complex head-and-shoulders bottom on a weekly time scale. The figure shows the target price found using the measure rule. Compute the formation height from the head low to the neckline and add the difference to the breakout price. The right shoulders often offer support during future declines.

are close together usually distinguishes the formation from a classic double bottom. Shoulder symmetry and a near horizontal neckline should put the finishing touches on the formation identification.

Once you take a position in the stock, set your stop-loss point. Many times the various shoulder troughs will act as support levels. If your head-and-shoulders formation is near the yearly low, then there is a very good chance that prices will either turn around at the head or decline slightly below it (by 10% or so) before bottoming out. From that point, prices climb higher.

If your formation is not within the lowest third of the yearly price range, then sell the stock once prices drop below the head. Prices falling below the head signal a formation failure and it is best to cut your losses instead of praying that they will turn around. They will not.

After an upside breakout, almost half the time (47%), the stock throws back to the neckline. Consider adding to your position or placing a long trade once prices stop declining. You should wait for prices to rebound on a throwback or else you could find yourself in a situation similar to that shown in Figure 19.2. Prices throw back to the neckline then continue down for over a week. Depending on when you bought the stock, you could have seen a near 10% price improvement if you had waited a few days.

Sample Trade

When the weather is nice, I like to take my bicycle out for a spin and give the automobile drivers something to aim for. It was on one of my bike trips that I met Melody. After I told her what I did for a living, she confessed that she was a nightclub dancer and made oodles in tips. I was unsure whether I bought her story, but she looked pretty enough (wearing a bike helmet and sun glasses, who can tell?).

Anyway, she told me about a trade she had made in the stock pictured in Figure 19.6. The stock intrigued her because a trendline drawn from the highest high in early October to just after the head marked a turning point. That is where prices moved up enough to pierce the trendline.

Melody knew that prices usually retest the low before beginning an extended move upward, so she followed the stock and watched it loop around and dip to 14. Then she glanced sideways and noticed the other dip at $14\frac{3}{8}$. That is when she uncovered the head-and-shoulders bottom.

A neckline connecting the rises between the two shoulders was impossibly steep; there was no way she could apply the traditional measure rule to determine a target price, so she decided to buy into the stock when prices closed above the right shoulder high.

This occurred in late May and she received a fill at $17\frac{1}{2}$. Taking a closer look at the graph, she saw two more shoulders, one during early February and the mirror image in mid-May, both at 16. Her simple head-and-shoulders bottom changed into the complex variety.

The realization did not affect her investment plans at all, but it made the situation more interesting. She wondered if another pair of shoulders would appear. Her suspicions were fulfilled during late July when another shoulder developed. This one at $15\frac{3}{4}$ mirrored the shoulder in mid-December 1993. Soon, prices began moving up. They climbed above the break-even point in mid-August and staged an upside breakout. Now she was able to apply the measure rule for the complex bottom and found the target was $22\frac{1}{8}$.

Since she did not need the money immediately, she held onto the shares as prices rose. She thought the stock had enough upward momentum to reach the old high at about $29\frac{1}{4}$, and she set her sights on that. As long as prices did not drop below the purchase price, she would stay in the trade.

She saw the stock building a base between 21 and 26 and wondered what to make of it. A downside breakout was a real possibility, so she raised her stop to 21—the height of the plateau in October—and at a price just below where the base seemed to be building.

In mid-June, just over a year after she placed the trade, prices zoomed up and reached her sell point. The stock sold at 29. The stock continued climbing, but she needed the money for a down payment on a house.

I was so engrossed with her story and the way she told it that I did not realize she had dismounted from her bicycle. She spoke of coming back to her place and making some new chart patterns, then playfully thrust her hips into mine.

I fell off my bicycle.

20

Head-and-Shoulders Tops

RESULTS SNAPSHOT

Appearance	Three-bump formation with center bump taller than the others
Reversal or consolidation	Short-term (up to 3 months) bearish reversal
Failure rate	7%
Average decline	23%, with most likely decline being 15%
Volume trend	Slopes downward with highest volume on left shoulder, followed by head and right shoulder, respectively.
Pullbacks	45%
Percentage meeting predicted price target	63%
Surprising findings	A down-sloping neckline or a lower right shoulder (versus left shoulder) predicts a larger decline, but results are not statistically significant.
See also	Head-and-Shoulders Tops, Complex

Of all the formations in this book, the head-and-shoulders top is perhaps the most popular. This stems, in part, from its reliability. With 93% of the formations breaking out downward and continuing to move down, there is no need to wait for a breakout before trading. In that regard, you can save yourself

290

more money if you own a stock and decide to sell or place a short sale sooner, garnering larger profits. Head-and-shoulders tops' popularity also stems from their recognizability. The characteristic three bumps with the higher center bump make the formation easy to spot.

Two surprising findings are that the slope of the neckline and a lower right shoulder predict a more drastic price decline after the chart pattern. Unfortunately, the results are not statistically significant, meaning that they may (or may not) be due to chance. They are still interesting nonetheless, and the Statistics section describes the findings in detail.

Tour

Figure 20.1 shows a good example of a head-and-shoulders top. The three bumps are clearly visible with the center bump being the highest of the three. The left shoulder usually appears after an extended uphill run. The entire formation seems to stand alone when viewed in the context of a year's worth of daily price data. This stand-alone characteristic makes the head-and-shoulders top easily identified in a price series.

Figure 20.1 shows the highest volume occurring during the head. More often the left shoulder will have the highest volume, followed by the head, with greatly diminished volume during formation of the right shoulder. The iden-

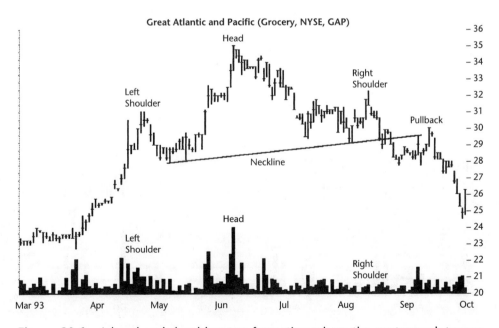

Figure 20.1 A head-and-shoulders top formation where the center peak towers above the other two. A pullback to the neckline occurs in almost half the formations.

tification guidelines are flexible because volume characteristics vary from formation to formation.

A trendline drawn along the bottoms of the two troughs between the three peaks forms the neckline. The line may slope in any direction but slopes upward about 52% of the time and downward 43% of the time with the remainder being horizontal. The direction of neckline slope is a predictor of the severity of the price decline. We see in the Statistics section that the neckline slope and the shoulder height are both related to the ultimate price decline.

Why do these formations form? Pretend for a moment that you are a big spender and represent what is commonly called the *smart money*. You are searching for a stock to buy and believe that Toll Brothers (Figure 20.2) represents an intriguing situation. You review the fundamentals and everything looks good, so you start buying the stock in mid-July as prices descend. Your buying turns the situation around: The stock begins rising.

Soon you have acquired all the stock you want and sit back and wait. As you expected, the company issues good news and the stock begins making its move. Other investors jump into the game and buy the stock, sending the price higher. As the stock rises above 10, you decide it is time to sell. After all, you have made 20% in about 2 weeks. Your selling causes the stock to pause then begin a retrace of the prior action.

Sensing weakness in the stock, you stop your selling and monitor the situation closely. Other momentum and buy-the-dip players, believing that this

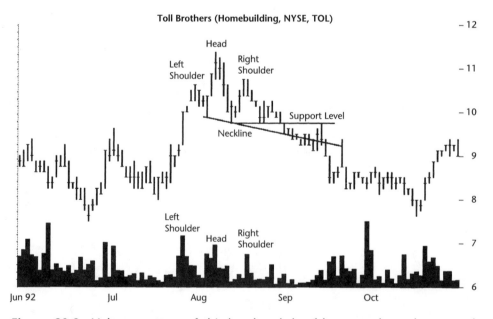

Figure 20.2 Volume pattern of this head-and-shoulders top obeys the general characteristics: highest on formation of the left shoulder and weakest on the right shoulder. The down-sloping neckline suggests an especially weak situation.

is a chance to get in on the ground floor of a further advance, buy the stock on the retrace. The decline halts and the stock begins rising again.

As it rises, other momentum players make a bid for the stock or buy it outright. Once the stock gets above 10, you begin selling it again, not heavily at first because you have a large number of shares to dump. Still, the market players notice your selling and the stock climbs just above 11 before heading back down.

You dump your remaining shares as the stock begins tumbling. Volume rises as other players sell their shares to unsuspecting buyers. The stock continues moving down and slides back below 10. Believing the stock oversold, demand picks up and sends the price moving up again for the last time.

You watch the action from the sidelines, content with the profit you have made. The stock climbs to $10\frac{3}{4}$ on the right shoulder. Lacking support, the rise falters on weak volume and the stock turns down. Investors versed in technical analysis see the head-and-shoulders top for what it is: a reversal. They quietly take their profits and sell the stock. Others initiate short sales by selling high and hoping the price falls.

Prices move down to the support level where prices declined the last time. The stock pauses at the support level for a week and makes a feeble effort to rise again. When the attempt falters, the stock moves down and pierces the neckline. Volume picks up and the stock tumbles. Eventually, prices decline back to where they began, just under 8.

In essence, the formation is a symbol of shares being turned more quickly as prices rise. Eventually the selling pressure squelches demand, sending prices tumbling.

Identification Guidelines

Are there certain guidelines that make identifying a head-and-shoulders top easy? Yes, and Table 20.1 lists them. The identification guidelines are just that, guidelines. The head-and-shoulders top formation can appear in a wide variety of shapes. Consider Figure 20.3. Shown is a head-and-shoulders top formation, but there are four shoulders and only one head. When a formation appears with more than the standard two shoulders and one head, it is called a complex head-and-shoulders pattern. Complex head-and-shoulders patterns for both tops and bottoms have their own chapters but many appear in this chapter's statistics. They are, after all, head-and-shoulder tops too.

The head-and-shoulders top formation usually appears at the end of a long uptrend. Sometimes, when the prior uptrend is of short duration, the reversal takes prices down to where they started the climb (see Figure 20.2). At other times, the decline is usually short (up to 3 months) or intermediate (3 to 6 months), or can signal a change in the primary bullish trend. The actual length of the decline cannot be predicted.

Table 20.1

Identification Characteristics of Head-and-Shoulders Tops

Characteristic	Discussion
Shape	After an upward price trend, the formation appears as three bumps, the center one is the tallest, resembling a bust.
Symmetry	The two shoulders appear at about the same price level. Distance from the shoulders to the head is approximately the same. There can be wide variation in the formation's appearance, but symmetry is usually a good clue to the veracity of the formation.
Volume	Highest on the left shoulder, followed by the head. The right shoulder shows the lowest volume of the three peaks.
Neckline	Connects the lows of the two troughs between the three peaks. The line can slope up or down. Often used as a trigger point (to buy or sell) once prices pierce the line.
Downside breakout	Once prices pierce the neckline, they may pull back briefly, then continue moving down.

Even though the formation shown in Figure 20.3 is somewhat odd, it does have a symmetrical appearance. The two left shoulders are at about the same price level as the corresponding two right shoulders. Each of the shoulders is approximately the same distance from the other and from its mirror opposite. In the chart pattern, the head is centrally located. The symmetrical appearance of a head-and-shoulders top formation is one of its key identifica-

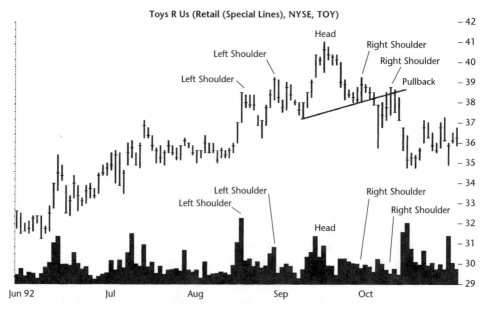

Figure 20.3 A complex head-and-shoulders top pattern. The chart shows the wide variation that a head-and-shoulders formation can take.

tion characteristics and helps separate any three bumps from a valid head-and-shoulders chart pattern.

Volume obeys the general characteristic: It is higher on the left shoulder than on the head and higher on the head than on the right shoulder. If you consider just the three inner peaks in Figure 20.3, the volume pattern changes somewhat since the left shoulder has volume diminished from that shown during the head. Even so, the volume on the left shoulder is still above the right shoulder.

The neckline, as shown in Figure 20.3, connects the two troughs between the three inner peaks. It slopes upward but need not do so (contrast with Figure 20.2). The neckline serves as a confirmation point. Once prices pierce the neckline, and assuming they do not pullback, prices continue moving down in earnest.

A pullback to the neckline occurs almost half the time. It usually takes less than 2 weeks to complete a pullback, but do not be fooled. The trend will resume downward shortly. However, a pullback does allow you one more opportunity to exit a long position or institute a short trade. Take advantage of it.

Focus on Failures

Failures of head-and-shoulders formations are rare, but they do occur. Figure 20.4 shows an example of a failure. The well-formed formation has a head centrally located between two shoulders. The left and right shoulders are at the same price level, 29⅛. Volume is highest on the left shoulder and lowest on the right, as you would expect.

Why do prices fail to pierce the neckline at point A and head down? The answer is not clear. The formation is perfect except that it fails to descend. It acts as a consolidation or continuation of the upward trend. Not shown in the figure, the prior two formations were descending triangles. These formations usually break out downward but these did not. Both had upside breakouts and both signaled a bullish uptrend. The two formations were clues to the strength of the rise, but one could also argue that the appearance of a head-and-shoulders formation would probably signal an end to the extended rise. It did not.

If there is a good side to this failure, it is that failures do not occur very often. Only 6% of the formations (25 out of 431) I looked at consolidate as the formation in Figure 20.4.

Statistics

Table 20.2 shows general statistics for the head-and-shoulders top formation. The head-and-shoulders top pattern is a plentiful one, occurring 431 times over the study period. In almost every occurrence it acts as a bearish reversal of

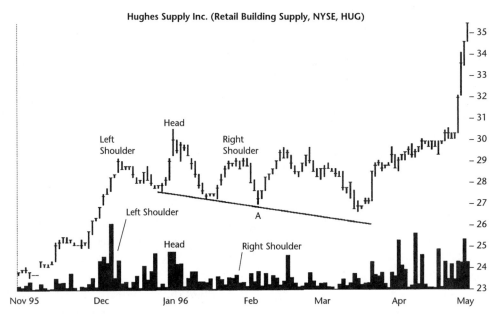

Figure 20.4 A rare head-and-shoulders consolidation. The formation fails to continue down after reaching point A. Symmetry and volume patterns offer no clue to the eventual failure.

Table 20.2
General Statistics for Head-and-Shoulders Tops

Description	Statistic
Number of formations in 500 stocks from 1991 to 1996	431
Reversal or consolidation	25 consolidations, 406 reversals
Failure rate	30 or 7%
Average decline of successful formations	23%
Most likely decline	15% to 20%
Of those succeeding, number meeting or exceeding price target (measure rule)	254 or 63%
Average formation length	2 months (62 days)
Average performance of lower right shoulder versus performance of lower left shoulder	24% versus 22%, but result is not statistically significant
Average performance of formations with down-sloping necklines versus up-sloping necklines	23% versus 22%, but result is not statistically significant

Note: With a 7% failure rate, you need not wait for the breakout before placing a trade.

the uptrend. Only 30 formations (7%) fail to continue moving down by more than 5% or break out upward. That statistic means that prices usually decline after a valid formation occurs and suggests that you need not wait for confirmation of a downside breakout. A discussion of this trading tactic follows in the Trading Tactics section.

Once prices pierce the neckline, they continue moving down another 23%, on average. However, a frequency distribution of declines suggests the most likely decline is less, about 15%. Figure 20.5 shows the relationship. The bell-shaped appearance of the chart is reassuring. I consider the tallest column the *most likely decline* because it has the highest frequency (the highest number of formations in that decline range).

I discuss the measure rule in the Trading Tactics section, but suffice it to say that the rule measures the height from the head to the neckline and subtracts the result from the point where prices pierce the neckline. Prices meet the target only 63% of the time. I consider values above 80% to be acceptable, so this method comes up a bit short.

On average, the formation is 2 months long (62 days), as measured between the left and right shoulder peaks. Of course, this understates the actual length of the formation since prices need time to rise up to the left shoulder and decline to the neckline. If you add the drop from the right shoulder to the

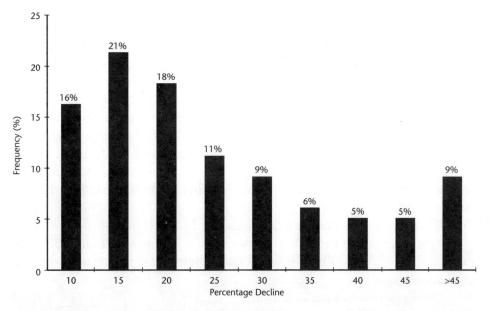

Figure 20.5 A frequency distribution of declines for successful downside breakouts in head-and-shoulders tops. The graph suggests the most likely decline is about 15%, below the average decline of 23%.

breakout point (that is, the neckline), then the average length rises to 79 days. I did not measure the time it takes prices to rise to the left shoulder peak.

Some analysts have suggested that the shoulder height implies a strong or weak technical situation. By that I mean if the left shoulder peak is higher than the right one, then prices are more likely to decline further than if the heights are reversed. Although I found this to be true, with a lower right shoulder decline of 24% and a 22% decline for formations with a lower left shoulder, the difference is not statistically significant. By that I mean the result could be due to chance, or it could mean that there is indeed some validity to the notion.

I examined the relationship between the two shoulder prices. Do short right shoulders mean a larger decline? I used a minimum price difference between the two shoulders of 5%. Although the performance results (34% average decline versus 19%) are significant, the sample size is not (I found only 11 or 12 samples out of 431 because identification depends on the shoulders being near in price to each other). Using a 4% price difference brings the results down to 25% and 22% and increases the sample size to 35. However, the results are nearly the same as that achieved without any qualifiers (those shown in the table). If you can make a blanket statement about this behavior, it might be that larger price differentials between the two shoulder prices results in different performance. Significantly lower right shoulders suggests a more substantial decline.

In a similar manner, some analysts have said that a down-sloping trend-line shows a weaker technical situation than an up-sloping one. This is also true, with losses averaging 23% versus 22%, but again, the difference is not statistically significant. Since so many have suggested that these relationships do exist and the statistics do not contradict that notion, then it is more likely to be a reliable indicator of pending price action.

Table 20.3 shows statistics related to breakouts. The vast majority (98%) of breakouts are downward, whereas only 9 formations move upward. However, there are 21 formations with downside breakouts that fail to move down by more than 5%. Even so, this only represents 5% of the formations with downside breakouts. The statistics suggest that a head-and-shoulders formation will not only break out downward, but that prices will continue moving down as well.

There are a large number of pullbacks, at 191 or 45%. Pullbacks are when prices drop below the neckline then return to it. Figures 20.1 and 20.3 show examples of pullbacks. On average, it takes slightly less than 2 weeks for the pullbacks to return to the neckline.

Once prices break out downward, it takes 3 months on average to reach the ultimate low. This seems to be a typical decline rate for bearish formations. Of course, sometimes the formations indicate a longer term trend change, but you will usually find that prices reach the ultimate low within 3 to 6 months (short- to intermediate-term trading implications).

Table 20.3
Breakout Statistics for Head-and-Shoulder Tops

Description	Statistic
Upside breakout	9 or 2%
Downside breakout	422 or 98%
Downside breakout but failure	21 or 5%
Pullbacks	191 or 45%
Average time to pullback completion	11 days
For successful formations, days to ultimate low	3 months (91 days)
Percentage of breakouts occurring near the 12-month low (L), center (C), or high (H)	L11%, C40%, H49%
Percentage loss for each 12-month lookback period	L22%, C22%, H21%

Note: Almost all the head-and-shoulders tops break out downward and reach the ultimate low in about 3 months.

A frequency distribution of the days to reach the ultimate low confirms the short-term implication of a head-and-shoulders top. The vast majority of formations (265 or 66%) are short term, with only 83 falling into the intermediate term, and 53 taking more than 6 months to reach the ultimate low.

If you consider where the formations appear over the prior 12-month price range, then you can get a feel for where the best performing head-and-shoulders patterns occur. First, I exclude all formations that begin within 1 year from the start of the study. Then the yearly price range is divided into thirds for each formation. Every formation sorts into one of the three bins, depending on the price at the breakout. The results show that most formations (49%) break out near the yearly high, suggesting that most head-and-shoulders tops appear at the end of an uptrend.

Do formations that have a breakout near the yearly high perform better (that is, decline further) than those breaking out near the yearly low? No. The performance percentages distribute evenly at about 22%. This means prices are likely to decline about 22% after a breakout regardless of where they occur in the yearly price range. In other bearish formations, we have seen that the best performing chart patterns occur near the yearly low.

Table 20.4 shows volume statistics. As I was searching for the formations, I made no assumptions about the volume pattern. However, an analysis of the statistics using linear regression shows there are definite trends. Almost two out of three formations (62%) have receding volume trends. This downward trend is clear in many of the charts that accompany this chapter.

When you look at the volume pattern of the three bumps, you discover that high volume usually accompanies creation of the left shoulder. The volume

Table 20.4
Volume Statistics for Head-and-Shoulders Tops

Description	Statistic
Number of successful formations showing downward volume trend	247 or 62%
Volume highest on which bump?	Left shoulder, 49%
Second highest volume on which bump?	Head, 51%
Volume lowest on which bump?	Right shoulder, 74%
Volume for breakout day and next 5 days compared with day before breakout	159%, 146%, 111%, 99%, 99%, 98%

Note: Volume is highest on the left shoulder and weakest on the right shoulder.

is higher than that shown during the other two bumps. Formation of the right shoulder usually shows the lowest volume. Volume at the head falls between the other two bumps—it is usually lower than the left shoulder but higher than the right one.

To make the volume assessments, I looked at each formation and logged the volume pattern for the three bumps. For example, I assigned the highest volume to one of the three bumps after looking at the chart pattern. This was also done for middle and low volume ranges. After reviewing all the stocks, I added up the numbers for the three categories (highest, middle, and lowest volume) for each of the three bumps (left shoulder, head, and right shoulder). The percentage numbers beside each entry in Table 20.4 tell how many bumps have the associated volume characteristics.

For example, left shoulders have the highest volume, with 49% of them falling in that category. Heads follow at 37% and right shoulders at 13%, all in the highest volume category. The only surprise in the figures is the number of hits in the lowest volume category. Seventy-four percent of right shoulders have low volume, whereas only 14% of left shoulders and 12% of heads show low volume.

Turning our attention to volume at the breakout, we find that the volume rises on the breakout day by 59% above the prior day (or 159% of the total). This is in line with other bearish formations. Shown in Table 20.4 are additional volume statistics for the week after the breakout. Notice how the volume drops off rapidly. Again, this decrease in volume is normal and emphasizes the belief that prices can fall of their own weight and do not need high volume to decline.

Trading Tactics

Shown in Table 20.5 are trading tactics, and Figure 20.6 shows an example of the measure rule as it applies to a head-and-shoulders top. If you ignore the backward volume pattern, the formation looks fine. Each of the three bumps

Table 20.5
Trading Tactics for Head-and-Shoulders Tops

Trading Tactic	Explanation
Measure rule	Compute the formation height by subtracting the value of the neckline from the highest high reached in the head, measured vertically. Subtract the result from the breakout price where prices pierce the neckline. The difference is the minimum target price to which prices descend. Alternatively, compute the formation height from the highest high to the daily low price in the higher of the two troughs. Subtract the result from the daily high price in the higher of the two troughs to get the target price. This method boosts the success rate to 69% and does not rely on the neckline or breakout point (useful for steep necklines).
Do not wait for confirmation	Once the right shoulder forms and *you are confident that a head-and-shoulders formation is valid,* sell your stock or sell short. With a 93% success rate, there is little need to wait for a confirmed breakout before placing a trade.
Short stop	For short sales, place a stop just above the lower of the two troughs or just above the neckline, whichever is higher.
Watch for pullback	Initiate a short sale or add to your position during a pullback. Wait for prices to begin falling again before placing the trade as prices sometimes pull back and continue moving up.

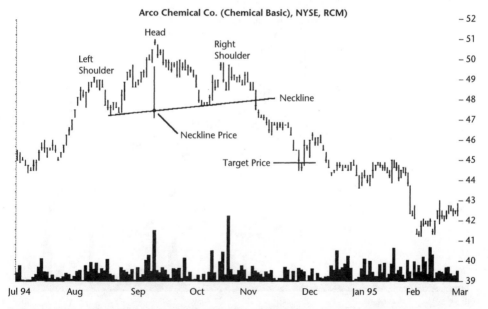

Figure 20.6 The measure rule as it applies to a head-and-shoulders top. Calculate the formation height by subtracting the neckline price from the highest high, measured vertically. Subtract the result from the high at the breakout. The result is the minimum target price to which prices decline.

appear rounded and the overall formation is symmetrical. The measure rule uses the formation height as a basis for computing the target price. In the head, measure vertically down from the highest daily high until you intersect the neckline. Subtract the value of the neckline from the highest high. The result gives the formation height. In the figure, the stock reaches a high price of 51 on September 13. Directly below that point is the neckline price at about $47\frac{3}{8}$. The difference of $3\frac{5}{8}$ is the formation height.

Once prices pierce the neckline, subtract the formation height from the daily high at the breakout point. In Figure 20.6, the high at the breakout is $48\frac{1}{2}$, leaving a target price of $44\frac{7}{8}$. Prices surpass the target when they decline below the value in late November. Since the target serves as a minimum price move, prices often continue moving down, as in Figure 20.6. However, only 63% of the formations meet or exceed the price target. I consider values above 80% to be reliable.

The measure rule, as just described, is the conventional way to compute a target price. However, it does have a flaw. Consider Figure 20.7. Prices during the right trough recession decline to $27\frac{3}{4}$, well below the higher trough at $31\frac{1}{4}$. A neckline joining the two is too steep. Prices never plunge through the neckline and it is impossible to compute a target price using the conventional method. Instead, compute the formation height by taking the difference

Figure 20.7 Head-and-shoulders top with steep neckline. There is no target price using the conventional measure rule because of the steep neckline. Alternatively, compute the formation height by subtracting the higher trough low (point A) from the highest high. Subtract the result from point A to get the target price. Prices meet or exceed the target 69% of the time versus 63% for the conventional method.

between the highest high in the head and the lowest low in the highest trough (point A on the chart) in Figure 20.7. After finding the formation height, subtract the value from point A to get the target price. In this example, the highest high is at $33\frac{5}{8}$ and the lowest low at the highest trough is $31\frac{1}{4}$, giving a height of $2\frac{3}{8}$. Subtract the result from $31\frac{1}{4}$ to get a target of $28\frac{7}{8}$. Figure 20.7 shows this value, and prices reach the target during mid-April.

The alternative method has two advantages. First, it can always be calculated and is somewhat easier to use since it does not rely on the value of the neckline. Second, it is more accurate, achieving a success rate of 69%, meaning that more formations exceed the price target using this alternative method rather than the conventional one.

Returning to Table 20.5, since the formation rarely fails, there is little need to wait for a confirmed breakout. Instead, once you are *sure* a head-and-shoulders top is forming and you want to maximize your profits, sell any shares you may own or sell short (as close to the right peak as possible). This action allows you to get out of a commitment sooner than waiting for the neckline to be pierced.

Occasionally, prices will rebound at the neckline and move higher. Either repurchase the stock at that point or close out your short. Since prices usually pierce the trendline on their way down, do not be too quick to repurchase the stock. It may bounce up at the trendline then continue down after moving horizontally or follow the neckline. Sometimes general market conditions or other companies in the same industry can provide a direction clue. If they show weakness, expect your stock to follow the crowd and prices to move lower.

If you sell short, place your stop-loss order either just above the neckline or above the lower of the two troughs, whichever is higher. Selecting a nearby resistance point usually works well.

If prices pull back to the neckline, consider adding to your short position. However, be sure to wait for prices to begin falling after a pullback. Occasionally, prices will pull back and continue rising.

Sample Trade

Kelly is not just a housewife; she is much more that. When her husband brings home the bacon, she not only fries it but cleans up the mess afterward. She balances the books and keeps tabs on their newborn.

She started investing years ago for fun. Now, it has become part of her daily life. In the spare moments between chores, she is often staring at the computer screen, reviewing the statistics of a prospective acquisition and letting her daughter bang on the keyboard.

Over the years she has been able to parlay their meager savings into a six-figure retirement portfolio. It was not easy and the mistakes were painful but she viewed each failure as a learning experience.

The stock pictured in Figure 20.7 posed an interesting situation for her. She was not keen on shorting a stock because her paper trades rarely worked out. Still, she kept her eyes open and searched for good investment candidates. This one piqued her interest.

The stock began its uphill run just before May 1993. It followed a gently sloping trendline upward until late January when it stumbled. The stock moved down to $26\frac{1}{2}$ before recovering, a drop of less than three points, but a sign of weakness. Kelly followed the stock closely and when the head appeared, she made a note on her program that it might turn into a head-and-shoulders top. "It just had that certain feel," she remarked. She was right.

The right shoulder plunge took prices lower than she expected but quickly recovered to near the left shoulder high. She drew a neckline below the two valleys and thought the line was too steep to serve as an anchor for the measure rule, so she used the alternate measure rule and computed a target price of just $28\frac{7}{8}$. This did not seem right either, so she used the right shoulder low to compute another target. This one turned out to be $21\frac{7}{8}$, or the height from the head to the right shoulder valley projected downward from the valley low. That target would take prices back to the July level and it seemed reasonable to her.

Still, something bothered her about the stock and she decided not to trade it. When the doorbell rang, she left her daughter alone briefly to answer it. Moments later, the phone rang. It was her broker confirming that the stock sold short. Kelly ran to the computer to see her daughter standing on the chair, beating on the keyboard with a wide but guilty grin on her face. Kelly hoped it was only gas, but, no, she had indeed sold the stock short at 31.

After spending some anxious moments reviewing the trade, Kelly decided to maintain the position. The number of shorted shares was just 100, an amount she could live with. Prices quickly retreated to the neckline where they found support. The stock bounced and when it moved above the right shoulder low, she got concerned. After a few days, the stock leveled out and moved sideways. In case this turned out to be the beginning of a measured move up, she placed an order to cover her trade at 29. That would leave her with a small profit but still allow her to participate if the stock declined.

Two weeks later, she had an answer. The stock tumbled for 5 days in a row, then just as quickly recovered, only this time it formed a lower high. The volatility was wearing her down so she placed an order with her broker to cover her position when prices reached the old low. She was taken out when prices descended to $22\frac{3}{4}$ on their way down to 20. After expenses, she made about 25% on the trade. Her daughter got a big kiss for her help.

21

Head-and-Shoulders
Tops, Complex

RESULTS SNAPSHOT

Appearance	A head-and-shoulders formation with multiple heads, shoulders, or both
Reversal or consolidation	Short-term (up to 3 months) bearish reversal
Failure rate	8%
Average decline	27%, with most likely decline being 20%
Volume trend	Downward
Pullbacks	64%
Percentage meeting predicted price target	67%
Surprising findings	Formations with down-sloping necklines or higher left shoulders perform marginally better.
See also	Double Tops; Head-and-Shoulder Tops; Horn Tops; Rounding Tops; Triple Tops

Except for appearance, there is not much difference between a normal head-and-shoulders top and a complex one. Add a dual head or a few extra shoulders to a regular formation and you have a complex head-and-shoulders top. Both formations have a volume trend that generally slopes downward between the shoulders. The left shoulders often have higher volume than the corresponding right ones.

The failure rate for complex head-and-shoulders tops is very low (8%) but slightly above the rate recorded for regular head-and-shoulders tops. Pullbacks have also moved up a notch and now appear in nearly two out of three formations.

The average decline at 27% is on the high side for a bearish formation. However, the most likely decline is just about evenly distributed from 10% to 30% (when viewed in 5% increments).

Two interesting findings deal with necklines and shoulder height. When the neckline, which is a trendline joining the lowest minor lows between the shoulders, slopes downward, the performance improves slightly from a decline of 26% to 27%. Likewise, when the outermost shoulder is higher on the left than the corresponding one on the right, the performance improves from 27% to 28%. In both cases, the differences may not be statistically significant (meaning they could be due to chance).

Tour

There are two basic varieties of complex head-and-shoulder tops, as illustrated in Figures 21.1 and 21.2. In Figure 21.1, the formation appears after an

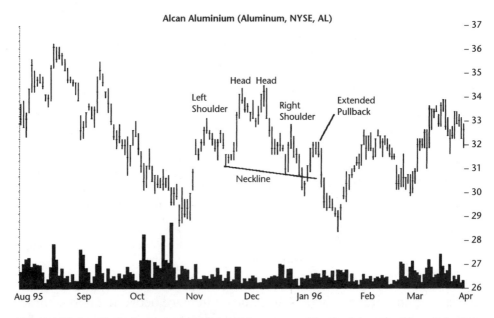

Figure 21.1 Complex head-and-shoulders top with dual heads. The stair-step pattern of a measured move up forms the left shoulder and head. The twin peaks take on the appearance of a horn top, and the resulting move down resembles another measured move, albeit stuttered.

extended bull run that begins in November 1992 at a low price of 15¼. The stock climbs to a high of 36⅝ by mid-July 1995, then melts back to 28⅝ by mid-October, forming a base for the head and shoulders. The stock rebounds, creating the left shoulder. It pauses at the 31–32 level by moving sideways, then spikes upward again in a sort of measured move thrust. The measured move up finishes shy of its target price by just over a dollar before the stock begins retracing its gain. The peak serves as the first head.

After moving down a bit, the stock pushes upward and tags the old high, then drops. Another head appears. Once prices slip from the head, they find support at the first shoulder trough and rebound. The right shoulder takes shape. After declining through the neckline, formed by a line joining the two shoulder troughs, prices quickly pull back and move higher. They turn away at the 32 resistance level and continue down in a straight-line run to 28⅜.

Computing a line using linear regression of the daily volume over the formation (outermost shoulder to shoulder) indicates volume recedes. Although it is difficult to tell from the chart in Figure 21.1, about two out of every three complex head-and-shoulders tops show a receding volume trend.

If you believe in the classic definition of a double top, you might consider the twin heads a candidate for that formation. However, several flaws eliminate this pattern as a candidate for a double top. First, the two peaks are too close together on the time line. For a classic double top, the peaks should be at least a month apart (my definition of a double top allows peaks to be closer together). Also, the recession between the two peaks should take prices down by 15% to 20%. Figure 21.1 shows a decline of just 5% from the highest peak, well short of the goal.

I could further complicate the comparison by pointing out that the two heads look like a horn top, but we are discussing complex head-and-shoulder formations. Let me say that you find such behavior quite often in technical analysis: Each formation can be viewed from several different perspectives. Some analysts might see a complex head-and-shoulders formation while others see a pair of measured moves—one the skewed mirror image of the other—while yet others might see a horn top. The results are the same so there is no need for concern: All point to a bearish situation.

Figure 21.2 shows a different type of complex head-and-shoulders top. Multiple shoulders with only one head is the more common of the two varieties. Pictured is the type of technical pattern that rips the heart out of novice investors. Imagine someone buying this stock in October, just before the rise begins. Prices quickly move from a low of about 13 to a high of 27⅞, a doubling of the stock price in a little over 3 months. On the way up, our novice investor is thinking that picking stocks is an easy game; his selections are turning to gold.

The first shoulder forms as prices touch 27⅞, then retreat to a low of 22. The decline undoubtedly upset our investor pal. He probably told himself that he would sell the stock once it returned to its old high.

Figure 21.2 Typical complex head-and-shoulders reversal. Multiple shoulders with a single head in a rather flat formation round out the pattern. The volume pattern emphasizes that volume is usually higher on the left side of the formation than the right.

In early January, prices zoom upward and make a smaller peak at 27½. Since the rise is so steep, our intrepid investor thinks, *why sell the stock when it is going to go higher?* He is right. Prices retrace a bit then move higher and form the head at a price of 28⅝. Once the head completes, things start to go wrong for our buddy. He is swayed by glowing predictions on the Internet of the stock moving up to 35 or 40 within a year.

At the top, prices round over and start down. They stop midway between the troughs of the two left shoulders before making one final attempt at a new high. Up to this point, there are several opportunities to sell the stock at a good price. Did our novice investor take them? Probably not. Always optimistic that prices will ultimately break out and reach higher ground, he does not see the budding complex head-and-shoulders formation for what it is: a warning.

When prices drop below the neckline, our novice investor has just 2 short days before things really get going. By the third day things are looking grim as the stock closes at 23, near the low for the day. Prices quickly unravel and ultimately reach a low of 15, just a few dollars above the purchase price. That is when our investor throws in the towel and sells the stock. Of course, this is near the low and the stock ultimately climbs to 30 a year later.

Identification Guidelines

How can our novice investor recognize the bearish reversal? Table 21.1 outlines some identification tips of a complex head-and-shoulders top.

Consider Figure 21.3, another example of a multiple shoulder chart pattern. After a decline from a head-and-shoulders formation just off the left side of the chart, prices decline until reaching bottom at the start of July. Then they rise up, haltingly, and form a new head-and-shoulders formation: a complex top. If you ignore the labels for a moment, the inner price action looks like a rounding top. This smooth price rollover is common for complex head-and-shoulder formations. Of course, the flat head shape for a multiple shoulder pattern (Figure 21.2) is also typical.

You can divide Figure 21.3 into a pure head-and-shoulders formation by ignoring the outer shoulders. For single-head formations, this is the easiest way to correctly identify a complex head-and-shoulders top. First locate a regular head-and-shoulders pattern then expand your view to include additional shoulders. In this example, the head rises above the surrounding shoulders. The two shoulders are usually equidistant, or nearly so, from the head. The price level of the left and right shoulders is very nearly the same. Thus, the

Table 21.1
Identification Characteristics of Complex Head-and-Shoulders Tops

Characteristic	Discussion
Shape	A head-and-shoulders top with multiple shoulders or, more rarely, two heads. The head is higher than the shoulders but generally not by very much.
Symmetry	The tendency for the shoulders to mirror themselves about the head is strong. The price level of the shoulders and time distance from the shoulder to head is about the same on either side of the head. The shoulders also appear to be the same shape: Narrow or wide shoulders on the left mirror those on the right.
Volume	Usually higher on the left side than on the right and is usually seen when comparing the shoulders on the left with corresponding ones on the right. Overall, the volume trend recedes.
Neckline	Connects the lowest left shoulder trough with the lowest right shoulder trough. When the line extends and intersects prices, that signals a breakout.
Downside breakout	When prices close below the neckline, a breakout occurs. For those cases with a steep, down-sloping neckline, use the lowest trough price as the breakout point.

Figure 21.3 A more rounded appearing complex head-and-shoulders top. Left shoulder 1 and right shoulder 1 could be considered part of the inner head-and-shoulders formation. The inner head-and-shoulders looks like a rounding top formation.

symmetry of a complex head-and-shoulders top is more pronounced than a regular head-and-shoulders formation.

In a regular head-and-shoulders formation, one shoulder may be higher in price than the other or one shoulder will be much further away from the head—a rather extended shoulder. That is usually not the case with the complex variety. Symmetry is paramount and a key identification element.

Moving to the outer shoulders, they also are equidistant from the head and are very nearly at the same price level as well. Continuing the symmetry example, the two peaks labeled left shoulder 1 and right shoulder 1 appear to be shoulders of the same formation, although further away than the inner grouping.

If you consider the inner quad of shoulders as part of the head, then what remains is a large, regular head-and-shoulders formation. This is denoted by left shoulder 1, right shoulder 1, and the large, rounded head (composed of five minor highs). Even the neckline supports this example as prices touch the line several times before dropping through it in a 1-day decline of about four points.

If you could zoom in on the volume pattern, you would see it is marginally heavier on the left side of the formation than on the right, at least for the formation bounded by the inner (higher) neckline. High volume on the left side of the formation as compared to the right is typical for complex head-and-shoulders formations and occurs about two-thirds of the time.

The neckline joins the lows of the lowest trough and is interpreted the same way as a normal head-and-shoulders top. Once prices pierce the neckline, a downside breakout occurs and prices move lower. Volume typically rises on a breakout and can remain high for several days, depending on the severity of the decline.

Focus on Failures

Complex head-and-shoulders patterns suffer two types of failures. Both are rare. Figure 21.4 shows the first type. I define a downside breakout as a close below the neckline, or in the case of steep necklines, a close below the lowest shoulder trough. Figure 21.4 shows prices declining below the neckline only once on May 8 but closing above it. From that point, prices rise and move above the highest head and an upside breakout occurs.

The formation itself is well formed. It has two heads at about the same level and two shoulders also near the same price level. Symmetry throughout the formation looks good, too, as the shoulders are equidistant from the head. Volume appears heavier on the left shoulder than on the right, as you would expect. Only during the decline from the right head to the right shoulder does

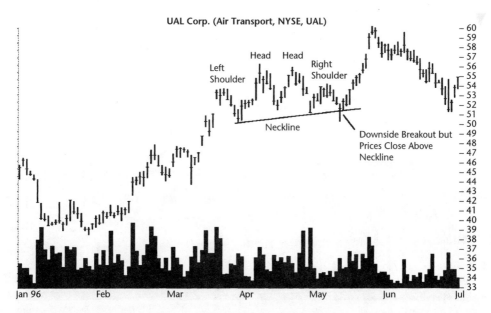

Figure 21.4 A complex head-and-shoulders failure to reverse. Prices fail to close below the neckline before moving above the formation top and staging an upside breakout.

volume rise. In short, there is no real indication that this formation will fail to continue moving down, but it does.

Figure 21.5 shows a slightly different picture. The multiple-shoulder formation appears less balanced. The shoulders are somewhat less even and not equidistant from the head. However, it is a complex head-and-shoulders top with a downside breakout. Unfortunately, prices fail to continue moving down. The stock suffers a 1-day drop of $2, but then rises in an ascending broadening wedge pattern. The wedge is a bearish pattern that breaks out downward but it too fails to descend very far. Within a few months, the stock is again making new highs.

Returning to the complex head-and-shoulders pattern, I regard the formation as a failure because prices fail to move down by more than 5% after the breakout. A 5% decline should take prices to 49⅝, but the actual decline is well above that.

Are there any clues to the failure of this formation? The volume pattern is flat. It shows no tendency to diminish over time. A receding volume pattern is not a hard-and-fast rule so I do not consider this pattern to be that unusual. To answer the question, I see no real clues as to why the formation does not continue moving down. A closer examination of the fundamentals on the company may provide some clues.

Figure 21.5 Another failure of a complex head-and-shoulders top. This one fails to decline more than 5% below the breakout point. An ascending broadening wedge takes shape in late November and December.

Statistics

As alarming as the two figures may appear (Figures 21.4 and 21.5), one has to balance failures with the realization that they do not occur very often. Table 21.2 shows that only 11 out of 141 formations fail to move down by more than 5%. That gives a 92% success rate. In the vast majority of cases I studied, the formation acts as a trend reversal. Once prices break out downward, they continue down by more than 5%. In their quest to reach the ultimate low, prices decline by an average of 27%.

The most likely decline is somewhat harder than usual to determine. Figure 21.6 shows a frequency distribution of declines with a 10% interval between bins. The figure shows the most likely decline is 20%. Subdividing the interval into 5% bins shows the frequency for many bins is within a few hits of the others. The 5% chart suggests the declines can range from 10% to 30%, almost equally.

The Trading Tactics section discusses the measure rule in detail, but it involves computing the formation height and subtracting it from the breakout value. The measure rule provides a minimum price target that hits 67% of the time. This is lower than the 80% I like to see, so one should consider the possibility of falling shy of the target before placing a trade.

Table 21.2
General Statistics for Complex Head-and-Shoulder Tops

Description	Statistic
Number of formations in 500 stocks from 1991 to 1996	141
Reversal or consolidation	15 consolidations, 126 reversals
Failure rate	11 or 8%
Average decline of successful formations	27%
Most likely decline	20%
Of those succeeding, number meeting or exceeding price target (measure rule)	87 or 67%
Average formation length	3 months (83 days)
Number of successful formations showing downward volume trend	89 or 63%
Average performance of formations with down-sloping necklines versus up-sloping necklines	27% versus 26%
Average performance of formations with higher left shoulder (farthest on left versus farthest on right) versus higher right shoulder	28% versus 27%

Note: The complex head-and-shoulders pattern takes longer to form and declines further than regular head-and-shoulder formations.

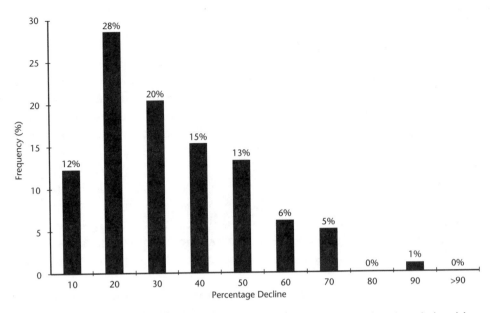

Figure 21.6 Frequency distribution of declines for complex head-and-shoulders tops. The most likely decline is 20%.

The formation is about 3 weeks longer (83 days total) than a regular head-and-shoulders formation. This should come as no surprise since it requires more time for another set of shoulders or heads to appear.

Almost two-thirds (63%) of the formations have a downward volume trend. A line formed using linear regression on the volume data makes the determination. Most of the time the line slopes downward and indicates volume is receding.

Some analysts suggest that a down-sloping neckline implies an especially bearish situation. I found this to be true, but the difference (with an average decline of 27% versus 26%) may not be statistically significant. In the calculation, I used the lowest of the two shoulder troughs to determine the slope of the neckline.

In a similar manner, high left shoulders, when compared to their right counterparts, suggest a more bearish outlook. Again, I found this to be true with formations that have higher left shoulders suffering a decline averaging 28% versus 27%. For this study, I used the outermost shoulders as the benchmark. Since the two numbers are so close to each other, the difference may not be meaningful.

Table 21.3 shows breakout statistics. There are only three upside breakouts, with the remainder being downward (138, or 98%). Once a downward breakout occurs, the formations must continue moving down by at least 5% or else they are 5% failures. Eight formations (6%) fall into this category.

Table 21.3
Breakout Statistics for Complex Head-and-Shoulders Tops

Description	Statistic
Upside breakout	3 or 2%
Downside breakout	138 or 98%
Downside breakout but failure	8 or 6%
Pullbacks	88 or 64%
Average time to pullback completion	10 days
For successful formations, days to ultimate low	3.5 months (110 days)
Percentage of breakouts occurring near 12-month price low (L), center (C), or high (H)	L6%, C47%, H48%
Percentage loss for each 12-month lookback period	L22%, C28%, H26%
Volume for breakout day and next 5 days compared with day before breakout	175%, 170%, 138%, 120%, 112%, 106%

Note: Nearly all the formations (98%) have downside breakouts.

Pullbacks, which are prices that break out downward but return to the neckline within 30 days, are quite numerous at 88 (64%) of formations, suggesting that if you miss the breakout, wait. A pullback may occur, allowing you to place a short sale at a higher price. Of course, if the stock fails to pull back, then look elsewhere for a more promising situation. Never chase the stock as you will buy into a situation that may soon reverse and go against you.

The average time for the pullback to return to the neckline is 10 days. Many of the formations have pullbacks occurring just a few days after a breakout. The average is skewed upward by several outliers that take over 3 weeks (but less than a month) before returning to the neckline.

On average, it takes $3\frac{1}{2}$ months to reach the ultimate low. When we combine this statistic with those in Table 21.2, we discover that these formations are wide, suffer a more severe decline, and take longer to reach the ultimate low. In that regard, the complex head-and-shoulders formation is more powerful than a regular head-and-shoulders reversal.

Most of the formations occur in the center third (47%) or upper third (48%) of the yearly price range. Only 6% of the formations break out near the yearly low. The results make sense in that the price trend rises to the formation, effectively elevating the breakout point out of the lower regions. If you filter the percentage loss for each of the formations over their yearly price range, you see that the largest declines occur in the center third of the price range. The formations in that category decline by an average of 28%. Quite close to this are formations with breakouts in the top third of the yearly price range, with an average decline of 26%.

Volume is unusually high for several days after a breakout. You can see the trend in Table 21.3. Volume starts out high, 75% above the prior day (or 175% of the total volume), but recedes to near the average by the following week.

Trading Tactics

The measure rule predicts the minimum expected decline. Look at Figure 21.7 as an example of the measure rule outlined in Table 21.4. Compute the formation height by subtracting the difference between the highest high ($31\frac{5}{8}$) from the value of the neckline directly below the highest high (27). Subtract the result ($4\frac{5}{8}$) from the breakout price ($25\frac{3}{4}$), which is where declining prices pierce the neckline. Prices drop below the target price of $21\frac{1}{8}$ in early March.

This is the conventional measuring rule and it is successful 67% of the time. That is below the 80% success rate I like to see for measure rules. The conventional method also has a flaw when the neckline slopes steeply. Under such circumstances, prices may never pierce the neckline and yet the stock is tumbling. Fortunately, the neckline rarely slopes steeply in complex forma-

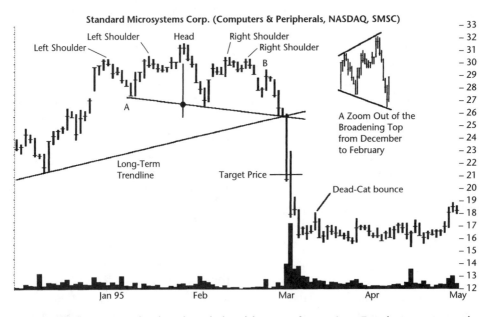

Figure 21.7 A complex head-and-shoulders top formation. For the measure rule, compute the difference between the highest high and the neckline, measured vertically, and subtract the result from the breakout price. A broadening top appears from December through February and a dead-cat bounce follows.

Table 21.4
Trading Tactics for Complex Head-and-Shoulders Tops

Trading Tactic	Explanation
Measure rule	Compute the formation height by subtracting the neckline value from the highest high reached in the head, measured vertically. Subtract the result from the breakout price where prices pierce the neckline. The result is the minimum target price. If the formation looks like a mountain suddenly appearing out of a flat base, prices may return to the base. See Figures 21.2 and 21.5.
Do not wait for confirmation	If you can determine that a complex head-and-shoulders top formation is completing, consider acting immediately. Place a short trade or sell any long commitments. This formation rarely disappoints and the decline is above average. Should prices rebound at the neckline, reestablish your position.
Short stop	Look for resistance areas about the neckline troughs. Place a stop just above the higher shoulder trough. The shoulder tops and head also represent good locations for stop-loss orders.
Watch for pullback	Place a short sale or add to the position during a pullback. Wait for prices to begin falling again before placing the trade as prices sometimes pull back and continue moving up.

tions. However, if you do run across a formation with a plunging neckline, use the lowest of the shoulder troughs as the breakout price. Compute the formation height in the normal manner, but subtract the height from the trough value to get a target price.

A slightly more conservative measure rule computes the formation height from the highest high to the higher of the neckline troughs. Then subtract the result from the higher of the neckline troughs and the result is the target price. This method results in 76% of the formations meeting the measure rule, which is still short of the 80% I like to see.

Using the chart pattern shown in Figure 21.7 as an example, the highest high is at $31\frac{5}{8}$ and the higher of the two neckline troughs is at point A, $27\frac{1}{2}$ (using the daily low price). This gives a formation height of $4\frac{1}{8}$ ($31\frac{5}{8} - 27\frac{1}{2}$) and a target price of $23\frac{3}{8}$ (or $27\frac{1}{2} - 4\frac{1}{8}$). Prices reach the target during the large 1-day decline on March 2.

If the head-and-shoulders formation does *not* occur after an extended upward trend—the situation shown in Figure 21.1—then prices will probably drop back to the low where the formation began. In Figure 21.1, the low just before prices start rising to the formation is about 28. That is the level to which prices return after the breakout.

At other times, the formation will suddenly shoot up from a base, then just as quickly return to the base. Figures 21.2 and 21.5 show examples of this situation.

Since the complex head-and-shoulders top is so reliable, once you are *sure* you have a valid pattern, take advantage of it. If you own the stock, sell it. If you do not own the stock, short it. For short positions, look for areas of strength—resistance levels—and place a stop-loss order just above that level. Common resistance levels are the shoulder troughs, shoulder tops, and head top. Should the price rise above the highest high, immediately cover the short position as it is an upside breakout and likely to continue soaring.

Be aware that prices sometimes break out downward, then regroup and rise above the neckline before plunging down again (see Figures 21.1 and 21.3). These extended pullbacks and regular pullbacks are good places to initiate a short sale or add to a position.

Sample Trade

Henry runs a small hedge fund. He considered buying into the stock shown in Figure 21.7 but needed more bullish evidence. Two weeks later he got his signal. Prices pushed up through a long-term, down-sloping trendline in August 1994. Other indicators he uses on a daily basis confirmed the buy signal, so he bought shares for his fund at an average price of about 17¼.

As the stock climbed, he followed its progress and checked periodically on the fundamentals. The ride up was not an easy one because the stock began acting oddly from October through early December. At one point during that period, it looked as if a broadening top was forming, but the price action changed enough that the formation fell apart.

The stock bounced between 21 and 25 several times then pushed its way to higher highs. Henry suspected the end was near, so he began taking a closer look at the fundamentals. He was so engrossed with his research on the company that he failed to notice a pattern forming. Over drinks with his fund manager friends, he shared with them what he had dug up about the company. The news was not good.

"So that's why it's making a broadening top!" one remarked. Henry furrowed his brow and pictured the price action in his mind and there it was, a broadening top, just like his friend had said.

The next day Henry pulled up the chart and looked at it more closely. He saw higher highs and lower lows (see the zoom out in Figure 21.7), characteristic of a broadening pattern. Coupled with his fundamental research on the company, he knew it was nearing time to sell, but not yet. He wanted to sell at the top, when prices tagged the top trendline.

In early February, when prices attempted to reach the previous high, they fell short, dipped down for a few days, and tried again (the two right shoulders).

The second rise was even shorter than the prior one, signaling weakness, so Henry started selling immediately.

The failure to sail across the formation and touch the top of the broadening formation meant it was a partial rise. A partial rise in a broadening top usually means one thing: A downside breakout will follow.

By the time the stock pulled back up to the base of the two right shoulders (point B), Henry had sold his holdings. As he was getting ready to leave his office for home, something on his computer screen caught his eye. The broadening pattern had changed into a complex head-and-shoulders top. There were the two left shoulders balancing the two right ones with a head perched in the center.

Henry discussed the new situation with his mentor and his fund manager buddies, then decided to short the stock. By the time prices reached the long-term up trendline, he had a tidy sum sold short.

Two days later, prices tumbled. They dropped 20% or $5 a share in 1 day and continued down. In less than a week, they were at 16 before finding some support, a plummet of 36%.

Henry had studied the behavior of dead-cat bounces, and he pulled out his notes and brushed up. He knew the stock would bounce upward, usually within a week, then trend lower.

True to form, prices moved up a bit (to $18\frac{1}{8}$), but it was not the smooth, rounded bounce he expected. In the coming days, prices moved lower, so Henry quit complaining, but he watched the situation closely.

The stock bottomed out at about 16 and trended horizontally. To him, it looked as if the stock was building a base and preparing for an upward move, so he covered half his short position.

In late April, when prices jumped up to $18\frac{1}{2}$, he immediately covered the remainder of his position. In the pub that evening with his buddies, he was all smiles. He was feeling so good that he decided to pick up the tab.

22

Horn Bottoms

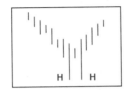

I first discovered this formation while pondering a result from my study of double bottoms. Double bottom formations with bottoms closer together perform better than those spaced widely apart. What would happen if you considered formations that have bottoms only a week or so apart? I tested the idea and discovered that the formation performs well. The failure rate at 11% is well below the 20% maximum rate I allow for reliable formations.

The average rise at 37% is below the usual 40% gains posted by other bullish formations. Such large gains do not happen overnight. A frequency distribution of the time it takes to reach the ultimate high shows most horn bottoms falling into the long-term category (taking over 6 months to reach the ultimate high).

I reviewed a number of criteria to improve the performance of horns. The criterion responsible for the most improvement is when the horn length is longer than most spikes over the prior year (at least twice as long). The average gain rises to 43%.

Tour

Figure 22.1 shows what a horn bottom looks like. After peaking in late December 1993, prices plummet from a high of $50\frac{3}{4}$ to the horn low at a base of $30\frac{3}{4}$. On the left side of the horn, prices have a large weekly price range of about $7. High volume makes the week appear like a one-week reversal (with the same attributes as a one-day reversal but over the course of a week), signaling a possible trend change.

The following week, prices close lower but nowhere near the left horn low. Then, 1 week later, prices spike lower again but close near the high of the week and just $\frac{1}{8}$ below the prior close. The horn bottom is complete: A double price spike separated by 1 week marks the turning point. From that point, prices move up and more than double from the horn low in about a year and a half.

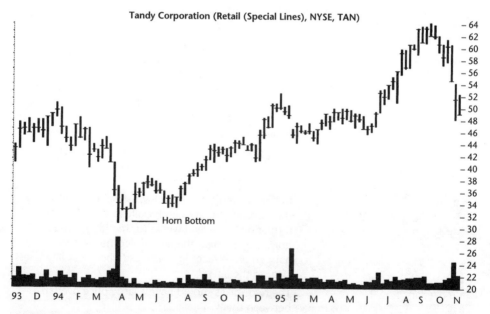

Figure 22.1   A good example of a horn bottom. Two downward price spikes, separated by a week, look like a steer's horn flipped upside down.

Identification Guidelines

How do you correctly identify horn bottoms? Table 22.1 shows identification characteristics. In essence, the characteristics define the shape of an inverted horn that is clearly distinguishable from the surrounding price action.

Consider Figure 22.2 that shows two horn bottoms. What might strike you first about the left formation is its similarity to Figure 22.1. The stock shown in Figure 22.2 tumbles from a price of almost 25 in August 1991 to a low of just 6½ at the right horn spike in less than 2 years. Then prices recover and move higher.

Horns are visible on weekly charts. Although they appear on daily charts, weekly charts make selection easier. For the formation on the left in Figure 22.2, the chart shows two long, downward price spikes separated by a week. The low of the center week stays well above either of the spike lows, emphasizing the inverted horn shape of the formation.

Looking back over the months, you can see that there are no downward spikes that come near the length of the horn spikes (as measured from the lowest low to the lower of the two adjacent weeks). The twin horns mark an unusual event, one that an investor should pay attention to.

Table 22.1
Identification Characteristics of Weekly Horn Bottoms

Characteristic	Discussion
Weekly chart, downward spikes	Use the weekly chart and locate two downward price spikes separated by a week. The two spikes should be longer than similar spikes over the prior year and be well below the low of the center week. It should look like an inverted horn. Abnormally long spikes result in better performance.
Small price variation	The price difference between the two lows of the horn is small, usually ⅜ or less, but can vary up to $1 or more for higher priced stocks.
Clear visibility	In a downtrend, the horn lows should be well below the surrounding lows, especially to the left of the formation for several weeks (or months). Usually, horns appear near the end of declines but also happen on retraces in uptrends (where visibility is less clear to the left).
Large overlap	The two spikes should have a large price overlap between them.
High volume	The left spike shows higher than average volume (54% of the time) and the right spike shows *below* average volume (52% of the time). However, these are only guidelines and volume varies greatly from formation to formation.

The price difference between the two horn lows is usually small, about ⅜ or less. Higher priced stocks can show larger differences (but on a percentage basis, the differences are minimal). In Figure 22.2, the difference between the two spikes is just $0.25 (for the left formation).

For the left formation, the horn appears after a downward price trend, allowing clear visibility to the left of the formation, as no downward trends or price outliers obscure the view. This is important in that the formation should stand alone and not be part of a congestion region. It should mark the turning point of a downward price trend.

Price overlap is quite good for the formation, with the two horn spikes nearly the same size but the left one shifts upward.

The formation shown on the right of the chart in Figure 22.2 is what a horn bottom looks like in an uptrend. There is a small price retrace, of 3 weeks' duration, just as the horn bottoms out. These few weeks separate the formation from the surrounding price action and allow easy recognition.

The two spikes share the same low price, 14½, and have good price overlap (as the right spike almost completely overlaps the left one). You can argue that the separation of the horn low from the surrounding weeks is not exceptional when compared with the pipe formations in early December and late June. That is certainly true, but most of the prices show remarkably even bottoms, not a jagged coastline.

The volume trend on this formation is unusual as both horns show below average volume. The left formation shows a different volume trend as both horns sport above average volume. The statistics say that the left side of the

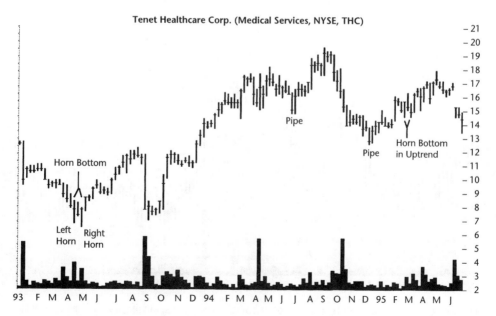

Figure 22.2 Two examples of horns, one in a downward trend and one in an uptrend. Notice that the second pipe formation calls the turn exactly.

horn bottom will have *above* average volume 54% of the time, whereas the right will have *below* average volume just 52% of the time. Since both figures are quite close to 50%, it really can go either way, so I would not place too much emphasis on volume.

Focus on Failures

Even though horn bottoms sport a low failure rate (at 11%), they still have failures. Consider Figure 22.3, a 5% failure or a horn bottom. A 5% failure is when prices start out in the correct direction but falter (rising by no more than 5%), turn around, and head back down. The twin, downward price spikes look good in that they are long and with good overlap. They form as part of a retrace from the high, and prices usually return to form a second high (a double top), or perhaps move even higher. If you believe that this stock will form a second top, then this formation is probably not worth betting on as the price appreciation potential is just not exciting enough.

If you look at this formation differently, you might suspect that it will form a head-and-shoulders top. The left shoulder is already visible in late May 1994 and another shoulder could form as part of a mirror image, probably in April or May of 1995. If that is the case, then you should also pass this one up as the right shoulder might top out at about 16. This assumes prices continue

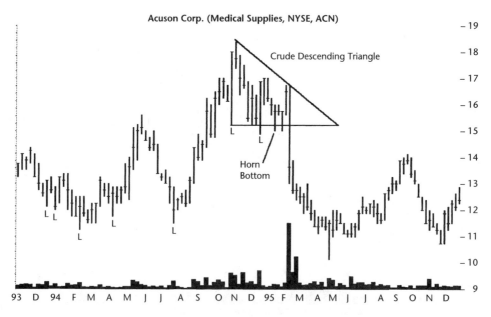

Figure 22.3 A horn bottom failure. Among other clues, similar length price spikes (marked L) suggest this formation might be suspect. The descending triangle suggests lower prices.

moving lower and probably stop dropping in the 10 to 12 range (forming the neckline) before moving up to the right shoulder. Since prices should drop, why buy now?

Another clue to this formation failure is the spikes themselves. If you look over the prior prices, you see several downward price spikes that rival the length of the horn. These are warning signs that this horn might not be anything special.

The visibility is poor because earlier prices block the view. Usually, prices have lows that move down in sync with the remainder of the prices (like that shown in the February to April 1995 decline). A horn appearing in a sharp decline should have good visibility to the left of the formation. In this case, the horn bottom has competing prices to the left of it, blocking its view. What this tells us is that prices seem to form a base while their tops are declining. In other words, a descending triangle is forming and the investor should be wary.

Taken together, there seems to be ample evidence that this horn might not work out as expected. But, statistically, how often do horn bottoms fail?

Statistics

Table 22.2 shows statistics for horn bottoms. The chart pattern is quite plentiful, occurring almost 300 times in 500 stocks over 5 years. Of these formations, 160 are consolidations of the prevailing trend, whereas the remainder act as reversals. A closer examination of the data shows that 88% of the reversals occur when prices are moving down—they reverse direction and head up after the formation.

Most of the consolidations are also in a downtrend, with 70% showing prices moving down over the prior month. The longer-term trend (over 3 months), however, is upward 65% of the time. In other words, the overall

Table 22.2
General Statistics for Weekly Horn Bottoms

Description	Statistic
Number of formations in 500 stocks from 1991 to 1996	296
Reversal or consolidation	160 consolidations, 136 reversals
Failure rate	34 or 11%
Average rise of successful formations	37%
Most likely rise	20% to 30%
Left, right horn volume versus 25-day moving average	146%, 116%
For successful formations, days to ultimate high	9 months (265 days)

price trend is up, then consolidates (moves down or retraces) for a month before continuing up.

The failure rate is quite low at 11%, well below the 20% maximum for reliable formations. Almost all the formations work as expected by moving up more than 5%. The average rise is 37%, with the most likely rise falling between 20% and 30%, a strong showing.

I computed the values using the average of the highest high and lowest low the week after the formation ends (the week following the right horn spike). This assumes that an investor buys the stock the week after noticing the horn and receives a fill at the midrange value. It also assumes that he sells out at the highest possible price (the ultimate high) before a significant trend change occurs (a price change of 20% or more).

Figure 22.4 shows a graphic representation of the price gains. It is created using a frequency distribution to eliminate any undue skewing of the average by large percentage gains. You can see in Figure 22.4 that the rightmost column is quite large, showing 11% of the formations with gains over 90%. The remainder of the chart takes on the appearance of a bell-shaped curve.

I classify the *most likely gain* as the column(s) with the highest frequency (not including the rightmost column). In Figure 22.4, these are 20% and 30%, so the most likely gain should fall in that region. However, the adjacent columns, 10% and 40%, are nearly as high, so the range might be wider. Of course, your results will vary.

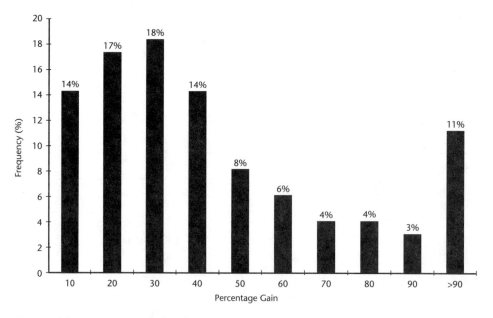

Figure 22.4 Frequency distribution of gains for horn bottoms. The most likely gains are in the 20% to 30% range if you ignore the rightmost column.

Volume for the horns, when compared to a 25-day moving average of volume, is 146% for the left horn spike and 116% for the right horn spike. These figures emphasize that there is quite high volume on the left spike and somewhat diminished volume on the right one, on average. A count shows that 54% of the left spikes have *above* average volume, whereas 52% of the right spikes have *below* average volume.

For those formations that move higher by more than 5%, it takes them 9 months to reach the ultimate high, on average. That is a comparatively long time for a bullish bottom.

Table 22.3 shows some interesting statistics of horn bottoms. The benchmark, the average gain for the formation, is 37% with a failure rate of 11%.

Table 22.3
Surprising Results for Horn Bottoms

Description	Average Rise (%)	Failure Rate (%)
Benchmark	37	11
Rise for horns with price differences between lows	38	
Rise for horns with no price difference between lows	36	
Performance of horns with lower right (R) spikes versus horns with lower left (L) spikes	L37, R40	
Rise when the right horn is an inside week	33	
Rise when right horn is an outside week	39	
Performance for high volume left (L) horns, right (R) horns, and both (B) horns	L38, R37, B37	13 for both right and left horns
Performance for low volume left (L) horns, right (R) horns, and both (B) horns	L37, R37, B35	
High left horn volume, low right horn volume	40	7
High right horn volume, low left horn volume	38	
Linear regression price trend: 3 months up	37	
Linear regression price trend: 3 months down	38	
Large price spike (2× average)	43	12
High volume left, low volume right, down-sloping 3-month price trends	34	14

When comparing the low price between the two horn spikes, those formations with a price difference show gains averaging 38%, whereas those with no price difference have gains of 36%. In essence, you can expect horns with uneven low prices to do better. Since horns with uneven low prices perform better, which is more profitable: formations showing a lower left horn or a lower right one? Horns with a lower right spike perform better, showing a 40% average gain, whereas those horns with a lower left spike have gains averaging 37%.

I also looked at the high prices and discovered that inside weeks perform poorly (with gains of just 33%). Inside weeks are just like inside days in that the high is below the prior high and the low is above the prior low. The price range is inside the range of the prior week (or day). I ignored the intervening week (that is, the week between the two spikes) in the comparison.

I checked on outside weeks, where the right horn high is above the left horn high and the right horn low is below the left horn low (no ties allowed). Horns meeting the criteria show gains averaging 39%. Again, the comparison ignores the center week.

For the following comparisons, I define high volume as being above the 25-day moving average and low volume as being below the 25-day moving average. Do high volume horns score better? Yes, but the difference is minimal. High volume on the left horn works best, showing gains of 38%, whereas low volume left horns have gains of 37%. Gains for horns with high or low volume on the right horn ties at 37%. In other words, those formations with high volume on the right horn show the same gains as those with low volume on the right horn. When volume is high on both horns, the chart pattern has an average gain of 37%, and horns with low volume on both spikes have gains of 35%. With high volume on both horns, the failure rate increases slightly to 13%.

Measuring the different combinations, high left and low right horn volume shows a 40% gain and a failure rate of 7%. The opposite combination, low left and high right volume, has gains of 38%.

I used linear regression on the closing prices to determine the existing price trend leading to the formation. Do horn bottoms perform better after prices have been trending down for 3 months or trending up? The results are a wash, with a 37% gain for those horns in a rising price trend and a 38% gain for those in a downtrend.

Do large downward price spikes perform better? Yes, with gains of 43% but the failure rate rises slightly to 12%. To arrive at this determination, I computed the spike length from the lowest low to the lowest adjacent low (on either side) over the prior year leading to the formation. I averaged the values together to get an average spike length and compared it to the horn length.

Think of the comparison using your fingers: I measured the difference between your middle fingertip and the closer of the two adjacent fingertips. Those horns that are at least twice the average length perform better than shorter ones.

Putting many of the tests together—high volume on the left horn, low volume on the right one, and a down-sloping price trend over 3 months—shows gains of 34% and a failure rate of 14%. Since these various factors are simply trying to tune the database for highest performance, your results will vary. Scanning the table for the best value shows that when horn spikes are abnormally long, at least double most spikes over the prior year, then performance improves.

Trading Tactics

Table 22.4 outlines trading tactics and begins with the measure rule. There is none. Since horn bottoms have no measure rule, there is little guidance that I can suggest on when to take profits or how well a formation will perform. However, once you identify a horn bottom using the guidelines outlined in Table 22.1, then buy the stock.

Perhaps the most important key to horn bottoms is that they should continue to look like horns (see "Clear visibility" in Table 22.1). Prices should climb after the twin horn spikes. If you need to wait an extra week or two to prove this occurs, then do so.

Separate the price trend leading to the formation into either an uptrend or downtrend. Horns that appear late in uptrends may mark the end of the upward price move. Prices continue moving higher (perhaps by 10% or so), then stop. Of course, if your horn appears at the start of an uptrend, then prices might well be on their way to a large gain.

Horns in downtrends are common. On the one hand, if the downtrend is just a retrace of the prevailing uptrend, then refer to the uptrend guideline. In

Table 22.4
Trading Tactics for Horn Bottoms

Trading Tactic	Explanation
Measure rule	None
Identify	Use the characteristics outlined in Table 22.1 to correctly identify a horn bottom. The week after the right horn is key. Prices should climb smartly and the weekly low should not be anywhere near the horn low (in other words, the horn should still look like a horn and not be encroached on by the succeeding price action).
Uptrends	Some horns appear near the end of uptrends, so watch for the trend to change.
Downtrends	Horns will usually not mark the end of the downtrend, but they will be close. Prices might continue to drift down for $1 or so (below the lowest horn low) then head upward.
Stops	If you can afford the loss, place a stop $1 below the lowest horn to reduce the chance that a retest of the low will stop you out.

such a case, if the horn appears after an extensive advance, then the uptrend may be nearly over. Invest cautiously or look elsewhere.

On the other hand, if the stock has been trending downward for a long time (for months anyway), then the end might be in sight. The horn probably will not mark the low exactly, but it should be close. Usually, horns appear a month or so before or after the actual turning point.

If prices are trending down and you see a horn forming, you might wait before buying the stock, just to be sure prices have really turned around. For uptrends, you probably should buy into the situation immediately since prices will only climb away from you and get more expensive.

Place a stop loss up to $1 or so below the lowest low. For low-priced stocks, this may mean taking a significant loss. In such a case, perhaps it is best to skip the trade and look elsewhere. The reason for placing the stop well below the lowest horn low is to allow prices time to turn around. Prices sometimes curl around and retest the low (moving $1 or so below the horn low) before recovering and trending upward.

Sample Trade

Mary saw the horn bottom forming in the stock pictured in Figure 22.5. To her the chart suggested prices would continue moving up. Prices certainly climbed above the right horn low (at 31) quite smartly, leaving the horn clearly visible on the weekly chart.

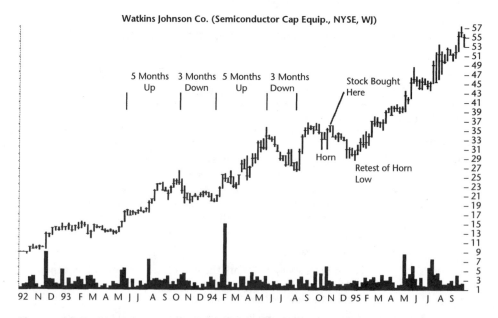

Figure 22.5 Horn bottom on weekly chart. Mary was stopped out during the throwback just before prices doubled.

Looking back at the entire price chart, she saw prices begin climbing in early October 1992 at a low of 8⅝. From that point, they soared to the current price in several waves. Waves pushing prices higher took between 4 and 5 months, whereas those moving lower took 3 months.

When the horn formed, the 5-month up pattern was in progress; that is what she hoped anyway. She bought the stock the week after the horn completed at 35. She hoped the horn marked an end to the short retrace and prices would resume their upward trend. She was wrong. When prices curled around, she placed a stop at 30⅞ — ⅛ below the lowest horn low. She suspected that this might not be low enough, but a 12% loss was all she was willing to tolerate.

In early December, her worst fears were confirmed. She was stopped out as prices plummeted from 33 to 29. Three weeks later the stock hit bottom at 28½ and turned around. From high to low, the decline lasted just over 3 months, as she predicted. Prices moved swiftly upward and topped out at 57, exactly double the low.

Did Mary sell too soon and pass up her chance to nearly double her money or did she use prudent money management to limit her losses? Those questions are ones we all face with eventually. Do you know the answer?

23

Horn Tops

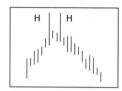

RESULTS SNAPSHOT

Appearance	Two upward price spikes separated by a week on the weekly chart
Reversal or consolidation	Either, with short-term (up to 3 months) bearish implications
Failure rate	16%
Average decline	21%, with most likely loss about 10%
Surprising finding	The failure rate drops to 6% when the volume on both spikes is below the 25-day volume moving average.
See also	Double Tops; Pipe Tops

As you look at the Results Snapshot statistics, you have to ask yourself one question: Why would you ever want to trade this formation? With a likely loss of just 10%, you probably would be a fool to short a stock based on this formation. However, if you trade enough and with luck, your returns should approach the average of 21%. The kicker is horn tops take less than 4½ months to reach the ultimate low, on average. Annualizing the returns gives a score of 58%, enough to warrant a closer look.

A surprising finding is that when the volume on both spikes is low, below the 25-day moving average, then the failure rate drops to 6% while still maintaining a 21% average decline. That is something to keep in mind if you trade this formation.

Tour

With many formations, there is usually a mirror image; with double bottoms, for example, there are double tops. So it is with this formation. Chapter 22 discussed horn bottoms and this chapter talks about horn tops. Having discovered the bottoms, I wondered if the tops would work out as well. First, though, what do horn tops look like?

Figure 23.1 shows an example of a timely horn top. If you read Chapter 22 on their bottom siblings, then horn tops should come as no surprise. A horn top is an inverted version of the weekly horn bottom. A horn top sports twin peaks separated by a week and is commonly found near the end of an uptrend. Volume is usually heavy at both peaks but not by a huge margin above the 25-day moving average. After the right price spike, prices drop lower and continue moving down, sometimes substantially.

In Figure 23.1 the stock begins its rise to the horn in mid-June 1993 at a price of $20\frac{3}{8}$. At the peak, prices reach a high of $32\frac{5}{8}$, a gain of 60% in 2 months. With such a sharp gain in so little time, a consolidation or congestion region is likely. Instead, the horn top marks a change in trend. Combined with the earlier top, the double top is a bearish signal.

After the twin peaks of the horn appear, prices drop to 26, then pull back to the formation base, generally following an up-sloping trendline. Then prices

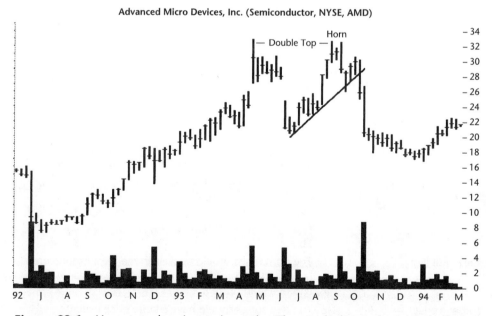

Figure 23.1 Horn top showing twin peaks. The stock drops almost in half after the horn top. Note the weekly time scale. The two peaks in April and August represent a double top.

head down again. In the beginning of January, prices reach bottom at $16\frac{3}{4}$ for a decline of almost 50%.

Identification Guidelines

Table 23.1 shows identification characteristics that make horn tops easy to recognize. Consider the horn shown in Figure 23.2. Use the weekly chart to facilitate identification. Look for twin price spikes that are separated by a week. The two spikes should be well above the surrounding prices (clear visibility) and a good distance from the high in the center week. If you look back over the price history for the year, the two spikes should stand out and be larger than most other spikes. In Figure 23.2, you can see that the price spike in late September is the only real competition (for the period shown, anyway).

The high-to-high price variation between the two spikes is usually small, about $\frac{3}{8}$ or less. Occasionally, some horn tops will show large price discrepancies, but these usually are associated with higher-priced stocks. In the study, no formation had a peak-to-peak price difference of more than $1\frac{1}{4}$. Figure 23.2 shows a price differential of $\frac{3}{8}$ point. It is unusual for the two peaks to end at the same price so expect some price variation.

Price overlap between the two spikes should be large. This guideline means that you should discard any formation that has a long left spike but a very short right one (or vice versa) or two spikes that have few prices in common. Figure 23.2 shows two long spikes with much of their length overlapping.

Table 23.1
Identification Characteristics of Horn Tops

Characteristic	Discussion
Weekly chart, upward spikes	Use the weekly chart and locate two upward price spikes separated by a week. The two spikes should be longer than similar spikes over the prior year and tower above the high of the center week. It should look like a horn.
Small price variation	The price difference between the two horn highs is small, usually $\frac{3}{8}$ or less, but can vary up to $1 or more for higher-priced stocks. Do not expect the horn highs to end at the same price; that only happens 20% of the time.
Clear visibility	The horn highs should be well above the surrounding highs and the best performing reversals appear at the end of a long uptrend.
Large overlap	The two spikes should have a large price overlap.
Low volume	For best performance, look for below average volume on both horn spikes.

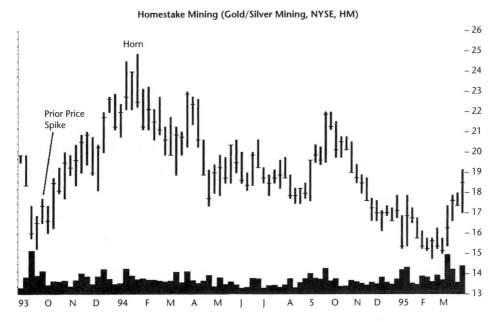

Figure 23.2 Horn tops with unusually tall price spikes. This horn exceeds the clearance of an earlier spike.

The final guideline is not really a guideline at all as much as it is an observation. When the volume on each spike is below the 25-day moving average, then the formation tends to have significantly fewer failures (the rate drops from 16% to 6%).

Focus on Failures

There are a variety of reasons why a particular formation fails. Some break out upward and never look back, whereas others begin moving down, falter, then recover and climb significantly. The latter case, the so-called 5% failures, are predominant with horn tops. Prices fail to continue down by more than 5% before recovering and heading higher. However, with a failure rate of 16%, the rate is still less than the 20% maximum for reliable formations.

Unfortunately, a 5% failure does not tell the complete story. With horn tops the most likely decline is just 10%, hardly enough to cover the cost of making a trade. Still, that performance is about par for bearish reversals in a bull market.

What can be learned from examining the failures? There are 30 failures. Of those formations, 15 precede a meaningful decline in the stock by an average of 2.7 months. Most warn about a coming decline by forming less than 2 months ahead of schedule. That is worth knowing. If a horn fails to call the turn in a stock you own, be alert to a possible trend change coming soon.

You can improve your investment performance if you consider the overall environment for the stock. Look at the horn top pictured in Figure 23.3. After trending down for a year, the stock pierced the down-sloping trendline, signaling a trend change, and moved higher. Then the horn top formed.

In situations like this, after a long downtrend, a stock usually bounces up, curls around, and retests the low (but not always). So when the horn formed, it probably signaled the price top before the retest. Although not shown in Figure 23.3, the stock did move lower, but it first bobbled up for a few months (to 63½). Ultimately, the stock dipped to 49⅛ before recovering.

Before you invest in this formation, you have to place emphasis on the piercing of the down trendline. It suggests that prices will rise (a piercing is one indicator of a trend change). With a price rise imminent, why would you consider shorting the stock? Even though the horn reversal suggests prices will decline (and they do, in the short term, but only by a dollar or so), does it merit a trade?

When there is serious conflict or doubt about a situation, then look elsewhere for a more promising trade. Sure, you might miss making a killing now and again, but you do not want to end up on death row after your trading capital runs out from all the losses you have been taking.

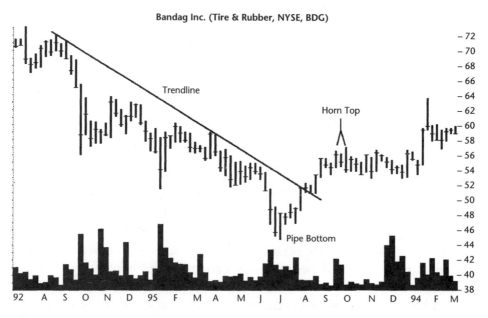

Figure 23.3 Horn top appearing after an extended downtrend. It is probably best to ignore such horn tops. A pipe bottom marks the turning point.

Statistics

Table 23.2 shows statistics for the horn top. I uncovered 188 formations in 500 stocks over 5 years. As far as formations go, horn tops probably rank as somewhat rare, but they are plentiful enough to be a viable trading vehicle.

The formation is almost evenly split among consolidations (92) and reversals (96). The best performing formations are reversals, in which the horn top accurately signals a trend change with prices moving lower.

The failure rate (16%) is good. I consider formations with values below 20% to be reliable. The average decline is 21% for successful formations. However, the most likely decline is just 10% as shown in Figure 23.4. A frequency distribution allows a presentation of the losses without the undue influence of large losses skewing the average. You can see that the highest column is the 10% category, followed by 15%. Figure 23.4 suggests that your losses will probably fall around these two numbers. Clearly 40% of the formations show losses totaling 15% or less. Of course, if you are an optimist, it also means 60% of the formations score better than a 15% decline. That is really not bad for a bearish formation in a bull market.

Table 23.2 shows the average horn volume. The left horn has slightly higher volume on average than the right spike, and they both exceed the 25-day volume moving average.

For those formations that move lower by more than 5% (anything less is a failure, and excluded), they reach the ultimate low in about 4½ months (134 days).

Table 23.3 shows the benchmark, 21% average loss for the 84% of formations in the study that move significantly lower (by falling more than 5%). The remainder of the table highlights different studies to determine the performance of various features of the horn top.

Do horns with uneven high prices perform better than those with the same high price? No. Horn tops in which the highest price is the same on both

Table 23.2
General Statistics for Horn Tops

Description	Statistic
Number of formations in 500 stocks from 1991 to 1996	188
Reversal or consolidation	92 consolidations, 96 reversals
Failure rate	30 or 16%
Average decline of successful formations	21%
Most likely decline	10%
Left, right horn volume versus 25-day moving average	138%, 125%
For successful formations, days to ultimate low	4.5 months (134 days)

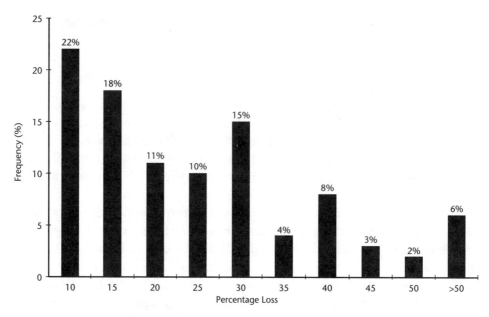

Figure 23.4 Frequency distribution of losses for horn tops. The most likely decline is 10%, with 40% of the formations showing declines of 15% or less.

Table 23.3
Surprising Results for Horn Tops

Description	Average Decline (%)	Failure Rate (%)
Benchmark	21	16
Decline for horns with price differences between highs	21	
Decline for horns with no price difference between highs	23	
Percentage rise for high volume left (L) horns, right (R) horns, and both (B) horns	L21, R22, B21	18 for both right and left horns
Percentage rise for low volume left (L) horn, right (R) horn, both (B) horns	L22, R21, B21	6 for both right and left horns
High left horn volume, low right horn volume	21	
Low left horn volume, high right horn volume	22	
Linear regression price trend 3 months up	22	20
Linear regression price trend 3 months down	20	
Large price spike (3× average)	25	43

Note: Large spike length showed the largest loss but nearly a tripling of the failure rate.

price spikes perform better, with losses averaging 23% versus 21% for formations with uneven high prices.

What are the volume characteristics of horns? The left spike, when accompanied by low volume (below the 25-day volume moving average), performs marginally better than when attended by high volume (22% versus 21%). The reverse is true for the right spike, with 22% losses for those with high volume versus 21% for those with low volume. Performance is 21% when both the right and left spike show high volume (and a similar result for those horns showing low volume on both spikes). When both spikes show below average volume, the failure rate decreases to 6%, well below the benchmark 16% rate. Different combinations such as high left and low right volume on the spike of a horn top show similar losses, namely 21%. The reverse, low left spike volume and high right spike volume, scores a 22% loss. For all the different combinations, there is not a large enough difference between the numbers to bother with a test for significance. Does it really matter whether the average loss is 21% or 22%? Probably not. Incidentally, the phrases *high volume* and *low volume* are comparisons with the 25-day moving average. High volume is when the formation is above the moving average, and low volume is when it is below the moving average. Think of the phrases not as high or low but as above average and below average.

I use linear regression on the weekly price data over a 3-month span to assess the price trend leading to the formation. For those horn tops with rising price trends, the average performance is 22% versus 20% for those with downward sloping trends. Again, not enough of a difference to get excited about.

Formations showing large price spikes outperform the benchmark with a 25% loss. Unfortunately, the loss accompanies a significant deterioration in the failure rate, which climbs to 43%. There are only 28 formations with spikes that are at least three times the average spike length over the prior year. In case you are wondering how spikes twice the normal size do, they show losses averaging 22% accompanied by a failure rate of 27%.

As you look over the values in the table, you can probably surmise that it really does not matter what the horn looks like or how much volume accompanies the formation. In many cases, prices decline, on average, about 20% to 22%. However, to reduce the risk of a failed trade, it is probably wise to choose formations with below average volume on both spikes (thereby reducing the failure rate from 16% to 6%).

Trading Tactics

Table 23.4 outlines trading tactics for horn tops. With a likely decline of just 10% (but an average decline of 21%), should you trade this formation at all? Sure, but it all depends on how it is used. If you own stock in a company that has zoomed upward and forms a horn top, it is time to consider taking profits.

Table 23.4
Trading Tactics for Horn Tops

Trading Tactic	Explanation
Identify	Use the characteristics outlined in Table 23.1 to correctly identify a horn top on the weekly charts.
Threat assessment	Look for an uptrend spanning many months. Such uptrends often show horns near the end of the trend. If the horn top appears near the end of a long *downtrend*, then it is best to avoid it. Watch out for horns appearing after a downward trend when the trend changes and starts moving higher. Prices may decline but the decline is usually short-lived (as in the rise between a double bottom).
Low volume	The failure rate declines to 6% if below average volume appears on both spikes. This is worth considering.
Trend change	A horn top usually signals an approaching trend change, usually in less than 2 months.

Perhaps the first and most important trading tactic is to be sure that you have a valid horn top. Table 23.1 can assist you in your identification. After you have correctly identified the horn, look at the surrounding price pattern. Is the stock trending higher and has it been moving higher for months now? If so, then the horn may signal an approaching top. Sometimes the horn calls the turn exactly while at other times it is off by a few months (usually it precedes the turn but sometimes it lags).

If the horn appears on a downtrend, that is fine. The formation is simply implying that the trend will continue moving down. However, should the horn appear after an extended downtrend, then the possibility of further declines may be in jeopardy. This is especially true if the horn appears after a long downtrend when prices are beginning to move up again (they are retracing some of their losses). Often the retrace signals a trend change. You will be buying into a situation in which you believe prices will fall and retest the low, but prices will dip slightly then head higher.

Be cautious when selling short after a long downtrend and be especially cautious if the downtrend has ended and the horn seems to mark the end of an upward retrace. Do not expect prices to fall far. They do occasionally but the majority of the decline has already passed.

In the Statistics section I point out the interesting result that spikes with volume below the 25-day moving average show substantially lower failure rates while keeping the average decline at 21%. That is worth considering before you place a trade.

Even if a horn top fails and prices either drop by less than 5% or move directly higher, there is a chance that the horn is a premature signal of a bearish trend change. Therefore, whenever you see a horn top, be aware that the end of an uptrend may be just a few months away.

Sample Trade

You might be saying, "Those bromides are all fine and good, but how do I really trade it?" Consider the situation in Figure 23.5 faced by Sandy. She watched the complex head-and-shoulders formation take shape in a stock she owned. Volume on the far left shoulder was higher than during the head, as expected, and volume on the far right shoulder was further diminished. All in all, it was setting up to be a dire situation. When she spotted the horn top forming on the right shoulder, she knew the end was near.

Two weeks after the right horn spike appeared, she sold her holdings in the stock for a tidy profit. But she was not finished. The following week, she shorted the stock at $34\frac{1}{4}$. Her calculations using the measure rule for the head-and-shoulder formation indicated a decline to 16. This was higher than the 12 predicted by the measure rule because she used her sell point instead of the breakout point (which was not reached yet so she had no idea what it was).

With the stock selling at 34, a drop to 16 seemed too optimistic. Still, she watched with glee as the stock plummeted. In rapid order it fell to about 25 before meeting support. Sandy scanned the weekly chart looking for support

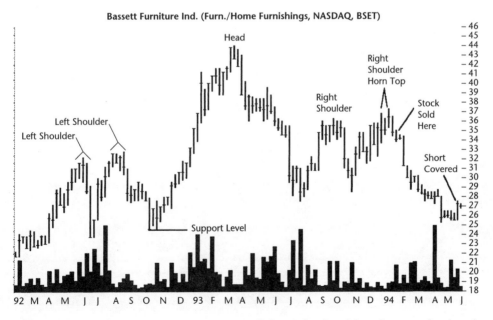

Figure 23.5 A horn top appears as part of the right shoulder of a complex head-and-shoulders formation.

levels and noticed one during October at about 24½ and one during June at around 23¾. Together, these two levels and the round number of 25 probably spelled a difficult time for the stock to continue lower.

When the stock headed back up in late May, she decided to close out her position at 27. She pocketed about $7 a share in just over 4 months. When she returned to the chart a year later, she saw that it did descend lower as the head-and-shoulders formation predicted. During early November, it reached a low of 20⅛, still well above the calculated 16 target she used and the 12 predicted by the measure rule. The flip side of this is that after she sold the stock, it climbed to 30¾, just 10% below her sell point.

24

Inside Days

RESULTS SNAPSHOT

Upside Breakouts

Appearance	A daily price range narrower than the prior day
Reversal or consolidation	Short term (up to 3 months) bullish consolidation
Failure rate	56%
Average rise	13%, with most likely rise between 0% and 5%
Surprising findings	Many, for both up and down breakouts. See Table 24.3 in the Statistics section.

Downside Breakouts

Appearance	A daily price range narrower than the prior day
Reversal or consolidation	Short term (up to 3 months) bullish reversal
Failure rate	51%
Average decline	10%, with most likely loss between 0% and 5%
Surprising findings	Many, for both up and down breakouts. See Table 24.3 in the Statistics section.

This formation had me perplexed for the longest time. The question I was struggling to answer is, how do you measure success or failure of this 2-day formation? The answer seems obvious now, but it was not when I started researching this chart pattern.

The theory behind the formation says an investor can expect a large price move *the day after* an inside day; that is how I ended up measuring success or failure. You can see in the Results Snapshot that the performance (the failure rate) is essentially random—near 50%. About half the formations have large price moves immediately after an inside day and half do not.

Some analysts may argue that if you try to depend on a large move the very next day, you are subject to disappointment. One must be open-minded and have patience, a large move will surely come along eventually. My response is, how long should I wait? Two days? A week? A month? When will the large price move occur?

Yes, several of the formations *do* experience a large price move 2 or more days after an inside day, others do not. I decided to measure the performance improvement when a large move is expected within *2 days*. The results? The upside failure rate improves to 46% (from 56%), whereas downside failures decrease to 43% (from 51%). That is an improvement but still well shy of the 20% maximum for reliable formations.

If I waited a week for a large price move, there would be even more improvement. Of course, waiting a year would show an even larger improvement. So I ask again: How long should I wait? I settled on the more conservative measure and expect a large price move the next day. You are certainly free to continue the analysis for various time periods to see how the pattern performs.

I separated inside days into two types: those with price trends moving upward (upside breakouts) and those moving lower after the inside day (downside breakouts). The determination of whether the formation is a reversal or not depends on the trend before and after the formation. Inside days with upside breakouts usually continue the upward, short-term trend, whereas those with downside breakouts seem to mark the end of the upward trend (acting as reversals).

The average move is small (13% and 10%) and the most likely gain or loss is less than 5% for each breakout direction. With other types of formations, any move less than 5% classifies as a failure (the so-called 5% failure). However, since the price moves from inside days are usually of small impact and duration (many post lower lows the day after the inside day only to begin moving higher; or the reverse: a higher high followed by a downward move). Thus, the average gain or loss includes the many small moves as well as the larger ones.

Tour and Identification Guidelines

Table 24.1 outlines the identification characteristics and Figure 24.1 shows numerous examples of inside days. An inside day is so-called because the daily price range is inside the range of the prior day. At least, that is how I chose to

Table 24.1
Identification Characteristics of Inside Days

Characteristic	Discussion
Lower high	The daily high must be below the prior daily high. No ties allowed.
Higher low	The daily low must be above the prior daily low. No ties allowed.
Daily range	The daily high cannot equal the daily low. In other words, there must be some sort of daily price range.

interpret the definition. Some technical analysts allow ties of the daily high or low, but I do not. I also imposed a further restriction: The inside day needs a daily price range. In other words, the intraday high and low cannot be the same price. There is no real significance to this except for thinly traded stocks. Thinly traded stocks have hundreds of inside days over the 5-year period under study. It is bad enough that even with the stipulations shown in the table, the number of formations is well over 100 for many stocks in the database. In the Statistics section, I detail how I trimmed the number of formations to a more manageable level.

The many black dots in Figure 24.1 highlight inside days. Although I designate the inside day to be the day with the narrower price range, the chart pattern is really a combination of 2 days. As an example, consider the inside day highlighted by the text in the figure (late October).

Figure 24.1 Numerous examples of inside days, which are highlighted by the black dots. The one in late October marked the start of a measured move up formation.

The first day of the chart pattern has a high of 50¾ and a low of 48½. The following day—the inside day—the range is 50 to 48⅝. The inside day has a lower high and a higher low than the prior day, and the daily price range is not zero (meaning that the high and low are different values).

The primary belief is that there will be a large price move after the inside day. You can see in Figure 24.1 that the day after the chart pattern prices move up smartly. One could argue that the inside day acts as a reversal of the downward price trend (while the inside day that happens 3 days before is a consolidation of the downward trend—prices continue moving down after the formation). Prices rise from a close of 49¼ to 54⅛, pause for a week, then continue up to reach a high of 59 ⅛ in late November. Astute readers might recognize the price pattern as a measured move up.

One has to ask the obvious question and that is, is an inside day a real chart pattern or is it just a name attached to a random event? That is a good question and one for which I am not sure I have the answer. If you believe in the strict version of the theory, that a large price move follows the day after an inside day, then the formation is just a random event. With failure rates over 50%, it is more accurate to say a *small price move follows the day after an inside day*.

If you are not so strict and simply say that a large price move follows (with no time limit), then the price pattern works out better. This is really no surprise when you consider that we begin with a comparatively narrow price range. Eventually we will get either a wide price range or prices will move up or down. The real question is, what does the term *large price move* mean?

I define the term to mean that prices the day after an inside day either climb or descend beyond the high or low posted the day before the inside day (of the 2-day formation, that is the day with the larger price range). If this does not happen, then a wider intraday price range, one that appears to be a multiple of the inside day's range, is also acceptable. If both these conditions are not met, then the formation is a failure.

Focus on Failures

When considering a formation such as an inside day, the normal gauges of failure really does not apply. The notion of a 5% failure, when prices move less than 5% in the direction of the breakout, is meaningless when the formation lasts just 2 days and the ultimate move might constitute a higher high or lower low *the very next day*.

Instead, I chose to rate the formation on how well it obeys the theory that prices make a *large* move *the day after* an inside day. Why the time limit? Two reasons really. First, eventually a stock is going to make a large move, so placing a time limit in which to expect a move makes sense. Second, we are in the business of making money. Our job is to find formations that make the most money in the shortest possible time, so a time limit in which a formation must perform also makes sense.

Exactly what constitutes a failure (alternatively, what does a *large* move mean)? As mentioned in the Identification Guidelines section, a failure is when prices do not move very far the day after an inside day. Figure 24.2 highlights two failures. The first failure comes after an inside day in late January. The inside day has a price range of 15¼ to 14¾. The following day the range is exactly the same. Clearly, a large price move does not immediately follow the inside day. The second failure is similar in that the daily price range does not change much from the inside day, nor do prices move very far. Yes, the low is lower than the inside day but by less than ³⁄₁₆—not a very compelling move.

Contrast the two failures with the move following the inside day in mid-August. Prices gap (a breakaway gap, incidentally) upward and the daily *low* is above both the *highs* of the prior 2 days (which makes up the inside day formation). This inside day leads to a large price move.

What about a formation that is not so obvious? For that I needed to establish some rules. I consider the formation a success if the day after an inside day has a higher high or lower low than the day before the inside day (and not by just a little either). In other words, a price trend should develop. If prices fail

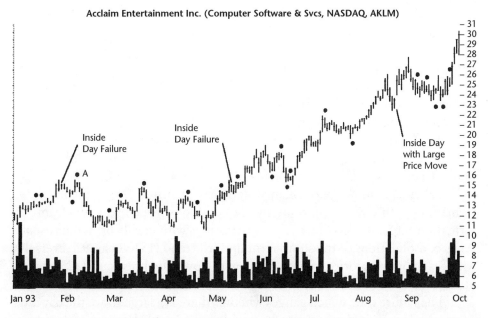

Figure 24.2 Two failures among the many inside days (black dots). A large price move does not follow the two inside days and so they are failures. A breakaway gap appears after the August inside day.

to move higher, then a larger intraday price range, one that is a multiple of the inside day, constitutes a winning combination.

For example, point A in Figure 24.2 shows what I consider to be a large price move after the inside day. The daily low of 14½ matches the low of the day before the inside day and the high matches the inside day's high. The price range *looks* like a large price move when compared with the inside day.

Perhaps my rules are too strict because the failure rates are abnormally high. In the next section, Statistics, I discuss the numerical results.

Statistics

Figures 24.1 and 24.2 illustrate one important fact: Inside days are plentiful. They are so numerous that I chose to limit the number of formations I would examine (many stocks have over 100 formations in 5 years). Fortunately, this formation is easily recognized by the computer with complete accuracy.

Instead of tabulating the performance of just five stocks (for about 500 formations), I chose to spread the selections over many stocks. To do this I limited the number of formations to 10 per stock by counting the number of formations in the stock and skipping the appropriate number.

For example, if a stock has 20 formations, I tabulate every other formation. A stock with 100 formations means that I use every tenth pattern. Not only does this technique spread the formations over the 5-year span, but it enlarges the number of stocks from about 5 to 52. The large number of formations tabulated and the spreading of the formation in both time and across many stocks ensure that the sample pool is diverse and representative of the performance of any one formation.

I separated the formations into those with prices trending up after the formation (upside breakouts) and those with trends moving down (downside breakouts). An upside breakout means a higher close or a higher high the day after the inside day. A downside breakout means a lower close or a lower low. If none of the three (high, low, or close) change, then I examine additional days until a trend determination can be made.

Table 24.2 shows performance statistics for inside days. I included 243 formations with upside breakouts and 277 with downside breakouts from 520 formations in 52 stocks over 5 years. Formations with upside breakouts usually act as consolidations of the short-term upward trend (151 versus 92 reversals), whereas a slight majority of formations with downside breakouts (123 consolidations versus 154 reversals) mark a reversal of the upward trend.

The failure rate, which gauges whether there is a large move the day after an inside day, is 56% and 51% for upside and downside breakouts, respectively. I consider failure rates below 20% to be acceptable, so this is well into

Table 24.2
General Statistics for Inside Days

Description	Upside Breakout	Downside Breakout
Number of formations in 52 stocks from 1991 to 1996, limited to 10 formations per stock	243	277
Reversal or consolidation	151 consolidations, 92 reversals	123 consolidations, 154 reversals
Failure rate	137 or 56%	141 or 51%
Average rise/decline of successful formations	13%	10%
Most likely rise/decline	0–5%	0–5%
For successful formations, days to ultimate high/low	2 months (65 days)	22 days
Percentage of formations occurring near 12-month low (L), center (C), or high (H)	L24%, C24%, H52%	L17%, C34%, H49%
Percentage gain/loss for each 12-month lookback period	L27%, C6%, H11%	L11%, C11%, H8%
Volume day before to day after versus 25-day moving average	140%, 83%, 93%	140%, 83%, 93%
Percentage gain/loss for volume 1.5× 25-day moving average	10%	13%
Percentage gain/loss for volume 0.5× 25-day moving average	22%	9%

the twilight zone. Thus, it is more accurate to say that most formations make a small move the day after an inside day.

The average gain is only 13% and the average loss is 10% for the two breakout types. This is well below the 40% for upside breakouts and 20% for downside breakouts that formations commonly share. The reason for this poor showing is probably because of the way the ultimate high or low is determined. In the case of the ultimate high, the rule is that when the trend changes, the ultimate high is the highest high posted between the formation and the trend change. Additionally, if prices break out upward then dip below the formation low, that truncates the period used (the reverse is true for downside breakouts).

With a formation as short as an inside day, there is not much latitude before prices move below the formation low. Most other formations have a wider price range that allows the stock plenty of room to recover before dropping below the formation low and calling an end to the search for the ultimate high. The narrow formation height sometimes penalizes performance.

Both upside and downside breakouts have likely gains of less than 5%. Figure 24.3 shows a frequency distribution of the gains (formations with upside breakouts) and losses (downside breakouts) for the inside day chart pattern. Both upside and downside breakouts have the highest column in the zero to 5% range. Almost half (49%) of the formations with downside breakouts have losses less than 5%. Two-thirds (or more) of the formations have returns less than 10%. Such meager returns suggest it is unwise to depend on this formation for any substantial lasting move.

Oddly enough, it takes almost three times as long to reach the ultimate high after an upside breakout (65 days) than the low in the downside breakout (22 days). A review of the data shows that there are a number of long duration climbs to the ultimate high. The large numbers unfairly pull the average upward. Removing all triple-digit durations (of which there are 13) results in an average climb to the ultimate high of just 13 days. A similar computation for the ultimate low reveals prices reach the low in 17 days.

Do inside days occur near the yearly high, low, or somewhere in between? A frequency distribution of the closing price to the prior yearly price range reveals that those formations with upside breakouts occur predominately in the upper third of the price range. A similar situation exists for downside breakouts with 49% of the formations residing within a third of the yearly high.

Mapping the performance onto the yearly price range is only revealing for upside breakouts. The best performing inside days with upside breakouts

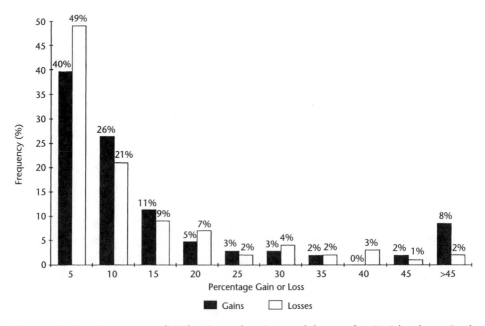

Figure 24.3 Frequency distribution of gains and losses for inside days. Both upside and downside breakouts from inside days have moves typically less than 5%.

are those with closing prices within a third of the yearly low. They have gains averaging 27%. The worst performing upside gain is for those with closing prices in the center third of the yearly price range. They have average gains of just 6%. Downside breakouts are unexciting, scoring losses within 3% of each other. The numbers suggest that if you are going to trade inside days, then you might pay attention to where they occur in the yearly price range. Choose ones with upside breakouts near the yearly low.

The volume pattern is what you would expect. The day before an inside day shows the highest volume at 140% of the 25-day moving average. A higher number of shares change hands when a large price range occurs as compared to the inside day when the volume drops to 83% of the average.

I looked at the performance for inside days with high and low volume separated by their breakout direction. For inside days with upside breakouts and volume that is half the 25-day moving average, they score gains of 22%, well above those inside days with volume 50% (1.5×) above average. However, the reverse is true for downside breakouts. Inside days with high volume perform better than those with low volume. Therefore, the breakout direction and volume pattern can be a clue to the performance of inside days.

Table 24.3 lists surprising findings for inside days. The failure rate explains the first finding, that of whether the formation lives up to expectations. The belief is that a large price move follows an inside day. Over half the formations fail to show such a move.

The next several table entries determine whether the breakout direction is predictable. Does the closing price the day before the inside day predict the breakout direction? No. I divided the intraday price range into three parts, 25%, 50%, and 25% of the range. Then I tagged in which part the closing price resides. I looked to see if an upside or downside breakout relates to whether the closing price is in the top 25% or bottom 25% of the daily price range. The results hover around 50%—essentially random.

Table 24.3
Surprising Results for Inside Days

Description	Results
Do inside days predict a large price move the next day?	No
Does the closing price of day before inside day predict breakout direction?	No
Does the closing price of the inside day predict the breakout direction?	Yes
Does the closing price of the inside day versus prior day predict breakout direction?	Yes
Do inside days result in larger price ranges the next day?	56% have larger ranges
The smaller the daily price-range ratio between the day before and the inside day, the larger the rise or decline	N/A

I applied the same test to the inside day instead of the day before and the results change. When the close is within 25% of the daily high, 61% of the formations have upside breakouts. When the close is within 25% of the daily low, 60% of the formations break out downward.

Next, I compared the close of the inside day with the prior day's price range. When the price of the inside day closes within 25% from the prior day's high, an upside breakout occurs 58% of the time. That result is not much better than a random event (50%). However, when the close is within 25% of the prior day's low, a downside breakout occurs 70% of the time. Thus, *if you have an inside day that closes near the prior days' low, expect a downside breakout.*

Do inside days result in large price ranges the next day? The average daily price range is $1.05 the day before the inside day, then it drops to $0.47 during the inside day and climbs to $0.64 a day later. A frequency distribution of the results says 44% of the days after an inside day have an equal to or smaller daily price range. Alternatively, 56% have larger daily price ranges.

The last finding in the table deals with the ratio of two daily price ranges. I computed the daily price range the day before the inside day and divided it by the daily price range of the inside day. Then I compared the ratios with the ultimate gain or loss. A scatter plot of the results indicates that chart patterns with smaller ratios perform better than those with larger ones. Figure 24.4 shows

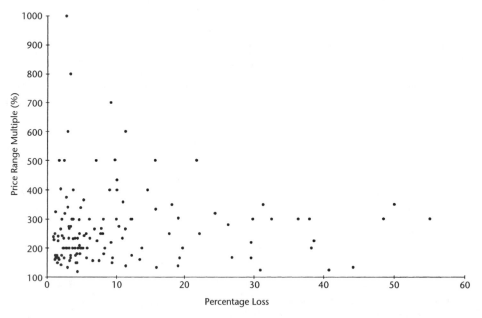

Figure 24.4 Price range versus ultimate loss. The graph shows the ratio of the price range the day before to the inside day's range compared with the resulting percentage decline for downside breakouts. The graph suggests smaller price ratios perform better.

what I mean. Of the two charts, one for upside and one for downside breakouts, the figure shows the more pronounced effects of the two; it is for inside days with downside breakouts.

At first, Figure 24.4 looks like a random splattering of dots. But, upon reflection, you can see that as the price-range ratio gets smaller, performance improves. By this I mean that there are more dots in the lower portion of the graph extending to the right than in the left portion extending upward. The graph for upside breakouts is similar, but the effect is less prominent.

Why is this the case? I compare the situation to symmetrical triangles. Those formations are like coils, tightly winding until the spring releases and prices shoot upward or downward in an explosion of activity. An inside day is just a 2-day triangle.

The analysis considers the ratios of the price range for the inside day with the prior day. What if the real effect is the formation height? Do shorter formations perform better than taller ones? Here the effect is just the reverse. Formations with downside breakouts have a scatter plot that is essentially random with dots all over the chart. However, the chart of upside breakouts shows a slight tendency for shorter formations to perform marginally better than their taller counterparts. By *shorter formation*, I am talking about the height (daily price range from high to low) of the day before the inside day. Using inside days instead of the day before shows an essentially random relationship for both upside and downside breakouts.

Trading Tactics

Without degenerating into a discussion of the random walk and the likelihood of tomorrow's price being higher is just 50–50, there are scant trading tactics that I can offer, certainly not enough to fill a table. If you still need a bromide, then let me say this: If you are going to rely on an inside day to place a trade, then trade in the direction of the trend. Wait for prices to stage a breakout by closing either above the top or below the bottom of the inside day. If the breakout is upward, then go long; if it is downward, then short the stock, run to your favorite place of worship, and pray!

In the Statistics section I briefly mention the next two suggestions. *The best performing inside days, with upside breakouts, occur in the lowest third of the yearly price range* (with gains averaging 27%, well above the 13% average). Downside breakouts show no meaningful performance difference wherever they break out in the yearly price range. *Pay attention to the volume characteristics of inside days.* Upside breakouts on *low* volume and downside breakouts on *high* volume often perform better than other combinations. See Table 24.2 and the Statistics section for more information.

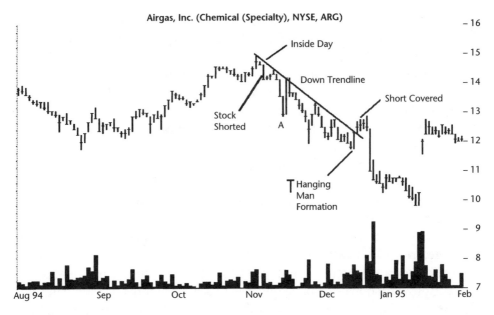

Figure 24.5   Inside day with a hanging man formation. Nathan successfully position traded this inside day for a $2,000 paper gain. A hanging man formation appears in mid-December.

Sample Trade

Nathan has a conservative job in the banking industry but in his spare time he likes to take out his aggression by paper trading stocks with the hope of one day becoming a full-time position trader. When he saw the inside day develop in Airgas, he decided to paper trade it from the short side (see Figure 24.5). With the knowledge that the closing price of an inside day might suggest the breakout direction, he believed that the stock would tumble—or so he hoped. The day after the inside day, he sold the stock short and received a fill at 14½.

As predicted, the stock closed lower for the day but quickly retraced its progress over the next 3 days. Just as he was about to cover his position and get out, the stock reversed direction and turned down. Three days later it slipped below 13, for a tidy paper gain on his 1,000 shares.

Then, the stock jumped upward (point A on the chart) but Nathan was not aware of the sharp move until well into the following day. He drew a down-sloping trendline along the minor daily highs and saw that the up-move had but just barely pierced the trendline. This signaled a possible trend change. However, when he got a quotation from his broker, the stock was already moving back down.

He flipped a coin and decided to hold on to the position a little longer. At the end of the trading day, the stock closed lower, back below the trendline. Realizing that his decision was little more than a crap shoot, he decided that should the stock pierce the up-trendline and close above it, he would cover his short.

Each day he plotted the stock and watched its progress. In mid-December, when the stock closed above the trendline after a hanging man formation, Nathan decided it was time to check out. He covered his short and received a fill at 12$7/16$, making him about two grand richer. "Paper trades are easy!" he snorted.

25

Island Reversals

RESULTS SNAPSHOT

Tops

Appearance	Prices gap up to the formation then gap down at the same price level, leaving an island.
Reversal or consolidation	Short-term (up to 3 months) bearish reversal
Failure rate	13%
Average decline	21%, with most likely decline less than 10%
Volume trend	Downward
Pullbacks	65%
Percentage meeting predicted price target	78%

Bottoms

Appearance	Prices gap down to the formation then gap up at the same price level, leaving an island.
Reversal or consolidation	Short-term (up to 3 months) bullish reversal
Failure rate	17%
Average rise	34%, with most likely rise being 20%
Volume trend	Downward
Throwbacks	70%
Percentage meeting predicted price target	85%

The performance of island reversals is perhaps surprising only for its mediocrity. Failure rates for both tops (13%) and bottoms (17%) is quite good, below the 20% threshold that I view as the maximum allowable for reliable formations.

For tops, the average decline is a very respectable 21%, but the most likely decline is less than 10%. This suggests you would not want to make a habit of trading this formation. For bottoms, the average rise is 34%, reasonable for bullish formations but still not up to the caliber of other bottom reversals. The most likely rise is less than 20%, about average for bullish formations.

Pullbacks and throwbacks are prevalent, suggesting that the gap after the island completes closes quite quickly. Investors can make use of this behavior to delay their investments until the pullback or throwback completes and prices resume their breakout direction.

Tour

Figure 25.1 shows what island reversals look like. The first island, shown on the far left, is a one-day reversal. In the study of islands, I did not tabulate such narrow formations, but the figure shows an example of a small reversal. The center formation is an island bottom. Prices gap downward in mid-September, reach a new low in early October, then gap upward later in the month. The

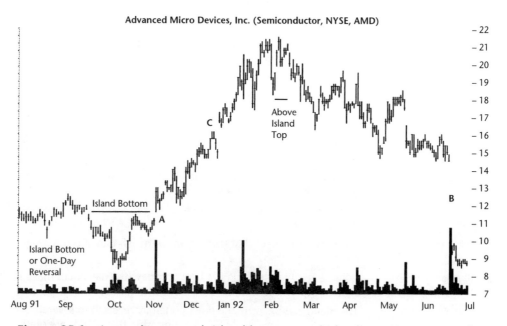

Figure 25.1   A one-day reversal, island bottom, and island top. You can see the price change that results after each reversal.

two gaps appear at about the same price level, 11½. From that point, prices climb quite rapidly and reach a high of 21½, well above the 11¼ price posted the day before the breakout. Notice that the breakout is on very high volume. The last island highlighted on the chart is near the top. It is an island top and prices head down from about 20 to less than 8. This formation is a traditional island top because of its compact size. I did not count it in my tabulations because the gap on the right is less than the ¼ point I used to filter such formations. Still it does emphasize a trend reversal with excellent timing. Not highlighted is a very large island top. The island bottom shares the left gap (point A) while the right gap is the large price decline in mid-June (point B). The large island is almost 8 months long.

Identification Guidelines

Island reversals are easy to identify and Table 25.1 shows the identification characteristics. Both types of reversals, tops and bottoms, are set off by gaps. The first gap is usually an exhaustion gap (or a breakaway gap if the move is strong enough) and the second one is a breakaway gap. The gaps appear at or near the same price level but are typically not the same size. The large gap marked as point B in Figure 25.1 (on the far right) makes this clear. That gap has a size of almost 5 while the one on the left (point A) is only ⅜ wide.

As far as identification goes, the gap in mid-December 1991 (point C) should not be paired with the gap in late October (point A) since they are not at the same price level. Even though the price pattern looks like an island

Table 25.1
Identification Characteristics of Island Reversals

Characteristic	Discussion
Shape	Gaps set off both island tops and bottoms and share all or part of the same price level. Most times, prices move away from the gaps leaving the island with a clear view of the opposing gap (the left gap usually does not close quickly).
Rising trend	Tops have prices that lead up to the left gap and fall away from the right gap.
Falling trend	Bottoms have prices that lead down to the left gap and rise away from the right gap.
Volume	Volume is usually high on the breakout day (the day prices make a second gap and form the island) but need not be.
Time	The island can be from one day (a one-day reversal) to several months long. Some analysts have suggested that islands are quite short, up to a week or two, with relatively flat price zones, but I placed no such restrictions on them.

because it is set off by gaps, it is not an island reversal by the traditional definition. The gaps must overlap prices or be quite close to one another. In this study, all islands have price gaps within ⅛ of one another and are at least ¼ point or larger. In addition, I did not consider one-day reversals (islands composed of 1 day) as part of this study. I believe that such islands are too difficult on which to base an effective trading policy.

Consider Figure 25.2, which shows several island reversals. The first two islands happen as part of a retrace in a downtrend. The small island tops last for about a week before prices resume their downward plunge.

The island bottom forms after an extensive decline that sees prices drop from a high of 36½ to 12 in less than 5 months. The exhaustion gap occurs on very high volume and prices that day have a very large 3½ point trading range. The gap remains open until prices gap upward in late January. Looking at the bottom formation overall, it looks like a complex head-and-shoulders bottom. Marked on the figure are the dual shoulders and duplicate heads. The volume for the head-and-shoulders pattern is what you would expect: highest on the left shoulder, diminished on the head, and quite low on the right shoulder. Only after prices gap upward does volume spike higher for 2 days before recovering and trending downward.

The island top on the right of the figure is somewhat difficult to spot because of the large gap on the left that matches the small one on the right. It

Figure 25.2 Several island reversals, some with short durations and some with longer durations. The island bottom is also a complex head-and-shoulders bottom that retests the neckline in April.

only takes a few days for prices to reach their high before easing down. When prices gap lower at the end of March, volume does not budge. This may signal a weak trend and it turns out that prices do not make consistent new highs for at least a year.

Focus on Failures

Failures come in all manners of depiction. Look at Figure 25.3, a chart of a large island top. This failure is typical of many formations, especially those with small declines. The island is unusual as it forms after a region of consolidation. The first gap is a breakaway gap since it breaks away from the consolidation region on high volume and prices move up. The second gap is an exhaustion gap that closes quickly.

The figure shows a 5% failure. Prices head lower after the second gap on the right, but decline by no more than 5% before recovering and moving substantially higher. Why? There is a common law, for lack of a better term, that says a reversal will only travel as far as the prior rise. In other words, a reversal has to have something to reverse. In Figure 25.3, you can see that prices consolidate for 2 months. When the island top appears, what is there to reverse? The rise from December to mid-February, when prices rise from roughly 55 to 65, unwinds. Prices move steadily lower at first then plunge and end back at

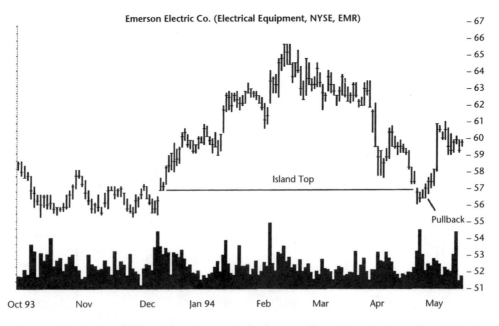

Figure 25.3   Long island top that fails because prices drop by less than 5%. A reversal needs something to reverse.

56. Beyond that, the prior year's worth of support at that level is just too extensive to allow any further decline. *There has to be something to reverse.* Remember that before you take a position in a stock, especially something such as an island reversal that is known to be light on performance.

Figure 25.4 shows another failure. The island bottom is clearly visible on the chart. The two gaps separate the main body of the island from the mainland with plenty of clear ocean. Over the course of the formation, the first gap remains open. The second gap closes about a week after prices throw back to the breakout point. Then prices continue lower.

How could you have known that this island bottom would rise by less than 5% before sinking? The question is irrelevant because of throwbacks. For island bottoms, throwbacks occur 70% of the time, on average. This high rate allows an investor the luxury of waiting before investing. Once the stock throws back to the formation, wait for prices to recover. Assuming they do, jump in and buy the stock.

In the situation shown in Figure 25.4, the stock did not recover; it continued down. Had the investor been paying attention, he would not have gotten himself into this money-losing situation in the first place.

Is there another reason to suspect this formation? Sure, and it is called a trendline. If you draw a down-sloping trendline along the peaks, beginning with the tallest one, you quickly discover that the minor peak after the island

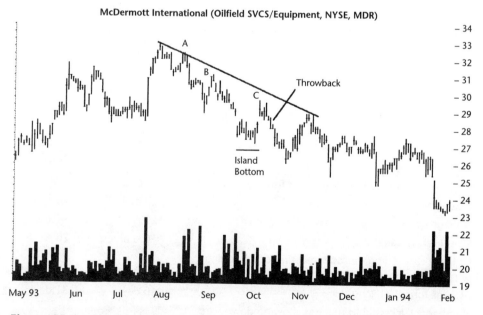

Figure 25.4 An island bottom failure. Wait for prices to close above the trendline before investing in this island bottom. Since prices do not close above the trendline (at point C), skip this trade.

bottom (point C) falls well short of the trendline. Trendlines are known for their ability to support or resist price declines and advances, respectively. In this case the trendline acts as resistance to the rising trend. It repels the advance and prices turn lower.

In other words, the investor should have waited for prices to close above the trendline before buying the stock. Even if he mistakenly connects points A and B with a trendline and extends it downward through point C, it should give him pause. Although prices pierce the trendline, they fail to close above it. If they cannot close above it, how will prices rise?

Statistics

Table 25.2 shows general statistics for island reversals. I searched all 500 stocks for island tops and bottoms and located 245 tops and 278 bottoms over 5 years of daily price data. The failure rates are good at 13% and 17%, both below the 20% level that I consider a maximum for reliable formations.

The average decline (21%) and rise (34%) are about what you would expect for bearish top and bullish bottom reversals. The island bottoms could be a bit stronger to lift them up with some of the better performing bottoms (they gain about 40%). However, the real worry is the most likely decline and rise. For tops the likely decline is 10% or less and for bottoms, the likely gain is less than 20%. Figures 25.5 and 25.6 illustrate this. Both figures show a frequency distribution of losses or gains. I use a frequency distribution to remove any unwanted skewing of large numbers that affect an average. The tallest column then becomes what I term the most likely decline (for tops) or rise (for bottoms).

Table 25.2
General Statistics for Island Reversals

Description	Tops	Bottoms
Number of formations in 500 stocks from 1991 to 1996	245	278
Failure rate	32 or 13%	46 or 17%
Average decline/rise of successful formations	21%	34%
Most likely decline/rise	10% or less	20%
Of those succeeding, number meeting or exceeding price target (measure rule)	166 or 78%	198 or 85%
Average formation length	40 days	31 days
Number of successful formations showing downward volume trend	188 or 77%	205 or 74%

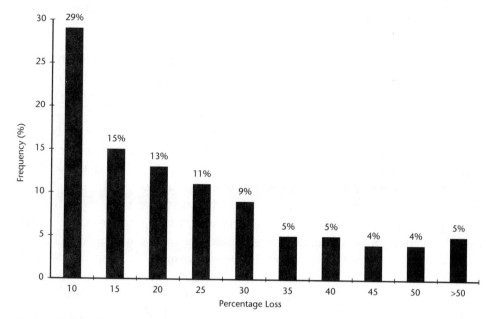

Figure 25.5 Frequency distribution of losses for island tops. Note that the most likely loss is less than 10%.

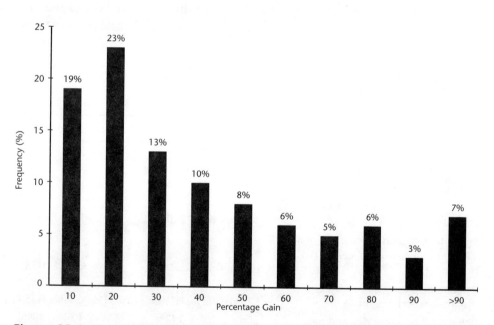

Figure 25.6 Frequency distribution of gains for island bottoms. Island bottoms have a likely loss of 20%.

Figure 25.5 shows the column with the highest frequency as having a loss of up to 10%. You can see that almost 60% of the formations have gains averaging less than 20%. That is a sobering thought. The figure warns you not to expect too much of a decline from an island top in a bull market.

Figure 25.6 shows a graph of gains for island bottoms. The most likely gain is the highest column at 20% but the 10% column follows closely. In this case, 42% of the formations (or almost half!) have gains of less than 20%.

Most measure rules use the height of the formation, so I computed the target price for each successful formation and tabulated whether the pattern hit its target. Both tops and bottoms do quite well, with 78% and 85%, respectively, reaching their predicted prices. I consider values over 80% to be reliable, so these are close enough for comfort. Of course, if the formation is not very tall, then it is comparatively easy to make the grade. This is especially true when just 2 days' worth of prices compose an island (the days have gaps on either side).

The average formation length is quite short, about a month or so for both tops and bottoms. Again, the number of small duration islands influences the duration. Still, when you review all the data, the formations are generally quick to reverse. About half of all islands (43% for tops and 50% for bottoms) last 2 weeks or less.

Over the course of the formation, 77% of the tops and 74% of the bottoms show a receding volume trend. I use the slope of a line found using linear

Table 25.3
Additional Statistics Related to Island Reversals

Description	Island Tops	Island Bottoms
Pullbacks/throwbacks	160 or 65%	195 or 70%
Average time to pullback/throwback completion	8 days	9 days
For successful formations, days to ultimate low/high	3.5 months (72 days)	6 months (178 days)
Percentage of islands occurring near 12-month price low (L), center (C), or high (H)	L19%, C37%, H44%	L34%, C28%, H38%
Percentage change for each 12-month lookback period	L28%, C22%, H19%	L31%, C33%, H35%
Volume for breakout day and next 5 days compared with day before breakout	306%, 187%, 141%, 120%, 126%, 113%	201%, 124%, 88%, 84%, 86%, 86%
Performance for high volume breakouts versus low volume breakouts	22% versus 16%	33% versus 39%

regression on the volume data to derive this conclusion. In many instances, the declining volume trend is clearly visible on the chart.

Table 25.3 lists additional statistics. Island tops have pullbacks 65% of the time, whereas bottoms have throwbacks to the gap 70% of the time. In both cases the numbers are quite high and suggest a trading tactic to make use of this behavior (that is, wait for the pullback or throwback). I discuss Trading Tactics in the next section.

The average time to a pullback or throwback is a short 8 or 9 days for tops and bottoms, respectively. This is slightly shorter than other chart patterns.

For successful formations, the time to the ultimate low or high varies quite widely between tops and bottoms. For tops, it takes 72 days to reach the low, but 6 months for bottoms to climb to the ultimate high. Perhaps this should not be so surprising since it often takes longer to move further.

I separated the formations into three categories, depending on their breakout price within the yearly range. Most of the island tops and bottoms occur in the highest third of the yearly price range. Although that may sound strange for a *bottom*, it is not. That is because I define an island bottom to be when prices decline to, then rise away from, the formation. Tops, on the other hand, have prices that lead up to, then down from, the formation.

When we substitute performance into the same three categories, we discover that island tops occurring in the lowest third of the yearly price range perform best with losses averaging 28%. The performance suggests that weak situations (an island near the yearly low) get weaker (move down even further). Bottom performance is about evenly split and ranged from 31% to 35%.

The table shows volume statistics. Clearly, the breakout day, which is the day prices gap away from the formation, shows very high volume. For tops the volume remains high through the following week but with bottoms it quickly calms down and remains quiet.

I did a study to see if high volume breakouts push prices further. For island tops, the answer is yes, as those formations with volume 125% of the prior day show losses averaging 22%, whereas formations with volume 75% of the prior day have losses of just 16%.

For bottoms, the reverse is true. A low volume breakout scores better with a 39% rise, whereas those formations with high volume have gains of 33%. In both cases, the 125% (high volume) and 75% (low volume) benchmarks are arbitrary designations.

Trading Tactics

Table 25.4 outlines trading tactics. The first trading tactic is not really a tactic at all; it is the measure rule, which assists investors in gauging whether a trade is worth risking. Consider the island bottom shown in Figure 25.7. The high-

Table 25.4
Trading Tactics for Island Reversals

Trading Tactic	Explanation
Measure rule	Compute the formation height by subtracting the lowest low from the highest high in the formation. Add the difference to the highest high for island bottoms, and subtract the difference from the lowest low for island tops. The result is the target to which prices should rise (for bottoms) or fall (for tops).
Wait for pullback or throwback	Island reversals show a reluctance to continue moving in the direction of the breakout. Prices usually reverse direction and quickly fill the gap before recovering and resuming their original trend. Wait for the pullback (tops) or throwback (bottoms) to complete and prices to resume their original direction before investing.
Watch trendlines	Trendlines, when pierced, often signal a trend change. Should an island reversal appear near a trendline, wait for prices to close beyond the trendline before investing.

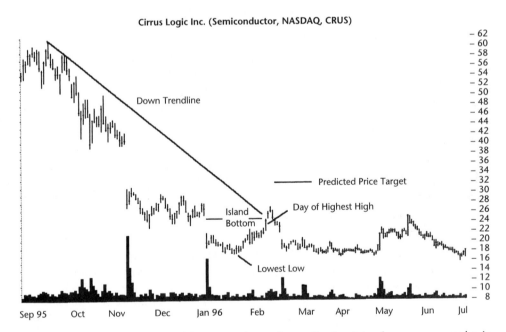

Figure 25.7 A failed island bottom. Sometimes the best trade you can make is none at all.

est high in the formation is $24\frac{5}{8}$ (which is just below the gap in early February, not the larger gap in mid-February) while the low is $17\frac{1}{2}$. Add the difference of $7\frac{1}{8}$ to the highest high to get the predicted price target. In this case, the target is $31\frac{3}{4}$, a target not reached before the formation fails.

Since pullbacks and throwbacks occur a majority of the time and since island reversals have a low failure rate but poor performance, it is wise to wait for the retrace. It usually occurs a week or two after the second gap. If a pullback or throwback does not occur quickly (in less than a month), then move on to the next trading situation.

When a pullback or throwback occurs, do not invest immediately. Wait for the retrace to complete and for prices to turn around and resume their original direction. Sometimes prices retrace to the formation, then continue moving in the adverse direction.

In the Focus on Failures section of this chapter I discuss the use of the trendline in detail, so there is not much added here. However, both up and down trendlines can show a trend change. Wait for prices to *close* above a down trendline or below an up trendline before pulling the trigger. Many times prices will near the trendline and be repulsed, so you want to make sure that the piercing does, indeed, signal a change in trend.

Sample Trade

Consider the situation faced by Clarence as illustrated in Figure 25.7. He watched the semiconductor company's stock plummet. During November and December, the stock formed a type of island consolidation. He knew it was not a reversal because the two gaps did not line up across from each other. Then another island formed in January to early February.

Since prices gapped down to the second formation then gapped up away from it, he knew he was dealing with an island bottom, a better investment choice for performance than an island top. He used the measure rule to gauge the likely price to which the stock would climb. The target represented nearly a 30% rise in price, large enough to risk a trade.

Before he bought the stock, he made a few checks. He saw that the trend was down, as the stock had fallen from a high of $61\frac{1}{8}$ to the island low of $17\frac{1}{2}$. Clarence drew the trendline from the highest high downward and saw it go through the right island gap. This was a good sign as prices had moved above the line and closed there. It signaled a trend change.

Still, something did not feel right about the stock. It had made a new low and the semiconductor industry as a whole was soft. Did the island bottom really mark a turning point or would the stock simply rise up, spin around, and retest the low? He was unsure, so he decided to wait and see if prices threw back to the formation. If they threw back then continued higher, he would buy the stock. Three days after the upside breakout, the stock threw back and closed the gap. Now, Clarence knew, all the stock had to do was move higher. It did not. The stock continued moving down and in less than a week had slipped below the trendline again. He decided to look elsewhere for a more promising situation.

Looking back at the stock well over a year later, he saw that it reached a low of 8 and never rose above 27¼, the high just after it pierced the trendline. He realized that sometimes the best trade you can make is none at all.

26

Measured Move Down

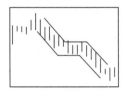

RESULTS SNAPSHOT

Appearance	Prices move down, retrace, then move down again. The two down legs are nearly equal in both price and time.
Reversal or consolidation	Intermediate-term (up to 6 months) bearish reversal
Failure rate	22%
Average decline	36%, with most likely decline between 25% and 40%
First leg decline	25% in 54 days
Corrective phase rise	16% in 39 days (40% to 60% retrace of prior decline)
Last leg decline	27% in 60 days
Measure rule	43% of second legs are longer than first leg price decline.
Surprising finding	The corrective phase should be in proportion to the first leg decline.
Synonym	Swing measurement
See also	Flags and Pennants

The measured move down, or swing measurement as it is sometimes called, is an exciting formation because it vividly tells you how far down it is going. Unfortunately, with a failure rate of 22%, it is also more risky. I consider formations with failure rates less than 20% to be reliable. That is not to say that this one is unreliable, especially since it has a 36% average decline, which is well above the usual 20% decline for bearish reversals. For this formation even the most likely decline is high but wide at 25% to 40%.

When we examine the two down legs of this formation, we find that they are nearly the same length, 60 days versus 54 days, with declines of 25% versus 27%. On a percentage basis, the second leg seems longer, but on a price basis, the second leg is 8% shorter. Remember that as prices fall, they have to travel less far to make the same percentage decline. This helps explain why only 43% of the second legs exceed the first leg price decline (in other words, the measure rule).

A surprising finding that helps with gauging the veracity of the formation and its performance is the size of the corrective phase. A large first leg price decline should also show a large corrective phase retrace. If the corrective phase falls short of the usual 40% to 60% retrace, then beware. Be prepared to exit the trade well before reaching the target price.

Tour

Figure 26.1 shows what a typical measured move down looks like. The decline from the high (point A) to the start of the retrace (point C) is called the *first leg*. The retrace is commonly referred to as the *corrective phase* and the remaining

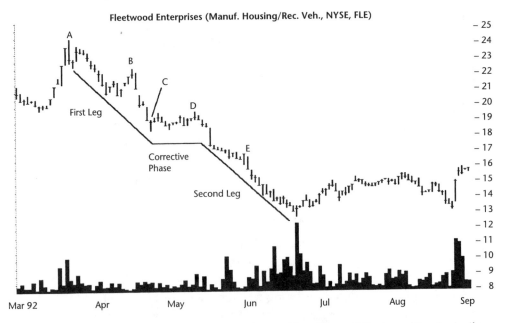

Figure 26.1   A typical measured move down. The slope of the trendline is similar for both legs. Points A, B, and C mark a nested measured move.

decline to the low is called the *second leg*. The first and second legs are nearly the same size, but their behavior is described in more detail later in the Statistics section.

The corrective phase is simply an upward retrace of the downtrend. It is a place for the stock to catch its breath and for novice investors to buy into the situation. They purchase the stock and push it up, believing the decline is at an end. Do not be fooled; the decline is only half over. That is the beauty of this formation. Before you buy a stock after a long decline, consider that it might be making a measured move down and that the decline is not over. Paying attention might save you some big bucks.

Returning to Figure 26.1, you can see the two legs following a trendline that has nearly the same slope. This is not always the case, but a surprising number of formations obey this dictum. Further, a channel—two parallel lines that follow prices down—can encompass the two legs. Although the example in Figure 26.1 is weak on the first leg, you can see how the second leg follows a top trendline, connecting points D and E and extending down.

Lastly, the three points marked A, B, and C mark another measured move down. This one is more compact and it is not uncommon to find nested formations like this. Sometimes, you get one measured move right after another.

Identification Guidelines

Table 26.1 highlights identification characteristics for the measured move down chart pattern. The first leg occurs as prices reach a new high and a trend change begins. Prices decline leaving a price peak on the chart. From there,

Table 26.1
Identification Characteristics of the Measured Move Down

Characteristic	Discussion
First leg	Usually begins from a new high. Prices decline rapidly in a straight-line fashion. Avoid declines that curve (they are rounding turns, scallops, or saucers).
Corrective phase	Prices can move horizontally but usually rise and recover from 40% to 60% of the prior decline before resuming the downtrend. If the corrective phase nears or rises above the first leg high, look elsewhere.
Second leg	The *slope* of the first leg down trendline often carries onto this leg. Both legs usually fit inside their own trend channels.
Avoid	For cascading measured moves, use the first retrace and not later ones as they get progressively closer to the end of the trend. Avoid horizontal, saw-tooth consolidation regions and measured moves that rise from a flat base. Make sure the measure rule does not predict prices will fall below zero.

prices continue moving lower, usually in a straight-line run. Most times you can draw two parallel lines, one connecting the minor highs and one joining the minor lows, forming a down-sloping trend channel. The corrective phase stops the decline. Prices can move horizontally but usually retrace a significant portion of their losses, say, between 40% and 60%.

When the second leg begins, the downturn resumes. Prices usually follow the slope set by the first leg but this varies from formation to formation. Of course, the two legs will not share the same trendline since the corrective phase offsets them. Even so, the second leg usually fits inside its own trend channel as prices decline in a straight-line fashion. The second leg decline approximates the price decline set by the first leg and the time it took to accomplish it.

There are several guidelines that you should follow when searching for the measured move down. Avoid formations that show a rounded first leg, where prices move lower but curve around in a sort of rounding turn, scallop, or saucer. The trend should be a straight-line decline.

During the corrective phase, prices should not rebound (or come close) to the high set by the first leg. If prices near or rise above the first leg high, then avoid the formation.

Watch for consecutive measured moves in a declining price trend. The downtrend eventually will end, so it is best to trade on the first or second measured move and avoid the rest.

Occasionally, the prevailing price trend will be horizontal. Prices rise up and reach a high then begin down in the first leg. When prices return to the base, they bounce. This bounce, wrongly interpreted as the corrective phase of a measured move down, is really a minor high in a consolidation trend. Prices return to the base and may bounce several more times before beginning a sustained move upward. The overall picture looks like a horizontal saw-tooth formation. Avoid measured moves that spring from a horizontal trend.

The last caveat is to consider the measure rule. I discuss the measure rule in the Trading Tactics section of this chapter, but the measure rule says the second leg will approximate the price move of the first leg. If the first leg has a large decline, you may find that the predicted price is very close to zero or perhaps even negative. Obviously, the stock is not going to go negative and probably will remain far above zero, so you might look elsewhere for a more promising trade. Examples of these idiosyncrasies follow in the Focus on Failures section.

Figure 26.2 shows two examples of the measured move down formation. The first one, marked by points A, B, C, and D, begins after a long price rise. The stock moves up from $43\frac{1}{8}$ in late November 1994, to $59\frac{5}{8}$ in early July. Then, prices decline following a down trendline and stay within the trend channel until mid-August, when they reach a low of $51\frac{1}{2}$. The corrective phase begins on volume that is high but not unusually so. Prices move up and retrace 68% of the decline before tumbling again. In the second leg, prices move below the low (point B) and continue lower to point D. Then it is over.

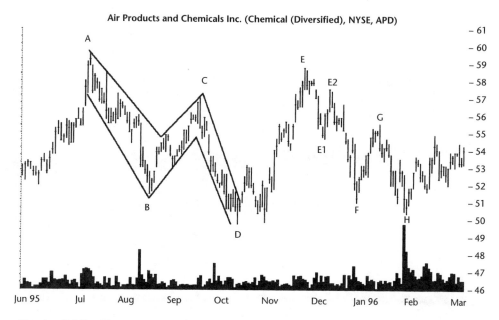

Figure 26.2 Two measured moves. Notice how they fit neatly inside a trend channel. With measured moves, the price decline from C to D nearly matches the decline from A to B.

The second leg is steeper than the first leg and covers the ground in about half the time (36 days versus 19 days). In addition, the second leg is slightly shorter than the first one (the first leg declines by 8⅛, whereas the second one falls 7¼).

Another measured move occurs in mid-November and ends at about the same level as the first formation in late January (see points E, F, G, and H). If you look closely at Figure 26.2, you can see another measured move that forms in the first leg from point E to point F. Points E1 and E2 mark the corrective phase.

Focus on Failures

What constitutes a failure of a measured move down? Early in the study of this chart pattern, I decided that if prices do not dip below the first leg low, then the formation classifies as a failure. Admittedly, this is subjective and it depends to a large extent on the size of the corrective phase, but it does weed out the weaker situations.

There are a number of identification mistakes that I want to point out. Figure 26.3 shows the first one. The semiconductor maker's stock reaches a high, along with a host of other chip makers' stocks, in the summer and fall of 1995. The stock forms a head-and-shoulders top in August and September

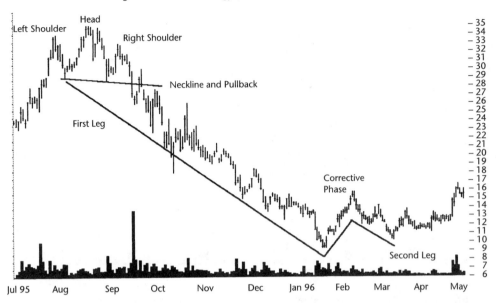

Integrated Device Technology (Semiconductor, NASDAQ, IDTI)

Figure 26.3 A head-and-shoulders top leading to a measured move down. The head-and-shoulders top forms the basis for the large decline. The corrective phase is small in comparison to the large first leg decline. The measure rule for the measured move formation predicts prices will go negative. Think the stock will make it?

before burning out. In a near straight-line run, the stock tumbles from a high of 33½ to a low of 9⅛.

If this decline marks the first leg of a measured move down, how far will prices fall in the second leg? That depends on how far up the corrective phase brings prices. The corrective phase rises to a high of 15¼. I discuss the measure rule later, but it says the second leg approximates the price decline of the first leg. If we run through the computations, we discover that the predicted decline is minus 9⅛. Even if the company were to declare bankruptcy, its stock price would never go negative, there is no way that prices are going to decline that far.

Another key to this failure is the size of the corrective phase. Usually, prices recover 40% to 60% of the first leg decline, but this one does not come close (about a 25% retrace). With larger price declines, the corrective phase is proportionally larger too. However, the formation in Figure 26.3 does not show such behavior.

Figure 26.4 shows another situation: the flat base problem. Prices are essentially flat from the start of February. By that I mean the minor lows all share the same value—about 40. When prices move up in August and reach a minor high in September, it is nothing unusual. Although the prior minor highs do not ascend to this height, there is no reason to suspect that a measured move will follow.

Anadarko Petroleum Corp. (Petroleum (Producing), NYSE, APC)

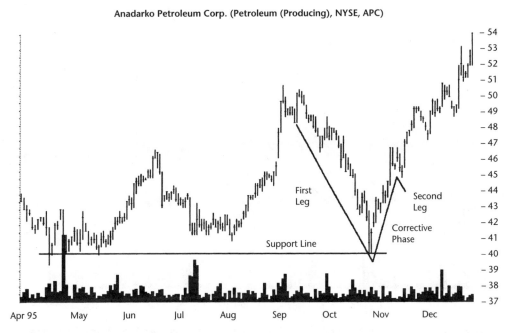

Figure 26.4 A measured move from a horizontal base. These formations rarely work out as anticipated.

When prices decline to the base at 40 and bounce, a naive investor might think a measured move down is forming. The corrective phase in late October and early November sees prices rebound quite a ways up the first leg before curling over and heading down. If the investor sells short at this point, it will be a costly mistake. Prices quickly skyrocket to 60 by May from the second leg low of 44⅞. Why does this formation fail? The strong support level at 40 curtails any meaningful decline below that point. In other words, there is nothing to reverse.

Figure 26.5 shows the last failure, a case of mistaken identity. After a long, extended rise, a retrace can be expected, maybe even a trend change that takes prices drastically lower. When prices turn down in early January, a decline is long overdue. If you connect the minor lows in the uptrend, you discover that prices pierce the up trendline in mid-December. This piercing supports the theory that the trend is changing. It is not conclusive, but it does tilt the scales in that direction. Throughout the month of December prices essentially move horizontally before perking up and making a new high just before prices plummet. The failure to continue moving higher is another clue to a trend change. The final clue is when prices descend and drop below the prior minor high reached in late October. It even tumbles below the support level at 12⅝ before recovering.

The corrective phase of the measured move down sees prices recover quite far, representing a retrace of 85%. That is well above normal and should

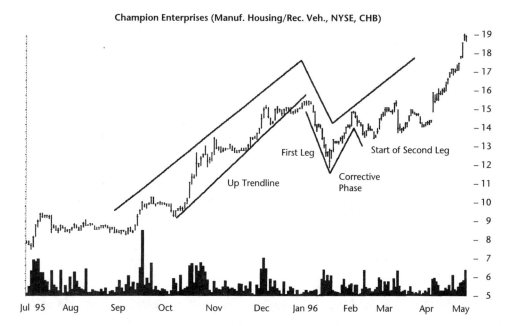

Champion Enterprises (Manuf. Housing/Rec. Veh., NYSE, CHB)

Figure 26.5 This measured move down is really the corrective phase of a measured move up.

flag a potential problem. With such a large retrace, prices will probably decline to at most the prior low and stall (because the second leg is slightly smaller than the first one). It did not even go that far. Prices declined to the prior minor high at 13½ and held steady for a week before moving higher.

Why did this formation fail? The choice of a measured move down for this situation is poor because of the extent of the corrective phase. If we look at the larger picture, we discover that the first down leg is nothing more than the corrective phase of a measured move *up!*

Statistics

Table 26.2 shows the only statistics for this formation. I uncovered 622 formations in 2,500 years of daily price data. Such a large number of formations means they are common, offering plenty of investment opportunities.

Of the formations I uncovered, the vast majority (88%) are reversals of the upward trend; the remainder are consolidations. Consolidations typically occur as part of a long downtrend. Sometimes the formations are small when compared with the total down move, whereas others are part of two or three cascading formations in the same bear run.

For measured moves, I define a failure to be when prices do not decline below the low established in the first leg. I did multiple passes to be sure that I located as many of the failures as I possibly could. This amounted to 22% of

Table 26.2
General Statistics for the Measured Move Down

Description	Statistic
Number of formations in 500 stocks from 1991 to 1996	622
Reversal or consolidation	77 consolidations, 545 reversals
Failure rate	134 or 22%
Average decline of successful formations	36%
Most likely decline	25% to 40%
Average formation length	5 months (153 days)
First leg price decline	25% in 54 days
Corrective phase price rise	16% in 39 days
Second leg price decline	27% in 60 days
Corrective phase percentage retrace	40% to 60%
Percentage of formations starting near 12-month price low (L), center (C), or high (H)	L0%, C6%, H93%
Measure rule	43% of second legs are longer than first legs

the formations. The failure rate is quite close to the 20% maximum that I deem acceptable for reliable formations.

The average decline amounts to 36%, as measured from the highest high reached in the first leg, through the corrective phase, to the lowest low in the second leg. Since you probably will not be able to identify a measured move down until sometime in the second leg, your average decline is likely to be considerably less than 36% (probably about 20% since the corrective phase brings prices up). The most likely decline is between 25% and 40%. Figure 26.6 shows the results of a frequency distribution of declines for all successful formations. Notice the center of the graph has four columns of about equal height. If you ignore the catch-all column on the right of the figure, the four center columns have the highest frequency. As such, I consider them to be representative of what you can expect to earn from this formation. Again, let me remind you that the decline measures from the highest high in the first leg to the lowest low in the second. Once you identify a measured move down, a significant portion of the decline may already have occurred.

The average formation length is 153 days (about 5 months). The first leg averages a price decline of 25% in 54 days; the corrective phase posts an average gain of 16% in 39 days, and the second leg declines by 27% in 60 days. You can see in Table 26.2 that the two legs are nearly the same in percentage decline and time.

How much does the corrective phase recover? On average, about 40% to 60% of the first leg decline. Figure 26.7 shows a frequency distribution of the

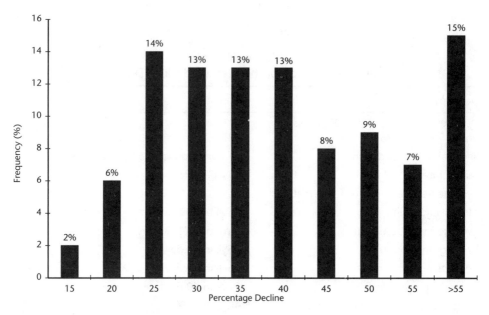

Figure 26.6 Frequency distribution of declines for the measured move down. Ignoring the right column, the most likely decline is between 25% and 40%.

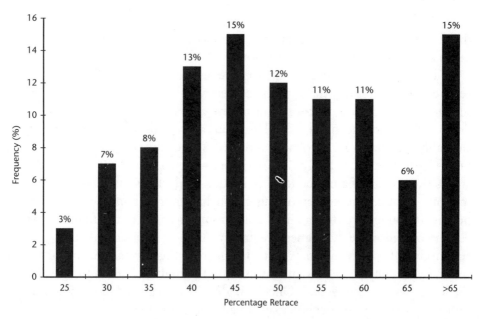

Figure 26.7 Frequency distribution of the percentage price retrace. The corrective phase typically retraces between 40% and 60% of the prior decline.

percentage price retrace shown by the corrective phase when compared with the first leg decline. The highest column, the one on the right, is excluded because it is a catch-all column for large percentage retraces. Ignoring the right column, the 45% column is tallest but is closely joined by the columns from 40% to 60%. Thus, I conclude that the corrective phase retrace is most likely to fall within the 40% to 60% range.

Due to the nature of the measured move down, the chart pattern usually forms near the yearly high. A frequency distribution of the formation start (the highest high in the first leg) when compared with the prior yearly price range shows that 93% of the formations begin in the highest third of the yearly price range. Many of the other formations are ones that occur as prices slide down a trendline and create several measured moves down in a row.

I counted the number of formations meeting or exceeding the measure rule and discovered that only 43% of the formations have second legs that are equal to or longer than the first legs. I consider values above 80% to be reliable. This means you should not depend on the target being met. The 80% benchmark hits when the second leg down move is equal to two-thirds of the first leg.

Trading Tactics

Table 26.3 outlines trading tactics and the measure rule. Use the measure rule to help predict how far prices will decline. Refer to Figure 26.8 during the discussion of its computation. In the figure, four points outline the measured move: A through D. First, tabulate the height of the first leg (shown by points A and B) by subtracting the lowest low (42) from the highest high ($52\frac{7}{8}$). This gives a difference of $10\frac{7}{8}$. Subtract the difference from the highest high in the corrective phase (point C at $47\frac{3}{4}$). The result is a target price of $36\frac{7}{8}$. Prices meet the target on December 7.

Once you suspect that a measured move down is forming, probably just after the corrective phase completes and prices start down, short the stock. Use the measure rule to predict the price target, but expect prices to come up short. Place a stop-loss order $\frac{1}{8}$ above the corrective phase high (the corrective phase is a source of support and resistance). For a more conservative target, follow the measure rule using two-thirds of the first leg height. Prices reach the new target 80% of the time. For example, two-thirds of the first leg height in Figure 26.8 is $7\frac{1}{4}$. Subtracting this value from the corrective phase high gives a closer target of $40\frac{1}{2}$. Cover your short if prices rebound off a support zone or approach the measure rule target.

After a measured move down completes, the corrective phase often spells a resistance zone for future moves. Prices pause on the approach to the

Table 26.3
Trading Tactics for the Measured Move Down

Trading Tactic	Explanation
Measure rule	The second leg is about 10% shorter than the first leg, so expect the actual price to fall short of the target. Compute the length of the first leg from the highest high to the lowest low (at the start of the corrective phase). Subtract the result from the highest high reached in the corrective phase to get the target price (which is met 43% of the time). For a more conservative target, use two-thirds of the first leg height. This shortened height means that prices hit the target 80% of the time.
Short during second leg, stop loss	Short the stock as soon as it becomes clear that a measured move is in progress. If prices rise above the corrective phase high, then close out your position. Prices occasionally will rise up to the corrective phase high a second time before ultimately declining, so put your stop about $\frac{1}{8}$ (or more) above the high.
Close out	Cover your short when the price drops to a support area and meets resistance to a further decline, especially if prices near the measure rule target.
Support/resistance	The corrective phase shows future support or resistance.

corrective phase low and at the high. Figure 26.8 has these zones labeled. If you are nimble, you can anticipate this rise and trade long once the measured move down completes. Sell if prices run into trouble during the corrective phase and begin heading lower. In a bull market you can generally expect prices to eventually push through the corrective phase resistance and move up to the old high.

Sample Trade

People are nasty; just ask Eddy. He is an airline reservation agent. Between the company monitoring his phone calls to be sure he peddles a car and hotel when appropriate and the people screaming at him from the other end of the phone, it is a tough living. There is nothing he can do about equipment problems or the weather, but people do not seem to care. Even the full moon gets into the act as that is when the crazies call.

What he would really like to do is invest in the stock market. He does it now but to a limited extent because of his cash-flow problem. Fortunately, with a few clicks of his computer mouse he can flip to the Internet and monitor his latest stock pick when he is not busy.

That is how he uncovered the situation shown in Figure 26.8. He watched the stock climb from a low of about 10 in June 1994 to a high of $53\frac{5}{8}$ in Octo-

Figure 26.8 Measured move down followed by corrective phase. Eddy made $5 per share trading this (points A–D) measured move down.

ber 1995. Every so often, he would draw trendlines along the bottoms of the minor lows and notice how the upward trend seemed to be accelerating (the trendlines grew steeper over time).

Since he knew this could not last, he was ready for a trend change, which occurred on November 14 when prices pierced the trendline, moving down. Instead of shorting the stock immediately, he decided to wait for a pull-back. Much to his surprise it never came. Prices moved steadily lower until they reached a support level at 42. From that point on, prices rose higher for the next week and a half. Then, they dropped sharply, tumbling $3 in one session.

When prices fell, they pierced a small up trendline, drawn along the bottoms of the climb from points B to C. Eddy recognized what was happening when he drew the trendline on his chart. The chart pattern was making a measured move down, so he shorted the stock that day and received a fill at 42.

He used the measure rule to compute the predicted price move and placed an order with his broker to cover the short at the predicted price (36⅞). Just 3 days after he placed the trade, the stock was covered. He made about $5 a share or 12%.

If you look at Figure 26.8, you can see that prices rose to the level of the corrective phase bottom (point B), then retreated 2 days after Eddy completed his trade. Later on you can see that prices also stopped rising at the top of the corrective phase. The corrective phase is a zone of support and resistance.

27

Measured Move Up

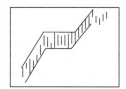

RESULTS SNAPSHOT

Appearance	Prices move up, retrace, then move up again.
Reversal or consolidation	Long-term (over 6 months) bullish reversal
Failure rate	23%
Average rise	68%, with most likely rise between 30% and 60%
First leg rise	43% in 87 days
Corrective phase decline	14% in 45 days
Second leg decline	37% in 65 days
Percentage meeting predicted price target	57%
See also	Flags and Pennants

The measured moved up formation is the reverse of the measured move down. The measured move up sports a 23% failure rate, slightly higher than the 20% maximum I consider reliable formations to possess. However, the average gain is an astounding 68%, which is misleading. The value represents the price difference between the lowest low in the first leg and the highest high in the second leg. Obviously, this is a best-case scenario and you can expect your results to be a little better than half that rate. Why? The reason stems from being able to identify the formation promptly. When the chart pattern enters the corrective phase, where prices retrace their gains, only then can one suspect a measured move is forming. Only after prices start moving up again, at the start of the second up leg, should an investment be placed.

By the Results Snapshot statistics you can see that the second leg averages a 37% gain. Since an investor probably would not take a position in the stock until after the second leg begins, the gain will probably be about 30% or so.

Tour

In the preceding paragraphs I mentioned a number of terms. Figure 27.1 outlines a measured move up formation with the various components labeled. The first leg is composed of a rise in price that follows a trendline. Many times a trendline drawn on either side of the minor highs and lows constructs a channel.

The corrective phase retraces a substantial portion of the rise, usually 35% to 65%, before prices resume rising. In Figure 27.1, the corrective phase begins in late January and extends through most of February. Prices retrace 55% of the first leg price move. Once the correction completes, prices climb even more rapidly during the second leg. You can see that prices bow upward instead of touching the trendline in a sort of rounding-over maneuver before

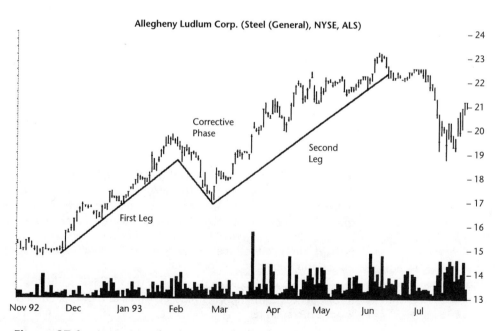

Figure 27.1 A measured move up. The second leg gain nearly matches the gain posted by the first leg.

topping out in June. The rise constitutes what is commonly called the second leg. It is the rise from the corrective phase to the end of the formation.

Once the formation completes, prices sometimes drop back to the level of the corrective phase. In this example, you can see that prices dropped to just below the top of the corrective phase (in July) before recovering. Of course, sometimes prices do not stop there at all. A trend change occurs and prices simply tumble and return to the base of the formation or, worse, continue moving down.

Identification Guidelines

Table 27.1 lists the identification characteristics for this formation. The formation usually, but not always, begins when prices bottom out after a downtrend. The declining price trend can range all over the scale. In Figure 27.1, for example, prices reach the November lows after shooting up in a bull run that starts in December 1991 and ends 2 months later. Then prices meander—essentially moving horizontally with a slight downward bend. Six months later, they decline from a high of about $18\frac{1}{4}$ to a low of $14\frac{3}{4}$.

Consider Figure 27.2 where the price decline is short—barely a month long. Over the longer term (not shown in the figure), prices are rising. They

Table 27.1
Identification Characteristics of the Measured Move Up

Characteristic	Discussion
Downward trend	A downward price trend that lasts from a few weeks to over a year usually precedes the start of the formation. The formation begins a trend change that usually starts from near the yearly low.
First leg	Most times prices follow a trend channel upward before entering the corrective phase.
Corrective phase	Prices decline, usually between 35% to 65% of the first leg move, before heading upward again. The retrace is usually proportional to the first leg rise: Large retraces follow large rises. Sometimes the corrective phase resembles a saw-tooth pattern (a few sharp rises and declines in a row) before prices break away and zoom upward. This saw-tooth pattern usually associates with a long price climb leading to the formation.
Second leg	Prices rise, loosely following the slope of the trendline set by the first leg. Prices commonly fit inside a channel as they rise, but this is not a prerequisite.
Avoid	Avoid formations where the retrace travels too far down the first leg. Anything beyond an 80% retrace is probably too far and too risky to invest in.

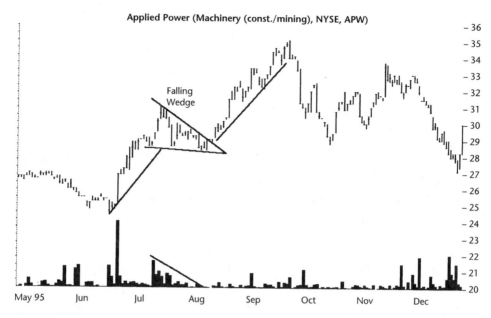

Figure 27.2 A falling wedge marks the corrective phase in this measured move up formation. Note the receding volume trend of the wedge.

begin climbing in November 1993 at a price of 14½ and reach a preformation high of 27 in May 1995—a near double. The figure shows that the first leg has a slight bow to it in the early part of the rise. However, you can extend the up trendline and draw a parallel one connecting the minor highs and see that the first leg fits inside a trend channel. The second leg does even better. The bottom trendline touches several places and a parallel top trendline (not shown for clarity) also intersects the minor highs nicely.

In this case, a falling wedge composes the corrective phase. This formation makes trading the measured move easy since it predicts a price rise. Once prices break out from the wedge, buy into the stock and ride the upward move. If you bought the stock following this procedure, you would make somewhere between 15% and 20%, depending on when you traded the stock. That is not a bad return for a hold time of about 6 weeks. Also note the very distinctive down-sloping volume trend for the falling wedge.

The slope of the two trendlines, along the bottoms of the legs, are nearly the same. It is somewhat surprising how often this holds true. However, just because there is a wide variation in the trend slope is no reason to eliminate a formation from consideration.

In this example, the corrective phase sees prices retrace their prior gains by 40%, within the usual 35% to 65% range for measured move up formations. Sometimes when the rise leading to the start of the formation is extensive, the corrective phase becomes long and choppy, resembling a saw-tooth formation marked by quick rises and sharp declines. In such a case, it might be prudent to wait for prices to rise above the high established during the first leg before investing. That way you can avoid the most common measured move up failure.

Focus on Failures

What exactly is a measured move up failure? I define a failure of a measured move up chart pattern to be when prices do not rise above the prior leg high. The definition is a subjective measure. With deep corrective phases, even a rise to the old high can be a substantial move. Still, I feel the benchmark is a good one, so that is the one used in the statistics.

Figure 27.3 shows the most common type of measured move up failure. The stock forms a double top that kills the second leg rise. The failure is clear since prices rise to 37⅝, just ⅛ below the prior high before heading lower. Certainly the second leg does not near the price move of the first leg as do most well-behaved measured moves. Why does this particular formation fail? The figure shows a choppy, horizontal saw-tooth pattern leading to the first leg rise. The first leg soars above the two tops of the saw-tooth and moves up smartly. Then prices round over and start correcting. The figure, at this point, reminds me of a mini bump-and-run reversal. However, the bump phase just does not meet the two-to-one height ratio of the lead-in phase. Still, it does give you pause about investing in this situation.

Figure 27.3 A measured move up that fails after turning into a double top.

The second leg starts rising with no significant change in volume. This is a warning sign. There is a common Street axiom that says rising prices need high volume but falling prices can decline of their own weight. This formation appears to be an example of that axiom. Since there is little upward buying pressure to push prices higher, they fade out just below the prior top then tumble. The resulting decline sees prices fall below the start of the first leg.

Before we move on to statistics, I want to alert you to some identification problems. You want to avoid formations that have corrective phases that descend too near the first leg start. I do not have a set amount for this, but I would probably steer away from formations that retrace more than 80% or so of the prior upward move.

In addition, if the first leg does not follow a straight course upward or if it fails to stay within a well-defined trend channel (as does the first leg in Figure 27.3), you might want to look elsewhere for a more promising situation. Sometimes when a chart formation does not *feel* right or look right, then it is giving you a warning to stay away. Since this is a common chart pattern, you can easily find another opportunity.

When prices rise steadily for a long time, say over a year or more, then begin a measured move up, the corrective phase might be excessively choppy. I mentioned this behavior in the Identification Guidelines section and in Table 27.1, but it is something to keep in mind.

Also, do not be too quick to buy into the situation. Remember that the corrective phase should be proportional to the first leg rise. By that I mean prices should fall anywhere from 35% to 65% of the first leg move before beginning the second leg. If prices only fall 15% before turning up, then it might be a false breakout.

Sometimes prior peaks are a key to how far prices retrace. These minor highs are often places of support. When prices decline to that level, they pause and move horizontally for a time before continuing down or rebounding. Volume is often a key to the level of support you can expect from these types of situations. A prior peak with high turnover will give more support to a stock on its way down. That is not to say that the stock will not burn through the support, just that it might take more of a push to fall off the cliff.

Statistics

Table 27.2 shows comparatively few statistics for measured move up formations. I located 501 formations and of these formations, 69% act as reversals of the prevailing trend. This means prices are heading steadily down before the start of the first up leg. The remaining 156 formations occur as part of the upward trend.

The failure rate at 23% is higher than the 20% maximum I like to see. The implication is that about one out of four formations fail to rise above the

Table 27.2
General Statistics for the Measured Move Up

Description	Statistic
Number of formations in 500 stocks from 1991 to 1996	501
Reversal or consolidation	156 consolidations, 345 reversals
Failure rate	114 or 23%
Average rise of successful formations	68%
Most likely rise	30% to 60%
Average formation length	6.5 months (197 days)
First leg price rise	43% in 87 days
Corrective phase price decline	14% in 45 days
Second leg price rise	37% in 65 days
Corrective phase percentage retrace	35% to 65%
Percentage of formations occuring near 12-month price low (L), center (C), or high (H)?	L79%, C21%, H1%
Measure rule	57% of second legs are longer than first legs

first leg high before trending down. As mentioned in the Focus on Failures section of this chapter, many failures occur while prices are advancing and forming a second top. They stall out and turn lower, leaving a double top formation.

For those formations that work as expected, the average gain is 68%. As explained earlier, this may sound like an outsized gain and it is. Since you probably will not be able to (or want to, for that matter!) buy into a measured move before the end of the corrective phase, the second leg (37% gain) better represents the performance of the formation.

Figure 27.4 shows the results of a frequency distribution of gains for successful formations in this study. I define the most likely gain as being represented by the highest columns. Since the column on the right is a catch-all column, it is excluded from the analysis. The remainder of the chart indicates that the most likely gain is between 30% and 60%, with a tendency to gravitate toward the upper end of the range. Since over a quarter of the formations have gains over 100%, you might find a situation in which your gains are well above the most likely gain. Remember, I compute the gains from the lowest low in the first leg to the highest high in the second leg. If you invest near the start of the second leg, you should reduce your expectations accordingly.

For a better gauge of the expected gains, consider the performance of the various components. The first leg has a 43% average gain in about 3 months. The corrective phase brings prices down by 14% in 45 days, whereas the last leg sends prices higher by 37% in about 2 months. Your likely gain, depend-

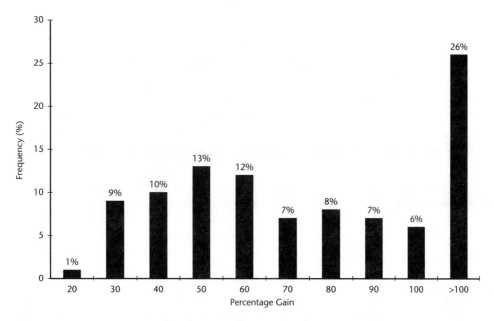

Figure 27.4 Frequency distribution of gains for the measured move up. Excluding the tallest column, the most likely rise is between 30% and 60%.

ing on when you take a position in the stock, will probably be near the second leg gain.

I took a close look at the corrective phase retrace by doing a frequency distribution of the percentage retrace for all successful formations. I graphed the results using a 1% interval ranging from 20 to 80. I wanted to see if there was any truth to the belief that the retrace would be one of the Fibonacci ratios on a percentage basis. The Fibonacci ratio is the ratio between any two successive numbers in a Fibonacci sequence. The Fibonacci sequence begins with the values of zero and one and successive numbers are the sum of the prior two (as in 0, 1, 2, 3, 5, 8, 13 and so on). Once the sequence develops, two important ratios between pairs and the inverse of alternate pairs become clear: 0.618 and 0.382. The theory says that, on a percentage basis, support at the 62% and 38% retracement levels is common.

If there is any truth to the average retrace being a member of these values, then a frequency distribution would illustrate it. I do not show the graph because there are too many columns to be clearly presented, but the results are easily described. The overall graph resembles a bell curve with noticeable peaks. The first peak is at 35% and it towers above the surrounding ones. The next few peaks, which are the tallest on the graph, fall at 47%, 50%, and a somewhat smaller one at 52%. As we advance up the scale, we find another cluster in the 62% to 64% range, with 62% being the highest. Other peaks toward the outer ends of the graph are at 28% and 79%. If we boil down the results, we find that the most common retraces during the corrective phase occur at 35%, 50%, and 62%, close to the predicted values of 38% and 62%.

A frequency distribution of the start of each successful formation in the yearly price range shows that most of the formations begin life within a third of their yearly low. Only 21% of the formations begin in the center third of the yearly price range. The significance of this should be obvious but I state it here anyway: If you think you have a measured move up occurring within one-third of the yearly high, then you are probably wrong. Avoid those measured moves that do not occur near the yearly low.

Slightly over half (57%) of the formations fulfill the measure rule. The measure rule conveniently leads us into the Trading Tactics section.

Trading Tactics

Table 27.3 shows trading tactics for measured move up formations. The measure rule predicts the level to which prices will rise. To estimate the target price, compute the height of the first leg. I use the measured move up formation shown in Figure 27.5 as an example. Locate the highest high in the first leg. Usually this is somewhere near the beginning of the corrective phase, and point A indicates this in the figure. From this value ($21\frac{1}{8}$), subtract the lowest low ($14\frac{1}{8}$) in the first leg, shown as point B. The difference (7) is the height of the first leg. Add it to point C ($18\frac{3}{8}$)—or the lowest low in the corrective phase—to arrive at the target price. In this case, the target price is $25\frac{3}{8}$. Prices reach the target just 10 trading days after the corrective phase ends.

On a *price basis*, the second leg is about 10% *longer* than the first leg, on average, even though it represents a 37% price change versus 43% for the first leg. (This anomaly is due to rising prices. If the percentages are the same, the price move will not be.) However, just 57% of the formations have second legs

Table 27.3
Trading Tactics for the Measured Move Up

Trading Tactic	Explanation
Measure rule	Calculate the height of the first leg from highest high to lowest low. Add the difference to the lowest low in the correct phase. The result is the expected target price. Decide if the predicted move is worth the risk of a trade.
Yearly low	Choose formations that start (have their lowest low during the first leg) in the lowest third of the yearly price range. Avoid those forming near the yearly high.
Buy	Take a position in the stock sometime after the corrective phase completes and prices rise during the second leg.
Support/resistance	The corrective phase shows future support or resistance.

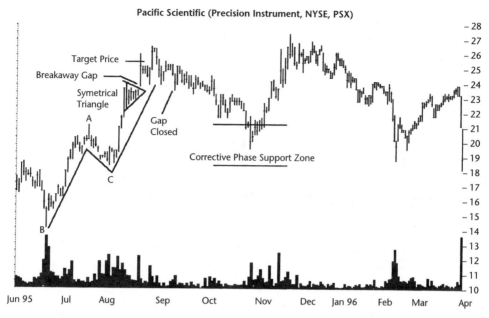

Figure 27.5 Measured move up formation with symmetrical triangle. Michelle rode this measured move up in a stock she owned. She sold when the breakaway gap closed. A symmetrical triangle shows a typical volume trend.

that are equal to or longer than the first legs. In other words, slightly over half the successful formations fulfill the measure rule. I consider values above 80% to be reliable, so the measured move up formation falls well short of the mark.

Once you calculate the target price using the measure rule, ask yourself if the gain is large enough to justify a trade. If the answer is yes, then look at the chart again. Are there areas of resistance on the way to the target price where the stock might get hung up? If so, you might need to lower your target. If you are lucky and significant resistance is above your target, you can move your price upward to just below the resistance zone. In all likelihood the stock will shoot into the resistance zone, so you will have ample opportunity to close out your position.

When selecting a formation to trade, it is best to choose those that start near the yearly low. In my analysis of these chart patterns, only two appear within the upper third of the yearly price range. The vast majority (79%) are near the yearly low. After prices leave the corrective phase, then buy the stock. To gauge the breakout point, draw a down-sloping trendline along the minor highs in the corrective phase. Once prices *close* above the trendline, then buy the stock. As the stock approaches the target price, do not be too quick to sell. If prices are on a roll, go with the flow and wait for prices to start declining. Obviously, if prices pause near but below the target price, then it might be wise to sell.

Once prices begin moving down, they sometimes return all the way down to the corrective phase before meeting any meaningful support. They may pause at the top of the corrective phase or rebound at the bottom of it. Sometimes, prices just sail right on through. Whatever the case, be aware that if you do not sell near the target price and decide to hold on, you might lose all your gains.

Sample Trade

Michelle is an engineer. Over the years, she has developed a thick skin to take the ribbing from her college colleagues in a male-dominated profession. Even when she ventured into the professional environment after college, the ribbing continued. Make no mistake: She is pretty and they just wanted her attention. I saw this firsthand when I stopped by her office with a question. She was not there at the time, but her desk blotter had the scribblings of love notes from dozens of men. Of course, I added my own. But I digress.

If you were to give a Rubic's cube to Michelle, she would not necessarily solve it. First, she would want to take it apart to see how it is constructed. This inquisitiveness coupled with her ability to solve tough problems in a unique way makes her special even among engineers. She is also an investor with the same qualities.

Michelle had a unique way to take advantage of the situation shown in Figure 27.5. She already owned the stock but believed it was running out of steam. During the prior November to February period (not shown), she saw the stock form a double top. Prices declined from a high of $24\frac{1}{8}$ to the low of $14\frac{1}{8}$ at the start of the measured move.

Unfortunately, as a novice investor, she was unable to pull the trigger and sell it after prices confirmed the double top. She rode the decline down to the low and saw 41% of her gains evaporate. When the stock began moving up, she breathed easier. Still, she vowed to do better the next time. As the stock started its climb, she saw the increase in volume. The increase meant that the run would be an extended one, as there seemed to be enough enthusiasm to send prices higher.

All bull runs must pause now and again and this situation was no different. Michelle saw the stock pause and consolidate for nearly a month during July. She looked back at the chart and noticed that the stock had reached a zone of resistance where there were several old highs that stalled prices near the 21 level. Volume picked up and when prices shot upward, she immediately recognized the measured move formation. Did she sell? No. She hung on for the ride. Michelle calculated that the stock would rise to $25\frac{3}{8}$, a new yearly high. She suspected that the stock might find resistance at the old highs of 24, and that is exactly what happened. A symmetrical triangle formed in the stock. The formation obeyed the rules for symmetrical triangles, lower highs and higher lows with a receding volume pattern, and she was confident that she had correctly identified it.

Since there was no way to tell which direction the stock would break out of the triangle, she sat tight. Then prices gapped out the top. Was the gap a breakaway gap or an exhaustion gap? She reasoned that since the gap appeared just after a region of consolidation, it was most likely a breakaway gap, so prices would continue rising, but how far? She hoped the triangle represented the halfway mark of an up move. She knew that symmetrical triangle formations sometimes act like half-mast formations, so she expected a climb to 28 (see the measure rule for Symmetrical Triangles). To her it sounded like a long shot, but one worth waiting for. Her calculated price target of $25\frac{3}{8}$ was met the day prices jumped out of the triangle.

About a week after prices left the triangle, they reached a new high then fell back. When prices closed the gap in the first part of September, she decided to sell her holdings. Fortunately, the next day prices zoomed upward and she was able to sell her shares at $24\frac{1}{2}$, near the daily high of $25\frac{1}{8}$. As she watched, the stock tumbled back to the middle of the corrective phase, right in the center of the support zone. Then, the stock recovered. As the stock climbed and posted a new high, she wondered if she had sold too soon. She felt better after reviewing the chart 6 months later and seeing prices hovering in the $15 range.

28

One-Day Reversals

 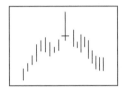

RESULTS SNAPSHOT

Tops

Appearance	A large 1-day upward price spike with prices closing near the low
Reversal or consolidation	Short-term (up to 3 months) bearish reversal
Failure rate	24%
Average decline	19%, with most likely decline being 10%
Volume trend	Heavy volume on reversal day but recedes quickly
Pullbacks	71%
Synonyms	Climax Day, Selling Climax

Bottoms

Appearance	A large 1-day downward price spike with prices closing near the high
Reversal or consolidation	Short-term (up to 3 months) bullish reversal
Failure rate	17%
Average rise	26%, with most likely rise between 10% and 15%
Volume trend	Heavy volume on reversal day but recedes quickly
Throwbacks	61%
Synonyms	Climax Day, Selling Climax

One-day reversals (ODRs): The only surprise in the Results Snapshots is that the formations perform so well. Sure, the 24% failure rate for tops is above the 20% maximum I arbitrarily assign to reliable formations, but it could be worse. The average loss for tops at 19% is quite close to the average of 20% for all bearish formations. However, bottom reversals, with gains averaging 26%, are well short of the usual 40% for bullish patterns. The most likely rise is 10% to 15%, about what you would expect. I suspect that by the time you place a trade after this formation, it will be too late and your return will be unremarkable.

Pullbacks are prevalent (happening in 71% of the ODR tops) and suggest you might wait for them before investing in an ODR top. Throwbacks are a bit weak, however, so do not depend on seeing them in ODR bottoms.

Tour

The ODR top shown in Figure 28.1 marks the crest of an unbalanced head-and-shoulders top. It appears after a long climb that begins in January. The ODR has a closing price near the daily low and the spike itself is longer than many of the spikes over the preceding year.

Figure 28.2 shows what the bottom version of the ODR looks like. It appears after a downtrend that in this case is not very long. The downtrend

Figure 28.1   A one-day reversal top appears as a large spike with a closing price near the daily low. It marks the head of an unbalanced head-and-shoulders top.

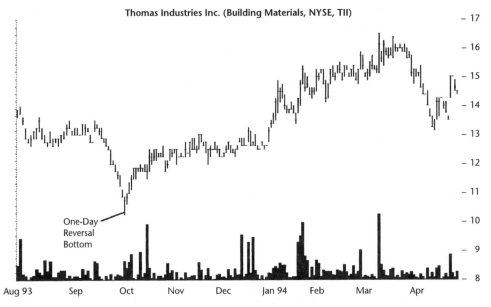

Thomas Industries Inc. (Building Materials, NYSE, TII)

Figure 28.2 A one-day reversal bottom appears after a downtrend. Note the large downward price spike with a closing price near the daily high.

begins just 2 months before the reversal. The ODR bottom has a closing price near the daily high and accompanies high volume, and the spike is longer than other spikes throughout the prior year.

Why do ODRs form? When I see a large price spike, I think of one thing: stop running. Imagine a series of stop-loss orders placed consecutively below the current price. It does not take much of a downward move to trigger the first stop. If the number of shares being sold is large enough, coupled with the assistance of short sellers, traders, and market makers, the price may drop even further. When that happens, the next stop triggers and so on. The price tumbles until enough buying demand comes on-line to stop the cascade. This stop running (or gunning the stops) is intentional.

Once it is over all the people wanting to sell their shares have already sold, so there is overwhelming buying demand. The price recovers to near where it started the day. At the close, a long thin line appears on the bar chart. It is an ODR, where prices start the day about where they end, but in the interim, prices plummet several points. The selling pressure abates leaving only buying demand to carry prices higher over the coming days.

The same scenario applies to ODR tops. Prices quickly rise but finish the day near the lows. Afterward, overwhelming selling pressure takes prices lower.

Identification Guidelines

How do you identify ODR tops and bottoms? Table 28.1 highlights some characteristics to assist you in your selection process. First, start with a price trend. In many cases, the ODR occurs at the end of the trend, so the trend is usually a long drawn out affair (over several months). Some ODRs occur after prices move for only a few weeks, so it varies from formation to formation.

For ODR tops look for a rising price trend; for ODR bottoms, the trend should be declining. Do not make the mistake of picking an ODR top in a declining price trend or an ODR bottom in a rising price trend. Although these spikes might act as consolidations, it is best to limit your selections to reversals and depend on a trend change.

Figures 28.1 and 28.2 show an ODR top and an ODR bottom. In Figure 28.1 you can see part of the upward trend that begins at a price of $5.70 nearly a year before the reversal. Figure 28.2 shows a much shorter and sharper decline. A zoom-out of the figure shows an upward trend that begins in November 1992 and peaks in August. Then, the stock moves horizontally and tumbles for 2 weeks down to the ODR.

Both figures show large price spikes that seem to poke well beyond their peers. The daily range exceeds anything on the charts up to that date. The spikes seem to stand alone with good visibility to the left.

Another key identification guideline is where prices close. For tops the closing price should be at or near the daily low. Bottom reversals show just the opposite: The closing price should be near the daily high. The closing price near the end of the range suggests prices are likely to continue in the new direction. For tops the direction is down and for bottoms it is up. Although the next day's trading range may cover some of the ODR, prices commonly close, and the range moves, in the predicted direction.

Table 28.1
Identification Characteristics of One-Day Reversals

Characteristic	Discussion
Price trend	For ODR tops, look for a price uptrend over several weeks or months. For ODR bottoms, the price trend should be down.
Large spike	Both tops and bottoms sport tall price spikes. The spikes should be twice as large, or more, as the average spike over the prior year.
Close near end	For tops the closing price should be near the low of the day, and for bottoms it should be near the high. By *near*, I mean within one-third of the daily range.
Volume	Volume is usually higher on the reversal day than the prior day and can be unusually strong.

The last guideline is volume. Usually, an ODR, either a top or bottom, shows high volume, certainly volume that is above the prior day. This is clear in Figure 28.2, where the high volume lasts for several days as prices climb, but is less outstanding in Figure 28.1. Volume seems to be higher on bottoms than on tops, supporting the belief that rising prices need a push while declining prices can fall of their own weight.

Focus on Failures

Unfortunately, failures occur too often with these formations. Failures such as those shown in Figures 28.3 and 28.4 are typical. Figure 28.3 shows an ODR top failure. The price trend is up, the ODR spike towers above the surrounding prices, the closing price is near the daily low, and there is high volume— all the ingredients needed for a successful ODR. It works. Two days later, prices drop from an ODR high of 39 to a low of $35\frac{1}{2}$.

If investors were to try to take advantage of this situation, they may not recognize an ODR until the next day or even later. Therefore, I compute performance using the lowest price in the ODR to the ultimate low. In this case, the ODR low is $37\frac{1}{8}$, rendering a price decline of 4%. I consider declines of less than 5% as failures (the so-called 5% failure).

Figure 28.4 shows a similar situation with an ODR bottom. Here, the downward spike is obvious. Volume attending the spike is high and prices close

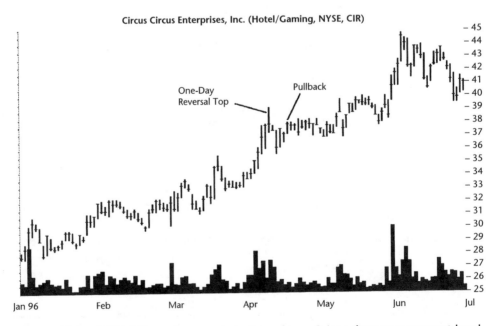

Figure 28.3   A 5% failure of a one-day reversal top. Prices drop to a support level then recover.

American Brands, Inc. (Tobacco, NYSE, AMB)

One-Day Reversal
Bottom Failure

A

Jul 92   Aug   Sep   Oct   Nov   Dec   Jan 93   Feb

Figure 28.4   A one-day reversal bottom fails after prices rise by less than 5%.

near the high for the day. The situation suggests prices will move higher and they do for nearly 2 months, then they begin moving lower again. From the daily high at the ODR to point A, the ultimate high for this formation, prices climb by less than 4%. This performance qualifies as a 5% failure.

The reason for failure in each case is similar. Can you guess what it is? They both stumble across support or resistance barriers that they cannot penetrate. Figure 28.3 has significant support at the 35½ level, whereas Figure 28.4 has resistance in the 43 to 44 range. The movement stalls at the zones and reverses, setting up for the eventual failure. The lesson to be learned from these two failures is that you should always look to see how far you expect the move to go. Consider the areas of support and resistance before making a trade.

Statistics

Table 28.2 shows statistics for ODR tops and bottoms. ODRs are not as plentiful as some other formations, but that is not to say they are scarce. On the contrary, I uncovered 235 tops and 331 bottoms in the stocks I examined.

Almost a quarter (24%) of the ODR tops and 17% of the ODR bottoms fail. Prices continue moving in the same direction after the formation as before (in other words, 5% failures, where prices briefly move in the expected direction then reverse). When they do work, ODR tops have average declines of 19%, whereas ODR bottoms rise by 26%.

Table 28.2
General Statistics for One-Day Reversals

Description	Tops	Bottoms
Number of formations in 500 stocks from 1991 to 1996	235	331
Failure rate	56 or 24%	57 or 17%
Average decline/rise of successful formations	19%	26%
Most likely decline/rise	10%	10% to 15%
Percentage of pullbacks/ throwbacks	71% or 165	61% or 202
Average time to pullback/ throwback completion	13 days	16 days
Days to ultimate low/high	2 months (66 days)	3 months (96 days)
Percentage of ODRs occurring near 12-month price low (L), center (C), or high (H)	L6%, C17%, H77%	L35%, C34%, H31%
Percentage gain for each 12-month lookback period	L20%, C22%, H17%	L30%, C23%, H28%
Volume for ODR day and next 5 days versus day before ODR	182%, 110%, 77%, 62%, 69%, 72%	214%, 107%, 86%, 75%, 74%, 74%
Number of ODR days with volume above prior day	170 or 72%	285 or 86%
Number of days with twice prior day's volume	93 or 40%	176 or 53%

Figure 28.5 illustrates the results of a frequency distribution of losses or gains for ODR tops and bottoms, respectively. By far, the tallest columns are those situated near the 10% and 15% categories. These categories signify the most likely returns for ODRs. Almost half (49%) of the tops decline by 15% or less, an alarming result if you short a stock expecting a long decline. Bottoms perform marginally better, but that is scant comfort when the study period encompasses a raging bull market.

Pullbacks at 71% and throwbacks at 61% are reassuringly high (especially pullbacks). However, they take somewhat longer than usual to complete at 13 and 16 days, respectively (normal completion time is about 10 to 12 days). If you are considering shorting a stock showing an ODR top, you would probably be wise to wait for a throwback before investing. After the throwback, wait for prices to head down again before selling short.

The time it takes to reach the ultimate low or high is brief, at 66 and 96 days for ODR tops and bottoms, respectively. This coincides with the small average losses and gains for the two formation types. Small returns take a correspondingly shorter time to reach their price targets than do larger gains.

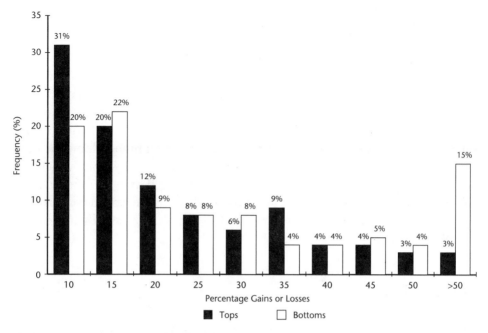

Figure 28.5 Frequency distribution of returns for one-day reversals. The chart suggests that the most likely return is less than 15%.

If we divide the prior year's price range into three parts, we discover that ODR tops predominantly form within a third of the yearly high. This is no surprise, really, because the chart pattern forms after an extended up move.

ODR bottoms form near the yearly low but not decisively so. You can see that the range splits evenly around 30% and change. This surprised me. I expected bottoms to appear near the yearly low, not spread evenly across the range. The results suggest that ODR bottoms happen after a short price retrace, not an extended downtrend.

If we substitute the performance into the yearly range, we discover that the best performing tops occur in the center of the yearly price range (with declines averaging 22%), whereas bottoms outperform near the low (a 30% rise). The results are close enough to each other that nothing meaningful results, but you can use the information to select better ODR candidates. Choose ODR bottoms near the yearly low and ODR tops in the center third of the yearly price range for best average performance.

Table 28.2 shows volume numbers for the two formation types. Both show heavy volume on the reversal day that quickly diminishes. Since this is an average, I counted the number of ODR days with volume above the prior day. For ODR tops 72% are higher, whereas 86% of ODR bottoms have higher volume. If you set the benchmark to twice the prior day's volume, the scores drop to 40% for tops and 53% for bottoms, meaning that high volume usually accompanies ODRs—well, higher than the day before the ODR at any rate.

Trading Tactics

I do not recommend trading ODRs. Although their average return is acceptable, the most likely return is just too small at less than 15%. I consider these values just too skimpy to risk a trade. Coupled with a high failure rate, for ODR tops anyway, one should look for a more promising formation. However, that is not to say that these formations are not useful. They are. If you are considering buying a stock and see a large upward spike on high volume, beware. Prices will likely head lower. The same applies to downward spikes, which signal a bullish reversal. Again, that is worth knowing if you see one of these spikes in a stock you own. A large downward spike may cause you concern, but it is really a bullish event. Prices generally move higher, especially if the close is near the daily high.

Sample Trade

Consider how Jim used an ODR top in a stock he owned (see Figure 28.6). Jim likes to ski. When he left for his ski trip in mid-February, the stock was making new highs. He was having so much fun that he forgot to check in with his broker and was unaware of the 22% decline (from 25 to 19⅝). When he returned from his trip and got back into his daily routine, the news awaiting him was shocking.

Figure 28.6 One-day reversal top formation following a pipe and a broadening formation. Jim used the one-day reversal top as the final sell signal. Highlighted is a pipe top (pretend it is on the weekly scale) and a broadening bottom.

On a weekly scale, the stock made a pipe top suggesting prices would tumble and they did. As Jim followed the stock each day, it appeared to be making a sort of broadening formation. His experience told him that a break-out from a broadening bottom (a bottom since prices were trending down to the formation) could occur in either direction, so he was sure to stay close to his charts. The day after he saw the ODR top appear on high volume, he decided that the price was the best he could do. The pipe, broadening formation, and ODR were all clues pointing to the same conclusion: The stock was going down. He sold that day at $22\frac{3}{8}$, well above his purchase price of $10\frac{5}{8}$.

In Jim's case, he was not trading the formation itself. Instead, he used the information to protect profits in a stock he already owned. In August the stock reached a low of $11\frac{3}{8}$, about half the price at which he sold.

29

Outside Days

RESULTS SNAPSHOT

Upside Breakouts

Appearance	A daily price range wider than the prior day; breakout is upward
Reversal or consolidation	Short-term (up to 3 months) bullish consolidation
Failure rate	25%
Average rise	32%, with most likely rise less than 10%
Surprising findings	Many. See Table 29.3.

Downside Breakouts

Appearance	A daily price range wider than the prior day; breakout is downward
Reversal or consolidation	Short-term (up to 3 months) bearish consolidation
Failure rate	42%
Average decline	17%, with most likely decline less than 10%
Surprise findings	Many. See Table 29.3

Outside days are mirror images of inside days. Outside days are characterized by a wider price range, one that is both higher and lower than the prior day.

The formation comes in two varieties: those with upside breakouts and those with downside ones.

Upside breakouts, as the Results Snapshot outlines, sport a failure rate of 25%, just above the maximum 20% rate that I consider acceptable. The average rise is a subpar 32% with a likely rise of less than 10%. Downside breakouts perform substantially worse in some respects. Their failure rate is exceedingly high at 42% with an average decline of 17%. The average decline is not bad for a bearish formation but the most likely loss is less than 10%. With likely gains or losses of less than 10%, you have to consider whether this formation is worth trading. Meager gains coupled with a high failure rate suggest that this is probably one formation to avoid.

Tour and Identification Guidelines

Table 29.1 lists identification characteristics for outside days. This formation is easy to identify and it is also common. Figure 29.1 shows what I mean. I have identified over a dozen outside days in the chart (each dot highlights an outside day). An outside day is just as it sounds: The daily price range is outside the prior day. By that I mean the high is higher than the prior high and the low is below the prior low. In essence, an outside day looks like a 2-day broadening formation; the price range broadens out.

The combination of the wide outside day with the comparatively narrow day before implies one thing: a price move. Traders, once they spot an outside day, wait for prices to move above the high or below the low. That becomes the direction they trade. For example, the first outside day shown in Figure 29.1 begins with a $\frac{3}{4}$ point difference between the high and low of the day before (46 to 46$\frac{3}{4}$). The outside day widens the range to 46$\frac{7}{8}$ and 45$\frac{7}{8}$. The following day, the day after the outside day, prices make a new high but the stock closes unchanged. A trader would be wise to wait for a definitive breakout—a close either above or below the outside day's high or low.

Two days later a breakout results when prices move decidedly lower and close at 45$\frac{1}{2}$, comfortably below the low of the outside day. A downward

Table 29.1
Identification Characteristics of Outside Days

Characteristic	Discussion
Higher high	The daily high must be above the prior daily high. No ties allowed.
Lower low	The daily low must be below the prior daily low. No ties allowed.
Daily range	The day before the outside day must have a daily range. In other words, the daily high cannot be the same as the daily low.

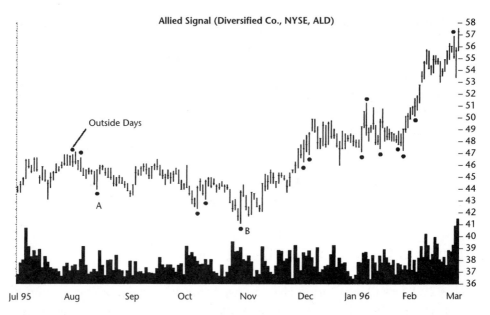

Figure 29.1   Numerous outside days highlighted by black dots. Point A suggests prices will move higher and they do, but only briefly. Point B is a more timely buy signal.

breakout appears, telling astute traders that prices should continue moving down. And that is just what happens. The stock reaches a low of 41⅛ in late October.

Before you get too excited about this formation, look at point A on the chart in Figure 29.1. It highlights an outside day too. A day later prices close above the high posted by the outside day and it appears the stock is moving up. The breakout signal is correct, too, as prices close even higher the next day. But that is all. From that point on, prices tumble.

Let us say you buy after the breakout (2 days after the outside day; the first day after the outside day suggests an upward price move so you buy the next day) and happen to receive a fill at 46. During September you have a handful of days to sell the stock at a small profit or break-even. Your first real chance to make a tidy sum is during the holidays in late November. On May 1 the stock climbs to over 60. That is not a bad move from 46, but during the interim you would need the fortitude to wait out a decline to 41 (a 10% paper loss).

By now you might be asking yourself if this formation really works. Take a look at point B. This outside day calls the turning point exactly. Imagine getting in at the low, 41⅛, and riding it up to 60. That is almost a 50% move. Of course, it also requires perfect timing, a quality that eludes most of us.

Scan the various figures in this chapter and decide for yourself whether this formation is trustworthy. Perhaps there are lessons to learn if we focus on the failures.

Focus on Failures

Since this formation has no definitive breakout direction, one cannot assign a failure to a particular chart pattern simply because it breaks out in the wrong direction. Instead, I wait for what I call a 5% failure. If a chart pattern breaks out upward, for example, moves up by less than 5% before turning around and tumbling, then the formation is a 5% failure. This also applies to downside breakouts. If a stock breaks out downward but travels down less than 5% before heading up substantially, it is a 5% failure.

Figure 29.2 shows an example of a 5% failure. After a sharp run up beginning in late April, the stock takes a breather in mid-May and essentially moves horizontally for just over a week before continuing up. It is during this pause that the stock forms an outside day. The stock trades within a very narrow range, 26⅛ to 26. The following day, the outside day, the stock has a price range of 26⅜ to 25⅞. The wider range, both above and below the previous day's range, classifies the new day as an outside day.

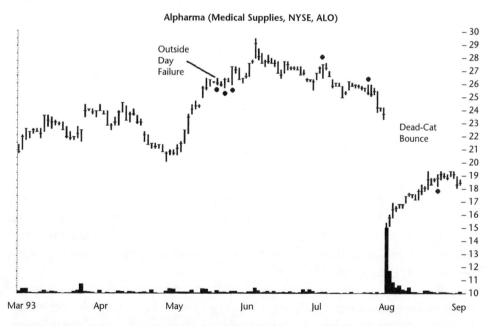

Figure 29.2 The outside day suggests a downside breakout but prices move down by less than 5% before recovering. The result is a 5% failure. Later, a dead-cat bounce drops prices drastically before they bounce.

The next day the stock closes lower, suggesting a downside breakout. However, the stock, although posting a lower low the following day, closes higher. If investors sell their holdings on the belief that a downward trend change is at hand, they are disappointed in the short term. The stock moves up, in the process creating three outside days in a row, peaking in early June at $29\frac{3}{8}$. The outside day is a 5% failure because the stock only drops about $\frac{3}{8}$ before recovering.

Look what happens 3 months later. The stock falls off a cliff and splashes $9 lower, a massive, 1-day decline of 38%. The stock executes a dead-cat bounce and ends up closing even lower 4 months later (typical for a dead-cat bounce).

During the rounding over of the stock, there are a total of five outside days, three of them predicting a decline. The last outside day with a downside breakout (suggesting lower prices) is just over a week before the tumble.

We discuss statistics in a moment, but let me reference the failure rate. For upside breakouts, the formation is above the 20% maximum permissible rate with 25% being failures. For downside breakouts, the formation performs even worse: 42% are failures. Of the two, the upside breakout is more reliable than the downside one, but still below par.

I searched through the formations in the 51 stocks that I catalogued, and I could find no consistent guide to determining whether a formation is going to fail or not. With a bull market from 1991 to 1996, the 5-year period under review, it is no wonder that upside breakouts fail less frequently than downside ones.

At first I thought these formations occurred at short-term turning points but that was rejected when I highlighted all formations in a stock (not just 10 per stock as I have in the study). Outside days seem to appear all over the place. I am inclined to think that these chart patterns are just random events with no real value. With that in mind, let us look at the statistics.

Statistics

Table 29.2 shows general statistics for outside days. I programmed my computer to identify every outside day and it soon became apparent that there were too many to log. Not only did they clog my screen but they would have overloaded my spreadsheet as well, so, just like inside days, I limited the number of outside days I would review.

The computer counts the number of formations in a stock and skips as many as necessary so that I end up with 10 widely space formations per stock. For example, if a stock has 150 formations (which is not unusual, let me assure you) over a 5-year span, the computer selects the first 1, skips the next 14, then selects another and so on until it has 10 identified. Selecting the formations in this manner spreads them out over time and using only 10 per stock diversifies

Table 29.2
General Statistics for Outside Days

Description	Upside Breakout	Downside Breakout
510 formations in 51 stocks from 1991 to 1996, limited to 10 formations per stock	268	242
Reversal or consolidation	148 consolidations, 120 reversals	133 consolidations, 109 reversals
Failure rate	67 or 25%	101 or 42%
Average rise/decline of successful formations	32%	17%
Most likely rise/decline	10%	10%
For successful formations, days to ultimate high/low	4 months (120 days)	1.5 months (49 days)
Percentage of outside days occurring near 12-month low (L), center (C), or high (H)	L21%, C25%, H54%	L33%, C29%, H38%
Percentage gain/loss for each 12-month lookback period	L49%, C32%, H32%	L14%, C20%, H17%
Volume day before to day after versus 25-day moving average	86%, 112%, 115%	86%, 112%, 115%
Percentage gain/loss for volume 1.5× 25-day moving average	37%	18%
Percentage gain/loss for volume 0.5× 25-day moving average	29%	20%

them over a number of different stocks and industries as well. I believe that the 510 formations I ended up using are a representative sample of the entire database.

Since chart patterns with upside breakouts might perform differently than downside ones, I analyzed them separately. The pattern splits almost evenly between upside breakouts, with 268 formations identified, and downside breakouts, at 242 formations. In both cases, they act as consolidations of the short-term price trend.

The failure rate, at 25% for upside breakouts and 42% for downside ones, is above the maximum 20% that reliable formations possess. Failure is measured by first observing the direction of the breakout. When prices start a new trend, the breakout direction is easy to ascertain. When the breakout direction is less clear, the closing price is the key along with a higher high or lower low. Eventually, the stock will close above or below the outside day and that becomes the breakout direction. Then the ultimate high or low is found by determining when the trend changes, typically with a significant price move in an adverse direction. If prices fail to move higher than 5% before reversing direction and dropping through the outside day's low (for upside breakouts) or high (for downside ones), then the formation is a failure. In short, prices must move more than 5% in the breakout direction to classify as successful.

The average rise or decline is 32% for upside breakouts and 17% for downside ones. Both figures are a bit shy of the benchmark; a well-performing bullish formation typically scores about 40%, whereas bearish formations return about 20%. So, not only is the failure rate higher than it should be, the performance is subpar too.

A frequency distribution of the gains and losses gives a better perspective on what an average investor can expect to earn. Most of the formations have gains of just 5% to 10%. A few larger gains pull the overall average upward.

Figure 29.3 shows the results of the frequency distribution for both types of breakouts. The tallest column represents the gain or loss with the highest frequency. This turns out to be the first column (up to a 10% return) for both types of breakouts. Adding the columns with similar breakout directions together, we see that 56% of the formations with downside breakouts have losses less than 15%. Upside breakouts perform marginally better with 52% of the formations having returns of 20% or less. In essence, your chances of having a poorly performing formation is comparatively high.

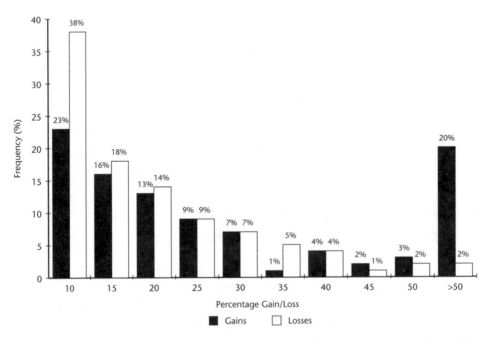

Figure 29.3 Frequency distribution of gains and losses for outside days. The tallest column shows the most likely return, the one with the highest frequency, and it is 10% for both gains and losses.

For successful formations, it takes 4 months (120 days) to reach the ultimate high and 49 days to reach the ultimate low, on average, for upside and downside breakouts. That sounds about right. It takes upside breakouts about twice as long to travel twice as far.

Where in the yearly price range do outside days occur? Those with upside breakouts usually occur within a third of the yearly high. This is also true for downside breakouts, but the range is closer to a third for each. Mapping performance over the three ranges, we discover the best performing outside days are those with breakouts within a third of the yearly low. They have gains averaging 49%. Downside breakouts are more evenly split, but the center third of the yearly price range performs best with losses averaging 20%.

A review of the volume statistics turns up no surprises. The day before the outside day scores 86% of the 25-day volume moving average. The outside day shows slightly higher volume, 112% of the average, and the following day registers 115%. I did not separate the volume statistics according to breakout direction.

Do outside days showing a large number of shares traded mean a more powerful move? Yes, and no. Formations with upside breakouts having volume over 1.5 times the 25-day moving average (that is, at least 50% above normal) show gains of 37%, above the 32% registered for all formations with upside breakouts. Downside breakouts are similar, with losses of 18% versus 17% after ignoring volume.

In comparison, low volume shows a different trend. Upside breakouts perform worse (with a 29% gain) but downside breakouts perform better, with losses of 20%. For this test, formations with volume levels 50% below average qualify.

Table 29.3 shows some surprising results for outside days. Does the closing price the day before the outside day predict the eventual breakout direction? Yes, and no. I divided the daily price range into three segments, the upper and lower segments representing 25% of the price range with the center section representing 50%. Then I compared the closing price in the upper or lower segments with the breakout direction. When the stock closes within 25% of the daily high the day before the outside day, the stock shows an upside breakout 46% of the time—less than correctly selecting the side of a coin flip. However, when the price closes within 25% of the daily low, an upside breakout occurs 61% of the time. I admit that this is a strange result, but that is what the statistics show. By the way, this is for all formations, even those with 5% failures, not just those with successful breakouts.

Does the closing price of the outside day predict the breakout direction? Using the same methodology, an upside breakout when the outside day's close is within 25% of the daily high predicts correctly 66% of the time. Similarly, a downside breakout when prices are within 25% of the daily low is correct 62% of the time.

Table 29.3
Surprising Results for Outside Days

Description	Results
Does closing price of day before outside day predict breakout direction?	Maybe
Does the closing price of the outside day predict the breakout direction?	Yes
Does closing price of outside day versus prior day predict breakout direction?	Yes
Do outside days result in larger price ranges the next day?	17% have larger price ranges
The smaller the daily price-range ratio between the day before and the outside day, the larger the rise or decline.	Result is random
Shorter formations are more powerful.	True, for upside breakouts only

Does the closing price of the outside day versus the prior day predict the breakout direction? This is a bit confusing so let me explain. I divided the day before the outside day into three sections: 25%, 50%, and 25% of the daily price range. Then I compared the closing price of the outside day with those three sections. When the outside day's closing price is higher than 25% from the daily high of the prior day, then an upside breakout correctly signals 65% of the time. Similarly, a downside breakout happens 62% of the time. I do not attach any cosmic importance to this finding simply because the outside day is wider than the prior day, so a close 25% from the prior day's high (low) or higher (lower) is comparatively easy to reach.

Of the three findings, I place the most importance on the belief that *the close of the outside day predicts the breakout direction*. If the close of the outside day is within 25% of the daily high or low, then prices are likely to move higher (upside breakout) or lower (downside breakout), respectively.

Do outside days result in larger price ranges the next day? No. Only 17% of the formations show a wider price range the day after an outside day. This is really no surprise since an outside day by definition is a wide animal, so it is only natural that the daily price range narrows somewhat the next day.

With *inside days*, there appears to be a relationship between the daily price range of the 2-day formation with the ultimate gain or loss. Smaller daily price-range ratios perform better than larger ones. With outside days there appears to be no such relationship. A scatter plot of the results shows the relationship to be random.

The last surprising finding is that smaller formations appear to be more powerful. Figure 29.4 shows the relationship. I computed the height (the difference between the intraday high and low) for the outside day and drew a scat-

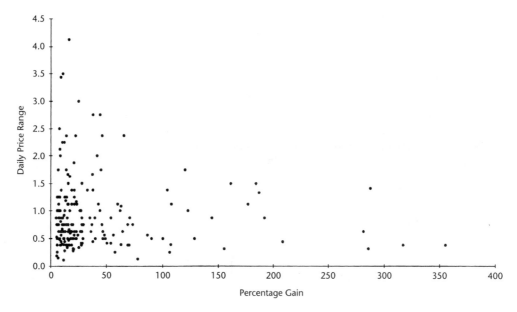

Figure 29.4 Scatter plot of daily price range versus percentage gain. Shorter formations perform better by scoring larger gains. This applies to upside breakouts only.

ter plot of the range with the resulting percentage gain (for upside breakouts only). The chart shows that shorter formations have larger price gains. For example, the highest gain from a formation with a daily price range over $2 is less than 75%, while the best gain for formations under $2 is over 350%. Many comparatively short formations have gains over 100%.

As you look at the figure, you can count the number of dots over 100%. There are 20. There are 185 short formations (meaning a daily range of less than $2) with upside breakouts, so the chances of any given short formation scoring an outsized gain is small—about 11% (that is, 20/185). If your outside day has a price range of just $0.50, then the likelihood of showing a gain over 50% is about one in three (33%). That is not bad, but the bottom line is: Don't hold your breath. The relationship for formations with downside breakouts is random.

Trading Tactics

There are few trading tactics for outside days, so I do not present them in table form. The first real question you need to answer is if you want to trade this formation at all. Almost half the formations (42%) with downside breakouts fail. Upside breakouts perform better (25% failure rate), but they still fall short of the benchmark 20% maximum for reliable formations. Do you *really* want to trade this one?

If the answer is still yes, then stick to outside days with upside breakouts. Remember that a closing price within the top 25% of the daily price range during the outside day correctly predicts an upside breakout two out of three times (but does not address the failure rate, so be careful). If the outside day happens to have a narrow daily price range, say less than $0.50, that is also an advantage. Shorter formations with upside breakouts perform better. Justin's trade in the Sample Trade section also poses additional ideas.

Sample Trade

Justin is a successful doctor. When he is not seeing patients, he toys with new investment techniques both on paper and in real-time. After reviewing the outside day formation, he derived five rules that the formation had to meet before he would invest in it.

1. *The formation must have an upside breakout.* This is due primarily to the poor showing of downside breakouts coupled with the larger gains possible with upside breakouts (32% gain versus 17%).

2. *The formation must be near the yearly low.* Outside days within a third of the yearly low handily outperform (49% average gain versus 32%) the other two ranges (center third and highest third).

3. *The outside day must have volume 50% above the moving average.* High volume outside days score larger gains (37% versus 29%) than low volume outside days.

4. *The daily close must be within 25% of the daily high.* This suggests an upside breakout that, in turn, suggests prices will climb.

5. *The daily price range must be less than or equal to fifty cents.* Outside days with a narrow price range perform better than those with a very wide daily range.

Justin knew that it was only a matter of time before the formation appeared in a stock he was familiar with and that met his five rules. He was not going to chase the formation and search for it in stocks he did not know. In early November, the formation finally appeared in a stock he followed (Figure 29.5).

Working the five rules backward, the outside day has a daily price range of $0.32 (17.13 – 16.81), well outside the prior day's high (17) and low (16.94). This satisfies rule five. The stock closed at the daily high, meeting condition four. Number three passes as well since the 25-day volume moving average (up

Figure 29.5 Outside day with upside breakout. Justin bought the stock after the outside day appeared and broke out upward. He more than doubled his money. The day he bought was an inside day.

to, but not including the outside day), is about 95,400 shares, whereas the volume during the outside day is 273,600 shares. This is well above the 50% minimum (that is, 50% above the moving average or 143,100 shares). The formation must be near the yearly low, rule two says. The yearly high up to this point is 21.31 and the low is 15⅛. The close, at 17.13, just slips beneath the 17.19 level that marks the lowest third of the yearly price range. The first rule says that the formation must have an upside breakout.

All Justin could do at this point was wait. While waiting, he plotted the stock quotation each day and 2 days later, another outside day appeared. This did not seem to contradict his analysis so he ignored it and waited for a clear breakout signal. He received the signal when prices moved above the outside day's high and closed there. The following day, he bought the stock at 17½, the low for the day. When he checked in with his broker, he recognized the new chart pattern as an inside day and hoped that this meant the stock would continue higher. Eventually, that is just what happened.

Since Justin is a long-term investor and believed in the fundamentals of the company, he saw no reason to take profits anytime soon. There were bumps along the way, sure, but as a buy-and-holder, he was unconcerned. On the weekly chart, he drew up-sloping trendlines, then had to redraw them as the stock climbed even faster in 1995. Then prices pierced the upward trendline, moving down. To Justin, this was a big negative and coupled with some changes at the company of which he disapproved, he decided to sell. In late January 1996, he sold the stock at 41, below the daily high of 42 but well up from the daily low of 38¼. He more that doubled his money on the trade even though it took just over 3 years to do it.

Justin was early. If he had held onto the stock for 4 more months, he could have sold at 66. Of course, a month after that the stock was down to 45.

30

Pipe Bottoms

RESULTS SNAPSHOT

Appearance	Two adjacent, downward price spikes on the weekly chart
Reversal or consolidation	Long-term (over 6 months) bullish reversal
Failure rate	12%
Average rise	47%, with most likely rise being 20%
Surprising findings	See Table 30.3
See also	Horn Bottoms

After researching the performance of horn tops and bottoms, the natural thing to do is to remove the intervening week and test the pattern again. That is where the pipe formation comes from. Pipes bottoms are an exciting discovery with a low failure rate (12%) and a high average rise (47%).

I conducted an in-depth study of pipe bottoms on *daily* price charts and came up disappointed. The statistics show that daily pipes have a failure rate of 18% with an average gain of 33%. Both numbers are respectable but what really bothers me is the most likely gain, which is just 10%. Almost half the formations (45%) have gains less than 20%. However, there are a number of large gains; almost a quarter of the formations (23%) have gains over 50%.

I began to believe that an investor trading daily pipes would either pick a formation that fails or one that has such a small gain as to be unprofitable, so I discarded the research and looked at the *weekly* chart. As you can see from the preceding numbers, the performance is quite good. Even the most likely rise holds up well, being 20% (but it can range from 10% to 40% almost equally). Almost 40% of the formations have gains over 50%. Not only is this formation worth exploring further, it just might be an outstanding performer worth adding to your technical toolbox.

Tour

Figure 30.1 shows a pipe formation and the price appreciation that results. The chart is on the weekly scale and you can see that prices begin dropping in mid-October, 1993, down to the pipe pattern. Prices make a straight-line run downward from a high of 29 to the left pipe low of $20\frac{1}{2}$. Volume picks up during the left pipe spike and is even higher the following week. The two downward price spikes, of almost equal length and overlapping, mark a turning point, a signal that the decline is over.

From the low, prices move up smartly and reach a new high of $44\frac{7}{8}$ in early November, which is a climb of almost 120% in just 9 months. For this formation, such large gains are not unusual. Almost 20% of the pipes have gains over 90%.

Figure 30.1   A pipe bottom on the weekly chart. Pipes commonly form after a retrace in an uptrend or at the bottom of a prolonged downtrend.

Identification Guidelines

How do you correctly identify pipe bottoms? Table 30.1 outlines the identification characteristics. Although there are a number of guidelines to consider, they are really quite obvious. Consider the pipe shown in Figure 30.2. The first guideline suggests that you use weekly charts. Although pipes appear on daily charts, they do not perform as well as pipes on weekly charts. Two, adjacent downward price spikes compose the pipe bottom, and it looks like two parallel lines on the chart. The price difference from the left low to the right low is minimal. A significant number of formations (414 or 94%) have low-to-low price differences of $.25 or less. Figure 30.2 shows no difference in the two pipe lows.

The pipe spikes should appear as a large price drop and wide price range for 2 weeks in a row. The week before and after the pipe should have low prices near the top of the pipe. This makes the pipe stand out on the price chart as an easily recognizable formation. For example, the pipe shown in Figure 30.2 has a prior week low of $11\frac{5}{8}$, somewhat near the left pipe high of $12\frac{9}{16}$ (certainly

Table 30.1
Identification Characteristics of Pipe Bottoms

Characteristic	Discussion
Weekly chart	Pipe bottoms on the daily price chart exist, but pipes on the weekly charts perform better. Use the weekly chart.
Two downward adjacent spikes	Locate two downward price spikes that are next to each other.
Low-to-low price variation	The price difference between the two lows of the pipe is small, about $0.25 or less, but you should allow more variation for higher priced stocks.
Large spikes	Prices should spike down unusually far during the 2 weeks, more than most downward spikes during the year. The pipe stands alone as the prior week and the following week have low prices that are near the pipe highs.
Large overlap	The 2 weeks composing the pipe should have a large price overlap between them.
High volume	Not a prerequisite, but most pipes show above average volume on at least one or both spikes.
Obvious pipe	The pipe should be obvious on the chart. If it does not stick out like a sore thumb, then you should look elsewhere. The best performing pipes appear at the end of downtrends.

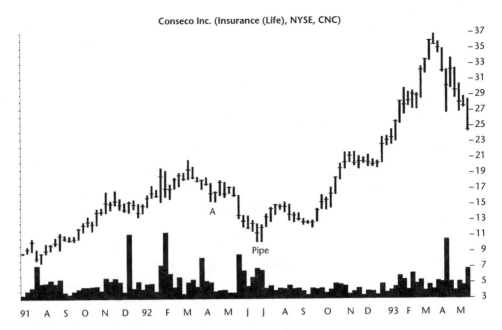

Figure 30.2 Another example of a pipe bottom on the weekly chart. Point A is another pipe bottom with less spectacular results.

well above the low of $10^{5}/_{16}$). The right side does even better. It sports a low of $12^{1}/_{4}$, near the right pipe high of $12^{1}/_{2}$.

The spike decline should be unusual. The length should be well above the average downward spike length over the past year. It must appear as a large decline on the price chart, not just another 2-week blip in a sea of long downward price spikes. The pipe has a large price overlap. This is clear in Figure 30.2 as the left side of the pipe is just slightly taller than the right side. As a selection guideline, what you do not want to see is a large left side and a short right side.

The volume for the week of each pipe spike is usually above average but need not be. Pipes with above average left volume and below average right volume perform better than all other combinations. However, I would not exclude a pipe simply because it does not obey the volume characteristics.

The last guideline is perhaps a summation of all others. The pipe must be unusual enough to jump out of the price chart. Usually, this is because pipes form at the end of a decline and mark the turning point, such as that shown in Figures 30.1 and 30.2. Less frequently, pipes act as a consolidation of the upward trend. They spike downward for 2 weeks, then prices continue rising.

If you look closely at Figure 30.2, you should be able to see another pipe. I have made it easy for you by marking it as point A. The pipe is not quite as well defined as the other pipe and the price appreciation is certainly not as spectacular. Prices rise from the right pipe low of $15^{3}/_{8}$ to a high of $18^{1}/_{8}$ before prices resume their downward trend. This particular formation just clears the 5% failure cut with a gain of 5.5% (as measured from the average of the high and low price the week following the right pipe to the ultimate high, which happens to be the same day in this case).

Focus on Failures

Pipes do not have a breakout point, thus there are no upside breakout failures. With pipe bottoms, there is only the 5% failure. A 5% failure is when prices do not move higher by more than 5% before reversing the trend. Figure 30.3 shows two such failures. The two pipes in April and May show good definition. They look like pipes, but they do not act like pipes. After the pipes complete, prices should move up smartly, but they head lower instead. Why? Volume on the left spike of both pipes is below the 25-day moving average of the volume. However, the right side shows higher than average volume in both formations. Still, the volume pattern is unconvincing, as it usually appears most brisk at pipe bottoms. As a contrast, look at the pipe on the far left side of the chart. Both spikes show volume that is well above average.

Perhaps the best clue to the failures lies buried in the guidelines outlined in Table 30.1. Prices should drop unusually far during the 2 weeks, *more than*

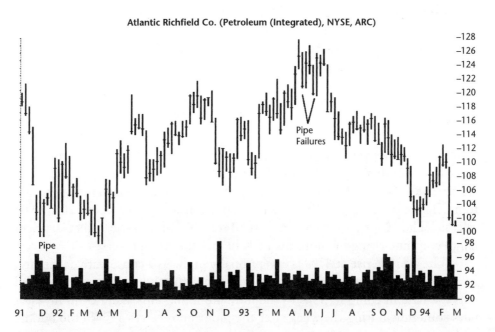

Figure 30.3 Pipe bottom failures. Clues to these two pipe failures are in the spike lengths and volume trend. The best performing pipes form when prices are trending down.

most downward price thrusts during the year. As you look at the chart, you can see several downward, 1-week spikes (December and February, for example) that nearly equal the length of the two pipe formations. The entire chart seems filled with ragged price spikes of varying lengths. For this reason, you should be skeptical of investing in these two pipes.

Incidentally, before we leave Figure 30.3, it is a good time to illustrate a somewhat common feature of pipes. Since pipes often appear at the end of a downward price trend, prices sometimes rise up, loop around, and retest the low. The pipe in early December 1991 is an example. Prices top out at 124½ (not shown) in late October then plunge downward. In just 6 weeks they reach the pipe low of 99⅛. Prices bounce upward, round over, and fall back on themselves, forming a new low at 98⅛. The retest of the original low completes in late March.

Pipe bottoms seem to exhibit support at their lows. Rarely do prices drop more than ½ point or so below the pipe low before recovering and beginning an extended upward trend. The ½ point is not an absolute rule as it depends on the price of the stock (the one shown in the chart is a $100 stock and it drops $1 below the prior low).

So even though you may buy into a stock above the top of the pipe and watch prices fall, hold on. Do not sell until prices drift below the pipe low. I discuss trading tactics later in this chapter.

You might ask why the March 1992 low is not a pipe formation. The reason is the same as the one cited earlier. The downward price spikes do not descend far enough to differentiate them from normal price behavior. The two downward price thrusts are not obvious enough to qualify them as a pipe (and the volume is weak too).

Statistics

Table 30.2 shows general statistics for pipe bottoms. These formations are so plentiful (442) that I stopped searching at 200 stocks. Most of the formations are reversals (60%), whereas the remainder are consolidations of the prevailing trend. The failure rate at 12% is quite good. I consider values below 20% to be reliable. The 52 formations that fail are of the 5% failure variety, that is, prices fail to continue rising by more than 5% before the trend reverses.

The average rise at 47% is exceptionally high. As a conservative measure, I averaged the high and low price the week after the right pipe spike and used it as the base in computations to the ultimate high. This assumes an investor buys sometime during the week after the pipe and receives a fill in the middle of the weekly price range.

I use a frequency distribution of gains to find the most likely rise (see Figure 30.4). If you ignore the rightmost column for a moment, the figure shows that the first four columns are almost the same. The 20% column has the

Table 30.2
General Statistics for Pipe Bottoms

Description	Statistic
Number of formations in 200 stocks from 1991 to 1996	442
Reversal or consolidation	179 consolidations, 263 reversals
Failure rate	52 or 12%
Average rise of successful formations	47%
Most likely rise	20%
Left pipe volume versus 25-day moving average	130%
Right pipe volume versus 25-day moving average	117%
For successful formations, days to ultimate high	9.5 months (296 days)

highest frequency, followed by 30% and 40%. Thus, you might believe that the 20% column represents the most likely gain. You can see from the chart how the tall right column, with gains over 90%, pulls the average upward. If you sum the values over 50%, you discover that 39% of the formations have gains over 50%. That is quite good.

The left and right pipe volume numbers are 130% and 117%, respectively, of the 25-day volume moving average. These values emphasize that volume is higher on the left spike and diminished on the right spike but still above average.

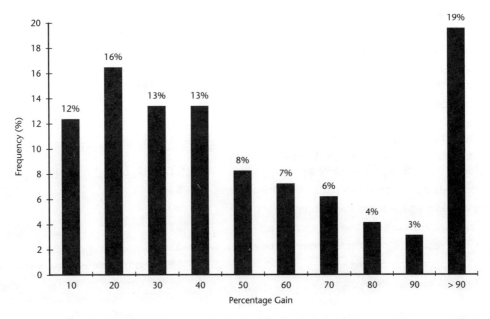

Figure 30.4 Frequency distribution of gains for pipe bottoms. The most likely gain is 20%, but it may be pulled higher by the tall right column.

The time from the right pipe spike to the ultimate high is long, almost 10 months. This follows what we have seen in other formations. Small gains complete quickly but an average rise of 47% takes time.

Table 30.3 shows a number of unusual results for weekly pipe bottoms. I did not use any of the ideas presented in the table while searching for pipe bottoms. The reason is that I did not want to fit the results to the data. So, I located the formations then found what parameters worked best (I verified the results in out-of-sample tests).

The benchmark is a 47% gain, measured from the average of the high and low prices the week after a weekly pipe bottom to the ultimate high. The gain assumes you buy the stock sometime during the week after seeing a pipe and sell just before a major trend reversal. Changing the starting point to the right pipe low boosts the average gain to an amazing 60% and expands the most likely gain to a range between 20% and 50%.

Most pipe bottoms, by choice, have little or no difference between the low prices composing each spike of the pipe. I divided the results into those that have a difference between the two lows and those that do not. Pipe bottoms with a price difference have a 49% gain, whereas those with no difference show gains averaging 43%.

Table 30.3
Surprising Results for Pipe Bottoms

Description	Average Rise (%)	Failure Rate (%)
Benchmark	47	12
Rise for pipes with price difference between lows	49	
Rise for pipes with no price difference between lows	43	
Percentage that lower left (L) pipes work better than lower right (R) pipes	L50, R47	
Right pipe as inside week	50	
Percentage of high volume left (L) pipes, right (R) pipes, both (B) pipes that score better	L51, R47, B51	
Percentage of low volume left (L) pipes, right (R) pipes, both (B) pipes that score better	L42, R47, B44	
High left pipe volume, low right pipe volume	53	28
High right pipe volume, low left pipe volume	40	
Linear regression price trend: 3 months up	41	
Linear regression price trend: 3 months down	51	
Large price spike (5× average)	58, 33 samples	12
Large price spike (4× average)	55, 62 samples	11
High volume left spike, low volume right spike, down-sloping 3-month price trends	52, 28 samples	25

Since a pipe with an uneven low price works better, which works best, a lower left or right side? It turns out that pipes with a lower left spike show superior gains at 50% versus 47%. If a lower left spike works best, what of the high price? I did not do a thorough analysis of the various combinations but did examine how an inside week performs. An inside week is one in which the high is below the prior high and the low is above the prior low. In essence, the price range is inside the prior week's range. When the pipe bottom is an inside week, it scores a gain of 50%.

How does volume play into the performance? I looked at volume on each of three categories: volume on the left side of the pipe, on the right side, and on both sides. High volume on the left side and both sides perform best, accompanying pipes with gains averaging 51%. Low volume on the three categories show that the performance is best on pipes with low volume on the right side, scoring a 47% rise.

Knowing that the left side with high volume and the right side with low volume score best, how does the combination perform? The combination scores an average gain of 53%, well above the 47% benchmark. If you are unfortunate to locate a pipe with the opposite volume combination (low left volume and high right), then the average performance sinks to just 40%.

When searching for this formation, I noticed it often forms near the end of a downward price retrace, so I examined the data to be sure that this is indeed the case. I measured the price trend by using linear regression on closing prices for the 3 months leading to the pipe. When the price trend is upward, the average gain is a paltry 41%. Downward price trends do much better with gains averaging 51%. These results imply that the best gains occur after prices have been moving down for quite some time. It is as if the formation is signaling a climactic end to the decline. After the pipe, prices move upward and score outsized gains.

Lastly, I observed that large gains follow large downward spikes. I measured the average spike length over the course of a year by looking at every adjacent 3-week period. If the center week is the lowest, I subtract the difference from the low to the lowest low of the adjacent weeks. This is like measuring the smallest difference in length between your middle three fingers. I added the difference to all the other spike differences and computed the average. Then, I compared this average spike length with pipe spike length. When the pipe spike is at least five times the average spike length, the resulting gain is 58%, but there are only 33 formations that make the cut. Dropping the multiple to four times the average lowers the average gain to 55%, but 62 formations make the grade.

Lest you try to read too much into these statistics, let me warn you that while the average percentage gain may rise, the failure rate usually rises too. Table 30.3 shows some of the failure rates (those left blank were not measured). For example, if you combine the best of the volume characteristics with a downward price trend over 3 months, you discover an average gain of 51% for pipes showing those characteristics (only 28 formations qualify) but the failure rate zooms to 25%, above the 20% maximum failure rate for which I consider a formation reliable.

Trading Tactics

Table 30.4 lists pipe trading tactics. Perhaps the most critical feature of a pipe bottom is what happens in the third week. While you can easily spot two adjacent downward price spikes, toss the formation aside if prices do not rise the third week. The third week, the week following the second pipe spike, should leave a well-defined dual spike visible on the price chart. The 4-week pair (which includes the weeks before and after the pipe) is V-shaped and is even more clear when combined with a downward price trend.

As mentioned in Table 30.4, a downward price trend is usually where you will see these formations, at least the best performing ones. Prices move down, reach the pipe bottom, then turn around and start climbing. Figures 30.1 and 30.2 are good examples of this behavior.

Once you have identified a pipe bottom on the weekly scale, buy the stock. Since a stock will often retest the most recent low before starting on a sustained journey upward, be prepared for it. Place a stop-loss order ½ point (to allow room for the retest to drift below the pipe low) below the lowest pipe. If hit, then prices are probably going to continue down. In such a case, close out your position and send a letter home asking for more money!

Table 30.4
Trading Tactics for Pipe Bottoms

Trading Tactic	Explanation
Downward plunge	Many of the best performing pipes show a downward price trend leading to the formation. Pipes often occur at the bottom of a retrace in an upward price rise or mark the end of an extended price decline.
Buy	After a pipe bottom passes the identification characteristics shown in Table 30.1, buy the stock.
Stop loss	Pipes act as support zones but prices sometimes dip up to ½ point below the pipe low, so use that as your stop-loss point. Raise your stop as prices climb.
Watch for throwback	While not a throwback per se (because the weekly scale is being used and throwbacks happen in one month or less), be aware that prices sometimes retest their lows and drop slightly below the pipe low before beginning a sustained upward climb.

Sample Trade

One way to learn how to trade pipe bottoms is to review what Peter did. Peter is one of the more intelligent software engineers I know. Not only is he smart, but he is personable as well. He is very helpful and friendly unless management turns the screws and demands that work actually be done on time. Then the pressure seeps in and tempers flare. When the pressure gets too intense and Peter feels the need to take a break, he does not take a walk as most other people do. Instead, he invests in the stock market. Since he has an Internet connection in his office, he is on-line in just seconds. The situation shown in Figure 30.5 intrigued him. Prices had been moving horizontally since April 1992, forming an extended base on which an upside breakout of significant proportions would evolve, he hoped.

Over the shorter term prices began trending down in mid-January 1994. They reached a low the week of April 4, 1994, accompanied by above average volume. Had this downward price spike been alone, it might have signaled a one-day reversal (one-week reversal really, since we are on the weekly scale). However, another downward spike appeared the following week. Prices did not drop to the low of the prior week ($38\frac{3}{8}$) but they came close at $38\frac{5}{8}$. The dual spikes were long enough to set them apart from the surrounding price

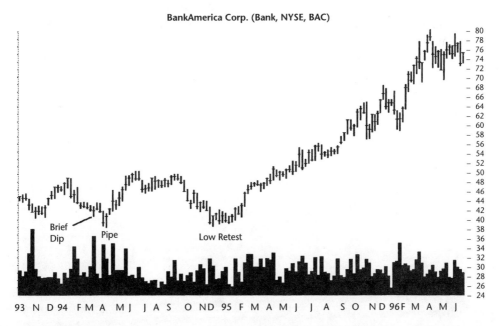

Figure 30.5 Pipe bottom with preceding brief price dip and following low retest. Peter bought this stock the week after the pipe completed and sold it for a 71% gain 2 years later.

action, certainly longer than the brief, 1-week, dip in mid-March. The following week prices moved up smartly, leaving a clear pipe bottom visible on the chart. At the end of that week, Peter bought the stock and received a fill at 42. He set a stop loss at 37⅞, ⅛ below a whole number. Peter placed the stop there because he knew that whole numbers are sometimes support areas. Placing the stop just below 38 would give the stock every opportunity to turn around and move higher.

As Peter watched the stock, he was pleased that it was working out so well. The real test, he knew, would be when the stock approached the top of its trading range. Over the prior 2 years, it had reached a high of 55½ and a low of 40½. If you exclude 3 months when prices shot higher then fell back down, the range was tighter with a high about 49. Peter knew that 49 and 55½ were the keys. If prices pierced those levels, then they would probably continue moving higher.

Peter watched the stock and when it reached a high of 50¼ and fell back, he knew this run was not the one that would send the stock higher. He saw prices crumble again and hoped that it was only a retest of the low and not the start of a new downside breakout.

During late November, prices reached a low of 38⅝, tying one of the pipe lows. Then prices moved modestly higher. Peter decided to double his position and bought more stock. In early February, prices broke out of their congestion zone and zoomed higher. From that point on, there was no looking back.

Prices continued rising in an almost straight-line bead until April 1996. Then, after setting a new high (80⅜), prices backtracked. Expecting a retrace in an uptrend, Peter held onto his shares. He watched the shares sink and when they reached 72, he gave up and sold. Prices dipped to 69¾ before beginning upward again. Peter sold too soon (as it continued moving substantially higher). Still, he made $30 a share or 71% in about 2 years.

31

Pipe Tops

RESULTS SNAPSHOT

Appearance	Two adjacent upward price spikes on the weekly chart
Reversal or consolidation	Short-term (up to 3 months) bearish consolidation
Failure rate	18%
Average decline	21%, with most likely decline between 10% and 20%
Surprising result	A 3-month downtrend (minimum) leading to the formation results in the best performance, with losses averaging 24% and an 11% failure rate.
See also	Horn Tops

If you compare the above statistics with horn tops, you will not find much difference because the two formations are similar, even in appearance. Still, the 18% failure rate for pipe tops is quite good, below the 20% maximum for formations that I consider reliable. The average decline is 21% with a likely loss between 10% and 20%. This is an improvement from horn tops, which show the most likely loss to be just 10%. The best performing pipe tops are those with price trends at least 3 months long leading down to the formation. The pipes appear as part of a retrace in a downtrend and perform much better than other combinations. They score average losses of 24% with a smaller failure rate of 11%.

Tour

Figure 31.1 shows what pipes look like and how they perform. There are three pipe formations shown in the figure, all of them tops, all warning of an impending trend change. The pipe on the left occurs while prices are still rising and acts as part of the consolidation of the trend. I consider it a failure because prices climb significantly above the pipe top before tumbling.

The center pipe really marks the turning point. It towers above the surrounding hillside and prices on either side of it fall away. The resulting formation looks like an upside down V.

The pipe on the right is the last one before prices really begin tumbling. It flags the last chance to exit your holdings or place a short at a good price. From the high at 39¼, prices tumble to below 13 by the end of this study—a 67% loss.

Identification Guidelines

Table 31.1 outlines the guidelines for correctly identifying pipe tops. First, use weekly charts as they make pipes easy to spot. You should see two adjacent upward price spikes. The twin spikes should be unusual in that they should be well above the surrounding prices and taller than most other price spikes

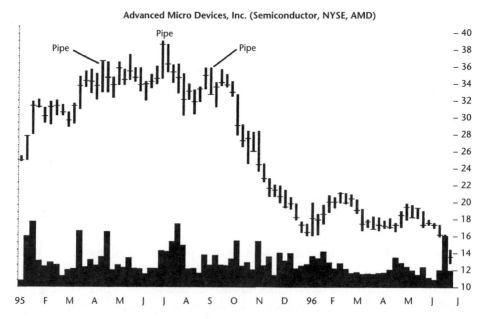

Figure 31.1 Three pipe tops. The first one is a failure because prices rise significantly above the pipe top.

Table 31.1
Identification Characteristics of Pipe Tops

Characteristic	Discussion
Weekly chart, upward spikes	Use the weekly chart and locate two adjacent upward price spikes. The two spikes should be longer than similar spikes over the prior year and tower above the surrounding prices.
Large overlap	The two spikes should have a large price overlap between them. Do not pair a tall spike with a short one.
Small price variation	The price difference between the two highs is small, usually $\frac{3}{8}$ or less, but can vary up to $1 or so for higher-priced stocks.
Upward retrace in downtrend	The best performing formations appear at the top of a retrace in a prolonged downtrend.

throughout the year. Also, the two spikes should show a large overlap between them; one spike should not be significantly shorter than the other and they should have many prices in common.

The peak-to-peak spike price difference should be small, usually less than $\frac{3}{8}$. In the study, only a handful of formations have tip price differences of $1. The vast majority (88%) have differences of $\frac{3}{8}$ or less.

If you look at enough pipe tops, you will discover that many form as part of an upward retrace during a downtrend such as that shown in Figure 31.2.

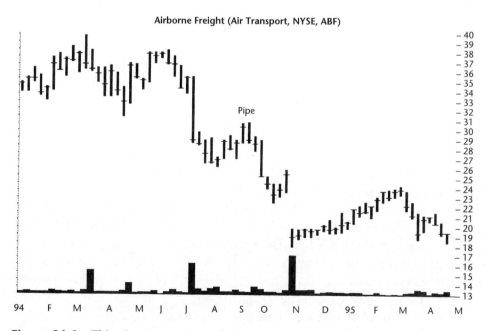

Figure 31.2   This pipe top appears during a retrace in a long-term downtrend, as do some of the best performing pipes.

You can see that prices peak in mid-March at a price of $39\frac{7}{8}$, then move down for just over a month before recovering. The second top does not last long before prices start moving down again. Prices take a sharp 1-day drop from $35\frac{1}{2}$ to 29 and move down even further before recovering. The upward retrace sees prices bounce to a high of $30\frac{7}{8}$ from a low of $26\frac{1}{4}$. That is when the pipe forms.

The twin highs of the pipe are just $\frac{1}{8}$ apart and are well above the surrounding high prices. Except for the spike in mid-March, the price spikes are unusually tall when compared with other spikes throughout the prior year. Since the pipe spikes both share the same low price, the two spikes exhibit a large price overlap.

The pipe signals a resumption of the downtrend. In less than 2 months, prices drop to a low of 18 before recovering slightly.

Focus on Failures

The vast majority of failures occur when prices decline by less than 5% before resuming their upward trend. These 5% failures do not happen that often, only 18% of the time for pipes, but their occurrence is significant enough to warrant a review of the situation.

Many failures occur when prices are trending up. The uptrend ranges from several months to over a year and the pipes seem to signal a coming trend change. Sometimes they do and prices drop, but by less than 5%. At other times, the drop is more severe, but it is in the future, from 2 to 5 or more months ahead. In between the pipe and the drop there are higher prices.

Sprinkled among the uptrend failures are those related to downtrends. Pipes usually appear at the end of a long downtrend or shortly after the trend changes and begins moving up. Instead of an upward retrace in a downtrend, the pipe marks the turning point for higher prices.

Consider Figure 31.3, a pipe top in a stock that has been moving sideways for about a year. Upward breakouts from these long, flat consolidation areas typically mark the beginning of a long rise, as in this case. For many chart formations, even those that have a measure rule to predict what the eventual price will be, there is still one overriding rule: There must be something to reverse.

You can see that the consolidation region narrows over time, reminiscent of a long, symmetrical triangle. Even the volume pattern supports the formation by receding most of the way along the chart pattern. Since the boundaries of a symmetrical triangle mark lines of support and resistance, the possible decline from the pipe base to the triangle boundary is just 5%, not a very compelling investment. In essence, there just is not much of a climb to reverse.

However, in all fairness, if the pipe correctly predicted a downside breakout from the triangle, I would be telling you a different story. Since it is difficult or impossible to predict the breakout direction from a symmetrical

Alex Brown Inc. (Securities Brokerage, NYSE, AB)

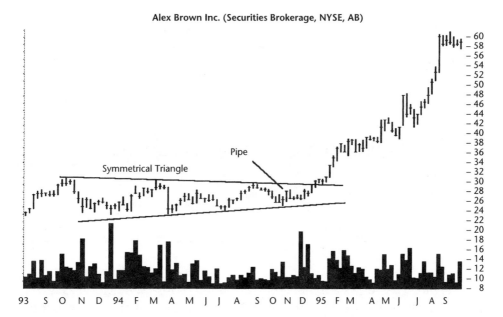

Figure 31.3 This pipe top forms near the end of a long symmetrical triangle. An investor should wait for a downside breakout before trading this pipe.

triangle, it is best to wait for the actual breakout. If investors waited for prices to pierce the bottom trendline after the pipe appeared, they could have saved themselves from a loss. As it is, the pipe shown in Figure 31.3 is a failure of prices to decline. Prices reached a high of $60\frac{3}{4}$ in September, more than double the price where the pipe forms.

More often than not, a pipe acts as a consolidation of the trend, so you should not depend on it acting as a reversal. Although a reversal does happen 46% of the time, you should invest believing that prices will continue in the direction of the prevailing trend. If the trend is upward, then prices will continue moving higher. Prepare for the worst; hope for the best.

Statistics

Table 31.2 shows general statistics for pipe tops. I uncovered 443 formations in just 150 stocks before I decided that my spreadsheet was full enough. Of these formations, 54% act as consolidations of the prevailing trend, whereas the remainder act as reversals. The failure rate, at 18%, is just under the 20% threshold I consider the maximum allowed for reliable formations. Most of these failures are of the 5% variety, in which prices begin heading lower but soon turn around and climb significantly higher (after falling by less than 5%). The average decline is 21%, about what you would expect from a bearish chart pattern.

Table 31.2
General Statistics for Pipe Tops

Description	Statistic
Number of formations in 150 stocks from 1991 to 1996	443
Reversal or consolidation	238 consolidations, 205 reversals
Failure rate	80 or 18%
Average decline of successful formations	21%
Most likely decline	10% to 20%
Left pipe volume versus 25-day moving average	123%
Right pipe volume versus 25-day moving average	123%
For successful formations, days to ultimate low	4 months (123 days)

Figure 31.4 shows a frequency distribution of losses. The chart suggests that the most likely decline is in the 10% to 20% range. You can see that the first three columns are nearly equal in height. Together they represent 55% of the formations. In essence, over half of the formations have declines of 20% or less on average. In a statistical anomaly, the volume for both weeks of the pipe average 123% of the 25-day volume moving average. In a moment, we will see that volume—either high or low—plays an insignificant part in whether the

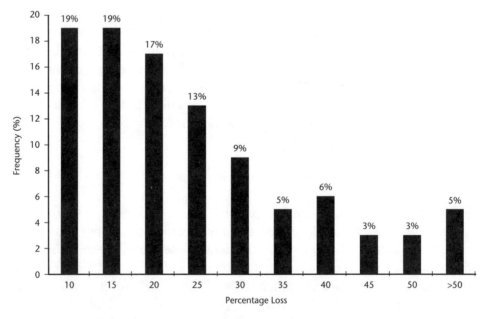

Figure 31.4   Frequency distribution of losses for pipe tops. The graph emphasizes that the most likely decline is in the 10% to 20% range.

decline is large or small. For those formations that decline by more than 5%, it takes about 4 months to reach the ultimate low.

Table 31.3 explores some surprising facets of pipe tops. The benchmark, which comprises all formations that work as expected, has an average decline of 21% with an 18% failure rate. When we separate pipes into those with price differences between the highs from those that reach the same high price, we discover that the average loss is 23% for those pipes with no price difference. The average loss from pipe tops with different high prices is 21%.

Volume, as mentioned in the preceding section, does not appear to be a significant determinant to the performance of pipes. With high volume on the left and right side of the pipe spikes, the performance ranges from 19% to 22%, respectively. Low volume on the spikes results in similar, although slightly better, performance, at 21% to 23%. The different combinations, however, do make a difference. For those formations with high volume on the left spike and low volume on the right, the loss is 18% while the failure rate drops marginally to 16%. When you flip the volume around, that is, low left volume and high right spike volume, the average loss amounts to 24% but the failure rate also climbs, to 22%.

I used linear regression to assess the 3-month price trend leading to the formation. When the price trend is up, the chart pattern scores an average decline of 19%. However, when the trend is down, the decline averages 24%

Table 31.3
Surprising Results for Pipe Tops

Description	Average Decline (%)	Failure Rate (%)
Benchmark	21	18
Decline for pipes with price difference between highs	21	
Decline for pipes with no price difference between highs	23	18
Percentage of high volume left (L) pipes, right (R) pipes, both (B) pipes that score better	L19, R22, B21	
Percentage of low volume left (L) pipes, right (R) pipes, both (B) pipes that score better	L23, R21, B23	
High left pipe volume, low right pipe volume	18	16
Low left pipe volume, high right pipe volume	24	22
Linear regression price trend: 3 months up	19	
Linear regression price trend: 3 months down	24	11
Large price spike (4× average)	22	

with only an 11% failure rate. When contemplating pipe tops for shorting, consider looking for a declining price trend.

I also examined pipes for their height, as measured from the lowest high of the two spikes to the highest high of the two adjacent weeks. Spikes that are four times or more higher than the average spike (computed over the course of a year) result in a 22% decline, admittedly not very exciting, especially since the benchmark is 21%.

Trading Tactics

Table 31.4 outlines trading tactics for pipe tops. The performance of pipes depends on the prevailing trend. For larger percentage losses, look for pipes that appear in downtrends. Pipes will usually appear in an upward retrace of a long-term decline. Try to find pipes where the decline is evident but just starting. What you do not want to do is invest near the end of a downtrend. Of course, trying to determine when a trend will end is something of an art. However, if the stock has been trending down for many months (such as a year or more), then you should probably look elsewhere.

In long-term uptrends, the pipe might signal the end of a trend. Sometimes it is premature by a few months, so do not be in too much of a rush to sell the stock short. At other times, a review of the surrounding price patterns might be rewarding. Double or triple tops sometimes show pipes on one of the tops, calling the turn exactly.

For many uptrends, the pipes represent periods of short-term weakness. Prices will move down for a month or two (sometimes more) before resuming the uptrend. The decline might be 10% to 20% but seldom represents a significant percentage change. Still, they can be profitable if you are careful (and lucky).

Table 31.4
Trading Tactics for Pipe Tops

Trading Tactic	Explanation
Downtrends	The best performing pipes occur during downtrends. Prices bounce upward, form a pipe, then resume their downward trend.
Watch for trend end	Do not invest if the pipe appears after a long downtrend. The pipe may signal the end of the trend.
Long-term uptrends	Look at long-term uptrends. If a pipe appears in an uptrend of a year or more, then the pipe might signal a trend reversal. Be careful as the pipes sometimes are premature by 2 to 5 months.
Uptrend retrace	Pipes often appear in uptrends. They mark short-term weakness where the trend reverses and moves down. These can be profitable short-term moves.

Sample Trade

Johnny is a civil servant working in one of the state offices. He handles most of the paperwork for companies just getting started. Most are sole proprietorships that go bust in less than a year but there are exceptions. He tries to use his daily contacts to further his investment acumen. Discussions with customers have helped him spot profitable trends and have helped him avoid costly mistakes.

His interest turned to the steel industry when he learned that the federal government was thinking of punishing foreign producers for dumping steel in the United States. He learned about the trend from comments made about how prices for steel products were dropping rapidly. Companies using the cheap steel thought the decline was great but the steel companies did not agree. That is why they started jumping up and down on their favorite politicians.

When Johnny saw the situation depicted in Figure 31.5, he formed a unique plan to profit from the pipe top. He measured the percentage gain from the base (point A in the figure) to point B, the first minor high. The rise was 34% (that is, $(19\frac{3}{4} - 14\frac{3}{4})/14\frac{3}{4}$). Then he calculated the amount of the retrace from points B to C, which turned out to be 14%.

As he watched the price climb from point C to the pipe, he whipped out his calculator and discovered that the percentage change was 36%, quite near the 34% gain of the first push. He suspected and hoped that the pipe top marked the start of a downward retrace that would take prices lower, probably around 15% lower. So, he sold the stock short and received a fill at $22\frac{1}{4}$. He put

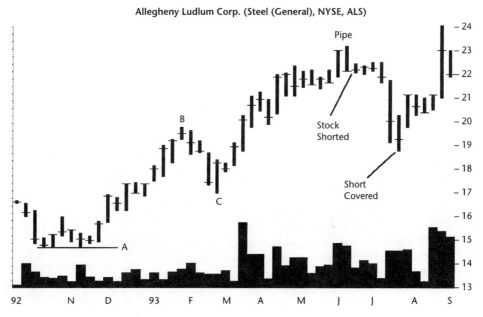

Allegheny Ludlum Corp. (Steel (General), NYSE, ALS)

Figure 31.5 This pipe top appeared at the end of a rise-retrace pattern that saw prices climb by 35% and fall by 15%.

an order to close out his position should the stock decline by 15% to 19. On the other side, he placed a mental stop-loss order at 23¼, slightly above the right pipe high at 23³⁄₁₆.

The stock moved horizontally for several weeks then tumbled. When it reached 19, his short was covered and he made about $3 a share in 5 weeks. Meanwhile, the stock bottomed out at 18¾, just below his target and an amount similar in size to the earlier retrace.

Lest you get too excited about this rise-retrace type trade, let me caution you. Although I have used this maneuver profitably, many times things do not turn out quite so neatly. Be careful and make use of stop-loss orders, especially if you are shorting a stock. Search for support and resistance zones to help gauge the ultimate decline.

32

Rectangle Bottoms

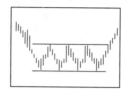

RESULTS SNAPSHOT

Upside Breakouts

Appearance	Prices trend down to the formation then oscillate between two horizontal trendlines before breaking out upward.
Reversal or consolidation	Long-term (over 6 months) bullish reversal
Failure rate	0%
Average rise	46%, with the most likely rise about 20%
Volume trend	Upward
Premature breakout	12%
Throwbacks	61%
Percentage meeting predicted price target	93%
Surprising finding	Actual breakout is opposite that shown by premature breakouts 75% of time.
See also	Rectangle Tops

Downside Breakouts

Appearance	Prices trend down to the formation then oscillate between two horizontal trendlines before breaking out downward.

Reversal or consolidation	Short-term (up to 3 months) bearish consolidation
Failure rate	4%
Average decline	19%, with most likely decline between 10% and 15%
Volume trend	Downward
Premature breakout	17%
Pullbacks	70%
Percentage meeting predicted price target	65%
Surprising findings	Actual breakout is opposite that shown by premature breakouts 75% of time.
See also	Rectangle Tops

Like other formations without a classic definition of a top or bottom, I decided to give rectangles a definition by separating them based on the price trend approaching the chart pattern. If the trend is downward, then the formation is a bottom. If the trend is up, then the formation classifies as a top. The distinction is perhaps arbitrary, but it does help with searching for reasons to a given breakout direction.

This chapter concerns itself with rectangle bottoms. Bottoms have two breakout directions: up and down (no surprise, right?). The Results Snapshot lists the more important statistics. The failure rate for rectangles with upside breakouts is 0%. Do not get too excited as the sample size is small (41 formations). I do not believe that upside breakouts never fail. They do, it just did not happen on my shift. One thing is clear, though: They are reliable. The average rise is 46%, above the usual 40% gain for bullish formations. The most likely rise at 20% is about what you would expect. With such a large gain, it is no surprise that the formation meets its price target 93% of the time. I consider anything above 80% to be reliable.

Rectangles with downside breakouts perform almost as well. They have a 4% failure rate. That is very good as I consider reliable anything below 20%. The average loss is 19%, just shy of the usual 20% for bearish formations. Pullbacks score well, appearing 70% of the time. That score is high enough on which to base a trading tactic. After a downside breakout, short the stock then add to the position once a pullback returns to the formation and begins moving down again (always wait for the downside move because prices might continue climbing).

A surprising finding is that a premature breakout is opposite the genuine breakout direction 75% of the time. We explore this further in the Statistics section.

Tour

Figure 32.1 shows an example of a rectangle bottom. The short-term price trend is upward (for 3 days anyway) leading to the formation, but I discard it. I look at the intermediate-term trend, which is down, and view the decline a few days before the formation start as an overshoot. This commonly happens just before prices oscillate between the support and resistance zones.

The chart pattern forms after prices loop around during the October 1994 to January 1995 period and retrace some of their gains. Prices drop quickly from the support zone at 57 to 52½, then they bump up against the top of the rectangle resistance zone at 56 and slink back to find support at 54.

Prices bounce off the two zones like a Ping-Pong ball ricocheting off players paddles. Up and down, up and down prices boomerang on volume that is rising. Soon, one player sneezes and the ball shoots past him. Prices move up, pausing only a day before moving higher on heavy volume. Prices quickly climb and enter another congestion zone; this time it is a descending triangle with an upside breakout.

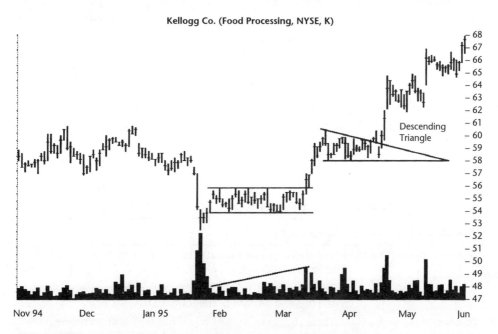

Figure 32.1   A rectangle bottom shows an intermediate-term downtrend leading to the formation with an upside breakout. After the breakout, prices move into a descending triangle and burst upward out of this formation as well.

Identification Guidelines

Table 32.1 shows a few identification guidelines for rectangle bottoms. While reviewing the guidelines, consider how they apply to the rectangle shown in Figure 32.2.

The price trend leading to the rectangle bottom is downward, which is what separates rectangle bottoms from their top brothers. I usually use the intermediate-term price trend when considering whether prices are trending up or down. This is subjective and varies from formation to formation. As shown in Figure 32.1, I ignore the few days just before the formation starts, choosing to use the prevailing longer trend instead. Prices bounce between two levels, setting up a support zone at the bottom and a line of resistance at the top. If you connect the minor highs with a trendline, it should be horizontal or nearly so. A similar line drawn below the bottoms forms a parallel trendline. The two trendlines bound the price action. Occasionally, one of the lines will not be exactly horizontal or will break near the end, which is fine as long as the slope is not too steep to disturb the overall picture.

At least two touches of each trendline are required for a valid rectangle. Figure 32.2 shows three alternating touches. Touches need not alternate, but you should have at least two clearly defined minor highs and two minor lows coming close to or touching the trendlines. Except for the brief punch through the top in early December, prices stay within the two boundary lines until breaking out downward on light volume in mid-January.

The volume pattern is somewhat random but it does seem to track the breakout direction. For Figure 32.1, the volume pattern is up and so is the breakout. Figure 32.2 shows high volume at the start of the formation and light volume just before the downside breakout. I caution against trying to predict the breakout direction by looking at the volume trend. Although it does track

Table 32.1
Identification Characteristics of Rectangles Bottoms

Characteristic	Discussion
Downward price trend	The short- or intermediate-term price trend leading to the formation is down.
Horizontal trendlines	Two horizontal, or nearly so, trendlines bound prices along the top and bottom of the formation.
Touches	There should be at least two touches of each trendline (at least four touches total).
Volume	Volume follows the breakout direction. For upside breakouts, the volume trend is upward; downside breakouts show a receding volume trend.

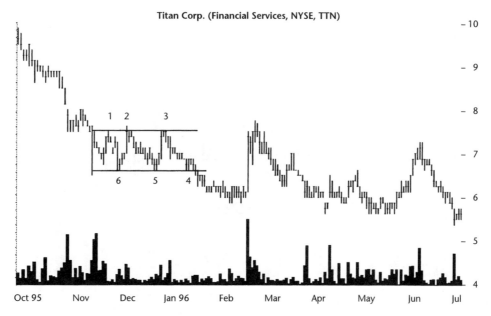

Figure 32.2   A rectangle bottom appears in a downtrend. Prices fall out the bottom then retrace to the rectangle top before moving lower.

the breakout direction more often than not, the chances of it going with the breakout direction is just above picking the correct side of a coin toss.

Focus on Failures

Figure 32.3 shows a rectangle bottom in a downtrend. Since most rectangle bottoms act as consolidations of the prevailing trend, the breakout is expected downward. Prices drop away from the support line at 54¾ and 2 days later pull back to the formation. Prices move horizontally for several days before ultimately climbing above the top of the rectangle. When prices pierce the top rectangle trendline and close above it, I consider the downtrend to be over.

Since the initial decline moves just 3% down, the formation is a failure. Formations that do not move in the breakout direction by more than 5% are what I call 5% failures. Although this formation ultimately moves lower, it does so only after closing above the formation top. If you sold this formation short expecting a price decline, you may be stopped out for a loss. Certainly, your worry would climb along with prices.

Failures do occur, as Figure 32.3 illustrates, but rectangles are reliable. Out of 95 formations, just two are failures. That observation conveniently brings us to the Statistics section.

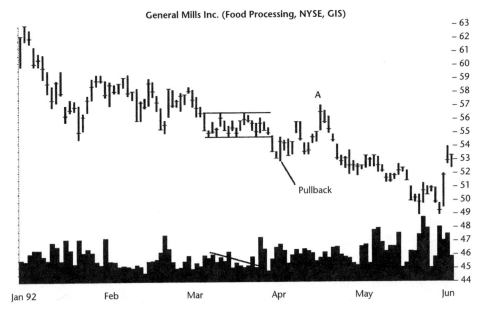

General Mills Inc. (Food Processing, NYSE, GIS)

Figure 32.3   Rectangle bottom in a downtrend. This is one of a handful of rectangle failures. Prices break out downward and move less than 5% before closing above the formation top.

Statistics

Table 32.2 shows general statistics for rectangle bottoms. With prices leading down to the formation qualifying the chart pattern as a bottom, only the breakout direction is uncertain. I divided the statistics according to the breakout type: upside and downside breakouts.

Of the 95 bottoms studied, I found slightly more rectangles acting as consolidations (54) of the prevailing price trend than reversals (41). Expect the breakout direction to follow the trend leading to the formation. If, upon entry, prices are moving down, expect them to continue moving lower after the breakout 55% of the time. That result is not much above a coin toss but it is useful.

As mentioned in the Focus on Failures section, just two formations fail, placing the failure rate at 4% for rectangles with downside breakouts or 2% for rectangle bottoms overall. Let me emphasize that because I did not find any failures of rectangle patterns with upside breakouts does not mean there are none. I just did not find any in the stocks I was looking at. However, as a rule, rectangle bottom formations rarely fail, but they do have premature breakouts, so be careful.

The average gain for upside breakouts is 46% and downside breakouts lose 19%. The first number is above the usual 40% gain, whereas the second is below the 20% posted by other bearish formations.

Table 32.2
General Statistics for Rectangle Bottoms

Description	Upside Breakout	Downside Breakout
Number of formations in 500 stocks from 1991 to 1996	41	54
Reversal or consolidation	41 reversals	54 consolidations
Failure rate	0%	2 or 4%
Average rise/decline of successful formations	46%	19%
Most likely rise/decline	20%	10% to 15%
Of those succeeding, number meeting or exceeding price target (measure rule)	38 or 93%	34 or 65%
Average formation length (start to breakout)	3 months (84 days)	3 months (87 days)
Number showing downward volume trend	19 or 46%	29 or 54%
Performance when volume is trending down or up	Down 43%, up 49%	Down 17%, up 22%
Volume for breakout day and next 5 days compared with day before breakout	163%, 167%, 106%, 91%, 91%, 133%	171%, 201%, 141%, 124%, 121%, 133%

I use a frequency distribution of gains or losses to compute the most likely rise or decline. Figure 32.4 shows the most likely gain for rectangle bottoms with upside breakouts. You can see that the graph looks quite irregular overall. Even though the tallest column is 60%, that cannot represent the most likely gain (it is just too high and is above the average, too). I consider the second tallest column, 20%, to be representative of what an investor can expect to earn. The reason for the irregular looking graph is the sample count. With just 41 samples to spread over 10 categories, the numbers can throw off the frequency distribution. Oddly enough, the tallest column has the highest number of samples—10. The 20% column has 8 samples and the others have 4 or less.

Figure 32.5 shows a similar situation for rectangle bottoms with downside breakouts. The two tallest columns, 10% and 15%, represent the most likely losses. The first two columns have 12 and 13 samples, respectively, whereas the other columns have 6 samples or less. Again, due to the small sample size, the figure may or may not be accurate. However, the results from both Figures 32.4 and 32.5 are about the same as other bullish and bearish formations.

A discussion of the measure rule occurs in the Trading Tactics section, but it involves adding or subtracting the rectangle height from the breakout direction. The result is the minimum expected target price. For upside break-

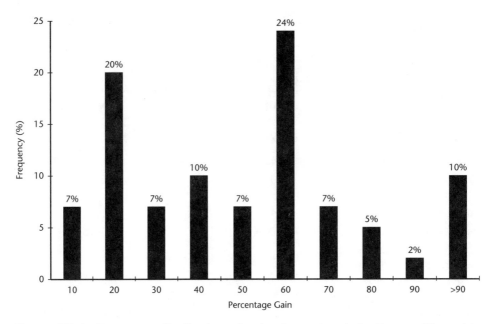

Figure 32.4 Frequency distribution of gains for rectangle bottoms with upside breakouts. Due to the small sample size, I consider the 20% column to be the most likely gain an investor can expect to receive.

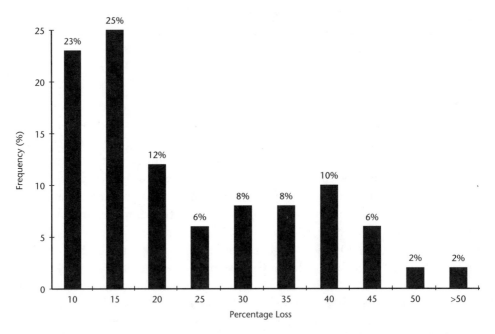

Figure 32.5 Frequency distribution of losses for rectangle bottoms with down-side breakouts. The two tallest columns represent the most likely loss.

outs, almost all (93%) of the rectangles meet or exceed their targets. For downside breakouts, only 65% reach their targets. I consider values over 80% to be reliable, so rectangles with downside breakouts fall short.

The average formation length is the same for either breakout direction, about 3 months. Those formations with an upside breakout have a receding volume trend 46% of the time, whereas those with downside breakouts show receding volume 54% of the time.

If we separate the formations by their volume trend, we discover that upside breakouts having an upward volume trend perform better (a 49% gain) than those with a receding volume trend (gains of 43%). The same is true for rectangle bottoms with downside breakouts. Those with an upward volume trend score losses of 22%, whereas receding volume trends have losses of 17%. Thus, if your formation has an upward volume trend, expect a slightly better push to the ultimate high or low.

Shown in Table 32.2 is the volume trend for the day prices move above or below the rectangle trendline boundary and the next 5 days. For upside breakouts, the volume is high for a few days then returns to about normal. Downside breakouts show unusually high volume for the following week. I double-checked the statistics and could not find anything wrong with them, so I guess that is just the way the 54 chart patterns act. Your results, of course, may vary.

Table 32.3 shows premature breakout statistics for rectangle bottoms with both upside and downside breakouts. Premature breakouts are rare, occurring only 5 times (12%) in upside breakouts and 9 times (17%) in downside ones. The volume pattern is not significantly different from a genuine

Table 32.3
Premature Breakout Statistics for Rectangle Bottoms

Description	Upside Breakout	Downside Breakout
Number of premature breakouts occurring in genuine breakouts	5 or 12%	9 or 17%
Volume at premature breakouts versus 25-day moving average	Down 224%	Up 217%, down 121%
Number of formations with premature breakouts having both upside and downside premature breakouts	0	2 or 18%
Number of premature breakouts in same direction as genuine breakout	0	4 or 36%
Number of premature breakouts in different direction from genuine breakout	5 or 100%	7 or 64%

breakout to help with identification. Volume, incidentally is compared with the 25-day moving average. Premature downside breakouts have more than double (224%) the average volume, whereas premature breakouts in formations with downside breakouts are above average (217% for upside premature breakouts and 121% for downside premature breakouts) too. Just two formations have premature breakouts in both directions. These just happen to occur when the real breakout is downward.

The last set of statistics in the table suggests premature breakouts are on opposite sides to the real breakout. A premature breakout is when prices close outside the formation boundaries but quickly rejoin the formation. The real breakout comes later as prices soar away from the formation, usually without returning.

Table 32.3 shows that most genuine breakouts are on opposite sides of the premature breakout. Only 36% of downside breakouts have breakouts in the same direction, whereas most of the others are on opposite sides. Combining the statistics indicates that 75% (12/16) of the genuine breakouts are on the side opposite the premature breakout.

Table 32.4 shows breakout statistics. Rectangle bottoms with downside breakouts show the most likelihood of prices returning to the formation (70%). Upside breakouts have throwbacks occurring 61% of the time. Both numbers are good. The average time to complete a throwback is 11 days and for a pullback it is 9 days, which is about the same as other formation types. The time to reach the ultimate high is a long 9 months for upside breakouts but a short 2½ months for downside breakouts. This makes sense as a large gain takes more time to travel further.

Where in the yearly price range do most breakouts occur? Most upside breakouts happen in the center third of the yearly price range. Downside breakouts occur in the lowest third of the yearly price range. I expected upside breakouts to show the highest population in the upper third of the price range

Table 32.4
Breakout Statistics for Rectangle Bottoms

Description	Upside Breakout	Downside Breakout
Throwback/pullback	25 or 61%	38 or 70%
Average time to throwback/ pullback completion	11 days	9 days
Days to ultimate high/low	9 months (275 days)	2.5 months (78 days)
Percentage of breakouts occurring near 12-month price low (L), center (C), or high (H)	L19%, C50%, H31%	L56%, C32%, H12%
Percentage gain for each 12-month lookback period	L45%, C49%, H36%	L21%, C16%, H16%

since the breakout is at the top of the formation. Mapping the performance over the yearly price range shows that those with upside breakouts do best when they break out in the center third of the yearly range, scoring an average return of 49%. It is also odd that those near the yearly high do worst, with gains averaging 36%. Usually, the momentum players grab the stock near the yearly high and bid it up.

The best performing downside breakouts are those that occur within a third of the yearly low, with losses of 21%. It seems that a stock having a tough time only sees things get worse after a downside breakout from a rectangle. This follows the belief that you should short stocks making the new low list and not those making the new high list.

Trading Tactics

Table 32.5 lists trading tactics for rectangle bottoms. The first tactic is to determine the predicted price target using the measure rule. The rule first finds the height of the formation by subtracting the lowest low from the highest

Table 32.5
Trading Tactics for Rectangle Bottoms

Trading Tactic	Explanation
Measure rule	Measure the height of the rectangle by subtracting the value of the trendlines from each other. For upside breakouts, add the height to the top trendline; for downside breakouts, subtract the value from the bottom trendline. The result is the expected minimum price move. For a maximum price target, measure the *length* of the rectangle and extend it vertically above the top trendline (for upside breakouts) or below the bottom one (downside breakouts). The price then becomes the maximum expected move.
Wait for breakout	Since you cannot be sure in which direction a rectangle will break out, wait for prices to *close* outside the trendline before trading in the direction of the breakout.
Tall rectangle scalp	If the rectangle is tall enough, sell or sell short near the top trendline and buy or cover near the bottom trendline.
Throwbacks, pullbacks	If you have a downside breakout, watch for a pullback and short the stock or add to your short position once prices begin descending again. Use the same technique for an upside breakout: Wait for the throwback then initiate or add to your position when prices rise.
Other	Watch for rectangles forming as the corrective phase of a measured move formation and adjust the target price accordingly. Rectangle reversals sometimes appear as flat bottom formations

high. In essence, just subtract the value of the two trendlines from each other. Figure 32.6 shows an example of this. The top trendline is at a value of $12^{7}/_{16}$ and the bottom one is at 11. The difference, $1^{7}/_{16}$, is the formation height. Add the height to the value of the top trendline to get the upside break-out target ($13^{7}/_{8}$) and subtract it from the value of the lower trendline to get the downside breakout target ($9^{9}/_{16}$). Some analysts suggest measuring the length (not the height) of the rectangle, flipping it vertically, and adding or subtracting it from the top or bottom trendline to get the maximum price move (for upside and downside breakouts, respectively). This sounds a bit far-fetched, but it is a handy guideline. Use it with caution as I have not verified how well it works.

Since you cannot predict the breakout direction with complete accuracy, wait for the breakout before investing. Place the trade after prices *close* outside the rectangle trendlines, then trade with the trend. If the formation is tall enough, consider placing an intraformation trade near the two trendlines. Short at the top when prices begin descending and cover when they rebound off the bottom trendline (do not cover too soon as prices may continue moving down). Go long at the bottom and sell at the top trendline when prices begin falling. Again, wait for a direction change as prices may stage an upside breakout.

Throwbacks and pullbacks allow investors another opportunity to place a trade, add to their position, or get out with a smaller loss. Take advantage of it but wait for prices to complete their throwback or pullback before placing a trade or adding to a position. The reason is that prices may continue in the adverse direction instead of returning to the trendline and rebounding.

Sometimes, rectangle bottoms form as the corrective phase of a measured move formation. See Measured Move Down for information on how to take advantage of the situation. Occasionally a rectangle will mark the end of a substantial decline and appear like a flat bottom before prices rise.

Sample Trade

Figure 32.6 shows a paper trade I made recently. The rectangle bottom appeared after prices dropped from a high of $20^{5}/_{8}$ in October 1997. The drop was a painful one but it did not occur all at once. Prices dropped quite rapidly to 15 where they moved horizontally for 8 months. Then the second half of the decline took over and prices reached a low of about 11.

Prices bounced off the low several times, like a boy taking his first steps on a trampoline. They were tentative, shaky, with not much enthusiasm. Then in mid-October 1998, prices touched the bottom trendline and moved quickly across the formation to tie the September high at $12^{3}/_{8}$. A few more oscillations and the two trendline boundaries became apparent.

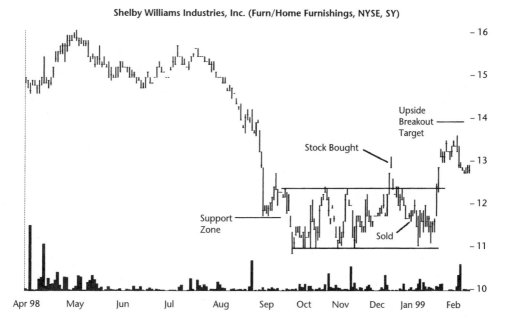

Shelby Williams Industries, Inc. (Furn/Home Furnishings, NYSE, SY)

Figure 32.6 Rectangle bottom followed by upside breakout. The measure rule applied to this rectangle bottom computes the formation height as the difference between the trendlines. Adding the difference to the value of the top trendline gives an upside breakout target of 13⅞.

If you look at the overall picture, you might think that prices would continue down—a downside breakout (following the downward trend). I could not tell which direction prices would go, so I decided to wait for the breakout. If the formation acted as a consolidation, then the breakout would be downward. However, with a two-step downtrend from the high at 20⅝, this reminded me of a measured move down with a really long corrective phase. I thought it might break out upward. If the rectangle was taller, I would try an intraformation trade (buy at 11⅛, sell at 12⅜, then reverse).

In early December, prices pierced the top trendline and closed above it; the rectangle staged an upside breakout. I noticed the breakout the day after it happened and called in my trade. I received a fill at 13, midrange for the day.

I estimated that a support zone had formed at 11¾, so I placed a stop at 11⅝. Prices had stopped at this level just before the chart pattern formed and again just before the December breakout. A better stop would have been just below the lower rectangle trendline because both trendlines act as support or resistance zones. However, I did not want to take such a large loss (15%+).

Even paper trades go wrong and that is what happened here. A day after buying the stock, prices returned to the rectangle formation to do more work. Prices slowly, agonizingly, moved lower until hitting my stop in late December. I took a paper loss of 11%.

It turns out that I placed a trade on a premature breakout. The statistics suggest that after an upside premature breakout, the genuine breakout direction should be down. Well, that did not work out either. Prices shot out the top of the formation. As I write this, they are hovering about 13, my purchase price last time. I suspect prices might throw back to the formation again. If that happens and they start moving up again, perhaps I will buy the stock for real.

33

Rectangle Tops

RESULTS SNAPSHOT

Upside Breakouts

Appearance	Prices trend up to the formation then oscillate between two horizontal trendlines before breaking out upward.
Reversal or consolidation	Long-term (over 6 months) bullish consolidation
Failure rate	2%
Average rise	52%, with the most likely rise between 20% and 30%
Volume trend	Downward
Premature breakout	11%
Throwbacks	53%
Percentage meeting predicted price target	91%
Surprising finding	The actual breakout is opposite that shown by premature breakouts 65% of the time.
See also	Rectangle Bottoms

Downside Breakouts

Appearance	Prices trend up to the formation then oscillate between two horizontal trendlines before breaking out downward.

Reversal or consolidation	Short-term (up to 3 months) bearish reversal
Failure rate	0%
Average rise	20%, with most likely decline being 20%
Volume trend	Downward
Premature breakout	23%
Pullbacks	55%
Percentage meeting predicted price target	77%
Surprising findings	The actual breakout is opposite that shown by premature breakouts 65% of the time.
See also	Rectangle Bottoms

Rectangle tops with upside breakouts fail 2% of the time. The average rise is an astounding 52% with a likely gain between 20% and 30%. These numbers are excellent. With such a large gain, it is no surprise that the measure rule works out well with 91% of the formations hitting their price targets.

Downside breakouts tell a similar tale, but one that is not quite as rosy. Downside breakouts have a 0% failure rate not because they are excellent performers, but because I did not find any that failed. I am sure there are rectangle tops with downside breakouts that fail to move down by less than 5%. The average loss is 20% with a strong likely decline of 20%, too. This is unusual but it suggests there are few large declines to skew the average. A glance at the frequency distribution shows that the assumption is correct. The percentage of formations with downside breakouts meeting or exceeding the price target is 77%, just below the 80% threshold that I consider reliable.

The only surprising finding deals with premature breakouts. When a premature breakout occurs in a rectangle top, the probabilities suggest that the genuine breakout occurs on the opposite side. This relationship is not as strong as for rectangle bottoms but it comes close.

Tour

Figure 33.1 shows an example of a rectangle top. Prices begin their upward trek in June 1992 at 14 and reach the rectangle in May of the following year. Then prices consolidate for over a month, bouncing between overhead resistance at 24⅝ and support at 23⅝. A trendline drawn across the minor highs is horizontal as is the one connecting the minor lows. There are a number of touches of both trendlines suggesting a reliable formation. At the start, prices overshoot both up and down by peeking outside the two trendlines. This is not

Williams Companies Inc. (Natural Gas (Diversified), NYSE, WMB)

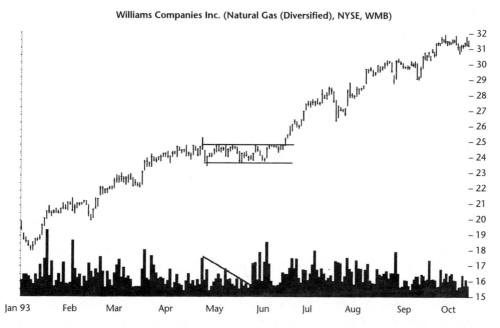

Figure 33.1   Rectangle top with an upside breakout performs well in this uptrend.

a problem because it occurs too early in the chart pattern before it can be recognized as a rectangle.

The volume pattern begins in the typical manner—receding. However, about two-thirds of the way to the breakout the pattern changes. Volume gets heavier as if building pressure for the upcoming release. Then, mysteriously, volume subsides as prices move horizontally just below the top trendline for over a week. When prices pierce the top trendline, volume picks up but not remarkably so. Volume just builds on the expanding trend that is developing since prices began sliding along the trendline top.

Prices climb away cleanly. There is a slight, 3-day dip in late June when it looks as if prices are trying to throw back to the formation top, but the buying pressure is just too strong. The retrace stops and prices turn around and continue moving up.

Why do rectangles form? A rectangle chart pattern is a struggle between the haves and the have-nots. Those that own the stock but want to sell have identified a price at which they are willing to part with their shares. When the price reaches that level, they sell, forcing the price down. When prices fall, they quit dumping the stock. On the other side is another group of investors who want to acquire the stock. They place buy orders at what they perceive to be the fair value. When prices fall to their target price, the buy orders overwhelm supply and the price rises. If this struggle goes on long enough, prices bounce between one extreme and the other. Over time, you can draw a horizontal trendline along the peaks and another along the valleys as a rectangle formation takes shape. Eventually, one of the sides runs out of ammunition. If the people selling their shares run out first, buying demand overwhelms supply and the price pierces the top trendline. If the buyers spend all their money and back away from the table, prices drop through the bottom of the rectangle. In either case, the shares continue in the breakout direction because of growing demand (the price moves upward) or increasing supply (the price tumbles).

Identification Guidelines

Table 33.1 shows identification guidelines for rectangle tops. Over the short to intermediate term, the price trend should be leading up to the formation. This upward trend is what distinguishes the formation from rectangle bottoms. The distinction is arbitrary; I wanted to see if there is any difference in the way the two perform.

As a rectangle forms, prices rise to a resistance level and fall back to a support area for another try. If this pattern continues, the minor highs can be joined with a trendline drawn along the top of the formation, and another trendline can be drawn below the minor lows. The two trendlines are horizontal or nearly so. If there is a slight tilt to the trendline, do not worry. A slight tilt is fine as long as it does not disturb the overall appearance of a congestion region.

To qualify as a rectangle, prices must touch each trendline at least twice. The touches need not alternate from one trendline to the other, but the minor highs and lows must be distinct. You do not want to see two touches along the top as part of the same minor high. Instead, look for two distinct hills and two valleys at a minimum.

The volume trend varies from formation to formation but usually recedes. Many of the charts accompanying this chapter show such a trend. Figure 33.2 shows what a rectangle top looks like. Prices are trending up lead-

Table 33.1
Identification Characteristics of Rectangle Tops

Characteristic	Discussion
Rising price trend	The short- to intermediate-term price trend leading to the formation should be up.
Horizontal trendlines	Two horizontal (or nearly so) trendlines outline the price action, one above the minor highs and one below the minor lows.
Touches	There should be at least two touches of each trendline (at least four touchs total).
Volume	Volume usually recedes until the breakout.

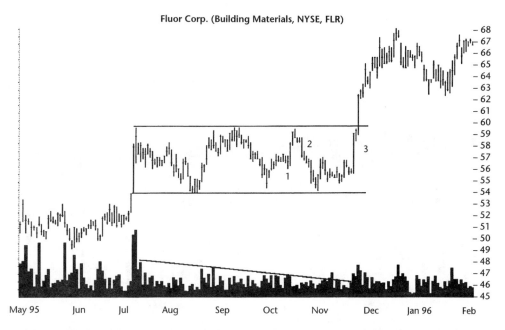

Fluor Corp. (Building Materials, NYSE, FLR)

Figure 33.2 A rectangle top with receding volume trend. Although most rectangles exhibit receding volume, do not automatically exclude those with rising volume trends. Three profitable trading opportunities are marked where prices cross from one side to the other.

ing to the rectangle. Then they bounce between support at 54 and overhead resistance at 59½. The wide, tall rectangle has plenty of trendline touches. If you are lucky, you might be able to get three or four trades from this formation (as marked by the numbers on the figure). Each side-to-side pass represents a price change of about $5, plenty of profit opportunity to be of interest to the more adventurous trader.

The volume pattern trends downward over the formation. Near the end, the volume spurts upward propelling prices higher until they break out and zoom to new highs. The statistics reviewed later in this chapter suggest that the majority of rectangles have receding volume trends. That is true but it may be difficult to see. I would not exclude a rectangle formation simply because the volume trend is not rising.

Focus on Failures

Of the nearly 300 rectangles I reviewed, just 5 fail. After separating rectangles into tops and bottoms, the top variety has just three failures. Figure 33.3 shows an example of a failure. Prices break out of the formation at 35⅝ and move upward to a new high of 37. However, they stall in mid-April before turning

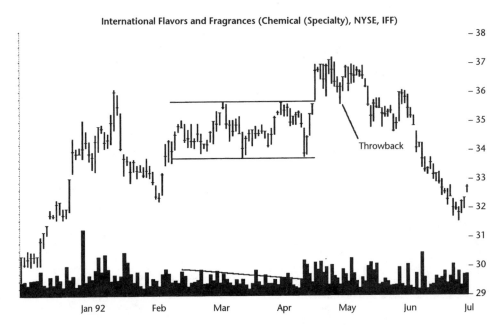

Figure 33.3 A 5% failure of a rectangle top. Prices follow the existing trend upward but only for a little gain before heading back into the rectangle and shooting out the other side.

around and throwing back to the formation. Once prices choose a new direction, they head down at a good clip. The brief climb represents a 4% price change. I consider anything less than a 5% move in the breakout direction to be a failure. The failure confirms when prices close beyond the side opposite the breakout. It is what I call a 5% failure.

I flag 5% failures because I want a method to catalog poorly performing chart patterns. Look at this another way: Had you bought this stock when it left the rectangle top, you would be upset when it throws back to the formation and continues lower. You might even take a loss if you are not quick on the trigger. Fortunately, rectangle failures are rare. I uncovered no failures in rectangle tops with downside breakouts. That does not mean they will never occur. It just means I did not spot any in the stocks under review.

Statistics

Table 33.2 shows a number of statistics related to rectangle tops. When combined, I uncovered just over 200 rectangles in 500 stocks over 5 years' worth of daily price data. Most of the formations are consolidations of the prevailing trend, especially for downside breakouts that have 140 consolidations.

Upside breakouts have a 2% failure rate, an exceedingly low value. Downside breakouts do even better with no formations failing. I consider zero fail-

Table 33.2
General Statistics for Rectangles Tops

Description	Upside Breakout	Downside Breakout
Number of formations in 500 stocks from 1991 to 1996	140	62
Reversal or consolidation	140 consolidations	62 reversals
Failure rate	3 or 2%	0
Average rise/decline of successful formations	52%	20%
Most likely rise/decline	20% to 30%	20%
Of those succeeding, number meeting or exceeding price target (measure rule)	125 or 91%	34 or 65%
Average formation length (start to breakout)	3 months (97 days)	3 months (85 days)
Number showing downward volume trend	89 or 64%	44 or 71%
Performance when volume is trending down and up	Down 55%, up 48%	Down 20%, up 19%
Volume for breakout day and next 5 days compared with day before breakout	164%, 164%, 119%, 105%, 112%, 96%	168%, 158%, 115%, 112%, 107%, 93%

ures to be a statistical anomaly. I am sure that if I looked at more stocks I could come up with a few failures. However, for both breakout directions, the low failure rates underscore that rectangles are reliable formations.

For upside breakouts, the average rise is 52%. This is well above the usual 40% gain. For downside breakouts, the decline averages 20%. The most likely gains and losses range from 20% to 30%. These values are also strong numbers, especially for upside breakouts.

Figure 33.4 shows a frequency distribution of gains for rectangles with upside breakouts. I exclude the catch-all category ">90%" and conclude that the tallest columns (20% and 30%) represent the most likely gains. The rightmost column illustrates why the overall average is 52% (because a large number of outsized gains pull up the average). When you consider all the columns, you may conclude that your gains will probably be better than 20% or 30%. For gains up to 30%, only about a third of the formations (38%) fall in that range. The remainder have gains over 30%, a mouthwatering return indeed.

Figure 33.5 shows a frequency distribution for rectangles with downside breakouts. This figures shows that 66% of the formations have losses amounting to 20% or less. That is a warning, suggesting that your return from rectangles with downside breakouts may be less than you hope. The figure also shows why the most likely rise is the same as the average rise. There are no tall columns in the upper range to distort the average.

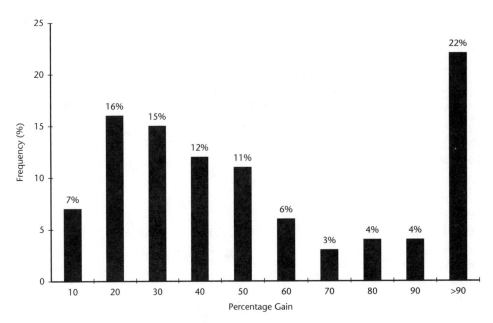

Figure 33.4 Frequency distribution of gains for rectangle tops with upside break-outs. The most likely gain is in the range of 20% to 30%, but several large gains (over 90%) overshadow the results.

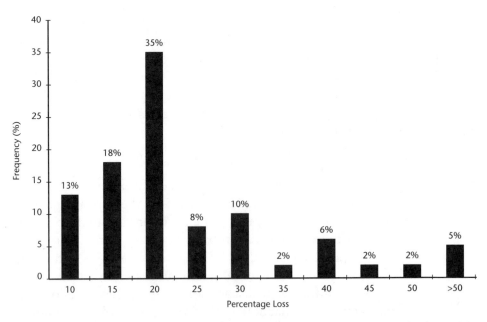

Figure 33.5 Frequency distribution of losses for rectangle tops with downside breakouts. Two out of three formations have losses less than 20%.

A discussion of the measure rule occurs in the Trading Tactics section of this chapter, but it involves computing the height of the rectangle and adding or subtracting it from the breakout point. The result is the expected target price. For upside breakouts, 91% of the formations meet or exceed their price targets, whereas only 65% of rectangles with downside breakouts make theirs. I consider values above 80% to be reliable.

The average formation length is about 3 months for both breakout types. Over 3 months' time 64% of upside breakouts and 71% of downside breakouts show receding volume trends. Some analysts suggest that a receding volume trend is key to a sound rectangle. When I examined this hypothesis, I discovered that rectangles with upside breakouts and a receding volume trend outperform their rising volume counterparts with gains of 55% versus 48%. Downside breakouts are more evenly matched with losses at 20% versus 19%.

Table 33.2 shows the results of a comparison of breakout volume with the day before the breakout. I used the day before the breakout instead of the average volume because of the receding volume trend. The day before the breakout may be the lowest value in the series and an average volume would probably involve a higher unfair comparison. Even so, volume is high on the breakout day and remains high through the following week for both breakout types.

Table 33.3 shows statistics related to premature breakouts. I define a premature breakout to be when prices close outside the rectangle trendlines and yet return to the formation. For upside breakouts, there are 15 formations with premature breakouts and 14 associated with formations that eventually breakout downward.

The volume during a premature breakout is higher than the 25-day moving average of the volume, as you would expect. This means it is difficult or impossible to distinguish a premature breakout from a genuine one. Table 33.3 shows that premature upside breakouts in formations with a genuine

Table 33.3
Premature Breakout Statistics for Rectangle Tops

Description	Upside Breakout	Downside Breakout
Number showing premature breakouts	15 or 11%	14 or 23%
Volume at premature breakout versus 25-day moving average	Up 184%, down 130%	Up 146%, down 132%
Number of formations with premature breakouts having both upside and downside premature breakouts	2 or 12%	0
Number of premature breakouts in same direction as genuine breakout	5 or 29%	6 or 43%
Number of premature breakouts in different direction from genuine breakout	12 or 71%	8 or 57%

upside breakout have volume that is 184% of the average. Downside premature breakouts in the same formation type have volume that is 130% above the average. Only two chart patterns have up and down premature breakouts in the same formation.

Does a premature breakout signal the direction of the actual breakout? Both breakout types suggest a premature breakout is opposite the genuine breakout direction. A genuine upside breakout follows a downside premature breakout 71% of the time. Downside breakouts are not so reliable: Only 57% of the formations with premature upside breakouts later show genuine downside breakouts. If we combine the premature breakout statistics and compare it with the total, we find 65% of the premature breakouts are on the opposite side of the actual breakout.

Table 33.4 shows statistics related to genuine breakouts. Throwbacks to the formation top and pullbacks to the bottom occur in 53% and 55% of the formations, respectively. The numbers are not high enough to suggest a trading tactic to take advantage of them.

Both breakout directions complete their throwbacks and pullbacks in 11 days, which is about average for these types of retraces. No formation has a throwback or pullback more than 30 days after the breakout. Any price retrace after a month I consider due to normal price action, not a throwback or pullback.

For upside breakouts, it takes about 8 months to reach the ultimate high and almost 3 months for downside breakouts to bottom. If you are a long-term investor of a rectangle top with an upside breakout, be prepared to wait for the long term before cashing out. For downside breakouts, a short-term play is in order.

Where in the yearly price range do most formations occur? Both breakout types occur in the highest third of the yearly range. Mapping performance over the range shows that the best performing upside breakouts have gains of

Table 33.4
Breakout Statistics for Rectangle Tops

Description	Upside Breakout	Downside Breakout
Throwback/pullback	74 or 53%	34 or 55%
Average time to throwback/pullback completion	11 days	11 days
Days to ultimate high/low	8 months (244 days)	3 months (82 days)
Percentage of breakouts occurring near 12-month price low (L), center (C), or high (H)	L3%, C21%, H76%	L18%, C36%, H46%
Percentage gain for each 12-month lookback period	L22%, C51%, H56%	L20%, C21%, H19%

56% when they break out from formations near the yearly high. Downside breakouts are about evenly split across the three categories.

Trading Tactics

Table 33.5 explains trading tactics for rectangle tops. The measure rule predicts the minimum target price. First, compute the height of the rectangle by subtracting the value of the lower trendline from the upper one. Add the difference to the top trendline for upside breakouts and subtract it from the bottom trendline for downside breakouts. The result is the target price.

For an example of the measure rule and how it applies to rectangles, consider the rectangle top pictured in Figure 33.6. The top trendline has a value of $38\frac{3}{4}$, whereas the bottom one perches at $33\frac{3}{4}$. The difference of 5 is the height of the rectangle. If this rectangle were to break out downward, then the target price would be $28\frac{3}{4}$ or the lower trendline value minus the formation height. Since the breakout is upward, add the height to the top trendline, giving a target price of $43\frac{3}{4}$. Prices reach the target about a month after the breakout.

I have read that to compute the *maximum* price move, one physically measures the *length* of the rectangle and applies it to the top trendline for upside breakouts or subtracts it from the bottom trendline for downward

Table 33.5
Trading Tactics for Rectangle Tops

Trading Tactic	Explanation
Measure rule	Measure the height of the rectangle from trendline to trendline. For upside breakouts, add the height to the top trendline; for downside breakouts, subtract it from the bottom trendline. The result is the minimum expected move. For a maximum price target, measure the *length* of the rectangle and extend it vertically above the top trendline (for upside breakouts) or below the bottom one (downside breakouts). The price becomes the maximum expected move.
Consolidation	More than two out of three rectangles act as consolidations of the prevailing trend. Expect the breakout to continue the trend.
Wait for breakout	Since you cannot be sure in which direction a rectangle will break out, wait for prices to close outside the trendline before trading in the direction of the breakout.
Tall rectangle scalp	If the rectangle is tall enough, sell or sell short near the top trendline and buy or cover near the bottom one.
Other	Watch for rectangles forming as the corrective phase of a measured move up formation and adjust the target price accordingly. Rectangle reversals sometimes appear as flat top formations

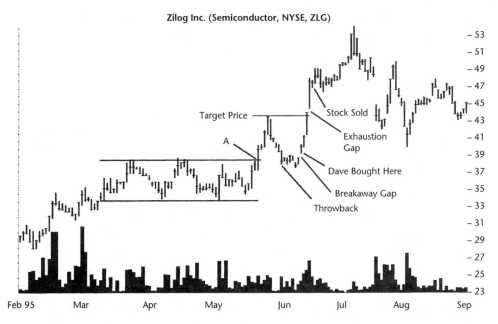

Figure 33.6   Rectangle top with breakaway gap and exhaustion gap. Dave traded this formation after buying it once the throwback completed.

breakouts. When using my computer, the technique comes close to the ultimate high. On paper, the results are less accurate. I have not tested this method extensively and cannot vouch for its accuracy. However, one has to wonder how measuring a formation (in inches) can accurately translate into a price move, but who knows, the system might work or at least prove helpful.

Returning to Table 33.5, the breakout direction is usually in the direction of the prior trend. For Figure 33.6 the direction is upward and that is the direction in which the breakout occurs. Once prices close outside a formation, then a breakout (or premature breakout) occurs. If the breakout is upward, go long or cover your short. If the breakout is downward, then short the stock or sell your position. If the rectangle is tall enough and providing you discover it quickly enough, you can trade the formation as it swings from trendline to trendline. Short or sell at the top trendline and cover or buy at the bottom trendline. Keep an eye on the price trend leading to the formation in case a breakout occurs. If the stock moves outside the rectangle trendline and you are losing money, close out your position. You might also want to get on the bandwagon and trade in the direction of the new trend.

If the breakout turns into a premature breakout when prices return to the rectangle proper, do not panic. There is still a chance that prices will resume their original breakout direction. Again, if the trade goes against you by shooting out the other side of the rectangle, then close out your position and do it quickly. If you hesitate, you may have another opportunity to add to your position or close it out if the formation pulls back or throws back. Take advantage of it especially if you are losing money. Often, prices will return to the formation boundary then turn away. If you do not get out during the pullback or throwback, then it is likely your losses will grow. Do not pass up the second chance and do not hope that prices will continue recovering. They will not!

Before placing a trade in a rectangle formation, see if the chart pattern is part of a larger pattern. Sometimes, the rectangle is the horizontal part, called the corrective phase, of a measured move up formation. Knowing that a rectangle is a subpart of a measured move allows you to get a better gauge on the expected price move. When the rectangle top is a reversal of the prevailing price trend, the resulting formation resembles a flat top. Suspect that a reversal might be under way if the price trend leading up to the rectangle is unusually steep.

Sample Trade

Dave is an artist. It is tough making a living and he wants to move to the computer world and become a graphics artist. He has been playing around with some hardware and software that duplicate the feel of a brush on various textures but wants to get the latest versions.

Recognizing chart patterns comes easily to him. With his keen eye, he has been on the prowl for a lucrative stock play. That is one reason he stumbled across the rectangle shown in Figure 33.6, but he did not spot the rectangle in a timely fashion. The only reason he noticed it is because of the throwback. Throwbacks and pullbacks are peculiar enough with their hooking retrace that they are easy to spot. One has only to look back and identify the associated formation.

Dave computed the formation height and applied it to the top of the rectangle to get the expected minimum price move. Did he pull the trigger when prices threw back to the formation? No, he waited. He followed the stock closely and when it gapped up (a breakaway gap), he bought and received a fill at 40. Each day the stock moved higher and in 3 days it had reached the target price of $43\frac{3}{4}$. The next day the stock gapped again (exhaustion gap) signaling an impending end to the rise. The next day prices faltered, and that is when he sold and closed out his position at $47\frac{1}{2}$. He netted over $7 a share or 18% in less than a week.

He took half his profits out of the market and upgraded his tools. With the remainder, he kept trolling the markets looking for another opportunity.

34

Rounding Bottoms

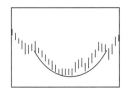

RESULTS SNAPSHOT

Appearance	A long, rounded upward turn in prices
Reversal or consolidation	Long-term (over 6 months) consolidation
Failure rate	38%
Failure rate if waited for upside breakout	5%
Average rise	54%, with most likely rise being 20%
Percentage meeting predicted price target	36%
Synonyms	Rounding Turns, Saucers
See also	Bump-and-Run Reversal Bottom; Cup with Handle; Head-and-Shoulders Bottom, Complex; Scallops, Ascending and Descending

Rounding bottoms, rounding turns, and saucers are synonyms for the same formation. The pattern differs from the cup-with-handle and scallop formations in subtle ways, so be sure to study those formations if you are unsure about identification.

   If you consider that this formation acts as a consolidation of the prevailing trend and anything acting contrary to that is a failure, then the failure rate for this pattern is very high at 38%. However, if you consider upside breakouts only (a breakout being when prices move above the left saucer lip), then the failure rate drops to just 5%. I consider failure rates above 20% to be alarming. The chart pattern sports a 54% average gain with a likely rise of 20%. Almost a quarter of the formations have gains over 90% and that pulls the average upward. The large gain masks the performance of the most likely rise. With a deep cup formed over many months, it makes sense that the measure rule would have trouble predicting accurate price targets. Prices fulfill the measure rule just 36% of the time for successful formations with upside breakouts.

Tour

Figure 34.1 shows an example of a rounding bottom on a daily scale. I would not call it a good example because the bottom is too irregular. In mid-May there is an out-of-pattern downward price decline that ends with prices quickly rebounding. In late June prices jump up then fade back down. The June rise is not uncommon so do not get too excited when it happens in a stock you own. Prices should return to near the base of the rounding bottom before continuing to rise. The volume trend takes on the appearance of being rounded if you ignore the four annoying spikes in the center.

A rounding bottom marks a struggle between buying demand and selling pressure that is nearly equal. Through the first part of the formation, the

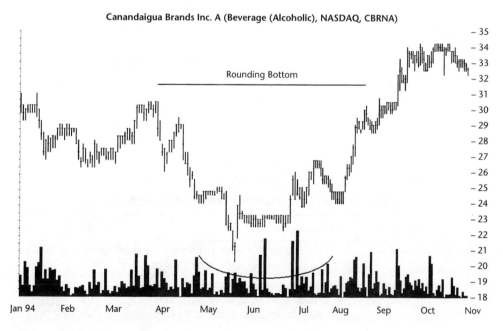

Figure 34.1 A rounding bottom on a daily scale. The bottom takes a brief dip in mid-May and a quick rise in late June.

sellers have the upper hand as they drive prices lower. Eventually, the forces come into balance and the stock bottoms out and moves horizontally. Later still, buying demand picks up and the stock inches upward. The climb is not always a smooth one. Sometimes, a large upward demand spike occurs sending the price skyrocketing, but in a month or so prices head back down and plane out slightly above where they left off. Then they resume their climb. When the stock reaches the old high, selling pressure usually drives prices lower, forming a handle. Prices recover and break through the old high and push higher still.

Identification Guidelines

As chart patterns go, rounding bottoms are easy to identify. Table 34.1 lists guidelines for their identification. Since rounding bottoms are often quite long (in this study, the longest is over $2\frac{1}{2}$ years), I usually use the weekly scale to make identification easy. I search for a price pattern that looks like a bowl or saucer. Once I discover the pattern, a quick glance backward finds prices trending upward for quite a while. The rounding bottom is usually a gentle retrace of some of the gains.

Consider Figure 34.2. The most recent up leg of the climb to the formation begins in late December 1991 on very high volume. Prices climb from a weekly low of about 4 to a high of $9\frac{5}{16}$, a gain of 235% in about 3 months. Then the stock eases over. Prices move lower and retrace much of their gains. The decline is not a quick straight-down affair. Rather, the stock moves lower on its way to $4\frac{3}{4}$ by curving around and flattening out.

Once prices reach the low, they move hesitantly higher by traveling horizontally for several weeks before beginning an accelerated climb. Prices reach the level of the left saucer lip and do not pause. They keep climbing until they reach 13 and then 16 before backing down to 11.

Table 34.1
Identification Characteristics of Rounding Bottoms

Characteristic	Discussion
Weekly scale	I use the weekly scale to identify these behemoths, although you can use the daily scale if you wish.
Rounded bowl shape	The price trend curves gently usually over many months and usually after an upward price trend. Connect the weekly low prices to visually construct a saucer or bowl shape in your mind.
Curving volume trend	The volume trend sometimes mimics the price trend by appearing as a bowl.

Figure 34.2 This is a good example of a rounding bottom on the weekly scale. Notice the bowl-shaped volume trend.

A rounding bottom does not require a handle, which is a price consolidation area that commonly forms immediately after the right saucer lip, but most times you will see one. After reaching the lip of the saucer, prices usually drop and consolidate before heading higher. A handle is typical behavior when prices reach an old high. The rise falters as tepid demand or excessive selling push prices lower; then, the two highs act as a resistance zone. Sometimes, prices make several attempts before pushing through the resistance and moving higher; sometimes, prices just give up and roll back downhill.

The volume trend usually echoes the price trend by rounding upward too. You can see this in Figure 34.2 although it is not as pronounced as it sometimes is.

Focus on Failures

To be fair, the preponderance of failures are probably due to semantics. When studying this formation, I discovered that most act as consolidations of the prevailing trend. After moving upward, prices round down, swing around, and head back up. I label those chart formations that do not fit this template as failures. Figure 34.3 shows an example of such a failure; it acts as a reversal of the primary trend. Prices trend down beginning on the left side of the chart to the base of the rounding bottom. Then, prices swing around and begin a new trend upward.

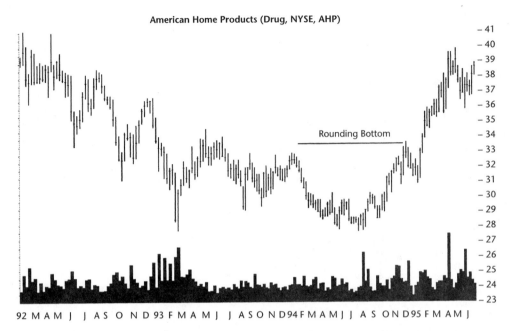

American Home Products (Drug, NYSE, AHP)

Figure 34.3 Rounding bottom that acts as a reversal of the trend.

The formation is a rounding bottom, but it does not act like a consolidation. If you had shorted this formation with the expectation that prices would continue down, you probably would have wound up with a loss. Thus, I consider this formation and others like it as failures.

Another type of failure, called a 5% failure, is when prices move in the intended direction after the formation completes but fail to travel more than 5% before turning around and heading substantially in the opposite direction. Only 11 of the formations with upside breakouts are 5% failures. This means once a formation breaks out upward, there is a good chance it will continue moving up.

Statistics

Table 34.2 shows general statistics related to rounding bottoms. I uncovered 243 formations in 2,500 years of daily price data. Of the formations I discovered, about 67% are consolidations of the prevailing trend and the rest are reversals.

The failure rate is exceedingly high at 38%. As explained in the Focus on Failures section, I label every formation that is not a consolidation of the trend a failure and include 5% failures too. If we consider only formations that break out upward, the failure rate drops to a more palatable 5%, which is very good.

Table 34.2
General Statistics for Rounding Bottoms

Description	Statistic
Number of formations in 500 stocks from 1991 to 1996	243
Reversal or consolidation	163 consolidations, 80 reversals
Failure rate	93 or 38%
Failure rate if waited for upside breakouts	11 or 5%
Average rise of successful formations	54%
Most likely rise	20%
Of those succeeding, number meeting or exceeding price target (measure rule)	50 or 36%
Average formation length	8.5 months (259 days)

Obviously, the statistic suggests a trading tactic: Wait for prices to climb above the right saucer lip before buying the stock (watch out for handles too; buy after the handle forms and prices move up).

The average rise of successful formations is 54% compared with a usual gain of 40% in other bullish chart patterns. However, the most likely rise is 20%. Figure 34.4 shows a frequency distribution of gains for successful round-

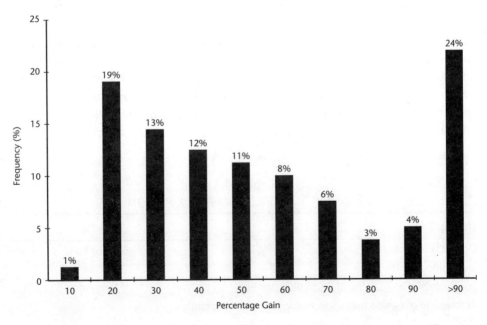

Figure 34.4 Frequency distribution of gains for rounding bottoms. Almost a quarter of the rounding bottoms have gains over 90%.

ing bottom formations. You can see that the highest column is 20% (if you ignore the rightmost one for the moment). I consider it to represent the most likely gain an investor can expect to receive. This is a conservative measure since the many large gains (each over 90%) shown in the rightmost column tend to pull the overall average upward.

Rounding bottoms do not have measure rules. However, that did not stop me from checking on how one would perform. I simply computed the formation height from the right saucer lip to the lowest low in the formation and added the difference to the right saucer lip. The result is the expected minimum price. About a third (36%) of the formations meet or exceed their price targets. I consider values above 80% to be reliable, so the measure rule essentially does not work for this formation—just like the pundits said.

The average formation length is a hefty 8.5 months (259 days). If you are looking for a formation to trade, you might look elsewhere. This one takes too long to form before the action really gets going. Still, if you have a rounding bottom in a stock you own or discover one reaching the right lip, the Trading Tactics section of this chapter gives you some suggestions on how to tame the beast.

Table 34.3 outlines statistics related to breakouts. Most of the formations (209) have upside breakouts, whereas the others are downside ones. After the breakout, 11 months typically pass from the right saucer lip to the ultimate high. That is a long time to wait, but during that time prices climb an average of 54%.

I sorted the formations into three categories depending on their position within the yearly price range. It turns out that most formations have the right saucer lip (the breakout point) in the upper third of the range. Only three formations (or 2%) have breakouts from the center third of the price range. This should not be too surprising because of the nature of this formation. Since it is an exceedingly long chart pattern, the saucer lips naturally are the highest points on the yearly price chart. In Table 34.3, I did not show the performance related to the three categories since the highest third of the yearly price range contains all but three of the formations. The performance for that category is

Table 34.3
Breakout Statistics for Rounding Bottoms

Description	Statistic
Upside breakout	209 or 86%
Downside breakout	34 or 14%
For successful formations, days to ultimate high	11 months (334 days)
Percentage of upside breakouts occurring near 12-month price low (L), center (C), or high (H)	L0%, C2%, H98%

56%, very near the overall average of 54% (the three formations occurring in the center third of the price range have gains of 45%).

Trading Tactics

I considered removing trading tactics for this formation but changed my mind. Although I do not recommend trading this formation on a consistent basis (because it takes too long to form), there is one key trick to improving your performance: Wait for prices to close above the right saucer lip before investing. But before discussing trading tactics further, consider the measure rule outlined in Table 34.4. The measure rule helps estimate the potential profit. To apply the measure rule and help you visualize its use, consider the chart shown in Figure 34.5. Subtract the lowest low in the saucer from the right saucer lip. In Figure 34.5, the low is 25 and the right saucer lip is (arguably) $31\frac{7}{16}$, giving a formation height of $6\frac{7}{16}$. Add the height to the value of the right saucer lip to get the target price. In this case, the target is $37\frac{7}{8}$ and prices reach that level in late January.

A word of caution about the measure rule: It essentially does not work since only one in three formations meets its target. Rely instead on support and resistance zones as you try to estimate how well the formation will perform and balance your potential profit against the inherent risk.

I consider rounding bottoms to be one of the more treacherous formations. Take another look at Figure 34.5. In judging when the breakout occurs, you should use the left saucer lip. Unfortunately, this rounding turn has no left lip. How do you gauge a breakout? That is the situation I faced. I learned that in such circumstances I needed to wait for the handle to form and prices to

Table 34.4
Trading Tactics for Rounding Bottoms

Trading Tactic	Explanation
Measure rule	Subtract the lowest low from the right saucer lip. Add the difference to the value of the right saucer lip to get the target price. This is the minimum price move to expect. The measure rule only works about a third of the time, so be conservative and lower your target.
Wait for price rise	Wait for prices to rise (close) above the left saucer lip before buying.
Watch for handle	Many times prices will reach the level of the left saucer lip then dip to form a handle. Buy when prices rise above the right saucer lip (or pierce a handle trendline moving up).

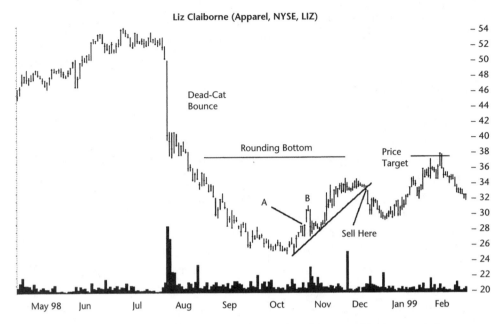

Figure 34.5   A treacherous example of a rounding bottom that has no left saucer lip. The rounding turn forms after disappointing earnings send the stock into a dead-cat-bounce.

climb above the handle high (or right cup lip). When it did (point A), or so I thought, I paper traded the stock and bought in, just as it crested (point B). That turned out to be a minor high. Prices dropped the next day then slowly recovered making another handle. A good place to sell is when prices pierce the up trendline in early December.

Sample Trade

How do you use the trading tactics to improve your investment performance? Consider what Glen did with the situation shown in Figure 34.6. It was his dream to become a day trader but he had neither the trading capital nor the necessary skills for the job. He decided to get there one trade at a time.

In December, as he was flipping through his charts, he came across what appeared to be a mild double bottom. On the daily chart the two bottoms in August and November were barely discernible. Was it a valid formation and should he buy the stock now? Glen decided that the retrace between the two bottoms was not high enough and the two bottoms not clear enough to be worth considering. He justified his action by thinking that if he was having a hard time spotting the formation, then others would have the same trouble. If no one spots the formation, then prices will not rise.

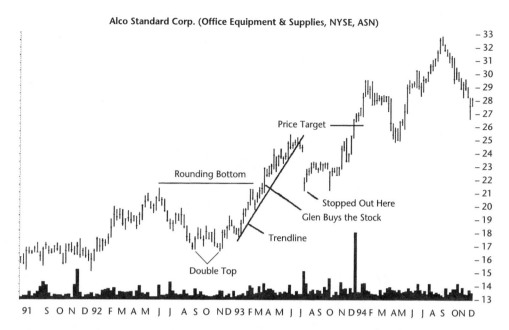

Figure 34.6   The double bottom formation is barely discernible within the rounding bottom on the weekly scale.

When he flipped to the weekly chart, it changed the characterization of what he was seeing. On his screen was an obvious rounding bottom. The volume pattern supported the conclusion: receding as prices declined and rounding up as prices rose. So, he decided to wait for the rounding bottom to stop near the prior saucer lip at about $21\frac{3}{8}$. When it paused for 2 weeks in February, he knew the formation was primed. The question then became, what was it going to do next? The only way to find that out was to wait.

The following week prices dropped. He waited until prices closed above the right saucer lip and headed higher. He knew that to buy earlier risked a downturn in the stock from which it might not recover for a long time. If the stock ventured above the right saucer lip, then the probabilities suggested a continuing push higher.

When prices hit 22, he bought. He looked back at his chart and decided to put a stop-loss order $\frac{1}{8}$ below the saucer lip, just below a support level. He decided that if the stock hit his stop, in all likelihood it was going down. Content with his investment decision and trading plan, he was confident that his career change to day trading was a simple step away. He was even more confident as the stock climbed. He began looking through brochures from several companies that offered seminars on day trading. Then the stock declined and closed below the up trendline. It was a warning sign that anyone could have missed. Glen certainly did.

The following week when he received a call from his broker saying prices had hit his stop-loss order, he was shocked. Glen booked a loss of about a buck a share. As he watched the stock, he became even more upset. It turns out the stock sold at the low for the week.

Three years later, after day trading was over for the day, Glen happened to review this trade. He decided to pull up the chart and gasped at what he found. The stock peaked at 66, exactly triple his purchase price.

35

Rounding Tops

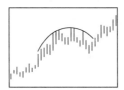

RESULTS SNAPSHOT

Appearance	As prices move up, they curve around then breakout upward.
Reversal or consolidation	Long-term (over 6 months) bullish consolidation
Failure rate	19%
Failure rate if waited for upside breakout	6%
Average rise	41%, with most likely rise between 20% and 40%
Percentage meeting predicted price target	69%
Surprising finding	Most of the time prices rise after a rounding top completes.
Synonyms	Domes, Rounding Turn
See also	Bump-and-Run Reversal, Top; Head-and-Shoulders Tops, Complex

When is a top not a top? When it is a rounding top or dome and prices break out upward. That is the real surprise with this formation as most of the rounding tops have upside breakouts. The failure rate is 19%, a sliver below the maximum rate of 20% that I consider reliable formations to possess. If you wait for an upside breakout, then the failure rate drops to 6%. At first, I set the breakout point as being one-third up the formation. I considered that a 30% retrace after the dome rounds over as a sign of an upside breakout. Prices pierce many down-sloping trendlines by that rise and it also gives other investors time to recognize the trend change (so they help push up the price). However, the results were just too unreal to use (a 0% failure rate and average climb of 58%). The computation neglected other formations that began moving up but ultimately ended lower. I reworked the figures using the dome top as the breakout point. The results are more in line with other formations. Rounding tops have an average gain of 41%, with a likely rise between 20% and 40%.

Tour

Figure 35.1 shows a rounding top on the daily time scale that appears irregular with its many price spikes. The stock begins its upward trek in early February. When prices summit in mid-May and start rounding over, the climb amounts to a gain of 22%. In a series of steps prices decline and reach their low before turning up in September. Once prices make the turn, they rapidly climb above the old high and soar to over 71 by the time this study ends.

The reason a rounding turn occurs is not difficult to explain. Prices move up on bullish enthusiasm confirmed by high volume at the start. Knowing that prices are climbing, sellers hold on to their shares a bit longer. This forces demand to climb along with the share price. However, as prices rise, buying demand tapers off and eventually catches up to supply. Prices round over at the

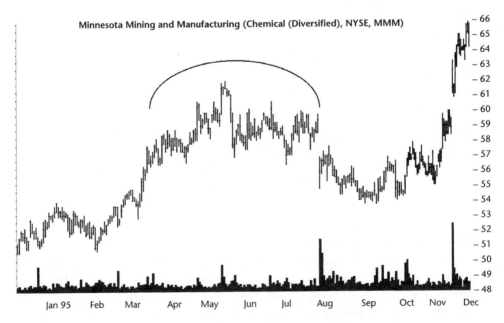

Figure 35.1   A rounding top on the daily time scale.

top. Since the shares are fetching a premium to intrinsic value, more sellers appear. The smart money starts selling, too, and the price drops.

Once investors discover the upward price momentum has turned, selling pressure increases, forcing the price down. Volume may pick up as more traders try to dump their shares as prices decline. Eventually, the decline ends when nervous novices toss in the towel and sell their holdings. When all those who considered selling their shares have sold, the smart money jumps in and buys the stock.

Identification Guidelines

Table 35.1 outlines the characteristics that rounding tops possess. Using either the daily or weekly time scale, prices start moving up from the base of the dome formation. As they move up, they bend over and round off at the top, then continue their rounding turn until they head down and retrace much of the prior rise. Buying demand often cuts the decline short before prices return to where they started.

Like the rounding bottom formation, rounding tops have the same volume pattern, but with rounding tops they are opposite the dome shape. By that I mean volume is lowest at the center of the formation and higher at either end. This is just a guideline, not an inviolable rule. Many times you will see an irregular volume trend over the life of the formation. Pay it no heed; it is still a rounding top. What is important is that prices round over and a bowl-shaped volume trend just adds evidence to the veracity of the chart pattern.

Figure 35.2 shows two examples of a rounding top on the weekly time scale. The first one begins at a low price of $12\frac{1}{16}$ in late December 1991. Prices rise at a gentle rate then the weekly highs begin rounding over near the top. By late April prices are heading down again, retracing some of their gains. Prices only decline to 14 before heading up on their way to the second formation.

Table 35.1
Identification Characteristics of Rounding Tops

Characteristic	Discussion
Daily or weekly scale	These formations are often long enough to appear on the weekly charts as well as the dailies.
Rounded half-moon shape	The price trend curves beginning from the lower left upward to the top of the dome then rounds over and moves down again. At the formation end, prices sometimes bottom somewhat higher than where they started.
Curving volume trend	The volume trend sometimes appears rounded too, but inverted from the dome. In other words, volume is occasionally higher on either end and shallow in the center.

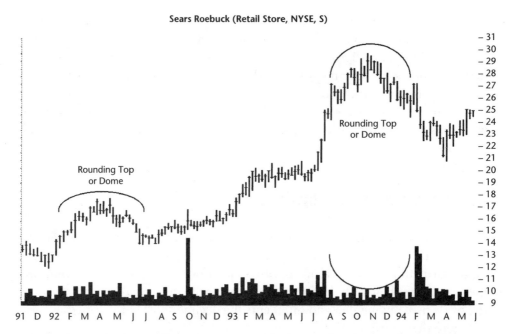

Figure 35.2 Two rounding tops on a weekly time scale. The gentle rounding over gives way to a rising trend most of the time. Note the rounding-appearing volume trend on the right formation.

The second dome is not as rounded as the first, but the volume pattern is characteristic of rounding tops. Volume is higher at either end of the formation than at the center. Overall, the volume pattern looks like a wide bowl on the chart.

The price pattern of the second dome finishes higher than where it begins, just as did the first one. From the low of $20^{13}/_{16}$, prices climb to a high of $53^{7}/_{8}$ a few weeks before the end of this study in July 1996. That is a gain of about 260%. The first rounding top has a rise of 210% as measured from the low in June 1992 to the high reached during the second rounding top in October 1993.

Focus on Failures

As I was searching for rounding tops in the stock charts, it quickly became obvious that they act as consolidations of the prevailing trend. The statistics confirmed my hunch. Thus, I consider everything that is not a consolidation of the prevailing trend to be a failure. The reason for this is the same one posited for the bottom variety. If you buy into a situation believing that prices will leave the formation in the same trend as they enter, you will probably be upset when prices reverse. Reversals are rare, happening less than 20% of the time, but they do occur.

Figure 35.3 shows an example of a rounding top failure. For 5 months prices rise on their way to the start of the formation. Then prices dip for a few weeks just before the rounding top begins. A person investing in this formation would expect prices to continue moving higher, resuming the intermediate-term uptrend. However, they would be wrong. Prices reverse and head lower. From the high reached in the rounding top to the low just 3 months later prices decline by 60%.

I could find few technical clues as to why this formation did not perform as expected. The 2-week decline leading to the start of the formation is significant as it drops below the intermediate-term trendline, part of which is shown in the figure. Prices recover and move along the trendline during mid-October through early November, then rise above it smartly until tumbling below it in mid-January. The first trendline piercing during late September serves as a warning that the end is approaching. Investors were getting nervous about holding the stock. Eventually, this nervousness translated into higher volume as prices plummeted.

I consider an upside breakout to occur when prices rise above the dome top. Usually prices continue moving higher by more than 5%. When they do not, it is called a 5% failure. Just six formations (6%) fail to move higher than 5% before plunging. This suggests that once prices break out upward, they continue moving up.

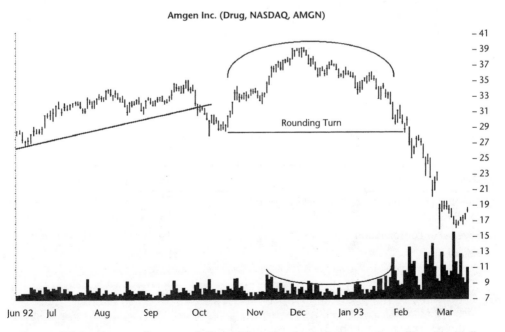

Amgen Inc. (Drug, NASDAQ, AMGN)

Rounding Turn

Jun 92   Jul   Aug   Sep   Oct   Nov   Dec   Jan 93   Feb   Mar

Figure 35.3 A rounding top failure. The piercing of the up trendline (partially shown) before the formation began is a clue to the failure of this formation to continue moving up.

Statistics

Table 35.2 contains general statistics for rounding tops. Rounding tops are somewhat rare, occurring only 165 times in 500 stocks over 5 years. Most of the formations act as consolidations of the prevailing trend; the remainder are reversals. As explained in the Focus on Failures section, I consider reversals to be failures of the formation to move in the intended direction. As such, they comprise most of the failures. If you wait for an upside breakout or for prices to rise above the dome high, then the failure rate drops to 6%. That is well below the 20% maximum that I consider reliable formations to have.

The average rise of successful formations is 41% as measured from the dome top to the ultimate high (when the primary trend changes). This is about average for bullish formations.

Figure 35.4 shows that the most likely rise ranges from 20% to 40%. The graph shows the results from a frequency distribution of gains. The tallest columns are the ones with the highest frequency. I consider them to represent the most likely rise. Usually the chart looks more like a bell-shaped curve, but this one appears irregular with spikes at 80% and 90%. I think the irregular pattern is due to the scarcity of formations. If there were more successful rounding tops, the pattern would appear smoother.

Although rounding tops do not have a measure rule, that did not stop me from checking to see if an acceptable gauge is available. I calculated the formation height from the dome high to the right side low and added the result to the dome high. Only 69% of the formations have prices that move above the calculated target price. I consider values above 80% to be reliable, so this chart pattern falls short. The Trading Tactics section discusses use of the measure rule in more detail.

Table 35.2
General Statistics for Rounding Tops

Description	Statistic
Number of formations in 500 stocks from 1991 to 1996	165
Reversal or consolidation	134 consolidations, 31 reversals
Failure rate	31 or 19%
Failures after upside breakout	6 or 6%
Average rise of successful formations	41%
Most likely rise	20% to 40%
Of those succeeding, number meeting or exceeding price target (measure rule)	59 or 69%
Average formation length	6 months (182 days)

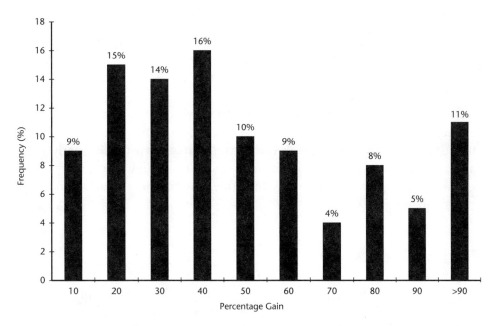

Figure 35.4 Frequency distribution of gains for rounding tops. The most likely rise ranges between 20% and 40%.

The average formation length is 6 months, rather long as far as formations go. This length reinforces the belief that rounding top formations readily appear on weekly time charts.

Table 35.3 shows statistics related to breakouts. I consider prices to break out of the formation when they rise above the dome high (upside breakouts). When you filter the breakouts into the two types, you find that there are 101 upside breakouts and 64 downside ones.

I did not consider a rounding top breakout to be that significant except for the direction. The majority of breakouts are upward, contrary to the popular belief that domes represent tops; prices should fall after a rounding top occurs. That is not what I found with over 100 formations supporting the conclusion. I feel safe basing the performance statistics on those formations with upside breakouts.

Table 35.3
Breakout Statistics for Rounding Tops

Description	Statistic
Upside breakout	101 or 61%
Downside breakout	64 or 39%
For successful formations, days to ultimate high	1 year (371 days)
Percentage of breakouts occurring near 12-month price low (L), center (C), or high (H)	L0%, C5%, H95%

For successful formations with upside breakouts, it takes about a year (371 days) to reach the ultimate high. That is a long time for a 41% average gain. We have seen with other formations that large percentage gains take longer to reach the ultimate high. Rounding tops are no exception but the rise is perhaps more gentle.

If you split the yearly price range into thirds to see where the breakout resides, you discover that nearly all break out within a third of the yearly high. Just four formations (5%) break out in the center third of the yearly price range. With most formations having breakouts in the highest category, there is no need to map performance over the three ranges. The formations meet the average, gaining 41%.

Trading Tactics

Table 35.4 shows trading tactics for rounding tops. The measure rule estimates the minimum expected price target. Although a measure rule is not supposed to exist, I found that it works 69% of the time. I view values over 80% to be reliable, so in that regard, it comes up short of the mark. When using the rule, be sure to look for resistance areas. They are the areas where the price rise is likely to stall, forcing the measure rule to underperform. To use the measure rule, subtract the lowest low from the highest high in the formation, which gives the formation height. In Figure 35.5, point A shows the lowest low at $45\frac{5}{8}$, whereas point B depicts the highest high at $49\frac{7}{8}$. Add the difference, $4\frac{1}{4}$ (the formation height), to the highest high (point B) to get the target price. In this case, the target is $54\frac{1}{8}$, met in early July.

There are several ways to profit from rounding tops. The suggested method is to wait for the breakout, prices to climb above the dome high. Since prices are already climbing, they continue moving up 94% of the time. That is a reassuring number but no guarantee of success. If you like to take more risk,

Table 35.4
Trading Tactics for Rounding Tops

Trading Tactic	Explanation
Measure rule	Compute the formation height by subtracting the right dome low from the formation high. Add the difference to the high to get the target price.
Buy on breakout	Buy when prices close above the dome high.
Buy above 30% retrace	For a more risky but profitable trade, buy when prices rise above the right dome low by at least 30% of the formation height.
Right low support	The right dome low shows support. If prices throw back to this level and continue down, sell.

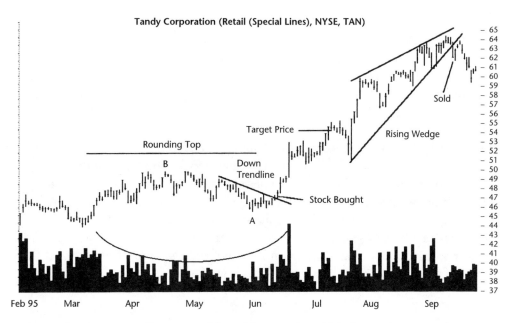

Figure 35.5 A rounding top with a rising wedge. This formation turned into a profitable opportunity for Sharon. She bought into the situation and sold after the rising wedge breakout.

buy at a lower price (one-third of the formation height, above the right dome low). I use the 30% retrace amount since a rise of that magnitude usually breaks a down-sloping trendline that sometimes forms as prices decline during the rounding turn. A breakthrough of a trendline or even a 30% retrace is usually strong enough to command attention from other investors (they jump on the uptrend) and minimizes the chance of a downside breakout.

If you purchase a stock after a rounding turn completes and see prices rise for a month or so, curl around, and fall below the right dome low, sell the stock. Most likely it is going to continue down. Watch for a bounce at the right dome low as that area sometimes acts as a support zone. As always, look for other areas of support to gauge how far the decline may go.

Sample Trade

Sharon is a high-energy player. She is the one you see careening out of control when skiing down the expert slope. She is the one you see night after night relaxing in a bar after work, surrounded by men. In other words, she is fun to be with, the life of the party.

Her investment style mirrors her lifestyle. When she spotted the rounding top pictured in Figure 35.5, she waited for just the right moment to buy. At first, she thought it might be a head-and-shoulders top but the two shoulders and head were at about the same price level and the volume pattern was all wrong.

In mid-June, when prices began heading up and pierced the down-sloping trendline, she bought the stock and received a fill at 47. Then she held on and watched the stock daily. As prices rose, she noticed that the oscillations from minor high to minor low seemed to be narrowing. To her, these oscillations indicated that a rising wedge was forming, but the volume pattern was abnormal. With a rising wedge, the volume pattern tends to recede over time.

In early September, Sharon grew alarmed because the volume trend began to decline drastically. Her studies showed a tendency for a severe drop-off in volume just before a rising wedge breakout, so the day after prices pierced the lower wedge trendline, she sold the stock at 62.

Her analysis was perfect. After she sold the stock, prices pulled back to the lower wedge trendline and hung on for 2 more days before tumbling. At the start of the new year, the stock reached a low of 34⅛.

36

Scallops, Ascending and Descending

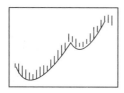 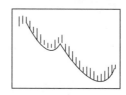

RESULTS SNAPSHOT

Ascending

Appearance	Prices peak, retrace, and curve around then form a higher peak. The price pattern looks like the letter J.
Reversal or consolidation	Long-term (over 6 months) bullish consolidation
Failure rate	25%
Average rise	33%, with the most likely rise between 20% and 30%
Volume trend	Upward but looks like the letter U—highest at the ends of the formation
Percentage meeting predicted price target	71%
Surprising finding	Consecutive scallops in a trend get shorter and narrower.
See also	Cup with Handle; Head-and-Shoulders Bottom, Complex; Rounding Bottoms

Descending

Appearance	Prices peak, curve downward and around, then form a lower peak. The price pattern looks like the letter J reversed.

Reversal or consolidation	Short-term (up to 3 months) bearish consolidation
Failure rate	3%
Average decline	24%, with the most likely decline about 20%
Volume trend	No discernible volume trend
Percentage meeting predicted price target	52%
See also	Head-and-Shoulders Bottoms, Complex; Rounding Bottoms

The classic definition of scallops refers to the ascending variety only, where you find repeated saucer-shaped formations in a rising price trend. I reasoned that if there is an ascending variety, there probably is a descending variety. I decided to find out, but before I discuss the two types of formations in detail, I think it is worth reviewing the major findings.

For ascending scallops, the failure rate at 25% is above the 20% maximum that reliable formations possess. Descending scallops have a failure rate of just 3%. Why the big difference in failure rates? The difference is because I use the highest high on the right side of the formation to calculate the percentage change to the ultimate high or low. For ascending scallops, this penalizes performance since the right edge is much higher than the left. For descending scallops, it helps performance because the right side is well above the formation low and the ultimate low.

The percentage rise for ascending scallops is 33%, respectable but mediocre when compared to other bullish formations. For descending scallops, the declines average 24%; that is quite good (we usually see a 20% decline for bearish patterns). The measure rule is weak in both species and especially so with the descending variety—only 52% of the chart patterns reach their price targets.

One surprising finding is that consecutively ascending scallops get narrower and shorter, on average, when compared with prior scallops in a series. For example, in a line of four ascending scallops, the first one will be wider and taller than the last one. The relationship for descending scallops is unknown because of a dearth of consecutive formations.

Tour and Identification Guidelines

Table 36.1 outlines identification guidelines for both ascending and descending scallops. One difference between the two types is the price trend leading to the formation. As the name implies, ascending scallops appear when prices are

Table 36.1
Identification Characteristics of Ascending and Descending Scallops

Characteristic	Discussion
Price trend	Prices should be rising leading to ascending scallops and declining toward descending scallops.
J shape	Both ascending and descending formations have two price peaks with a rounded recession in between. The ascending variety has a higher right peak, whereas the descending scallop has a higher left peak. Ascending scallops look like the letter J and descending scallops look like a reversed J.
Volume	Ascending scallops often show a U-shaped volume trend that gets heavier over time, but there is no discernible volume trend for descending scallops.

moving higher over the intermediate- to long-term trend, that is, over 3, 6, or more months. The descending variety occurs when prices are moving steadily down.

Figures 36.1 and 36.2 show examples of ascending and descending scallop formations, respectively. Figure 36.1 shows three ascending scallops with the first one being an especially large one. It looks like a rounding bottom except that the minor high, where the formation ends on the right (in mid-April), is well above the minor high on the left (during early December). This is typical for ascending scallops—the right side should be above the left. However, it is

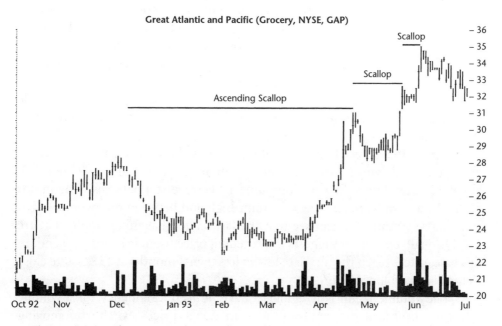

Figure 36.1   Three ascending scallops. The formation resembles the letter J.

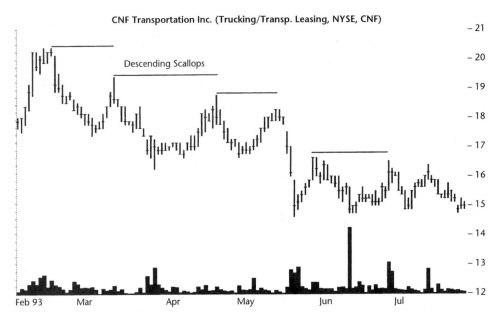

CNF Transportation Inc. (Trucking/Transp. Leasing, NYSE, CNF)

Figure 36.2   Four consecutive descending scallops.

all right if the two peaks are close to each other in price. This often signals an end to the series of scallops and the rising price trend.

The J-shaped pattern appears on the smallest scallop in Figure 36.1. I highlight this formation with some consternation. When hunting for scallops, one should look at the price lows, not the highs. If you connect the minor lows of the first two formations, you see that prices have a bowl shape. The bowl shape is not clear in the smallest formation unless you trace along the highs.

The smallest formation in Figure 36.1 also has the best volume pattern— a U-shaped trend. This is common for ascending scallops but should not be viewed as a requirement. The first scallop does not have an easily recognizable bowl-shaped volume trend but it is there. The volume spikes are higher near the formation ends than in the center.

Figure 36.2 shows four descending scallops. You can see that the overall price trend is downward. It starts on the left at about 20 and saucers down to about 15. The descending scallops appear like reverse J patterns. The minor high on the right is below the left minor high and between the two peaks is a rounded recession. You can see that the last scallop has minor highs that are nearly equal. This often suggests the receding price trend is nearing an end. In this case, prices reach the ultimate low in less than 2 months at $13\frac{5}{8}$, quite close to the last bowl low of $14\frac{3}{4}$.

The volume trend is irregular. I have noticed a tendency for a volume spike to appear near the center of the formation as prices switch from moving downward to upward. In Figure 36.2 you can see the spikes in late March and mid-June.

Focus on Failures

Scallops suffer from what I call *5% failures*. A 5% failure is when prices break out in the intended direction but fail to continue moving in the same direction by more than 5%. They double back and head in the opposite direction, sometimes causing an investor to lose money. Figures 36.3 and 36.4 show examples of failures. There is nothing wrong with the ascending scallop in Figure 36.3 in the April–May period. Prices round up nicely and continue higher while the volume pattern is bowl-shaped if you disregard the twin spikes in early May. However, the late June formation marks the high for the stock. Again, there is really nothing wrong with the pattern. The J shape is pronounced and smooth. The volume pattern is somewhat rugged but higher on either end than in the center. The narrowness of the formation is a clue to its failure. It is about 2 weeks wide, which is quite narrow for scallops (the average width is about 2 *months*). From the high at 19, the stock heads down in a choppy manner until the end of the study (mid-July 1996) where it is at 13½.

Descending scallop failures are similar to the one shown in Figure 36.4. The formation sometimes acts as a reversal of the downward trend since prices move up substantially after the formation ends. The price trend leading to the formation is downward. This is not entirely clear from the figure, but the stock reaches a high of 36⅝ in late September 1993, then prices move down until

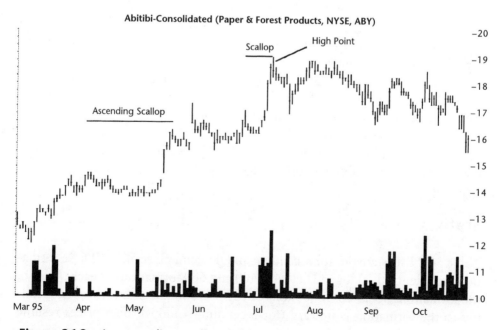

Figure 36.3   An ascending scallop failure in late June. Most scallops act as consolidations of the trend but the narrow ascending scallop in late June marks the high for the stock.

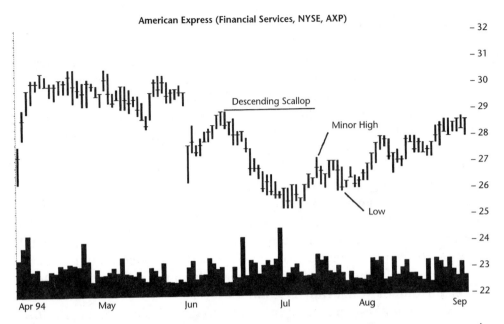

Figure 36.4   A descending scallop failure. This descending scallop acts as a reversal.

they reach a low of 25¼ in early July. After the formation reverses, prices climb and reach a high of 50¾ in early April 1996.

If you measure from the right minor high to the ultimate low (as marked on the figure), the decline is less than 5%—a 5% failure. The only thing that stands out about this formation is that it occurs well into a downtrend implying a trend reversal is likely.

We see in the Statistics section that most descending scallops form near the yearly low, suggesting the trend has been moving down for some time. This downward trend coupled with a poor measure rule showing, where about half the formations fall short of their price targets, leads one to believe that the performance may be worse than the statistics suggest. In short, be careful about investing in a descending scallop that forms well into a downtrend.

Statistics

Table 36.2 lists statistics for ascending and descending scallops. These formations are plentiful—I logged between 400 and 600 formations of each. Most of the formations act as consolidations of the prevailing trend. If the trend leading to the formation is upward (for ascending scallops), then prices resume their uptrend shortly after the formation ends.

I log a failure if prices move in an unexpected direction for too long. For ascending scallops, a failure occurs when prices move downward and slip below

Table 36.2
General Statistics for Ascending and Descending Scallops

Description	Ascending Scallops	Descending Scallops
Number of formations in 500 stocks from 1991 to 1996	613	414
Reversal or consolidation	492 consolidations, 121 reversals	310 consolidations, 104 reversals
Failure rate	151 or 25%	14 or 3%
Average rise/decline of successful formations	33%	24%
Most likely rise/decline	20% to 30%	20%
Of those succeeding, number meeting or exceeding price target (measure rule)	327 or 71%	206 or 52%
Average formation length	2 months (57 days)	1.5 months (49 days)
Days to ultimate high/low	8 months (231 days)	3.5 months (101 days)
Percentage of scallops occurring near 12-month price low (L), center (C), or high (H)	L2%, C14%, H84%	L51%, C34%, H15%
Percentage gain for each 12-month lookback period	L56%, C40%, H31%	L24%, C23%, H27%
Consecutive number of formations	2 = 67%, 3 = 38%, 4 = 18%, 5 = 8%, 6 = 3%, 7 = 2%, 8 = 1%	2 = 62%, 3 = 27%, 4 = 9%, 5 = 3%, 6 = 1%, 7 = 0%

the formation low without first moving 5% above the right formation edge. Failures for descending scallops are similar in that prices need to rise above the right edge high without first dropping by more than 5%. The failure rates—at 25% and 3% for ascending and descending scallops, respectively—measure from the high reached in the right scallop edge to the ultimate high or low. As explained earlier, this measurement penalizes ascending scallops and assists descending ones. The measurement accounts for the different failure rates and explains the subpar 33% gain and exceptional 24% average loss for the two chart patterns. Despite these variances, I consider the measurement method to be acceptable since the right minor high, when completed, is easy to identify and serves as a good reference point.

I compute the most likely gain or loss by using a frequency distribution of the gains and losses. Figure 36.5 shows a graph of the gains and Figure 36.6 shows a graph of the losses.

In Figure 36.5 the two highest columns represent the most likely gain because they have the highest frequency. Even though the *average* gain for all successful formations is 33%, the *most likely* gain rests between 20% and 30%.

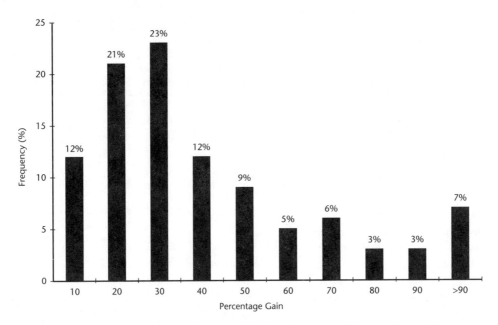

Figure 36.5 Frequency distribution of gains for ascending scallops. The most likely gain is between 20% and 30%.

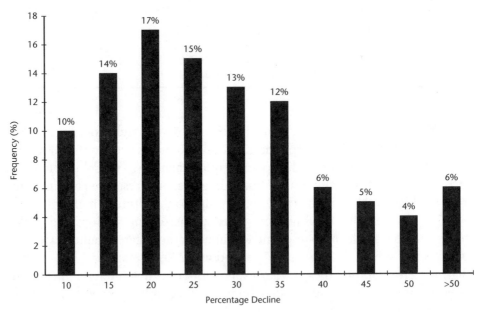

Figure 36.6 Frequency distribution of losses for descending scallops. The most likely loss is 20%.

Figure 36.6 shows a distribution of the losses. The tallest column, at 20%, represents the most likely loss since it has the highest frequency. However, the two adjacent columns are quite close to the tallest one so the likely decline may range between 15% and 25%. I view these figures as representations of what you might expect to make if you trade these formations.

I discuss the measure rule in the Trading Tactics section, but it involves computing the height of the formation and adding the result to the right edge high or subtracting it from the lowest low in the formation. The result is the minimum price target. For ascending scallops, 71% of the formations meet or exceed their predicted price targets, whereas only 52% of descending scallops meet theirs. I view values above 80% to be reliable, so scallops fall short of the benchmark. What does this mean? If you buy a stock and see a scallop develop near the beginning of the price trend, prices will likely meet the target. However, if the trend has been in existence for a long time (say, over 4 months), then there is a greater chance that prices will not meet the predicted target. Of course this depends on the overall market. Declines during a raging bull market may be short-lived, so factor in the market accordingly.

The average formation length is quite short, less than 2 months for both types of scallops. Some, such as that shown in Figure 36.1, will be longer than average and some will be shorter, but overall, there seems to be a tendency for the formation to last between 1 and 3 months.

The time it takes to reach the ultimate high or low is about double that for ascending scallops than for descending ones. Coupled with the average rise or decline, this suggests the declines are steeper, more violent, and the rises more drawn out and sedate. It also suggests investors should be patient, at least for ascending scallops, and let the stock play out before selling.

Where in the yearly price range do the formations occur? For ascending scallops, most of them occur within a third of the yearly high as measured from the high at the right end of the formation. For descending scallops, most occur within a third of the yearly low. Overlaying the performance on the yearly price range, we discover that ascending scallops occurring within a third of their yearly low perform best, with a 56% average gain. I hasten to add that there are only 8 formations in this category, well short of the 30 samples needed to make definitive conclusions. However, the other two categories have enough samples and suggest that the lower they occur in the yearly price range, the better performance will be. Descending scallops, on the other hand, are mixed. Performance is essentially flat, ranging between 23% and 27%.

I included a tabulation on the number of consecutive formations in a stock. In essence, I wanted to know how likely it is that a second, third, or fourth (and so on) formation would occur in a trend. It turns out that it is quite common to have more than one scallop in a single uptrend or a single downtrend. In other words, about two-thirds of the time a second scallop appears after the first one (in the same trend). A third scallop will appear about a third to a quarter of the time. Table 36.2 shows the remainder of the percentages. Why is this significant? If you are considering shorting a stock that shows three cascading scallops, there is a good chance that you will be making a mistake. Only 9% of the formations have four descending scallops in a row and that suggests the end of the downtrend is near. The more scallops you find, the higher the likelihood the end of the trend is approaching.

Do ascending scallops change their shape as they climb? I measured the width of each scallop and where it occurs in a series of consecutive scallops (over a single uptrend). Figure 36.7 shows the results. Only four points are shown because the sample size diminishes beyond four scallops in a row. The first scallop has an average width of 62 days but by the time the fourth scallop in a series appears, the width decreases to 47 days, on average. So, if you discover a narrow ascending scallop well into an uptrend, you might consider avoiding the stock. Otherwise, you might be investing near the top.

Do ascending scallops become flatter as they climb? Figure 36.8 shows the result of the analysis. The first scallop has an average height, as measured from the highest high to the lowest low, of about 18%. This drops to 14% by the time the fourth scallop in a row appears. Again, I graphed only four points because of the rarity of trends containing more than four ascending scallops in

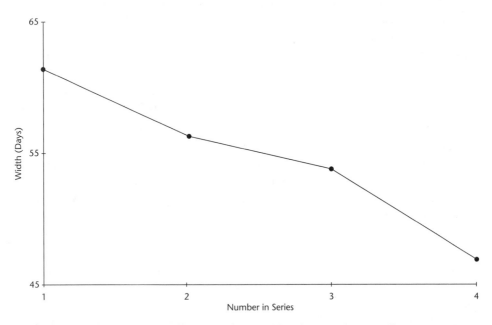

Figure 36.7 Graph showing narrowing width of ascending scallops over time. The more consecutive ascending scallops that appear in an uptrend, the narrower they become. If you see a narrow ascending scallop forming after a long uptrend, you might avoid taking a position in the stock.

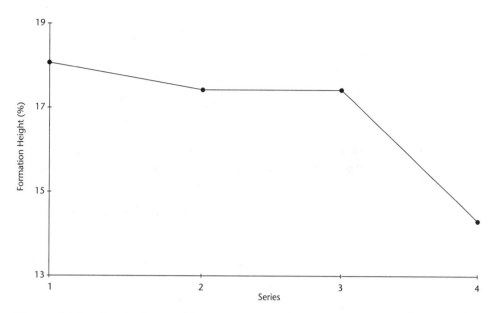

Figure 36.8 Graph showing formation height of ascending scallops. Ascending scallops become slightly flatter as they climb.

a row. I tried to apply the analysis to descending scallops without success. Only three points are available (because of the sample size) and the results are inconclusive.

Trading Tactics

Table 36.3 shows trading tactics for ascending and descending scallops. The first trading tactic is to determine how far prices are likely to move once the formation completes. This is called the measure rule because it involves measuring the formation height and applying it to the breakout point.

The measures for both ascending and descending scallops begin by computing the formation height in the same way. Subtract the lowest low reached in the bowl from the high reached on the right side of the formation. Once you have the height, add the value to the highest high on the right side of the formation for ascending scallops or subtract it from the lowest low for descending scallops. The result is the minimum expected price target. An example makes the calculation clear. Consider the ascending scallop that forms during late September as shown in Figure 36.9. Apply the measure rule to this formation by subtracting the formation base from the right side high. Point B shows the base low at 12½ and the right side high, point A, is 16. The difference of 3½ is the formation height. For ascending scallops, add the difference to the right-side high (point A) to get the target price of 19½. Prices meet the target

Table 36.3
Trading Tactics for Ascending and Descending Scallops

Trading Tactic	Explanation
Measure rule	Compute the height of the scallop by taking the difference between the right-edge high to the lowest low in the formation. For ascending scallops, add the difference to the highest right-edge high, and for descending ones subtract the difference from the lowest low. The result is the minimum expected price target.
Lip retrace	Once prices crest the right lip high, prices fall. If they drop below the bottom of the formation in an uptrend, then the formation is a failure and you should avoid the stock or close out your position. Likewise, if prices rise significantly above the top of the right edge in a downtrend, then the formation is also a failure.
Buy point	Take a position in the stock once prices drift below the right-edge high. For ascending scallops, wait for prices to bottom out. For descending scallops, sell short immediately once prices reach the right-edge high and head down.
Stops	Ascending scallops: $\frac{1}{8}$ below the lowest low. Descending scallops: $\frac{1}{8}$ above the right lip high.
Avoid	Be careful of shorting a stock showing a descending scallop that forms many months into a downtrend. The downtrend may be near the end.

in late April (not shown on the chart). If the scallop is descending, then subtract the difference from the formation low (point B) to get the target price. In such a case, the target would be 9 ($12\frac{1}{2} - 3\frac{1}{2}$).

In both cases, the formation height uses the *right-side high, not the left*. For ascending scallops, this makes the measure rule much harder to fulfill because the right side is much higher than the peak on the left. For descending scallops, the measure rule is easier to meet because the right side is lower than the left side. Still, ascending scallops meet their targets more often than descending ones by 71% to 52%. This statistic implies that the descending variety form near the end of the trend—something you should keep in mind if you intend to short a stock containing a descending scallop.

Once a scallop completes, prices decline. They retrace all or a part of their gains (that is, from the right-edge high to the bowl low) before heading higher (in the case of ascending scallops) or continuing down (for descending scallops). In Figure 36.9, you can see that the retrace after the first scallop brings prices down to the height of the left scallop lip at $14\frac{1}{4}$. The retrace after the center scallop sees prices return to near the bowl low.

For ascending scallops, once prices crest on the right side and begin declining, wait for the decline to end. In some cases, another scallop will form and it will be relatively easy to buy during formation of the bowl. For descending scallops, you will want to sell short as soon as the right side peak becomes obvious and prices head down.

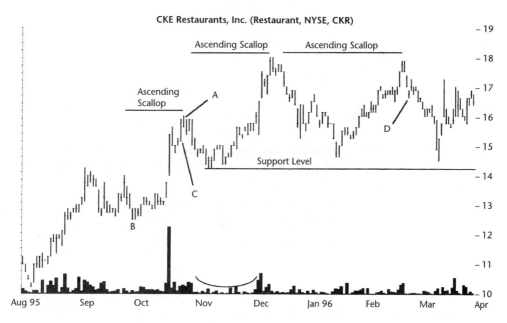

Figure 36.9 Three consecutive ascending scallop formations. Kristy bought the stock at point C once prices rose above the top of the ascending scallop. The last scallop has a V-shaped bowl and a right rim that almost makes it to the high of the left side. She sold at point D.

Stop-loss points should be ⅛ beyond the support or resistance level. In Figure 36.9 place a stop-loss order at 12⅜, or ⅛ below the formation low (point B) for the first scallop. If the loss from the purchase point is too large, consider moving the stop to just below the left peak. As you can see in Figure 36.9, the left peak is an area of support, but it varies from formation to formation.

For descending scallops, place the stop for short trades ⅛ above the right peak. In Figure 36.2, the scallop on the left would have a stop placed at 19½.

Sample Trade

How do you trade these formations? Sometimes it helps to have inside information. That is what Kristy's boyfriend is doing time for in a low-security prison. She has become the primary trading arm of the relationship, a hobby she had long before her beau came along.

Kristy was intrigued by the scallop formation shown on the left in Figure 36.9. The V-shaped look to the bowl concerned her as did the poorly shaped volume pattern. But she liked the prospects for the restaurant company and her fundamental analysis was thorough and tasty.

Before she bought the stock at point C, she computed the estimated gain and compared it to the risk of a loss. The targeted rise was to 18¾ (she calculated using the right-side peak 3 days earlier). The risk point was 14, the high of the left side and a massive support area reached in early 1994. At her purchase point of 15¼, the risk was 1¼ (15¼ – 14) and the potential reward was 3½ (18¾ – 15¼). The nearly three to one ratio was high enough to risk a trade.

She felt gratified when prices closed at the high for the day, suggesting prices the following day would move higher still. When she looked at the stock the next day, prices did reach a new high but closed lower. As she posted her daily quotes for the stock, the declining price trend over the next week or two concerned her, but not unduly so. Kristy recognized the rounding turn of another scallop forming and saw that her stop held.

Day by day she followed the stock and did not like the third scallop in the series (the rightmost one). The bowl shape was irregular and the volume pattern was unconvincing. When prices stopped at the old high before collapsing, she knew the rise was at an end. She pulled the plug on the operation at 16¾, shown as point D in the figure.

In the short term, Kristy was right in that prices headed lower. They moved down until reaching the low of the bowl but then rebounded. By mid-June, they had nearly doubled, reaching a high of 28¾, 10 points above the target price of 18¾. Still, on her 1,000 shares, she cleared almost $1,500 on the trade.

37

Shark-32

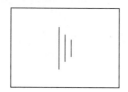

RESULTS SNAPSHOT

Upside Breakouts

Appearance	A 3-day symmetrical triangle with consecutively lower highs and higher lows. Breakout is upward.
Reversal or consolidation	Short-term (up to 3 months) bullish consolidation
Failure rate	41%
Average rise	32%, with most likely rise between 10% and 15%
Volume trend	Downward
Throwbacks	64%
Surprising finding	Horizontal symmetry improves results.
See also	Triangles, Symmetrical Bottoms; Triangles, Symmetrical Tops

Downside Breakouts

Appearance	A 3-day symmetrical triangle with consecutively lower highs and higher lows. Breakout is downward.
Reversal or consolidation	Short-term (up to 3 months) bearish reversal (55% of formations) or consolidation
Failure rate	44%
Average decline	21%, with most likely decline less than 10%

Volume trend	Downward
Pullbacks	58%
Surprising finding	Horizontal symmetry improves results.
See also	Triangles, Symmetrical Bottoms; Triangles, Symmetrical Tops

Despite this formation being only 3 days long, I applied the 5% failure rule to its performance. A 5% failure occurs when prices move less than 5% in the breakout direction before reversing and moving significantly in the new direction. For sharks with upside breakouts, the failure rate is exceedingly high at 41%. The failure rate is even worse for downside breakouts at 44%. I consider formations to be reliable if the failure rate is below 20%. The reason for the poor showing is, in part, because of the compactness of the formation. Prices break out in one direction, reverse course, and shoot out the opposite side of the formation, scoring a failure. With larger chart patterns, the stock has more opportunity to resume the original breakout direction before making it to the other side of the pattern.

The average rise from upside breakouts is 32%, well below the 40% posted by well-performing formations. Downside breakouts perform in line with their bearish cousins, scoring a 21% average decline.

I used a frequency distribution to compute the most likely gain or loss. Both types of breakouts have likely gains or losses of about 10%. These results are typical for many formations and suggest that you have to be ready to pull the trigger quickly if you want to keep any profit.

Shark-32 patterns with both breakout types show a receding volume trend over the 3 days, just as any other symmetrical triangle (sharks are very short symmetrical triangles).

Some analysts say that sharks appearing symmetrical about the horizontal axis perform better than those that are not symmetrical. I found this to be true generally for both breakout directions. I explore this further in the Statistics section later in this chapter.

Tour and Identification Guidelines

The narrowing highs and lows of a shark-32 pattern remind me of a spring being wound tighter and tighter. Eventually the spring releases and prices shoot out of the formation. That is the theory, anyway, but the reality shows that prices quickly return, causing a failure. More about failures later.

As far as formations go, this one is easy to identify and quite common. I offer no table of identification guidelines because it is so simple. Locate a 3-day price pattern that looks like a short symmetrical triangle, that is, a chart pattern having lower highs and higher lows on each of 3 consecutive days. No ties allowed and the shortest day should have a nonzero price range (that is, the high and low cannot be the same price).

Figure 37.1 illustrates what I am talking about. If you look closely, the tops slope downward and the bottoms slope upward, forming a 3-day symmetrical triangle. Each succeeding high is below the prior day's high and each succeeding low is above the prior day's low. Together, they form a 3-day, triangular-shaped shark fin, hence the name *shark-32*.

The volume trend is nearly always downward. This is sometimes not clear, but I used linear regression to compute the slope of the line over the 3-day formation. All three chart patterns shown in Figure 37.1, for example, have downward volume trends.

At first you may be skeptical that the formation on the right has a downward volume trend. Think of it this way: If you substitute dots instead of volume bars in the figure then draw a line so that it is equidistant from the three dots, you will find that the slope of this line is downward (higher on the left). In essence, this is linear regression, a mathematical way of placing the line evenly between the dots. The slope of the resulting line gives the volume trend.

Focus on Failures

The shark-32 formation sports a very high failure rate, so finding failure examples is easy. Figure 37.2 shows a shark formation failure. Regardless of what you call this formation—a reversal or consolidation of the prevailing trend—

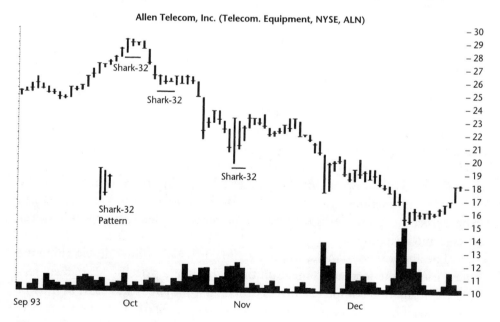

Figure 37.1 Three shark-32 patterns. Each has lower highs and higher lows on 3 consecutive days.

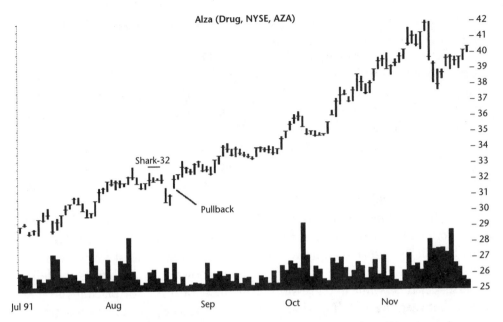

Figure 37.2 A shark-32 failure. Prices break out downward, pull back, and move substantially higher from this shark-32. The downward plunge takes prices less than 1% lower, a so-called 5% failure.

once prices break out of the formation, they should continue moving in the same direction without reversing substantially.

First some definitions: A breakout is when prices close outside the formation. Since the first day has the widest price range, it is the benchmark to gauge a breakout. A breakout occurs if prices close above the first day's high or below its low. Expect prices to continue moving in the breakout direction.

However, throwbacks to the triangle apex from the top or pullbacks from the bottom are both permissible. Throwbacks or pullbacks occur over half the time (sometimes both occur, but I only consider to be valid those in the breakout direction). Occasionally, prices throw back or pull back then keep moving. If a throwback drops below the first day's low or a pullback rises above the first day's high (and closes there), then the formation is a failure.

Figure 37.2 shows a shark-32 pattern in a rising price trend. Since the shark pattern functions as a consolidation of the trend most of the time, we can expect prices to continue rising after the pattern completes. It does not; prices reverse and head down.

The apex of the triangle, where two imaginary trendlines drawn along the boundaries of the formation meet on the right, is at a price of $32\frac{1}{8}$. Two days after the formation completes, prices drop to a low of $30\frac{5}{8}$ and close at the low for the day. The next day prices move even lower to $30\frac{7}{16}$. The first day of the formation has a low of $31\frac{3}{4}$, so prices have clearly broken out downward (the close of $30\frac{5}{8}$ is below the first day's low of $31\frac{3}{4}$). We can expect prices to continue heading down, but they stop and pull back to the triangle apex. The decline, as measured from the breakout day low to the ultimate low, is just 0.6%.

Since the breakout direction is unknown ahead of time, an investor must wait for prices to close above or below the triangle before taking a position in the stock. Thus, I use the breakout day high or low to determine the gain or loss because that is the first day in which an investor would likely take a position.

You can see in Figure 37.2 that an investor selling short the day after the breakout would have gotten creamed. Prices pull back to the triangle apex the next day and 2 days later they move above the top of the triangle. When that happens, the formation fails. Prices continue up until mid-January when they reach a high over 55.

There is a saying that large formations are stronger than smaller ones. This adage certainly appears to be the case with this formation. It is even more pronounced after factoring in the high failure rates. The larger symmetrical triangles have failure rates that are about one-tenth the rate of sharks.

Statistics

Table 37.1 shows general statistics for the shark-32 pattern. Since chart patterns perform differently depending on their breakout direction, I separated the formation into two categories: upside and downside breakouts. These formations are plentiful enough that I only examined 100 stocks over 5 years to log almost 300 patterns. You can see in the table that most act as consolidations of the short-term price trend with downside breakouts having slightly more reversals.

The failure rate for both breakout directions is just over 40%. This is double the 20% maximum I consider acceptable, suggesting that you should

Table 37.1
General Statistics for Shark-32 Formations

Description	Upside Breakout	Downside Breakout
Number of formations in 100 stocks from 1991 to 1996	160	139
Reversal or consolidation	111 consolidations, 49 reversals	63 consolidations, 76 reversals
Failure rate	66 or 41%	61 or 44%
Average rise/decline of successful formations	32%	21%
Most likely rise/decline	10% to 15%	Less than 10%
Number showing downward volume trend	146 or 91%	119 or 86%

stay away from this chart pattern. The average rise is 32% for upside breakouts and the decline for downside breakouts averages 21%. These statistics are both worse (40% average gain) and better (20% average loss) for typical bullish and bearish formations. The frequency distribution in Figure 37.3 shows the most likely gain or loss for the shark-32 pattern. The tallest column is the one with the highest frequency and the one I consider to be the most likely gain or loss. For upside breakouts, the most likely gain is about 10% to 15%, with a quarter of the formations having gains over 50%. Fifty percent is quite large and is responsible for boosting the overall average up to 32%. I do not consider the right column to be representative of what a typical investor can expect to receive, so I disregard it.

For downside breakouts, the most likely loss is 10%; that is the tallest column on the graph. A third of the formations have losses under 10%, so if you are considering shorting a shark-32 pattern with a downside breakout, you might reconsider.

As mentioned earlier, I performed linear regression on the 3-day volume series and discovered that the slope of the regression line is downward over the course of the formation.

Table 37.2 shows breakout-related statistics for the shark-32 pattern. The shark-32 pattern differs from a symmetrical triangle in that the breakout for a

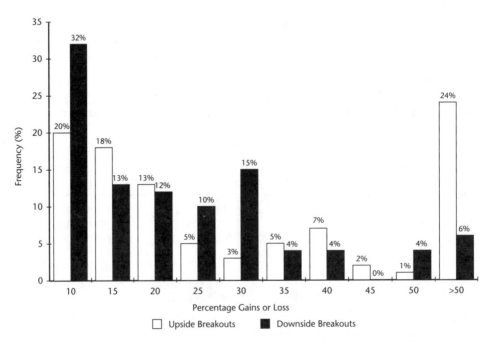

Figure 37.3 Frequency distribution of the most likely gain or loss for shark-32 chart patterns with upside and downside breakouts. The likely return is less than 10% or 15%.

Table 37.2
Breakout Statistics for Shark-32 Formations

Description	Upside Breakouts	Downside Breakouts
Days to breakout	8 days	8 days
Throwback/pullback	102 or 64%	80 or 58%
Average time to throwback/pullback completion	8 days	8 days
For successful formations, days to ultimate high/low	6.5 months (192 days)	2 months (66 days)
Percentage of breakouts occurring near 12-month low (L), center (C), or high (H)	L9%, C27%, H64%	L29%, C35%, H35%
Percentage gain/loss for each 12-month lookback period	L32%, C41%, H31%	L18%, C21%, H23%

shark pattern, by definition, comes after the formation completes. For symmetrical triangles, the breakout usually occurs well before the triangle apex. For the shark pattern, 8 days typically lapse before prices close above the highest high or below the lowest low posted during the first day of the pattern (the widest of the 3 days).

Throwbacks occur when prices return to the triangle apex after an upside breakout. Throwbacks happen 64% of the time and are too infrequent to base a trading plan on, but they do give an investor another opportunity to take a position in the stock. Unfortunately, not all throwbacks (and pullbacks, too) rebound and continue moving up. Figure 37.2, for example, shows a pullback that, after returning to the shark pattern, fails to continue moving down again. Pullbacks occur after a downside breakout when prices return to the triangle apex, which happens 58% of the time.

The average time for a throwback or pullback to return to the price level of the triangle apex (the center of the shortest day in the shark-32 pattern) is 8 days. This is a day or two earlier than most formations. If you miss the initial breakout, you might have another chance to invest or add to your position within the coming week.

I determine the ultimate high or low by a significant change in trend, usually 20%, but stop short if prices return to the shark-32 pattern and cross to the other side.

The number of days to reach the ultimate high or low varies depending on the breakout direction. For upside breakouts, prices reach the ultimate high over 6 months later. For downside breakouts, prices reach the ultimate low in about 2 months. I measure both from the breakout point.

Where in the yearly price range does this formation occur? Most of the shark-32 patterns (64%) with upside breakouts form within a third of the yearly high. For downside breakouts, the pattern distributes more evenly with 35% appearing within a third of the yearly high or midrange. Mapping performance onto the yearly price range, the picture changes somewhat. The best performing patterns for upside breakouts are those that land in the center third of the price range. They score an average gain of 41%. For downside breakouts, the best performing formations begin tumbling within a third of the yearly high; they post losses averaging 23%.

The last statistic concerns symmetry. Shark-32 patterns that are symmetrical about the horizontal axis perform better than those that are not. The following formulas measure symmetry:

Symmetry = 0.10 to 0.50   (A variable number that determines how symmetrical the pattern needs to be.)

Apex Price = (H + L)/2   (This is the third or smallest day in the formation.)

Base Height = H[2] – L[2]   (This is the daily range from the highest to the lowest during the first day.)

To be symmetrical, a shark-32 pattern must satisfy the following equation:

Apex Price ≤ H[2] – (Base Height * Symmetry)

Apex Price ≥ L[2] + (Base Height * Symmetry)

In essence, all we are doing is making sure that the middle of the narrowest day is within a given distance from the center of the widest day. The distance I tested ranged from 0.10 to 0.50 in steps of 0.02. A value of 0.50 means that 50% of the price lies above the center and 50% lies below—perfectly symmetrical. I ran all successful formations through the various combinations for both upside and downside breakouts. Those formations with upside breakouts and symmetry values between 0.40 and 0.50 perform better than their nonsymmetrical counterparts. They have gains that range from 31% to 34%, whereas their nonsymmetrical counterparts have returns of 30% to 32%. For downside breakouts, the best performing symmetrical range is narrower at 0.44 to 0.50. The symmetrical sharks have losses ranging between 21% to 25%, whereas the nonsymmetrical sharks have a flat 20% return.

I consider the performance improvement to be marginal and the formation needs to be almost perfectly symmetrical to show any meaningful improvement. Still, it is an interesting finding.

In case you are wondering what a nonsymmetrical triangle looks like, look back to Figure 37.1. With a symmetry setting of 0.44, only the middle formation is symmetrical. The other two have first days in which the low price is too far down (look at the distance between the two tops and two bottoms of the first and second days—they are uneven and thus asymmetrical).

Trading Tactics

If your worst enemy tells you this is *the* formation to trade, ignore him; he is trying to lead you into bankruptcy. With a failure rate nearly the same as a fair coin toss, why risk a trade? Since you might ignore my advice and trade this one anyway (or perhaps you have found a way to make it work), Table 37.3 lists a few helpful suggestions about the shark-32 formation.

If you add up the number of consolidations and the number of reversals listed in Table 37.1, you will find that the shark-32 pattern usually acts as a consolidation of the prevailing trend. Knowing this, you should anticipate a breakout in the direction of the short-term trend. Figure 37.4 shows this type of behavior. The price trend is moving downward when the formation appears. After the formation completes and prices drop below the first day's low, they continue moving down.

The best performing shark-32 patterns are symmetrical about the horizontal axis, or nearly so. Run the daily high and low prices through the formulas shown in the Statistics section using symmetry values of 0.44 or higher. If you are lazy and want to take an easier approach, visually find the midpoint of the first and third days' price range. If the two points are close to one another, then the shark-32 is symmetrical.

Since you cannot be sure in which direction the breakout will occur (but lean in the direction of the prevailing trend), always wait for the breakout. I determine that a breakout occurs when prices either close above the shark's first day's high or below the first day's low.

Once prices break out, be aware that there is a better than even chance of a throwback (upside breakouts) or a pullback (downside breakouts). Prices

Table 37.3
Trading Tactics for Shark-32 Formations

Trading Tactic	Explanation
Profitable suggestion	Save your money and do not trade this one.
Trade with the trend	Since the shark pattern is usually a consolidation, expect a breakout in the direction of the prevailing price trend.
Symmetry	Choose only near symmetrical patterns.
Wait for breakout	The breakout direction is unknown, so wait for prices to close above or below the first day's (the widest of the 3 days) high or low, then trade with the trend.
Watch for throwback, pullback	More than half the time, a throwback from the top or pullback from the bottom occurs. Place a position or add to it once prices resume their original course.
Half-mast formation	Sometimes the pattern appears midway through a price move.
Stops	Place a stop-loss order $\frac{1}{8}$ above (downside breakouts) or below (upside breakouts) the tallest day in the chart pattern.

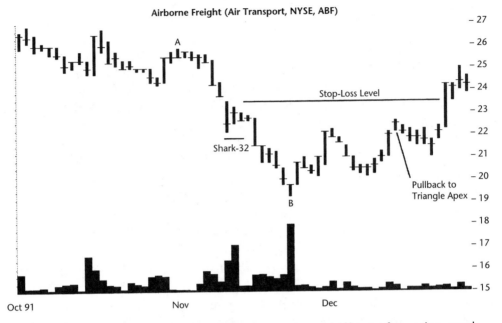

Figure 37.4 The shark-32 pattern sometimes acts as a half-mast formation, marking the midpoint of a move. Here, it bisects the move from points A and B in a consolidation of the downward trend.

return or come close to the center of the 3-day formation (the triangle apex). When prices return to their original breakout direction, that is the time to either place a trade or add to it.

Take a look at Figure 37.4. Notice anything peculiar? The formation apex (at 22⅞) positions neatly between the minor high—point A at 25⅞, and the minor low—point B at 19¼. The shark-32 pattern acts as a midpoint or half-mast formation. This is useful in trying to gauge the length of the ultimate move.

If you walk back into your computer room and find that your young son has placed a trade in a shark-32 formation while you were away, do not panic. Place a stop at the other end of the formation. For example, in Figure 37.4, you would place a stop at 23⅞, or ⅛ above the highest high in the formation (since the trend is moving down). If the trend was moving up, the stop would be placed ⅛ below the lowest low in the shark-32 pattern. That way, when 40% of the formations fail, you will not lose too much money.

38

Triangles, Ascending

RESULTS SNAPSHOT

Appearance	Triangle shape with horizontal top, up-sloping bottom
Reversal or consolidation	Short-term (up to 3 months) bullish consolidation
Failure rate	32%
Failure rate if waited for upside breakout	2%
Average rise	44%, with most likely rise being 20%
Volume trend	Downward
Premature breakouts	25%
Breakout distance to apex	63%
Throwbacks	58%
Percentage meeting predicted price target	89%
See also	Head-and-Shoulders Tops; Triple Tops

Have you ever heard someone say, "I just happened to be in the right place at the right time?" Perhaps you have even said it yourself. Investing is a lot like that—being in the right stock just before it takes off. That is one of the reasons the ascending triangle is one of my favorite formations. You can make a bundle of money if you trade it properly. But before we get to trading tactics, let us look more closely at ascending triangles.

The Results Snapshot shows the important findings. The ascending triangle has a poor failure rate of 32%. However, if you wait for an upside breakout, then the failure rate drops to just 2%.

For upside breakouts, the average rise is a strong 44%. A frequency distribution of the gains suggests that the most likely gain is 20%. With such a strong showing, prices fulfill the measure rule 89% of the time. I consider values above 80% to be reliable, so this chart pattern stacks up well.

Tour

Figure 38.1 shows a good example of an ascending triangle. A horizontal trendline drawn across the minor highs and an up-sloping trendline connecting the minor lows form the characteristic triangular pattern. Volume diminishes as prices bounce between resistance at the top and support at the bottom. A premature breakout gives a hint of the coming action; less than 2 weeks later, prices break out again and move higher.

Why do ascending triangles form? Imagine you are the manager of a large mutual fund. Over the years your fund has purchased a few hundred thousand shares of the company shown in Figure 38.1. After seeing the stock

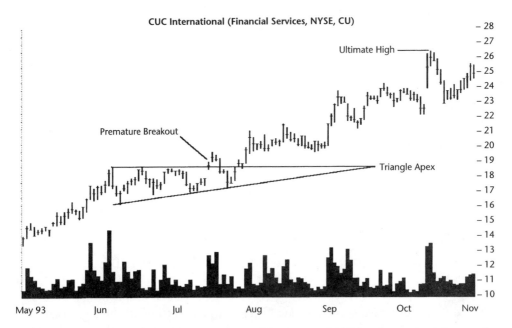

Figure 38.1 A good example of an ascending triangle. The horizontal top and up-sloping trendline on the bottom mark the boundaries of this bullish formation. The premature breakout on high volume is often indistinguishable from the real breakout. The volume trend is downward until the premature breakout.

rise for almost a year, you are getting nervous about continuing to hold the stock. You believe the stock is trading well above its fair market value and you have spotted a more promising situation in another company.

You tell the trading department to dump all your shares as long as it receives at least 18½. For 2 days, starting on June 4, 1993, the trading department sells shares. Since your fund has a large block of shares to get rid of, the price cannot climb much above 18½ without the fund selling shares and forcing prices back down. The selling puts a ceiling on the stock. Word gets around that you are selling and other institutional investors jump on the bandwagon and sell too. Their aggressive selling satiates demand and the stock starts declining. It tumbles to a low of 16¼ on June 9, where buying demand halts the decline. Buyers, viewing the price of the stock as a steal, demand more shares. The buying pressure turns the decline around and prices start rising—quickly at first but more slowly as more investors become willing to sell their shares. When the stock hits 18½ again on June 16, your fund sells more shares, effectively halting the advance. The stock struggles at that level for 3 days. Again, the selling pressure forces prices down and they cross to the other side of the now-forming ascending triangle. Prices rebound one last time, and hit the sell zone and stay there for about a week before being turned away by an excess supply. A call from the trading department confirms that the stock has been completely sold.

Without an overhanging supply to halt the stock's rise, prices gap up on increasing demand and soar to 19¼. Your fund is out of the picture, but the forces of supply and demand are not finished with the company. Others still selling their shares force the stock price back down into the triangle proper. Prices race to the other side of the triangle, rebound off the lower trendline, then march back up out the top. Prices dance along the top trendline for a day, then catapult higher and move up.

If I had to sum up the price action of an ascending triangle, I would say it forms because of a supply of shares available at a fixed price. Once the supply depletes, shares quickly break out of the formation and move higher. If demand continues to be strong, prices rise. Otherwise, the stock collapses back on itself and either regroups for another try or continues down.

Identification Guidelines

Finding an ascending triangle in a chart of daily price data is simple, perhaps too simple. I recently read a tutorial in a popular magazine in which nearly half the illustrations purporting to be triangles were incorrectly identified. If you have any doubt about the validity of a chart pattern, others may share those doubts. If others do not see the same shapes you do, chances are the pattern will not work as you expect. Under those circumstances, where there is some doubt about correct identification, do not trade the formation. Save your money for a trade where you are sure the formation is valid. I discuss identification problems later in this section.

The triangle pictured in Figure 38.1 is nearly a classic example of an ascending triangle. The horizontal top line of resistance repels prices and they rebound off a steadily rising support line below. The two narrowing lines, one horizontal and the other sloping up, outline a triangular shape. The ascending trendline predicts a rise in prices, hence the name *ascending triangle*.

Table 38.1 lists ascending triangle characteristics. The top horizontal trendline should have prices that approach and withdraw at least twice (in other words, two distinct minor highs). Similarly, the up-sloping trendline should be supported by two distinct minor lows. The two trendlines meet at the triangle apex, but prices usually break out of the formation well before then.

Table 38.1
Identification Characteristics of Ascending Triangles

Characteristic	Discussion
Triangle shape	Two price trendlines, the top one horizontal and the bottom one sloping up, form a triangle pattern. The two lines join at the triangle apex.
Horizontal top line	Prices rise up to and fall away from a horizontal resistance line *at least twice* (two minor highs). Prices need not touch the trendline but should come reasonably close (say, within 1/8). The line need not be completely horizontal but usually is.
Up-sloping bottom trendline	Prices decline to and rise away from an up-sloping trendline. Prices need not touch the trendline but should come close (within 1/8). At least two trendline touches (minor lows) are required.
Crossing pattern	Prices should cross the chart pattern several times; they should not leave a vast amount of white space in the center of the triangle.
Volume	Volume is heavier at the start of the formation than near the end. Volume is usually low just before the breakout.
Premature breakouts	Somewhat prone to premature breakouts, both up and down. Volume on a false breakout is also heavy, just as the genuine breakout.
Upside breakout	Volume is heavy (but need not be) and continues to be heavy for several days.
Price action after breakout	Once prices pierce the horizontal resistance line confirming a breakout, prices move up and away from the formation. Throwbacks to the formation top are common. If prices continue to climb rapidly, volume will probably remain high. For downside breakouts, volume is high at first and usually tapers off unless the price decline is rapid, in which case volume will probably remain high.

As the triangle forms, volume is heavy at first but tapers off until the day of the breakout. Often volume is abnormally low a few days before the breakout, as if the formation is gathering strength for the final push. When the upside breakout comes, volume can rise substantially and usually does, but heavy volume on a breakout is not a prerequisite.

How can you be sure the breakout is not a premature breakout? You cannot. A premature breakout is a close outside the boundaries of the two trendlines. After a few days, prices return to the confines of the triangle and eventually break out for good by soaring above the top trendline. Volume on premature breakouts is indistinguishable from normal breakouts and both occur at about the same distance to the triangle apex.

Once a triangle has a genuine breakout on the upside, what is the behavior like? Prices rapidly climb away from the triangle but occasionally throw back to the top of the formation. Volume is usually heavy, supporting the rise, and continues to be heavy as momentum gathers speed. Once prices level out, volume returns to normal. If prices rise over several weeks, the volume pattern usually appears erratic and heavy when compared to earlier in the year.

What about support and resistance? If you consider the triangle as the momentary intersection of two trendlines, you can guess where support and resistance will be. It will be along the two trendlines. Figure 38.2 shows an example of this on the weekly time scale. Notice the generally down-sloping

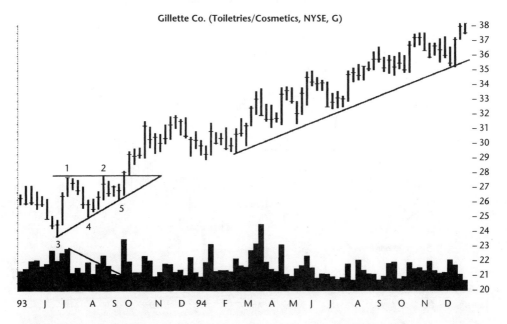

Figure 38.2 Ascending triangle on weekly time scale. The price rise generally follows the up-sloping support line of the triangle. The numbers count the minor high and low touches of the trendline.

volume trend from the formation start to the week before the breakout. Volume spikes upward on the breakout then generally declines as prices round over and approach 1994. Prices start climbing again, essentially hugging the trendline started by the ascending triangle. The upward trend continues for several years following the triangle-initiated support line. Although the match between the sloping trendline and the slope of the later price action is not exact, the trend is clear. The triangle sports two minor high touches of the top trendline and three on the bottom, numbered in the figure. Trendline touches and prices crossing the triangle are important selection criteria.

By now you may feel comfortable with correctly identifying an ascending triangle. However, there are some situations that may fool investors new to the formation. Figure 38.3 shows the first one. Cover up the right half of the figure and ask yourself if what you see on the left looks like an ascending triangle. The horizontal line, arbitrarily drawn to rest on top of the central peak, extends to the left and right until it intersects prices. Although the lower trendline has several instances where prices decline to and bounce off of the up-sloping line, the top trendline does not have such a situation. Only in the center of the formation do prices rise up to and decline away from the horizontal trendline. The intersection of prices with the horizontal trendline on the left coincidentally touches a daily high. Otherwise, the price trend is one

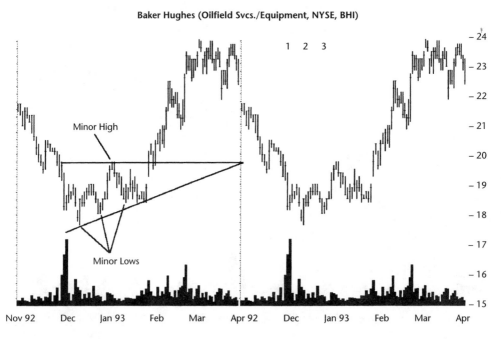

Figure 38.3 Two views of an incorrectly identified ascending triangle. What looks like an ascending triangle on the left clearly is not on the right. The three downward spikes in December, identified by the numbers near the top of the figure, mark a head-and-shoulders bottom with a horizontal neckline, not a triangle.

that has been declining for several days in a row. At the start, there is no minor high supporting the horizontal trendline.

The same can be said of the formation's right side. There is no minor high on which the horizontal trendline can rest. Looking at the right side of the chart. Does this still look like an ascending triangle? I can hear you asking me to lower the horizontal trendline until it touches the two minor highs in early to mid-December (below number 1 and midway between numbers 2 and 3). That is not a bad guess, but it is still wrong. What you are really looking at is a head-and-shoulders bottom. The left shoulder has a large volume spike (under number 1). Located under number 2, the head shows a smaller volume spike. The right shoulder shows volume that recedes even further (number 3). A true ascending triangle has at least *two* minor highs forming the top trendline and at least *two* minor lows forming the bottom.

Figure 38.4 shows another example of a falsely identified ascending triangle. This chart has too much white space in the central portion of the triangle. A well-defined ascending triangle has prices that bounce from one side of the formation to the other as it nears the apex. Take a good look at the figure. This represents one of the most common identification mistakes. Novices will find a rounding bottom and draw a horizontal line across the top and another tangent to the bottom price action then yell, "Eureka! An ascending triangle!" Wrong.

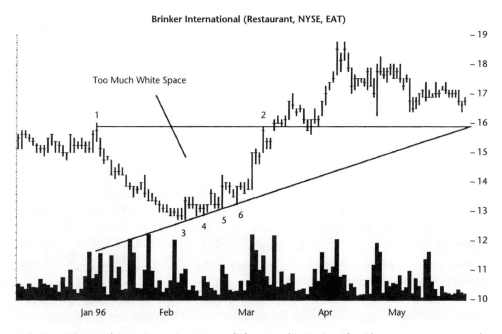

Figure 38.4 This pattern is not a valid ascending triangle. There are not enough crossings between the two trendlines to illustrate a valid triangle construction. The minor highs and lows are numbered.

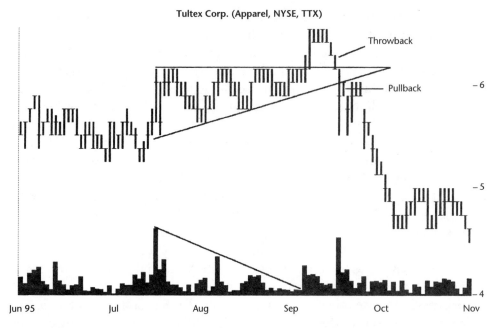

Figure 38.5   An excellent example of a correctly constructed ascending triangle. The number of minor highs and lows is good and there are plenty of crossings from the top trendline to the bottom. The volume trend is downward too, until the upside breakout.

Contrast Figure 38.4 with Figure 38.5. In Figure 38.5 notice the number of times prices move from one side of the triangle to the other. Even though prices do not rise very far before throwing back to the triangle apex and moving down, it is still a nicely formed ascending triangle. Also note the generally decreasing volume, especially near the breakout.

Focus on Failures

Figure 38.5 shows the first failure type: a 5% failure. Strictly speaking this is not a 5% failure (because prices climb by 6%), but it is typical of what one looks like. A 5% failure is when prices break out and move less than 5% higher before curling around and moving below the formation low. In this case, prices leave the formation at $6\frac{1}{8}$ and reach a high of $6\frac{1}{2}$—a 6% move, far enough away for the chart pattern to be a success. For ascending triangles, 5% failures are rare, occurring just 2% of the time.

Figure 38.6 shows the more common failure type when prices break out downward and continue moving down. I have numbered the minor highs and lows to help with identification. The top trendline is horizontal and the bottom one slopes up. As you run through the identification characteristics in Table 38.1, there is only one thing that looks odd with this ascending triangle: the

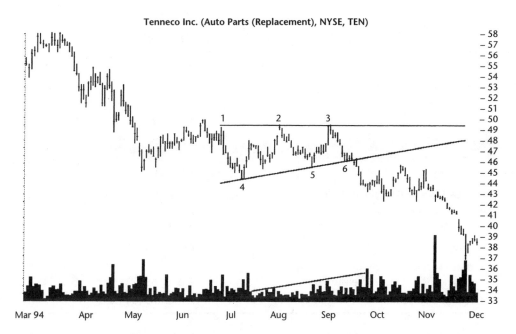

Figure 38.6 A classic ascending triangle failure. Prices break out downward and continue moving down. The numbers show the trendline touches.

volume pattern. The volume trend in this chart pattern slopes up. I usually ignore the volume pattern because I stumble across many instances when I have a perfectly valid chart pattern but the volume trend is wrong. That is the case here. I would not throw out the formation just because of the volume trend, but I would take one additional step before investing: I would wait for the breakout. If you wait for the breakout, you will pass up losing opportunities such as this one. You will learn in the Statistics section that a third of the ascending triangles break out downward.

Statistics

Table 38.2 shows the general statistics for ascending triangles. There are fewer ascending triangles than I expected in the 500 stocks I examined—725. That is less than two each over the 5-year period. Several stocks have from three to six triangles, whereas many others have none. Still, the number of triangles examined allows their statistical performance to become clear. The vast majority (529) of ascending triangles act as consolidations of the prevailing trend. The other 196 are reversals.

Do ascending triangles ascend? Yes. More than two out of three (68%) have a meaningful rise after an upside breakout. However, if one waits for a breakout (a *close* above the horizontal trendline), the failure rate improves significantly. Even if an investor buys on a premature upside breakout, the likelihood

Table 38.2
General Statistics for Ascending Triangles

Description	Statistic
Number of formations in 500 stocks from 1991 to 1996	725
Reversal or consolidation	196 reversals, 529 consolidations
Failure rate	230 or 32%
Failure rate if waited for upside breakout (5% failure)	13 or 2%
Average rise of successful formations	44%
Average decline of failed formations	21%
Most likely rise	20%
Breakout distance to apex	63%
Of those succeeding, number meeting or exceeding price target (measure rule)	439 or 89%
Start to breakout	2 months (64 days)

of making a successful trade rises from 68% to 85%. Just 2% of the upside break-outs curl around before soaring less than 5% (the 5% failure rate). The implications of this are obvious: Wait for an upside breakout from an ascending triangle before buying the stock.

Those triangles that perform as expected show an average rise of 44%, whereas those that fail tumble by an average of 21%. I did a frequency distribution of the gains to better judge what the gain would be for a typical stock. Figure 38.7 shows that most of the gains occur in the 11% to 20% range. Almost half the formations (49%) have gains less than 30%. The large column on the right pulls the average upward.

I plotted the average price rise versus the distance to the apex. I wanted to verify the claim that the most powerful breakouts occur two-thirds of the way to the triangle apex. Figure 38.8 shows the results. The chart resembles a bell-shaped curve tilted on its side, suggesting that the further away from the average breakout of 63%, the weaker the breakout becomes.

One surprise with ascending triangles is the high number that meet the measure rule (89%). I discuss the measure rule further in Trading Tactics but it describes a way to predict the minimum price move. You simply compute the height of the triangle at the start of the formation and add the result to the price level of the horizontal trendline. The result is the expected minimum price rise. Almost 9 out of 10 ascending triangles hit their price targets. However, the 89% value is misleading. The average height of the formations in the database is just 10% of the stock price. This means the predicted price target is only 10% higher than the breakout price, so it is relatively easy to

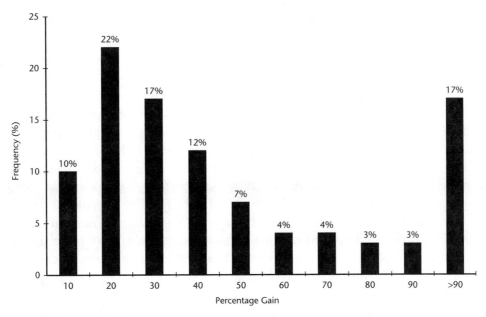

Figure 38.7 Frequency distribution of gains for ascending triangles. The most likely gain is 20%, but the rightmost column skews the average gain upward.

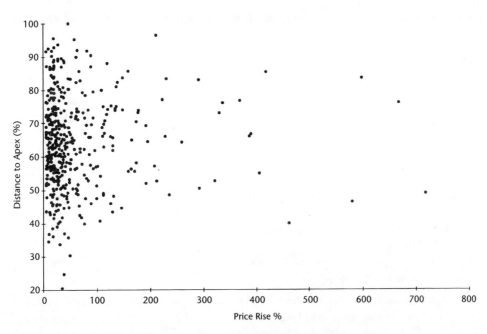

Figure 38.8 Scatter diagram of average price rise versus distance to apex. The most powerful breakouts occur two-thirds of the way to the triangle apex.

meet the target. Perhaps the biggest surprise of all is that the 89% figure is not higher.

Another unexpected discovery is the relatively high number of premature breakouts, shown in Table 38.3. One of every four formations has either a premature upside or downside breakout (or both). There are slightly more premature upside breakouts (22%) than downside ones (12%). The volume is above average, at 175% and 106% of the 25-day volume moving average of upside and downside premature breakouts, respectively. The above average volume makes a premature breakout look just like a genuine breakout and they occur about the same distance from the apex as normal breakouts (60% and 63%, respectively). I noticed a tendency for a premature breakout to echo on the other side of the formation with another premature breakout. Just over a third (36%) of the formations that have premature breakouts have both up and down premature breakouts.

Do premature breakouts predict the direction of the genuine breakout? If you exclude horizontal breakouts, premature upside breakouts occur with genuine upside ones 40% of the time, and downside breakouts 46% of the time. Likewise, downside premature breakouts pair with genuine upside and downside breakouts 42% of the time.

What does all this mean? Nothing. When you have a premature breakout, either up or down, the final breakout can still go either way. That is the

Table 38.3
Premature Breakout Statistics for Ascending Triangles

Description	Statistic
Number of premature breakouts (up or down)	184 or 25%
Number of premature upside breakouts	163 or 22%
Number of premature downside breakouts	88 or 12%
Volume at upside premature breakout as percentage of 25-day moving average	175%
Volume at downside premature breakout as percentage of 25-day moving average	106%
Upside premature breakout distance to apex	60%
Downside premature breakout distance to apex	63%
Number of upside and downside premature breakouts	67 or 36%
Premature breakout up, genuine breakout up	65 or 40%
Premature breakout up, genuine breakout down	75 or 46%
Premature breakout down, genuine breakout up	37 or 42%
Premature breakout down, genuine breakout down	37 or 42%

Note: Premature breakouts are indistinguishable from real breakouts and offer no clue as to the direction of the genuine breakout.

conclusion I reached after reviewing the statistics shown in Table 38.3 and several others not included. *Premature breakouts do not predict the final breakout direction or success or failure of the formation.*

Putting premature breakouts aside, what about the genuine breakout? Both upside and downside breakouts occur nearly the same distance to the apex, 63% and 68%, respectively (Table 38.4). In only 13 instances does an upside breakout result in failure (a 5% failure, from Table 38.2). Five percent of the downside breakouts move down by less than 5%, curl around, and soar upward. The overall result means that if the formation has an upside breakout, it will continue up. If it has a downside breakout, it likely will continue down.

Almost two out of three times (62%) an ascending triangle will break out upward and 33% of the time it will breakout downward. Those statistics are not as good as other formations, but there are ways to improve on the win/loss record as we see in Trading Tactics.

Throwbacks occur when prices break out upward and quickly return to the formation. Pullbacks are similar except that the breakout is downward and prices rise back to the up-sloping trendline. Throwbacks at 58% of formations with upward breakouts are more prevalent than pullbacks at 49% of formations with downward breakouts.

The statistics reveal that, on average, throwbacks and pullbacks complete in about 2 weeks (15 and 13 days, respectively). Since this is the average, prices generally start returning to the triangle before this period. For successful formations, prices reach the ultimate high in 6 months (186 days), on average. A frequency distribution of the time between an upside breakout and the ulti-

Table 38.4
Breakout Statistics for Ascending Triangles

Description	Statistic
Upside breakout distance to apex	63%
Downside breakout distance to apex	68%
Downside breakout but success	33 or 5%
Upside breakout	450 or 62%
Downside breakout	238 or 33%
Horizontal breakout	37 or 5%
Throwback	262 or 58%
Pullback	117 or 49%
Average time to throwback completion	15 days
Average time to pullback completion	13 days
For successful formations, days to ultimate high	6 months (186 days)

Note: If the formation breaks out upward, it continues to rise.

mate high is somewhat puzzling. The majority of stocks (224 or 45%) take less than 3 months to reach their ultimate high followed by 96 (or 19%) for inter-mediate-term moves and 35% (175) for durations over 6 months. Although I consider an ascending triangle to have short-term investment implications, a stock could have a price move lasting much longer.

Table 38.5 outlines a study of volume for ascending triangles. Using linear regression, I examined the volume characteristics from formation start to the day before the breakout. In 68% of the cases, the volume trends downward over the period. Linear regression is a fancy way of computing a line that best fits the points such that the distance from each point to the line is minimal. Specifically, I used the slope of the linear regression line to determine the volume trend.

Table 38.5 shows a comparison of the average breakout volume with the 25-day moving average of the volume ending the day before the breakout (I did not want the actual breakout volume influencing the moving average). Notice that the day *after* an upside breakout is the highest volume day (176% or 76% above the moving average). It suggests that once people discover an upside breakout, they buy the stock, forcing the volume to spike the day after the breakout. From that point on, volume recedes but is still comparatively high a week later.

Some analysts say throwbacks are more likely after a low volume break-out. I checked this and found that it is not true. A throwback occurs after a high volume breakout 54% of the time and after a low volume breakout 46% of the time. It is more accurate to say that a throwback is more likely to occur after a *high* volume breakout.

Do high volume breakouts push prices higher? Not really. When the breakout volume is over 50% above average, prices rise by 42%. When the breakout volume is less than 50% below the 25-day moving average, a 43% rise results.

Table 38.5
Volume Statistics for Ascending Triangles

Description	Statistic
Number showing downward volume trend	495 or 68%
Volume for breakout day and next 5 days compared with 25-day moving average	130%, 176%, 151%, 144%, 128%, 121%
Percentage of throwbacks after high volume breakout versus low volume breakouts	54% versus 46%
Performance of high volume breakouts versus low volume breakouts	42% versus 43%

Note: The trend of volume is downward until the breakout day when it spikes upward.

Trading Tactics

Now that you can identify ascending triangles and know their behavior, how do you trade them? Before I give an example of a trade, I discuss trading tactics and the measure rule (see Table 38.6).

The shape of the ascending triangle suggests prices will rise, but how far? If you compute the height of the formation and add the result to the price of the horizontal trendline, the result is the minimum predicted price. This is called the measure rule.

An example makes the calculation clear. Consider the stock shown in Figure 38.9. Calculate the height of the formation by subtracting the low (14 at the sloping trendline) from the high ($17\frac{5}{8}$ denoted by the horizontal trendline) at the formation start. The difference is $3\frac{5}{8}$. Add the result to the highest high—the value of the horizontal trendline—and you get a target price of $21\frac{1}{4}$. Prices reach the target on July 16, 1992, when they climb to a high of $21\frac{5}{8}$, about 6 weeks after the upside breakout.

A more visual and conservative approach is to draw a line from the start of the formation (the top left corner) parallel to the up-sloping trendline. The value of the line the day prices break out of the formation becomes the target

Table 38.6
Trading Tactics for Ascending Triangles

Trading Tactic	Explanation
Measure rule	Compute the height of the formation at the start of the triangle. Add the result to the price of the horizontal trendline. The sum is the minimum price target.
Wait for confirmation	Buy the stock the day after a breakout (when prices close above the top trendline by at least $\frac{1}{8}$). If you miss it, hope for a throwback then buy when prices resume the breakout direction after the throwback completes.
Sell on measure rule	For short-term traders, sell when prices *near* the target price (see measure rule) or when prices pierce a support trendline. For intermediate- and long-term traders, hold the stock until fundamentals or market conditions change.
Sell on downside breakout	If you own the stock and it breaks out downward, sell. If you do not own it, sell it short. Should the stock pull back, that is another opportunity to sell, sell short, or add to your short position.
Short sales	If you short the stock and an ascending triangle appears, you have a one in three chance that it will break out downward. Cover the short immediately if it breaks out upward.

Note: Buy the stock after a confirmed breakout (the stock closes above the triangle top) and sell when it nears the target price.

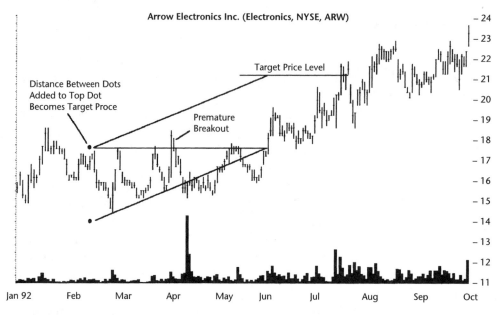

Figure 38.9   Measure rule applied to ascending triangles. There are two ways to predict the price move of an ascending triangle. Compute the formation height by subtracting the low from the high at the start of the formation (denoted by the two circles). Add the result to the price marked by the top trendline. The combination is the price to which the stock will climb, at a minimum. Alternatively, draw a line parallel to the up-sloping trendline beginning with the left top corner of the formation. At the point where prices break out of the formation, the price level of the line becomes the target price.

price. The figure shows the new line. Be careful when determining where the formation begins since tagging the beginning of the formation too soon will cause an abnormally high price target.

Since a third of the formations break out downward, you must wait for an upside breakout before investing. Once prices close above the top trendline, buy the stock. Although you will be buying at a higher price, the chances of having a failure are small (2% versus 32% if you do not wait).

Once prices rise, use the measure rule to estimate gains. Since the measure rule is not perfect, be ready to take profits once prices near the target. Use past resistance zones to fine-tune the prediction.

If prices break out of the triangle downward, then sell your holdings immediately. This is also a time to go short. Look for prices to drop up to 20%. If a pullback occurs, wait for prices to resume their downward direction then add to your short position. Close out the trade if the fundamentals improve or if prices pause at a support zone.

Sample Trade

Dan is an investor with a few years of experience. He is new to technical analysis and discovered ascending triangles by accident. After doing some research to familiarize himself with the formation, he found that if he delayed buying a stock until after a breakout, he would increase his chances of success. However, he would also give up part of his gains as the fastest portion of the rise occurs at the start. That was a trade-off he was willing to make.

Dan took an interest in the company shown in Figure 38.10 when he noticed an ascending triangle forming in the stock. He believed that the breakout was nearly at hand when volume suddenly sank to 23,400 shares on August 19. Two days later, on higher volume, prices crossed the triangle and peaked out the top. For the next few days, prices balanced themselves on the top horizontal trendline and waited for demand to send them higher. The decisive breakout occurred on August 26, even though volume was tepid. Dan grabbed his calculator and computed the breakout distance to the apex and discovered that the breakout occurred at the 70% mark. This signaled a potentially strong breakout.

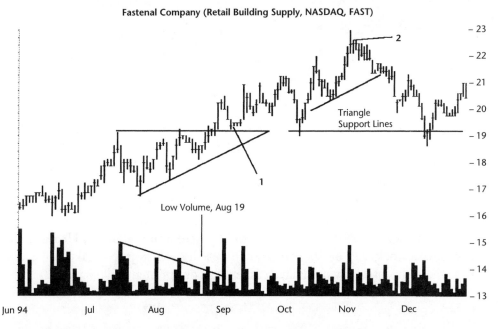

Fastenal Company (Retail Building Supply, NASDAQ, FAST)

Figure 38.10   Trading an ascending triangle. Dan bought 500 shares of the stock at point 1 after the stock threw back to the formation. He sold it at point 2, the day after the stock hit the price target of 22½. Note the down-sloping volume trend during creation of the formation and the two support lines parallel to the two triangle borders.

However, volume told a different story. Although volume had been steadily receding throughout the formation as one would expect, there was not enthusiastic volume on the breakout. With this stealthy signal, Dan decided to wait before buying the stock.

Believing that a profitable opportunity was at hand, he computed the target price to see if it afforded a profitable move. At the formation start, the horizontal trendline marked the high for the stock at 19¼. At the same point, the up-sloping trendline marked the low. At the start of the formation, the lower trendline was at 16⅜. This predicted nearly a three-point climb, or a 15% move from the 19¼ launch price. To Dan, the small move was not terribly exciting, but it was much better than the interest rates the banks were paying.

Two days after the breakout, the stock started declining and returned to the top of the formation. That is when Dan pulled the trigger and bought 500 shares at the high for the day, 19½ on September 2, 1994. Immediately, he placed a stop-loss order to sell the stock should it decline below the lowest low of the formation. The formation low occurred on July 25, 1994, at a price of 16¾. He told his broker to sell the stock ⅛ below this, or 16⅝. That would limit his loss to a steep 15%, but it was also slightly below the nearest support level (the bottom of which was also at 16¾). He reasoned that there was a decent chance that if the stock declined, growing demand would repulse prices and not trigger his stop.

Then he waited and watched the stock. It peaked at 21¼ on September 26 before leveling off and heading back down. Since the stock was not near the price target of 22½, Dan decided to hold on. The stock continued sinking until it found support at the horizontal triangle trendline at 19 on October 5. At that point, the stock started moving up again. On Halloween, the stock reached his price target by hitting a daily high of 23. He decided to sell the stock the next day and received a fill at 22½.

Dan evaluated his results and reviewed the trade. He had a net gain of $1,450 or almost $3 a share. That is a 15% gain in 2 months or almost a doubling of his money if he kept up the performance for the entire year. He also decided that he was lucky as he sold near the top. When the stock returned to the support level in early October, it could have continued down. He decided that once a stock rises by 10%, he should raise his sell stop to break-even even though, in this case, it would have cashed him out prematurely.

39

Triangles, Descending

RESULTS SNAPSHOT

Appearance	Triangle shape with horizontal bottom and down-sloping top
Reversal or consolidation	Short-term (up to 3 months) bearish consolidation
Failure rate	45%
Failure rate if waited for downside breakout	4%
Average decline	19%, with most likely decline between 10% and 20%
Average volume trend	Downward
Premature breakout	22%
Breakout distance to apex	69%
Pullbacks	64%
Percentage meeting predicted price target	67%
See also	Head-and-Shoulders Tops

The Results Snapshot shows performance results for descending triangles. The failure rate at 45% is well above the 20% cutoff for reliable formations. However, if you wait for a downside breakout, then the failure rate drops to just 4%.

The average decline, at 19%, is about what you would expect from a bearish formation. The most likely decline, at 10% to 20%, is evenly distributed across the range. Premature breakouts occur in nearly a quarter of the formations (22%), so that is something to watch out for.

Tour

Figure 39.1 shows a descending triangle that is typical in many respects. Prices rise to meet a down-sloping trendline on the top of the pattern and fall back. Then, they rebound off a horizontal trendline along the base of the formation. The volume pattern is unusual for a descending triangle. Normally, volume recedes as the breakout approaches, but this one appears to have a V-shaped trend—higher at the beginning and end and weaker in the center. The breakout is downward and occurs on low volume. A bearish breakout can have high or low volume but volume is usually heavy. After the breakout, prices pull back to the triangle boundary before continuing down.

Why do descending triangles form? The descending triangle shown in Figure 39.1 begins forming in October 1994 as part of a consolidation in a downward trend. Imagine you believe the fair value of this stock is $7\frac{3}{8}$ but is overvalued at prices much above that. You tell your broker to buy the stock

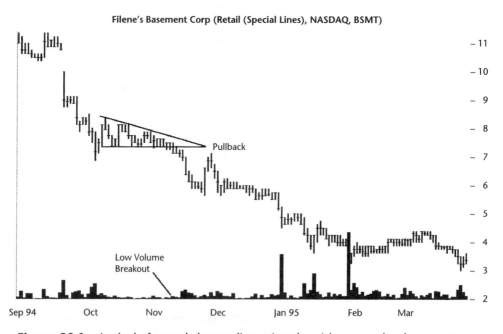

Figure 39.1 A nicely formed descending triangle with unusual volume pattern. Typically, volume trends downward and is quite low just before the breakout. Also shown is a pullback, repulsed by the horizontal resistance level.

should it fall to $7\frac{3}{8}$. After reaching a minor high at $8\frac{3}{8}$ on October 11, the stock begins declining for a few days. It descends and reaches the buy price 2 days later. Your broker buys the stock.

You are not alone. Other investors, believing the stock is retesting the low that occurred a week earlier, also buy the stock. Together, the buying puts a momentary floor on the stock. For the next 2 days, the stock returns to the $7\frac{3}{8}$ level before buying demand pushes the price higher. This time the stock does not climb as high as the prior minor high; it only reaches a value of $8\frac{1}{8}$ before turning down. Again, when the stock reaches a low of $7\frac{3}{8}$, buying demand increases enough to halt the decline at that level and to send the stock moving back up. During the next 2 weeks or so, you and other investors buy the stock. Enthusiasm for the stock quickly wanes and a series of lower highs outline a down-sloping trend. The floor, at $7\frac{3}{8}$, becomes the horizontal support level.

Eventually, investors buy enough of the stock and have either run out of money to buy more or decide they already own enough. The stock slips below the support line on November 9, and closes at the low for the day at $7\frac{1}{8}$. The stock hovers near that price for a few more days before continuing down in earnest on higher volume.

Quick-footed investors, realizing that the floor is no longer holding firm, sell the stock. The price begins declining rapidly now but soon levels off. For a few days, selling pressure meets buying demand and the decline halts, turns around, and begins moving up. It nears the base of the triangle and the smart money quickly disposes of any remaining shares in their portfolios. The pullback completes and the stock rounds over and starts heading down again. In 3 months' time the stock reaches the ultimate low of just under 3 before leveling out. That is a decline of 60%.

Identification Guidelines

Descending triangles have distinctive chart patterns making them easy to identify. Consider the triangles shown in Figure 39.2. A descending triangle appears during March and April 1993 and marks the end of a long rise started in late 1992. On above average volume, the stock moves up in early March then quickly rounds over and heads down. It declines to a low of about $29\frac{1}{2}$ where it finds support. Prices bounce back up again, not carrying as high this time, then return to the support level. As April dawns, the stock bounces one last time before falling through the support line and heading down on high volume.

Like a ball bouncing along the floor, each bounce from the support line is less high than the previous bounce, giving the formation a down-sloping appearance along the top. The support region at $29\frac{1}{2}$ is flat. These two ingredients, a down sloping trendline on the top and a horizontal support line on the bottom, are the two main characteristics of descending triangles. A receding volume pattern throughout the formation rounds out the picture.

Figure 39.2 Two descending triangles. The March triangle forms after a long climb beginning in late 1992. The nicely formed chart pattern has a receding volume trend especially in the latter half of the formation. The July formation is a failure since it does not immediately descend as expected. Nearly half of descending triangles break out upward.

The July formation is also a descending triangle although not as well formed. The volume pattern rises through the first half of the formation before moving downward toward the triangle apex. Prices momentarily move down out of the formation on August 3 and stay below the horizontal support line for 2 more days. Then, prices start rising. They sail up through the base of the formation and shoot out the top, reaching a peak of 30⅛ in late August. Prices start moving down, slowly at first, then plunge down on exceedingly high volume. The stock declines to a low of 23¹³⁄₁₆ on December 21, 1993, a decline of about 15%. Using the same ultimate low point, the first triangle shows a decline of almost 20% from its horizontal support line.

I am sure that if you owned stock in this company and sold during either of the descending triangles, you would be pleased. Although the second formation is a failure because it rises above the triangle top, prices do start down within the month. Sometimes failed formations prematurely alert you to a trend change, as the July example shows.

Table 39.1 outlines the identification characteristics for descending triangles. The triangular-shaped appearance makes the descending triangle easy to identify. Prices rebound from the base of the formation following a horizontal trendline, whereas prices along the top obey a downward-sloping trend. Volume throughout the formation also follows a downward trend especially as

Table 39.1
Identification Characteristics of Descending Triangles

Characteristic	Discussion
Triangle shape	A triangular-shaped pattern bounded by two trendlines, the bottom one horizontal and the top one sloping down, that intersect at the triangle apex.
Horizontal bottom support line	A horizontal (or nearly so) base acts to support prices. Prices should touch the base at least twice (at least two minor lows that either touch or come close to the trendline).
Down-sloping top trendline	A down-sloping price trend that eventually intersects the horizontal base line at the apex. Prices should rise up and touch (or come close to) the sloping trendline at least twice, forming two distinct minor highs.
Volume	Volume recedes and tends to drop off just before the breakout.
Premature breakouts	Are rare but occur on high volume making them appear like genuine breakouts.
Downside breakouts	Usually occur on very high volume that diminishes over time. However, prices can also break out on low volume.
Price action after breakout	Prices usually move down quickly, reaching the ultimate low in a straight-line fashion. Pullbacks occur about two-thirds of the time.

it nears the breakout day. Volume on that day is typically very high when compared to the prior day. After a breakout, prices drop away from the formation quickly and reach their ultimate low rapidly. Since the impact of a descending triangle is short to intermediate term, prices soon recover.

Support and resistance appear along the two trendlines. Throwbacks to the top of the formation usually stop at the sloping trendline, whereas pullbacks to the bottom halt at the horizontal trendline. After a breakout, prices often follow the sloping trendline down. During the recovery process after a descending triangle, prices rise to meet the level of the horizontal trendline then pause. Sometimes it takes several tries before prices push up through the horizontal resistance line.

Triangles, as a group, are easy to spot. However, there are some situations that dictate a careful approach. Figure 39.3 shows such a case. It is an example of what looks like a descending triangle, but is not. The volume trend does not conform to the usual pattern for a descending triangle. Volume should recede as the breakout nears. In Figure 39.3 volume rises along with prices at the start of the triangle, then tapers off at the top when prices round over. However, volume climbs as prices descend then shoots up the day after the breakout. Comparing the volume at the start and end of the formation, you can see that the trend—although somewhat downward—does not recede over time. It is more of a bowl shape.

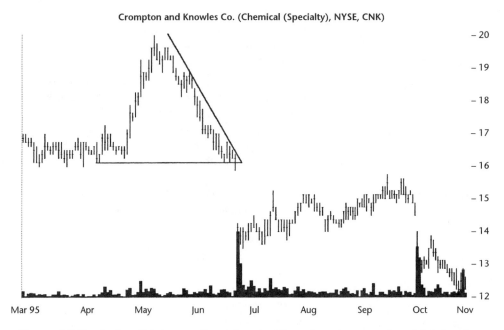

Figure 39.3   An invalid descending triangle. There is only one minor high leaving too much white space in the center of the formation. Prices should cross from side to side several times forming at least two minor highs and lows.

Volume for many formations is not a crucial factor, and you should not attach too much significance to it. However, a volume pattern that is not characteristic for a chart pattern raises a warning flag. Coupled with other factors, it might cause you to bypass the stock and look elsewhere for a more promising situation.

The price picture is even worse. Only one minor high composes the entire triangle. Well-formed descending triangles have prices that cross from side to side several times. There is no massive amount of white space in the center of the triangle. Contrast Figure 39.3 with Figure 39.1.

Focus on Failures

A 45% failure rate is shameful, but that is what descending triangles have. Figure 39.4 shows an example of a failure. Perhaps the first thing you notice is that prices rise; they shoot out the top of the triangle. Why? I can only speculate an answer to the question but Figure 39.4 does provide some clues. First, the triangle appears in a rising price trend. In almost two out of three cases, prices continue in the direction of the existing trend. In this case, that trend is upward.

Figure 39.4 shows a premature upside breakout in the beginning of February. It may sound silly, but that is a strong clue that prices will continue

Banc One Corp (Bank, NYSE, ONE)

Figure 39.4   A descending triangle failure. Since descending triangles act as consolidations of the trend, this one breaks out upward.

upward. If you bought the stock the day after the breakout, you may question the veracity of that comment. A day later, prices start a throwback that does not stop at the top trendline. Prices continue down and almost touch the lower trendline before resuming their uphill trend.

Still, waiting for a downside breakout before shorting a stock or selling an existing holding is always a wise course with these formations. Imagine that you sold your holdings once you recognized the chart pattern as a descending triangle. You would have missed out on the rise to 40—a 20% mistake.

The volume pattern for this formation is difficult to decipher. As prices rise, so does volume; as prices descend, volume recedes too. If you were to run the volume data through a linear regression formula, you would find that the slope of the resulting line tilts downward. In other words, volume recedes, just as in a well-behaved descending triangle.

Statistics

Table 39.2 shows general statistics for descending triangles. Fewer valid descending triangles appear in the database than do ascending triangles. Almost two out of three (422 out of 689) are consolidations of the current trend. This simply means that if the price trend is downward going into the triangle, it is still moving downward after leaving it.

Table 39.2
General Statistics for Descending Triangles

Description	Statistic
Number of formations in 500 stocks from 1991 to 1996	689
Reversal or consolidation	267 reversals, 422 consolidations
Failure rate	309 or 45%
Failure rate if waited for downside breakout	27 or 4%
Average decline of successful formations	19%
Average rise of failed formations	42%
Most likely decline	10% to 20%
Of those succeeding, number meeting or exceeding price target (measure rule)	256 or 67%
Start to breakout	2 months (61 days)
Start to apex	3 months (87 days)

Note: Only about half the descending triangles work as expected and two-thirds of those reach their predicted price targets.

In theory, descending triangles are wonderful formations because the top trendline predicts the breakout direction: downward. However, only 55% of the descending triangles work in this fashion. That is a little better than a coin toss and certainly not good enough on which to base a trade. However, if you wait for the breakout to occur, your chances of success rise to 96%. Unfortunately, the downside move is not terribly exciting at 19%, just a little behind other bearish formations that typically show a decline of 20%. To derive the most likely decline, I did a frequency distribution by sorting the percentage decline for each formation and grouping the values into 10 bins. Figure 39.5 makes it clear where most of the declines occur: the 10% to 20% range. That is what I call the most likely decline.

Descending triangles with upside breakouts do quite well, soaring 42% above the breakout price. The numbers suggest that you should trade with the trend. If prices break out upward, go long. If your triangle has a downside breakout, then short the stock.

For those stocks with descending triangles performing as expected, 67% meet or exceed their price targets. That is to say they decline below the predicted price. I consider values above 80% to be reliable, so descending triangles fall short.

On average, it takes about 2 months (61 days) before the triangles have a breakout. The overall formation length from start to the triangle apex where the two trendlines meet is 87 days.

Table 39.3 shows the statistics for premature breakouts. Only 22% of the formations have premature breakouts in either direction. A premature break-

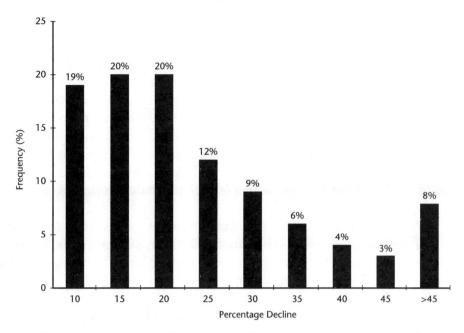

Figure 39.5 Frequency distribution of declines after a downside breakout from a descending triangle. There are relatively few large declines that distort the average decline. The most likely decline is in the 10% to 20% range.

Table 39.3
Premature Breakout Statistics for Descending Triangles

Description	Statistic
Number of premature breakouts (up or down)	151 or 22%
Number of premature upside breakouts	38 or 6%
Number of premature downside breakouts	137 or 20%
Volume at upside premature breakout versus 25-day moving average	127%
Volume at downside premature breakout versus 25-day moving average	143%
Number of upside and downside premature breakouts	24 or 16%
Premature breakout up, genuine breakout up	15 or 39%
Premature breakout up, genuine breakout down	12 or 32%
Premature breakout down, genuine breakout up	72 or 53%
Premature breakout down, genuine breakout down	42 or 31%
Upside premature breakout distance to apex	71%
Downside premature breakout distance to apex	64%

Note: Premature breakouts are indistinguishable from real breakouts and offer no clue as to the direction of the final breakout.

out is when prices close outside the formation boundary but quickly return within a few days (they should not venture very far, either). A genuine breakout soars outside the formation and usually continues in the breakout direction. A premature breakout is just a few days long, whereas a throwback or pullback often takes over a week before prices near the trendline again.

Upside premature breakouts are exceedingly rare, occurring only 6% of the time on above average volume. Downside premature breakouts are more likely at 20%, and display volume that is 43% above the average (or 143% of the total).

Of the formations having premature breakouts, only 16% have both upside and downside premature breakouts. The next four lines in the table try to determine if there is a relationship between premature breakouts and the direction of the final breakout. About half the formations (53%) with premature downside breakouts later break out upward. The other variations have substantially fewer hits. The table does not show the few remaining premature breakouts associated with horizontal breakouts.

The last two table entries try to determine if there is a way to eliminate premature breakouts by knowing that they break out sooner than genuine breakouts. The answer is no. Although premature downside breakouts occur, on average, about 64% of the way to the apex, it is close enough to the 69% genuine breakout distance that you will not be able to tell the difference. Since the volume pattern is also the same for premature and genuine breakouts, there is no way to differentiate a premature breakout from a genuine one.

Where do the most powerful breakouts occur? I graphed the distance to the apex versus the percentage decline but the graph shows a random relationship. However, some analysts have suggested that the most powerful breakouts occur about two-thirds of the way to the triangle apex.

Table 39.4 shows the statistics for genuine breakouts. Upside breakouts occur at nearly the same location as downside breakouts: 70% and 69%, respectively. Only 4% of the formations have downside breakouts that fail to continue falling, and a similar number of formations that break out upside continue down. To put this another way, prices continue moving in the direction of the genuine breakout. If the breakout is down, for example, prices continue dropping.

Upside breakouts occur 41% of the time, downside breakouts 54% of the time, and the remainder are horizontal—prices run flat and pierce the apex. Since descending triangles are supposed to descend, these statistics are alarming. The 54% downside breakout value is little better than the flip of a coin and warns you not to anticipate the breakout direction.

For formations with upside breakouts, throwbacks occur 39% of the time. Pullbacks from downside breakouts do much better, having a 64% rate. The pullback rate is a little too low to depend on it while trading; in other words, do not depend on a pullback before shorting the stock.

Table 39.4
Breakout Statistics for Descending Triangles

Description	Statistic
Upside breakout distance to apex	70%
Downside breakout distance to apex	69%
Downside breakout but failure	27 or 4%
Upside breakout but success	19 or 3%
Upside breakout	283 or 41%
Downside breakout	370 or 54%
Horizontal breakout	36 or 5%
Throwback	109 or 39%
Pullback	236 or 64%
Average time to throwback completion	12 days
Average time to pullback completion	12 days
For successful formations, days to ultimate low	2 months (66 days)
Percentage of breakouts occurring near 12-month low (L), center (C), or high (H)	L33%, C32%, H35%
Percentage loss for each 12-month lookback period	L21%, C17%, H17%

Note: Prices continue moving in the direction of the breakout, but do not try to anticipate the breakout direction.

Both throwbacks and pullbacks complete in 12 days, on average, after the breakout. I arrive at this value by removing any throwback or pullback that occurs more than 30 days after the breakout. Prices returning to the apex after a month are due to normal price action, not a throwback or pullback.

On average, it takes slightly over 2 months (66 days) to reach the ultimate low after a downside breakout. A frequency distribution of the results shows that the majority (72%) reach the ultimate low within 3 months, qualifying the formations as having short-term investment implications.

Where in the yearly price range do breakouts occur? Most downside breakouts happen when prices are within a third of the yearly high, but the other two-thirds are close. Mapping performance over the yearly price range shows that the best performing triangles have breakouts near the yearly low, scoring declines of 21%. The other two ranges perform less well. The number suggests that stocks having trouble (they are near the yearly low), continue to do poorly. In other words, do not short a stock making new highs; instead, look at those making new lows.

The last statistics table (Table 39.5) concerns volume. The volume trends downward for most descending triangles (72%) as measured using the slope of the linear regression line from the triangle start to the day before the breakout. I compared the breakout volume with a 25-day moving average of the volume. The table lists the results. The heaviest volume occurs the day after a breakout,

Table 39.5
Volume Statistics for Descending Triangles

Description	Statistic
Number showing downward volume trend	494 or 72%
Volume for breakout day and next 5 days compared with 25-day moving average	158%, 168%, 136%, 136%, 135%, 123%
Percentage of high volume breakouts subject to pullbacks versus low volume breakouts	56% versus 44%
Performance of high volume downside breakouts versus low volume downside breakouts	18% versus 17%

Note: The trend of volume is downward until the breakout day when it spikes upward.

suggesting that end-of-day traders notice the breakout then jump on the trend the following day. Volume remains heavy throughout the next week.

Do pullbacks occur after low volume breakouts? No. I used 50% above and below the 25-day volume moving average as the benchmark for high and low volume, respectively. Then, I sorted the pullbacks according to the breakout volume. Most pullbacks (56%), occur after a high volume breakout, not a low volume one.

Lastly, I determined that there is no significant relationship between high volume downside breakouts and large price moves. To check this, I separated downside breakouts with high volume and their corresponding price moves from their low volume counterparts. The average decline for high volume breakouts is 18% and for low volume breakouts, 17%. So, do not get too excited if you have a high volume downside breakout; it does not mean that your stock will fall any further than a low volume breakout.

Trading Tactics

Table 39.6 shows trading tactics for descending triangles and it begins with the measure rule. As you would expect, the measure rule tries to predict the value to which prices decline after a downside breakout. Compute the height of the formation by subtracting the price of the lower trendline from the upper one at the formation start. Then, subtract the height from the value of the lower horizontal trendline. The result is the target price.

Compute the height of the triangle shown in Figure 39.6 by taking the difference between the two trendlines (marked by the black dots). The value is $1\frac{7}{8}$ (that is, $9\frac{1}{4} - 7\frac{3}{8}$). Subtract the height from the value of the horizontal trendline, or $7\frac{3}{8} - 1\frac{7}{8}$, giving a predicted price decline to $5\frac{1}{2}$. Prices reach the target the day after the breakout, a 25% decline in 2 days. Since the measure

Table 39.6
Trading Tactics for Descending Triangles

Trading Tactic	Explanation
Measure rule	Calculate the height of the formation by subtracting the value of the lower trendline from the upper one at the formation start. Subtract the height from the value of the lower trendline to get the predicted minimum price decline. Alternatively, draw a line parallel to the down-sloping trendline starting at the lower left corner of the formation. The value of this line *where prices break out of the formation* becomes the target price.
Always wait for confirmation	Since this formation is nearly as likely to break out upward as downward, always wait for the breakout to occur. After a downside breakout, sell short immediately or after prices pull back to the triangle base and start moving down again. Another way to play the formation is to wait for an *upside* breakout then *buy* the stock. The most likely rise is about 25% with an average gain of 42%—high enough that it is probably worth betting on.
Sell on downside breakout	If you are a short-term trader, sell immediately should the stock suffer a downside breakout. The likelihood is that prices will continue down. For intermediate- or long-term holders who do not want to sell, consider adding to your position once prices near the measure rule target. Use support levels to help predict the ultimate low.
Cover on measure rule	For short-term traders, cover your short positions when prices *near* the target price (see measure rule).

Note: Sell short on the pullback to the triangle base and cover when it nears the target price. Alternatively, consider buying the stock after an upside breakout.

rule suggests the minimum price move, the final decline is often larger. In this case, the stock reached a low of 4.69 in mid-April 1994 for a total decline of 36%.

An alternative approach that eliminates the cumbersome math, is to draw a line parallel to the down-sloping trendline starting at the lower left corner of the formation. The value of the line where prices break out of the formation becomes the target price.

Waiting for a downside breakout to occur is paramount since the failure rate is so high. If you do not wait for a downside breakout before shorting the stock, prices could quickly rise away from you in an upside breakout. However, shorting a stock is not for the faint of heart and entails substantial risk. If you miss the initial breakout, you can always short after a pullback. A pullback is also a good time to add to your short position. Wait for prices to resume falling before shorting. Cover your position when prices approach the target price or until the picture changes (either fundamentally or technically).

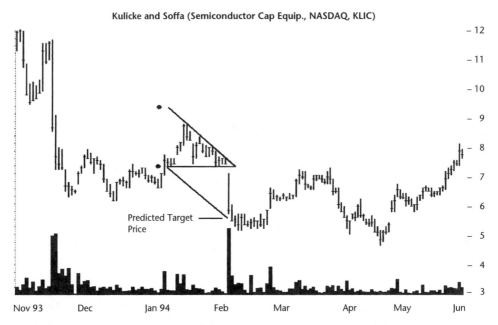

Kulicke and Soffa (Semiconductor Cap Equip., NASDAQ, KLIC)

Figure 39.6   Measure rule applied to descending triangles. There are two ways to predict the minimum decline. Take the difference between the two trendlines at the formation start (denoted by the black dots) and subtract the result from the value of the lower trendline, or draw a line parallel to the down-sloping trendline beginning at the lower left corner. The value of the line when prices break out of the formation becomes the target price. Both methods show a target price of $5\frac{1}{2}$.

Since a downside breakout can take prices down rapidly, the pullback typically allows you to enter the trade at a higher price than if you bought the day after a downside breakout. If the stock fails to pull back, look elsewhere for another opportunity. Do not chase the stock down in price should a pullback not occur. If the stock declines and you still decide to short the position, then you are probably entering near the low and setting yourself up for a disappointment.

If you are long the stock and are an intermediate- or long-term holder, do not worry about descending triangles. I used to get concerned about them when I saw them forming in a stock I owned. But since, on average, they only decline 19% in 2 months, that is just not enough to worry about or take action on. Of course, if you do not want to suffer through such a decline (which could go much lower), consider selling the stock on the downside breakout and buying it back after it fulfills the measure rule. Remember, the measure rule suggests a *minimum* price move and yet prices meet the target only two-thirds of the time. In other words, if you sell the stock, it might not decline as far as you expect.

Sample Trade

Jacob is a novice investor. He has an MBA and works in the insurance industry, which has acclimated him to risk. Still, shorting a stock is not his first choice. The stock shown in Figure 39.7 interested him. We talked in mid-September, a few days before the breakout, and discussed the situation. We ran through the qualifiers. The volume trend looked good: generally downward as you would expect until a few weeks before the breakout when it deviated from the normal pattern. The number of touches from side to side was good, and the minor highs and lows were distinct. We both concluded that this was a valid descending triangle in the making.

Jacob told me he was nervous about shorting the stock since it could turn around and climb away from him. I suggested that a stop placed at the top of the triangle would limit his risk and get him out if things did not work out. Still, he was uncomfortable shorting and really wanted to own the stock at a lower price, so I suggested buying the stock after it fulfilled the measure rule.

He computed the height of the triangle and discovered that the minimum downside move would take the stock to 12½. As Jacob watched the stock each day, he saw it break out downward and begin declining. The first time it

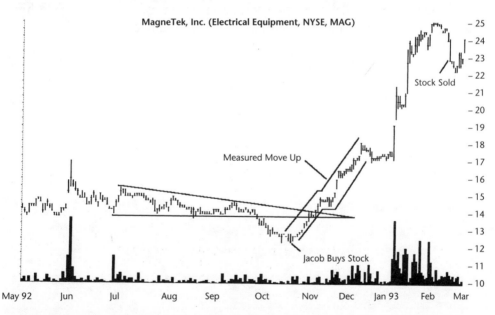

Figure 39.7 A descending triangle followed by a measured move up. Instead of opening a short position, Jacob bought into the stock after the descending triangle fulfilled the measure rule. He raised his stop as prices climbed and was eventually stopped out at 23 for a $2,000 profit. A measured move up formation helped him gauge the rise.

reached the target price and recovered a bit, he suspected the stock was near its low. At least, that is what he hoped.

On October 19, 1992, Jacob bought 200 shares of the stock at the close of $12\frac{1}{2}$, exactly the target price he predicted earlier. He placed a stop-loss order at $11\frac{1}{8}$, slightly below the prior December's low of $11\frac{1}{4}$, a support level. Then, he looked at the possible reward and believed the stock would rise to its old high of 17. He sat back and waited.

It didn't take long for the stock to bottom out and start its climb. In mid-November when it turned down for 2 days, Jacob hoped this was the beginning of a measured move up. He calculated the difference from the low near where he bought the stock to the most recent high and came up with a value of $2\frac{5}{8}$. He added this to the current closing price and computed a new target price of $17\frac{1}{2}$. This was quite close to his original price target of 17.

Over the next few days, the stock started moving up again. By early December it had hit his new price target and the measured move was complete. Jacob decided to raise his stop-loss point to 16, the top of a support layer. If the stock sold at 16, he would have a gain of 28%, a respectable return. The results pleased him so far, but he worried that prices would hit his stop as the stock consolidated.

Just after the new year the stock started climbing again and he held on for the ride. He kept raising his stop until he was taken out at 23, to which the stock declined in mid-February 1993. After expenses, this trade made him nearly $2,000, substantially more than his initial estimate.

40

Triangles, Symmetrical Bottoms

RESULTS SNAPSHOT

Downside Breakouts

Appearance	Prices trend down then form lower highs and higher lows following two sloping trendlines that eventually intersect. The breakout is downward.
Reversal or consolidation	Short-term (up to 3 months) bearish consolidation
Failure rate	2%
Average decline	19%, with most likely decline being 10%
Volume trend	Downward
Premature breakout	16%
Pullbacks	57%
Percentage meeting predicted price target	57%
Surprising findings	Triangles with high volume breakouts show larger losses. Pullbacks are more likely to occur after a high volume breakout.
Synonym	Coils
See also	Diamond Tops and Bottoms; Head-and-Shoulders Bottoms; Shark-32; Triangles, Ascending; Triangles, Descending; Triangles, Symmetrical Tops

Upside Breakouts

Appearance	Prices trend down then form lower highs and higher lows following two sloping trendlines that eventually intersect. The breakout is upward.
Reversal or consolidation	Short-term (up to 3 months) bullish reversal
Failure rate	3%
Average rise	41%, with most likely rise being 20%
Volume trend	Downward
Premature breakout	16%
Throwbacks	43%
Percentage meeting predicted price target	79%
Surprising findings	Triangles with high volume breakouts show larger gains. Throwbacks are more likely to occur after a high volume breakout.
Synonym	Coils
See also	Diamond Tops and Bottoms; Head-and-Shoulders Bottoms; Shark-32; Triangles, Ascending; Triangles, Descending; Triangles, Symmetrical Tops

I separated symmetrical triangles into two types: those with prices trending up to the formation and those with prices trending down. The way you invest in each type may vary, so I wanted to collect the most beneficial statistics for investors. This chapter deals with symmetrical triangle bottoms, where prices trend down to the formation.

The failure rates at 2% and 3% are surprisingly small. Once a breakout occurs, prices tend to keep going and do not suffer from a 5% failure (that is, a quick reversal). The average move after a breakout is about what you would expect for bullish and bearish formations. Downside breakouts show losses averaging 19%, whereas upside ones gain 41%.

Symmetrical triangle bottoms with upside breakouts hit their price targets more often (79%), continuing a trend that we have seen in other formations: Bullish patterns perform better than bearish ones. For downside breakouts, prices meet or exceed the measure rule prediction 57% of the time. The measure rule predictions are shy of the 80% minimum for reliable formations.

One surprising finding, and it may not be a surprise at all, is that breakouts on high volume perform better than those on low volume. However, the differences are not statistically significant, meaning that they *may* be due to chance.

Throwbacks and pullbacks are more likely to follow high volume breakouts than low volume ones. However, the sample size is small so do not attach too much significance to the result.

Tour

Figure 40.1 shows a good example of a symmetrical triangle. It appears in the fall of 1995 when many of the semiconductor and semiconductor capital equipment stocks were being electrocuted. The chart pattern occurs in a downtrend with prices falling from a high of $94\frac{3}{4}$ to a low of $24\frac{3}{4}$ by mid-1996.

The triangle has two trendlines bounding prices on the top and bottom. The minor highs and minor lows narrow over time, forming the distinctive triangular shape. The volume trend also recedes until the breakout nears and bursts upward on the breakout day. Prices bounce from one side of the chart pattern to the other, filling the triangle with a sturdy, solid mass of price movements.

Identification Guidelines

Surprisingly, symmetrical triangles are one of the more tricky formations to identify. Table 40.1 outlines the selection guidelines for them. For symmetrical triangle bottoms, prices trend down to the formation. Symmetrical triangle tops, on the other hand, have prices leading up to the formation. Even though a bottom may appear near the yearly high, I classify it as a bottom if prices decline into the formation. Figure 40.2 shows another example of a symmetrical triangle bottom.

Table 40.1
Identification Characteristics of Symmetrical Triangle Bottoms

Characteristic	Discussion
Downward trend	For bottoms, prices trend down to the formation but can break out either up or down.
Shape	Prices follow two sloping trendlines, the top one sloping down and the bottom one trending up so that they intersect at the triangle apex, sometime in the future. The trendlines need not be the same length.
Touches	There should be at least two minor highs and two minor lows touching the trendlines (in other words, at least four trend reversals).
Volume	Usually recedes throughout the formation, but can be spiky, and is often very low just before the breakout.
Premature breakout	Has at least one close outside the triangle but prices soon return within the triangle borders.
Breakout direction	Unknown ahead of time. You must wait for the breakout before investing. A breakout has prices moving away from the triangle, not quickly returning as in a premature breakout.
Duration	Typically longer than 3 weeks, at a minimum. Formations 3 weeks or less better classify as pennants.

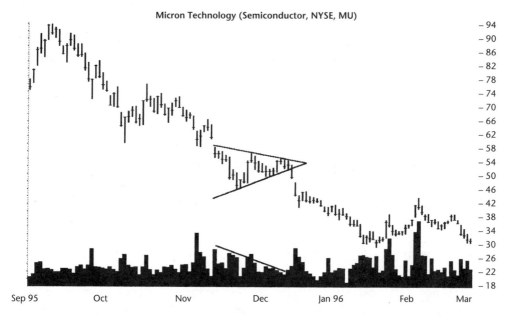

Figure 40.1 A symmetrical triangle bottom in a downtrend. Prices enter from the top and leave following the same trend.

Figure 40.2 shows a large symmetrical triangle with a downside breakout, pullback to the lower triangle trendline, and prices that fall away from there. Two sloping trendlines bound the price action; the top trendline slopes down and the bottom one slopes up. Neither trendline is horizontal or nearly so; they both have a decent measure of slope to them. This is an important distinction

Figure 40.2 A large symmetrical triangle with a downside breakout and pullback.

because triangles with horizontal trendlines classify as either ascending or descending triangles. The trendlines join at the triangle apex on the right, distinguishing the formation from the family of broadening formations.

The term *symmetrical* applies to the shape of the formation. Often, the angles of the two trendlines with the horizontal are quite close to one another, making it look symmetrical about the horizontal axis. However, this is not a prerequisite, only an anomaly.

There are three minor highs and three minor lows shown in Figure 40.2, as marked by the numbers. The terms, minor high and minor low mean that prices form a small peak or trough that is distinguishable from the surrounding price action. Prices drop away from either side of the minor high, for example.

I cannot stress how important it is to have at least two minor highs and two minor lows in the formation. Many times a rounding bottom may tempt you to create a symmetrical triangle out of it. The price action seems to narrow over time but there is really only one minor high. Figure 40.3 is a good example. The pseudotriangle forms beginning with the minor high at point A and drops rapidly to the minor low at point B. Then prices meander up along the lower trendline before crossing to point C. There are not enough price crossings of the triangle to suggest a reliable formation. Although prices touch both trendlines several times, there is too much white space filling the center of the formation. The difference between this figure and the prior one is clear.

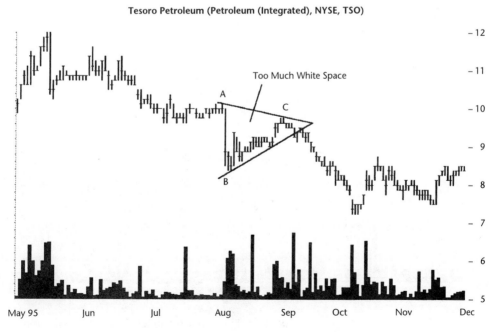

Figure 40.3 An invalid symmetrical triangle bottom. There are not enough price crossings to fill the triangle, leaving white space predominating.

The volume trend is predominantly downward but irregular in appearance. I would not eliminate a symmetrical triangle just because the volume trend is abnormal. Many times perfectly valid triangles appear on unusual volume.

Once you think you have correctly identified a symmetrical triangle bottom, think again. Look to the left of the formation and search for another smaller minor low. This might be the left shoulder of a head-and-shoulders bottom formation. At other times, you will be cutting off the right half of a diamond bottom. Since symmetrical triangles usually form part of those formations, it may pay to take a broader view. If you discover a head-and-shoulders, diamond, or other formation that uses a symmetrical triangle, ignore the triangle and focus on the investment implications of the other formation. Doing so will help you determine the breakout direction and ultimate price move.

Focus on Failures

Figure 40.4 shows what a failure looks like in a symmetrical triangle (the left triangle). I call this type of failure a 5% failure because prices fail to continue moving in the breakout direction by more than 5% before reversing. The figure shows a well-formed symmetrical triangle during February and March with two minor highs and three minor lows, all of them touching (or coming close to) their respective trendlines. The two trendlines intersect and the formation

Figure 40.4 Two symmetrical triangles. The one on the left has an upside breakout that fails to rise by more than 5%. The formation is a 5% failure. The triangle is part of a double or triple top.

stands alone. By that, I mean it is not part of another formation. Or is it? The left peak in conjunction with the first minor high in the triangle might mark the beginning of a double top (or, if you include the second, lower, peak in January, it might be a triple top). Since prices do not fall below the lowest low between the two peaks before reaching a higher high, the formation does not confirm and is not a double (or triple) top.

However, the higher high forming as part of the throwback to the triangle apex (late March) could extend the double top into a triple top. Once prices tumble below the low formed between the three peaks, a triple top is confirmed and prices head downward, pulling back briefly (twice) to just above the formation low before continuing down. The pullback forms another symmetrical triangle, as shown in Figure 40.4.

The big picture explains why the triangle fails. No matter whether you call this a nested triple top or a multiple top (or whatever), the word *top* in the phrase is a big clue. If it is a triple or multiple top, the breakout direction is down. The triangle breaking out upward instead of downward in this situation is suspicious. Before you invest, make sure you take a wider view; flip over to the weekly chart and see if a different situation arises from the one shown on the daily chart. Defer to the weekly chart if you see a conflict.

Statistics

Statistics for symmetrical triangles are many and varied. Table 40.2 shows the first batch. As mentioned earlier, I separated the triangles into two types: those with prices trending down to the formation from those appearing in uptrends. This chapter deals with symmetrical triangle bottoms, where the trend is downward, leading to the formation.

Table 40.2
General Statistics for Symmetrical Triangle Bottoms

Description	Upside Breakout	Downside Breakout
Number of formations in 500 stocks from 1991 to 1996	63	83
Reversal or consolidation	63 reversals	83 consolidations
Failure rate	2 or 3%	2 or 2%
Average rise/decline of successful formations	41%	19%
Most likely rise/decline	20%	10%
Of those succeeding, number meeting or exceeding price target (measure rule)	48 or 79%	46 or 57%
Average formation length	2 months (55 days)	2 months (53 days)
Breakout as percentage of distance to apex	79%	74%

Bottoms have two breakout directions, up and down, and each table shows statistics related to each direction. There are slightly more triangles with downside breakouts (83) than upside ones (63). Since the entry direction is downward, triangles with upside breakouts are reversals of the trend and those with downside breakouts are consolidations. For both types, the failure rates are similar, 3% and 2%, which is very low considering I view failure rates above 20% to be excessive.

When these formations work, their performance is about what one would expect: 41% for bullish breakouts and 19% for the bearish variety. The most likely gain or loss is more modest at 20% to 10% for upside and downside breakouts, respectively. I tabulate the most likely gain or loss using a frequency distribution of gains and losses, as shown in Figures 40.5 and 40.6.

Figure 40.5 shows that the tallest column, 10%, has the highest frequency. Almost half the formations (42%) have declines of 15% or less, so invest carefully in symmetrical triangles showing downside breakouts. The numbers suggest the downturn will be momentary and you should expect continued gains. Of course, the stock, the industry, and the general market will dictate your results.

Figure 40.6 shows the tallest column at 20%, followed closely by the 40% column. The irregular appearance is due to the small sample size but generally follows the pattern for other chart types. It is interesting that three-fourths of the formations with upside breakouts have gains over 20%. That explains why the average, at 41%, is well above the most likely rise. I suspect that the most

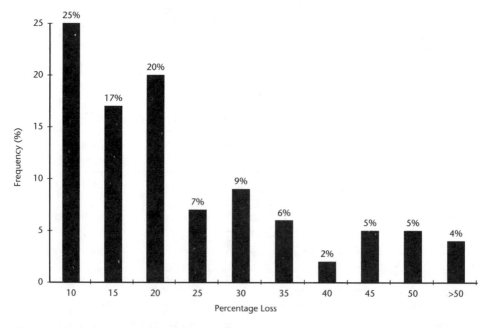

Figure 40.5   Frequency distribution of losses for symmetrical triangles with downside breakouts. The most likely loss is the tallest column, 10%.

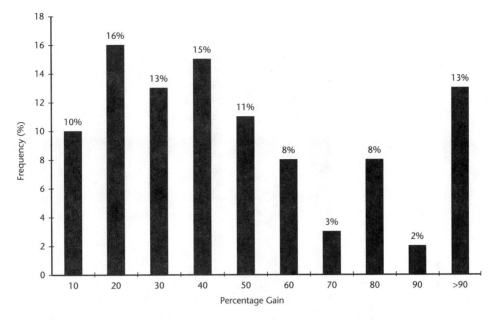

Figure 40.6 Frequency distribution of gains for symmetrical triangles with upside breakouts. The graph suggests the most likely gain is about 20%. The irregular appearance of the series is due to the small sample size.

likely rise figure understates the performance and that actual trading results should be better.

The measure rule predicts the move from a triangle after a breakout. It can be measured in two ways, but for statistics, I chose to use the formation height added to the formation high or subtracted from the low to derive a target price. This is explained in more detail in the Trading Tactics section of this chapter, but 79% of the symmetrical triangles with upside breakouts meet or exceed their targets, whereas 57% with downside breakouts hit theirs. I consider values above 80% to be reliable so symmetrical triangle bottoms come up short.

The average formation length at about 2 months is nearly the same for both types.

I have been watching symmetrical triangles form in stocks I follow for years now and I was under the impression that they act like their ascending and descending triangle brothers when it comes to the breakout point. Symmetrical triangles break out much later, on average, than I expected. Figure 40.7 shows a frequency distribution of symmetricals with the two types of breakouts.

On average, the breakout point is similar, about three-fourths of the way to the triangle apex (where the two sloping trendlines meet). As I look at the figure, the surprising thing is how few breakouts are near the two-thirds mark. Only 15% of the triangles with downside breakouts pierce the trendline by that point, whereas a scant 5% of triangles with upside breakouts step up to the

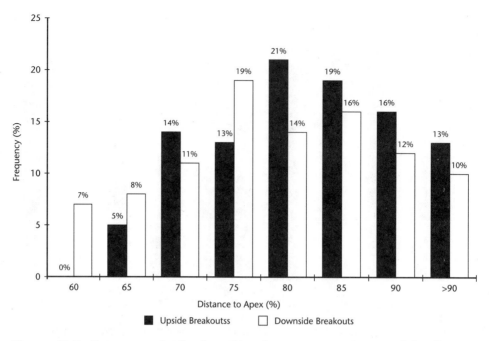

Figure 40.7 Frequency distribution of breakouts as a percentage of the distance to the apex. Most breakouts occur about 75% to 80% of the way to the triangle apex.

plate. Most breakouts occur 75% to 80% of the way to the apex. The good news about this is that it gives you a longer opportunity to trade the triangle internally: Buy or sell at the trendlines then take the opposite position as prices cross to the other side without worrying about a breakout until the apex nears.

Table 40.3 highlights statistics for symmetrical triangles with premature breakouts. Comparatively few symmetrical triangles have premature breakouts (16%) for both breakout directions. A premature breakout is when prices *close* outside the trendline boundary but quickly return to the triangle formation before reaching the apex. The table shows the different types of premature breakouts along with a comparison of breakout volume. Volume is above average, making premature breakouts indistinguishable from genuine breakouts. However, premature breakouts do break out slightly sooner (71% versus 79% and 72% versus 74%).

Table 40.4 shows statistics related to genuine breakouts. About half the formations have either throwbacks (43%) or pullbacks (57%) to the trendline or triangle apex. These complete in less than 2 weeks (12 and 11 days) and none takes more than a month to loop around. Anything longer than a month I consider to be normal price action and not a throwback or pullback.

Once a breakout occurs, it takes about 5½ months to reach the ultimate high after an upside breakout and less than half that time to reach the ultimate low after a downside breakout. Most of the upside breakouts (48%) occur in the center third of the yearly price range. Downside breakouts have the break-

Table 40.3
Premature Breakout Statistics for Symmetrical Triangle Bottoms

Description	Upside Breakout	Downside Breakout
Number of premature breakouts (up or down)	10 or 16%	13 or 16%
Number of premature upside breakouts	0	8 or 10%
Volume at upside premature breakout	0	79% of 25-day moving average
Number of premature downside breakouts	10 or 16%	7 or 8%
Volume at downside premature breakout	123% of 25-day moving average	161% of 25-day moving average
Of formations showing premature breakouts, number having both upside and downside premature breakouts	0	2 or 15%
Upside premature breakout distance to apex	0	72%
Downside premature breakout distance to apex	71%	72%

out price within a third of the yearly low. Mapping performance over the yearly price range, we find the best performing triangles with upside breakouts happen in the upper third of the range. Downside breakouts perform best from the center third of the yearly range. The sample sizes are small, especially for the high category in upside breakouts (five samples), so interpret the numbers cautiously.

The last statistics table (Table 40.5) concerns volume. The vast majority of formations (73% and 82%) have receding volume trends as measured by the slope of a line plotted using linear regression. Since the volume trend recedes and can become very low just before the breakout, I compared the breakout day volume with the prior day. Once a breakout occurs, the volume shoots

Table 40.4
Breakout Statistics for Symmetrical Triangle Bottoms

Description	Upside Breakout	Downside Breakout
Throwbacks/pullbacks	27 or 43%	47 or 57%
Average time to throwback/ pullback completion	12 days	11 days
For successful formations, days to ultimate high/low	5.5 months (163 days)	2.5 months (74 days)
Percentage of breakouts occurring near 12-month low (L), center (C), or high (H)	L42%, C48%, H10%	L51%, C27%, H22%
Percentage gain/loss for each 12-month lookback period	L42%, C37%, H67%	L18%, C23%, H16%

Table 40.5
Volume Statistics for Symmetrical Triangle Bottoms

Description	Upside Breakout	Downside Breakout
Number showing downward volume trend	46 or 73%	68 or 82%
Volume for breakout day and next 5 days compared with day before breakout	169%, 172%, 142%, 127%, 110%, 122%	245%, 250%, 218%, 162%, 147%, 145%
Are low volume breakouts more subject to throwback/pullback?	No	No
Performance of high volume breakouts versus low volume breakouts	48% versus 40%	18% versus 12%

upward for both breakout directions (169% and 245% of the prior day's total). Volume remains high throughout the week.

Are low volume breakouts more likely to pull back or throw back? No. It is just the opposite: High volume breakouts are more likely to throw back or pull back. For upside breakouts, one formation (4%) follows a breakout on volume 50% below the 25-day moving average, whereas 15 formations (56%) follow breakouts with volume that is 150% of the 25-day moving average. Downside breakouts show a similar trend with 4 or 9% appearing after a low volume breakout and 12 or 26% appearing after a high volume breakout. As you can see, the sample size is small but the results follow what we have seen for other formation types.

Do high volume breakouts propel prices farther? I use the same 50%/ 150% volume benchmark to denote low or high volume and gauge performance for those formations that fall within the two volume categories. In both downside and upside breakouts, high volume breakouts result in better performance than those on low volume. However, the differences are not statistically significant, meaning that they could be due to chance (alternatively, they could be accurate). Again, the sample size is small.

Trading Tactics

Table 40.6 outlines trading tactics. There are two types of measure rules for symmetrical triangle bottoms. Figure 40.8 shows the first one. Compute the formation height from highest high (point B at $9\frac{3}{4}$) to lowest low (point A at $8\frac{3}{8}$). Either add the difference of $1\frac{3}{8}$ to point B or subtract it from point A, depending on the breakout direction. In this case, the breakout is upward, so the target price becomes $11\frac{1}{8}$ (that is, $9\frac{3}{4} + 1\frac{3}{8}$). Prices reach the target in less than a month.

Table 40.6
Trading Tactics for Symmetrical Triangle Bottoms

Trading Tactic	Explanation
Measure rule	Compute the formation height by subtracting the lowest low from the highest high. For upside breakouts, add the difference to the highest high or for downside breakouts, subtract the difference. Alternatively, symmetrical triangles can be halfway points in a move, so project accordingly.
Trade with trend	As consolidations, prices usually leave the triangle in the same direction as when they enter.
Wait for breakout	Always wait for the breakout in case the triangle reverses.
Intrapattern trade	If the triangle is wide and long enough, sell or go short at the top trendline and buy or cover at the bottom one. Cover at the breakout if it goes against you or stop trading once prices near the apex.

Figure 40.8 Measure rule for symmetrical triangle bottoms. Use the measure rule to predict the target price. Subtract the low (point A) from the high (point B) and add the difference to the high (point B). The actual trade results in a gain of 27% in 1 month.

Some symmetrical triangles act like larger versions of pennants. They are half-mast formations and mark the halfway point in a move (like a measured move up or down formation). Had the triangle broken out downward, it might have continued down and fulfilled the measure rule. In such a case, the measure from point C (on the left at 11⅞) to point A should be subtracted from the value of point B. The result is the target price of 6¼. Point C is the start of the move leading to the triangle and the measure rule applies just as in a measured move up or down formation.

Use one or both measure rules as appropriate to the situation. The first method, using the formation height, is the more conservative of the two and more likely to be fulfilled.

It is difficult or impossible to determine in which direction prices will break out. Generally, they continue the prevailing trend. By this I mean prices exit following the intermediate-term price trend that leads to the formation. Even in Figure 40.8, although the formation acts as a short-term reversal of the downward trend, the longer-term trend is upward (it is not visible in the figure). Prices begin rising in early February from a price of 6 and reach a high of 11⅞—about double—by early September.

Since you cannot reliably determine the breakout direction, it is always best to wait for a breakout. Occasionally, prices squeeze out the triangle apex and have no breakout at all. This is a rarity, but it does happen. Once prices break out, trade with the trend: Go long if prices break out upward and short on downside breakouts.

I have noticed that even when prices break out in an adverse direction (a reversal of the prevailing trend), they quickly reverse again and resume the original trend. This means, for example, in an upward trend they break out downward and fall by 10% or 15%, then head back up and finish much higher. This behavior for reversals is something to watch out for, especially for downside breakouts in a raging bull market.

Another way of trading triangles is to buy near the lower trendline and sell near the upper one, then go short. Occasionally, a symmetrical triangle is wide enough and long enough that you can profitably trade it in this manner, but you have to be nimble. If you are inexperienced, be sure to practice this on paper before trying it with real money.

Sample Trade

Can you make money on symmetrical triangles? Yes. Consider the trade I made in the stock shown in Figure 40.8. There were a number of factors that led me to this stock, including a rising rig count, rising oil prices, cold weather, and related political events (OPEC tightening and possible oil boycott against Nigeria). All of these factors suggested the price of oil during the winter would continue rising and demand for the oil field services industry would remain strong.

Another factor was that the stock price was riding along the bottom of a trend channel. The method used to create the trend channel is somewhat complicated but it involves drawing a line using linear regression on the closing prices then plotting two lines parallel to the regression line, each two standard deviations away. Figure 40.8 shows the upper line of the channel. I did not draw the lower line, but it intersects point A and is parallel to the top channel line. The trend channel suggests prices would move from one side of the channel to the other.

Since the upside breakout was on weak volume, I decided to hold off and wait for a throwback. This was a risky maneuver, but it worked out. On December 1, I bought the stock and received a fill at 9⅛.

The apex of a symmetrical triangle is often a place of support or resistance. You can see this on the chart. Prices declined to the apex and stayed there for 3 days. As predicted, the stock took off and climbed after that. Even though the stock fulfilled the measure rule, I suspected that it would continue crossing to the upper channel line. The stock stalled out midway across the channel, pausing at the linear regression line (not shown, but it is equidistant between the top channel line and point A). This is often the case and I was anticipating such a pause.

In about a week, prices started moving up again and quickly made a new high. When prices touched the top of the trend channel, I considered selling but did not for tax reasons. I decided to hold off until the new year—just 2 trading days away. On January 2 I sold the stock and received a fill at 11⅝. The delay in selling dropped my return from nearly 40% to 27%. Still, that is not a bad return for a hold time of 1 month!

41

Triangles, Symmetrical Tops

RESULTS SNAPSHOT

Downside Breakouts

Appearance	In a rising price trend, prices form lower highs and higher lows following two sloping trendlines that eventually intersect. The breakout is downward.
Reversal or consolidation	Short-term (up to 3 months) bearish reversal
Failure rate	6%
Average decline	20%, with most likely decline being 15%
Volume trend	Downward
Premature breakout	19%
Pullbacks	59%
Percentage meeting predicted price target	62%
Surprising finding	Premature breakouts occur a bit sooner than genuine breakouts and sometimes on light volume.
Synonyms	Coils
See also	Head-and-Shoulders Tops; Shark-32; Triangles, Ascending; Triangles, Descending; Triangles, Symmetrical Bottoms

Upside Breakouts

Appearance	In a rising price trend, prices form lower highs and higher lows following two sloping trendlines that eventually intersect. The breakout is upward.
Reversal or consolidation	Short-term (up to 3 months) bullish consolidation
Failure rate	5%
Average rise	37%, with most likely rise being 20%
Volume trend	Downward
Premature breakout	14%
Throwbacks	58%
Percentage meeting predicted price target	81%
Synonym	Coils
See also	Head-and-Shoulders Tops; Shark-32; Triangles, Ascending; Triangles, Descending; Triangles, Symmetrical Bottoms

Those of you familiar with symmetrical triangles might wonder how I separated them into tops and bottoms. I use the price trend leading to the formation. Symmetrical triangle tops have prices that trend up to the formation, whereas bottoms have prices leading down. I separated them by price trend in the hope that it would allow prediction of the breakout direction. Alas, it did not. This chapter concerns itself with symmetrical triangle tops.

The failure rates for symmetrical triangle tops are low at 6% and 5% for the two breakout directions. This compares favorably with the maximum 20% rate I consider reliable formations to possess.

Downside breakouts shows losses of 20%, about average for bearish formations. Upside breakouts, however, underperform with gains of 37% instead of the usual 40% for bullish chart patterns. But they are solid performers according to the measure rule (81% hit their targets). I consider values above 80% to be reliable. Downside breakouts fall short with only 62% meeting or exceeding their price targets.

An interesting finding is that premature breakouts occur about 71% to 76% of the way to triangle apex (versus 78% to 79% for genuine breakouts) and sometimes on quite light volume.

Tour

Figure 41.1 shows an example of a symmetrical triangle top. Prices rise to the start of the formation and make a new high. Then prices cross the formation from side to side, making lower highs and higher lows. After nearly 2 months, the trends are in place. A down-sloping trendline drawn along the tops connects the minor highs, whereas an up-sloping trendline on the bottom supports the minor lows.

The volume trend recedes although it is spiky in places. Prices attempt to leave the formation in late June but get sucked back in. They try again and with higher volume shoot out the top of the triangle but quickly throw back, curl around, and head lower.

Why do symmetrical triangles form? With tops, they usually form near the yearly high and that poses their first challenge. Prices zoom up making higher highs on succeeding days. Eventually, selling pressure quenches demand for the stock and prices turn down. The momentum players, sensing a change in trend, quickly sell some of their holdings, putting additional pressure on the stock. Prices fall to a level where prior support set up by a peak months earlier or various other factors entice investors to view the stock as a bargain. The price is shooting up, they reason, so why not join the trend especially now that it is at a cheaper price?

Such rationalizations increase demand and send the stock up again but this time the momentum players that missed a chance to sell earlier do so now.

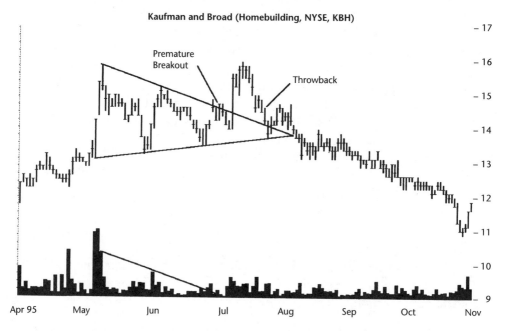

Figure 41.1   A symmetrical triangle top. Prices trend up to the formation.

Others, believing that there may not be enough upward momentum to carry the stock to the old high, sell too. The selling pressure halts the price rise at a lower level and turns it around.

Value investors seeing the stock drop, and since the fundamentals have not changed, buy it on the way down. Some add to their positions at a lower price and others buy it for the first time. The buying may force prices to move horizontally for a bit instead of straight down. Eventually, though, a higher low forms not so much from anxious buyers, but from a dearth of sellers.

Throughout the trend, volume is decreasing. Fewer and fewer shares are being traded and it becomes easier for the stock to change direction. Eventually, though, a large buy order comes in and prices rise. When they pierce the top trendline, they may begin to take out the orders that investors have placed to buy when prices rise above the trendline. This additional buying cascades and prices soar on heavy volume.

If demand is strong enough, prices continue rising. About half the time, though, prices spin around and head back to the triangle boundary—a throwback. There prices meet support at the top trendline or at the level of the triangle apex. Usually, prices rebound and continue in their original direction. Sometimes, though, prices continue down, signaling an end to the upward trend (such as that shown in Figure 41.1).

Identification Guidelines

Table 41.1 lists identification guidelines for symmetrical triangle tops.

Consider Figure 41.2, a symmetrical triangle with a premature upside breakout. The overall shape of the formation is triangular and defined by two trendlines: One slopes downward from the top and the other slopes upward from the bottom so that they join at the apex.

Numbers mark the minor highs and lows, which touch or come close to each trendline at least twice. That is important as the touches should be distinct individual hills (minor highs) and valleys (minor lows).

The volume pattern has a downward slope to it. Turnover may increase when prices rise and decline when prices fall, but the overall trend is receding. Let me say it is unusual for a symmetrical triangle to not have a receding volume trend, but that does not mean it will not happen. Even when volume does taper off, it may not be noticeable unless you run linear regression and look at the slope of the resulting line. However, more than 80% of the triangles do show a receding volume trend, high enough to make you consider any deviations carefully.

In a historical price series, a premature breakout is when prices close outside the formation trendlines (either above or below) but quickly return, usually within a few days. Not only do prices return, but they do so before the triangle

Table 41.1
Identification Characteristics of Symmetrical Triangle Tops

Characteristic	Discussion
Shape	A triangular shape forms within the confines of two trendlines, one sloping up and the other down so that they intersect at the triangle apex. The trendlines need not be the same length.
Touches	There should be at least two distinct minor highs and two minor lows that touch the trendlines (in other words, at least four trend reversals).
Volume	Usually recedes throughout the formation but can be irregular and is often very low just before the breakout.
Premature breakout	Has at least one close outside the triangle but prices soon return within the triangle borders before reaching the triangle apex. Breaks out a bit sooner than genuine breakouts and sometimes on light volume.
Breakout direction	Unknown ahead of time. A breakout has prices moving well away from the triangle, not quickly returning as in a premature breakout. If they do return (a throwback or pullback), prices generally bounce off the trendline or apex.
Duration	Typically longer than 3 weeks, at a minimum. Formations 3 weeks or less classify as pennants.

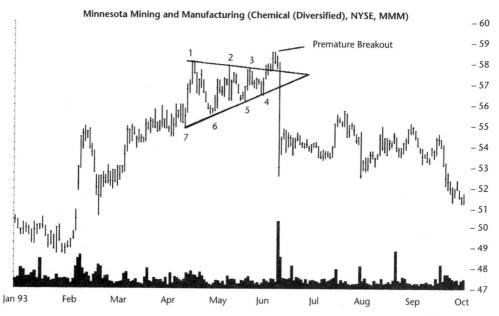

Figure 41.2 A symmetrical triangle top with a premature breakout. Prices close outside the triangle but return before the apex. In this instance, prices not only return but shoot out the other side. Numbers mark the various trendline touches. A dead-cat bounce sees prices tumble $5 in 1 day then bounce up and eventually move lower.

564

apex. We see in the Statistics section of this chapter that a premature breakout sometimes occurs sooner than a genuine breakout and on light volume.

Genuine breakouts, in comparison, usually soar well beyond the formation. If prices throw back to the top or pull back from the bottom, they do so either after the triangle apex or touch the trendlines and rebound. Sometimes, though, prices do return for more work within the triangle confines, then burst back out, occasionally in the adverse direction.

When considering a triangle such as that shown in Figure 41.2, prices break out downward because of a trend change. After establishing the breakout direction, it is easy to label the brief breakout on the top as a premature one. Prices ease out of the formation top and quickly return, albeit on their way to the other side. The upward momentum of the premature breakout is unsustainable and prices drop $5 in one session, forming a dead-cat bounce. Prices continued down, eventually reaching a low of 46⅜, a drop of 20%.

Figure 41.3 shows two triangle formations. The one on the left is not a valid symmetrical triangle. The left triangle forms beginning from the minor low at point A and rises to the minor high at point B. Then prices decline following the top trendline and reach the minor low at point C. Notice that there is only one minor high (point B) and two minor lows, but the second minor low, point C, is not included in the triangle. Not only is there a minor high and low missing, but the bottom trendline is drawn incorrectly as well. The white

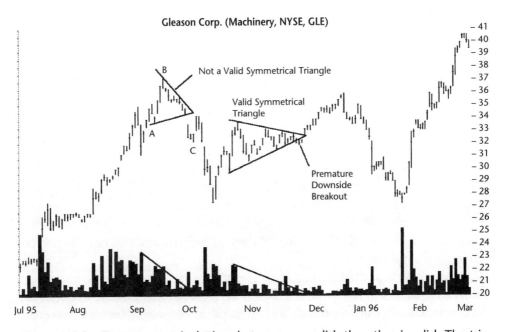

Figure 41.3 Two symmetrical triangle tops, one valid, the other invalid. The triangle on the right shows a premature downside breakout followed by a valid upside breakout. The triangle on the left is bogus.

space in the center of the triangle is often a clue to an improperly identified formation. Prices should cross the formation and fill the space.

The second triangle shown in mid-October has plenty of minor highs and lows that touch the two trendlines. It is a valid symmetrical triangle but it has a kicker. Just before the triangle apex, prices move outside the triangle trend-line boundaries, pull back, and move sharply higher.

I do not consider this downward poke to be a downside breakout because the breakout direction is predominantly upward (that is the direction in which prices moved furthest). I call the 3-day downside move a premature breakout. A premature breakout, either upward or downward, must have a daily close outside the triangle trendlines and must eventually return to the chart pattern.

The volume trend is predominantly downward in both chart patterns. Volume is 60,100 shares at the start of the October triangle but recedes until the day before the breakout, when only 4,600 shares trade. Quite a decline.

Before you pronounce a chart pattern to be a symmetrical triangle, look to the left of the formation. Is there a minor high that mirrors the one on the left? If so, then you might be looking at a head-and-shoulders top.

A mirror image of the symmetrical triangle, one that is back to back with the one you have selected, probably represents a diamond top or bottom. When one of the trendlines is horizontal, then the formation is an ascending or descending triangle. All these other formations are ones that you need to search for. Many are more powerful than a symmetrical triangle and give a better gauge to the ultimate price move.

Focus on Failures

If you have searched for other patterns and are sure a symmetrical triangle is valid, how can you be sure it is going to work as expected? You cannot. Look at Figure 41.4. It is a symmetrical triangle with a downside breakout. The break-out pulls back to the lower trendline, begins drifting down again, then just as quickly returns to the triangle apex. It brushes by the formation and moves horizontally for a month before resuming the intermediate-term uptrend.

Figure 41.4 shows what I call a 5% failure. A 5% failure is when prices break out and move less than 5% before turning around and moving substantially in the other direction. Fortunately, 5% failures are rare with symmetrical triangles. However, as you can see, they do happen, and you need to protect yourself from them.

As you look at the figure, you can see that prices initially break out downward after having moved up from the lows in August. Most of the triangles act as a consolidation of the trend, so that is the direction to bet on. Since the trend is upward leading to the formation, prices should shoot out the top, but they do not. When they go against the grain, ask yourself if that is the natural flow. Is there a fundamental reason prices are moving down? If you do not

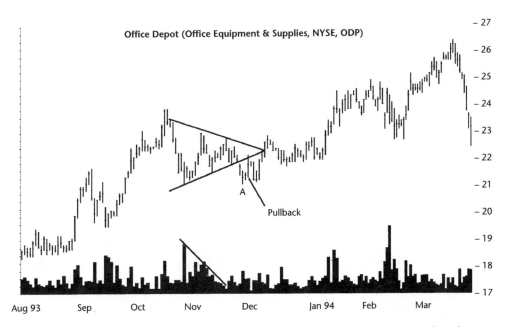

Figure 41.4 A symmetrical triangle that is a 5% failure. Here prices break out downward and pull back to the formation, curl around the apex, and eventually move higher. The formation is a 5% failure because prices decline less than 5% (to point A) before reversing.

know the answer, then do not make a trade. If you decide to short a stock, make sure you use a stop to limit your losses. Move your stop downward as prices decline so that you catch as much of the move as possible.

Statistics

Table 41.2 shows the first batch of statistics for symmetrical triangle tops. I separated the 400 or so formations I uncovered into tops and bottoms, depending on the price trend leading to the formation. Tops have prices trending up; bottoms have them moving down. Then I separated the chart patterns into those with upside and downside breakouts and list the figures separately.

I uncovered almost twice as many triangles with upward breakouts than with downward ones. Since the entry into the formation is from a rising price trend, those formations with upward breakouts act as consolidations of the price trend.

The failure rates, at 5% and 6% for the two breakout directions, are well below the 20% maximum that reliable formations share. Only 14 formations fail out of over 250, which is a very good score.

The average rise from an upside breakout is 37%, slightly below the usual 40% for bullish formations. Downside breakouts perform in line with

Table 41.2
General Statistics for Symmetrical Triangle Tops

Description	Upside Breakout	Downside Breakout
Number of formations in 500 stocks from 1991 to 1996	162	93
Reversal or consolidation	162 consolidations	93 reversals
Failure rate	8 or 5%	6 or 6%
Average rise/decline of successful formations	37%	20%
Most likely rise/decline	20%	15%
Of those succeeding, number meeting or exceeding price target (measure rule)	124 or 81%	54 or 62%
Average formation length	2 months (57 days)	2 months (50 days)
Breakout as percentage of distance to apex	78%	79%

expectations by declining 20% on average. The most likely gain is 20% and 15% for upside and downside breakouts.

Figure 41.5 shows a frequency distribution of losses, indicating where losses from most trades reside. In this case, there are few large declines so the most likely decline is also the tallest column (the one with the highest frequency). Almost half the formations (46%) have losses less than 15% and 77% have declines less than 25%. If you decide to short a stock, your losses might not be as large as you hope.

Figure 41.6 shows a frequency distribution of gains with the 20% column towering above the others. It is reassuring that only a third of the formations have gains less than 20%. To put it more optimistically, 65% of the formations have gains over 20%. With such large gains, you would expect the measure rule to perform well. It does, with 81% of the formations meeting or exceeding their price targets. I consider values over 80% to be reliable. Downside breakouts perform less well, with just 62% of the formations meeting their targets. I explain the use of the measure rule in the Trading Tactics section of this chapter.

The average formation length is about 2 months and both upward and downward breakouts exit close to 80% of the way to the apex. I took a closer look at the breakout distance to the apex and graphed the results in Figure 41.7 The figure shows that most formations have breakouts that hover around 80% to 85% of the way to the apex. I originally thought that most symmetrical triangles had breakouts that were about two-thirds of the way to the apex, just as do ascending and descending triangles. But symmetrical triangle formations break out later. This gives an aggressive investor more opportunity to profit

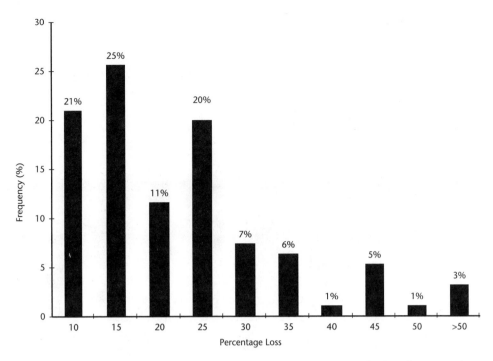

Figure 41.5 Frequency distribution of losses for symmetrical triangle tops. Note that the most likely decline is 15%.

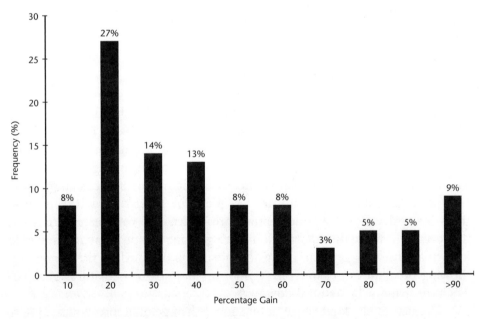

Figure 41.6 Frequency distribution of gains for symmetrical triangle tops. The most likely gain is 20%.

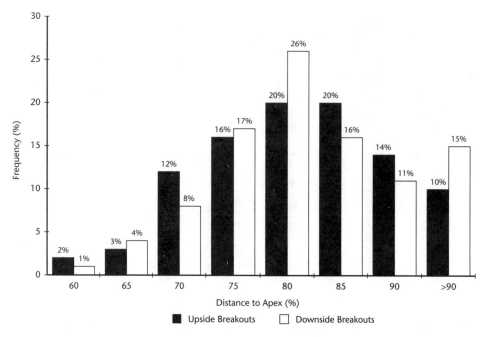

Figure 41.7 Frequency distribution of the breakout distance to the apex. Most formations break out 80% to 85% of the way to the apex.

from the intraformation swings: Buy or cover your short at the lower trendline and sell or sell short at the top trendline.

Table 41.3 shows various statistics related to premature breakouts. A premature breakout is when prices close outside the formation boundary but quickly return to the chart pattern, usually within a few days. Premature breakouts are rare, occurring less than 20% of the time for both breakout directions.

Premature upside breakouts are more plentiful (16%) in genuine downside breakouts than in upside ones (3%). Volume at an upside premature breakout is below average, at 88% of the 25-day moving average, but is 116% when it appears in formations where the genuine breakout is downward. Downside premature breakouts are less plentiful, at 12% and 10%, respectively for upside and downside genuine breakouts. The volume pattern is just the reverse: heavy in those formations with genuine upside breakouts and light in formations with genuine downside breakouts. A third of the formations showing premature breakouts have both up and down premature breakouts when the genuine breakout is downward.

Premature breakouts occur a bit sooner than genuine breakouts (71% to 76% of the way to the apex versus 78% or 79%). If you see a breakout occur earlier than normal accompanied by light volume, you should consider passing up the trade.

Table 41.4 outlines breakout statistics for symmetrical triangle tops. Throwbacks and pullbacks occur about 58% or 59% of the time. That statis-

Table 41.3
Premature Breakout Statistics for Symmetrical Triangle Tops

Description	Breakout Upward	Breakout Downward
Number of premature breakouts (up or down)	23 or 14%	18 or 19%
Number of premature upside breakouts	5 or 3%	15 or 16%
Volume at upside premature breakout	88% of 25-day moving average	116% of 25-day moving average
Number of premature downside breakouts	20 or 12%	9 or 10%
Volume at downside premature breakout	229% of 25-day moving average	66% of 25-day moving average
Of formations showing premature breakouts, number having both up and down premature breakouts	2 or 9%	6 or 33%
Upside premature breakout distance to apex	76%	74%
Downside premature breakout distance to apex	72%	71%

Note: Premature breakouts occur sooner and sometimes on lighter volume.

tic is not quite enough to include in your trading plan, but throwbacks and pullbacks give you the opportunity to add to your position. On average, they take just short of 2 weeks to return to the trendlines or triangle apex.

It takes almost three times as long to reach the ultimate high as the ultimate low. That is a bit longer to travel not quite twice as far than is shown by other chart types.

Table 41.4
Breakout Statistics for Symmetrical Triangle Tops

Description	Upside Breakout	Downside Breakout
Throwbacks/pullbacks	94 or 58%	55 or 59%
Average time to throwback/pullback completion	13 days	11 days
For successful formations, days to ultimate high/low	6.5 months (192 days)	2 months (70 days)
Percentage of breakouts occurring near 12-month low (L), center (C), or high (H)	L7%, C22%, H71%	L10%, C30%, H61%
Percentage gain/loss for each 12-month lookback period	L29%, C35%, H40%	L23%, C20%, H20%

Where in the yearly price range do breakouts occur? Both breakout directions have the majority of breakouts within a third of the yearly high. This is perhaps not surprising since, by definition, prices rise up to the start of the formation. Such a rise should help boost the breakout into the higher reaches of the yearly price range. Mapping performance onto the yearly price range shows that breakouts near the yearly high do well, with gains averaging 40%, whereas when breakouts occur in the lowest third of the price range they score just 29%.

Downside breakouts split evenly at about 20% each, with the lowest range outperforming with losses averaging 23%. The numbers reinforce the belief that you should short stocks making new lows, not new highs. Those making new highs tend to continue rising.

Table 41.5 shows volume statistics for symmetrical triangle tops. The vast majority, over 80% in each case, have a downward volume trend as measured by the slope of a linear regression line of volume. You can see in the table that the day after the breakout usually scores the highest volume. It seems that once investors see the breakout on their charts in the evening, they trade on the news the next day.

Are low volume breakouts more susceptible to throwbacks or pullbacks? No and yes. I rated a low volume breakout to be 50% of the 25-day moving average and a high volume breakout as 150% of the moving average. For upside breakouts, only 6% of the formations throw back after a low volume breakout, whereas 56% throw back after a high volume breakout. For downside breakouts, the results split at low volume, 24%, and at high volume, 20%. In both cases, the sample size is small and that perhaps explains the conflicting results.

Table 41.5
Volume Statistics for Symmetrical Triangle Tops

Description	Breakout Upward	Breakout Downward
Number showing downward volume trend	131 or 81%	79 or 85%
Volume for breakout day and next 5 days compared with day before breakout	167%, 170%, 161%, 137%, 124%, 136%,	153%, 173%, 154%, 132%, 117%, 132%
Are low volume breakouts more subject to throwback/pullback?	No	Yes
Performance of high volume breakouts versus low volume breakouts	38% versus 35%	21% versus 20%

Do high volume breakouts result in large price moves? A high volume upside breakout carries prices 38% higher, whereas a low volume breakout only sees prices climb by 35%, on average. For downside breakout, the results are closer at 21% and 20%, respectively. The results are statistically significant only for downside breakouts. This means the upside breakout results may or may not be due to chance.

Trading Tactics

Table 41.6 shows trading tactics for symmetrical triangle tops. The first trading tactic is to estimate how far prices will move. Figure 41.8 shows an example of how the measure rule applies to a symmetrical triangle top formation.

The triangle has a low at the start of the formation of $18\frac{7}{8}$ (point B). Subtract it from the high, point A, at $23\frac{1}{2}$. The result is the triangle height, or $4\frac{5}{8}$. For upside breakouts, add the height to the highest high to compute the target price ($28\frac{1}{8}$). For downside breakouts, subtract the height from the lowest low for the downside price target ($14\frac{1}{4}$). The target price serves as a minimum and prices should exceed the target, especially for upside breakouts.

When you compare the number of reversals to triangles that act as consolidations of the prevailing trend, you find that consolidations win easily. Knowing that, the best trading methodology is to anticipate a breakout resuming the

Table 41.6
Trading Tactics for Symmetrical Triangle Tops

Trading Tactic	Explanation
Measure rule	Compute the formation height by subtracting the lowest low from the highest high. For upside breakouts, add the height to the highest high; for downside breakouts, subtract the height from the lowest low. Alternatively, symmetrical triangles can be halfway points in a move, so project accordingly.
Trade with the trend	As consolidations, prices usually leave the triangle, resuming the intermediate-term price trend.
Wait for breakout	Always wait for the breakout in case the triangle reverses, then trade with the trend.
Stops	Place a stop-loss order $\frac{1}{8}$ above the triangle high (downside breakouts) or below the triangle low (upside breakouts). If this is too wide, use a closer support or resistance point and adjust the stops as prices move in your favor.
Intrapattern trade	If the triangle is wide and long enough, sell or sell short at the top trendline and buy or cover at the bottom one.

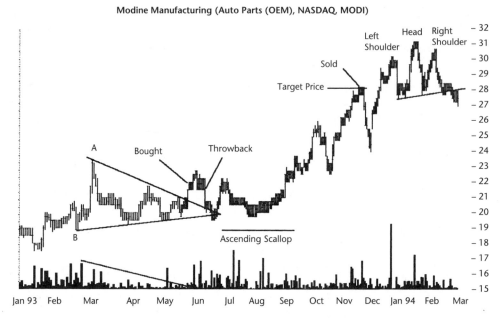

Figure 41.8   A symmetrical triangle top followed by an ascending scallop and a head-and-shoulders top. To use the measure rule, subtract the low (point B) from the high (point A) to get the formation height. For upside breakouts, add the height to point A and for downside breakouts, subtract it from point B. The result is the expected target price.

direction of the intermediate-term price trend. If prices were rising leading to the formation, they should break out upward and continue up.

However, since these chart patterns do reverse about a third of the time, it can pay to wait for the actual breakout. Once prices close outside the trendline, take a position in the stock by trading with the trend (go long on an upside breakout and short on a downside one).

Place your initial stop just above the highest high or below the lowest low in the triangle. In Figure 41.8, place the stop at 18¾, or ⅛ below point B. Many times, if prices reverse, they either stop at the trendline or triangle apex. When they fall below the lowest low or rise above the highest high, then you know prices are moving against you and it is time to close out the trade.

If the triangle is tall enough, consider making an intraformation trade. Buy when prices touch or near the bottom trendline and begin moving up, or sell short as they round over at the top. If you are lucky, you will be in the correct direction for the breakout and can let the trade ride.

As prices move in the breakout direction, move your stop to capture more of the profit. That way, even if the formation flames out quickly, you will have captured a measure of profit.

Sample Trade

Father Flannigan is a priest who tends his flock in a church near where I live. He is your typical man-of-the-cloth conservative. In his trading he likes to play it safe and tries not to be greedy.

He first noticed the symmetrical triangle shown in Figure 41.8 in mid-May, just as prices touched the lower boundary. He reviewed the identification guidelines and convinced himself that he had identified the triangle properly.

The day after prices closed outside the top trendline, he placed an order to buy the stock and received a fill at $21\frac{3}{4}$, about midrange for the trading day. Immediately after a phone call confirmed the order, he scurried into the church and said a prayer for divine intervention leading to a profitable trade.

His prayers seemed answered in the days that followed as prices rose steadily to a high of $22\frac{3}{4}$ before trouble set in. Prices began heading down and Father Flannigan wondered what he could do to change matters. He called his broker and placed a stop-loss order at $18\frac{3}{4}$, $\frac{1}{8}$ below the lowest formation low (shown as point B).

As prices descended, he spent more time in church asking for forgiveness for his sins and a little help with the trade. A crack of thunder announced that He was not pleased and prices threw back to the triangle apex and a little below. Prices hovered there for 3 days then began climbing slowly at first, but rapidly gaining momentum.

Now that the throwback was complete, Father Flannigan computed the target price using the measure rule and came up with $28\frac{1}{8}$. He called his broker, canceled his stop, and placed a limit order to sell his shares should prices reach the target.

For almost 2 weeks, things were looking up as prices climbed to $22\frac{1}{4}$ then stalled. Again, prices faded down to the triangle apex at 20 and moved horizontally for a few weeks in the heat of August. Then they rounded up in a small ascending scallop formation and Father Flannigan went to the church and counted his blessings—all three hundred shares worth.

Nervousness in mid-October forced the shares to tumble from a high of 26 down to $22\frac{1}{2}$. Father Flannigan tried to place a stop-loss order but his broker would not allow both a stop-loss and a limit order to sell the shares at the same time, so he quietly watched his stock from his laptop while sitting in a pew.

In late October prices began recovering and he breathed easier. In mid-November prices finally reached his limit price and his shares sold at $28\frac{1}{8}$, days before it tumbled to 24.

42

Triple Bottoms

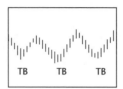

RESULTS SNAPSHOT

Appearance	Three distinct minor lows at about the same price level
Reversal or consolidation	Short-term (up to 3 months) bullish reversal
Failure rate	4%
Average rise	38%, with most likely rise being 20%
Volume trend	Downward
Throwbacks	70%
Percentage meeting predicted price target	73%
Surprising findings	Formations with a third bottom above the second one perform better with an average gain of 48% versus 31%. Formations with higher volume on the right bottom, when compared to the center one, have gains averaging 40% versus 28% for the reverse combination.
See also	Broadening Bottoms; Broadening Formations, Right-Angled and Descending; Broadening Wedges, Descending; Head-and-Shoulders Bottoms; Head-and-Shoulders Bottoms, Complex; Triangles, Descending

One of the surprising things about triple bottoms is their low failure rate: 4%. For some reason, I expected it to be higher. If one plays by the rules and waits for an upside breakout, then few triple bottoms fail to continue moving up, many times substantially. The average rise is 38% with a likely gain of 20%, about what you would expect from bullish formations.

Almost three out of four formations (70%) throw back to the breakout point. This is somewhat misleading because the breakout point can be far removed from the final trough—an average of almost 6 weeks away. But the time is well spent as prices climb from the third recession to the breakout or confirmation point.

Just for kicks, I measured the average gain for those formations with a third bottom *above* the low posted by the second one. The gain is 48%, whereas those with a third bottom *below* the second one score gains averaging just 31%. The differences are statistically significant but it may surprise you to learn the average price difference between the two bottoms is only 35 cents.

Volume is important to performance. When the volume on the center bottom is below that of the last bottom, the formations have gains averaging 40%. With the reverse situation where the center bottom has the higher volume of the two, performance dwindles to 28%. I explore statistics later in this chapter.

Tour

Figure 42.1 shows an example of a triple bottom. Prices descend to the 37 area three times and each time, they turn away; the level marks a zone of support preventing future declines. The sharp V-shaped recession, especially during the last valley, is typical for triple bottoms. The rounded-looking rise from the first valley to the second is also characteristic of triple bottoms but not a strict requirement.

The price level of the three valleys is nearly the same, in this case, within $\frac{3}{8}$ of one another. That is a key element of triple bottoms as we see in the Identification Guidelines section.

Each chart formation is unique with characteristics that distinguish it from other patterns, and the one in Figure 42.1 is no exception. The stock reaches a low in mid-October 1992, after trending down for 5 months. Then prices retrace their losses and stray into new high territory before heading down to the first triple bottom low. Support reached during formation of the first low is set up by the peak back in May 1992. Prices climb to the 37 area several times from January to May but fail to burst through the resistance.

The multiple hits on the ceiling are in no small measure responsible for the support the triple bottom encounters. As prices descend to 37, investors willing to part with their shares at the lower level are scarce. When someone does offer to sell, buyers snatch the stock believing they are getting a good bargain. And they are right. Prices do not meander at the 37 level for long. If you

Figure 42.1 A somewhat unusual triple bottom as it forms in the middle of a rising price trend. Prices eventually rise to $67\frac{1}{2}$ from the confirmation level of $46\frac{1}{2}$.

look closely at Figure 42.1, each valley floor is a 1-day downward spike, albeit small but visible.

The start of the formation, from the first to the second bottom, looks like a broadening top, right-angled and ascending with its horizontal bottom and up-sloping top trendline. However, there are not enough price crossings to really validate the formation. It always makes me nervous when I see plenty of white space in a formation (such as that shown between the first and second bottoms). When the rise between the second and third troughs fails to come anywhere near the up-sloping trendline, the jig is up.

Prices stop rising at the same point, about 46, making the triple bottom look like a double top. This, too, fails to come to fruition when prices reach the 37 support zone and turn around. The double top remains unconfirmed and it just becomes another two bumps on the price chart.

The convoluted creation of a triple bottom helps explain why the formation is so scarce, but I discuss statistics later. First, how do you identify a triple bottom?

Identification Guidelines

Table 42.1 outlines the guidelines for identifying triple bottoms. I think most technical analysts will tell you that not any three bottoms will do for a triple bottom. The three bottoms are usually large and well separated with generally

Table 42.1
Identification Characteristics of Triple Bottoms

Characteristic	Discussion
Three large, distinct bottoms	Look for three minor lows, well separated and distinct. The bottoms are usually large but sharp, and the price rise between them often appears rounded but need not be.
Same price	The price variation among the three bottoms is minor. The center bottom should not be significantly below the other two, otherwise it is a head-and-shoulders bottom.
Downward volume trend	The overall volume trend is usually downward but may be high in each of the three bottoms. Volume is usually highest on the first bottom and weakest on the last one.
Confirmation point	Prices must rise above the highest high in the formation (the confirmation point) or the chart pattern is not a triple bottom.
Weekly chart	Since triple bottoms are usually large price formations, look at the weekly chart to help identify the longer variety.

rounded rises in between. The lowest price in each bottom is at about the same level. If the center price is lower than the other two, then you might be looking at a head-and-shoulders bottom. When the bottoms are successively lower in price, it might be one of the broadening series of formations (broadening bottoms; broadening formations, right-angled and descending; broadening formations, right-angled and ascending if the bottoms are flat but the tops form successively higher peaks; and broadening wedges), so consult the appropriate chapter on those formations.

The volume trend usually recedes over the course of the formation. Since the formation tends to be long, the volume pattern appears ragged or irregular at times. Each of the three bottoms usually shows volume that peaks above the days leading to the bottom with the first bottom usually having the highest volume of the trio. In the Statistics section of this chapter we delve into the volume pattern more thoroughly.

Now that we have reviewed most of the guidelines, what does a triple bottom look like? Figure 42.2 shows a good example of a triple bottom. Notice the three downward price recessions. They are distinct and separated with the rally between each bottom quite pronounced. Prices rise from the low of about 35 to the confirmation line just over 40. The confirmation line is the highest high reached during the chart pattern. It serves as the breakout point, the point to which prices must rise before any three minor lows become a true triple bottom. When prices rise above the confirmation line, the formation confirms and prices should continue rising.

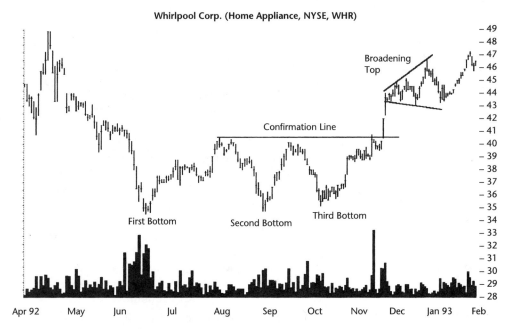

Figure 42.2   A triple bottom with three widely spaced, distinct troughs. A broadening top appears in mid-November.

You can see in Figure 42.2 that the three bottoms are at nearly the same price. Only the last bottom falls short of the goal. As we see in the Statistics section, this often signals a better performing formation. This triple bottom is the beginning of a large, extended move that takes prices from a low of $34\frac{1}{2}$ to a high of $73\frac{1}{2}$ in 16 months.

The volume trend in this formation is downward with the largest concentration of high volume on the first bottom. The center bottom has subdued volume and is even lower on the third bottom in early October. Volume spikes upward as prices rise to the confirmation point in mid-November. Then, prices consolidate for about a week before attempting to pierce the old resistance line at $40\frac{1}{2}$. On above average volume, prices push through the old barrier and quickly jump three points, build a broadening top formation, then continue higher.

Triple bottoms are usually large enough to be visible on weekly charts such as that shown in Figure 42.3. The three minor lows are evident in the weekly chart. The first rally peaking in early May marks the high point that later becomes the confirmation level. The climb between the second and third bottom is suspiciously flat, but rarely does any chart pattern fit the ideal shape. In this instance, each bottom is successively lower than the prior one. A lower low price on the last bottom is a clue to impending underperformance. That is exactly what happens as prices climb above the confirmation point of $21\frac{3}{8}$ to reach a high of 26 before heading back down. Although the 22% gain is below average, it is still better than taking a loss.

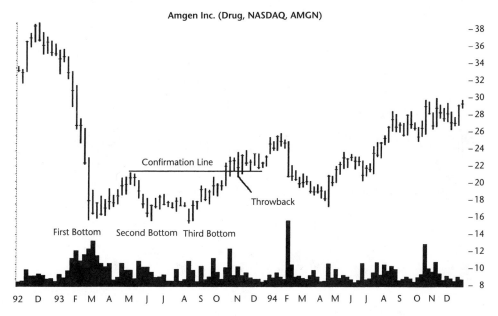

Figure 42.3 Triple bottom on the weekly scale. Many triple bottoms are visible on the weekly scale due to their long duration.

Investors not selling at the high see their investment dwindle to 17⅜ by late April 1994. If they hold their shares, the stock rebounds and does much better, topping out at 66½ in early March 1996.

The throwback to the confirmation line could encompass any number of weeks beginning in late October 1993. Prices pierce the confirmation line, moving up, then throw back to it within a month. Prices returning to the confirmation line beyond the 30-day time limit classify as normal price action, not throwbacks.

Focus on Failures

Once prices reach the confirmation line, they usually have been rising for well over a month, on average, since the third bottom. Prices often pierce the resistance line but double back, hesitating before continuing up—most of the time. In some cases, prices rise above the confirmation point by less than 5% before throwing back and continuing down. When that happens, it is called a 5% failure. In this study of triple bottoms, all chart patterns must stage an upside breakout (a rise above the highest high in the formation) before being labeled a triple bottom. Since all formations have upside breakouts, only 5% failures remain to wipe the warm glow of a successful investment from a novice investor's face. Fortunately, 5% failures are rare. Only five (4%) fail to continue moving up. Figure 42.4 shows an example of such a failure.

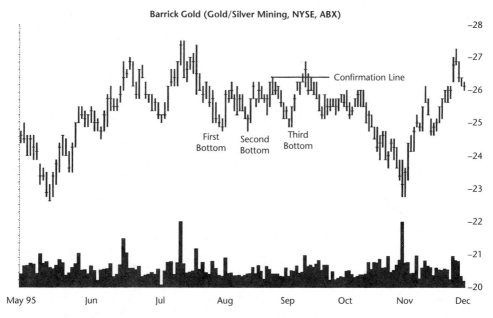

Figure 42.4 A triple bottom failure. This triple bottom fails to make a convincing upward run. It is a 5% failure since prices fail to rise by more than 5% before tumbling.

The triple bottom is immediately suspicious because it does not occur at a bottom. Prices round up beginning in mid-May, curl around, and head back down, retracing their gains by November. On a short-term basis, prices move down from a high of $27\frac{1}{2}$ in mid-July to the first bottom at $24\frac{3}{4}$. The formation is a triple bottom since prices rise above the confirmation point in mid-September. But the rise is brief—only 1 day has a close above the confirmation line before prices tumble.

What are the signs of a budding failure? In this situation, the curved rise leading to the triple bottom suggests a rounding top. The volume pattern is suspiciously flat, but an irregular or abnormal pattern is common and should not automatically disqualify a formation. Perhaps the most likely failure is not one of performance but of identification. Are the three bottoms well separated, each a significant minor low in its own right? Are the low prices near to one another without the center bottom being meaningfully below the other two?

As you look at the formation, it should take on a striking appearance and almost say to you, "Yes, I am a triple bottom!" There should be something familiar, a special quality that distinguishes a valid triple bottom from any other three-lump configuration. If it does not scream, "Buy me!" then you should probably look elsewhere.

One last point. If you discover four or five triple bottoms in a stock, then you are probably making an identification mistake. This is a rare formation, appearing only 122 times in 2,500 years of daily price data.

Statistics

Table 42.2 shows the first batch of statistics for triple bottoms. As mentioned earlier, triple bottoms are comparatively rare. I uncovered only 122 of them in 500 stocks over 5 years. Most act as reversals of the prevailing trend.

The failure rate for triple bottoms is only 4%, very good for a bullish bottom. All measurements begin at the confirmation point—the highest high between the three bottoms. Prices have to rise above this point or the formation is not a triple bottom. Then prices have to continue rallying by more than 5% or the formation is a 5% failure. With such a low failure rate, once prices rise above the confirmation point, they continue moving up (but they do throw back, so watch for it). A formation also fails when prices decline below the lowest low. With such a hefty decline needed before the formation fails, that may help explain the low failure rate.

The average rise above the confirmation point is 38% with a likely gain of 20%. The most likely gain derives from the frequency distribution of gains shown in Figure 42.5. Although the 20% column has the highest frequency, the surrounding columns are almost as high. It might be wise to suggest that the most likely gain could range anywhere from zero to 50%. The frequency of gains over 50% tapers off quickly, though.

Table 42.2
General Statistics for Triple Bottoms

Description	Statistic
Number of formations in 500 stocks from 1991 to 1996	122
Reversal or consolidation	41 consolidations, 81 reversals
Failure rate	5 or 4%
Average rise of successful formations	38%
Most likely rise	20%
Of those succeeding, number meeting or exceeding price target (measure rule)	85 or 73%
Average formation length	4 months (122 days)
Days between bottoms	1 & 2, 61 days; 2 & 3, 60 days
Formation end to upside breakout	42 days
Throwbacks	86 or 70%
Average time to throwback completion	9 days
For successful formations, days to ultimate high	7.5 months (221 days)
Percentage of breakouts occurring near 12-month low (L), center (C), or high (H)	L19%, C33%, H48%
Percentage gain for each 12-month lookback period	L39%, C38%, H36%

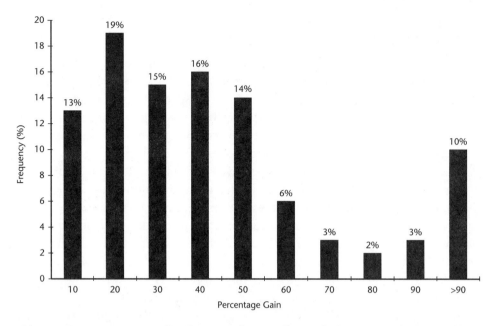

Figure 42.5 Frequency distribution of gains for triple bottoms. The most likely rise is 20%, the column with the highest frequency. However, the 10% through 50% columns are almost as high. This suggests the most likely rise may be higher than 20%.

The measure rule predicts how far prices will climb after the breakout. In the Trading Tactics section I explain this in more detail, but suffice it to say 73% of the formations meet their price targets. This is somewhat low, as I consider 80% a minimum reliable benchmark.

The average formation length is about 4 months, which makes triple bottoms one of the longer chart patterns. The formation length also makes triple bottoms visible on the weekly charts, so be sure to inspect them for another perspective before making a trading decision.

I tallied the days between the three bottoms and they are nearly the same: 61 days separate the first and second bottoms and 60 days separate the center and last bottom (measured from the lowest low in each bottom). I am not suggesting that a triple bottom has equally spaced bottoms. Some analysts say there is a tendency for the first two bottoms to be wider apart than the last two. Figure 42.2 shows an example of this. The first low is further from the center bottom than the last one. By contrast, Figure 42.4 shows the reverse with the last valley further away from the center than the first one.

After the last bottom, how long does it take to reach the breakout point (the confirmation line)? On average it takes 42 days—about a month and a half. Be patient. If the formation is a true triple bottom, prices will rise above the confirmation point and continue rising significantly from there. If you jump the gun and buy after the third bottom but before confirmation, there is a high likelihood that you will not be buying into a triple bottom. Prices probably will not rise to the confirmation point before tumbling below the lowest low. Remember, true triple bottoms are rare, and you need to see the whites of their eyes before pulling the trigger.

Once prices rise above the confirmation line, they usually return to the breakout point before turning around and rising again. These throwbacks occur often enough—70% of the time—that you should consider taking advantage of them. The throwback may be just a 1-day downward spike or hover near the confirmation point for several days, but it occurs with regularity. Once a throwback occurs, wait for prices to begin climbing again before placing a trade or adding to your position. Waiting for prices to rally removes the possibility they will continue down after the throwback and not rebound at all. The average time to complete a throwback is 9 days with none taking longer than 27 days. I consider loop backs beyond a month to result from normal price action, not from a throwback.

For those formations that work as expected (that is, the ones that do not fail), it takes over 7 months to reach the ultimate high. This is not surprising since a 38% average gain does not happen overnight. Most triple bottoms have confirmation points occurring within a third of the yearly high. For a *bottom* formation, does this not sound odd? Consider that the confirmation point is the highest point in the formation. If the yearly range is narrow or if the three bottoms begin in the center of the yearly price range, then it should come as no surprise that the confirmation point pokes into the upper tier. Mapping performance onto the yearly price range, we discover that the three ranges are about evenly split. Formations that have confirmation points in the lowest third of the yearly price range score best with a 39% average gain, whereas those in the upper third have gains of *only* 36%.

Table 42.3 shows volume statistics for triple bottoms. Almost two-thirds (61%) of the formations I studied have a downward volume trend. Other analysts suggest that the highest volume happens on the left bottom and is followed by the center one with the weakest volume on the right bottom. My analysis says this pattern is true in only 28% of the formations, but it occurs more frequently than any other combination. Applying this volume trend as a litmus test to performance indicates that the 34 qualifying formations have gains of 28% as compared with gains of 38% for all successful formations.

When comparing the volume level of the middle and last bottoms, and when the center bottom shows less volume, the average gain rises to 40% versus 28% for the traditional volume pattern cited earlier. The difference between the two is statistically significant. When the center bottom volume is above the last bottom, performance diminishes to 35%. Therefore, the volume pattern is important to performance.

How does the breakout volume stack up? Volume is 163% of the prior day's volume but quickly tapers off. Volume by the end of the week is well below the volume reading the day before the breakout.

Table 42.3
Volume Statistics for Triple Bottoms

Description	Statistic
Number showing downward volume trend	74 or 61%
Number of formations having consecutive receding volume on each low	34 or 28%
Average rise of patterns with consecutive receding volume on each low	28%
Average rise of patterns with center bottom below volume of third bottom	40%
Average rise of patterns with center bottom above volume of third bottom	35%
Volume for breakout day and next 5 days compared with day before breakout	163%, 124%, 87%, 83%, 78%, 72%

Trading Tactics

Table 42.4 shows trading tactics and begins with the measure rule. The measure rule predicts the minimum price move. To use the measure rule, subtract the lowest low from the highest high reached in the formation, then add the difference to the highest high. The result is the expected minimum price move. For example, consider the triple bottom shown in Figure 42.6. The lowest low occurs on the first bottom at $21\frac{1}{4}$. Prices reach the highest high during the rally from the first bottom to the second. The confirmation point is the highest high in the formation because prices must rise above this level before the formation confirms as a true triple bottom. In this example, the confirmation point is $25\frac{3}{4}$. The difference between the high and the low, $4\frac{1}{2}$, is the forma-

Table 42.4
Trading Tactics for Triple Bottoms

Trading Tactic	Explanation
Measure rule	Compute formation height from highest high to lowest low in the formation. Add the height to the highest high. The result is the expected minimum price move.
Wait for confirmation	Since most triple bottom formations continue heading down, always wait for prices to rise above the highest high reached in the formation (the confirmation point).
Wait for throwback	Seventy percent of the formations throw back to the breakout price, so consider waiting for the throwback before investing or adding to your position.
Stop loss	Place a stop-loss order $\frac{1}{8}$ below the lowest low. Raise your stop as prices rise.

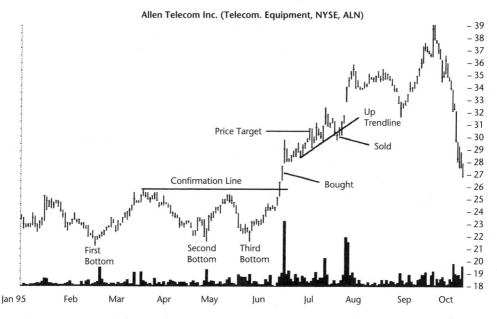

Figure 42.6 This triple bottom acts as a consolidation of the upward trend. Russell rode this triple bottom up but exited too soon. Several months after he sold, the stock was trading near 16.

tion height. Add the height to the confirmation point to get the target price, namely, 30¼. Prices hit the target in early July.

When is a triple bottom not a triple bottom? When prices fail to rise above the confirmation point. Always wait for confirmation. On average, it takes about a month and a half to get there but it is well worth the wait. The longest time it took to reach the confirmation point in the formations I looked at is 134 days—almost 5 months. Was the gain worth waiting for? Yes, prices rose by 82%! By the way, 13 formations reached their confirmation points in less than 10 days.

If you invest before the formation confirms, prices will likely resume their original trend. If the prevailing trend is down, prices will likely tumble below the support level shown by the three bottoms. At other times, prices will remain flat for an extended period (up to a year or more). Once prices pierce the confirmation point, should you invest? Not necessarily. Many, but not all, formations throw back to the confirmation price level. This is perhaps not so much a throwback in the traditional sense as it is a meandering down of prices. They pause at the breakout point and move sideways for a time, gathering strength for the push upward. That is when you often see a 1-day downward spike that tags the confirmation price—a throwback—if it occurs within 30 days after confirmation.

At other times, prices return to the confirmation point quickly, usually in less than 2 weeks but certainly no more than a month. It is at these times that you should invest or add to your position. However, do not do it immediately. The time to jump in is once prices flip around after the throwback and start heading up again. Otherwise, you risk throwing good money after bad as prices throw back and continue moving down. Do not let me scare you. This rarely happens (only 4% of the time), but it does happen.

If you are so unlucky as to misidentify a triple bottom or perhaps to catch the 4% that do fail, then be sure to place a stop-loss order about ⅛ below the lowest low. The three lows mark a point of support, so you will want to be just under that to give the stock every opportunity to rebound before being taken out.

If the decline to the stop point is too far, place your stop ⅛ below a nearer support zone. Raise your stop as prices rise, that way you will be cashed out at the first sign of trouble.

Sample Trade

Russell is an engineer working in the telecommunications industry. He once told me that the half-life of an engineer's knowledge is 10 years. "After twenty, there's nothing left! That's when it's time to hide from management." Before his time comes, he hopes to have a nest egg of funds accumulated from investing in stocks he is familiar with.

He likes to think he knows the telecommunications industry well enough to invest in it. He is a player, an investor who might be in a stock for a week or two, while at other times he takes a longer view. Occasionally, his positions last for years; these are the most profitable.

He invested in the stock shown in Figure 42.6 well before the triple bottom appeared. Even though the stock climbed from his $14 purchase price nearly a year before, seeing the triple bottom thrilled him. He believed that the formation would act as a consolidation of the upward trend. He was right. A day after the stock pierced the confirmation line, he bought more, receiving a fill at 27. His analysis suggested prices would rise to 30¼, fulfilling the measure rule. Russell believed the stock could do better and secretly he hoped for more.

After the purchase he waited. As the stock climbed, he logged into his broker at the end of the trading session each day and plotted the daily price change. Over time, he was able to draw an up trendline that skirted the daily lows as the price ascended (see Figure 42.6).

He drew a second trendline from the third bottom low upward (not shown). As he extended the two lines, they intersected on July 20. On that day, prices closed below both trendlines. Time to sell.

That evening, Russell phoned his broker and placed a market order to sell his holdings in the company the next day. The following day word came that his shares traded at 30¼. Much to his surprise, he met the measure rule prediction exactly.

He knew that he had done the right thing by selling, since a trendline penetration is not something to take lightly. Unfortunately, in this instance, he was wrong. The stock turned around and continued moving up. Soon, news came that earnings would be 40% above the prior year. This sent the stock gapping up (breakaway gap), eventually reaching a high of $39\frac{3}{8}$. Four months after reaching the high, the stock was trading at $16\frac{1}{8}$.

Russell left a lot on the table getting out at 30 and watching the stock coast to 40, but the feel of green in his pocket is a whole lot better than riding the stock down to 16.

43

Triple Tops

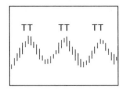

RESULTS SNAPSHOT

Appearance	Three distinct minor highs at about the same price level
Reversal or consolidation	Short-term (up to 3 months) bearish reversal
Failure rate	15%
Average decline	21%, with most likely decline being 10%
Volume trend	Downward
Pullbacks	84%
Percentage meeting predicted price target	47%
Surprising finding	A formation with a third top above the second one performs better, with an average loss of 22% versus 17%.
See also	Broadening Formations, Right-Angled and Descending; Broadening Tops; Broadening Wedges, Descending; Head-and-Shoulders Tops; Head-and-Shoulders Tops, Complex; Triangles, Ascending

The failure rate at 15% for triple tops approaches the 20% maximum I consider permissible for reliable formations. Still, there are a number of formations that perform worse, so there is no reason for concern. To take a more optimistic view, there is an 85% chance that prices will decline by more than 5%. The average loss is 21% with a likely decline of only 10%. So, if you are depending on the triple top formation to score an outsized decline, the probabilities are against you.

The pullback rate at 84% is one of the highest I have seen. This means you will have another opportunity to either sell your holdings before the real decline begins or add to your short position. It suggests some hesitancy for prices to break away.

Before you place a trade in a security showing a triple top, think about a short decline. Only 47% of the formations meet their price targets, whereas reliable readings are above 80%. It is comparatively unlikely that prices will decline by more than the formation height.

One surprising finding about triple tops is when the price of the highest high in the third top is above the second top. Formations with this configuration have losses of 22% versus 17%. The differences are statistically significant meaning that the results likely are not due to chance.

Tour

Figure 43.1 shows a triple top on the daily scale. The figure reminds me of a roller coaster as prices climb the first hill. Then it is over the top to glide down the slope and up to the next high and over the third one as well. After the final high, prices decline for the intermediate term pausing at the confirmation point while deciding which route to take.

A head-and-shoulders top forms, warning investors of further declines. Prices pull back to the triple top confirmation point, forming the left shoulder, peak at the head, and rise to form the right shoulder. Prices piercing the neckline seal the fate of the formation. Prices tumble in a straight-line fashion until they reach a low of 37, a decline from the triple top high of 50.

The three peaks of the triple top form at about 50 and have two valleys between them. The lowest valley low marks the confirmation point, the level to which prices must decline to confirm the validity of the formation. After confirmation, prices usually pull back to the confirmation point before crashing down further.

Identification Guidelines

Table 43.1 outlines identification guidelines for triple tops. When searching for a triple top or verifying that the three bumps you are looking at on a price chart belong to the formation, look at the highest high in each peak. The peaks should be near one another in price. A center peak that towers above the other

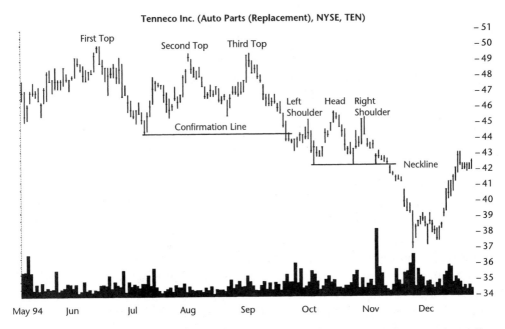

Figure 43.1 Triple top on the daily scale. A triple top has three peaks and a pull-back usually follows. A head-and-shoulders top forms at the confirmation point signaling further weakness.

Table 43.1
Identification Characteristics of Triple Tops

Characteristic	Discussion
Three large distinct tops	Look for three minor highs, well separated and distinct. The tall peaks are often sharp spikes that contrast with more rounding-appearing valleys.
Same price	The price variation among the three tops is minor. The center top should not be significantly above the other two, otherwise it is a head-and-shoulders top. There is a tendency for smaller triple tops to be one of the broadening family of chart patterns, especially the right-angle variety, so pay attention to the price lows, too.
Downward volume trend	The volume trend is usually downward but may be hard to read. Often the volume pattern is flat except near each of the three peaks. The first peak often has the highest volume.
Confirmation point	Prices must decline below the lowest low in the formation (the confirmation point) or it is not a triple top.
Weekly chart	Since triple tops are usually large price formations, look at the weekly chart to help identify the longer variety.

592

two suggests the pattern is a head-and-shoulders top. When the tops consistently inch upward, the activity suggests a broadening top. While looking at the three peaks, do not ignore the lows. The formation may be a right-angled descending broadening top or even a descending broadening wedge if the three peaks are moving down slightly in price.

In the case of a right-angled broadening top, you can probably make money on the triple top formation even before the broadening top breaks out. At least with a broadening formation, you can anticipate when it will be time to close out your position (do so when prices approach the lower, down-sloping, trendline).

The three peaks in a triple top usually are sharp and pointed looking, with rounded-appearing valleys in between. There are wide variations in this pattern, so do not be too critical. Make sure the three well-separated peaks are not part of the same congestion pattern. Each top should be a part of its own minor high, a distinct peak that towers above the surrounding price landscape.

The overall volume trend is usually downward and lackluster, but this varies from formation to formation. Volume on the three peaks, especially the first one, is higher than in the valleys.

To see what a triple top looks like, examine Figure 43.2. The three peaks are pointed, well separated, and distinct. The three minor highs are obvious and that is important in any formation. If other investors do not recognize a

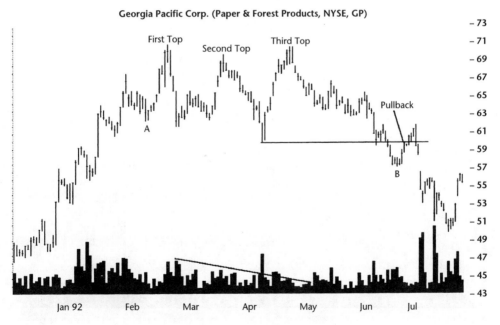

Figure 43.2   This triple top shows three distinct widely spaced tops at nearly the same price level.

chart pattern for what it is, they will not try to take advantage of it. If they do not buy or sell appropriately, the pattern will fail. Chart patterns are a self-fulfilling prophecy that depend on the crowd behaving the same way.

All three peaks are at about the same price level with the center peak a bit recessed from the other two. This is common as quite a number (31% or higher if ties are allowed) of triple tops have a lower center peak.

The receding volume trend is clear in the figure with the first peak witnessing the highest volume of the three.

An interesting development in this formation is a trendline drawn below the lows (not shown but it connects points A and B on the chart). With another trendline drawn horizontally across the three tops, the formation takes on the appearance of a right-angled descending broadening top. In many triple tops, the broadening formation also appears. This does not diminish the validity of the triple top, it just makes both formations easier to trade (because you can buy or sell at the trendlines and take advantage of partial rises or declines).

Figure 43.3 shows a triple top on the weekly chart. Even though the average triple top sports a 21% decline, prices occasionally fall much further. The chart is an example of this. You can see that the triple top marks the peak in the stock. From the high of $32^{15}/_{16}$, the stock plummets to $4^{3}/_{4}$, a stomach-churning decline of 86% in 2 years.

The chart also suggests some lessons. Sometimes the buy-and-hold strategy does not work. Whether you sold a bit early or a bit late, anything would

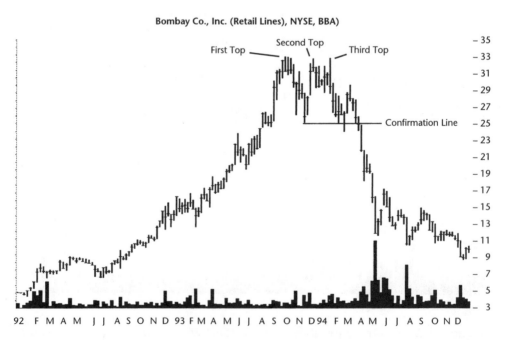

Figure 43.3   Triple top reversal on the weekly scale. The triple top marks the high point for the stock.

have been better than riding the stock all the way up and all the way back down. Do not laugh; I have done it myself but not with this stock. It is probably a mistake we all have made at one time or another and hope never to make again. Unless you use stops, you will probably make it again. You will watch all your profits evaporate as a stock declines while you continue hoping it will turn around. Then, just after you get disgusted enough to sell, prices bottom and start recovering.

Focus on Failures

As mentioned earlier, the failure rate of triple tops at 15% is comfortably below the 20% maximum that I consider reliable formations to maintain. I classify a failure of a triple top to be when prices reach the confirmation point and continue moving down by less than 5% before turning around and heading meaningfully higher. This is a key point. Prices must decline to the confirmation point, the lowest low reached in the formation. If prices do not decline to that level, then the three-bump formation *is not a triple top*—it is just a collection of minor highs (or, perhaps, some other formation).

Since a downside breakout is an identification prerequisite, that leaves only 5% failures. Figure 43.4 shows a typical example of a 5% failure. The three

Figure 43.4 A triple top failure. This is an example of a 5% failure where prices fail to continue moving down by more than 5% before turning around. Strong industry trends were instrumental in turning around the stock.

tops are distinct minor highs that form after a 2-month spurt upward. It is not surprising that the stock needs a rest and decides to retrace some of its gains— a common occurrence. From the high, the stock backtracks about four points before moving up again. The lowest low is just a smidgen below the confirmation point, which validates the formation, before prices begin climbing again.

Had you sold this stock short at the confirmation point of $20\frac{1}{4}$, you should have covered your trade once prices climbed above the highest high in the formation, in this case $23\frac{7}{8}$. This would have kept losses to a rather large 18%, but that is certainly better than hoping for a decline while watching it rise to 33!

It is often difficult to determine exactly why a stock fails to perform as expected. Often the fundamentals are the key. In this case, the oil-field services sector was improving due to an increase in exploration activity and deep water drilling. In late January, the Federal Reserve cut two key interest rates by $\frac{1}{4}$ percent, giving hope that the health of the overall economy would improve.

On the technical front, if you draw trendlines along the three tops and the minor lows, the formation takes on the appearance of a descending broadening wedge since the three tops are at consecutively lower prices. With the wedge, it is difficult to predict in which direction the breakout will occur. The fundamentals suggest the breakout will be upward, and that is exactly what happens. The formation serves as a resting place for the stock as it gathers strength for the next up leg.

One could view the formation as the corrective phase of a measured move up formation. The price prediction of the measured move fulfills quickly when prices climb to $28\frac{7}{8}$ in late April.

Statistics

Table 43.2 shows general statistics for triple tops. There are 122 formations in 2,500 years of daily price data, making the formation a rare one, indeed. Most act as reversals of the primary trend, meaning prices continue moving down after reaching the confirmation point.

The failure rate is 15%, below the maximum 20% that I consider reliable formations to possess. For those formations that do not fail, prices decline by an average of 21%. Figure 43.5 shows that the most likely loss is 10%. I use a frequency distribution of losses to get a bead on how an investor is likely to do with this formation. Of course, if you trade this formation often enough, your results should approach the average, but the chart suggests losses from a triple top are meager. Over half the formations have losses less than 20%.

The measure rule helps predict the target price to which the stock should fall, at a minimum. Unfortunately, the 47% of formations that reach their targets are well short of the 80% benchmark. This poor showing is in concert with the meager likely decline of 10%. A 10% loss is often not enough to exceed the formation height, which composes the measure rule. A more

Table 43.2
General Statistics for Triple Tops

Description	Statistic
Number of formations in 500 stocks from 1991 to 1996	122
Reversal or consolidation	25 consolidations, 97 reversals
Failure rate	18 or 15%
Average decline of successful formations	21%
Most likely decline	10%
Of those succeeding, number meeting or exceeding price target (measure rule)	49 or 47%
Average formation length	4 months (110 days)
Days between tops	1 & 2, 56 days; 2 & 3, 55 days
Formation end to downside breakout	40 days
Pullbacks	103 or 84%
Average time to pullback completion	8 days
For successful formations, days to ultimate low	3.5 months (101 days)
Percentage of breakouts occurring near 12-month low (L), center (C), or high (H)	L48%, C42%, H11%
Percentage decline for each 12-month lookback period	L18%, C22%, H24%

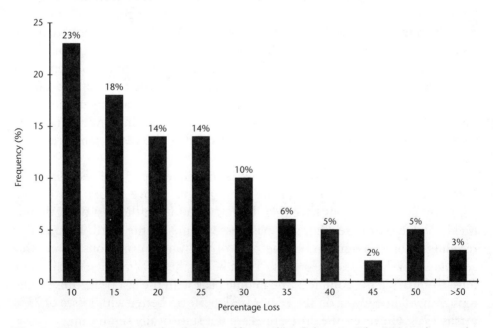

Figure 43.5 Frequency distribution of losses for triple tops. The 10% column, the column with the highest frequency, represents the most likely decline. Over half the formations have losses less than 20%.

detailed explanation of the measure rule appears in the Trading Tactics section of this chapter.

The average formation length is about 4 months, long enough to appear on weekly charts. It is always a good idea to consider different time frames when viewing chart patterns and before making trading decisions.

Like triple bottoms, the three tops in triple tops are about the same distance apart, in this case, 56 and 55 days between peaks. You can see from Figure 43.4 that equidistant peaks are not always the norm. Since the values are averages, your results may vary.

Before a three-peak formation becomes a triple top, prices must decline below the confirmation point (which is the lowest low in the formation). After the third peak, it takes approximately 40 days to reach the confirmation point. Once prices pierce the confirmation point, they often pull back. On average, prices return to the confirmation point 84% of the time, taking just 8 days to make the journey. As I was tabulating the results, I noticed several formations with prices returning to the breakout point within a day or two before moving on. These quick returns contribute to the short average—the normal pullback duration is about 11 days (for all tops, not just triple tops). From the confirmation or breakout point, it takes an additional 3½ months to reach the ultimate low, on average.

Where in the yearly trading range do triple tops occur? The confirmation point usually rests in either the lowest third of the year range (48% of the time) or in the center third (42% of the time). Only 11% of the formations are in the upper third. The reason for this is because the confirmation point (or breakout point) is the lowest price in the formation; usually low enough to keep it out of the upper range. Mapping the performance over the yearly price range, we discover that the best performing formations have breakouts in the upper third of the price range. Those in the top tier have declines averaging 24%, whereas those with breakouts in the lowest third of the yearly range result in declines of 18%.

Table 43.3 outlines volume statistics for triple tops. The declining volume trend appears only 58% of the time, not far above a coin toss (50%). Some say most triple tops have their highest volume on the first peak, diminished volume on the second, and even less volume on the third. I found this receding volume pattern to be true 25% of the time. Formations having this volume trend show losses averaging 19%, below the 21% average for all triple tops. Comparing the volume at the middle peak with the last peak, those triple tops with volume lower on the center peak perform better with losses of 23% versus 19%. However, the differences are not statistically significant.

Table 43.3 shows volume on the day of the breakout and up to a week later. When compared with the day before the breakout, the volume zooms to 188% of the prior day's value then tapers off but remains high. The numbers suggest that once prices begin declining, momentum kicks in and helps propel prices lower.

Table 43.3
Volume Statistics for Triple Tops

Description	Statistic
Number showing downward volume trend	71 or 58%
Number of formations having consecutive receding volume on each high	30 or 25%
Average decline of patterns with consecutive receding volume on each high	19%
Average decline of patterns with center top below volume of third top	23%
Average decline of patterns with center top above volume of third top	19%
Volume for breakout day and next 5 days compared with day before breakout	188%, 142%, 113%, 109%, 104%, 110%

Trading Tactics

Table 43.4 outlines trading tactics starting with the measure rule. Use the measure rule to help gauge how far prices will decline. Begin with computing the height of the formation by subtracting the lowest low from the highest high reached in the chart pattern. Subtract the difference from the lowest low to arrive at the predicted price. The predicted price serves as the expected minimum move. Unfortunately, the measure rule for triple tops only works 47% of the time, meaning that prices usually fall short of their targets.

Table 43.4
Trading Tactics for Triple Tops

Trading Tactic	Explanation
Measure rule	Compute the formation height by subtracting the lowest low from highest high in the formation. Subtract the height from the lowest low. The result is the expected minimum price move.
Wait for confirmation	Since most three-top formations continue moving up, always wait for prices to decline below the lowest low reached in the formation (the confirmation point). Once confirmed, prices usually continue moving lower.
Wait for pullback	The vast majority of triple top formations have pullbacks so if you miss the breakout, place or add to your short position once prices begin heading back down after the pullback.
Stop loss	For short positions, place a stop-loss order $\frac{1}{8}$ above the highest high.

Figure 43.6 makes the computation more clear. The lowest low of the formation occurs in late December when prices touch $17\frac{3}{4}$ briefly. The last peak harbors the highest high, $23\frac{3}{8}$. The difference, $5\frac{5}{8}$, is the formation height. Subtract the height from the lowest low to arrive at a target price of $12\frac{1}{8}$ (that is, $17\frac{3}{4} - 5\frac{5}{8}$). The figure shows prices reaching the target in mid-June.

To better gauge the veracity of the result, you might look at the predicted decline in percentage terms. From the confirmation point (the lowest low) of $17\frac{3}{4}$, a $5\frac{5}{8}$ point decline is a loss of 32%. Figure 43.5 indicates that only 21% of the formations have losses over 30% (total the columns to the right of 30%). This suggests the chance of prices declining 32% is just one in five.

In such a situation, and in most cases, you should look at support levels. Prices indicate support when they decline to a level then rebound. For example, the stock paused at the $16 level during July and August 1991 (not shown in Figure 43.6). This created the support level where the stock paused during April. Eventually, the stock worked through the support and tumbled to a lower support level.

In a roaring bull market, triple tops are often deceiving. Three price bumps appear and prices do not decline to the confirmation point before soaring up and away. Thus, an important guideline in using triple tops is to wait for prices to fall below the confirmation point. Let me say this more definitively:

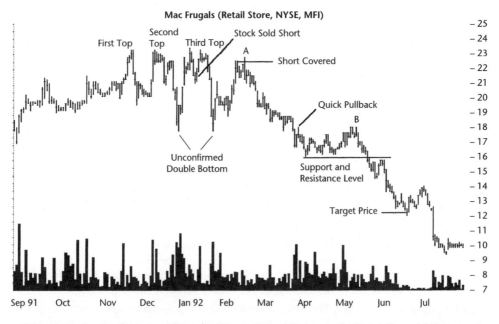

Figure 43.6   Triple top with unconfirmed double bottom. Danielle sold this stock before it reached the confirmation point then panicked at the unconfirmed double bottom. The stock eventually declined 56%. A descending scallop appears between points A and B.

You must wait for prices to fall below the confirmation point! If you decide to short a stock making a triple top before the breakout, you might get lucky and watch prices tumble, but you are pushing your luck. In many cases, you will be setting yourself up for a loss.

Pullbacks occur 84% of the time so if you miss the original breakout, you can often place your trade during the pullback. Figure 43.6 shows a quick pullback occurring just 2 days after the breakout (I define a breakout as being when prices close below the confirmation point). Just over a month later, investors have other opportunities (because prices rise to the breakout point) to add to their position before the decline really begins.

Should the trade go against you, place a stop-loss order ⅛ above the highest high. Since the three tops establish a resistance zone, prices will not hit the stop order until the resistance burns through. Sometimes a fourth peak will appear before prices move down.

Sample Trade

Danielle is in charge of the family finances. To boost the return on their savings, she has taken to playing the stock market. Her first few trades were tentative but profitable. That gave her enough courage to undertake the trade featured in Figure 43.6.

She is a brilliant, anxious, high-energy person who is comfortable taking more risks than most people, so it came as no surprise when she jumped the gun and sold the stock short in early January. She simply did not want to wait for prices to decline to the confirmation point. She explained that she wanted to maximize her gains and once prices were clearly heading down, she placed the trade and received a fill at 21½.

The day after she shorted, the stock turned around and headed back up, making a fourth peak. Instead of covering her loss, she decided to hang on. It was a good call as prices flipped around and headed back down. Seven days later they reached the confirmation point of 17¾ but stalled.

To Danielle, it looked as though the triple top became a multiple top and later developed into an unconfirmed double bottom. Each day as prices climbed and her gains dwindled, she became more nervous holding onto her short position.

Eventually, emotions overcame her desire to hold the stock and she covered her position at 22¼, suffering a minor loss of less than a point. A week or so after she bailed out, the stock was lower and it kept moving down.

The stock paused at the $16 support level for over a month, then continued down. Eventually, the stock bottomed out at 9⅜, comfortably below the predicted price and well below her entry point at 21½.

Danielle made two mistakes with this trade. First she did not wait for prices to pierce the confirmation point. Had she waited, she would have seen the false double bottom (it never confirmed as a true double bottom because prices did not rise above the highest high between the two bottoms).

Furthermore, she was not patient enough for the trade to work out. When a trade goes against you, most times it is wise to quickly close out a position, especially if it is a short sale where losses can be unlimited. However, there are times, such as this trade, where a bit of patience is necessary along with a properly placed stop. Since the three peaks represent a resistance zone, it is wise to place a stop just above the highest high, then wait for prices to hit it. Had Danielle waited, the trade would have worked out better than her analysis predicted.

44

Wedges, Falling

RESULTS SNAPSHOT

Appearance	A downward price trend bounded by two intersecting, down-sloping, trendlines
Reversal or consolidation	Short-term (up to 3 months) bullish consolidation
Failure rate	10%
Failure rate if waited for breakout	2%
Average rise	43%, with most likely rise between 20% and 30%
Volume trend	Downward
Premature breakout	27%
Throwbacks	47%
Percentage meeting predicted price target	88%
Surprising finding	The most powerful breakouts occur between 50% and 80% of the distance to the apex (centered around 65%).
See also	Pennants

There are no outstanding surprises among the statistics shown in the Results Snapshot. The failure rate for falling wedges is low at 10%. This low failure rate, coupled with an average rise of 43% and a likely rise of between 20% and 30%, suggests it is a profitable formation to trade. However, it is also quite rare.

The percentage of falling wedges meeting the predicted price target, at 88%, is very high but then the benchmark is easy. Prices need only rise above the top of the formation to hit the target.

My statistics show the most powerful breakouts occur at 50% to 80% of the distance to the apex (the center of this range being two-thirds of the way to the apex). By *powerful*, I mean that stocks falling within the range show larger gains, on average.

Tour

Figure 44.1 shows a falling wedge. Prices began declining in January 1992 from a high of 75¼ to the wedge start at 52¼. Prices recovered somewhat—a retrace in a downtrend—rounded over and headed lower. Prices tagged a new low in late July and bounced upward again. This time, the upward momentum did not carry quite as far as before. Another up and down oscillation occurred during mid-August just before prices finally reached a new low.

If you draw a trendline along the bottom of the minor lows and another along the tops, you see the familiar shape of a falling wedge. Falling wedges are rare formations that have price movements bounded by two down-sloping trendlines. When drawn on the chart, the picture looks like a wedge tilted downward.

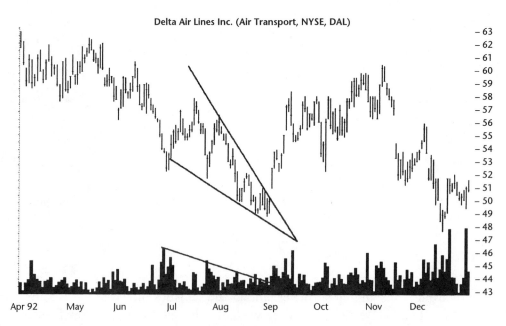

Figure 44.1   A falling wedge bounded by two down-sloping trendlines.

Once prices break out upward, they rise and quickly climb above the top of the formation. Many times prices continue moving up and score outsized gains.

Identification Guidelines

Table 44.1 shows identification guidelines, of which there are few. As mentioned before, two trendlines outline the price action. Both trendlines slope downward, with the top trendline having a steeper slope than the bottom one. Eventually, the two trendlines intersect at the wedge apex. You can see this in the wedge pictured in Figure 44.2. This wedge forms as part of a consolidation pattern in an uptrend. Prices oscillate from one trendline to the other several times before breaking out of the narrowing price pattern in mid-June.

I usually regard five touches as the minimum necessary to safeguard a good formation. The reason for the multiple touches is that the price pattern creates several minor highs and minor lows, each succeeding one narrower than the last. Having a five-touch minimum prevents a price pattern that resembles a rise and gradual decline from being labeled as a wedge. There needs to be several, opposing, touches of the trendline as prices progress through the formation. For example, Figure 44.2 shows six touches of the trendlines, five of which occur on the opposite side of the previous touch.

The minor highs and lows are descending even as they narrow. Down-sloping trendlines outlining the minor highs and lows are another key to correct identification of a falling wedge. Avoid a horizontal or near horizontal bottom trendline as the formation is most likely a descending triangle. For a falling wedge, both trendlines *must* slope downward.

Taken together, the wedge should have a minimum duration of 3 weeks and seldom does it last over 4 or 5 months. The formations in this study, for

Table 44.1
Identification Characteristics of Falling Wedges

Characteristic	Discussion
Two down-sloping trendlines	Draw two trendlines, one along the tops and one along the bottoms. The trendlines must both slope downward and eventually intersect.
Multiple touches	Most formations have at least five touches, three along one side and two along the other. Be skeptical of formations with fewer than five touches.
Three-week minimum	A falling wedge has a minimum duration of 3 weeks. Anything less is probably a pennant. Formations rarely exceed 4 months long.
Volume trend	Volume usually trends downward until the breakout.

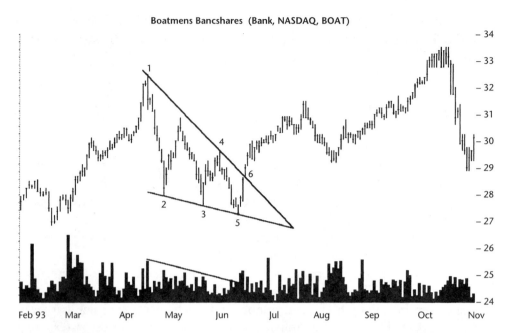

Figure 44.2   A falling wedge with six trendline touches. Several alternating touches of the trendlines are needed to form a reliable falling wedge.

example, have durations from 3 weeks to 4 months. Durations shorter than 3 weeks are probably pennants.

The volume trend should be downward. This is not an inviolate rule; it is only a guideline that usually rings true. For this study, 7 out of every 10 formations show a downward volume pattern.

Once prices pierce the upper trendline, they continue higher. Figure 44.2 shows prices staging a breakout in mid-June and reaching the ultimate high in early October. The rise, at 17% from the breakout, is well below the average rise of 43%.

Why do falling wedges act as they do? About two-thirds of the formations act as consolidations of the prevailing trend. Like the wedge shown in Figure 44.2, prices are heading upward when they run into turbulence. Investors pause from their buying spree and sit on the sidelines. Prices retrace their gains by creating the wedge, oscillating in ever-narrowing patterns, until the buying enthusiasm resumes. Volume supports this lack of enthusiasm as it recedes. When buying momentum resumes, prices and volume shoot upward again after the breakout.

Think of a falling wedge not as a pattern of weakness, but one of strength. Think of the formation as a spring winding tighter and tighter. As a spring tightens, it shrinks, and so too do prices and volume in the falling wedge. During a breakout, the pent-up force releases, and prices burst through the formation boundary and zoom upward.

Focus on Failures

In a perfect world there are no failures, but even with a 10% failure rate, you occasionally come across one. Like many formations, falling wedges have two types of failures. The first I call a 5% failure (see Figure 44.3). The falling wedge acts as a reversal of the upward trend. Although not shown on the chart, prices began rising in early December 1994. During creation of the chart pattern, prices move lower in a narrowing channel. After the breakout, prices climb and reach a high of $45\frac{3}{8}$, less than 5% above the breakout price of $43\frac{1}{4}$. From the high, prices head down and reach the ultimate low in late October at a price of $36\frac{3}{8}$. The inability of prices to continue rising more than 5% after a breakout constitutes a 5% failure. In the 125 formations studied, only two suffer 5% failures. The others are failures such as that shown in Figure 44.4.

Of the 12 failures found in this study, 10 are of the variety shown in Figure 44.4. Prices break out downward and continue down. If you could zoom away from the chart, you might recognize a large head-and-shoulders formation with each shoulder and head lasting from 3 to 4 months. The chart shows the rounded-appearing right shoulder. The latter part of the shoulder takes on the appearance of a falling wedge.

The top trendline is sloping more steeply than the lower one. Together, they both slope downward and eventually join some distance to the right.

Figure 44.3 An example of a falling wedge 5% failure. Prices do not move more than 5% above the breakout point before heading down again.

Figure 44.4 Another falling wedge failure. Prices continue down after this down-side breakout. Sometimes it is best to wait for the upside breakout before buying.

There are a number of alternating touches of the two trendlines. The volume trend is irregular but recedes according to the slope of the linear regression line of volume.

In short, the formation passes the various identification guidelines discussed earlier (see Table 44.1). Why, then, do prices breakout downward? You might pin the blame on the head-and-shoulders formation that connotes weakness. Of course, if prices moved higher then there would be nothing to say, nothing to blame. I could find no reason to explain this failure and the others like it. Fortunately, they are rare and if you play the percentages, it will happen only once every 10 trades.

Statistics

Table 44.2 shows general statistics for falling wedges. To find enough falling wedges, I had to search my alternate database too. Together, I only found 125 of these rare chart patterns. Most of them (62%) act as consolidations of the prevailing price trend. This means once the formation completes, prices resume rising just as they were before the formation began.

The failure rate at 10% is quite low and is even better if you wait for an upside breakout. Then the failure rate drops to 2%. Only 2 out of 125 formations fail to continue higher by more than 5% before ultimately turning down. Although falling wedge formations seldom fail, they are not easy to identify

Table 44.2
General Statistics for Falling Wedges

Description	Statistic
Number of formations in 500 stocks from 1991 to 1996	92
Number of formations in 297 stocks from 1996 to 1998	33
Reversal or consolidation	77 consolidations, 48 reversals
Failure rate	12 or 10%
Failure rate if waited for upside breakout	2 or 2%
Average rise of successful formations	43%
Most likely rise	20% to 30%
Of those succeeding, number meeting or exceeding price target (measure rule)	101 or 88%
Average formation length	1.5 months (44 days)

and they are rare, so you might factor those variables into your trading plan. I suggest waiting for the breakout before placing a trade.

The average rise is a very high 43%. However, the most likely rise is between 20% and 30% as shown in Figure 44.5. I construct the graph by using a frequency distribution of the percentage gains for successful formations. If you ignore the right column showing gains over 90%, the two highest columns

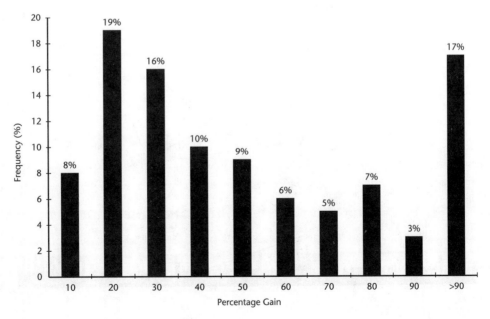

Figure 44.5 Frequency distribution of gains for falling wedges. The most likely gain is in the 20% to 30% range but the many gains over 90% pull the average upward.

are at 20% and 30%. These two columns have the highest frequency and represent the most likely gain. The chart shows the effect on the average by the outsized gains (those over 90%); they pull the average up to 43%.

I discuss the measure rule at length in the Trading Tactics section of this chapter. Suffice it to say that the measure rule says prices will rise above the top of the wedge, at a minimum. Since meeting this rule does not usually entail a large price move, prices easily reach the target. Almost all the formations (88%) with upside breakouts have prices that meet or exceed the measure rule (prices rise above the top of the formation).

The average length of a falling wedge is about 1½ months. The duration varies from 20 days to 125 days (about 3 weeks to 4 months).

What does a premature breakout look like? Consider Figure 44.6, which has both upside and downside premature breakouts. I define a premature breakout to be when prices close outside the formation trendline then return to the formation. During November, for example, prices rise above the top trendline and stay there for a few weeks. Then prices plunge through the formation and shoot out the other side. The downside premature breakout lasts only 2 days before returning to the formation. Again, prices move above the top trendline then sail back below it. Eventually, prices move up and away from the top trendline without returning to the formation. This is when the genuine breakout occurs. Until that point, the other outliers are premature upside or downside breakouts.

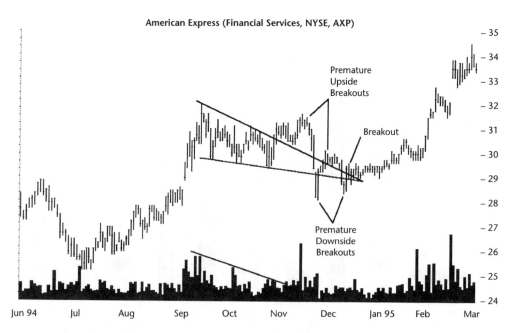

Figure 44.6 A falling wedge with premature upside and downside breakouts. Premature upside breakouts do not occur very often.

Table 44.3
Premature Breakout Statistics for Falling Wedges

Description	Statistic
Number of premature breakouts (up or down)	34 or 27%
Number of premature upside breakouts	15 or 12%
Number of premature downside breakouts	25 or 20%
Premature breakout up, genuine breakout down	3 or 2%
Upside premature breakout distance to apex	61%
Number showing above average volume on premature upside breakouts	53%

Table 44.3 shows statistics for premature breakouts. Thirty-four formations (27%) experience premature breakouts. Most of them (20%) are downside breakouts; the remainder (12%) are upside breakouts. Some formations have both types of premature breakouts (see Figure 44.6).

What is the likelihood that you will buy on an upside premature breakout only to have the formation break out lower? Only three formations (2%) fall into this category.

Is there a way to tell a premature breakout from a genuine one? No. Premature upside breakouts occur 61% of the way to the apex, whereas genuine breakouts happen at the 65% point, on average.

The volume trend also offers no clue. For premature breakouts, 53% experience above average volume (using a 25-day moving average of the volume) compared with the same percentage for genuine breakouts. In short, premature upside breakouts look just like the real thing.

Table 44.4 shows genuine breakout statistics. On average, breakouts occur 65% of the way to the wedge apex. A scatter plot of the breakout-to-apex distance versus the ultimate gain shows the most powerful breakouts occur at

Table 44.4
Breakout statistics for Falling Wedges

Description	Statistic
Upside breakout distance to apex	65%
Upside breakout	115 or 92%
Downside breakout	10 or 8%
Upside breakout but failure	2 or 2%
Throwbacks	54 or 47%
Average time to throwback completion	12 days
For successful formations, days to ultimate high	7 months (206 days)
Percentage of breakouts occurring near 12-month price low (L), center (C), or high (H)	L44%, C32%, H23%
Percentage gain for each 12-month lookback period	L47%, C42%, H36%

50% to 80% of the apex distance. This range centers on 65% where the average breakout resides.

Upside breakouts occur in 115 formations (92%) and the remainder of the formations (8%) have downside ones. Only two formations have an upside breakout and fail to continue upward by more than 5%.

Throwbacks for upside breakouts occur 47% of the time. This is a bit too low to pin an investment strategy on (such as wait for a throwback before investing). The average time for prices to complete the throwback and return to the breakout price is 12 days.

For successful, upside breakouts, prices reach the ultimate high in 206 days, on average. The ultimate high is the highest point reached before an extended (20% or more) downward trend change occurs.

Where in the yearly price range do the formations occur? Most (44%) have breakouts in the lower third of the yearly price range. Mapping the percentage gain onto the yearly price range, we find that those formations with upside breakouts occurring in the lower third of their price range do best, with a 47% rise. Those with breakouts in the top third have average gains of only 36% and so perform worse.

This is at odds with the results from other bullish chart patterns. Usually, the best performing formations are those that have breakouts near the yearly high. The momentum players grab hold of the stock and bid it up. With falling wedges, that is not the case. Why falling wedges behave this way is a mystery. Perhaps a larger sample size would firm up the results.

Only a few statistics (see Table 44.5) relate to the volume of falling wedges. Most (72%) show a downward volume trend. I determine this by viewing the slope of the linear regression line of volume tabulated over the formation. A receding volume trend is apparent in many of the figures that accompany this chapter.

Table 44.5 shows the breakout volume statistics for the breakout day until a week later. Volume is high on the day of the breakout and trends downward, as you would expect, but it rises the last 2 days. Usually, the volume trend continues moving downward throughout the week after a breakout. This suggests upside buying momentum increases once investors see the turnaround is at hand.

Table 44.5
Volume Statistics for Falling Wedges

Description	Statistic
Number showing downward volume trend	90 or 72%
Volume for breakout day and next 5 days compared with day before breakout	138%, 122%, 117%, 104%, 106%, 111%
Percentage of low volume breakouts versus high volume breakouts subject to throwback	40% versus 42%

Are low volume breakouts more likely to throw back? No. It is more likely that high volume breakouts will throw back and the results follow a pattern we have seen in other formations. For falling wedges, the differences are slight, but 40% of the throwbacks occur after a low volume breakout, whereas 42% happen after a high volume breakout. Incidentally, high and low volume is 150% and 50%, respectively, of the 25-day volume moving average.

Trading Tactics

Table 44.6 suggests some trading tactics for falling wedges, beginning with the measure rule. The measure rule for falling wedges is simple as there is no computation involved. The minimum predicted price is the highest reached in the formation. Figure 44.7 makes this clear.

The highest price is just as the formation starts in early June at $48\frac{5}{8}$, and it becomes the target price. After the breakout, prices hesitate and attempt a throwback to the formation trendline, but cannot quite reach it. After that, it is straight up. Prices reach the target in early August. The old high is a place of resistance and it takes about 2 weeks before prices are able to push decidedly above that level. Prices move higher until hitting 51 before stumbling and entering an extended downtrend.

Since 90% of the formations result in an upside breakout, there is little need to wait for the breakout before buying the stock. However, since prices are trending down, it is probably to your advantage to wait for the upside breakout. By waiting, you might receive a lower price than if you buy earlier, thereby increasing your chances of success. After a breakout, 98% of all falling wedges continue rising by more than 5%. Also, since falling wedges are not the easiest formations to identify, waiting before buying may allow any identification mistakes to become apparent.

If you want to buy the stock but it rises too far before you have a chance to pull the trigger, you might have another opportunity. Almost half (47%) of

Table 44.6
Trading Tactics for Falling Wedges

Trading Tactic	Explanation
Measure rule	Prices should rise to the top of the formation, at a minimum.
Buy after breakout	Since prices are trending down, it is best to wait for the upside breakout before buying.
Buy after throwback	If you miss the breakout and still want the stock, buy after a throwback or add to your position after a throwback once prices resume rising.
Watch for dip	Twenty-seven percent of formations show a dip just before the breakout. This is another reason to wait for the upside breakout before buying.

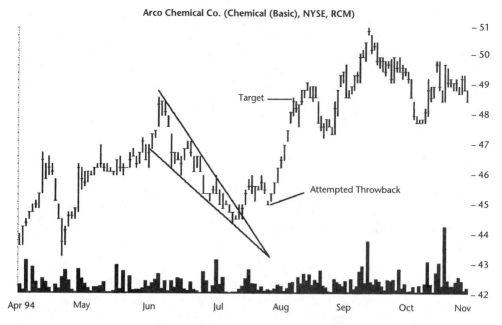

Figure 44.7   Measure rule for falling wedges. The highest price in the formation becomes the target price to which the stock will climb at a minimum.

the falling wedges experience a throwback. Should this occur in a stock you are following, wait for the throwback to reach the breakout price. Then, prices should turn around and move higher. Wait for the turnaround before buying as some stocks pause and move horizontally before continuing down.

As I was researching this formation, I noticed an interesting quirk. Sometimes just before the breakout, prices drop below the bottom trendline, circle around, then head up. Figure 44.8 shows an example of this behavior. You can see in the figure that in early January, prices break out downward, circle around, then move higher. In late April, prices rise to $44\frac{1}{4}$, well above the low of $27\frac{3}{4}$.

Sometimes the downside breakout takes the form of a premature downside breakout. Prices might drop below the trendline for a few days then reenter the formation only to zoom out the other side and stage an upside breakout. In either case, the real action is upward. Over a quarter (27%) of all falling wedges show this momentary downward spin. That is another reason to wait for the breakout before investing.

Sample Trade

Clint is the CEO of a small company that specializes in software for chambers of commerce. It is a cut-throat business because market growth is limited. The only way to increase revenue is to take business away from a competitor. Once a company entrenches itself with a chamber, it is almost impossible to pry it loose. But Clint has had some success because of the breadth of his offerings and some skilled marketing ploys.

When Clint is not worrying about his business or pitching his wares to a prospective customer, he plays the stock market hoping to make enough extra income to someday buy out his closest competitor. He recently added multimedia to his demo and that is what alerted him to the company shown in Figure 44.8.

From July to September of 1995, the stock made a head-and-shoulders top pattern. Clint watched the stock stumble, then saw the falling wedge form. He hoped that the new chart pattern marked the limit of the downside move and that he could buy in at a good price with a mouthwatering chance of prices rising to the old high.

When the stock punched through the bottom wedge trendline, he knew the wedge was a failure, so he waited to see what prices would do next. He saw them curl around and make a mini head-and-shoulders bottom and he penciled in a neckline joining the rises between the two shoulders. The neckline followed the slope of the lower wedge trendline.

Once prices pushed above the neckline and above the wedge apex, he placed an order with his broker and received a fill at 30. Clint's timing was excellent. Two days after he bought, prices were already in the mid-thirties and

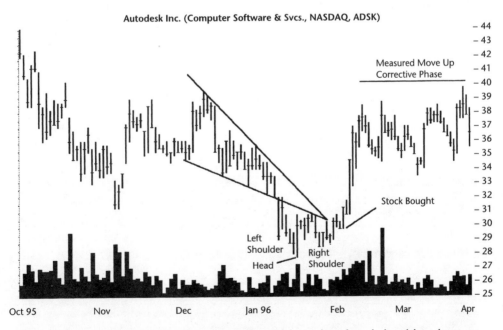

Figure 44.8 A failed falling wedge followed by a head-and-shoulders bottom, then a measured move up. More than one-fourth of falling wedges drop below the bottom trendline then quickly turn up and head higher. A small head-and-shoulders bottom appears as prices swing around the apex.

climbing. He saw prices go horizontal in mid-February through March and wondered if this was the corrective phase of a measured move up formation. That is the way he decided to play it.

The base of the measured move was at the head, $27\frac{3}{4}$, and the top of the corrective phase was at $38\frac{1}{2}$. The height was the difference between the two or $10\frac{3}{4}$. Projecting the height upward from the corrective phase bottom of $33\frac{1}{2}$ gave him a target of $44\frac{1}{4}$. He phoned his broker and placed a limit order to sell his holdings at that price.

When he was out on the road, he took along his laptop so he could dial into his broker and follow the price action of the stock. The chambers of commerce he dealt with were all on the Internet so getting a connection was never a problem.

In mid-April the stock left the corrective phase and started climbing again on the second leg up. In late April, an e-mail message from his broker told him prices reached his target and the stock sold at $44\frac{1}{4}$. In the days that followed, he smiled at his luck. Not only did he hit the high exactly, but the stock tumbled below 30 by the start of July.

"A few more trades like that and I'll be giving Microsoft a run for their money," he chuckled. "Now, if I could only find a way to keep my wife from spending it!"

45

Wedges, Rising

RESULTS SNAPSHOT

Appearance	An upward price trend bounded by two intersecting, up-sloping, trendlines
Reversal or consolidation	Short-term (up to 3 months) bearish reversal
Failure rate	24%
Failure rate if waited for breakout	6%
Average decline	19%, with most likely decline being 15%
Volume trend	Downward until breakout
Premature breakouts	22%
Pullbacks	53%
Percentage meeting predicted price target	63%
Surprising findings	The average decline of successful formations with receding volume trends is 21% versus 15% for upward volume trends. Only 38% of formations have high volume downside breakouts.
See also	Pennants

As formations go, the rising wedge is one of the poorer performing chart patterns. It sports a failure rate of 24%, which falls to 6% if you wait for a downside breakout. The average decline is 19%, just a bit below the usual 20% decline for other bearish chart patterns.

One interesting finding concerns the volume trend. Successful formations with a receding volume trend outperform those with a rising volume trend; the losses are 21% and 15%, respectively. This means if you restrict your selections to those showing receding volume throughout the formation, you should do better. On the flip side, you will also be passing up many formations in which you could trade profitably.

Only 38% of the formations have high volume downside breakouts. Apparently, prices can fall of their own weight even on low volume.

Tour

Figure 45.1 shows an example of a rising wedge. For years, the stock moved in a nearly horizontal trading range between about 25 and 31. The rising wedge chart pattern formed near the bottom of that range. Prices came off the prior high, rounded about, and headed up in October.

It was not clear from the chart pattern until well into the formation that a rising wedge was forming. The side-to-side oscillations bounded by the two rising trendlines gave a clue to the outcome. The receding volume trend bolstered the case that the pattern was indeed a rising wedge.

Figure 45.1   A rising wedge with two up-sloping trendlines. The volume trend usually slopes downward.

During mid-December, prices did not break down out of the of the formation so much as just meander lower. There was high volume on December 16, which probably marked the actual breakout, but it only lasted 1 day.

Prices attempted a pullback to the lower formation trendline but did not quite make it. Prices moved lower, recovered to post a new high, then withdrew to make another minor low during April. The April low marked the beginning of a new uptrend that lasted beyond the end of this study in mid-1996. By that time, the stock reached $58\frac{5}{8}$.

Identification Guidelines

Rising and falling wedges are among the most difficult formations to identify. However, there are some guidelines that can make identification easier and Table 45.1 lists them.

Refer to the rising wedge in Figure 45.2 as I discuss the guidelines. You probably first notice the two up-sloping trendlines. Both lines must slope upward and no near-horizontal trendlines are allowed (a horizontal top trendline indicates an ascending triangle).

Prices are moving upward, forming higher highs and higher lows, but two trendlines bound the price action. Rarely do prices move outside the two trendlines until the final breakout. However, you sometimes see premature breakouts, like that shown in Figure 45.2. A premature breakout is when prices close outside either trendline and later return to the formation.

You may think that the bottom loop from the breakout point to the pullback is just a premature downside breakout, but prices do not return to close

Table 45.1
Identification Characteristics of Rising Wedges

Characteristic	Discussion
Two up-sloping trendlines	Draw two trendlines, one along the minor highs and one along the minor lows. The trendlines must both slope upward and eventually intersect.
Multiple touches	Well-formed rising wedges have multiple touches of the two trendlines. Be skeptical of wedges having fewer than five touches (three on one side and two on the other).
Three-week minimum	A rising wedge has a minimum duration of 3 weeks. Anything less is a pennant. Formations rarely exceed 3 or 4 months long.
Volume trend	Volume usually trends downward throughout the formation.
Breakout volume	Breakout volume can be either heavy or light but is generally below average.

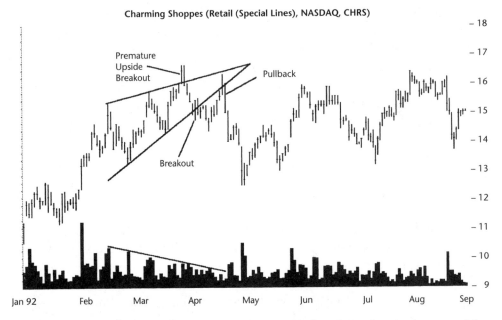

Figure 45.2   Rising wedge with premature upside breakout. A premature upside breakout occurs about twice as often as a downside one.

inside the formation. Thus, the actual breakout occurs just 3 days after prices return to the formation from the premature upside breakout.

A well-formed rising wedge has multiple touches of the trendline boundaries. Figure 45.2 shows three top touches and three bottom ones (including the piercing of the premature and actual breakout points). Fewer than five touches, three on one side and two on the other, should cast the formation in a dim light. It might not be a rising wedge at all.

A rising wedge with multiple touches takes time to form. Prices make new minor highs and minor lows as they bounce from trendline to trendline. It takes over 3 weeks for the formation to take on the wedge appearance. Formations shorter than 3 weeks are pennants. On the other hand, rising wedges do not last long. Typically, the apex—where the two trendlines meet—marks the end of the formation. Prices usually break out about two-thirds of the way to the apex. Rising wedges rarely last more than three months (the longest one in this study is 145 days—almost 5 months).

The receding volume pattern is another key element in correctly identifying a rising wedge. Most of the time, volume trends downward and becomes especially low just before the breakout. However, this is not an absolute rule, but the statistics show that formations with receding volume trends perform much better than those with rising ones.

If you are caught in a situation with a rising volume trend but price action narrows over time, then ignore the volume trend. Review the other guidelines (especially the number of touches) to make sure the chart pattern resembles a rising wedge. If there is doubt, do not invest until the stock breaks out of the formation. Not trading a wedge until after the breakout is almost always a wise course of action.

Rising wedges can form anywhere. You might expect them to form at the end of a long uptrend and that is indeed the case most of the time. Occasionally, prices are heading downward and a rising wedge forms as a sort of retrace against the downward trend. After the breakout, prices resume falling.

The narrowing price action and receding volume trend of a rising wedge are signs of weakness. Prices push to new highs, just above the last minor high, then pull back. On the minor low, weak buying enthusiasm catches the stock before it drops below the prior low and turns things around.

The volume trend usually is not exuberant enough to push prices above the top trendline for long and stage an upside breakout. Sometimes you do get a premature upside breakout (which, interestingly enough, occurs about twice as often as a downside one), but prices quickly rejoin the formation. Prices later descend out the bottom of the wedge and stage a downside breakout.

There is still buying demand for the stock since about a third of the formations descend less than the lowest point in the wedge. For the remainder of the patterns that do push lower, they, too, do not fall far. The average decline from a rising wedge is just 19%.

Focus on Failures

With poor measure rule performance and a small average decline, it should come as little surprise that rising wedges have higher failure rates than other formations. Consider Figure 45.3, a 5% failure in a rising wedge. Prices that drop by less than 5% before moving higher I call 5% failures. However, these types of failures are rare, occurring only 6% of the time.

You can see in Figure 45.3 the chart pattern forms after a downward price move of nearly 2 months' duration. The wedge appears to be a retrace in a downward price trend. The formation is part of the second up-leg in a measured move up chart pattern. Not shown is the first up-leg but the decline between the two up-legs begins in late September, and a portion of it shows in the figure.

Thus, one might have reason to suspect that this formation might not work out as expected. Prices move up and touch the top trendline then bounce to the other side. Prices cross from side to side as they rise and form a narrowing price channel.

Prices drop out of the pattern 68% of the way to the apex, about where you would expect them to. Volume is unusual as it is trending upward, but begins receding the week before the breakout. It is exceptionally low just before the downside breakout.

Once prices close below the lower trendline, investors usually sell, helping drive prices down. However, volume is low on this breakout. Prices need

Figure 45.3   An example of a rising wedge 5% failure. Prices fail to move down by more than 5% before rebounding.

not have high volume to recede; sometimes they can fall on their own weight. Almost two out of three formations in this study have breakouts with below average volume.

If you shorted the stock after the downside breakout, you would have visited the woodshed. No sooner do prices drop out of the formation than they turn around and head higher. In less than 2 weeks, prices rise above the wedge top. In another 3 months, prices finally break out of their consolidation zone and really begin climbing. In July, they reach a new high of over 95.

Figure 45.4 shows a different type of failure: Prices break out upward and continue rising. Of the two failure types, this is the most prevalent. The figure shows a well-formed rising wedge. It has many alternating touches of the two trendlines. Volume is uncharacteristically rising and irregular—a warning sign. The wedge forms as a sort of consolidation of the upward trend. Although the figure does not show this, prices start climbing in October 1993 and reach a peak the following January. Then the trend reverses and moves lower executing a long ascending scallop. As prices recover, they form moderately higher highs and higher lows—a rising wedge.

When prices gap (breakaway gap) above the top trendline, it signals the end of the rising wedge. Prices move horizontally for almost 5 months before jumping upward again.

For this failure, as in about 30% of the cases, the volume trend is upward. Certainly the three large volume spikes occurring on days when prices close higher should be a warning. Still, there is no guarantee that high or rising volume interferes with the performance of a rising wedge.

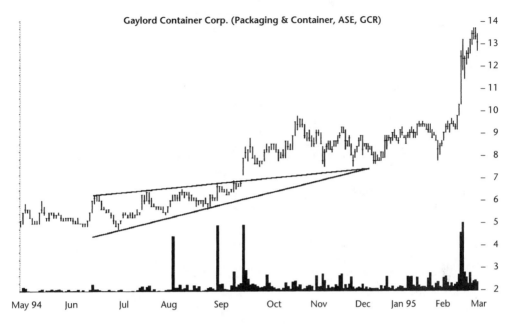

Figure 45.4   A failed rising wedge followed by a long ascending scallop that takes shape from October to February. This is the most prevalent type of failure for rising wedges. Prices break out upward and continue rising.

Statistics

Statistics help define the average formation and can help you gauge what to expect from a rising wedge. Table 45.2 shows general statistics. Compared with falling wedges, rising wedges are plentiful, occurring 179 times in 500 stocks over 5 years. A slight majority (54%) of them act as reversals of the prevailing trend.

The failure rate is 24%, above the maximum 20% rate that I consider reliable formations to possess. If you wait for a downside breakout before investing, then the failure rate drops to 6%. The average decline, at 19%, is near the low end for bearish reversals, which usually score about 20%. The most likely decline is 15%, shown in Figure 45.5. I created the graph by doing a frequency distribution of losses. The highest column, at 15%, is the most likely decline. If you add the values of the first two columns, you discover that nearly half (47%) of the rising wedges have declines less than 15%. Such meager declines pose the question, why waste time trading this formation?

If we separate the successful formations by volume trend and gauge their performance, we discover an interesting result. Those formations with a downward volume trend (as measured by the slope of the linear regression line) perform better than those with an upward volume trend. The performance difference, at 21% versus 15%, is statistically significant, meaning that the results are probably not due to chance.

Table 45.2
General Statistics for Rising Wedges

Description	Statistic
Number of formations in 500 stocks from 1991 to 1996	179
Reversal or consolidation	82 consolidations, 97 reversals
Failure rate	43 or 24%
Failure rate if waited for downside breakout	11 or 6%
Average decline of successful formations	19%
Most likely decline	15%
Average decline of formations with down-sloping volume trend	21%
Average decline of formations with up-sloping volume trend	15%
Of those succeeding, number meeting or exceeding price target (measure rule)	92 or 63%
Average formation length	1.5 months (44 days)
Downward volume trend	132 or 74%
Average volume for breakout day and next 5 days compared with day before breakout	131%, 113%, 107%, 114%, 100%, 113%
Above average volume breakouts (using 25-day moving average)	52 or 38%

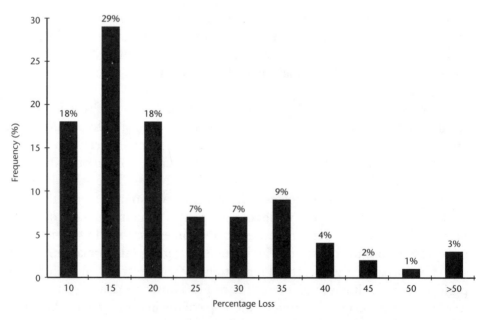

Figure 45.5 Frequency distribution of losses for rising wedges. The most likely gain is 15% and nearly half the formations have gains less than 15%.

In the Trading Tactics section of this chapter I explain the measure rule but it is quite simple: The lowest price in the formation becomes the target price. Even so, only 63% of the formations decline to the start of the wedge (the lowest price). I consider values over 80% to be reliable.

The average formation length is 44 days. Rising wedges typically last from 3 weeks to 4 months, so they appear best in daily charts.

The volume trend, which turns out to be a good indicator of the reliability of the chart formation, slopes downward 74% of the time. I measured this by finding the slope of the linear regression line calculated using volume data from the start of the formation until prices moved outside the trendline boundaries.

Table 45.2 shows the average breakout volume. It is highest the day after the breakout, at 131% of the prior day, and tapers downward but remains high up to a week later. Like falling wedges, the volume pattern is irregular. Usually, the pattern trends downward with each day having a lower volume than the preceding one but that is not the case here. Although volume begins to recede, it bounces up twice over the next 5 days.

Since large numbers can sway averages, I looked at each formation and computed the volume moving average up to the day before the breakout. Then I compared the result with the volume on the day of the breakout. In only 38% of the cases does above average volume accompany the breakout day. This follows the belief that downside breakouts can fall on their own weight (without high volume).

Table 45.3 shows premature breakout statistics. A premature breakout is when prices close outside the trendline then return within the formation boundary. Figure 45.2, for example, shows an upside premature breakout. Premature breakouts, either up or down, occur 22% of the time in this study. The results divide into downside breakouts (9%) and upside breakouts (16%). Some formations have both upside and downside breakouts.

Only 3% of the formations have a premature downside breakout with a genuine breakout upside. This is reassuring since it is difficult or impossible to distinguish a premature downside breakout from a real one. Should you

Table 45.3
Premature Breakout Statistics for Rising Wedges

Description	Statistic
Number of premature breakouts (up or down)	40 or 22%
Number of premature downside breakouts	16 or 9%
Number of premature upside breakouts	29 or 16%
Premature breakout down, genuine breakout up	6 or 3%
Downside premature breakout distance to apex	60%
Percentage showing above average volume on premature downside breakouts	56%

mistakenly sell short on a premature breakout, your chances of success are still high.

How far to the wedge apex do premature breakouts occur? On average, they break out 60% of the way to the apex. This compares with genuine breakouts occurring 61% along the way. In other words, premature breakouts look like the real thing.

The average premature breakout volume seems to confirm this belief. Breakout volume is above average 56% of the time. Although this may appear to be a low number, it contrasts with 38% of regular breakouts showing above average breakout volume. Volume for premature downside breakouts is 113% of the 25-day volume moving average.

Table 45.4 shows breakout statistics. The formations in this study have breakouts 61% of the way to the apex. The apex is where the two trendlines meet in the future. A scatter plot of the distance to the apex versus the resulting loss is inconclusive. Although falling wedges seem to have the most powerful breakouts about two-thirds of the way to the apex, the relationship with rising wedges appears to be more random.

Most of the breakouts from rising wedges occur downward (82%). Eleven (6%) have downside breakouts but prices turn around and move higher. Since this failure rate is so small, it should not be of major concern. Once prices break out downward, they continue lower nearly all the time.

Pullbacks occur 53% of the time. This is a bit too low to plan an investment strategy around. However, if you want to trade a wedge and miss the breakout, you might have a second chance should prices pull back to the formation. Once prices begin heading lower, after the pullback, sell the stock short. Pullbacks occur quickly, on average just 10 days after the breakout. Any pullback occurring over 30 days is not a pullback at all; it is just normal price behavior.

Table 45.4
Breakout Statistics for Rising Wedges

Description	Statistic
Downside breakout distance to apex	61%
Upside breakout	32 or 18%
Downside breakout	147 or 82%
Downside breakout but failure	11 or 6%
Pullbacks	78 or 53%
Average time to pullback completion	10 days
For successful formations, days to ultimate low	2.5 months (78 days)
Percentage of breakouts occurring near 12-month price low (L), center (C), or high (H)	L15%, C18%, H68%
Percentage gain for each 12-month lookback period	L21%, C17%, H19%

The days to the ultimate low, at 78, is quite brief. The low value coincides with the small average loss (19%). Generally, the longer it takes to reach the ultimate low, the larger the loss.

A frequency distribution of the breakout price reveals 68% of the formations have breakouts in the highest third of the yearly price range. Mapping performance over the yearly price range, we find that the best performing formations are those with breakouts in the lowest third of the yearly range. However, all three ranges are quite close in value. The results support the belief that weaker stocks fall further.

Trading Tactics

Table 45.5 shows trading tactics for rising wedges. The measure rule for rising wedges is opposite that for falling wedges. The measure rule says that prices should decline to the start of the formation (the lowest low), at a minimum. Even though the predicted decline is usually small, only 63% of the formations meet the benchmark. I view a score of 80% as being reliable, so this formation comes up short.

Figure 45.6 shows one application of the measure rule. The well-defined rising wedge passes all the identification guidelines outlined in Table 45.1. An investor willing to short the stock would use the measure rule to gauge the profitability of the trade. In this example, the target price is the lowest price in the formation, or 29¾. Prices drop through the target just over a week after the breakout.

To improve the chances of investment success, sell short after a downside breakout. Prices must close outside the formation trendline before you place a trade. Following this guideline for the stocks in this study lowers the failure rate from 24% to 6%. The trade-off is that you might be giving up some profit as you will be making a trade after prices begin moving down. Still, I will take a small profit over a loss any day.

Table 45.5
Trading Tactics for Rising Wedges

Trading Tactic	Explanation
Measure rule	Prices should fall to the bottom of the formation, at a minimum.
Sell after breakout	Wait for the downside breakout (prices should close outside the bottom trendline) to improve the chances of a successful trade.
Sell after pullback	If you miss the breakout and still want to trade the stock, sell short after a pullback, once prices turn down.
Take profit quickly	Since the decline is meager, be ready to pull the trigger and close out the trade.

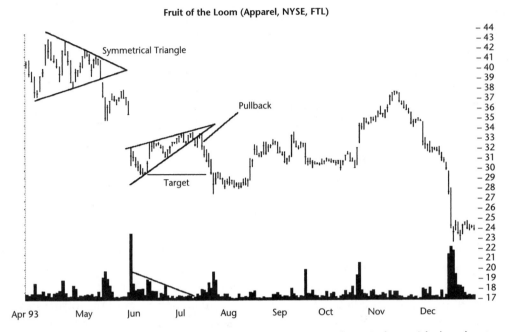

Figure 45.6 Symmetrical triangle precedes rising wedge. A downside breakout from the symmetrical triangle suggests prices will fall. The measure rule for rising wedges is simply the lowest price in the formation, shown here at 29¾.

If you miss the breakout, perhaps you can jump in on the pullback. About half the formations (53%) pull back to the bottom trendline, so there is an even chance that you can place a trade. After prices pull back, wait for them to start falling again. Sell short only after prices begin moving down to help protect yourself from a stock that pulls back and continues rising.

The last guideline in the table suggests taking profits quickly. The average decline is 19% with a likely decline of just 15%. So, in all likelihood, the stock will decline only briefly before recovering. If the stock looks like it is making a turn upside, then close out your short position.

Even for short-term (long side) traders, I do not suggest they sell their holdings if they see a rising wedge in a stock they own. Of course, if the fundamentals suggest otherwise, then sell your holdings and look elsewhere for another opportunity.

If you are considering shorting the stock, check the fundamentals and make sure there is a good reason for the stock to weaken. Just because you *hope* it will go down is no reason for the stock to comply.

Sample Trade

Joe is a midlevel manager at a large corporation. One of the qualities in which he is gifted is patience. He handles stress easily and does not let small problems bother him. In his spare time, he likes to trade stocks and has developed a keen sense to make short sales work for him.

After returning from vacation, Joe discovered the situation shown in Figure 45.7. He missed the initial downward breakout but still wanted to short the stock.

Viewing the chart from a longer-term perspective, Joe believed that the formation was an upward retrace in a long-term downtrend (not shown in the figure). At a minimum, he believed the stock would withdraw back into its base at about 30. He would consider closing out the trade at that point and not before unless prices rose against him. So, he set a stop-loss order at the top of the formation at $36\frac{3}{4}$, about $\frac{1}{4}$ point above the formation high.

If the stock continued in his favor, then it would be completing a downward measured move. Joe estimated that the measured move formation would take the stock to 28 and perhaps lower.

When the stock pulled back to the bottom trendline and headed down the next day, Joe sold the stock short and received a fill at 36. He reviewed the measure rule that said the stock would fall to the bottom of the formation for a decline of about 6% from the purchase price.

Joe watched the stock closely and was gratified to see prices soon drop below the measure rule target of $33\frac{3}{4}$. Then the stock rebounded. As the stock climbed at the start of December, Joe reevaluated his short position. From what he was able to gather, the fundamental and technical situation had not changed so he decided to sit tight.

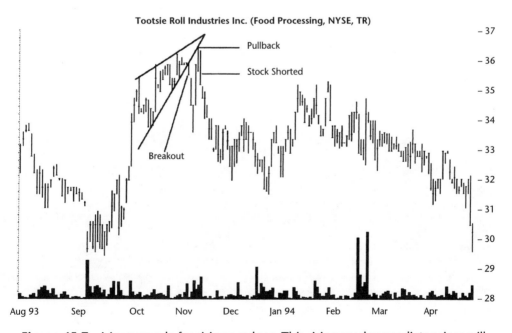

Figure 45.7 Measure rule for rising wedges. This rising wedge predicts prices will fall to $33\frac{3}{4}$ and they do, in just 2 days.

Even as the stock climbed above 35, Joe believed he was right. The tenacious attitude served him well on this trade and the stock soon began heading down again. In May, the stock reached his target price of 30 and Joe considered closing out his position, but did not.

The stock moved sideways for about 4 months then dropped down again. It reached a low of 25.43 in mid-December and headed back up. Joe closed out his short position at 27, just a week after it made a new low. On the trade, Joe made almost $9,000, or about 25%, on his 1,000 shares in about a year.

46

Weekly Reversals, Downside

RESULTS SNAPSHOT

Appearance	On the weekly scale, a higher high, lower low, and closing price below the prior weekly low
Reversal or consolidation	Short-term (up to 3 months) bearish reversal
Failure rate	37%
Average decline	18%, with most likely decline being 10%
Percentage meeting predicted price target	73%
Surprising findings	Failures become more likely as the time from the closest peak lengthens. A wide weekly price range results in better performing reversals.
See also	Weekly Reversals, Upside

Perhaps the most remarkable feature of the downside weekly reversal formation, if you can call it a formation, is its high failure rate at 37%. One out of three downside weekly reversals fail! I consider failure rates below 20% to be acceptable, so this chart pattern should serve as a warning: Perhaps you should skip this one.

The average decline is 18% with a likely loss of 10%. The average decline is a little less than what you would expect (20%) from a well-performing bearish reversal. The reversal does have some interesting statistical findings. First, weekly reversals usually occur near a price peak and quite often near a major peak (signaling a change in the primary trend). The further from the peak the reversal occurs, the more likely it is to end in failure. This makes intuitive sense because prices are already sliding down the trend before the reversal hits and takes them closer to the ultimate low.

As I was researching weekly reversals, I came across an analyst who suggested that the best performing reversals are those with large weekly price ranges and high volume. I investigated and discovered that a large weekly price range does indeed improve performance. However, there are not enough formations to determine if a wide price range *and* high volume produce superior results. I discuss this in the Statistics section of this chapter.

Tour

What do downside weekly reversals look like and why do they form? As an overview, Figure 46.1 shows two examples of a downside weekly reversal. The first reversal on the left comes just two weeks after the stock peaks. It marks the start of an extended downtrend that sees prices decline from their high of $37\frac{3}{8}$ to a low of $10\frac{3}{8}$, a plunge of 72%! The second weekly reversal occurs further from the twin peaks in early December 1992. Since prices are already declining, it serves as confirmation that prices will continue falling. I write that state-

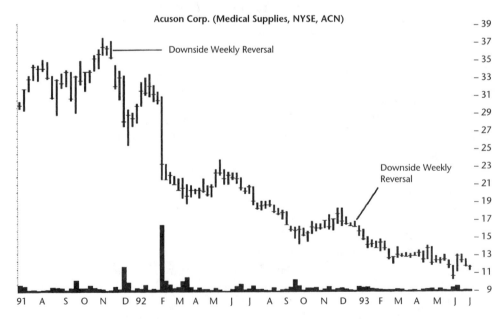

Figure 46.1   Two downside weekly reversals. The one on the left is a timely downside weekly reversal. Both reversals occur just a few weeks after a high.

ment with some trepidation because I only consider weekly reversals to be valid when they occur on or near an uptrend.

For example, the reversal on the left is close enough to the end of the uptrend to be a part of it (imagine prices moving up the week after the reversal . . . you would hardly notice the down draft). With the reversal on the right, it is a bit harder to write-off 3 or 4 weeks of declining prices. When considering the long-term trend, the decline is over a year long.

Why do downside weekly reversals form and why do they work? As prices climb following an upward trend, momentum typically increases in the early stages of a rise then diminishes before reversing. Prices follow. If the change in momentum is sharp, occurring in the span of a week, or sometimes even just a day, then a weekly reversal can occur. In the early part of the week, prices are chasing momentum higher. Prices make new highs, perhaps on a daily basis, bubbling upward from buying pressure as investors bid up the stock. Announcement of surprisingly bad earnings, poor same-store sales numbers, or some other fundamental or technical change occurs, buying enthusiasm dwindles, and selling pressure escalates. The momentum shifts from upward to downward. If the fundamental or technical winds are strong enough, prices dive and by the end of the week close below the prior week's low.

The weekly high price, after being carried upward by the rising momentum earlier in the week, forms a new high, but by week's end the trend reverses. The smart money, sensing the changing trend, takes flight and dumps the stock, contributing to the sharpness of the momentum change. As prices head down, the selling intensifies, driving down the stock still further.

Identification Guidelines

Table 46.1 outlines the identification guidelines for downside weekly reversals. Use the weekly charts to make identification easy. Look for downside weekly reversals in an uptrend; they warn that the upward trend is about to reverse. About half the time, the weekly reversal occurs exactly on the peak: The trend is upward and it makes a new high then prices plunge. In such a situation, the reversal is easy to spot and easy to believe. But what about the other 50% of the time when the reversal occurs after the peak?

If the reversal occurs well into a downtrend, ignore it. The trend may continue down or it may be near the bottom but it is best not to rely on the signal. For those reversals occurring near the end of the uptrend, you have to decide if they are reversals of the uptrend or consolidations of the downtrend.

Confused? Take another look at Figure 46.1. The reversal on the left occurs in a downtrend, but it is only 2 weeks from the end of the uptrend, so I view it as significant. The other reversal, as explained previously, occurs on the upward retrace (the secondary trend) in a long downtrend (the primary trend)

Table 46.1

Identification Characteristics of Downside Weekly Reversals

Characteristic	Discussion
Weekly chart	Look for weekly reversals on weekly charts.
Upward trend	Prices should be in an uptrend. Ignore downside weekly reversals when the predominant trend is downward. In a retrace after an uptrend, as long as the reversal occurs near the peak (less than 5 weeks away and near in price) then I consider it valid.
Higher high, lower low	Prices must be higher than the prior week's high and lower than the prior week's low. Ties not allowed.
Lower close	Prices must close below the prior week's low.

and is 3 or 4 weeks into the downtrend resumption, so it does not signal a reversal. Ignore it.

To help identify downside weekly reversals, I programmed my computer to use linear regression on the daily *high* price over 40 trading sessions—about 2 months' worth of *daily* prices. It correctly selected weekly reversals near enough to the uptrend to be significant and ignored those further down the trend.

Lest you be deceived into thinking linear regression is all you need to program, Table 46.1 shows that other characteristics are important too. On the weekly chart, the current high must be above the prior week's high price; the weekly low must be below the prior week's low, and the closing price must also be below the prior week's low. In this regard, the week is *wider* than the prior week with the closing price signaling the direction prices will move.

Figure 46.2 shows three weekly reversals, two of which are significant. The first reversal (on the left) occurs as prices are peaking on an uptrend. The high forms a price peak that is above the other prices over the last 3 months. The low and close are below the prior week's low and close. It is a valid downside weekly reversal and it warns of a new downtrend beginning. The center reversal occurs in the midst of a downtrend. Since prices are obviously heading down, ignore the reversal signal. The last reversal, the one on the right, occurs 5 weeks after prices peak. However, the high price has not declined much from the peak, so I consider it to be a valid downside weekly reversal. As you can see in Figure 46.2, prices meander lower for the next 6 months.

Focus on Failures

The failure rate of downside weekly reversals is an alarming 37%. The breakout direction is assumed to be down, since a lower low occurs, so false breakouts are not a problem. However, 5% failures, where prices fail to continue moving down by more than 5%, are *the* problem. Figure 46.3 shows what a 5%

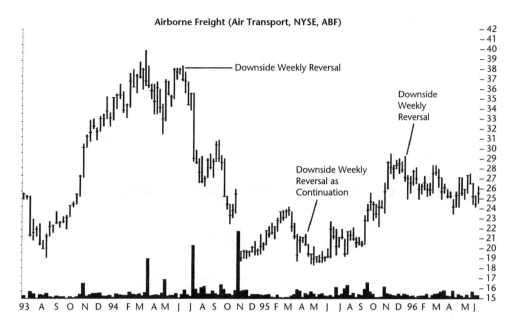

Figure 46.2 Three downside weekly reversals. A higher high, lower low, and a close below the prior week's low are key elements of a weekly reversal. The reversal should occur in or near the end of an uptrend.

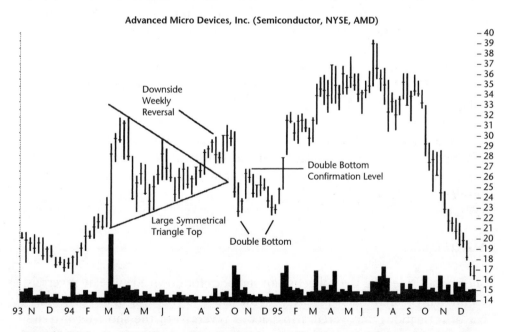

Figure 46.3 A 5% failure of a downside weekly reversal. The upside breakout from the symmetrical triangle top serves as a warning of strength and the weekly reversal as a throwback attempt.

failure looks like. You can see in the figure that prices break out upward from the large symmetrical triangle top, then make a downside weekly reversal. However, instead of trending down as prices should after a downside reversal, they plateau for an additional 2 weeks then climb. Once a higher high and higher low occurs, the downside weekly reversal is a failure.

An investor seeing the weekly reversal forming in the stock and taking advantage of it would probably be pleased. Eventually, just 5 weeks after the reversal signals, prices move significantly lower by descending from 31 to 22. Then prices form a double bottom that confirms in early January when prices climb above the confirmation price of $26\frac{3}{4}$. As you can see, prices continue moving up and peak at $39\frac{1}{4}$ before tumbling and trading at 13 by the end of the study.

Had an investor recognized the symmetrical triangle early enough, he or she may have regarded the downside weekly reversal with skepticism. The short decline looks like a throwback attempt to the top triangle trendline. In such a case, the top trendline is an area of support that often repels prices.

It is difficult to state a general reason why downside weekly reversals fail. When evaluating the veracity of the reversal signal, look for prior zones of support. If there is no support zone near the weekly low price, then the weekly reversal will probably work out fine.

Sometimes, a downside weekly reversal fails because it runs across a support zone that it cannot penetrate. At other times, it is an up-sloping trendline, connecting the low prices, that the reversal cannot pierce. Be sure to look for both situations and trade accordingly.

Market and industry forces play a part in the success of a downside weekly reversal. If stocks are in a raging bull market, the reversal signal is more likely to be wrong. Similarly, if the industry is doing well, that would suggest a short-lived decline.

Since a wide weekly price range often accompanies a downside weekly reversal, there is usually a fundamental reason why the stock has tanked. Finding the reason for the move can give you enough confidence to short the stock or sell a long-term holding.

Statistics

Shown in Table 46.2 is a collection of statistics for downside weekly reversals. I limited my search to 200 stocks from the usual 500 because of the large number of formations uncovered. Most act as reversals of the short-term trend, whereas many of the consolidations are 5% failures. Just over a third (37%) of the formations fail to continue moving down by more than 5% before trending higher.

The average decline of successful formations is 18%, whereas the most likely decline is 10%. I determine the most likely decline by using a frequency

Table 46.2
General Statistics for Downside Weekly Reversals

Description	Statistic
Number of formations in 200 stocks from 1991 to 1996	412
Reversal or consolidation	151 consolidations, 261 reversals
Failure rate	153 or 37%
Average decline of successful formations	18%
Most likely decline	10%
Of those succeeding, number meeting or exceeding price target (measure rule)	189 or 73%
For successful formations, days to ultimate low	3 months (80 days)
Percentage of reversals occurring near 12-month low (L), center (C), or high (H)	L15%, C18%, H67%
Percentage loss for each 12-month lookback period	L21%, C16%, H17%
Average volume week before and after versus week of reversal	51%, 80%

distribution of losses and Figure 46.4 shows a graph of the results. I refer to the tallest column in the chart as the *most likely decline* simply because it has the highest frequency. It is worth noting that combining the first two columns shows that over half the formations have losses less than 15%, so, even though your weekly reversal may not end in a 5% failure, the likelihood of having a large loss is not very high. About one in five (21%) reversals have losses over 25%. That is a comparatively poor showing for a bearish reversal.

At first, I did not tabulate a measure rule for the formation but changed my mind. I use the difference between the weekly high and low and subtract the value from the weekly close. Almost three out of four (73%) formations meet their target prices. This is shy of the 80% value I consider reliable.

It takes about 3 months to reach the ultimate low, which is the lowest low before a significant trend change occurs. This statistic (as well as other performance statistics) uses the closing price during the week of the weekly reversal to the ultimate low. I used the closing price as a proxy for the price an investor would likely pay.

Most downside weekly reversals occur in the highest third of the yearly price range. Again, I use the closing price as the benchmark. Mapping performance on top of the yearly price range, we find that the lowest third of the range performs best with losses averaging 21%. The other two ranges are about evenly split at 16% and 17%. The values suggest that a poorly performing stock (one that is near its yearly low) suffers comparatively larger declines after a downside weekly reversal.

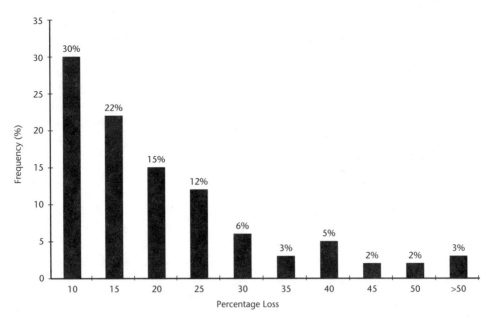

Figure 46.4   Frequency distribution of losses for downside weekly reversals. Over half the downside weekly reversals score losses less than 15%.

I compared the volume of a weekly reversal with the week before and the week after. The weekly reversal has volume that is about double the prior week but it tapers off quickly. The following week has only 80%, on average, of the shares traded during the weekly reversal. When comparing the volume during the weekly reversal with a 25-week moving average of the volume, I found 52% of the formations have above average volume.

Many technical analysts attribute a significance to volume. A high volume breakout, they reason, pushes prices further than a low volume one. I have found that sometimes this is true and sometimes it is not. As it applies to downside weekly reversals, the belief is that a large weekly price range coupled with high volume suggests a significant trend change. I investigated this claim and Table 46.3 shows the results.

The table needs some explaining. It represents how downside weekly reversals perform for the criteria of volume and price range. The column headings are multiples of the volume level when compared with the 25-week moving average. The row headings show the size of the weekly price range, expressed as a percentage of the closing price during the downside weekly reversal. Shown in parentheses are the number of formations meeting the criteria (the sample size). When the number of samples drops below 30, the percentages become suspect.

For example, in the second row, third column under "0–1×" is the value 11%. Those formations having volume between 0% and 100% of the 25-week moving average and a weekly price range between 5% and 10% (during the

Table 46.3
Average Percentage Loss from Formations Meeting Criteria of Volume
and Weekly Price Range

Price Range (%)	Benchmark (%)	Volume			
		0–1× (%)	1–2× (%)	2–3× (%)	3–4× (%)
0–5	6 (58)	5 (36)	8 (20)	11 (2)	0 (0)
5–10	10 (183)	11 (92)	10 (75)	6 (8)	3 (2)
10–15	16 (73)	12 (35)	19 (28)	19 (5)	15 (4)
15–20	20 (40)	22 (14)	15 (13)	24 (9)	4 (1)
20–25	24 (13)	31 (4)	21 (4)	17 (2)	19 (1)

Note: Shown is the average percentage loss from formations meeting the criteria of volume (columns) as a multiple of the 25-week moving average and the weekly price range (rows) expressed as a percentage of the closing price. Performance improves with a wider price range but the jury is still out on whether high volume is beneficial. Shown in parentheses are the number of formations meeting the criteria (the sample size).

week of the reversal) score losses averaging 11%. Another example is the 24% listed in the intersection of the 2–3× column with the 15–20% row. The value says downside weekly reversals have average losses of 24% if their volume is between two and three times as large as the moving average and the weekly price range is between 15% and 20% of the closing price. Only nine formations make the cut, so the sample size is very small despite having over 400 formations to qualify.

I used the benchmark column to evaluate the other columns. The benchmark column is essentially all the formations (regardless of volume) sorted into the weekly price ranges. I removed a few formations because they have excessively wide weekly price ranges and some start too close to the beginning of the study (there was not enough data to calculate a 25-week moving average). Duplicate entries are not allowed.

Do formations with high volume and a large weekly price range perform best? Yes. It is clear from the table that the weekly price range is important to performance. As you scan down most columns, the general trend is one of increasing performance. As you scan across the rows, it is not entirely clear whether volume improves performance. The diagonal, which shows a higher weekly price range and increasing volume, seems to indicate performance improves but the sample size is often too small to be too definitive.

Not shown in either of the two statistics tables is the finding that failures become more likely as the time from the nearest peak lengthens. I examined all failures and counted the weeks from the nearest price peak (zero if the weekly reversal happened to be the highest minor peak). Then I did a frequency distribution of the results. On a percentage basis, a graph of the result shows a line with an up-sloping trend. The sample size diminishes below acceptable levels in the last 3 weeks out of the 5-week series, so I avoid any formal conclusions. However, if the trend is valid, it suggests that you should avoid taking a position in a stock with a downside weekly reversal too far along a downtrend (say, more than 3 to 5 weeks from the prior peak).

Trading Tactics

I offer no specific trading tactics for downside weekly reversals. The measure rule, if you can call it that, is the formation height subtracted from the closing price. The formation height is simply the weekly low subtracted from the weekly high on the week of the reversal. I use the closing price of the same week. My statistics show that prices meet the target 73% of the time using this measure, short of the 80% I consider reliable.

With a 37% failure rate, it is probably not worth shorting a stock showing a downside reversal—it is just too risky. Instead, I would use the formation as supplementary evidence of a trend change. If prices slip below a moving average, the relative strength index moves out of overbought territory, or some other technical indicator signals a trend change, then the weekly reversal adds value.

Use the weekly reversal as a *warning* of a *possible* trend change, especially if you own the stock. The probability suggests the stock will decline but it may only be a short retrace in an uptrend. Only when a change in the primary trend occurs should long-term stock holders take action. Supplement the sell signal from the downside weekly reversal with other fundamental and technical information before pulling the trigger.

Sample Trade

Maggy decided to trade the weekly reversal shown in Figure 46.5. On the weekly chart she noticed the broadening top formation taking shape. When a weekly reversal appeared, she decided to sell the stock short and received a fill at 43.

The downside weekly reversal pierced the bottom trendline of a small descending broadening wedge that formed in late December. The downside wedge breakout coupled with a partial rise to the top of the broadening top suggested to her that prices would not only cross to the other side of the broadening top, but pierce the lower boundary was well. That is how she decided to play it.

You can see that the stock moved horizontally for 2 weeks before sinking. By mid-February, the stock had crossed to the lower boundary and pierced it as expected. Due to the downside breakout of the broadening top, she believed

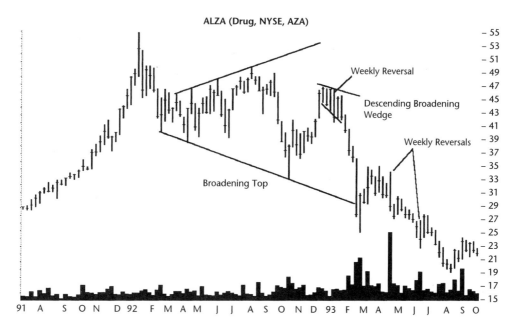

Figure 46.5   Broadening top formation with weekly reversals. The partial rise on the broadening top formation is a clue to the downside breakout and coupled with the descending broadening wedge means the stock is a good candidate to short.

the stock would eventually continue moving down and that gave her the confidence to ride out the turbulence in March 1993.

Additional weekly reversals added to her confidence and kept her in the trade. When the stock bounced off the August low of 19¼, she took notice. The stock climbed to 24½ then retraced to 20⅞. To her, the decline to the second low looked like a Fibonacci retracement (61.8% of the rise from 19¼ to 24½) so she decided to sell the following week at 21½. She made nearly 50% on the trade.

47

Weekly Reversals, Upside

RESULTS SNAPSHOT

Appearance	On the weekly scale, a higher high, lower low, with closing price above the prior weekly high
Reversal or consolidation	Short-term (up to 3 months) bullish reversal
Failure rate	23%
Average rise	44%, with most likely rise being 20%
Percentage meeting predicted price target	84%
Surprising findings	Reversals with moderately high volume (50% above the moving average) perform best but performance deteriorates as volume increases. A wide weekly price range improves performance.
See also	Weekly Reversals, Downside

The Results Snapshot shows a quick synopsis of the statistical results for upside weekly reversals. The formation performs substantially better than its brother, the downside weekly reversal. The upside variety sports a failure rate of 23%, still above the 20% maximum that I consider reliable formations should meet. Its average rise at 44% is quite high until you consider the most likely gain is 20%. The difference between the two values suggests there are a significant number of large gains pulling the average upward. A frequency distribution of the gains, which is where the most likely gain comes from, suggests meager gains are the norm.

How can you gain 44% in 3 months? Normally, you cannot. A frequency distribution of the days to the ultimate high shows that most formations (47%) reach the high in 3 months or less. The next highest category, at 38%, is for those formations with *long-term* gains (taking over 6 months to reach the ultimate high). The large number of quick but small gains are why the most likely gain is so low. It is not a contradiction at all, just a warning that this formation either performs poorly or very well. There is little middle ground.

The percentage of upside weekly reversals meeting their price targets at 84% is above the 80% reliability threshold. The high value should not come as a complete surprise since most bullish formations score well. The results are helped, in part, by each stock participating in a bull market over the 5 years under study.

I compared the gains for successful upside weekly reversals when their volume is half the 25-week moving average to reversals having volume 50% above the average. The performance associated with the low volume variety show gains of 38%; the higher volume reversals have gains of 44%. The difference between the two results is statistically significant. However, when raising the volume benchmark to two, three, and four times the moving average, performance steadily declines. Another study of all formations, both successful and unsuccessful ones, supports the deteriorating performance results as volume increases.

Performance improves with a wider weekly price range. The results range from an average gain of 15% for those formations with a narrow price range to 57% for those with a wider range.

Tour

Figure 47.1 shows two upside weekly reversals. The one on the left is less successful than the one on the right. The left one comes amidst a downtrend and correctly signals a reversal of the trend. However, the reversal does not last long. Prices hobble up then move sideways for 2 months before declining again. The second reversal works much better. It forms when prices score the lowest low on the chart but close higher. Prices climb steadily for about a month, retrace some of their gains then climb in a stair-step fashion. Prices eventually move from a low of $12\frac{5}{8}$ to a high of 37—a gain of almost 200%. The first reversal, by contrast, shows a gain of 31% from low to high. If you use the closing price during the weekly reversal, then the gains moderate to 160% and 13%, respectively. I use the closing prices as the starting point in all calculations involving performance. This gives a somewhat more realistic flavor to the performance.

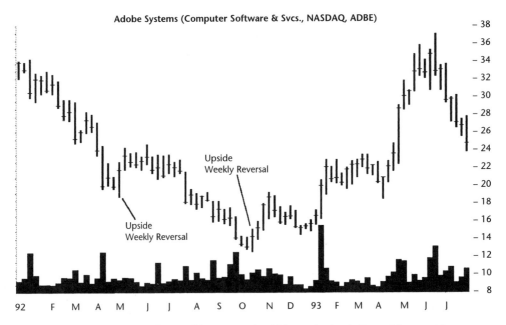

Figure 47.1 Two upside weekly reversals. Although the left upside weekly reversal correctly signals a trend change, the right one is more prescient.

Sometimes, such as the upside reversal shown on the left, the formation is premature. At other times, such as the one on the right, the reversal is quite timely. When it is early, it is usually by only a few weeks to a month or so, not 5 months premature (to the bottom) such as that shown in Figure 47.1.

The large weekly price range and closing price are two clues to a change in trend. A lower low, higher high, and a close above the high of the prior week suggest prices will rise. Usually, they do and sometimes quite far.

Volume, as you can see in Figure 47.1, can be spotty. Neither reversal has high or low volume; the number of shares traded is about midrange. This is not unusual as many well-performing upside weekly reversals have low or average volume during the week of the reversal.

Identification Guidelines

Table 47.1 shows identification guidelines for upside weekly reversals. The first order of business in correctly identifying an upside weekly reversal is to use the weekly chart to look for a reversal in a downtrend. The reversal appears as a weekly high above the prior week's high, a low below the prior week's low, and a weekly close above the prior week's high. In essence, you are looking for a wider price range than the week before with a close above the prior high price

Table 47.1
Identification Characteristics of Upside Weekly Reversals

Characteristic	Discussion
Weekly chart	Use weekly charts.
Downward trend	Prices should be in a downtrend or near the end of a downtrend. Ignore upside weekly reversals when the predominant trend is upward unless they occur during a correction of the upward trend.
Higher high, lower low	Prices must be higher than the prior week's high and lower than the prior week's low. Ties not allowed.
Higher close	Prices must close above the prior week's high

(not just a higher closing price, but one that is above the prior high). Once you have located all the ingredients, you have found an upside weekly reversal.

Figure 47.2 shows what upside weekly reversals look like. The first one (on the left) does not occur at the bottom of the downtrend. It is almost 2 months late, but you can see how successful it is. Prices zoom from the close of 9½ to 32⅞. Although the reversal occurs in a 2-month uptrend, I consider it close enough to the low pricewise to be a valid buy signal.

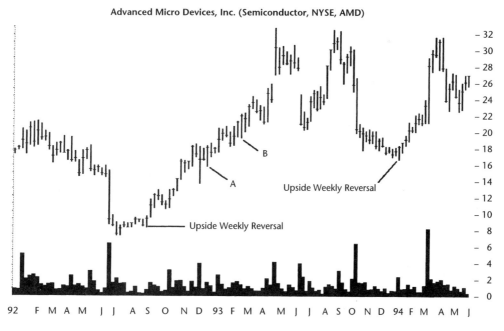

Figure 47.2   Successful upside weekly reversals. Points A and B, however, show upside weekly reversals that do not reverse. The price trend should be downward leading to an upside weekly reversal. The August 1992 reversal occurs after a long downtrend where prices are still near the low.

Contrast the reversal with points A and B in Figure 47.2. Both points are weekly reversals but prices do not reverse—they continue climbing. That is because the upside weekly reversal occurs in an uptrend and signals a continuation of the upward trend. The signals do not indicate how long the up trend will continue, however, so you should be cautious about taking a position. Sometimes, the reversal will occur near or at the end of the up trend.

Other upside weekly reversals appear during a retrace or consolidation of the upward trend (Figure 47.5 shows an example of this). The reversal signals the end of the correction and a resumption of the upward trend.

The reversal shown on the right in Figure 47.2 occurs at the valley floor. If you look closely, you can see the weekly high is above the prior week's high, the low is below the prior week's low, and the closing price is above the prior week's high as well. Prices rise 73% following the reversal, reaching a high of almost 32, then drop to find support at about 23. Prices do not make a new high until January 1995.

Focus on Failures

Not all reversals work out as expected. The failure rate at 23% is above the maximum 20% I consider reliable formations to possess. Consider the upside weekly reversal shown in Figure 47.3.

Many times, a down draft follows a brief spurt upward. When all is said and done, prices end near where they begin. An investor viewing the developing situation shown in Figure 47.3 might think the same thing. In June 1995, prices lift out of a 7-month consolidation region between 22 and 26 (partially shown) and reach a high of $39\frac{3}{8}$ several months later. That is a nice climb and one would expect a 40% to 60% retrace of the gain. If the trend reverses, then all gains could be lost and prices would return to where they began (to the 22 to 26 area). That is what happened. The bottom of the weekly reversal occurs right in the center of the consolidation region at 24. To me, the reversal suggests the decline is over and prices should climb, perhaps making a double top. It is a good investment opportunity except for one thing: The reversal fails.

Sure, prices hit a higher high the week after the reversal but close lower. The 7 weeks look like a diamond bottom, except that the diamond does not reverse—it consolidates. Prices drop out of the diamond and signal a resumption of the downward trend. The decline from the high near 40, the pause at 26, and the drop to a low of 16 should remind you of another formation—a measured move down. The diamond marks the corrective phase of the measured move down.

The upside weekly reversal in this situation is what I call a 5% failure. Prices move up by less than 5% before collapsing and heading significantly lower. In the nearly 500 formations I looked at, 5% failures occur 112 times or 23%. That statistic may sound low, but it is really quite high.

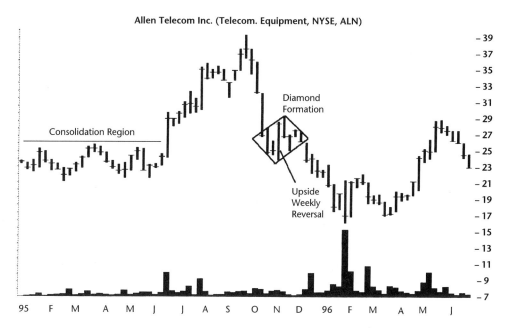

Figure 47.3 An upside weekly reversal 5% failure. The upside weekly reversal marks the bottom of the diamond bottom pattern that acts as a consolidation of the downward trend. The weekly reversal is a 5% failure because prices fail to continue moving up by more than 5%. The diamond is part of the corrective phase of a measured move down.

Many times it is difficult to pin down a generic reason why a particular type of formation fails. I looked at the statistics and noticed that the vast majority of failures occur with average or above average volume levels. Only 13% of the formations fail after showing low volume (volume during the reversal week that is 50% below the moving average). If you are considering buying a stock that shows high volume during the reversal week, you might look for other fundamental or technical factors to bolster your confidence of a successful trade.

Statistics

Table 47.2 shows statistics for weekly reversals. I uncovered 484 formations in 200 stocks spanning a 5-year period. Since these formations are common and since there is such a large number of them, I did not feel any need to search the other 300 stocks for additional formations.

Of the formations I uncovered, 137 act as consolidations of the trend, and the remainder act as reversals. Many of the consolidations turn out to be 5% failures. Almost a quarter (23%) of the formations are 5% failures.

Table 47.2
General Statistics for Upside Weekly Reversals

Description	Statistic
Number of formations in 200 stocks from 1991 to 1996	484
Reversal or consolidation	137 consolidations, 347 reversals
Failure rate	112 or 23%
Average rise of successful formations	44%
Most likely rise	20%
Of those succeeding, number meeting or exceeding price target (measure rule)	314 or 84%
For successful formations, days to ultimate high	7 months (218 days)
Percentage of reversals occurring near 12-month low (L), center (C), or high (H)	L30%, C38%, H32%
Percentage loss for each 12-month lookback period	L48%, C40%, H45%
Average volume week before and after versus week of reversal	59%, 82%
Percentage that high volume (50% above versus 50% below 25-week moving average) reversals perform better than low volume reversals	44% versus 38% gain but percentage deteriorates at higher volume

The average gain at 44% is comparatively high for bullish reversals. This contrasts with the most likely gain of 20%. Figure 47.4 shows a frequency distribution of gains that helps explain the discrepancy. The highest column is the one with the highest frequency. Twenty-one percent of the formations have gains between 10% and 20%. On the other end of the scale, 17% of the formations have gains over 90%. The relatively large number of outsized gains explains why the overall average is 44% (the high numbers pull the average up). More than a third of the formations (37%—the total of the first two columns) have gains less than 20%. It seems that you either do quite poorly or quite well with this formation. The way the bars in the chart orient (with the tallest ones clustered in the lower gains section) suggests your gains will be on the modest side.

By the way, the performance statistics in Table 47.2 use the closing price during the week of the reversal as the benchmark. The average rise, for instance, measures from the closing price to the highest high before a significant reversal occurs (or until the end of the data).

For those formations that work as expected, 84% meet their price targets. I created a measure rule for reversals that is similar to many other formations. Simply compute the height of the weekly reversal and add it to the closing price. The result is the target to which prices will ascend, at a minimum. In

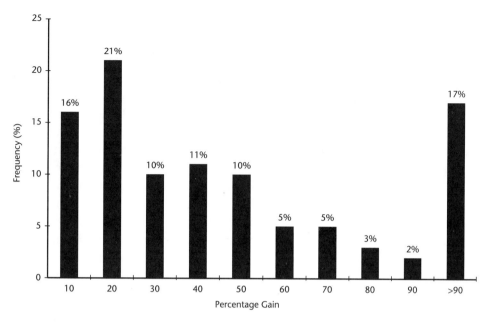

Figure 47.4 Frequency distribution of gains for upside weekly reversals. A third of the weekly reversals have gains of less than 20%.

some cases, the weekly price range is comparatively narrow, making the predicted target an easy shot.

It takes, on average, 7 months to reach the ultimate high. That is enough time for prices to climb an average of 44%.

Where in the yearly price range do upside weekly reversals occur? I divided the yearly price range into thirds for each formation and tabulated the results. The results were almost evenly split with the highest—38% of the formations—occurring in the center third of the price range. In essence, the formation can appear anywhere in the price range even though I use the closing price (which is at the top of the formation) as the benchmark. Even so, the low end scores well with 30% of the formations appearing within a third of the yearly low. Mapping the performance over the yearly price range, the statistics again show no significant trend. Those formations occurring in the lowest third of the range have gains averaging 48%, whereas those in the center third have gains of 40%.

Volume during the week of the reversal is above the adjacent weeks. The week before the reversal occurs has an average 59% of the shares traded during the week of the reversal. The week after the reversal, the volume drops to 82%.

I define high volume as being 50% above the 25-week moving average and low volume to be 50% below the average. When I sorted the *successful* formations (those that do not fail) into high and low volume categories, upside weekly reversals with high volumes score better than those with low volumes. The difference in the gains, 44% and 38%, respectively, is statistically significant. However, as I raised the high volume cutoff point to two, three, and four times the moving average, the performance steadily deteriorated (from 44% at 2×, to 38% at 3×, to 29% at 4×).

Some analysts suggest that high volume, when combined with a large weekly price range, results in a better performing weekly reversal. Table 47.3 shows the results of my study. I filtered the database of formations that have a weekly price range from 5% to 25% of the closing price and volume that is zero times (meaning that all formations qualify) to four times the volume of the 25-week moving average. The table lists the average gain for the formations followed by the number of formations meeting the criteria (the sample size) shown in parentheses. The percentage gains are suspect when the sample size drops below 30. The table shows values for *all formations, including those that fail* (which is different from the volume study just discussed) and the volume range, at up to four times the moving average, is larger than the earlier study.

In the benchmark column, you can see that as the weekly price range grows, the formations perform better, with gains starting out at 15% and rising to 57%. In the column, all formations qualify regardless of their volume level. The other columns generally support the notion of improved performance after a wide weekly price range (scan down each column).

In Table 47.3, it is difficult to see how volume influences performance. As you scan across each row, sometimes the performance improves and sometimes it does not. However, when you sum the percentage gains of each column (the last row in the table), it becomes clear that as volume increases, performance deteriorates.

Table 47.3
Average Percentage Gain from Formations Meeting Criteria of Volume and Weekly Price Range

Price Range (%)	Benchmark (%)	Volume			
		0–1× (%)	1–2× (%)	2–3× (%)	3–4× (%)
0–5	15 (48)	16 (35)	11 (9)	25 (2)	35 (1)
5–10	35 (196)	32 (101)	38 (69)	39 (23)	63 (1)
10–15	32 (112)	44 (34)	32 (59)	23 (16)	5 (3)
15–20	50 (47)	74 (13)	52 (24)	25 (4)	15 (4)
20–25	57 (22)	108 (6)	45 (11)	48 (4)	10 (1)
Sum:	1.89	2.74	1.78	1.60	1.28

Note: The numbers in the table represent the average gain for those formations meeting the price and volume ranges with the sample size in parentheses. Formations with a wide price range perform better than ones with a narrow price range. High volume impedes performance—if you trust the low sample numbers.

Since this conflicts with the commonly held belief that high volume should improve performance, the low sample counts may explain the discrepancy. The real test is whether a stock does well after you buy it.

Trading Tactics

I do not list trading tactics in the usual tabular format because they are so few. First, use the measure rule to estimate the target price to which the stock will climb. Simply subtract the weekly low from the weekly high during the week of the reversal. The difference is the formation height. Add the height to the weekly closing price to get the target to which prices will climb, at a minimum. Prices meet the target 84% of the time.

As an example, look at the upside weekly reversal shown in Figure 47.5. The high is at $21\frac{1}{8}$, the low is at $17\frac{3}{8}$, and the close is at 21. The height is the high minus the low or $3\frac{3}{4}$. Add the height to the closing price of 21 to get the target of $24\frac{3}{4}$. Prices hit the target about 3 months after the reversal.

The only other trading tactic is to be sure that the weekly reversal is on a downtrend—or reasonably close to the end of one. The one shown in Figure 47.5 occurs as part of a consolidation of the uptrend. Prices begin moving up in August 1993 to a minor high in January 1994. Then prices collapse from a high of 26 to a reversal low of $17\frac{3}{8}$.

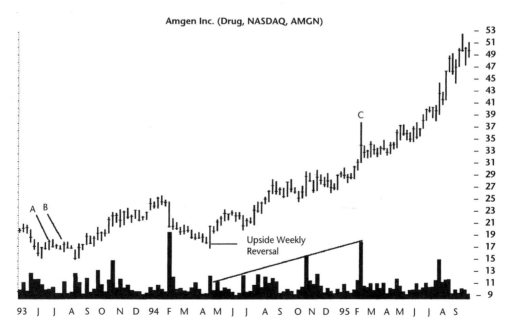

Figure 47.5 Trading an upside weekly reversal. Edward bought the stock the week after the upside weekly reversal and sold prematurely at point C.

In mid-July 1994, there is also another weekly reversal that is not high-lighted in Figure 47.5. The reversal happens after a quick price retrace and it marks the trend resumption. Earlier in the year, points A and B highlight two weekly reversals, both of which are failures. They occur in a minor downtrend and prices stabilize for about 2 months then move briefly lower. When prices decline below the low of the reversal, the reversal is a failure. Even though prices do climb into January 1994, the two reversals are disappointments because of the brief dip.

The two failures emphasize one final point. Do you really want to trade this formation? It sports an unacceptable failure rate of 23%, meaning it is risky. Also, the gains might be outsized (44%), but the statistics suggest the most likely gain will be about 20%. You can do better with less risk trading other formations. Or, better yet, use this as just one more tool in your toolbox of indicators you check before trading a security.

Sample Trade

Edward has a short fuse, a violent temper. Not only does he kill the messenger, he takes out the messenger's relatives as well. The people around him tiptoe gently as they pass his cube, but management likes him because he has a master's degree in engineering and seems to know his stuff.

I had the misfortune to be called in on a problem with my print redirector software he was using. After spending a few minutes looking at the data and performing a few tests, I concluded it was not a problem with my software. The fireworks display came early that year as Edward lit up. He ripped me up one side and down the other. I calmly walked away.

When the tables turned and he needed my help on one of his investments, he was very apologetic, almost submissive. He is new to trading and the upside weekly reversal seemed intriguing to him. He paper traded it with modest success and decided to try it for real. He invested in the stock shown in Figure 47.5. When the upside weekly reversal appeared, it fit his buy criteria, so he bought into the stock the following week at 20½. It pleased him to see the stock climb right after buying. As the weeks went by, the stock seemed to climb in stair-step fashion, moving up two steps and falling back one.

He drew a line along the volume tops and noticed it was following an upward-sloping trendline. Edward did not really know whether this was significant, but the high volume seemed to be on up days, whereas the lower volume clustered around days when prices declined. To him this suggested momentum was moving up, helping propel the stock higher.

When he checked on the stock in early February 1995, he noticed the high volume and large weekly price range (highlighted in the figure by point C). This concerned him. When he flipped to the daily price chart, the spike looked like a mountain: Prices quickly rose up to the peak and then declined. The volume picture generally echoed the price pattern.

The price and volume spikes looked to him like a one-day reversal (and a one-week reversal on the weekly scale). To Edward this suggested it was time to bail out. He pulled his ripcord and received a fill at 34¼.

The trade netted him a gain of 67%, an amount he bragged about for weeks. Just over a year later when he looked at the weekly chart, he saw the stock had topped out at 66½. He could have tripled his money.

Boy, was he pissed.

Statistics Summary

Notes and Definitions

This summary is an alphabetical list showing performance statistics for the chart patterns covered in this book. Various rankings of the top ten chart patterns follow.

Key to the tables:

NM = Not material as there were too few to be significant
NS = Not studied or does not apply to this formation
( ) = Numbers in parenthesis are declines
  * = Unusual values due to low sample count
P = Pullback
T = Throwback

Explanations of the column headings:

Failure rate	Percentage of formations that do not work as expected, including 5% failures. The numbers apply to formations once they stage a breakout (confirming the formation).
Reversal or consolidation	The letter R appears if the majority of formations act as reversals of the price trend and the letter C appears for consolidations. If both R and C appear in an entry, then the chart pattern has no overriding majority of either type.
Throwback, pullback	A throwback is an upside breakout that returns prices to the top of the formation or trendline boundary. A pullback is a downside breakout that returns prices to the bottom of the formation or trendline boundary. Both occur after a breakout and return within 30 days. The percentages for throwbacks apply to formations with upside breakouts only; pullback percentages apply to downside breakouts only.

Average rise or decline	I typically measure the average rise or decline from the price on the breakout day (using the daily high or low) that is closest to the formation. The ultimate high or low is the highest or lowest point before a significant change in trend (typically a 20% price change, measured high to low).
Likely rise or decline	Computed by measuring the individual percentage rise or decline for each formation and tabulating a frequency distribution of the results. The most likely rise or decline is the range with the highest frequency and usually excludes the rightmost column.
Rank by score	I separated each table entry into bullish (1 to 35) and bearish (1 to 32) formations then ranked them by their score. The score is the average rise or decline times the most likely rise or decline divided by the failure rate. The best rank is 1.

Summary of Statistics for All Chart Patterns

Formation	Failure Rate (%)	Reversal or Consoli- dation	Throwback Pullback (%)	Average Rise or Decline (%)	Likely Rise or Decine (%)	Rank by Score
Broadening Bottom, down breakout	6	C	NS	(27)	(15–20)	5
Broadening Bottom, up breakout	2	R	NS	25	10	13
Broadening Formation, Right-angled and Ascending, down breakout	9	R	P 72	(18)	(10)	17
Broadening Formation, Right-angled and Ascending, up breakout	6	C	T 44	32	20	14
Broadening Formation, Right-angled and Descending, down breakout	3	R	P 33	(19)	(10–15)	4
Broadening Formation, Right-angled and Descending, up breakout	19	C	T 23	27	20–30	24
Broadening Top, down breakout	4	R	NS	(23)	(10–20)	3
Broadening Top, up breakout	4	C	NS	34	10–15	15
Broadening Wedge, Ascending	6	R	T 7, P 21	(20)	(10)	13

(continued)

Summary of Statistics for All Chart Patterns (*continued*)

Formation	Failure Rate (%)	Reversal or Consoli- dation	Throwback Pullback (%)	Average Rise or Decline (%)	Likely Rise or Decine (%)	Rank by Score
Broadening Wedge, Descending, down breakout	41	R	P 36	(24)	(20)	25
Broadening Wedge, Descending, up breakout	37	C	T 40	46	20	27
Bump-and-Run Reversal Bottom	9	R	38	37	20	18
Bump-and-Run Reversal Top	19	R	P 39	(24)	(15–20)	15
Cup with Handle	10	C	T 74	38	10–20	20
Dead-Cat Bounce	10	R	NS	(15)	(5–25)	14
Diamond Bottom	13	R	T 43	35	15	21
Diamond Top	25	R	P 59	(21)	(20)	19
Double Bottom	3	R	T 68	40	20–30	4
Double Top	17	R	P 69	(20)	(10–15)	21
Flag, downtrend	12	C	P 20	(17)	(15)	16
Flag, uptrend	13	C	T 10	19	20*	26
Flag, High and Tight	17	C	T 47	63	20–30	16
Gap	NS	C	NS	Varies	Varies	35
Hanging Man, down breakout	22	C	NS	(16)	(5–10)	27
Hanging Man, up breakout	67	R	NS	40	10	33
Head-and-Shoulders Bottom	5	R	T 52	38	20–30	9
Head-and-Shoulders Bottom, Complex	6	R	T 47	37	20–30	10
Head-and-Shoulders Top, Complex	8	R	P 64	(27)	(20)	7
Head-and-Shoulders Top	7	R	P 45	(23)	(15)	11
Horn Bottom	11	C	NS	37	20–30	17
Horn Top	16	R or C	NS	(21)	(10)	23
Inside Day, down breakout	51	R	NS	(10)	(0–5)	32
Inside Day, up breakout	56	C	NS	13	0–5	34
Island Reversal, bottom	17	R	T 70	34	20	22
Island Reversal, top	13	R	P 65	(21)	(10)	20

(*continued*)

Summary of Statistics for All Chart Patterns (*continued*)

Formation	Failure Rate (%)	Reversal or Consoli- dation	Throwback Pullback (%)	Average Rise or Decline (%)	Likely Rise or Decine (%)	Rank by Score
Measured Move Down	22	R	NS	(36)	(25–40)	9
Measured Move Up	23	R	NS	68	30–60	12
One-Day Reversal, bottom	17	R	T 61	26	10–15	29
One-Day Reversal, top	24	R	P 71	(19)	(10)	26
Outside Day, down breakout	42	C	NS	(17)	(10)	30
Outside Day, up breakout	25	C	NS	32	10	30
Pennant, downtrend	34	C	P 17	(17)	(25)*	24
Pennant, uptrend	19	C	T 16	21	15–20	28
Pipe Bottom	12	R	NS	47	20	19
Pipe Top	18	C	NS	(21)	(10–20)	18
Rectangle Bottom, down breakout	4	C	P 70	(19)	(10–15)	8
Rectangle Bottom up breakout	0	R	T 61	46	20	32
Rectangle Top, down breakout	0	R	P 55	(20)	(20)	31
Rectangle Top, up breakout	2	C	T 53	52	20–30	1
Rounding Bottom	5	C	NS	54	20	6
Rounding Top	6	C	NS	41	20–40	7
Scallops, Ascending	25	C	NS	33	20–30	25
Scallops, Descending	3	C	NS	(24)	(20)	1
Shark-32, down breakout	44	R or C	P 58	(21)	(10)	29
Shark-32, up breakout	41	C	T 64	32	10–15	31
Triangle, Ascending	2	C	T 58	44	20	3
Triangle, Descending	4	C	P 64	(19)	(10–20)	6
Triangle, Symmetrical Bottom, down breakout	2	C	P 57	(19)	(10)	2
Triangle, Symmetrical Bottom, up breakout	3	R	T 43	41	20	5
Triangle, Symmetrical Top, down breakout	6	R	P 59	(20)	(15)	10
Triangle, Symmetrical Top, up breakout	5	C	T 58	37	20	11

(*continued*)

Summary of Statistics for All Chart Patterns (*continued*)

Formation	Failure Rate (%)	Reversal or Consoli-dation	Throwback Pullback (%)	Average Rise or Decline (%)	Likely Rise or Decine (%)	Rank by Score
Triple Bottom	4	R	T 70	38	20	8
Triple Top	15	R	P 84	(21)	(10)	22
Wedge, Falling	2	C	T 47	43	20–30	2
Wedge, Rising	6	R	P 53	(19)	(15)	12
Weekly Reversal, downside	37	R	NS	(18)	(10)	28
Weekly Reversal, upside	23	R	NS	44	20	23
Bullish pattern average				**38**	**20**	
Bearish pattern average				**(21)**	**(14)**	

In the following tables, I do not include the measured move up and measured move down formations because the average gain or loss is unrealistic. I calculated the returns assuming an investor notices the formation at the start of the chart pattern when a more realistic interpretation gauges results from the corrective phase (or the length of the second leg). In short, the average gain for a measured move up is probably about 37%, instead of 68%, and for the measured move down, expect an average loss of 20% instead of 36%.

Top Ten Best Performing Bullish Formations, Sorted by Score

Formation	Failures (%)	Average Rise (%)	Likely Rise (%)	Score
1 Rectangle Tops, up breakout	2	52	25	6.50
2 Wedges, Falling	2	43	25	5.38
3 Triangles, Ascending	2	44	20	4.40
4 Double Bottoms	3	40	25	3.33
5 Triangles, Symmetrical Bottoms, up breakout	3	41	20	2.73
6 Rounding Bottoms	5	54	20	2.16
7 Rounding Tops	6	41	30	2.05
8 Triple Bottoms	4	38	20	1.90
9 Head-and-Shoulders Bottoms	5	38	25	1.90
10 Head-and-Shoulder Bottoms, Complex	6	37	25	1.54

Note: The score column results from multiplying the average gain times the likely gain and dividing by the failure rate.

Top Ten Best Performing Bearish Formations, Sorted by Score

Formation	Failures (%)	Average Decline (%)	Likely Decline (%)	Score
1 Scallops, Descending	3	24	20	1.60
2 Triangles, Symmetrical Bottoms, down breakout	2	19	10	0.95
3 Broadening Tops, down breakout	4	23	15	0.86
4 Broadening Formations, Right-angled and Descending	3	19	13	0.791
5 Broadening Bottoms, down breakout	6	27	18	0.788
6 Triangles, Descending	4	19	15	0.71
7 Head-and-Shoulders Tops, Complex	8	27	20	0.68
8 Rectangle Bottoms, down breakout	4	19	13	0.59
9 Triangles, Symmetrical Tops, down breakout	6	20	15	0.50
10 Head-and-Shoulders Top	7	23	15	0.49

Note: The score column results from multiplying the average loss times the likely loss and dividing by the failure rate.

Top Ten Bullish Formations with Lowest Failure Rates

Formation	Failures (%)	Average Rise (%)	Likely Rise (%)	Score
1 Rectangle Bottoms, up breakout	0	46	20	0.09
2 Rectangle Tops, up breakout	2	52	25	6.50
3 Triangles, Ascending	2	44	20	5.38
4 Wedges, Falling	2	43	25	4.40
5 Broadening Bottoms, up breakout	2	25	10	1.25
6 Triangles, Symmetrical Bottoms, up breakout	3	41	20	3.33
7 Double Bottoms	3	40	25	2.73
8 Triple Bottoms	4	38	20	1.48
9 Broadening Tops, up breakout	4	34	12.50	1.06
10 Triangles, Symmetrical Tops, up breakout	5	37	20	1.90

Top Ten Bearish Formations with Lowest Failure Rates

Formation	Failures (%)	Average Decline (%)	Likely Decline (%)	Score
1 Rectangle Tops, down breakout	0	20	20	0.04
2 Triangles, Symmetrical Bottoms, down breakout	2	19	10	0.95
3 Scallops, Descending	3	24	20	1.60
4 Broadening Formation, Right-Angled and Descending	3	19	12.5	0.79
5 Broadening Tops, down breakout	4	23	15	0.86
6 Triangles, Descending	4	19	15	0.71
7 Rectangle Bottoms, down breakout	4	19	12.5	0.59
8 Triangles, Symmetrical Tops, down breakout	6	20	15	0.50
9 Wedges, Rising	6	19	15	0.48
10 Broadening Wedges, Ascending	6	20	10	0.33

Top Ten Bullish Formations with Highest Average Rise

Formation	Failures (%)	Average Rise (%)	Likely Rise (%)	Score
1 Flags, High and Tight	17	63	25	0.93
2 Rounding Bottoms	5	54	20	2.16
3 Rectangle Tops, up breakout	2	52	25	6.50
4 Pipe Bottoms	12	47	20	0.78
5 Broadening Wedges, Descending, up breakout	37	46	20	0.25
6 Rectangle Bottoms, up breakout	0	46	20	0.09
7 Weekly Reversals, Upside	23	44	20	0.38
8 Triangles, Ascending	2	44	20	4.40
9 Wedges, Falling	2	43	25	5.38
10 Triangles, Symmetrical Bottoms, up breakout	3	41	20	2.73

Top Ten Bearish Formations with Highest Average Decline

Formation	Failures (%)	Average Decline (%)	Likely Decline (%)	Score
1 Head-and-Shoulders Tops, Complex	8	27	20	0.68
2 Broadening Bottoms, down breakout	6	27	17.5	0.79
3 Broadening Wedges, Descending, down breakout	41	24	20	0.12
4 Bump-and-Run Reversal Tops	19	24	17.5	0.22
5 Scallops, Descending	3	24	20	1.60
6 Head-and-Shoulder Tops	7	23	15	0.49
7 Broadening Tops, down breakout	4	23	15	0.86
8 Shark-32, down breakout	44	21	10	0.05
9 Horn Tops	16	21	10	0.13
10 Triple Tops	15	21	10	0.14

Top Ten Bullish Formations with Highest Most Likely Rise

Formation	Failures (%)	Average Rise (%)	Likely Rise (%)	Score
1 Rounding Tops	6	41	30	2.05
2 Broadening Formations, Right-Angled and Descending	19	27	25	0.36
3 Scallops, Ascending	25	33	25	0.33
4 Head-and-Shoulders Bottoms, Complex	6	37	25	1.54
5 Horn Bottoms	11	37	25	0.84
6 Head-and-Shoulders Bottoms	5	38	25	1.90
7 Double Bottoms	3	40	25	3.33
8 Wedges, Falling	2	43	25	5.38
9 Rectangle Tops, up breakout	2	52	25	6.50
10 Flags, High and Tight	17	63	25	0.93

Top Ten Bearish Formations with Highest Most Likely Decline

Formation	Failures (%)	Average Decline (%)	Likely Decline (%)	Score
1 Pennant, trend down	34	17	25*	0.13
2 Scallops, Descending	3	24	20	1.60
3 Head-and-Shoulders, Tops, Complex	8	27	20	0.68
4 Diamond Tops	25	21	20	0.17
5 Broadening Wedges, Descending, down breakout	41	24	20	0.12
6 Rectangle Tops, down breakout	0	20	20	0.04
7 Broadening Bottoms, down breakout	6	27	17.5	0.79
8 Bump-and-Run Reversal Tops	19	24	17.5	0.22
9 Broadening Tops, down breakout	4	23	15	0.86
10 Triangles, Descending	4	19	15	0.71

Index of Chart Patterns

Broadening Bottoms, page 12

Broadening Wedges, Ascending, page 72

Broadening Formations, Right-Angled and Ascending, page 27

Broadening Wedges, Descending, page 87

Broadening Formations, Right-Angled and Descending, page 40

Bump-and-Run Reversal Bottoms, page 100

Broadening Tops, page 55

Bump-and-Run Reversal Tops, page 119

Pennants, page 213

Pipe Bottoms, page 417

Pipe Tops, page 429

Rectangle Bottoms, page 439

Rectangle Tops, page 453

Rounding Bottoms, page 466

Rounding Tops, page 477

Scallops, Ascending, page 487

Scallops, Descending, page 487

Shark-32, page 501

Triangles, Ascending, page 511

Triangles, Descending, page 529

Triangles, Symmetrical Bottoms, page 545

Triangles, Symmetrical Tops, page 560

Triple Bottoms, page 576

Triple Tops, page 590

Wedges, Falling, page 603

Wedges, Rising, page 617

Weekly Reversals, Downside, page 631

Weekly Reversals, Upside, page 642

Index

Numbers in bold type refer to chapters; numbers in italics refer to illustrations.